'With radical change in the air, Paul [...] for sustaining practical hope. Through [...] potentials, Auerbach advances a biting critique of the ideology, [...] class structures that sustain capitalism. And on this basis he presents an intriguing agenda for moving towards an egalitarian, solidaristic, democratically more substantive and culturally richer alternative.'

– **Sam Gindin**, *co-author of* The Making of Global Capitalism

'Here is a remarkable book that combines enormous wisdom, a deep historical and economic analysis, and a vision for a reconstructed socialist project which builds, not on fantasy, but on existing seeds within capitalism. Auerbach forensically analyses the errors of past socialist analysis and reconstructs a new vision founded on education and human development.'

– **Francis Green**, *Professor of Work and Education Economics, Institute of Education, University of London, UK, and author of* Skills and Skilled Work

'21st-century capitalism, without a socialist rival to temper its excesses, has degenerated into a dystopia of financial instability, economic stagnation and extremes of inequality. The resultant lack of opportunity has stunted the development of a generation in a way that resembles a return to feudalism more than it does Hayek's vision of a creative spontaneous order. Auerbach proposes instead a socialism that emphasises human development, equality and genuine democracy.'

– **Steve Keen**, *author of* Debunking Economics

'Paul Auerbach has written a book not for the converted, not for those in search of certainties or dogmas, but for those looking for intelligent arguments, proposals which are historically based and theoretically sound with the right dash of utopia to make the mix interesting and exciting – a book which puts at the centre of a major reform of society the pursuit of educational excellence for all. This is a book to be read slowly and carefully: the reader will emerge wiser and richer in the mind.'

– **Donald Sassoon**, *Professor of Comparative European History, University of London, UK, and author of* One Hundred Years of Socialism

'Paul Auerbach has written a brilliant and immensely important book. In the face of economic crisis, increasing inequality and looming environmental disaster we need more than defensive, "neoliberal light" policies or vague calls for radical change. Auerbach demonstrates how past socialist failures derive closely from a misreading of history. More importantly, his analysis points us in a new and promising direction. This ambitious book combines clear economic insight with a compelling vision for change. It will appeal to all who recognise the dangers and inequities of unfettered capitalism.'

– **Peter Skott**, *Professor of Economics, University of Massachusetts, Amherst, USA, and author of* Conflict and Effective Demand in Economic Growth

To Caroline, for everything

Contents

Acknowledgements   x

Introduction   1

Part I   Socialism and Central Planning   15

Introduction   15

1   Planning and Spontaneous Order   17
Planning as an aspect of rationality   17
Hayek and the constructivist fallacy   22
Social outcomes without planning?   28
Spontaneity and planning   32

2   The Giant Firm and the Plan   37
The Great Transformation   37
Modernity and the giant firm   39
The giant firm: size and complexity   42
The giant firm: the creation of management   48
Planning and the giant firm   54

**3   Technocratic Planning and the Emergence of a Socialist
      Orthodoxy**   66
Liberalism and the Great Transformation   66
The ideology of technocratic planning   70
Socialism and technocratic planning   85

4   Socialist Theory and Practice   97
Central planning and real existing socialism   97
Socialist calculation   110
Competitive dynamics in capitalism and socialism   115

5   Ironies of History: Markets, Planning and Competition   126
Postwar debates   127
The acceleration of competition   139
The demise of technocratic planning: the Alternative
Economic Strategy   143

Part II   Human and Economic Development   157

Introduction   157

6   **Education and Economic Growth: The Statistical and
    Historical Record**   161
    Education and growth: the statistical nexus   162
    How seriously do we take the results? I   170
    Interlude: technology as an elixir   175
    Education and industrial revolutions   178
    How seriously do we take the results? II   184

7   **Education as a Social Process**   191
    Human capital theory   191
    Educational development and external effects   194
    Education wars   202
    Radical prescriptions   212
    A missing element   223

8   **The Working and Living Environment**   225
    Learning in the working and living environment   226
    Employment and training   236
    Security and household planning   242

9   **The US as Exemplar and Paradigm**   249
    US history – the peculiar and the explicable   250
    Economic development and government enterprise   258
    Late Rome   270

10 **Economic Growth and Inequality**   277
    Why is growth desirable?   277
    Economic capacity and lags in economic development   282
    Inequality and national income   292
    Socialism vs. 'economic realities'   305

Part III   Socialism and Human Possibilities   317

Introduction   317

11 **Education in a Free Society**   319
    Hayek's dilemma   319
    Is it all a waste of time?   323
    Culture   335
    Strategies utopian and practical   341

12   Equality and Democratic Control   **364**
An overview   364
Economic policies for working and living in the world   367
Financial conundrums   378
Progressive taxation   395
Political economy: public affairs   399
The political economy of work   407

Conclusion   **422**

Notes   432

Bibliography   469

Index   511

Acknowledgements

I am grateful for advice and assistance from Mike C. Cole, John R. Davis, Sam Gindin, Francis Green, Hubert Kohler, Simon Mohun, Caroline Potter, Donald Sassoon, Peter Skott, Dimitris Sotiropoulos, Engelbert Stockhammer and Bob Sutcliffe.

A special word of thanks to Gilles Christoph for initiating this project and to Rachel Sangster for having faith in it.

Introduction

We live in dispiriting, pessimistic, cynical times. Present-day capitalism has generated a level of instability and dysfunction not seen since the interwar period of the twentieth century, with growing inequality of income and wealth, persistent high levels of unemployment and ever-diminishing prospects for young people. Political activity is widely perceived to be a game performed by an elite for its own benefit.

A major reinforcement for the existing way of doing things that, in spite of capitalism's manifest inadequacies, no alternative is on the table. In the absence of a positive vision of how society and the economy might develop in the future, it is unlikely that the present trajectory of capitalism will be derailed, no matter how acute the critique of contemporary developments. This book sets out a vision of an alternative political economy.

For much of the twentieth century, socialism in the form of central planning and state ownership of the means of production posed as the antipode to capitalism. When its real-life exemplifications in the Soviet Union and elsewhere collapsed, capitalism was seen to be without rival. Centrally planned socialism had failed as a practical concept and as an ideal, unable to replicate the dynamism and innovative energy of capitalism and identified with egregious violations of human and political rights.

The revised socialist agenda presented here will focus upon the upbringing and education of young people in the context of social equality. The creation of opportunities for the full development of human capacity across the population will form the basis for human liberation and democratic control of public affairs and working life. This approach to socialism differs markedly from typical dictionary definitions that are directed at state ownership of the means of production and central planning. It also distances itself from much of the tradition of social democracy. The latter has great accomplishments attached to its name, but has largely functioned as an attempt to alleviate capitalism's worst excesses: social democracy never posed an alternative trajectory of development or vision of the future to challenge that of capitalism.

1

The distinction between alleviationist and developmental approaches to social change is an important one, though any social movement is likely to be an amalgam of both. The epitome of the alleviationist approach in European socialism was the British Labour Party. Through much of its history, Labour Party rhetoric had been characterised by an emphasis on fairness and equality, but it addressed the realities of class power in Britain, from the school system to the House of Lords, only in the most feeble way. In the postwar period, its commitment to nationalisation was less a matter of pursuing a diluted version of the ideology of central planning than a pragmatic attempt to maintain high levels of employment. A general view emerged that the monies directed at the nationalised industries were a drain on the Treasury, carried out merely as concessions to a subgroup of workers tied to the Labour Party through the trade unions: the words on everybody's lips were about British decline. It was the perception, or delusion, of a path to development – of 'going somewhere' – that was Margaret Thatcher's greatest strength. There was a modicum of truth in her assertion that there was no alternative on offer at the time, either from other political parties or in the broader political and economic discourse, that was to the slightest degree convincing.

In the US, an extreme form of this alleviationist approach emerged, largely, though not exclusively, in the context of the Democratic Party, an organisation that did not even rhetorically challenge the presuppositions of capitalism. Alleviationism had its greatest success from the postwar years until the early 1970s in the form of a Keynesianism that extended beyond macroeconomic regulation of the economy to a range of social welfare measures. This period was characterised by rapid growth and relatively full employment across Western Europe and North America, accompanied by compression and then stability in the distribution of income: Keynesian regulation of the economy was credited with the success of capitalism during this golden age. When capitalism stumbled in the 1970s, alleviationist approaches failed as well. Since then, we have observed a renewal of capitalist ideology in an intensified form, partly because there has been no alternative on offer. No rival path to development has been forthcoming to challenge capitalism and the rich ideology used to support it.

Is there a socialist alternative? The socialism to be explored here, though having links to its long and, in many cases, distinguished tradition, is not to be identified with its historical association with state ownership and central planning. The optimism in the title of this book is in no way intended to imply any certainty about what will happen in the future. It does, however, signal a rejection of the 'no alternative' view and point to a socialist path to development.

The focus in this book on education and equality can easily be misunderstood. The expansion and transformation of education are key elements of the developmental form of socialism that will unfold here. But educational reform is viewed with suspicion in some progressive circles: it often functions in public policy initiatives as a substitute for dealing with economic and social inequality. Mainstream educational policy is commonly linked to attempts to blame much of the population for its inadequate intellectual preparation for participating in an economic race, if not with technology, then against other nations, in which 'we' are all supposedly involved. By implication, the on-going rise in inequality can be laid at the door of the losers in this race.

Education remains, however, the most powerful single public policy intervention for progressive reform and for the transformation of personal capacities. In recent years, progress in research and practice surrounding the psychological and cognitive development of young children is dispelling the fatalism associated with the ideology of IQ and the notion that the distribution of skills and attainments in society is simply a reflection of biological capacity. Public policy intervention in education can play a role in the release of the inherent potential of all individuals. It is a uniquely potent force for social transformation and the overcoming of class background.

Progressive formal education policy can thus be a vehicle for the promotion of equality, but it is not a palliative or a substitute for a focus on equality itself. With capitalism manifesting dramatic rises in inequality, it is common to see comments on this problem from prominent individuals that 'feel your pain' but warn against doing anything about it:

> If income could be redistributed without damping economic growth, there would be a compelling case for reducing incomes at the top and transferring the proceeds to those in the middle area and at the bottom. Unfortunately this is not the case. It is easy to think of policies that would have reduced the earning power of Bill Gates or Mark Zuckerberg by making it more difficult to start and profit from a business. But it is much harder to see how such policies would raise the incomes of the rest of the population. Such policies surely hurt them as consumers by depriving them of the fruits of technological progress.[1]

Alleviation of inequality, some experts assure us, can only take place at the cost of economic progress.

Such a view finds little confirmation in the historical record. Economic development is a social process involving the skills and initiatives of a broad base of the population rather than a gift bestowed by an entrepreneurial elite. Equality, far from being an obstacle to progress, is a creative force. It fosters a context in which formal education can flourish, and it offers opportunities to learn at work and in the broader world. Full employment and security permit both the adults and children in a household to plan and cultivate their capabilities. There is no dilemma posed by some presumptive trade-off between equality and economic progress.

We must resist the temptation, however, to simply accept the goals prominently displayed before us, such as economic growth, and claim that socialism is a way of 'doing it better'. Socialism here is perceived in terms of its ends and aspirations. At the level of individual well-being, it takes literally the commonly voiced notion that all children should have an opportunity to develop fully their range of human capacities, a demand usually tendered in a manner sufficiently vapid that no one could mistake such declarations for genuine statements of intent. The fulfilment of this goal implies an access to upbringing and education from the earliest stages of life that is not contingent upon, and, indeed, compensates for, limitations in household circumstances.

Socialism as presented here is thus truly radical, more so than conceptions associated with central planning. The transformational possibilities of socialism emerge from the notion that, in all societies, the mentality, repertoire of skills, knowledge and social attitudes of members of society are conditioned and contingent on social and economic institutions: they are not hard-wired biologically at or before birth. A central task for socialism is to engender in the population a facility for exercising democratic control over daily life and public affairs. The key public policy mechanism available for securing a social transformation of this kind is a programme, most especially from the preschool level to early adolescence, involving a substantial increase in the quantity and quality of resources devoted to formal education. Such a programme is not a fanciful or speculative one, as evidenced by the example of the elite's expenditure in this direction on their own children.

By itself, however, an aggressive public education programme is far from sufficient to permit the full development of a child's capacities: the household is the predominant and, at younger ages, the overwhelming influence on an individual's psychological and cognitive formation. The resources and the personal 'tutoring' that can be offered to children in households at the upper reaches of society will be difficult to replicate or compensate for in any programme of preschool and formal education, and most especially in societies evidencing high levels of social and economic inequality. Ambitious programmes of formal education must, therefore, be supported by a mitigation of household deprivation and insecurity if they are to have any chance of succeeding. Once we begin to view human beings not merely as commodities, but as individuals who plan and cultivate their own futures, deprivation and insecurity can be seen as factors that derange the ability of households to act as platforms in which formal education can take place in a fruitful manner.

The household and the general living environment are places of learning in themselves. An important part of a programme of equal opportunity involves efforts to extend generally the access to amenities, opportunities and stimulation accorded to the children of the well-off. The fact that children grow up in households and live in the world gives the lie to the notion that one can pursue a social strategy of equality of opportunity in, for instance, formal education, but care relatively little about equality of outcomes. Societies that generate highly unequal outcomes for households in the present will also be creating a disparate range of opportunities for the children in these households. The claim that one can offer equal opportunity to all but preserve highly unequal outcomes is simplistic, and most probably false.

A socialist focus on individual development also gives substantial weight to full employment. It is, first, a component of the secure environment necessary for the household to pursue long-term plans for the cultivation of the human assets of its members, including formal education. Second, work that makes full use of personal capacities is an essential aspect of human development: the workplace is an invaluable venue for skill enhancement and the cultivation of social citizenship. All employment should be associated with opportunities for the development of skills as a structural, and not incidental, aspect of the work environment.

In addition to personal development, however, the socialist perspective recognises the inherently social nature of human existence. Socialism is, therefore, intimately linked to the presence of a second aspect: democracy. In contemporary usage, the latter term has often been used merely to indicate the absence of overt terror from the state, rather than in its original meaning of 'rule by the people'. It is impossible to reconcile notions of democracy with the authoritarian structures and practices that individuals presently experience in their daily life at work. The restructuring of the work environment to give workers real decision-making power in the enterprise, and the engendering, or re-engendering, of collective organisation through labour unions, are necessary aspects of democratic practice.

Democracy must, therefore, embody substantial levels of participation in decision making in the working and living environment on a regular, even daily, basis. This notion of social citizenship should pervade the schoolroom from the earliest years and do battle against powerful contemporary pressures to focus education exclusively on vocational goals (especially for those from less privileged backgrounds). The school should be a mechanism for the cultivation of democracy, not only in the substance of what the child learns, but in the way the school conducts itself: a key goal should be a resolution of issues surrounding discipline by early adolescence. The educational process should be one that elides naturally into democratic decision making in the workplace, in daily life and in the broader political sphere.

The ability to exercise democratic control in the broader society embodies the need for a genuine voice for the mass of the population in the conduct of politics, traditional freedoms of speech and conscience, and transparency in the operation of political and economic affairs. The inequalities in income and wealth that pervade capitalist society have always manifested

themselves in elite control over political processes and the flow of information and opinion through the media. But in an even more direct manner,
capitalism impedes the development of a democratic polity. In the twenty-first century, the activities of multinational businesses and financial
enterprises have profound effects on our daily lives through the worldwide restructuring of the economy and destabilisation of the financial and
natural environment; enormous hidden transfers of wealth to tax havens
take place, abetted by respectable institutions, that affect the destiny of
nations, especially poor ones. The socialist asks: are these activities merely
private affairs, and will they ever be made amenable to democratic scrutiny
and control in the absence of a willingness to challenge the capitalist principle of the inviolability of private property?

A last, essential, but elusive aspect of socialism involves an undercurrent
of solidarity stretching across humankind. Even in the midst of conflicts
and problems within our own locality and nation, a socialist sensibility
compels an awareness of the implications of acts of public policy for human
beings worldwide and for those yet unborn. Thus, while the focus here
is on socialist policies in the richest countries, the implications of these
policies for the world's poorest will remain a central consideration in the
background. These policies are also important in the context of a range of
ecological issues, most especially those concerned with climate change.

The perspective above will inform our view of past efforts that have carried
the label of socialism and permit us to judge when reform programmes can
be viewed as truly radical. Part I, *Socialism and Central Planning*, reconsiders
the dominant path taken to socialist reform in the past – state ownership of
the means of production and central planning.

In Chapter 1, we see the genesis of the concept of planning in Enlightenment
thinking as co-extensive with rationality: it involved a reconsideration *de
novo* of all notions concerned with the functioning of the natural world and
of society, and a programme of reconstruction of ideas and institutions on
a rational basis. Planning as a dominant mode of regulation in society was
subsequently contested by notions of spontaneous order, as hinted at by
Adam Smith and then elaborated upon in modern times by, most especially,
Friedrich Hayek. Hayek contended that society was capable of organising
itself with an absence of central and conscious direction, and that inhibitions to this process of self-organisation of society were undesirable. The
notion of spontaneous order in Hayek's conception – that much of what
we value in our culture is the result of interactions between individuals at
ground level, without planning from above – is unexceptionable. But his
stronger notion that it is a virtue for society to have no sense of direction is
absurd and disingenuous. His preferred form of spontaneous order – market
capitalism – has always evolved, and continues to do so, in the context of
conscious coordination and planning (and often coercion) from the state
and other centralised agencies.

The continuing influence of the planning paradigm was, however, due not to its success in abstract debates but, as we shall see in Chapter 2, to the great transformation of economic and social life that took place in rich countries in the late nineteenth and early twentieth centuries. At the heart of this transformation was the emergence of giant firms that possessed characteristics departing significantly from their First Industrial Revolution progenitors. The new firms were seen to be the quintessence of modernity, dealing with an unprecedented range and complexity of tasks and creating organisational structures to cope with these tasks. Capitalism in its most modern manifestation was thus seen by many observers to be dominated not by the invisible hand of the marketplace, but by entities – giant firms – that planned and directed their own futures. What was often missed in the analysis of these developments was the extent to which giant firm planning was still embedded in a capitalist world of competition and finance.

For a broad range of observers, and especially socialists, as we will see in Chapter 3, Henry Ford's assembly line and state intervention during the Great War functioned as concrete exemplifications of how a whole economy might be planned, a perspective that developed into what will be called here the technocratic planning paradigm. The future socialist society could then be seen as 'one big factory', with the path already laid out by capitalism (albeit, for Marxists, with contradictions) in its most advanced aspects. While, for the mainstream of Anglo-Saxon free-market liberalism, capitalism was still to be characterised by markets and competition, in alternative perspectives, with both socialist and non-socialist variants, a new world had emerged: small firms and competition were atavistic remnants, with finance and marketing functioning purely as wasteful activities. An economy based on scientific and engineering principles was to be created, modelled on the planning and organisation taking place within the giant firm, but without the latter's gratuitous, wasteful elements. Adherence to this planning orthodoxy came to be the defining test of radicalism in socialist ideology: those having reservations about the submission of whole economies to the Plan were evincing a form of deviationism. Socialism became married to the planning paradigm, with social democratic reforms in education and social policy, even when highly successful, bereft of a unifying conception that linked them to a developmental strategy for society.

The Soviet attempt at planning and then the debate on socialist calculation are reviewed in Chapter 4. The failure of the Soviet economic experiment was not due to historical accident or contingent events, but resulted from weaknesses inherent in the concept of central planning as it emerged from the technocratic planning paradigm. In the debate on socialist calculation, a solution to the problems of centrally planned socialism was put forth: an alternative form of socialism was created that simulated the economic behaviour of a well-functioning capitalist free market. The ultimate demise of both these attempts at socialist construction – the Soviet centrally planned alternative to capitalism and the market socialist solution of economic theory – is to be located in their inadequate conceptualisation of capitalist economic development. They both foundered on their failure to understand the roles played by competition and finance in the fostering of dynamism, economic growth and development in capitalism.

Chapter 5 traces the collapse of the planning paradigm. It notes the widespread perception in the post-Second World War period of a growing corporatism and monopoly, a notion derived from the earlier technocratic planning paradigm of Chapter 3. This perception suggested to Western socialists and social democrats that a transition from the capitalism of the day to an economy subject to rational control and planning was feasible and a natural extension of contemporary developments. But this strategy fell into disarray because the growth of sophisticated planning and coordination within individual enterprises did not make for a world of controlled, monopoly capitalism but, on the contrary, engendered an increasingly competitive atmosphere in which national strategies for a centrally directed national economy were not viable: the collapse of the Alternative Economic Strategy of the Labour Party in Britain in the 1980s is an egregious example. The demise of socialist alternatives to capitalism in rich countries can be traced to the failure of these planning strategies in their various manifestations and the absence of an alternative radical vision of the future.

A key reason for the failure of the socialist project in all its variants in the twentieth century is thus seen in Part I to be rooted in its incorrect analysis of capitalist development. But the underlying principle remains a sound one: a socialist strategy, if it is not to be utopian (in the worst sense of the word), should emerge wherever possible from the possibilities and trajectories offered up by present-day society. Part II, *Human and Economic Development*, serves as a bridge to the revised socialist strategy of Part III. It argues that education and equality are not gratuitous luxuries that societies can indulge in when they are rich enough. On the contrary, and especially in the modern world, both these factors have played a central role in human and economic progress, and their cultivation for socialist purposes is congruent with a rational strategy for economic development.

A central issue in contemporary economic and social discourse concerns the links between levels of formal education and a nation's economic growth; it has spawned a vast statistical literature, as will be seen in Chapter 6. This literature contains a range of questionable presumptions buried within the empirical procedures typically used. One problematic element is the treatment of technological change as a discontinuous event, imparting to it a magical quality that can cure a range of economic ills, as if it were an elixir. Technological change, in both its genesis and its diffusion, is, in fact, a social process: the boundary between innovation and improvement is less clear than suggested by contemporary orthodoxy and the writings of Joseph Schumpeter. The review of the statistical literature is supplemented by a historical narrative that captures a range of considerations otherwise lost in discussions of this topic, including the manner in which education interacts with equality to promote economic, including technological, development. One fundamental disagreement here with the education–growth discussions typically found in both the public and academic spheres is their tendency to treat education as having value solely because of its efficacy in producing economic growth, even in the richest countries. For socialists and others wishing to show themselves to be practical and relevant in the current intellectual climate, the temptation to go along with this abnegation of the principles of human civilisation is to be resisted.

A broader vision of the role of education in society begins to be developed here and in subsequent chapters. Education is embedded in society. Mainstream considerations, however, are dominated, as will be seen in Chapter 7, by the theoretical perspective of the human capital literature. This individualistic approach is of limited use in understanding the complementary role that social context (including class) plays in formal education, with household wealth, fellow students and neighbourhood impinging on the educational process. In addition, individualistic approaches to the accretion of knowledge impede attempts to trace the societal impact of educational advance: the presence of external effects on learning will mean that the unfolding of the effects of enhanced education is likely to be manifest in society only with a substantial lag. By contrast, left-wing critiques have been equally inadequate, lurching from views in which education is seen to be a tool of capitalism to a range of utopian notions.

Missing from most discussions is the sense in which formal education in the modern world interacts with a broad range of other aspects of social functioning, as will be seen in Chapter 8. Classroom education is only one aspect of how individuals develop: many of the most important aspects of learning take place at work and in the process of living in society. Traditionally, individuals working and living in rich countries have been able to gain *in situ* advantages over others simply on this basis; there are good reasons for thinking that these advantages are dissipating more rapidly than heretofore. Public discussions concerned with learning in the workplace – training of various kinds – underline the class divides in society: for those headed for, or at, university, the discourse will often contain at least a perfunctory consideration of the role of this education in citizenship and of the need to acquire a broad-based range of skills for a lifetime of work. For the others – the majority of the population who do not pursue university education – education for citizenship is commonly not even broached as an issue, as if such individuals did not have the voting franchise. Acquisition of skills for this group, furthermore, is frequently discussed in terms of what suits the needs of employers, an approach which can, from the point of view both of the individual worker and of society, result in the cultivation of a skill base that is dangerously narrow from the perspective of a lifetime of work. Once we view the household as the fulcrum in which individuals can formulate their plans for both formal and *in situ* learning, an atmosphere of security and stability in which to pursue these 'investments' is conducive to the promotion of economic development. By contrast, a regime of Schumpeterian creative destruction can do long-term damage to the human aspect of this development by obviating the possibility of long-term household planning.

Many of the issues discussed above concerning public education, technological change and the role of the state can be exemplified in a US context. Chapter 9 contrasts the commonly held image (and self-image) of the US as a bastion of free enterprise with the key roles that were played by the state in the twentieth century in public education, technological advance and industrial enterprise. The mystique surrounding technological advance is contrasted with the substantive social context in which innovation has taken place in the US, with the development of the electronics industry used as an exemplification. The continuing and pervasive role that the US plays at both the academic and the popular level as the purveyor of doctrines of free enterprise worldwide often seems to have more to do with perpetuating this self-image than reflecting the historical realities that resulted in US economic ascendency in the twentieth century.

The long-term role of the US as a model of a successful economy is closely linked to its high levels of per capita income. The approach taken in Chapter 10 to national income and its growth is to disentangle its diverse aspects. First, as a measure of aggregate demand, it is used as a tool for economic stabilisation. In this role, the regulation of national income and its growth is a pressing consideration for dealing with unemployment and inflation. Second, national income in per capita form often serves as an index of social welfare. Its single-minded use for this purpose has long been criticised in the literature concerned with the economic development of poorer countries and, more recently, in the context of the dramatic increases in inequality that have taken place in many parts of the world. The primary focus here, however, is upon a third use of national income: it functions as an indication of a society's overall economic capacity to make social choices, with economic growth as a mechanism for expanding these choices. A misplaced emphasis on the conventional growth measure can lead to inappropriate, myopic social decisions, since some of the most potent ways of accelerating economic development in the long term, such as educational improvement, will yield their most significant benefits only with substantial lags. Typical approaches to economic growth also frequently pose a false choice between economic growth and equality, or see growing economic inequality as unfortunate merely from a welfare perspective. The alternative view offered here emphasises the role that inequality plays in limiting the ability of a society to make social choices: long-term growth in society's human capacity is thwarted when substantial sections of the population are subject to social and economic exclusion, while growing insecurity makes rational planning at the level of the household an impossibility. From a more positive perspective, economic equality and household security complement formal education programmes in the promotion of human and economic development.

In Part III, *Socialism and Human Possibilities*, a socialist agenda is presented focusing on human development, equality and democratic control, the latter functioning both in a traditional political context and at ground level, including the workplace. Strategies to fulfil this agenda emerge from the realities of present-day society and use, wherever possible, existing social and political mechanisms to facilitate reform.

Formal education is seen in Chapter 11 to be central both to human liberation and to the functioning of a democratic polity. The parameters of a socialist education programme for engendering an environment of genuine equal opportunity do not have to be plucked out of the air: they can be approximated from the resources that elite families devote to their children from birth, both in the household itself and in the context of the formal educational opportunities offered to these children. Such an approach is contrasted with the fatalism of the IQ literature, much of which posits a resigned acceptance to existing social and economic hierarchies based on pre-natal inheritance. In the fifth century, this fatalism and resignation had been linked by St Augustine to original sin; in the modern world, it is biology that predetermines one's fate. Both these approaches evince a distrust in the ability of social and political action to remake the world for the better, and thus stand in sharp contrast to the fundamental presumptions of socialist ideology and to a substantial scientific and empirical literature that finds no place for such fatalism.

Chapter 12 links the formal educational strategy of Chapter 11 with one that supports learning in the broader world and at work through the promotion of equality, household security and full employment. The pursuit of these economic goals complements strategies for the extension of democratic control in the broader society and at work. In all these contexts, difficult issues need to be resolved. What kind of measures can be taken in the domain of governmental activity and taxation to reverse the egregious levels of income and wealth inequality that have emerged in many countries? And how can full employment be secured in an economy that retains a substantial amount of decentralised economic activity and an active financial sector? How much worker control over enterprise decision making can take place without impinging on the fulfilment of goals for the economy and society as a whole? These and other issues will be confronted here, even if not fully resolved: the anchor and unifying aspect of all queries, however, is the focus on socialism as human development, equality and democratic control.

* * *

These central aspects of a socialist perspective – human development and education, equality and economic security, and democracy – coalesce when an important contemporary issue of public policy is considered: climate change. In discussions of this question, the public is often viewed as a recalcitrant, wild beast that must be manipulated in the right direction for its own good. Why, however, do I have every certainty that the overwhelming majority of readers of this book will support, and freely submit to, public policy measures that will be costly and inconvenient in the present in order to avoid a catastrophe in the future?

The facile and partly correct answer is that well-educated individuals will have an enhanced ability to follow the abstract arguments concerning the relationship between human activity, the changing climate and its likely effects on human functioning in the future. But to argue solely from the role of education in the engendering of rational approaches to public policy is to flatter the reader unduly. A component of at least equal weight is that most readers here (and certainly the author, despite his claims to origins as a working-class hero) are situated above the median level of income and are, in general, in a situation of relative economic security: whatever the disappointments or inconveniences brought about by the restrictions in consumption necessary to keep at bay, or at least slow down, climate change, I and most of my readers are in a position to make a rational calculation that such restrictions are preferable to the derailment of our lives and those of future generations that could be incumbent upon a large-scale change in the climate.

For much of contemporary society, and especially for many younger readers, policies to combat climate change might have highly unwelcome aspects: the restrictions and constraints on current consumption, and the insecurities generated by threats to current employment in activities linked to pollution, could be seen to threaten disruption of current modes of living not in the future, but in the present. Notions from well-heeled experts and politicians that 'we are all in it together' sit poorly when the likely sacrifices necessary for dealing with climate change will be distributed in a gravely uneven manner. The prerequisites for a rational, democratic public response to this impending, or even unfolding, crisis in the natural world are, therefore, not only a substantial rise in the knowledge base of the general population, but also the engendering of a sense of economic security and a presumption that the necessary sacrifices will be shared equally. A socialism concerned with human development and education, equality and economic security thus converges with the requisites of democracy and, perhaps, human survival.

The Conclusion responds to the question – 'why call it socialism'? It also discusses the reasons for the focus here on the socialist destiny of rich countries, despite the ultimate centrality for the future of humankind of the trajectory of development of 'the rest' – the poor nations of the world. It advances upon the proposition of Albert Einstein that 'the real purpose of socialism is precisely to overcome and advance beyond the predatory phase of human development'.[2]

Part I
Socialism and Central Planning

Introduction

Why did all attempts to build a socialist alternative to capitalism in the twentieth century fail? An extensive answer to this question will embrace a large number of considerations, but a blunt summary in a British context would be as follows: 'Much of the Left's energy has been dissipated by industrial experiments in planning ... it seems indisputable now that had the 1945 Labour government concentrated on rewriting the 1944 Education Act and reconstructing the university system, a genuine and lasting transformation of the society may well have been possible'.[1]

Perhaps the reader will find these words naïve: do they not merely substitute 'education' for 'planning' as a *deus ex machina* that will solve or obviate the complex problems of social transformation? The point, as we shall see, is well taken. In rich societies, a successful educational programme is the most powerful single public policy intervention for the promotion of equality and democracy. But the societal context in which formal education takes place is crucial, with high levels of social and economic equality helping to engender a flourishing environment for learning. In addition, learning, broadly conceived, will be seen in Parts II and III to encompass a range of experiences from birth, many of which take place outside the domain of formal education. These experiences emerge from living and interacting in the world, within the family and at work. An environment offering broad-based opportunities for learning in these contexts can be important in itself and complement the provision of formal education. A good system of formal education is, therefore, no replacement for the promotion of equality and opportunity in the living and work environment.

The quotation above was not presented to initiate a debate on the efficacy of any specific act of nationalisation, but as a vehicle for questioning why educational reform and human development played such a peripheral role in schemes for socialist transformation over the twentieth and twenty-first centuries. A significant part of the explanation can be found in socialist

15

ideologies in their dominant manifestations, Marxist and otherwise: education and human development were seen as merely part of the superstructure of a society, an aspect of social welfare provision and a secondary issue, one to be delegated to women. The primary concerns and defining questions for socialists focused on the substructure of the society: who owns the means of production, and how are societal resources allocated and distributed – by a market mechanism or by a central plan? The embrace of planning by socialist organisations worldwide was not an accidental or even a contingent event: the role of planning as an ideology and as a solution to society's ills was pervasive, not only for socialists but across the spectrum of political views from left to right, for much of the twentieth century.

It is socialism, however, that has maintained the strongest, almost tautological identification with planning in its various manifestations, but most especially with central planning. Socialism has suffered from a collapse of faith because it finds itself associated with this decrepit ideology. The high tide of free-market liberalism may have receded in recent years, but liberalism (often disguising a social Darwinist agenda) continues to present a coherent vision of the future that is unmatched by any existing socialist alternative.

1
Planning and Spontaneous Order

Two grand conceptions have emerged in Europe on how to organise society on a secular basis. In the early modern period, a conscious moulding of society and its institutions was seen as a logical extrapolation from the way rational human beings ordered their lives. In a later view, society was seen to behave as a natural system capable of self-regulation. In this chapter, these approaches – planning and its antipode, spontaneous order – will first be introduced. The remaining sections and much of the discussion in Part I will address the false presumption that these two notions are not only competing, but mutually incompatible.

Planning as an aspect of rationality

For Karl Marx, the ability of the human being to envision, organise and plan activities is a characteristic and distinctive property of the species to which it belongs:

> We presuppose labour in a form in which it is an exclusively human characteristic. A spider conducts operations which resemble those of the weaver, and the bee would put many a human architect to shame by the construction of its honeycomb cells. But what distinguishes the worst architect from the best of bees is that the architect builds the cell in his mind before he constructs it in wax. At the end of every labour process, a result emerges which had already been conceived by the worker at the beginning, hence already existing ideally. Man not only effects a change of form in the materials of nature; he also realizes his own purpose in those materials. And this is a purpose he is conscious of.[1]

This link between human rationality and planning had, however, already been formulated at the dawn of the Enlightenment in the seventeenth century. René Descartes' reflections in the *Discourse on Method* (1637) on how to reconstruct philosophy on a secure, rational basis were supported by analogy with the purposeful activity of the architect and the town planner:

> buildings undertaken and completed by a single architect are commonly more beautiful and better ordered than those that several architects have tried to patch up, using old walls that had been built for other purposes... ancient cities... are commonly quite poorly laid out compared to well-ordered towns that an engineer lays out on a vacant plain as it suits his fancy... [While] one does not see people pulling down all the houses in a city simply to rebuild them some other way... one does see that several people do tear down their own houses in order to rebuild them... Taking this example to heart... I could not do better than to try once and for all to get all the beliefs I had accepted from birth out of my mind, so that once I have reconciled them with reason I might again set up either other, better ones or even the same ones.[2]

The correct approach for Descartes, one that accords with reason, is congruent with planned, purposeful behaviour. It may well involve reconstruction *de novo*, as if 'on a vacant plain'.

The link in Western intellectual development between rational thought and the need for reconstruction *de novo* had been present at least as early as the late Renaissance, most prominently in a polemical context by Francis Bacon in his *Novum Organum* (*New Method*) of 1620. The stupendous and substantive achievements in natural philosophy (what we would now call the sciences) of the Enlightenment that followed were invariably characterised by a willingness to begin again, exemplified by the rejection of Aristotle's physics and Ptolemy's astronomy by Galileo. Cartesian philosophy emerged in the context of these scientific accomplishments (including those of Descartes himself); Descartes' implied dismissal of tradition in favour of reason accounts for his perpetual difficulties with political, and especially church, authorities, despite his protestations of adherence to the Catholic faith. In the eighteenth century, Enlightenment rejection of the edifying role of tradition in politics – of traditional institutions, modes of thought and practice – reached a consummation in the English-speaking world with Thomas Paine's *Rights of Man* (1791), written as a riposte to Edmund Burke's *Reflections on the Revolution in France* (1790). Britain emerges in this period, with David Hume and others, as the most articulate opponent of radical critiques of the established order and defender of existing political and legal institutions and social practices.[3]

Descartes' formulation of the link between rational thought, on the one hand, and the need for reconsideration and reconstruction of the foundations of all aspects of intellectual and practical activity, on the other, is the culmination and most articulate expression of the convulsion in Western thought that took place in the early modern period. Subsequently, in the wake of the French Revolution, applications of this Cartesian programme in the context of practical affairs represent early instances of a notion of *planification*: we see efforts to reform – to place in a proper, rational order and impose uniformity upon a range of social mechanisms that had emerged historically – weights and measures, the calendar and the law. These alterations to traditional practices imposed by the French Revolution played important roles in the promotion of capitalist development and were highly contested.[4] As in other cases to be discussed below, these changes, which permitted the expansion and deepening of markets, often took place in the wake of conscious administrative reform rather than as emanations of a spontaneous order. While the charming reforms to the calendar (with a month beginning in the latter part of April named *Floréal*) proved to be short-lived, juridical reforms imposed by the Revolution, such as the imposition of the civil legal code and the abolition of the remnants of feudalism, stimulated nineteenth-century continental economic development.[5]

Conceptions of planning – redesigning *de novo* in the social sphere and intervention in the traditional order of society, especially by the state – entered a new phase in the nineteenth century. Their most prominent advocates were not to be found in the early working-class movements, such as the Chartists in England, or among radicals on the European continent, such as Pierre-Joseph Proudhon or even Karl Marx and Friedrich Engels at the time of the Communist Manifesto (1847–8). Rather, it was Henri de Saint-Simon (1760–1825) and his disciples who, imbued with the successes of the pure and applied sciences of their day, were eager to partake in a social engineering of society with the intention of increasing society's productivity. In the France of the 1820s and 1830s, the role of Saint-Simonian ideology among engineers was a pervasive one.[6]

The Saint-Simonians came to be seen in retrospect as the chief progenitors of schemes for a planned economy. But, despite the fanciful aspects and the inflated language accompanying their ideas, Saint-Simonian notions of planning barely hint at the designs for controlling the economy that we will see materialise in the twentieth century in the form of technocratic central planning. Their concept of planning was firmly rooted in the nineteenth century, with a focus on an elite, meritocratic direction of society by the intellectual and productive classes, including industrialists and bankers. As in the case of the political economy of David Ricardo in England in the early nineteenth century, their enmity was directed at those idle groups, largely the landed classes, who stood in the path of the emerging industrial economy. Even when it developed a redistributionist tendency in the form of the advocacy of the abolition of inheritance, the Saint-Simonian movement was motivated more by a desire to promote the productive use of society's resources than by a reformation of the class structure and property relations in society: '[We] Saint-Simonians are opposed to the institution of private property simply because it inculcates habits of idleness and fosters a practice of living upon the labour of others.'[7]

From our current perspective, it would seem inappropriate to label Saint-Simonian ideas for intervention in the economy as either utopian or revolutionary. Stripped of rhetorical flourishes, the central notion involved banking sector coordination between (and within) industrial groupings, with the intention of providing inexpensive finance to firms. These ideas were to be reflected in the development of industrial banking in France in the form of the *Crédit Mobilier* and, even more importantly, in the industrial banks of nineteenth-century Germany.[8] Subsequently, these banks would play an important role in late-developing countries wishing to promote economic development.[9]

Saint-Simonian proposals for a rationalisation of industry deviated from the developmental nature of the overall strategy. Their purpose was to avoid the excesses that can emerge from the market economy – an anti-social depression of wages or the generation of industrial crises from overcapacity. But these policies, far from being an augury of socialist notions, were a manifestation of a defensive or even reactionary response to capitalism and its apparent destabilisation of traditional ways of life rather than a visionary, state-directed programme of economic change. The Saint-Simonians emerge less as the progenitors of twentieth-century technocracy, central planning and socialism than as an ideological antipode to British liberal ideology in the nineteenth century.[10] Saint-Simonian projects in France, often sponsored by the state for expansion and modernisation of roads, industrial and agricultural infrastructure, and, most especially, railways, were imitated throughout late-nineteenth-century Europe. Such a conscious, planned, but limited strategy of economic development would have been thought exceptional only in Britain at the apogee of liberalism.

The Saint-Simonian movement in France had no more direct access to political power in the nineteenth century than did the early socialists, but its influence was widespread in France's industrial revolution in the period up to the end of the Second Empire.[11] A striking example of *planification* in this period took place under that 'Saint-Simonian on horseback'[12] Napoleon III and his prefect Georges-Eugène Haussmann, who renovated Paris and made it over 'from a stinking and decrepitating rat-maze of slums into the epitome of everything we value about city life'.[13] Slums were demolished, boulevards and an integrated network of roads were created; at the height of Haussmanian activity, one in five Parisian workers was employed in construction. As we shall see, many of these reforms had contentious aspects, but those related to public health were the most indisputably beneficial: by 1869, Haussmann, beginning a process that was to continue for several decades, had constructed over 300 miles of new sewers in Paris, thereby reducing the incidence of the cholera that had literally plagued the city.[14]

At least one [British] authority downgrades the significance of these Parisian health reforms as 'much talk but little action'[15] in comparison with public action taken in Britain. But it was in Britain that ideological opposition to any form of state-directed intervention in the economy took its most articulate form, with two arguments that would resonate in the future. The first was concerned with a defence of liberty: the Medical Officer to the Privy Council, John Simon, reported on hostility to state intervention, with opponents claiming that it had 'interfered between parent and child [a reference to vaccination] between employer and employed [over sanitary measures in factories] and between vendor and purchaser [referring to legislation governing the quality of water and the adulteration of food]'.[16] For Herbert Spencer, a thinker admired by Hayek, 'The doctrine that it is the duty of the state to protect the public health... rests upon the assumption, that men are not fit to take care of themselves.'[17]

The second argument against intervention was that it interfered with nature, or with natural mechanisms for resolving problems: *The Times* reminded us in 1848 that 'the Cholera is the best of all sanitary reformers', and in 1852, at a meeting of the Institution of Civil Engineers, one advocate informed his audience that the role assigned to sewers 'should be left to nature'.[18] For Spencer, society itself was a natural phenomenon: 'Society, a living, growing organism, placed within the apparatuses of dead, rigid, mechanical formulas, cannot fail to be hampered and pinched.' Through the natural evolution of this living organism, 'existing social needs will be spontaneously met, though we cannot say how they will be met'; interference by the state would result in unintended consequences: '[Boards of Health] have, in sundry cases, exacerbated the evils to be removed; as, for instance, at Croydon, where, according to the official report, the measures of the sanitary authorities produced an epidemic, which attacked 1,600 people and killed 70... [W]hen... remedies applied by statesmen do not exacerbate the evils they were meant to cure, they constantly induce collateral evils; and these often graver than the original ones.'[19]

But such contentions – that the regulation of public health was a violation of natural liberty and that epidemics were natural remedies – progressively ceased to have an audience. In 1892, the last great cholera epidemic in the cities of Western Europe took place in Hamburg and killed 10,000 people: it was linked in the public's mind to that city's distinctively 'English', liberal tradition.[20] Public health measures, usually state-sanctioned and often in the context of urban planning, led to a decisive improvement in the health and longevity of the populations of rich countries from the mid-nineteenth century onwards. It was not until the availability of antibiotics in the mid-twentieth century that medical breakthroughs played any commensurate role in extending life span. Social and environmental planning of this kind eventually received broad-based support even in Britain. The opposition of figures such as Herbert Spencer was clearly of a rearguard nature.

Planning, broadly defined, has thus been defended as a manifestation of human rationality, a progressive development intrinsic to the Enlightenment project: structures emerging historically in a helter-skelter manner were to be reconstituted on a rational, logical basis. In the context of abstract systems, successes for the Cartesian programme of reconstruction *de novo* are evident in the emergence of sciences such as biology and physics in their modern form; practical applications of planning procedures in the Cartesian mould, such as urban planning and public health, have often extended human life and improved living conditions.

Given the extreme, and politicised, form in which the dichotomy between the market and planning is often posed, it is ironical that the implementation of explicit planning in the urban environment and in public health played a decisive role in supporting the claim that nine-teenth-century capitalism was eventually successful in improving the lives of ordinary people. Alongside the rises in real wages for the working class that emerged in this period are statistics on the health and bio-phys-iological state of this group that show much more ambiguous, and even contradictory, tendencies. It would appear that it was only as a result of substantial public investment in the latter part of the nineteenth century that the material well-being of working people achieved an unambigu-ously upward trajectory.[21]

Planning is, thus, an aspect of Enlightenment rationality and can claim indubitable achievements in the realms of science and public policy. The most grandiose expression of planning in the public realm is the utopian vision. As Zygmunt Bauman has suggested, even in this form, planning has a substantive, practical role:

> [Utopias] portray the future as a set of competing projects, and thereby reveal the role of human volition and the concerted effort in shaping and bringing it about ... It is ... the boldness of the utopian insight into the unexplored future, its ability to cut loose and be impractical, which sets the stage for a genuinely realistic politics, one which takes stock of all opportunities contained in the present.[22]

Hayek and the constructivist fallacy

We have seen that the arguments against planning enunciated in the nine-teenth century are, first, a defence of liberty – an opposition to planning as an arbitrary use of state power – and, second, an assertion that planning can interfere with nature, or (in a more subtle form) that planning prevents or interferes with natural or spontaneous mechanisms for resolving prob-lems or restoring order. Friedrich Hayek's career, spanning the greater part of the twentieth century, was devoted to an articulation and development of these two propositions. Hayek's discussion of these issues from a broad philosophical perspective will be dealt with in this chapter, with his critique of central planning to be addressed in Chapter 4.

Hayek's critique of planning, combined with a defence and conceptualisation of the market economy, is uniquely comprehensive; he was content to view his socialist colleagues as merely deluded, and dedicated his most famous book, *The Road to Serfdom*, to 'The socialists of all parties'.[23] His defence of capitalism shows the mutual interaction between the economic and legal systems of the market economy and offers an unambiguously favourable view of market societal organisation – a grand conceptualisation of capitalism as a form of spontaneously generated order. Far beyond the typical laissez-faire admonition to avoid governmental interference in the economy, Hayek's assertion of the presence of a spontaneous order in capitalism is accompanied by a celebration of its directionless character, of the inherent virtues of a society and economy without plans or goals.

Hayek's social thought centres upon a rejection of all aspects of the Cartesian programme of reconstruction *de novo*. He suggests that progress in the development of the principles of the law (or any kind of intellectual activity) takes place not by way of a reconsideration and reconstruction of foundations, but 'by our moving within an existing system of thought and endeavouring by a process of piecemeal tinkering, or "immanent criticism", to make the whole more consistent both internally as well as with the facts to which the rules are applied'.[24] Hayek here suggests a strategy of intellectual advance centred upon 'moving within an existing system of thought'; when dealing with practical issues he states that 'since we owe the order of our society to a tradition of rules which we only imperfectly understand, all progress must be based on tradition. We must build on tradition and can only tinker with its products.'[25]

These two statements together might lead one to the notion of Hayek as a conservative. In fact, the position he holds 'differs as much from true conservatism as from socialism'. As a liberal, he 'is not averse to evolution and change; and where spontaneous change has been smothered by government control, [I want] a great deal of change of policy'.[26] His vision of the good society is thus far bolder, and perhaps more peculiar, than a mere reaffirmation of the role of tradition. Rather, it consists of an assertion that the particular form of spontaneous order which has evolved in the West, most especially in Britain, is uniquely worthwhile: 'The possibility of men living together in peace and to their mutual advantage without having to agree on common concrete aims, and bound only by abstract rules of conduct, was perhaps the greatest discovery mankind ever made.'[27]

For Hayek, the source of society's most beneficial institutions, such as law and the market economy, is the interplay of social forces. The efficacy of a social order that emerges spontaneously and collectively over one imposed by one individual, or group of individuals, is due to the inherent limitations in the knowledge available to any one party: 'the concrete knowledge which guides the action of any group of people never exists as a consistent and coherent body. It only exists in the dispersed, incomplete, and inconsistent form in which it appears in many individual minds.'[28] Despite the fact that the knowledge accruing to any one individual is 'dispersed, incomplete, and inconsistent', and exists only in a specific, localised context, it is the relevant basis for the formation of rules governing a complex social order:

> appropriate rules of conduct are not derived from explicit knowledge of the concrete events we will encounter; rather, they are an adaptation to our environment, an adaptation which consists of rules we have developed and for the observance of which we will usually not be able to give adequate reasons … we can never rationally reconstruct … the whole system of rules, because we lack the knowledge of all the experiences that entered into its formation.[29]

In Hayek's view, the rules and conduct emerging from the partial and often non-explicit (tacit) and contextual knowledge of individuals operating through the spontaneous interplay of social forces will sometimes give adequate solutions to problems no individual mind could consciously solve, and 'thereby create an ordered structure which increases the power of individuals without having been designed by any one of them'.[30] The guiding force of a planner cannot serve as a substitute for this spontaneous solution because 'the knowledge which any individual mind consciously manipulates is only a small part of the knowledge which at any time contributes to the success of his action. When we reflect how much knowledge possessed by other people is an essential condition for the successful pursuit of our individual aims, the magnitude of our ignorance of the circumstances on which the results of our action depend appears simply staggering.'[31]

Thus, Hayek offers a defence for forms of governance and societal organisation linked to historically emerging traditions and traditional rules, as opposed to a constructivist approach in which rules of societal governance are consciously based on reason. The latter approach is impossible, because in the context of the inevitably limited knowledge of individuals, the kinds of traditions emerging from the spontaneous order are as good as we can do: 'The whole system of rules can therefore never be reduced to a purposive construction for known purposes, but must remain to us the inherited system of values guiding that society.'[32]

It appears, however, that it is the laws and traditions emerging from one particular society that have succeeded in forming the basis of Hayek's spontaneous order:

> The only country that succeeded in preserving the tradition of the Middle Ages and built on the medieval 'liberties' the modern conception of liberty under the law was England … The freedom of the British

which in the eighteenth century the rest of Europe came so much to admire...[was] a result of the fact that the law...was determined by courts independent of the power which organized and directed government.[33]

According to Hayek, we have emerging in England, perhaps uniquely, a system of judge and court-based case law, 'an adaptation which consists of rules we have developed and for the observance of which we will usually not be able to give adequate reasons'. But forms of law and governance from spontaneous, contextual decisions have emerged in a wide variety of cultures all over the world throughout human history. The reason for Hayek's privileging of its English manifestation appears to be its genesis in a particular set of economic formations: 'It is in the *ius gentium*, the law merchant, and the practices of the ports and fairs that we must chiefly seek the steps in the evolution of law which ultimately made an open society possible.'[34] We thus have a complete mutually reinforcing system made up of the interactive practices of free exchange, on the one hand, and context-based rules and juridical procedures, on the other, all combining to generate the liberal order of nineteenth-century Britain.

Hayek's fundamental principle is that individuals have, and invariably will have, only limited, partial knowledge and understanding of the social context and processes in which they are functioning. What emerges from this premise is Hayek's famous notion of unintended consequences, which has a dual aspect – a positive perspective, which suggests that, even in the context of such limited knowledge, a spontaneous social order might well emerge, without any design or intention of generating this order on the part of an individual or group of individuals; a negative aspect emphasises the inevitable failure of conscious, constructivist (planned) activity – broad-based social planning – due precisely to this lack of knowledge of the consequences of actions undertaken by individuals or groups desirous of acting as potential planners. Hayek's notion of limited knowledge acts as scissors to cut through the concept of social planning – one blade functions as an alternative perspective on how society can be organised in the presence of limited knowledge through a self-generating mechanism, and the other is a critique in general terms of the infeasibility of planning due to the planner's inevitably limited knowledge.

A consequence of the presence of limited knowledge on the part of any one individual or group of individuals is that, for society as a whole, an absence of goals, ends or direction is a virtue: 'it is thus due to the freedom of choosing the ends of one's activities that the utilization of the knowledge dispersed through society is achieved...The idea that the government can determine the opportunities for all, and especially that it can ensure that they are the same for all, is therefore in conflict with the whole rationale of a free society.' Indeed, 'the organization of society for a common purpose, which is fundamental to all socialist systems, is incompatible with individual freedom'.[35]

Hayek saw the battle for the legitimation of the spontaneously generated order as a conflict between philosophical approaches: 'scientistic philosophy...has done more to create the present trend toward socialism than all the conflicts between economic interests'.[36] The philosophical origins of his 'evolutionary approach' (Hayek's words) were in the eighteenth-century school of Scottish moral philosophers, including Adam Smith, who perceived the possibility of 'the formation of regular patterns in human relations that were not the conscious aim of human actions'.[37] By contrast, it was Descartes' successor Spinoza who most clearly articulated a rejection of the rules of morals and law grounded in tradition in so far as they could not be rationally justified.[38] Overall, however, it is Descartes and his constructivist fallacy that remain the central opponent:

> Since for Descartes reason was defined as logical deduction from explicit premises, rational action also came to mean only such action as was determined entirely by known and demonstrable truth... Institutions and practices which have not been designed in this manner can be beneficial only by accident. Such became the characteristic attitude of Cartesian constructivism with its contempt for tradition, custom and history in general... Yet the basic assumption underlying the belief that man has achieved mastery of his surroundings mainly through his capacity for logical deduction from explicit premises is factually false... Many of the institutions of society which are indispensable conditions for the successful pursuit of our conscious aims are in fact the result of customs, habits or practices which have been neither invented nor are observed with any such purpose in view. We live in a society in which we can successfully orientate ourselves, and in which our actions have a good chance of achieving their aims, not only because our fellows are governed by known aims or known connections between means and ends, but because they are also confined by rules whose purpose or origin we often do not know and of whose very existence we are often not aware.[39]

Hayek's discussion of later writers adds little to his general critique of planning centred around the Cartesian constructivist fallacy. According to him, the philosophers Georg Wilhelm Friedrich Hegel and Auguste Comte, with their focus on the movement of Reason, failed to achieve an understanding of 'the process through which the interaction of individuals produced structures of relationships which performed actions no individual reason could fully comprehend',[40] while the concept of central economic planning, which Hayek associated with Saint-Simon and his disciples, along with Comte, was 'based on the assumption that...a complete concentration of all relevant knowledge [in one place] is possible',[41] a critique we have met above. In the latter quotation, we see a rare reference by Hayek to Marx in a footnote, associating him with these Saint-Simonian doctrines.

Hayek thus offers a comprehensive critique of planning linked to the inherent limitations on the knowledge available to any one individual. In Hayek's critique of Cartesian constructivism, accretions to human knowledge come about not from a reconsideration *de novo* of foundational principles – intellectual revolutions – but by additions to the stock of existing explicit and implicit knowledge. This knowledge is widely dispersed throughout the community and is inaccessible to any one individual who might wish to pose as a societal planner. Advances, both intellectual and practical, inevitably take place in an incremental manner; a rational plan is impossible due to inherent limitations of knowledge available to the planner.

Of equal or greater significance, Hayek develops an alternative vision of societal organisation based on a spontaneously generated order not only of the economic system, but of its juridical foundations as well. Hayek's writings deal in great detail with the economic aspects of this spontaneous order, including the considerations surrounding the nature of competition, the theory of capital, the financial system and macroeconomic regulation. In his later years, his desire to round off his notion of an economy based on spontaneous order led him to advocate what were, in the context of twentieth-century institutions, radical changes, such as the introduction of a currency system based on private issuance.[42]

The juridical aspect of the spontaneous order is an important complement to Hayek's economic analysis. In the economic orthodoxy emerging after the Second World War, the outcomes emerging from a rigorous mathematical representation of a competitive market economy were seen to be optimally efficient, in the sense that no deviations from this competitive equilibrium were possible that would not be to the detriment of at least some individuals (this notion is known to economists as Pareto optimality). But this formal result is, in an important way, indeterminate, since the initial distribution of resources (including property) between individuals is taken as given: it will have to be determined exogenously – by some process outside of the economic system itself.[43] The distribution of resources and its associated legal apparatus were thus seen in this context as an outside, even arbitrary appendage to the economic system: there was nothing internal to the analysis (and by implication nothing inherent in capitalist society) to give legitimacy to the existent distribution of resources in society.

It has been common in the mainstream of economics to suggest that this element – the distribution of resources – could be separately determined by a (presumptively democratic) decision process in, perhaps, an egalitarian direction, while retaining the efficiency aspects of a market economy. Though problems arose even at a purely analytical level concerning whether these democratic decisions could be generated in a consistent way,[44] the issue of the 'initial' distribution of resources was on the table in mainstream economics: it could be subject to a social, that is to say, a political decision-making process without interfering with the efficiency characteristics associated with a market economy.

Hayek had a more principled view of these issues. He saw the legal system as an aspect of the spontaneous order that proceeds co-extensively (perhaps, one might say, dialectically) with a market economy – its structure of legal precedents emerges in a context of market exchange, and market exchange itself is encouraged by this form of legal environment. Thus, Hayek viewed the sphere of economic relations in capitalism and its legal system as inextricable, rather than separable, aspects of capitalism: they evolve together as part of a spontaneous process. His conceptualisation did not give an explicit justification for the existing distribution of resources, but, by implication, this distribution was legitimate because of the organic, necessary and interactive relationship between the juridical and economic aspects of the evolution of the market economy. The unification of these economic and juridical aspects in Hayek's social philosophy is supremely ambitious. Both these components interactively emerge as necessary aspects of an unplanned and natural historical process, one that makes efficacious, even optimal, use of human activity in a social setting, all the while taking into consideration the inherent cognitive limitations of *Homo sapiens*.

Hayek thus offers a defence of capitalism as comprehensive as Marx's critique of this mode of production. His seemingly rarefied discussion of the spontaneous order, making a virtue of aimlessness and lack of direction, has often had the effect of obliging progressive and social democratic approaches to public policy to be pursued in a defensive manner, under the guise of pragmatism and practicality. The only exception to this rule – the only class of goal-directed, consistent measures that, in the contemporary world, invariably escape the critique of being part of Hayek's 'fatal conceit' of attempting to plan – are free-market measures by right-wing governments designed, supposedly, to reinforce a pre-existing spontaneous order.[45] In the contemporary world, this form of state action has migrated in liberal ideology from an exceptional event to a norm of behaviour under the guise of neoliberalism, as we shall see in Chapter 3.

Social outcomes without planning?

The range of the issues surrounding Hayek's spontaneous order and the concept of planning can be sampled by returning to Descartes' substantive example – the organisation of a city. As we have seen, the city is an instance where planning has scored indubitable successes, but it is also where failure abounds.

Critics of city planning often view it as an aspect of state control and coercion: 'many state activities aim at transforming the population, space, and nature under their jurisdiction into the closed systems that offer no surprises and that can best be observed and controlled'. Haussmann's transformation of Paris, it has been argued, was primarily concerned with facilitating the repression of insurrections and 'could have been accomplished only by a single executive authority not directly accountable to the electorate'.[46] In this case (as in the renovations carried out by the city planner Robert Moses in New York City a century later), those displaced by the demolitions (invariably poor people) were not rehoused, and the delineation of the city into regions denoting class and levels of sanitation was exacerbated.[47]

In general, the legibility and uniformity emerging from the plan create the possibility that destructive forms of social engineering can take place, often with ruinous consequences to the natural environment.[48] When plans are executed by an authoritarian state and in the context of an incapacitated civil society, we can observe urban catastrophes such as the communist dictator Nicolae Ceauşescu's demolition and reconstruction of the centre of Bucharest in the 1980s.[49]

Even in instances less extreme than that of Ceauşescu's Romania, planning and the opportunity to reconstruct a city *de novo* can give an outlet to whimsical schemes and a warped imagination. For James Kunstler, the architect Le Corbusier was 'the Franco-Swiss avant-garde guru-fraud from the 1920s', whose *Plan Voisin* was a proposal 'to demolish a big hunk of Paris and replace it with *Towers in a Park* connected by freeways.... The [*Plan Voisin*] was the most conspicuous failure of all branches of modernism, be it in the arts, the practical professions, or social science.'[50] In Le Corbusier's plans for Paris and other cities, 'No compromise is made with the pre-existing city; the new cityscape completely supplants its predecessor... None of the plans makes any reference to the urban history, traditions, or aesthetic tastes of the place in which it is to be located. The cities depicted, however striking, betray no context; in their neutrality, they could be anywhere at all.'[51]

Le Corbusier is now, quite rightly, the *bête noire* of opponents of *planification* in the urban sphere, the most articulate of whom was Jane Jacobs, most notably in her book of 1961, *The Death and Life of Great American Cities*. A substantive focal point was her battle in New York City with Le Corbusier's brutal acolyte Robert Moses over the construction of a Lower Manhattan Expressway, which would have disembowelled several vibrant urban neighbourhoods. In contrast to the Le Corbusier dictum – 'The Plan: Dictator' – she put forth a naturalistic view of the city as a social organism: 'most city diversity is the creation of incredible numbers of different people and different private organizations, with vastly different ideas and purposes, planning and contriving outside the formal framework of public action... Cities have the capability of providing something for everybody, only because and only when, they are created for everybody.'[52] Although Jacobs herself was opposed to planning philosophies she regarded as anti-urban, she advocated state action and planning restrictions to promote the mixed uses of neighbourhoods that engendered vitality, and to deter the self-destruction of neighbourhoods that success and specialisation could naturally engender.[53] Nevertheless, Jacobs' vision of something resembling a spontaneous social order in an urban context has made her a favourite of the followers of Hayek; she was even cited by him late in his career.[54]

But class and power relations are central to the evolution of cities, and will colour our evaluation of both state planning and market activity in this context. The failures of state action in the sphere of urban planning observed by Jacobs in the 1960s were in part due to the internalisation by planners of the absurd notions of Le Corbusier, but were also a reflection of the class and racial tensions present in society, so that 'private enterprise – acting through the well-heeled builder and realtor lobby in Washington – [was] responsible for some of the more obnoxious features of the urban-renewal laws and for hamstringing public housing'.[55] State planning of the urban environment was involved in the dispossession and destruction of viable neighbourhoods and the construction of public housing monstrosities (I grew up in one of the more creditable examples in the borough of Queens in New York City). Much of this public housing was such a failure not because 'planning' interfered with some natural evolution emanating from a spontaneous order, and not wholly because of the intrinsic and inevitable failures of state action in this sphere, but, to a large extent, because the state was responding compliantly to the class pressures to which it was subject.

Hayek's approach to the urban question contained an unsurprising opposition to rent controls, but otherwise refrained from treating urban affairs solely in the context of his notion of spontaneous order. For Hayek, 'Civilization as we know it is inseparable from urban life.' It is an environment in which the 'close contiguity of life' and the resultant neighbourhood effects invalidate the assumptions underlying any simple division of property rights.[56] The price mechanism, therefore, 'reflects only imperfectly the benefit or harm to others that a property owner may cause by his actions... The value of any piece of property will be affected by the manner in which the neighbours use theirs and even more by the services provided and the regulations enforced by the authorities.'[57] Hayek appears to accept a Pigovian (after the early-twentieth-century economist Arthur Cecil Pigou) approach to the urban environment, in which the presence of external (or neighbourhood) effects is commonly used as a justification for state intervention.

Others have attempted to be more Hayekian than Hayek himself – to suggest that, even with the inevitable presence of these external effects in the context of the urban environment, a viable free-market resolution will emerge without the need for intervention by the state (except, of course, to guarantee and enforce rights to private property). A key resource in this regard has been an article by Ronald Coase in 1960:[58] apart from situations in which the presence of transactions costs plays a significant role in limiting negotiations between contesting groups (for instance, between a polluting factory and a widely dispersed public), there is no need for government intervention to guarantee an efficient economic outcome, even when external effects are present. Thus, in his famous example, a conflict between a rancher whose wandering cattle are damaging a contiguous grain-producing farm will resolve itself in an economically efficient manner: either the cattle rancher will pay damages to the farmer or, contrarily, the farmer will be obliged to bribe the rancher *not* to damage the farm.

This result was declared 'astonishing' by the free-market economist George Stigler, and has been used by others (often citing Jane Jacobs in the process) to declare that zoning and town planning in their various manifestations are undesirable:[59] a marketplace, unplanned solution emerges even in the presence of external effects. Pursuing the Coasian parable in the urban context, let us postulate a situation in which the affluent have developed a fashion for locations in the heart of the city, but that expansion beyond the present choice sites (for instance, in central Manhattan) and into contiguous areas has been inhibited by the presence (in the eyes of the rich) of negative external effects associated with existing poor tenants housed in these inner-city areas. Haussmann or Robert Moses-like expulsions by the state of these inner-city tenants to alleviate this situation may not take place for political reasons. A comparable result without any state intervention, however, emerges in the form of gentrification, whereby the landlords of existing poor tenants are 'bribed' to alleviate the negative external effects: the landlords' properties are purchased and their tenants expelled.

We thus have a Pareto-efficient solution in which slum landlords are made better off, because their properties are purchased at a premium, and affluent residents are no worse off, since the premium they pay for purchasing the slum dwellings is less than the increase in the value of their property. The market thus yields a solution to the issue of urban living and its associated external effects without state planning or intervention – the poor depart from the choicest inner-city areas. But, like all market solutions, it is one mediated by the income and wealth possessed by individuals. It is questionable whether such an outcome can be interpreted as a neutral, natural one emerging from a process of voluntary exchange, but for free-market advocates, the logical possibility of such a result is important, because it suggests that even in the urban context, where external effects are present, the marketplace yields an autonomous outcome, to the benefit of all decision makers (that is, property owners) without the encumbrance of planning.

Or does it?

The evocation of notions of spontaneous social order in the urban context suggests that decisions concerning the planning of a city can be avoided in favour of a decentralised popular mandate emerging from a spontaneous, market-like mechanism. But this is a myth. Fundamental to the urban designs of Le Corbusier and Robert Moses was the accommodation of the urban setting to the free flow of private cars, inevitably a low-density, Los Angeles vision of the city. Such a vision is ultimately incompatible with an environment in which the population has pedestrian and public transport access on a daily basis to shopping and service activities, and the rich level of social interaction envisioned by Jacobs. Her vision of forms of decentralised 'planning and contriving outside the formal framework of public action'[60] is a compelling one, but is no substitute for winning the battle of The Plan – what are the fundamental premises upon which the city is to be organised? The widening of streets and the lowering of population densities required by the vision of a city responsive to the needs of the car dictate that the resulting urban environment will treat the requirements of pedestrians and users of public transport as peripheral; by contrast, an environment of narrow streets and high-density living will be inconvenient and even dysfunctional for the car user. Choices – social decisions – will have to be made between alternative visions of the city, and these different visions are likely to be irreconcilable. These decisions cannot be avoided by evoking the presence of either a Hayekian spontaneous social order or a Coasian transactions-based equilibrium that will obviate the need to make these choices.

Spontaneity and planning

The notion that human society can function and evolve most fruitfully in the context of an unplanned environment that manages to coordinate and order itself in a spontaneous fashion – in the manner of a natural system – is a powerful one. It has even more force when this spontaneous order is identified with a real historical development – the array of economic and juridical institutions emerging in Britain from the Middle Ages.

This view of capitalism and capitalist history has been sharply contested. The list of reservations is well known: the evolution of the market and juridical environment has been mediated through class and power relations, manifested not merely through voluntary exchange, but through coercion and civil conflict. In England, the confiscation of the monasteries, the Enclosure Acts and the Civil War are often taken as emblematic examples of the importance of state power in the securing of the well-defined property rights so central to the emergence of a market economy. The growth of institutions supporting these property rights and the relative power of the merchant class in state decision making were substantially reinforced by the expansion of the Atlantic trade, a process deeply embedded with colonialism and slavery and thus not easily identified with Hayek's picture of trade as spontaneous and voluntary association.[61]

Hayek is correct to identify judge-based, common-law legal systems as particularly favourable to entrepreneurial and commercial interests.[62] But, as the perspicacious social theorist Karl Polanyi has pointed out, this is not invariably the case, so that different aspects of the spontaneous order may not be convergent: the judge-based law so prized by Hayek was used, on occasion, to support the victims of the emergent market economy,[63] so that, at times, a conflict may emerge between Hayek's support of the common law on a procedural basis and the failure of its judge-based actions to yield what he would consider the appropriate outcomes in terms of capitalist evolution.

For both Polanyi and Marx, the system of capitalism is inherently revolutionary and, for better or worse, a destroyer of tradition, so that neither Polanyi nor Marx ever referred to enemies on the right as conservative. Polanyi gives a picture of capitalism as a radical regime that has to be imposed by state action under the guise of laissez-faire, while much state action is seen by him to be a conservative, protective and spontaneous response attempting to regulate these developments:

> Administrators had to be constantly on the watch to ensure the free working of the system. Thus even those who wished most ardently to free the state from all unnecessary duties, and whose whole philosophy demanded the restriction of state activities, could but entrust the self-same state with the new powers, organs, and instruments required for the establishment of laissez-faire. This paradox was topped by another. While laissez-faire economy was the product of deliberate state action, subsequent restrictions on laissez-faire started in a spontaneous way. Laissez-faire was planned; planning was not.[64]

While many supporters of free-market policies have long admitted the need for active intervention on the part of the state to make such markets viable,[65] a focus on this fact can vitiate the polemical power behind the notion of markets as natural, spontaneous processes. In reality, market outcomes are dictated not just by individual preferences but by income, and what appear juridically as voluntary acts taking place in the context of market exchange (such as the departure from a residence by a poor person in the process of gentrification) may, in substance, be the equivalent of a state-induced expulsion. In the famous words of Anatole France, the law, in its majestic equality, forbids the rich as well as the poor to sleep under bridges, to beg in the streets and to steal bread.

And buried within the abstract prose and the grand vision of Hayek's spontaneous order is a set of concrete, and highly contentious, empirical propositions about capitalism and its history – that economic growth in capitalism has proceeded by yielding something approximating Pareto improvements in the population as a whole (and thus with minimal victimisation of any segment of the population), and that attempts through collective action to promote economic equality have invariably engendered stagnation.[66] By contrast, the Enlightenment principle of planning as an inherent aspect of human rationality has often been verified historically. In the nineteenth century, planned and coordinated interventions by the state in market economies can claim substantive accomplishments in areas such as public health. The claims by critics such as Herbert Spencer of the invariant failure of government intervention have not materialised.

Particularly threatening to the notion of the universal efficacy, or even existence, of a spontaneous order in the context of capitalist society is the important role that conscious planning and coordination has played, and inevitably plays, in the creation of markets themselves. Thus, the market for grain centred on Chicago, the quintessence of the economist's perfectly competitive market, came about when railroads interacted with the newly invented steam-driven grain elevators to generate substantial economies in the handling of grain. But these economies could be realised only when bushels of wheat ceased to be identified with individual farmers and were merged with those of others to become the economics textbook homogeneous product – wheat of a given quality grade. The grading, measurement and inspection necessary to make these developments work efficaciously only came about with the passage of a law in Illinois in 1859 giving the Chicago Board of Trade the legal capacity to administer and adjudicate these matters: the spontaneous factors effecting an expansion of the market for grain only fully emerged when they interacted with administered, conscious coordination underwritten by the state.[67]

Similar actions promoting the creation and expansion of markets have been undertaken by the state in substantively all capitalist economies, not necessarily because of any attachment to a constructivist ideology, but because, in late-developing societies most especially, there is often no other agency to do so. If, as we shall see in subsequent chapters, agency, conscious planning and the state have played central roles in the emergence and development of capitalism, Hayek's spontaneous order may appear to be more a utopian construction than a generalised description of historical reality.

And it is essential for Hayek that capitalism can be viewed as a system operating without agency if the constructivist fallacy of social justice is to be swept away: 'Since only situations which have been created by human will can be called just or unjust, the particulars of a spontaneous order cannot be just or unjust if it is not the intended or foreseen result of somebody's action…what is called "social" or "distributive" justice is indeed meaningless'. Furthermore, attempts at compromise are doomed to failure: 'The current endeavour to rely on a spontaneous order corrected according to principles of justice amounts to an attempt to have the best of two worlds which are mutually incompatible.' This approach to social justice is coupled with the rejection (cited above) by Hayek of any 'organization of society for a common purpose':[68] the lack of direction of the spontaneous order is a virtue.

* * *

The Enlightenment project of planning proposed to construct a future on the basis of reason, thus linking progress and human rationality. The successes of this project in the sciences are there for all to see. In the domain of public policy, planning is sometimes contrasted with its supposed opposite, the market, as a mode for channelling the allocation of resources. But the market/plan dichotomy lacks coherence: rich markets often need careful planning if they are to emerge, while from the opposite direction, as will be seen, successful planning is not a purely abstract, a priori procedure, but is invariably the product of social interaction, often in the context of competition and market relations.

In contrast to Hayek's view of the possibility of a society in which events unfold in a natural, spontaneous way without agency, contemporary social existence is replete with situations in which explicit decisions have to be made. In the context of the role of the car in an urban environment, for instance, the possibility of a resolution by way of a laissez-faire, spontaneous result emerging from the decisions of individuals is negligible. In other cases, such as that of the raising and educating of children, a purely individualistic, household-based organisation of this activity for society is logically conceivable, but few would consider it satisfactory as a general solution in the modern world. But how to resolve the question of the role of the broader society in child rearing and education – where to settle on the spectrum of possibilities, from pure household responsibility to Spartan collectivism – and what should be the form and content of this child rearing and education? No decisions are more fundamental to the cultural and economic trajectory of society, and yet a natural, autonomous mechanism or decision rule for resolving these questions is unavailable. Explicit social choices and the setting of goals are unavoidable, and take place most desirably in the context of publicly conducted and democratically reached decisions for these fundamental aspects of societal existence. Avoidance of making these choices and the setting of goals may simply mean a continuation of an established way of doing things, which is, in fact, a form of decision.

Hayek was correct, as we shall see, about the impossibility of operating a whole economy from a central plan. He would surely agree with Jane Jacobs that 'The main responsibility of [city] planning ... should be to develop ... [the city's] great range of unofficial plans, ideas and opportunities':[69] planning is an inherent aspect of rational behaviour by individuals, and successful public policy involves creating a social context for rational action to unfold successfully.[70] For Hayek, this social context contains almost a complete absence of collective or public action; for others, this latter component is of greater significance. But all shades of opinion are in agreement, at the beginning of the twenty-first century, that a key task of social policy is the channelling and coordination of the efforts, plans and initiatives of individuals and groups from below.

And yet we find that, at some point in the nineteenth century and carrying on well into the twentieth, much economic thinking, and socialist approaches overwhelmingly so, became dominated by the preposterous notion that an economy could be totally planned and directed from above. In the process, socialism has become aligned with other constructivist creations, such as Esperanto and 12-tone musical composition, and consigned to the realm of failed experiments. Earlier, it has been suggested that Hayek's tracing of the notion of central planning to Descartes' constructivism by way of Saint-Simon is at best a one-sided explanation. What, then, elevated the extraordinary conception of a central plan for a whole economy to be the focus of socialist thought about the future of society?

2
The Giant Firm and the Plan

State intervention in a range of public policy measures was well established by the late nineteenth and early twentieth centuries. The transmutation of this practice into the idea that it would be possible to direct whole economies by way of a central plan emerged from the concrete experience of modernity in a host of spheres. The driving force of this modernity and the major factor compelling attention and explanation in this period was the emergence of giant capitalist firms, because they changed the way people lived.

The Plan was made Flesh in the form of Henry Ford.

The Great Transformation

A transformation took place in the material existence of people living in Western Europe and North America in the half century before the outbreak of the First World War. Part of this development was due to the cumulative effects of the new ways of doing things emerging in the previous two centuries. From the seventeenth century, we see an 'industrious revolution'[1] that habituated a bourgeois class to an intensified pace of work to pay for the increasing range of material possessions on offer, including the products of imperialism and slavery, such as sugar, tea and coffee. The emergence of this class to a position of political power, or at least significant influence, generated changes in the juridical status of the majority populations in both rural and urban areas, abetting the creation of a pool of free labour across these societies.

In the early and mid-nineteenth century, a dispersion across continental Europe and North America of the British Industrial Revolution of the eighteenth century accustomed individuals of all classes to purchasing commodities such as cotton garments from the marketplace. An inexorable process of urbanisation began. The great majority of newcomers to this environment were entering into a context in which their own material survival was linked not to traditional institutions for the employment of labour, such as guilds and apprenticeship schemes, but to market exchange of their own labour with private employers, the remuneration from which was then used to purchase the necessities of life. In rural contexts, a money-based exchange economy for consumer and capital goods gradually became predominant. But it was not until the beginning of the twentieth century that rural areas of even advanced economies such as France and Germany were fully embedded in capitalist economic relations.

Even in the first stage of the Industrial Revolution, the slow accumulation of the changes of previous centuries resulted in much that was new and unprecedented. The new conditions are partially encapsulated in the rise in measured per capita income, first beginning in Britain in the 1820s but not clearly detectable to contemporaneous observers, with these developments delayed in continental Europe by about a generation. Whether these early increases in income are to be thought of as a genuine elevation in living standards is a contentious issue,[2] but the indubitable significance of these first-stage rises in money income is that the great majority of the population were drawn into the marketplace and the money economy, for both their remuneration and their purchase of the means of survival. By mid-century in Britain and a few decades later in continental Europe, the cumulative effects of rises in money income were sufficiently unambiguous to disconcert Marx and Engels. These improvements in material conditions were to shape the strategy and character of working-class movements across Western Europe in the latter part of the century, just when, as the *Communist Manifesto* of 1848 had predicted, the development of industry was leading to the creation of a proletariat which 'increases in number and becomes concentrated in greater masses'.

In the Great Transformation of the latter half of the nineteenth century, we see emerging in North America and Western Europe new standards of consumption, education, work and health. A part of this transformation was consequent on the continuation of long-term tendencies, such as a continuing rise in agricultural productivity even before the introduction to the farm of the internal combustion engine. Some of the rise in material standards was seen to be a result of the expansion of the liberal economy internationally, resulting in a decline in prices of raw materials and food. Even here the role of modernity in this process was evident, in the replacement of the sailing ship by motorised vessels and the transport of frozen meat to Europe from the Americas and the Antipodes. There were other dramatic changes in this period – the health interventions discussed in Chapter 1, resulting in a long-term decline in death rates, including infant mortality, state-sponsored education and the associated dissemination of mass circulation newspapers and other forms of printed culture – that generated significant alterations to daily life.

It is, however, the Second Industrial Revolution, linked to the emergence of giant firms within the Great Transformation, that was the most conspicuous element in altering material life and in ratifying and increasing the gap in military, economic and political power between the industrial powers and the rest of the world. An early example of the Second Industrial Revolution had been the emergence of the railway (or railroad, in American parlance), with its ability to alter the lives of individuals directly through its unprecedented capacity for land-based travel, and indirectly through its role in lowering the cost of distribution of commodities. Further innovations changing the world, such as the mass production of steel, electrical equipment and chemicals and the mass marketing of consumer products were identified with a modernity emanating from the giant firm, a process culminating in the consumer good most emblematic of the new era, the car.

The transformation in material conditions generated by the market economy – the outpouring of the 'immense accumulation of commodities' (in the words of the opening line of *Capital*) generated by capitalism – profoundly affected the consciousness of ruling groups and ordinary people. The emergence of giant firms and the Second Industrial Revolution permanently changed life in rich countries and became emblematic of modernity.

Modernity and the giant firm

The giant company erupted in the context of a confluence of events linking the opportunities emerging for the exploitation of mass markets with new technologies of mass production. Market domains expanded partially for political reasons – the unification of Germany in 1871 and the victory of the Union in the US Civil War in 1865, the maintenance of broad-based international economic stability under the *Pax Britannica* until 1914, and the conscious acts of market creation described in Chapter 1 by both state and business groups in many countries. Markets were enlarged as well by the revolutions taking place in sea and land transportation, and by transatlantic communication at the speed of light. Urbanisation, rising per capita income and (most especially in the US) a rapidly growing population in this period were all factors reinforcing the process of market expansion.

There also emerged a range of technologies lending themselves to the exploitation of these mass markets. But, as has been argued most explicitly by the business historian Alfred DuPont Chandler, this fit between market expansion and the new technologies of mass production did not emerge in an automatic or effortless manner. The organisational changes surrounding the creation of the successful giant firm were as innovative as any of their technological developments.[3] At one level, the issue was simply one of maintaining a sufficient scale of output in these capital-intensive industries. But the maintenance of scale often involved the conscious refinement of organisational mechanisms to deal with unprecedented challenges of

coordination and calculation – the imposition of a visible hand of management through vertical integration in capital-intensive industries to coordinate flows of inputs from suppliers and outputs to final users.[4] In many
cases, the use of this do-it-yourself strategy for the sourcing of inputs by
these pioneering firms was the only viable one, because alternative market
sources were simply non-existent.

Furthermore, a demand for the novel creations of these firms could not
be presumed, so that the marketing and advertising of these products was
not only an aspect of the firm's desire to make full use of its productive
capacity, but an intrinsic aspect of the innovative process. The link between
marketing and innovation in this period was put to one side, as we shall
see, by technocrats and socialists, who treated marketing and advertising as
wasteful activities, and by economic orthodoxy, with its emerging notion
of an ideal of perfect competition, in which no such activities would take
place.[5] Technocrats and socialists could be highly critical of these emergent
giants, but they were confident that the activities of big firms embodied and
exemplified the emergent path of the society and economy, and that the
future was a planned one.

The new entities were viewed as exemplifications of modernity and the
source of dynamism in capitalism for the half century prior to 1914: this
attitude persisted for much of the twentieth century. The US was seen by the
world, not in its own image of individualism and free-wheeling free enterprise, but as 'A nation of ... system builders ... imbued with a drive for order,
system, and control.'[6] The giant firm represented modernity in the sense
that its bureaucratic procedures and operation, including production, were
up-to-date and identified with formal techniques such as accounting and
applied science, techniques that were executed by specialists, often with
professional qualifications: the most highly qualified and ambitious candidates for a career in business sought work in these elite enterprises.

Emblematic of this new world was the emergence of an unprecedented
standardisation of the production processes and parts used within the giant
firm, with momentum in the direction of imposing such protocols within
whole industries. Even more characteristic of modernity, as far as the general
public was concerned, was the uniformity of the giant firm's final output,
most famously associated with Ford and the Model T and embodied in the
standardised packaging of goods. This notion of uniformity of characteristics became linked to an expectation on the part of the public of quality
control of products they purchased, including health regulation, such as the
pasteurisation of milk: in the US, Progressive Era legislation at the beginning of the twentieth century was an aspect of this general supposition that
the living environment could be made subject to rational control.[7]

The most important way in which the giant firm became coincident in the
public's mind with modernity was its identification with novelty: it was the
initiator of a range of notable innovations in the processes of production,

distribution and managerial organisation resulting in dramatic reductions in the costs of ordinary products. Many of these new business techniques were invisible to a general public, such as the development of the Gantt chart for the scheduling of projects within the firm, though some new techniques impinged upon daily life, such as the introduction of mass retailing or the mail order catalogue. Other innovations, in the form of new consumer products – processed foods, bicycles and aspirin – affected daily existence, as did the transformation of the urban environment through the electrification of cities and the substitution of trams and other motor-powered vehicles for the horse. At first, the public perception was that these discontinuities in the conduct of ordinary existence were down to the activities of the lone, heroic inventor. In the longer term, however, both reality and public perception converged: these substantive manifestations of modernity were seen to be products of the great corporate entities. The role of advanced-level technology and high science in the dramatic changes taking place in daily life only reinforced the public perception of a link between the giant firm and the dawning of a new age.

There was ambivalence about these giants: they were accused of monopolistic exploitation of consumers, ruthless practices against competitors and workers, and corrupt interactions with political forces. A ritualised nostalgia about the disappearance of small producers and retailers was pervasive alongside a conventional wisdom, perhaps linked to a popular dissemination of Darwinism, that small economic entities were atavisms to be swept away by history. To this day, the supposedly laggard behaviour of France and the UK in this period is often discussed in terms of the failure of these nations, in comparison with Imperial Germany and the US, to be at the centre of the changes incumbent upon the Second Industrial Revolution. Indeed, the annual growth rates of gross domestic product (GDP) from 1870 to 1913 of 2.83 and 3.94 per cent for Germany and the US substantially surpassed those of France and the UK over the same period (1.63 and 1.90, respectively), events with profound military and political implications. In per capita terms, however, the difference in growth rates over this period remains important but not quite so dramatic (1.63 and 1.82 for Germany and the US, respectively, versus 1.45 for France and 1.01 for the UK), so that by 1913 (using the US as a base of 100), we have levels of per capita income of 69 for Germany, 66 for France and 93 for the UK.[8]

It is possible, therefore, to exaggerate the economic success of Germany compared with France in terms of its effects on ordinary people's lives; even the achievements of the US in this period appear somewhat less stupendous in per capita terms. If, as was certainly the case, the giant firms of the US were the prime agents of modernity in this period, and were so perceived by social thinkers and the general public, the ability of other participants such as France or Japan[9] to adapt to that modernity and to refashion it to their own devices is an issue of major significance. A last, crucial element commonly neglected in the Second Industrial Revolution narrative, to be expanded upon in later chapters, is the role played by the development and expansion of state-funded education in all countries participating in the modernisation process.

The giant firm: size and complexity

The complexity of the issues confronting giant firms was of a new order of magnitude in comparison with enterprises from the First Industrial Revolution: they were not simply those of small enterprises writ large. Those controlling the destinies of these new giants had to create new administrative structures to manage the tasks facing them. They also had to develop new modes of operation to permit these giant vessels to change course when external events made this necessary, and, more dramatically, to create mechanisms that institutionalised the development of novelty, much of which would be imposed upon, and transform, the external environment. The new economic landscape, with a conspicuous and even dominant role for giant firms, brought forth a widespread reconsideration of the nature of economic and social life under capitalism, and not just among socialist theorists, as we shall see in the next chapter.

The emergent giants found themselves faced by a series of obstacles to their ability to function efficaciously. Indicative of the discontinuity generated by the emergence of the giant firm was the introduction in the US, Britain and other countries in the mid- and late nineteenth century of laws facilitating limited liability or corporate status, a disreputable practice associated in Britain with the South Sea Bubble of 1720. The size of the new firms made them conspicuously public as never before, and in literal terms they became, in the British sense, public companies, as their very magnitude increasingly necessitated the raising of equity finance from outsiders. Thus began a long-term process of separation of ownership and control among the great companies, by which the direction of enterprises moved from an owner-manager, the entrepreneur – a term tenaciously preserved even in the economic discourse of our day – to the complex web of family and institutional interests, financial influence and professional management characteristic of contemporary large firms. Both the size and the complexity of the new entities necessitated the creation of new forms of management. These firms were confronted with a broad range of new problems to be solved, so that hierarchal structures of control had to be arranged in which decisions, and the responsibility for them, could be allocated to individuals in a coherent manner. The tasks themselves were often of a sufficiently specialised nature that professional qualifications would be demanded of much of the managerial hierarchy.

The US railroads were singled out by Chandler as a key source for much subsequent managerial innovation.[10] By the very nature of the scale, complexity and technical sophistication of the railroads, the leading engineers of the day were attracted to this sector, and the problems they were confronted with, both managerial and technical, were unprecedented, involving a range of considerations that go beyond the mere fact of the size of these new entities. In the management of the railroad, as for other Second Industrial Revolution firms, a significant discontinuity with the textile mill of the First Industrial Revolution emerged: the new enterprises were not merely larger than their predecessors, but were also characterised by a radically different cost structure. For the textile mill, costs of production were dominated by variable costs (materials and labour used in the process of production). By contrast, for railroads and other highly capitalised Second Industrial Revolution enterprises, a central role was played by fixed capital – mostly track, rolling stock and their maintenance in the case of the railroads – which altered the long-term strategies of firms, because the presence of these high fixed costs meant that average total costs would rise to unacceptable levels at low levels of capacity utilisation.

Thus, while the First Industrial Revolution had already been characterised by an unprecedented strategic focus by the new firms on a high volume of production compared with their pre-capitalist predecessors in the textile sector, this focus on volume – on using the fixed plant to capacity – was magnified and became a central consideration for railroads and other Second Industrial Revolution enterprises. When coupled with the economies of production at large scale inherent in the industries characteristic of the Second Industrial Revolution, these volume effects substantially reinforced the tendency, already present from the First Industrial Revolution, for firms to pursue production and marketing strategies focusing on the mass market and on high levels of sales, even at the expense of profit margin.

The novel nature of the managerial tasks confronting these Second Industrial Revolution firms necessitated other changes in their internal mode of operation. The presence of high levels of fixed capital greatly complicated, even at a conceptual level, the calculation of the costs of a firm. For a First Industrial Revolution textile mill, with the bulk of its costs being variable costs, a calculation of costs could be readily made, since they were reflected in the outflow of cash on a short-term basis (measured in weeks): standard bookkeeping procedures were sufficient to keep track of the firm's progress. For the railroad, by contrast, the presence of high fixed costs meant that the rational calculation of costs becomes a far more abstract consideration – what proportion of fixed costs, including not only centralised expenditure on track building and maintenance and on rolling stock, but also on research and development (including monitoring new developments taking place outside the firm), marketing and general administration, are to be allocated to a rail journey between New York and Philadelphia, as compared with one between New York and Chicago? How are these costs to be allocated between passenger and commercial traffic, and to what extent does a contract with an oil company that guarantees high capacity utilisation over the next year justify, in a profit-maximising context, the offering of lower freight charges to such customers?

Furthermore, the long-lived capital goods being used by these new sectors had a value to the firm that was linked to a stream of cash flows stretching long into an uncertain future, so that intertemporal calculations (or conjectures) had to be made concerning, among other things, demand in the future for rail capacity, with an estimate of the costs of over- or underestimating this future demand. The complexities of making investment decisions on long-lived capital equipment were further exacerbated by the problems of technical change, which introduced questions concerning when an existing piece of equipment is deemed to be obsolescent and worth replacing – an economic, managerial issue and not a purely technical one.

All of these unprecedented managerial issues induced the highly skilled technicians of the US railroads to develop new methods for measuring the progress and status of the firm in the form of cost accounting. These new procedures were administered by specialists devoted to this field and replaced the straightforward bookkeeping practices characteristic of the First Industrial Revolution. These techniques for dealing with a railroad's fixed costs were not merely an extension of the practical bookkeeping that had been in place since late medieval Italy: they were novel conceptions for dealing with the costs of an activity at an abstract and conjectural level and then for finding a financial metric that permits rational, value-maximising decisions.

In addition to this array of managerial issues, the day-by-day technical difficulties of running a railroad in comparison with a cotton mill were unprecedented. The links between railway timetabling and the introduction of uniformity in time keeping[11] exemplify the demands for precision of Second Industrial Revolution entities, with the necessity for the synchronisation of rolling stock from different locations and its arrival at a common point, the maintenance and renewal of track, the repair of rolling stock and supplying it with fuel; there were issues concerning passenger amenities and the demands for high levels of safety and comfort for passenger travel. This need for synchronisation could be seen, as well, in other Second Industrial Revolution industries, most especially those using continuous process production techniques. The geographically dispersed workforce of the railroad had to be managed, remunerated, motivated and disciplined – a workforce far more heterogeneous in terms of the level and diversity of skills required than that of the textile mill.

These demands of a supposedly mundane, day-by-day kind posed challenges of coordination, and each demanded specialised attention. The marketing to, and bargaining with, the broad range of customers, from passenger traffic to a range of business customers, most especially the great oil producers, presented opportunities for high returns, but also problems of unprecedented complexity: on the demand side, what resources should be allocated to marketing and attracting new business from the range of potential customers, and how should one vary the price-cost margins charged to different groups: what kind of strategy of price discrimination should be pursued to maximise returns?

The challenges emerging in other Second Industrial Revolution enterprises were, if anything, greater than for the railroads, and necessitated further developments in the sophistication and complexity of their associated management procedures. The railroads faced obstacles in the achievement of efficiency because of the inherently abstract and conjectural aspects of having to deal with their substantial fixed costs, but other Second Industrial Revolution firms also faced this problem as well as a vast expansion in the heterogeneity of their activities that threatened to plunge the giant firm into a gaggle of confusion. But the large scale engendered by this range of activities also raised the possibility of gains in engineering efficiency. When tools and equipment and their specifications could be made common to the machine-building and body plant activities of a giant car company, a potentiality for cost saving was present, either from in-house production scale economies or in the purchasing of these items; improvement in coordination between these activities is likely to be forthcoming as well.[12] As we shall see, the movement for standardisation, both within and between firms, played a key role in the positing of 'the plan' as a rival to markets and competition as a vehicle for the achievement of efficiency and modernity.

Another aspect of this heterogeneity proved more troublesome to the giant firm: as it took on an increasingly diverse range of activities, it became more difficult to calculate their relative efficiency. To this day, the ideal form of evaluation of efficiency is that used by the First Industrial Revolution textile mill owner: 'management by walking around' permits a judgement to be made, in a hands-on fashion, of efficiency in the enterprise. In a giant car firm, however, how does one judge the relative efficiency of machine-building and body plant activities, much less compare their performance with the marketing and sales divisions?

There emerged two complementary approaches to a solution. The first of these was the continued development of the cost-accounting procedures described above to permit an evaluation in purely financial terms of the performance of physically incommensurate activities within the firm, such as those taking place in the machine-building and marketing divisions: the failure to pay adequate attention to this question, it has been suggested, was a leading cause for the difficulties of Ford in the 1920s.[13] At the beginning of the twentieth century, a second mechanism for dealing with the problem of efficiency within the giant firm was the development of scientific management. This doctrine, to be explored below, played various roles within the firm, but among its purposes was the creation of a standard for how workers *should* perform in the context of the firm's diverse activities, so that efficiency in different subdivisions could be compared.

Second Industrial Revolution enterprises, even for seemingly straightforward production goods industries such as steel, were faced with a range of interlinked production and marketing decisions of greater complexity than those faced by the textile mill or even the railroad. Thus, the innovation of new ranges of steel from different alloy mixtures, and the offering of new products, such as barbed wire and girders, suitable for the new skyscrapers of the great cities, had to be linked to a set of strategies for securing markets for these innovations once, or even before, they were created. For the consumer goods industries, the centrality of marketing as a managerial concern was even greater. A breakfast food manufacturer had to test demand – to discern, guess or estimate what would be acceptable to consumers, to design these novel creations in order to change what in many cases were millennial habits in favour of these products, and to maintain the loyalty of consumers in the face of new competition.

For most Second Industrial Revolution enterprises, the labour question also became a central issue: with great masses herded together in limited space, there was an immense potential for the coordinated use of this concentration by management, as well as a threat from labour's increased ability to generate disruption. The growing heterogeneity of the labour force in terms of its skills generated new challenges: the direction, coordination and remuneration of such a mixed group and issues surrounding in-house training were questions both for management and for the workforce and its organising elements, such as unions. These developments were taking place in a political and juridical context of extensions to the adult male franchise and of labour rights to organise and act collectively in the advanced sectors of the world economy. Theorists of planning (including socialists), modelling themselves on the procedures of the managers of giant capitalist firms, followed the latter in treating the activities of labour as something to be controlled and directed, rather than as creative forces in their own right.

In many sectors, the most striking element of discontinuity with the past was the decisive role of pure science in the development of technology. Recent discussions have tended to elevate the implicit role of science even in the development of the First Industrial Revolution, a period superficially dominated by empirical approaches to innovation.[14] In the Second Industrial Revolution, the situation was gradually transformed. Key US industries (non-electrical machinery, steel and vehicles) had been distinguished 'by an aversion to organized science-based research',[15] but in, for instance, chemical and electrical equipment manufacture, the role of science became unequivocal and lay at the heart of German, and eventually US, industrial dominance. The result was, for the first time, a popular identification of the scientific revolution of the seventeenth century with a transformation of daily life. As late as the early nineteenth century, as the cliché has it, the great mathematician Carl Friedrich Gauss would sit writing at a table with implements and illumination familiar centuries earlier: within a few decades, all this would change.

By the latter part of the nineteenth century, science would impinge upon the ordinary lives of individuals, with giant firms hiring a new range of personnel to direct, monitor and coordinate relatively abstract scientific research projects that were to be realised in a commercial context. In addition, there were considerations surrounding the marketing of new products and the legal complications surrounding the securing of property rights on them, implying the need for specialised professionals to deal with these issues. Legal protection becomes more critical as the ratio of science to craft rises in new invention, since new developments are no longer connected to the know-how embodied in individuals associated with the enterprise, but are contained, by definition, in objectively replicable procedures that can only be protected by law or secrecy. The emergence of science over craft did not take place on a once-and-for-all basis but, as we shall see, continues to unfold to the present day and plays an important role in the evolution of the competitive environment.[16]

The management of enterprises also grew increasingly complex in a Second Industrial Revolution context because of the transformation of financial affairs. The large size of the new entities, as we have seen, resulted in a qualitative rise in the amount of finance that had to be raised and the necessity to appeal to outside sources for these funds The textile mill of the first-stage Industrial Revolution had been, by contrast, a largely self-financed enterprise, with outside financing limited to short-term, self-liquidating loans from local banks to service inventories and liquidity needs. For the newly emerging giant firms, the range of sources of outside finance, in terms of both necessity and opportunity, was immensely greater. In addition to dealing with banks for short-term working capital, the giant firm, with its large fixed capital requirements, would issue shares and debt of various term lengths to the public, necessitating, in principle, a higher level of public disclosure, detail and accuracy in the firm's accounts than heretofore if these public offerings were to be marketable. In the US, it was common for the state to play a role in the financing of the railroads, almost invariably accompanied by claims of corruption and misallocation of resources, including unnecessary extension of lines. The cajoling and bribing of governmental bureaucrats and politicians, at both national and local levels, for subsidies and rights of way quickly took the railroads into a range of managerial decisions and interactions more complex than ever encountered by the textile mill.

The financing of the railroads and other large firms characteristic of the Second Industrial Revolution thus necessitated a transformation in the modes of firm finance, not only because of the absolute size of these entities, but also because of the increasing role of fixed capital. For giant firms, this need for long-term finance generated a range of strategies in different countries, with Britain and the US becoming associated with an equity-based stock market system of finance, while German firms characteristically had interlocking relationships with the banks to secure their needs for long-term lending facilities. These differing financial arrangements resulted in alternative forms of governance at the highest levels in these stock market and bank-oriented firms, arrangements that may well have affected their trajectory of development in the long term.

For practically all schools of thought analysing the emergence of the giant firm, however, the preferred solution has been to put questions concerned with finance to one side: economic orthodoxy claims to see through the mere veil of finance to the real factors allocating goods on the basis of consumer preferences and costs of production; technocrats and socialists dismissed activity emanating from the financial sphere as wasteful and dysfunctional. We shall see subsequently that the financial sphere has played a critical role in the resolution of both the theoretical and real-life battles between capitalism and central planning, and in the continuing trajectory of capitalist development to this day.

The giant firm: the creation of management

In order to deal with the array of difficulties, complexities and opportunities before them, the giant firms created a whole new set of administrative structures to respond to incipient managerial diseconomies of scale that threatened to swamp these large enterprises with inefficiency. Rather than accept the diktat of the long-run average cost curve (seen in the microeconomics textbooks given to students to this day), with its exogenously imposed regions of economies and then diseconomies of scale, this curve was reshaped by the pioneers of modern business. The ambiguities and tensions emerging from the allocation of prerogatives reserved for the centre and the levels of autonomy retained by the subdivisions persist to this day in great capitalist firms and were, as we shall see, reproduced in centrally planned economies.

The method developed by the US railroads to deal with both the top-level managerial challenges and the complex array of daily concerns in this sector was the introduction of new formal structures for directing the railroads and the development of specialised personnel to cope with the new array of tasks coming on stream. Top-level managerial tasks were in the hands of staff directly responsible to a board of directors and, in principle, the shareholders; line management was responsible for dealing with the day-by-day operations of the organisation, including, most crucially, daily interactions with the workforce. This formalisation of administrative responsibilities was a continuation and refinement of processes going on for several centuries in governmental, military and even ecclesiastical organisations. But the development of bureaucratic structures in large firms in the late nineteenth century took place with exceptional rapidity and played a central role in their substantive development: in the absence of these innovations, the productive forces of these new giants would have been stifled by diseconomies of scale resulting from the unprecedented managerial challenges of running these firms.

What characteristically emerged was a delineation of staff responsibilities into general management, marketing, finance, purchasing, research and development, a legal division, personnel – dealing with the labour force – and other tasks. The organisation chart of the giant firm was born. Employment within these subdivisions increasingly consisted of individuals with narrow specialisations within these areas and, most especially in the US, with newly emerging professional qualifications, as often as not linked to university study – the MBA, marketing, accounting and finance qualifications, and others of a similar nature from the late nineteenth century. These qualifications also facilitated the maintenance of a class separation between the staff and others in the company, both line and workers.[17]

For the giant firm, this coherent separation and delineation of tasks within the staff on the basis of real or imagined higher skills, most especially when combined with central direction by hired managers, promoted a perception of objectivity and scientific direction in the firm, the epitome of the modernism enunciated in the writings of the sociologist Max Weber. This perception of modernity was reinforced by the adaptation of recent developments in pure science into substantive innovations: in the public's mind, the repairing of clothes by a local seamstress was part of the traditional world of craft (even if executed by an electrified sewing machine), but electric lighting and toothpaste were linked to giant firms, science and modernity.

The dictum from Chandler is that a firm's internal structure will follow from the strategy it chooses to pursue. The innovations in railroad management discussed above were a far-reaching attempt to release the constraints dictated by managerial diseconomies of scale. The aim was to create an efficient form of governance for the giant firm in the context of a strategy that almost invariably involved confrontation with, exploitation of, and often creation of a mass market. In this new form of governance, as we have seen in the case of the railroads, staff and line functions were separated, with staff functions then delineated and allocated in a coherent way. In the case of many other Second Industrial Revolution enterprises, a more decentralised, multidivisional version of this management structure was developed. It served the purpose of accommodating firm strategies that involved products differentiated into market segments, either because of their inherent heterogeneity or because of the geographical dispersion of the markets in which they were sold. Thus, after the First World War, the centralised management structure of Ford reflected its strategy of focus on the production of the

Model T; for General Motors (GM), its multidivisional structure, in which its centralised staff functions were replicated in subdivisions such as Buick, Oldsmobile and Cadillac, was a reflection of its strategy to offer consumers a diversity of output.

These sophisticated management formations were made possible by two developments taking place simultaneously in the US. The first of these was the emergence of an advanced specialisation in cost accounting that attempted to evaluate the profitability not only of the company as a whole, but also of its disparate subdivisions, thus permitting semi-autonomous operation of these subdivisions. Several obstacles impinged upon the ability of the central staff of GM to use these new techniques to evaluate and rank the performance of the management of its various subdivisions, such as Buick and Oldsmobile, simply by treating them as profit centres. One obstacle to a profit-based measure of the performance of subdivisions was the presence of resources, such as the Fisher body plant and research and development that were common to all subdivisions. These centralised assets were key aspects of GM's overall competitive advantage through the exploitation of economies of scale across the whole firm. But in order to measure the profitability of each subdivision, the apportioning of the use of these common resources (for instance, research and development) to each subdivision had to take place; the accounting conventions for making these calculations were inevitably imprecise and possessed arbitrary characteristics. Even if, however, this obstacle could be overcome, the success of the Cadillac subdivision in a particular period might be a fortuitous and temporary reflection of economic prosperity rather than the skill of its management (rent rather than efficiency, in economists' terms).

A further obstacle to treating subdivisions as autonomous entities is that the subdivisions' management will invariably develop their own vested interests, in conflict with the goals of the centre: the centre may view a modicum of competition between Buick and Oldsmobile as desirable, but such rivalry could easily become too much of a good thing, as far as the centre is concerned. In more general terms, the creation of subdivided sources of control in the giant firm creates myriad ways in which organised groups within the company are motivated to depart from the centre's goals and give a distorted report on their own performance. Even with these limitations, however, the new management structures, which reached their most sophisticated form in the US, were successful in directing the trajectory of the giant firms that were transforming the economic landscape.

A second development that facilitated the emergence of sophisticated management formations, most distinctly in the US, was of personnel adequately trained to execute these managerial tasks. For the economic historian Alexander Gerschenkron, a characteristic of late-developing economies is that their deficit of skilled personnel impelled them to pursue a strategy of industrial development that involved centralised coordination within enterprises, and commonly with links to central government.[18] Like the proverbial education minister in nineteenth-century France, it was thought best to dictate from Paris what was to be taught at 3:00 P.M. in a distant schoolroom in France rather than rely upon an improvised lesson from a barely tutored peasant.[19] The great US firms, by contrast, had the option, when their business strategy deemed it appropriate, to construct a business architecture that attempted to combine the virtues of centralised control with decentralised flexibility and spontaneity. GM could give substantial leeway to the managers of the Buick and Oldsmobile subdivisions in their marketing and production strategies because giant firms in the US, in contrast to Gerschenkron's late-developing economies, were able to staff these subdivisions with personnel possessing explicit professional training for these tasks. The advantages accruing to the US in this sphere were due, at least in part, to the fact that it was emerging as a world leader in educational development, most especially in business and professional training.

The transformational aspects of the management of the giant firm took place not only in the fulfilment of its higher, staff-level tasks, but at the level of line management in dealing with day-by-day operations, including interactions with the workforce. The changes resulting on the shop floor were widely perceived, even by socialists, to be aspects of modernity, a continuation and qualitative development from the First Industrial Revolution, with the procedures and output of the giant firm associated with efficiency, uniformity and unprecedented quality control. These developments, as embodied in the term 'Taylorism', were accompanied by battles of a highly contentious nature concerning the work process. But for the purveyors of the new system, this battle with the obduracy of the labour force was of a piece with rational organisation and standardisation of processes and output in the firm.[20]

The 'American system of manufactures' of the mid-nineteenth century already embodied in incipient form an emphasis on high levels of uniform output produced using special-purpose machine tools and interchangeable parts;[21] mechanical engineers in the US played a pioneering role in the latter part of the nineteenth century in the setting of sector-wide standards for precision and compatibility. But the development of precision in industry was also advanced by the demands of science for accuracy. Here, Germany, because of the standardising services offered by its National Physical Laboratory, was seen to possess advantages over the US not only in pure scientific research, but also in the emerging chemical and electrical industries;[22] in the latter sectors especially, the battles over compatibility were particularly intense.[23] Thus, precise measurement and the standardisation of parts and processes were both an inherent characteristic of scientific rationality and a key aspect of competitive advantage: for C. A. Adams of the US Bureau of Standards in 1919, 'the degree of standardization in any nation is a measure of its civilization, certainly in the material sense of the word',[24] but for others it was also 'a fundamental characteristic of our modern economic system ... [the] rapid industrial growth of the last two decades, particularly in the United States, may be said to be based largely upon the partly unconscious, partly deliberate, extension and refinement of industrial standardization'.[25]

The exigencies of both scientific rationality and economic efficiency were thus seen to converge in the need for standardisation, symbolised in the US by the creation of the Bureau of Standards in 1902. Herbert Hoover, as US secretary of commerce in the 1920s, used his experience controlling waste and duplication in the First World War to promote, through the Bureau of Standards, the use of simplified practices in industry and a reduction in product variety. For Hoover, this was all part of a broader programme of 'associational reform' that involved efforts to reduce industrial waste through standardisation conferences and cooperative efforts in industry and the professions, with light-touch guidance and coordination from the state.[26] We thus see here two themes that will arise again in the next chapter: the impetus that the First World War gave to notions of the efficacy of central direction of economic activity, and the idea – an alien one to the economic orthodoxy of the twenty-first century – that the invisible hand of competition can result in inefficient, wasteful duplication that even the Republican Herbert Hoover would consider ripe for governmental correction.

Standardisation reached its apogee of public visibility with Ford and the Model T when, after introducing it in 1908, he announced in 1909 that this was to be Ford's sole model. But, while efficiencies to be gained from economies obtained through uniformity of output remained a focus of attention for socialists, Henry Ford's obsession with the Model T was eventually an aspect of his undoing at the hand of GM in the 1920s. Of lasting significance for all economies, both capitalist and socialist, was Ford's advance upon and exploitation of earlier developments in standardisation of tools, parts and equipment within the US automobile industry to create the moving assembly line at Highland Park in 1913 and 1914.[27] The flow-through production of the assembly line, inspired perhaps by the procedures of Chicago meat packers or by Ford's earlier employment in an electric power station, resulted in a dramatic lowering of the costs of production and of the selling price of the vehicle: 'The Ford men became known for designing the best special-purpose machines in the world, laying them out along with their materials-handling network for a smooth flow of parts through the plant ... A newsman describing the new Ford plant at Highland Park ... identified its salient feature as "System, system, system".'[28] And it is by way of these managerial developments that the US industry asserted its dominance over the world car industry in this period, rather than through any distinctive technological innovation (the exception being the design of the first practical electric starter).[29]

Henry Ford always denied being influenced by Fredrick Winslow Taylor, and others have suggested that the latter's direct impact on business practice has been exaggerated. But the publication in 1911 of Taylor's *Principles of Scientific Management* was a seminal event: the most general and elaborated exposition of this new version of the American System emerging in the early twentieth century.[30] As far as Taylor was concerned, the most contentious aspects of his programme – the notorious time and motion studies governing worker performance and the displacement of foreman autonomy with managerial, hierarchical structures – were only aspects of a broader set of reforms to the workplace. These reforms, including the installation of appropriate tools and their proper disposition on the shop floor, were to facilitate a smooth flow of production and the elimination of bottlenecks and the downtime of workers and machines.

These procedures, with developments in the standardisation and simplification of parts and procedures, all converged as part of an overall movement for rational control of the firm's activities through the use of cost-accounting procedures and the coordinated flow of this information to the management centre. The emergence of the techniques of cost accounting played a key role in the creation of the giant, vertically integrated firm that could function in a viable manner. But these developments can barely be separated from the *normative* approach to costs characteristic of Taylor's notions of the scientific management of the giant firm,[31] an issue that is deeply problematic for both Marxian economics[32] and economic orthodoxy. In the latter case, as every first-year economics student learns, the cost curves used to determine prices in the marketplace are presumed to represent, at each level of output, the minimal value consistent with the inputs used: inside of the firm there is no technical, or even managerial, problem to be solved – technical efficiency is axiomatically assumed. But this was precisely the problem confronted by the giant, vertically integrated firm, attempting to monitor its costs: in the act of pursuing a broad range of heterogeneous activities, many of them unprecedented in their form and scale, there was no possibility of 'using the market' as an alternative source or as a measure of the efficiency with which these activities were being pursued inside the enterprise.

The new techniques of cost accounting were necessary if giant firms were to make commensurate calculation of costs across a range of heterogeneous activities and be freed from being engulfed by managerial diseconomies of scale. Note that, in principle, it is not sufficient to have a set of accounting techniques that merely reflects the *relative* costs of pursuing activities within the firm, since such techniques could be consistent with a generalised inefficiency: what was needed was an absolute standard of the efficiency of an activity, and this is what the techniques of Taylor and others claimed to offer – the 'one best way' of pursuing an activity.

What came to be known as 'Taylorism' included a range of objective considerations for minimising effort for a given activity, such as the optimal placement of machinery on the shop floor. It is these techniques, whether evolved from a collective lore of best industrial practice or pretending to be the product of deep science and mathematical optimisation, which are the least controversial aspects of the Taylorist heritage. Especially in science-based sectors such as the chemical industry, production protocols for a wide variety of tasks were introduced, with strictly laid-out procedures and little room in principle for improvisation on the part of the workforce. This tendency was reinforced by the progressive substitution of science-based standards for experience and instinct in manufacturing – scientifically calcu-lated and calibrated levels of impurities, and at a later date, the introduction of statistical procedures for judging quality control in factories. Notions of scientific rationality thus converged with strict control of workforce activity and rational calculation of the firm's costs, even if these objective improve-ments in efficiency are not clearly separable from the more sinister aspects of Taylorism – those time and motion studies designed to eliminate shirking and extract the maximum amount of effort from labour on a sustainable basis. Rational calculation of a firm's costs facilitated the installation of Taylorist systems of piecework associated with work intensification.

In the broad range of manufacturing activity, this notion of strict proto-cols replacing improvisation on the factory floor (and control of work processes by, especially, skilled workers) often remained more of an aspir-ation on the part of management than a reality, but this very ambition has remained central to management ideology. Modernity came to be identi-fied, in both a positive and a negative sense, with regularity of production protocols and, to some extent, with the presumption that mass production, low cost and quality control could be secured with uniformity of output of the final product, from the Model T Ford to, at a later date, the McDonald's hamburger. The imposition of these uniformities was instrumental in the assertion of *control* over the firm's activities, including, most desirably, over a malleable, passively compliant workforce, with the unifying factor in all of these modernist tendencies the perception of the giant firm as a vast planning agency.

Planning and the giant firm

The notion of the enterprise as the fulcrum of plans and decisions has become a commonplace of managerial ideology. To plan is to attempt to foresee future constraints and opportunities, to put a measurement or at least a ranking upon them, and then to act in such a way as to bypass or minimise these constraints and to realise these opportunities in a manner consistent with the overall goals of the enterprise. Such an approach is in sharp contrast with the conception of the firm emerging from orthodox economics, in which, in the extreme form of the model of perfect competi-tion, the firm's response to a set of both exogenously given cost constraints and demand opportunities is passive. As we shall see, this passivity has remained a dominant aspect of orthodox theory even when it has attempted to cope with the challenges of explaining the eruption of giant Second Industrial Revolution firms: in contrast to the managerial conception, orthodoxy excludes the notion of the firm as a mechanism to facilitate planning – to control and even *create* the environment in which the firm functions.

The formation of the new structures of management to deal with both top-level managerial tasks and the day-by-day operations of the organisation is an important concomitant of planning in the conduct of the affairs of large firms. But these alterations in the structure of management were, following Chandler's dictum, a reflection of changes in strategy. The giant firms' forms of capital structure, governance and personnel, as we have seen, were qualitatively different from those of small enterprises because the range and scale of tasks undertaken by the new giants were unprecedented. This expansion in ambition – in the range and scope of what could be accomplished in an administered, planned way – was what most fired the imaginations of contemporaries. The giant firms spread their domain of competence across an unprecedented variety of activities, many of which were not pre-existing but the creations of either the research and development or the marketing division of the firm. But it was the increase in levels of vertical integration – the share of tasks that are done in-house – that emerged as the greatest challenge to the market-based view of the capitalist economy: the old-fashioned invisible hand of the marketplace had been replaced by the visible hand of administrative coordination. This description of the situation in the US at the beginning of the twentieth century dates from 1977,[33] but also captures why many contemporaneous observers had considered these developments to be so revolutionary.

The importance of the rise of large, vertically integrated firms was that these entities were epicentres of planning and an alternative to the market as a device for the production and allocation of resources in the economy. In the next chapter, these ideas will be seen to function as core beliefs for socialist planning until the latter's demise. Economic orthodoxy, by contrast, remained almost completely unmoved by these events. The dominant economic thinking, even today, tends to dismiss this planning perspective on the rise of these vertically integrated giants in favour of one in which this development is simply an extension of static exchange and contractual relations. Thus, in an article of 1937, 'The Nature of the Firm', Ronald Coase answers the question 'Why do firms exist?' by suggesting that

> The operation of a market costs something and by forming an organisation and allowing some authority (an 'entrepreneur') to direct the resources, certain marketing costs are saved. The entrepreneur has to carry out his function at less cost, taking into account the fact that he

may get factors of production at a lower price than the market transactions which he superseded, because, it is always possible to revert to the open market if he fails to do this.[34]

Firms internalise tasks when the cost of pursuing market exchange, for instance, the purchase of inputs, is higher than the cost of doing these tasks themselves. In the 1970s, the economist Oliver Williamson clarified the nature of these costs: in marketised, arm's-length relations between parties, the costs of writing a watertight contract may be prohibitive, and it may be preferable to indulge in a hierarchal, vertically integrated solution instead: 'product markets are subject to failure in various respects and … internal organization may be substituted against the market in these circumstances … The advantages of integration thus are not that technological (flow process) economies are unavailable to non-integrated firms, but that integration harmonizes interests (or reconciles differences, often by fiat) and permits an efficient adaptive, sequential decision process to be utilized.'[35] Such an approach elucidates why, for instance, a hospital may choose to have in-house cleaners who can be hierarchically directed to deal with a range of emergencies and contingent circumstances; the alternative would be to employ outside cleaners on a contract in which all these contingent circumstances must be explicitly written down. Note, however, that the imposition of a hierarchal form of governance does not yield a simple resolution to conflicts between the periphery and the centre. Whether in the context of the giant firm or of the Soviet economy, bureaucratic infighting merely replaces arm's-length disputes between firms over contractual arrangements.

The economics literature thus uses the prism of the conflict over the writing of contracts to perceive vertical integration and its historical development.[36] Yet this static approach does little to capture the revolutionary and tumultuous nature of the changes emanating from this period of economic history. Problems over transactions costs played a role in giant firm decisions in the direction of integration, but, overwhelmingly, the markets that Coase and Williamson posited as alternatives often simply did not exist:

the initial move forward into distribution and marketing by entrepreneurs in the new industries of the Second Industrial Revolution was that often suppliers and distributors had neither sufficient knowledge of the novel and complex products nor the facilities required to handle them efficiently … In the most technologically complex of the new industries – particularly chemicals, electrical equipment and nonelectrical heavy machinery – industrial customers had little or no knowledge of how to install, maintain, and repair or even use the new machines or materials. Here the new companies relied on direct sales.[37]

Overall, the act of integration by Chandler's giant firms was less a defensive one in response to market failure than a positive re-creation of the industrial landscape: 'In the years following World War I, growth was driven much less by the desire to reduce transactions, agency and information costs and much more by a wish to utilize the competitive advantages created by the coordinated learned routines in production, distribution, marketing, and improving existing products and processes'.[38] In the robust terms of the economist William Lazonick, 'what mainstream economists view as "market failures" I view as "organizational successes" '.[39]

The enhanced version of orthodoxy based on the presence of transactions costs does not successfully capture Chandler's historical narrative. This narrative, and the events of the late nineteenth and early twentieth centuries it encapsulates, are better conceived by viewing the firm as an entity pursing a series of 'learned routines' that are inherent in the processes of standardisation and mass production discussed above: 'For the history of industrial enterprise, learned routines are those involved in functional activities – those of production, distribution and marketing, obtaining supplies, improving existing products and processes, and the developing of new ones.'[40] Even more important are those routines that permit the enterprise to enhance its capabilities and to transform the environment in which it functions: 'The modern industrial enterprise, therefore, has not been simply scale intensive, capital-using, and natural-resource-consuming. It has also been knowledge-augmenting and learning-enhancing. By committing to the extensive long-term investment in human and organizational resources as well as physical assets, these large enterprises could exploit the complementarity between the large-scale investment in physical capital and the sustained capital formation in such intangible assets as human resources and technological knowledge.'[41]

Note here the continuity and the complementarity between the broad range of planned, long-term investment activities undertaken and internalised as routines by the firm and the one particular aspect of these activities – technological innovation – singled out for special attention by present-day economists: 'Although product pricing remained a significant competitive weapon, these firms competed even more forcefully through functional and strategic efficiency: that is, by carrying out processes of production and distribution more capably; by improving both product and process through systematic research and development; by locating more suitable sources of supply; by providing more effective marketing services; by product differentiation (in branded packaged products primarily through advertising); and by moving more quickly into expanding markets and out of declining ones'.[42]

This picture from the end of the twentieth century of the giant firm as a vehicle for planning – for organising and transforming its internal activities and the external environment – corresponds to the views of many observers at the beginning of the century. These commentators, including socialists, typically dealt in a positive manner with certain aspects of these processes, such as the rational organisation of the workplace, standardisation of inputs and production processes, and mass production, while often dismissing other activities of the giant firms, such as their financial and marketing activities, as peripheral and wasteful. The desirable aspects of planning could, it was postulated, be extricated from capitalist competitive relations. For Chandler, by contrast, the array of activities undertaken by these new firms has to be seen as part of an indivisible whole in the context of a capitalist pursuit of profit in rivalry with, in many cases, other giant firms.

A second, curious aspect of the attitudes of these early observers is that they, no less than the orthodox, market-oriented economists of the time, gave no special attention to what now appears to be the most revolutionary aspect of the planning activities of these giant firms, namely, their capacity for fundamental innovation of new technologies, products and processes. An exception here would seem to be the economist Joseph Schumpeter, famously touted as the 'prophet of innovation', who, as early as 1911, spoke about development as a 'spontaneous and continuous change...which forever alters and replaces the equilibrium state previously existing'.[43] But in this early writing he gave no indication that the period from the late nineteenth to the early twentieth century was anything but a continuity with the development of entrepreneurial capitalism from earlier times: he nowhere suggests that a revolutionary transformation was taking place, both in the structure of capitalism with the emergence of giant firms and in the outpouring of new technologies and innovations of all kinds. More significantly, Schumpeter, in these earlier writings, never indicates, as Chandler and others from a later period would do, that these two dramatic discontinuities from the past – the emergence of giant enterprises and the outburst of innovations – were connected, so that innovation and control of the environment are embodied in the management structure and goals of large firms in the context of rivalrous capitalist activity.[44] In 1928, the provenance of innovation is seen by Schumpeter either in competitive capitalism and the foundation of new firms or in a 'trustified capitalism', about which he is dubious, precisely because progress becomes 'automatized' and in the hands of bureaucratic managers rather than entrepreneurs.[45]

Schumpeter's famous later pronouncements focus on the role of monopolies in innovation, with relatively little emphasis on the continuing context of capitalist rivalry in this process, as in Chandler (or Hayek).[46] Furthermore, for Schumpeter, it is these discontinuous innovative thunderbolts from the monopolies that matter, almost exclusively, with only marginal consideration given to the important processes of diffusion and of incremental improvement of innovations, many of which emerge from competitive rivalry between firms and sometimes between nations:[47] as we shall see in Chapter 5, the writings of his acolyte John Kenneth Galbraith served to confirm opinion in the Soviet Union that their planned path, with its absence of overt competitive rivalry, was an appropriate one.

Lastly, Schumpeter's continuing focus in his later period on the role of the entrepreneur led him to suggest that the growing separation of ownership and control would sap capitalism of its dynamism, all this at the dawn of the golden age of capitalism: in 1947, the quintessence of a Schumpeterian thunderbolt – the invention of the transistor – came forth from AT&T, a managerially directed corporation (see Chapter 9). Thus, Schumpeter proved to be neither a prophet nor a particularly acute observer of contemporaneous events. But failure of economic orthodoxy, even in the immediate postwar period, to have broached the question of innovation, much less integrated it into its repertoire, meant that Schumpeter's Delphic pronouncements on this question were given prophetic status. As we shall see in Chapter 6, orthodoxy was soon to reverse this obliviousness with a vengeance and attribute almost all material progress to technological change.

Thus, it is difficult to find observers at the beginning of the twentieth century who had coherently developed the notion that the new planned structures of capitalism had institutionalised change, most strikingly in the context of new technologies. Marxist analysts (and Schumpeter, who credited Marx) were partial exceptions, but for Marxists, creative destruction was mostly to be seen in the negative context of the destabilisation of capitalism, as new technologies, with their labour-replacing characteristics, generated a long-term decline in the economy's rate of profit. In the more positive context of planning and rational organisation in a new socialist society, it was, rather, standardisation and mass production – the Fordist system – that were taken to be worthy of emulation. This failure by socialist theorists to focus in a serious way on the need to institutionalise processes of innovation was to prove a key weakness in the functioning of the centrally planned economy when Marxists were in control.

From the vantage point of the present, it is the great innovations of the late nineteenth and early twentieth centuries, especially those in the technological realm, that are the apogee of successful planning in this period. All these efforts, however, were ultimately at the service of the capitalist pursuit of profit. For those directing the affairs of the giant firms, innovations of a technical nature were no different from its marketing and advertising activities – they were merely aspects of a more general effort to exercise control over the economic environment to fulfil this goal. Thus, marketing and advertising were part of an attempt to relax constraints emanating from the existing market demand for its products, and were intended to complement the development of new products and their mass production. The Kellogg's company undertook in 1906 not only the task of the mass production and distribution of breakfast foods, but the transformation of the daily habits of a subcontinent in favour of their manufactured creations, novelties so remarkable that the words to describe them entered the language only in a tentative manner (my mother persisted in calling these products *dry* cereal, as opposed to a traditional *kasha* [porridge]). This gigantic undertaking could take place only in the context of a coordinated strategy of marketing and advertising, to inform, assure and cajole a mass public into changing the rhythm of their ordinary existence.

In a similar way, the technological changes largely brought about by the great firms in this period were also at the service of the firm's pursuit of profit. While the rich world outside the US was slow to assimilate the new breakfast foods, the innovations in chemical and electrical equipment manufacture from giant enterprises in Germany and the US attracted universal admiration. For the giant firms themselves, these innovations were all developed as part of planning strategy to lift the constraints of demand through the creation of new consumers' and producers' goods, and by innovations lowering the costs of production of existing products.

The need for a coherent, planned approach to innovation in the new era was reinforced by the growing predominance of pure science in the development of many commercial technologies. As a result, there was an inherent lengthening of the gap from relatively abstract scientifically based conceptualisations to the realisation of commercial benefits from these ideas. Furthermore, the heterogeneity of personnel and equipment that had to be coordinated within the firm greatly increased, including the need for legal personnel to protect scientifically based innovations from being appropriated by rivals. Lastly, with abstract knowledge emerging as a key resource for a firm's competitive advantage, giant firms organised themselves as monitoring stations for scientific and technological innovation.

And it was this *planned* development inside of the great firms that permitted not only an explosion of commercially viable new technologies, but their exploitation, development and improvement at a speed that was unprecedented.[48] In the US, the independent inventor was gradually displaced by the German example of the industrial research laboratory, in which, as Carl Duisberg, the director of Bayer, suggested, one would find 'not a trace of a flash of genius', but which had produced 2,000 different dyestuffs for Bayer on the eve of the First World War.[49] A major impetus for this in-house approach was a conservative one: the need to solve problems associated with existing technologies to which the companies were already committed.[50] The rise of the role of scientific, theoretical considerations in invention meant that suitably trained individuals (often with PhD qualifications in the appropriate discipline) would find themselves pursuing applied work in an industrial laboratory that had progressively less distance from the theoretical work undertaken in universities.

The incipient tension between the relatively short-term, profit-oriented time horizons of even the largest firms and the longer-term nature of fundamental scientific research was sufficiently contained in the first decades of the twentieth century: these firms emerged as the key sources of technological innovation. As we shall see in Chapter 9, a new and more complex arrangement came into place after the Second World War in the US, though the popular view of the matter never progressed beyond the image of the independent inventor embodied in Thomas Edison.

Yet even Edison found himself becoming immersed in systems building and the exigencies of pure science as the complexities of bringing the light bulb to fruition unfolded:

> Did Edison invent the incandescent electric lamp? He undoubtedly learned something from others, but he stood alone in his appreciation of the essential requirements, set his goals accordingly, overcame many obstacles that stalled his rivals, and developed not only a practical lamp but the associated components, such as improved generators and other hardware, that made a large-scale lighting system possible. And then he built the system.[51]

Edison's success in the construction of a complete system for the delivery of the light bulb did not result from having possessed at the outset a complete, integrated vision of the problems involved. It was, rather, the product of his initial accomplishment (a successful lamp), and then the tenacity and financial resources to sustain him and his fellow researchers through myriad complications as they emerged, including the need to design in-house the dynamo that would be used in the first lighting systems.[52] The long-term risky investments he undertook and the integration of complex components, including those that had to be developed in-house, made the Edison venture the standard in its day for not only technological progress, but also planning. Emil Rathenau, one of the creators of Germany's electric industry, recalled his impressions after seeing Edison's display at the Paris Electrical Exhibition of 1881:

> The Edison system of lighting was as beautifully conceived down to the very details, and as thoroughly worked out as if it had been tested for decades in various towns. Neither sockets, switches, fuses, lamp-holders, nor any of the other accessories necessary to complete the installation were wanting; and the generating of the current, the regulation, the wiring with distribution boxes, house connections, meters, etc., all showed signs of astonishing skill and incomparable genius.[53]

And Rathenau's son Walter was to become a key organiser of the centrally directed German economy during the First World War that, as we shall see in the next chapter, became the object of so much admiration on the part of the Bolsheviks. Lenin's obsession with electrification as a symbol of modernity was thus linked not only to its technological novelty, but to its acting as an illustration of the efficacy of the planning process. What was absent from Lenin's enthusiastic response was any notion of electrification as an exemplification of the innovative process itself – what lessons can be drawn on how to generate these new technologies? For Edison, the pursuit of electrification remained a capitalist venture. He undertook serious efforts to calculate the costs of the new technology vis-à-vis gas lighting,[54] and at early stages felt competitive pressure from other electrical manufacturers.[55] The security of his financial backing was linked to his past successes at making his ventures profitable;[56] Schumpeter's emphasis on the key role of finance in the innovative process receives an important confirmation in this history. The key role of finance in the process of innovation will prove, as we shall see in Chapter 4, a crucial aspect of capitalism's success in its battle with central planning, as well as its Achilles' heel.

Edison's electrification venture thus serves as an example of the confluence of the enhanced role of abstract science in innovation with the need for planning and coordination. Edison's practical understanding of electricity and other relevant matters proved sufficient in the initial development of the light bulb. But the integration of the device as part of a broader system – the generation of electricity from the new dynamos and the controversy he was involved in over the use of either direct or alternating current in long-distance transmission of electricity – brought the great artisan Edison closer to having to deal with notions as abstract as the partial differential equations of James Clerk Maxwell than he ever would have believed, or felt comfortable with. The production of light bulbs, the generation of electricity, including the production and procurement of the relevant equipment, the integration and production of power lines, and the political and legal complications of procuring rights of way and eminent domain were tasks of integration, planning and coordinated effort that had little precedent in earlier times. The very innovative nature of the product and its associated technology dictated, almost by definition, that many of the projects necessary for its consummation had to be carried out in-house. In only a few of these cases were the personnel, infrastructure or technology available outside of these firms that would have enabled a reversion to the open market as an alternative to the creation of the necessary technologies and their managerial structures.

In other giant firms, the key interventions were largely of a managerial and organisational nature. There were few strictly technological innovations in the development of Ford's assembly line, with the key intervention being the aggressive exploitation of the production of interchangeable parts, a practice over a century old. What was distinctive was Ford's careful coordination of all parts of the production process and its integration with a marketing strategy of very high volume of a uniform, well-made but inexpensive product – the Model T. This exploitation of the technology of parts standardisation must be seen in the broader context of Ford's desire for the imposition of standardisation, not only in inputs and production processes, but in product uniformity as well – all mechanisms for the maintenance of control in the context of mass production.

These developments were intimately connected, as we have seen, with notions of scientific management of the labour force. Scientific management was seen as a vital component in putting production on a rational basis: without a normative standard of how much a worker ought to produce in various contexts, the new cost-accounting techniques developed to aid the large firm in judging the relative efficiency of its disparate activities would be of limited use. Thus, the much-applauded aspects of this new world – the tight quality control of products, as well as the rationality, coherence and efficiency associated with the monitoring of costs in the giant firm – were, in the eyes of its creators, inseparable from the Taylorist regime of precise measurement and control of an often monotonous and authoritarian work process.

By contrast, the failure to achieve standardisation in parts, processes and products in contemporaneous British industries, and their maintenance of what appear to be low levels of market concentration in comparison, for instance, with their US counterparts, is not, as might be suggested by economic orthodoxy, a salutary preservation of competition in the British economy, but a retention of old-fashioned ways of doing things.[57] In the machine tool and electrical goods industries, the failure of any great firm, combination of firms or governmental agency to impose standardised specifications led to fragmented industries whose seemingly low concentration prevented firms, each with its idiosyncratic specifications and submarkets, from competing against each other in a meaningful way. As we have seen earlier in the context of the market for grain, an administered solution imposing uniformity of measurement, standards and quality often acts as a prerequisite for the creation of a market in its literal sense.

Even in situations in which technological innovation was not prominent, the desire to control and direct the trajectory of events was an important aspect of the emergence of these giants. For John D. Rockefeller, securing deals with the railroads at the expense of competitors was merely an aspect of bringing an order and predictability to the oil market that would be of general social benefit by permitting a general expansion of the sector. It was common for the great industrialists to defend their pursuit of greater market control by citing the wasteful aspects of competitive processes, remarks echoed by socialist thinkers. Implicit in such a notion is the ubiquitous presence of economies of scale in many sectors, so that any losses to the public due to monopoly control were to be more than compensated for by the potential for lower costs associated with the higher volumes of output within a single organisation. The exercise of control by a giant enterprise extended to using its influence in the political domain to create barriers to new competition, for the receipt of government contracts, and to prevent labour organisations from creating 'obstacles in restraint of trade'.

The characteristic aspect of the giant firm was, thus, the attempt to exercise control – over the range of links in the chain of production, distribution and innovation; over competitors, actual and potential; over consumers, with marketing and advertising; and over the labour force, with a refashioning of the work process. For the small groups of individuals directing the great enterprises, the very size of these firms meant that new solutions to the question of financing had to be introduced that did not simply cede sovereignty of the firm to a distant, dispersed and transitory share-owning public. It was not, however, merely the vast size of these enterprises and the longevity of the capital being used by these firms that necessitated the development of a whole new class of strategies for the financing of the firm: of equal significance is the fact that the planning horizon of these new entities, with their self-conscious attempts to control the future, was significantly longer than that of First Industrial Revolution firms. The political context of these giant firms posed both dangers and opportunities. Their large size made their efforts to control their environment conspicuous, and they sometimes achieved notoriety in the eyes of the public. On the other hand, the substantial resources available to them permitted them to develop methods for influencing or accommodating themselves to the power of the state, and for integrating the workforce into their desired regime of control and planning.

By the early twentieth century, the material lives of the populations of North America and Western Europe had been transformed, along with the emergence of an enhanced capacity of the nations in these areas to wreak destruction upon each other. The most conspicuous vehicle for this transformation was the giant firm, which was mass-producing products in unprecedented quantities and inventing utterly new ones. The key problems that these enormous entities had to solve were concerned with the planning and control of their activities: there were technical questions concerned with the standardisation of processes and products, managerial problems linked to coordination and control of the enterprise in the context of innovation (including problems of marketing, finance and dealing with competitors), and the integration of the labour force as a malleable input into the production process.

These giant firms, the fulcrum of modernity, had planning, coordination and control as the focus of their activities, and therefore posed a major challenge to an economic orthodoxy centred round competitive markets. This orthodoxy was, in essence, unaffected by the Second Industrial Revolution. Alongside this orthodoxy, there emerged a set of doctrines suggesting that a qualitative discontinuity with the past had taken place. The capitalism that was changing the world was perceived to be a planned capitalism functioning through the visible hand of administrative control, one that was relegating Adam Smith's world of invisible-hand competitive capitalism to the historic past. The simultaneous truth and fallaciousness of this new planning doctrine was to reveal itself throughout the twentieth century, as analysts of various kinds failed in their attempt to extract the rational planning element of big-firm capitalism from its embedded links to finance, marketing and competition. But the doctrine itself, whether true or not, was to be a major force guiding the trajectory of real-world events through its influence on socialist ideology.

3

Technocratic Planning and the Emergence of a Socialist Orthodoxy

The world of the late nineteenth century was one of continuous innovation and novelty that impinged, for better or ill, on the life of every inhabitant of the rich nations, and on a large part of those living in colonies or subject to the political and economic hegemony of the great powers. Novelties from the commercial sector transformed consumption, work and travel patterns, while weaponry emerging from the new technologies would bring misery and death to millions from August 1914, as it had already for many in colonial nations and subject areas. The ideology of liberalism, emanating most powerfully from the British Empire, saw the world through an unchanged vision of entrepreneurs, competition and free trade.

For people across the political spectrum who were convinced that a new world was emerging, it was a commonly held presumption that control and planning within the giant firm were inseparable from innovation and modernity. Aspects of this unfolding technocratic planning paradigm could be found politically on the right from social Darwinists – including the Robber Barons themselves and later from fascist writers – who viewed the emergence of dominant firms as a natural unfolding of capitalist competition, and from technocratic perspectives representing a range of political views. In a key development, notions of planning were fused with a bureaucratic perspective, most especially in the context of the state as a vehicle for economic development. This state planning view of modernity eventually absorbed the socialist tradition to the point of threatening to extinguish the latter's independent identity.

Liberalism and the Great Transformation

Liberal economic thought, dominant in the British Empire and having important representation in the US and on the Continent, presented to the world a unified and coherent set of propositions: capitalism, free trade and the laissez-faire state, all in the context of a gold standard guided from Britain, were the keys to general prosperity. In the bastions of liberal ideology, the US and Britain, there were contrasting political responses in the new era. In the US, Progressive era reformers in the early years of the century, while accepting the reality or even the inevitability of the new form of capitalism in its big business manifestation, were often willing to use an anti-big business rhetoric that in Europe would be identified with socialist politics. One aspect of the US progressive movement, identified with Theodore Roosevelt, advocated regulation of the great trusts. A more distinctly American approach to big business had been initiated with the passage of antitrust legislation: great enterprises such as American Tobacco and Rockefeller's Standard Oil were dismembered early in the century.

There emerged a widespread concern, most robustly in the US and persisting for much of the twentieth century, that capitalism was coming under the domination of monopolies. Monopoly was seen as the source of predatory policies of various kinds, including monopolistic or cartel price gouging in sectors of market dominance, bullying and intimidation of competitors, and vertical integration leading to the spectre of the control of raw materials by (foreign) cartels. The latter possibility had economic implications, in posing a threat to competitive entry, and political-security implications, in the context of nations preparing for the next war. An important contradiction to the US image (and self-image) as a focal point of support for liberalism and free markets is the fact that from 1875 (and probably from 1861) until the end of the Second World War, the US had the highest average tariff rates on manufactured products in the world.[1]

In Britain, by contrast, even when the free trade consensus was questioned politically after 1903 by Joseph Chamberlain, this withdrawal from liberal orthodoxy was more a defensive response to the deleterious effects on manufacturing in Britain of its high levels of capital export and of other nations' unfair tariff levels, rather than a questioning of the premises of that consensus.[2] Not until 1919 do we see some alarm expressed in Britain about the growing power of monopolies and trade associations.[3] The British government refused, at the beginning of the century and subsequently, to pursue anti-monopolies policies: there was even tepid governmental promotion of industry rationalisation (amalgamation) in the interwar period. These policies may be a reflection of the weaker presence of giant firms in the UK compared with the US, or they may indicate the view that competition (except in the form of free trade) was an imperfect, approximate form of regulation whose loss was of minimum consequence. The possibility exists, however, that in Europe in general, even in Britain, there was an awestruck admiration for the great behemoths emerging, most especially, in the US. Perhaps Britain was reflecting in its passive political behaviour a perception of the link between planning, large scale and modernity, even at the expense of competition, which in continental Europe frequently resulted in active support for cartels and rationalisation.

What is most striking, however, are not the ambivalent responses in the political world to these great changes in the functioning of capitalism, but the position taken by the great liberal economists of the age, who, when faced with the presence of giant firms, defended their traditional worldview by ignoring these entities. Alfred Marshall, the most influential economist in the English-speaking world, was well regarded for his practical approach to, most especially, industrial affairs. Not only do economics textbooks to this day reflect a stylised version of his formulations, but up to the end of the twentieth century prominent economists such as Milton Friedman and George Stigler were proud to be followers of Marshall. Yet in both his theoretical and more descriptive work, from the late nineteenth century to the 1920s, Marshall betrays little hint of the great eruption that had taken place in the business world, most prominently in the US and Imperial Germany, and of Britain's laggard development relative to these countries.[4] Marshall's perspective suggested a loosely competitive context,[5] with the size of the firm presumed to stay within bounds that permit competitive conditions to exist. While his analytical constructions could, in principle, have admitted the possibility of the emergence of giant firms dominating an industry, Marshall's 'representative firm', even after the First World War, continued to be a stylised representation of the British textile mill.

Marshall and other liberal economists were also unresponsive to the dramatic changes taking place in the internal direction and structure of the emergent great firms. The firm remained a black box, a vehicle for trading in a market economy, ruled by an entrepreneur and 'his' family, and going through a life cycle of expansion and decline, going from 'shirtsleeves to shirtsleeves in three generations'.[6] There is very little indication from Marshall or other liberal economists that, in the most dynamic sectors of the world capitalist economy, firm governance in giant enterprises was being transformed by innovations in management so dramatic as to create a discontinuity with the forms prevalent in the First Industrial Revolution.

For Marshall, the distinctive success of corporate business management in the US, impossible to ignore by 1920, is mystifyingly accounted for by 'a powerful process of natural selection [that] has thus called out the leaders of American industry ... who entered on life with the resolve that they would prove themselves to be abler and greater than their fellows by becoming rich'.[7] The unprecedented scale and diversity of activities that needed to be coordinated by the giant firm and developments in its internal workings and procedures (including standardisation) are considered. But we are admonished, in a section entitled 'Temptations of joint stock companies to excessive enlargement of scope', that there is a 'tendency of some joint stock companies and municipalities to make things, which it would perhaps have been better for themselves and for others that they should have bought ... a true balance of its advantages and disadvantages is perhaps never made out'.[8] Ironically, in the 1970s this counsel could have proved useful for firms in the midst of conglomerate *hubris*, but in 1920, this balancing of opposing forces – 'in almost every trade there is a constant rise and fall of large businesses, at anyone moment some firms being in the ascending phase and others in the descending'[9] – comes across as not so much a commonsensical weighing of countervailing tendencies as an obtuseness about how the leading exemplars of the industrial economy, especially in the US, had transformed the environment in the previous decades.

Most significantly, firms in the Marshallian context were seen to be passive respondents to the constraints of cost and demand rather than agents of change that might transform these constraints by managerial or technological innovation, often in the context of new products for which marketing and advertising had to be provided. When, in the interwar period, the new world of giant firms was obliquely recognised in the Marshallian tradition with the creation of imperfectly and monopolistically competitive market structures, the results were unsatisfactory.[10] These new versions failed to capture what had been most important about the events of the Great Transformation at the beginning of the century – that the emerging giant firm often functioned as a fulcrum of coordination and planning. Its central activities involved on-going endeavours to reshape the very parameters of cost and demand that continued to be taken as given, even in these updated versions of the Marshallian model. The attempts by the giant firm to exercise control over the environment in which it functioned would lead some epigones of planning to see this new entity and its activities as the basis upon which a whole economy could be organised; Marshall and mainstream liberalism never offered a coherent riposte to this view. The unimaginative response of the dominant economic ideology to the dramatic changes in the functioning of business affairs inaugurated in the late nineteenth century continued for much of the next hundred years, with even a reassertion of a strict competitive orthodoxy after the Second World War.

Why did orthodox responses to the Great Transformation prove to be so inadequate? One reason is the analytical intractability of the events themselves, whose key aspects were first well encapsulated not by a theorist but by a business historian, Alfred Chandler, as we have seen in Chapter 2, and then only in the period after the Second World War. The subsequent attempts to reformulate his conception within traditional orthodox categories of markets and transactions in the Coase–Williamson literature succeeded in capturing little of the revolutionary nature of the giant firm emerging at the beginning of the twentieth century. In the British case, perhaps this failure of economic analysis from Marshall and his successors was also a reflection of the dominance in British polity through much of the twentieth century of a financially oriented 'gentlemanly capitalism'[11] that responded in such a laggard fashion to the conditions permitting a Second Industrial Revolution in, especially, Germany and the US. The possibility exists, however, that this intellectual failure was itself a contributing factor to Britain's sluggish response to the Second Industrial Revolution.

Though the discussion in subsequent chapters postulates that the eventual demise of socialism in the twentieth century was linked to its inadequate conceptualisation of trends in capitalism, there is an element of mitigation to be found. Unlike liberal economics, the planning ideology with which socialism became identified represents an attempt to engage with and understand the dramatic events surrounding the Great Transformation; even when the analysis was faulty, important insights into the workings of the new economy emerged. By contrast, orthodox economics has continued to emphasise the efficacy of market relationships, an adherence that, like a stopped clock, has yielded correct, if deceptive, results upon occasion and functions as orthodoxy, or even common sense, in many parts of the world in the twenty-first century. It has led to a range of public policies in which financial returns are taken to be the unquestioned guide to, and measure of, economic development and progress; the economy as a whole is often seen to be a self-equilibrating spontaneous order, in which direction and regulation is necessary only to facilitate this natural state. These presumptions will be contested here and in subsequent chapters, but from a perspective that has only limited points of contact with the critique of this orthodoxy presented below.

The ideology of technocratic planning

Intellectual opposition to liberal economic thought was widespread in the Western world (as well as among subject peoples and in colonies), but was often accompanied by a rejection of modernity, whether from William Morris or the Catholic Church. However, from a disparate collection of individuals and movements there emerged as well an opposition to liberal ideology that embraced contemporary developments. With only limited deformation of the historical record, it is possible to isolate a range of positions associated with these non-liberal thinkers. This alternative to liberal thought is dubbed here the 'technocratic planning paradigm', embodied in four principles:

1. The liberal vision of competition between enterprises as a mode of regulation for the economy was seen to be obsolescent. This first principle emerged from an empirical generalisation: there had been an inexorable growth in the efficient scale of enterprises and of units of production in modern capitalism.
2. Planning was taken to be the relevant mode of regulation for the economy as a whole, and was to be modelled on the internal workings of the giant firm.

3. There was an embrace of an engineering perspective that viewed activities such as administration, marketing and, especially, finance as peripheral: all were waste, to be eliminated in a rational approach to the organisation of economic activity.
4. The above principles became associated with the notion of the developmental state – the state as a key actor in the process of economic development.

The long-term significance of the technocratic planning paradigm as a unified dogma is its manifestation in the theory and practice of centrally planned socialism. The emphasis in this section, however, is upon the non-socialist variants of the technocratic planning paradigm emerging contemporaneously with socialist views. The planning paradigm thus had a broad base of support across the political and ideological spectrum: its final flourish as a non-socialist doctrine, as we shall see in Chapter 5, took place with the publication in the 1960s of John Kenneth Galbraith's *New Industrial State*.

In the first principle of the technocratic planning discourse, we have a conflation of large-scale enterprise with notions of modernity and efficiency, and often with monopoly: industry, especially the leading sectors of the economy, was seen to be falling inevitably into the hands of a small number of dominant firms – monopolies – with competition identified with anarchy and redundant capacity, and small enterprises with old-fashioned and inefficient ways of doing business. The emergence and inevitable predominance of large firms in the leading sectors of the economy were seen through a Darwinian prism: the fittest had survived due to their inherent superiority and the intrinsic, especially technological, advantages of large scale. Thus, the steel magnate Andrew Carnegie became a disciple of Herbert Spencer, and in a Sunday school address, John D. Rockefeller declared:

> The growth of a large business is merely a survival of the fittest...The American Beauty rose can be produced in the splendor and fragrance which bring cheer to its beholder only by sacrificing the early buds which grow up around it. This is not an evil tendency in business. It is merely the working-out of a law of nature and a law of God.[12]

It was not just American captains of industry who voiced these views. In the US, the famous German-born American engineer and scientist Charles P. Steinmetz, a self-proclaimed socialist, acted as an apologist for his employer General Electric and similar giants. He explained that the new technologies, with their high levels of fixed costs, inevitably result in 'ruinous competition', with amalgamation and 'co-operation' the inevitable, and desirable, consequence; attempts to thwart these developments through antitrust activity are to 'act against the laws of nature'. His favourable view of Imperial

Germany's industrial development, if not its politics, was consistent with this perspective.[13]
Even tenacious critics of big business in this and later periods were likely to ruefully concede the validity of the empirical premises of the techno-cratic planning paradigm: 'under a system once broadly competitive, methods of producing many commodities have changed in favor of the large firm; the very competition that induces the most economical utiliza-tion of the means of production has induced the survival of firms so large and so few that perfect competition itself no longer survives in a number of industries'.[14] An acceptance of the empirical validity of this first principle was thus widespread, and not only from the spokespeople and apologists for big firms: monopoly power was sometimes defended as mitigating the wastefulness of a traditional, competitive capitalism that perpetuated the existence of redundant capacity in the form of firms too small to be effi-cient. Capitalism, it was often argued, blindly, imperfectly and slowly elimi-nates this redundant capacity in an unplanned way, but only at a high cost to human beings and to the overall efficiency of the economy. Thus, the first principle of the technocratic planning perspective was that there had been an inexorable growth in the efficient scale of enterprises and units of production, a tendency that was dictating a decline in the role of competi-tion between enterprises as a mode of regulation for the economy. This view underlined for many the inevitability of the rise of the 'big monopolies' and engendered an ambivalent response to this development.

The first principle of technocratic planning rejected as irrelevant the liberal conception of a competitive economy. By contrast, the second principle used the change in the economic landscape to offer a positive alternative to the liberal vision of capitalism: the world to come was to be dominated not by the invisible hand of competition but by a visible hand of planning and conscious coordination. Some of the impetus for an organised capitalism through amalgamations and cartel arrangements in nineteenth-century Germany, and later in other countries, was in response to economic back-wardness: an attempt to generate scale efficiencies and to conserve, through centralisation, the scarce human and institutional resources available for enterprise management (see Chapter 2). However, for a broad swathe of opinion, the most significant motivation for an acceptance of consolidation and organisation was that the planned, ordered economy offered a possi-bility of relief from the gyrations in prices, production and employment that seemed to be endemic to capitalism. In Germany, the major stimulus for consolidation took place in the wake of the depressed conditions after 1873, and this motive emerged as a common one in capitalism: *The Menace of Overproduction*, written by a wide range of representatives of US business, was published after the stock market crash of October 1929.[15] And in 1931, we read the following favourable interpretation of German procedures:

The aim of rationalisation is to eliminate that competition which results from faulty judgment of individual producers, from their miscalculation of the market, and to coordinate the efforts, first, of individual enterprisers within an industry; second, of the different industries within a country; and third, of the competing industries in two or more countries... Rationalisation, in its broadest sense, aims to eliminate errors of judgment due to faulty knowledge of market conditions by vesting the power to regulate production, fix prices and allocate territories in a central authority. Rationalisation represents the idea of enlightened leadership embracing an entire industry in its relation to other industries and to the national economy.[16]

In this pre-Keynesian period, there was little that was being offered by economic orthodoxy in terms of public policy to alleviate that most egregious of capitalist failures – outbreaks of mass unemployment. Here we see the notion that centralised coordination in capitalism might eliminate perturbations resulting from 'competition which results from faulty judgment of individual producers': scientific management was to be used in the mitigation of economic fluctuations;[17] in 1899, similar sentiments had been expressed by the revisionist Marxist theorist Eduard Bernstein. Less ambitiously, macroeconomic fluctuations, including the great downturn of the 1930s, were frequently viewed through the prism of an inevitable elimination of jobs and redundant capacity due to increases in efficiency. For technocratic planners, this process of rising productivity, manifesting itself in capitalism in such a wasteful manner, could be achieved more rationally through a planned, coordinated rationalisation.

In a more positive direction, rationalisation was linked to the development of scientific management and the dispersal of best-practice scientific and managerial technique, giving us a glimpse of a new economic order.[18] In Europe, the cult of technocratic expertise and efficiency – 'Americanism' – in the form of scientific management and corporate organisation reached its apogee in the period after the First World War, and technocrats in the US reciprocated this admiration by noting the active role of the German state in this process. At various times, interest groups along the whole political spectrum were represented in the rationalisation movement, including radical groupings on the left and right, as well as those who wished to use the cult of technical expertise as a device for mitigating social conflict.[19] Whereas, in the US, rationalisation took place within the corporate structure or, at most, industry groupings, in Germany it was present in coordinated activity at the national level. These developments unfolded most dramatically, and with significant influence on the Bolsheviks, as we shall see below, with Walter Rathenau's organisation of Germany's economy in the First World War.

In a document from a semi-official source in the US from 1929, we see how widespread envy of Germany's postwar movement in the direction of rationalisation had become,[20] and how this rationalisation process was identified with engineering efficiency in the form of standardisation:[21]

> Rationalization ... is standardization [and] scientific management ... carried out on a broad national, and in some cases, international basis ... Standardization as a conscious deliberate policy involves the rationalizing process, and to a certain extent all standardization is a manifestation and a part of rationalization. But the popular use of the term 'rationalization' is much broader:
>
> > In its broad German conception, rationalization includes standardization and simplification, reduction of waste and scientific management, labor-saving equipment, reduction of overhead cost, economy in selling, and finally, and highly important from our point of view, the consolidation of corporations with all allocation of production and the closing of uneconomic industrial units. There is a national committee that encourages standardization in all its ramifications throughout industry. (US Dept. of Commerce, Division of Simplified Practice, *Monthly News Bulletin*, 15 September 1927.)

Second, we see a welcoming to cartels and other anti-competitive activities as aspects of this rationalisation – this emerging from a country that had pioneered antitrust legislation:

> The revival of cartels, industrial mergers and combinations, pooling agreements, etc., are important features of the rationalization movement. So important a feature has this part of the movement become that it has come to occupy the center of the stage in many discussions of the program to eliminate waste on a national scale. An American Standards Association bulletin refers to it as:
>
> > the concentration of a country's economic resources in the hands of those industrial combinations most competent to use them, and the modernization of industrial plants and processes. Such rationalization postulates every form of cooperative activity from the formation of selling combinations to the actual amalgamation of business, to the end of eliminating all wastes arising through uneconomic types of competition. (*Sustaining Members Bulletin*, 14 February 1928.)

Third, we see positive remarks about the 'Russian Gosplan' at a time when the US did not have diplomatic relations with the Soviet Union:

> A similar conception [to that of Germany] of the marshalling of industrial resources, skill and energy underlies the Russian Gosplan. The recent

report of the British Liberal Party, 'Britain's Industrial Future,' lays down the tentative outlines for some such national coordination and unification of the nation's industries. There are, of course, considerable differences between these latter proposals and the rationalization movement as it is developing in Germany ... [b]ut in their technological features, all three are proceeding along similar lines.

Though these notions of national planning remained a minority view in the US, they emerged in the first decades of the twentieth century across a broad political spectrum that is only sampled here, extending far beyond radical socialism. The idea, as above, of 'eliminating all wastes arising through uneconomic types of competition' is a particularly startling one to twenty-first century readers, who live in an era in which the efficacy of competition is an unquestioned and universal proposition.[22]

The vision of a wholly planned economy had early roots in Saint-Simonian and Marxian notions, but there is little doubt that the striking example of the innovative activities of the giant enterprises in the US and in Germany was the key to the plausibility of the emergent vision of a planned economy. The construction of the administrative apparatus and procedures necessary to make these giants viable was seen to rival in ingenuity the substantive technological achievements within giant enterprises. These developments, along with the enhanced capacity of governmental bureaucracies, were at the heart of technocratic planning.

The practice of giant firms and state bureaucracies was to become the basis of the new ideology for a broad spectrum of non-liberal thinkers, both socialist and others. The notions of economic planning for a whole society, in both their technocratic and socialist versions, embodied many of the limitations to be found in the business literature. Most specifically, since the conceptualisation of firm-level planning in this era gave no explicit attention to decision making under uncertainty, central planning theorists largely ignored this issue as well, reinforced by the complacent notion that much or all of the uncertainty to which an individual capitalist firm is subject will disappear if the whole economy is subject to a plan. And socialists, using the great firms as a model, did not disentangle the 'capitalist' from the 'planning' elements in 'capitalist planning' – they did not successfully clarify those elements of the capitalist environment that were necessary and inextricable aspects of the ability of great firms to plan successfully. This proved to be, as we shall see in Chapter 4, a major failure for socialist theorists and for practitioners of planning, as well as for orthodox defenders of capitalism.

The third principle of the technocratic planning paradigm involved the embrace of an engineering perspective emerging from mid-nineteenth-century France and Britain. Engineers confronted practical problems of resource allocation for which, in their view, the contemporaneous political economy did not offer adequate solutions. Perhaps strongest in France, the tradition of engineering economics yielded energy-based distinctions between useful work and waste, and a quantitative expression of efficiency: 'Engineers do economics while others talk about it.'[23]

Engineering planning had a visionary aspect – the new economy is to be innovative and to be *engineered* in a planned, rational way, down to the finest details of its operation. A growing uniformity in the quality and specifications of output is, in general, a fundamental aspect of capitalist development and is co-extensive with the evolution of markets; standardisation of parts in production had been a developing trend since the eighteenth century. The convergence and the consummation of these two tendencies were seen in the Ford assembly line: its output was uniform, both in the sense of evidencing high levels of quality control and in the notorious limitation on the range of variants from the standard Model T (in terms of colour and availability of 'gizmos'): the latter constraint on product diversity was justified in terms of maximising the possibilities for scale economies through the elimination of gratuitous variations in peripheral aspects of the product.

The drive for standardisation of specifications for inputs used in production – in machine tool parts, electrical equipment and so on – became a rallying cry for the technocracy movement. The dogma of maintaining a uniformity of output (in the sense of limiting product differentiation) gradually disappeared from general discussions concerned with reforming capitalism: one reason might be the success that GM had over Ford in the 1920s in maintaining scale efficiencies in the presence of a broad range of car models. Uniformity of output continued to be upheld, however, in the Soviet planning context and in socialist critiques of capitalism.

The engineering perspective reached its fullest development as a purely economic doctrine in the technocratic movement in the US. In Germany, by contrast, the lessons to be learned from the emergence of giant enterprises were filtered through notions of national economic development using protectionism from the nineteenth-century economist Friedrich List, and in radical socialist Marxian currents. In the US, the host of the most prominent exemplars of the new capitalism, substantial antagonism to the rise of these giant firms emerged. For those willing to take a more favourable, or at least a more accommodating, view of these developments from a planning perspective, there was limited scope for doing so, given the strong association in US political discourse between planning and radical socialist ideas. The doctrine of technocracy, coalescing around the ambiguous figure of Thorstein Veblen, took a position in support of planning and opposed to market liberalism that was not perceived as politically radical or threatening by mainstream opinion.

Veblen's early work, *The Theory of the Leisure Class*, with its famous discussion of 'conspicuous consumption' by the well-to-do, was centrally concerned with the deleterious aspects of this expenditure. It was natural for his followers to focus, in this context, on firms' advertising and marketing activity as wasteful: it was unnecessary and gave impetus to profligate consumption.[24] Veblen viewed the activities of the business class so unfavourably that industrial consolidations were perceived to have, if nothing else, the virtue of reducing the volume of these activities: 'perhaps the greatest opportunity for saving by consolidation ... is in doing away with unnecessary business transactions and industrially futile manoeuvring on the part of independent firms that the promoter of combinations finds his most telling opportunity ... there is a saving of work and an avoidance of that systematic mutual hindrance that characterizes the competitive management of industry'.[25]

But for Veblen, the greater part of business activity is worse than parasitic. For him, material progress emerges from improvements in the arts of manufacture – the work of engineers and technicians, in spite of the 'sabotage' coming from the business community:

> The material welfare of the community is unreservedly bound up with the due working of this industrial system, and therefore with its unreserved control by the engineers, who alone are competent to manage it. To do their work as it should be done these men of the industrial general staff must have a free hand, unhampered by commercial considerations and reservations ... Yet the absentee owners, now represented, in effect, by the syndicated investment bankers, continue to control the industrial experts and limit their discretion, arbitrarily, for their own commercial gain, regardless of the needs of the community.[26]

Veblen was not a follower of Marx, and he has little to say about the working class. He presents a utopia that responds to the logic of technology. His writings are important because they represent a significant stream of opinion, one distanced from Marxist orthodoxy, which believed that the material progress generated by the Second Industrial Revolution could be detached from the business institutions that had been responsible for generating this progress. In a manner resembling that described by Marx, these institutions were acting as a fetter on the full use of the nation's productive capacity:

> a free run of production, such as the technicians would be ready to set afoot if they were given a free hand, would mean a full employment of the available forces of industry, regardless of what the traffic would bear in point of net profit from sales ... [but it] ... has not been had nor aimed at; nor is it at all expedient, as a business proposition, that anything of the kind should be allowed.[27]

The Engineers and the Price System ends with a chapter entitled 'A Soviet of Technicians', a designation that later took on a bitterly ironical twist with the trials and conviction of engineers for acts of sabotage in the Soviet Union of 1930 on charges that now are considered to have been without foundation. Veblen's quixotic proposals for an engineer-led utopia went nowhere. They ran up against the sociological reality in the US that discontent on the part of engineers themselves was not directed towards creating an independent power centre, a Soviet of technicians, that would oppose the reigning business culture. On the contrary, the engineers were embedded in that business culture, and any discontent on their part was focused on raising their status within it.[28]

A second issue concerning Veblen's new society is a strictly economic one: would the calculation of efficiency solely according to an engineering logic ever be possible, and are all aspects of business culture, including its financial institutions and mechanisms, mere impediments to the realisation of efficiency? This third principle of technocratic planning resulted in a rejection not only of a functional role for the financial sector, but also of other activities seemingly peripheral to the firm's production activities.

And here we see a further ambivalence on the part of much non-liberal opinion concerning the rise of the giant firm: its emergence was seen to be inevitable largely for technological reasons, but the technocratic planning aspect of non-liberal opinion, with its focus on engineering rationality, was temperamentally at odds with the Weberian identification of modernity with bureaucracy, to be discussed below. The administrative apparatus that invariably accompanied the vast expansion in the size and complexity of the activities of the giant firms (and of the state) compared with anything to be seen previously were an anathema to the technocratic view: bureaucracy, administration, not to mention marketing and finance, were *waste*. Somewhat contradictorily, payments to middlemen were also thought of as waste, obviating the possibility of considering using the market to alleviate bureaucratic stress inside an enterprise. The unresolved question of the efficacy of these peripheral economic activities persisted in the conduct of real existing socialism and played a part in the demise of the dream of an economy based solely on engineering considerations, one without the wasteful frills associated with commercial activity.

The fourth aspect of the technocratic planning approach emerged when the principles enunciated above were linked to the notion of the state as a key actor in economic development, an integration that was to become a central aspect of the ideology of the new Soviet state. By contrast, liberal opinion and its associated economic doctrines in the late nineteenth century had little to say explicitly about economic growth and development, and had no role for the state in any such process. The liberal notion that free trade and its incumbent specialisation of activities led to a generalised prosperity would, if anything, promote a withdrawal of state activity.

The late emergence of this fourth technocratic planning principle – the developmental state – is somewhat curious, since the pervasiveness and depth of bureaucracy had been evolving in a European context for half a millennium. The expansion of the scope and domain of governmental activity in modern Europe long precedes the emergence, in the latter part of the nineteenth century, of the giant enterprises that became the epitome of the new world of administration because of the unprecedented scale and diversity of private sector activities they needed to coordinate. Even well along the path of expansion of state activity, the court of Louis XIV of France in the seventeenth century, so centralising in its aspirations, was constrained by the physical infrastructure of roads and even the language diversity within the kingdom. By the late nineteenth century, the railway and telegraph, and then the telephone, had given the most liberal of Third Republic governments a direct access to, and power over, the people of France that the ministers of the Sun King could only have dreamed of. The introduction of the typewriter and office equipment and the continued development of the mechanics of data collection were complemented by the emergence of institutions for the training of a professionalised bureaucracy. These changes in the administrative capacity of the state were taking place in authoritarian St Petersburg as well as in liberal London, with little regard to the putative ideology governing state activity.

The extended capabilities of the bureaucracy were matched by developments in civil society that facilitated an expanded role for the state: urbanisation, a growing literacy in a uniform national language (Parisian French), the use of money in rural areas, and the substitution of the state for the church in the provisioning of activities such as schooling, the marriage registry and, in Britain, the Poor Laws and their successors. All of these factors made the administration and local execution of a new range of state activities, regulations and forms of taxation possible. The augmentation of state activity also created dependency and vested interests, as in the provisioning and the setting of standards for state education and of poor relief. The activities of the state and bureaucracy in London and Paris thus became tied to intimate aspects of civil life to an unprecedented degree.

A definitive perspective on the emergence of bureaucracy is most commonly linked to the work of Max Weber, with the publication posthumously in 1922 of *Economy and Society*. For Weber, the administrative mechanism was an aspect of the cultivation of rational decision making in both the public and commercial spheres. Professionally trained state personnel do not only receive instruction in the formal aspects of the tasks that they administer, but are inculcated with the spirit of a public mission to be fulfilled – they are the embodiment of the disinterested needs of the state, pursuing tasks for the advancement or, at very least, the balancing of the needs of society. The bureaucracy follows rules, protocols and routinised procedures that, in any given instance, can seem arbitrary or unfair in application, but generate the possibility of a society run rationally. In the absence of such rules and protocols, we return to a medieval context in which the concepts of corruption and favouritism cannot even be defined:

> The decisive reason for the advance of bureaucratic organization has always been its purely *technical* superiority over any other form of organization. The fully developed bureaucratic apparatus compares with other organizations exactly as does the machine with the non-mechanical modes of production. Precision [and] speed... are raised to the optimum point in the strictly bureaucratic administration... 'Equality before the law' and the demand for legal guarantees against arbitrariness demand a formal and rational 'objectivity' of administration... If, however, an 'ethos' – not to speak of other impulses – takes hold of the masses on some individual question, its postulates of *substantive* justice, oriented toward some concrete instance and person, will unavoidably collide with the formalism and the rule-bound and cool 'matter-of-factness' of bureaucratic administration... Bureaucracy is *the* means of transforming social action into rationally organized action. Therefore, as an instrument of rationally organizing authority relations, bureaucracy was and is a power instrument of the first order for one who controls the bureaucratic apparatus.[29]

These consciously constructed rules and procedures constraining the activities of the state and its bureaucracy play the same role in society as do the spontaneously generated, judge-based precedents emerging from the tradition supported by Hayek. In both cases, decision making is removed from democratic processes – from impulses that might take hold of the masses.

It is precisely under capitalism that bureaucracy has reached new heights, in part because improvements in transport and communications have facilitated this development. But bureaucracy and administrative procedures have also expanded their scope under capitalism because of the functional role they play in its operation. In contrast with the relatively autarchic economic relations of pre-capitalist society, market-centred economies make demands upon government for the maintenance of physical infrastructure such as roads, a legal framework for enforcement of contracts, and a role in the money and credit system that, at the very least, is not disruptive. Furthermore, imposition by the state of uniformity in measurement and quality standards has been instrumental in the making of markets, and the rising agglomeration of the population in cities highlighted the need for urban planning and the institution of professionalised policing to maintain 'order'.

As a result, any apparent conflict between the Hayekian and Weberian perception of these rules disappears in the contemporary world. As we

have seen in Chapter 1, traditional liberalism sanctions active intervention on the part of the state to make markets viable. In recent times, we
have seen a more ambitious tendency surface in the form of a neoliberalism
that 'enjoins everyone to live in a world of generalized competition ... [and
creates] a world in its own image through its power to integrate *all* dimen-
sions of human existence'.[30] In a form particularly manifest in Germany,
there has emerged an activist role for the state in a liberal context, an ordoliberalism that involves 'institutionalizing the market economy in the form
of an "economic constitution" ... in such a way as to develop the fullest, most
coherent form of market'.[31] Weberian bureaucratic rules, as in the ordinances
governing the European Union, are thus validated and legitimated by the
notion that they are merely providing support for an underlying Hayekian
spontaneous order. In the wake of this marriage between Weberian and
Hayekian principles, we can currently observe ever more ambitious forms
of bureaucratic activism, such as a range of international agreements –
the Trans-Pacific Partnership and the Transatlantic Trade and Investment
Partnership – which will override individual governments' procedures with
regard to intellectual property rights and labour relations. Interventions of
this kind have their legitimacy greatly enhanced when the new Weberian
protocols that will emerge from these treaties are seen to be merely the ratification of a Hayekian spontaneous order of free trade and investment.

The role of the state in its military dimension has played an important
role in the history of capitalism.[32] This fact often lacks a proper representation in the Anglo-Saxon world, perhaps because standing armies, with their
enormous expense, have not played a central role in the emergence and
maintenance of power in Britain and the US (the British building an empire
using mostly naval power and the US by defeating its weak southern neigh-
bour Mexico and otherwise subduing aboriginals).[33] For other nations in
Europe, the emergence of a professionalised military and the delineation of
clear hierarchical structures distinguishing the tasks of commissioned and
non-commissioned officers was a school for the development of modern
bureaucracy, and paralleled or even preceded such developments in the
commercial sector. The increasingly mechanised nature of modern warfare
led to growing links with big business – a military-industrial complex –
in which the cultivation of modern hierarchical structures was mutually
re-enforced. These developments reached their consummation with the
concept of total war after August 1914. In all countries, the scale and the
economic commitment were unprecedented, but it was in Germany that
the economic mobilisation for the war made the most notable impression on
social observers of all political persuasions both during and after the war.

Liberal theorising about the state in the late nineteenth century was
largely concerned with constraining the scope of its activities, rather than
analysing its functional role and its internal structure. In practical terms,
however, great changes were taking place, with the institution of civil

service examinations in Britain for administration both at home and across the empire, giving Britain, like other European countries, an administrative structure that was substantively autonomous from the nominal government of the day. Some contrast emerged between the British approach, which professionalised its civil service to the highest levels, and that in the US, where upper-level administrative posts were more commonly the subject of political appointment (ambassadorships) or direct election (the local dog catcher, or much of the judiciary). But these developments in the US progressively appeared as populist and politicised interventions into the normal operation of bureaucratic functions and professionalised activities.

The introduction of a professionalised civil service, a significant change in the practicalities of state administration, was not complemented with any serious reconsideration in liberal thought of the role of the state administration in public affairs: the purpose of the latter remained the facilitation of commerce and the minimisation of its own wasteful use of resources. As we have seen earlier, it is only with the writings of the British economist Pigou in the early twentieth century that a systematic rationale emerged in liberal opinion for the role of the state in the regulation of external effects, both positive and negative (such as pollution); this literature had no significant influence on public policy until after the Second World War. Only with the coming of the depression of the 1930s did the liberal John Maynard Keynes find a theoretical justification for an active role for the state in stabilising the overall level of economic activity in an inherently erratic capitalist system.

Both the Weberian conception of a society governed by a disinterested rule-following bureaucracy and the liberal notions of an individualistic market-based civil society served as alternatives to the growing threat posed by a legitimacy based on democracy – explicit social decisions emanating from universal male suffrage – which might well have moved in an egalitarian, socialist direction. But even in late-nineteenth-century Germany, this largest of socialist movements was unsuccessful at forming alliances outside of the urban working class to divert the path to destruction being taken by Junker militarism. Whatever the reasons for this failure, including successful state repression, these difficulties were exacerbated by an official Marxist ideology that, quite properly, emphasised international solidarity over nationalism, but also alienated small landholders and capitalists with its call for the abolition of private property and frightened a liberal constituency with its rhetoric of revolution and dictatorship of the proletariat. In the longer term, socialism as a democratic movement was greatly compromised when it became identified with, at best, a Weberian bureaucracy and at worst (in the Stalinist case) a homicidal one; by contrast, notions of democracy were tied to a resurgent and only slightly modified market liberalism.

Socialism became inextricably identified with bureaucracy when it became linked to the ideology of technocratic planning in the Soviet Union, beginning in the 1920s, where the state was seen to play a central role in economic development. The concept of the developmental state was a continuation of early modern mercantilist notions of the state's role in national strategies for economic security, which was then integrated with a new element – the state as a vehicle for late-developing economies. Friedrich List (1789–1846) promoted a national economic strategy for Germany in the nineteenth century that was a self-conscious attempt to create an antipode to the liberal ideology emerging from the British Empire. He viewed Britain's advocacy of universal free trade as self-serving – advocating for other countries a policy which it had not itself pursued in its developing phase, and which would leave developing countries unable to compete with Britain:

> The island kingdom borrowed from every country of the Continent its skill in special branches of industry, and planted them on English soil, under the protection of her customs system … Once possessed of any one branch of industry, England bestowed upon it sedulous care and attention, for centuries treating it as a young tree which requires support and care … in any nation already advanced in agriculture and civilisation, by means of moderate protection, its infant manufactures, however defective and dear their productions at first may be, can by practice, experience, and internal competition readily attain ability to equal in every respect the older productions of their foreign competitors … England has attained to wealth and power not by means of, but in spite of, her commercial policy. As well might they argue that trees have grown to vigour and fruitfulness, not by means of, but *in spite of,* the props and fences with which they had been supported when they were first planted.[34]

List's notions of state intervention were substantively limited to tariff policy, and there was an absence of economic justification in theoretical terms that could compete with the formidable apparatus of liberal economics from David Ricardo supporting free trade. But Listian notions of state control, when combined with the Saint-Simonian forms of state investment policy typically found in various countries in continental Europe, acted as practical alternatives to the free trade and laissez-faire ideology that was emerging out of the British Empire. Marx, however, with his anti-state and internationalist perspective, remained a fierce opponent of List:

> The nationality of the worker is neither French, nor English, nor German, it is *labour, free slavery, self-huckstering.* His government is neither French, nor English, nor German, it is capital. His native air is neither French, nor German, nor English, it is factory air. The land belonging to him is neither French, nor English, nor German, it lies a few feet *below the ground.* Within the country, money is the fatherland of the industrialist. Thus, the German philistine wants the laws of competition, of exchange

value, of huckstering, to lose their power at the frontier barriers of his country![35]

Germany emerged in the late nineteenth century as the antipode to British liberalism. This was only in part because of the state's substantive intervention in industrial development at the national and regional level or its tariff policies. More important was the fact that this most successful of large European economies appeared to be mounting an ideological challenge to, and even rejection of, British liberalism as a mode of economic regulation: the operation of cartels and restraints on effective competition in Germany were integrated into public policy.[36]

Technocratic planning emerged in response to the Great Transformation of the late nineteenth century, with some aspects of the technocratic programme becoming part of general political discourse in Europe only after the Great War; in Britain and the US it remained a fringe development, both politically and intellectually. The most important political response on the right to emerge out of technocratic planning was fascism. To the extent that we can attribute a common basis and coherent economic doctrine to Italian and German fascism, it can be characterised by a subordination of economics to political, especially military-expansionist, goals. In the Italian case, it took a particularly incoherent form: expansionary politics and irregular attempts to control aspects of the economy were combined with an adherence to liberal economic principles. Italy's decision to remain on the gold standard in the 1930s, when most of its economic and potentially military rivals had departed from it, limited the ability of the fascist regime to pursue an armaments policy that would correspond to its international ambitions.[37] In Germany, by contrast, the fascist regime imposed, from the time of its accession to power, a series of controls on business unprecedented in peacetime, with direct oversight over large firms and cartels and the financial sector; fascism inherited a technocratic distaste for finance and peripheral sectors (reinforced in the German case by the identification of these activities with Jews). Economic planning was an aspect of national security, including state-directed securing of sources of raw materials. These policies, combined with tight control on competing imports, were highly profitable for business and fulfilled the central goal of arming and militarising the economy.[38] In wartime, however, as we shall see in the next chapter, the regime's social Darwinist belief in the efficacy of rivalry between firms proved less successful than the planned approach of both the Soviet Union and the US. For fascist states in the 1930s, and for the Soviet Union as well, the positive reception these regimes often received abroad was commonly linked to a perception of their strong resolve to deal with the crisis of mass unemployment.[39] This contrast was particularly strong when the comparison was with the passivity, fatalism and dithering to be found in a Great Britain still in the grip of liberal economic ideology.

In the Soviet Union, as we shall see, the developmental state became the basis for a socialist strategy, most especially when combined with the technocratic presuppositions about the centrality of planning and coordination in modern capitalism. The technocratic planning vision and the coextensive socialist notions were thus addressing the vast changes that had taken place in the economic landscape since the late nineteenth century, the threats to the social order posed by economic instability, and the challenges faced by late-developing economies. If in many ways the solutions offered by the technocratic planning perspective were inadequate, its engagement with these issues, even in its failures, advanced the discourse more than the unimaginative response of liberalism.

Socialism and technocratic planning

The disparate socialist movement emerging in the early nineteenth century, with a range of political and social demands, converged on a small number of economic principles by the end of that century. Socialism in the late nineteenth century in the UK and the rest of Europe was often displacing a radical liberalism on a range of traditional positions, such as the extension of the voting franchise (liberals often supporting the maintenance of restrictions on voting), expansion of public education, anti-clerical and secular attitudes, feminism, support for ethnic rights (such as the Jewish Socialist Bund in Russia) and national independence movements (Polish socialist movements in Tsarist Russia). In other ways, socialism became identified with views discontinuous from the liberal tradition – a radical pacifism, internationalism and anti-colonialism increasingly at odds with dominant opinion in the period before the Great War. Even more striking was the creation, as in the German Social Democratic Party (SPD) in prewar Germany, of a 'society within a society' of worker organisations dedicated to mutual assistance, education and social interaction, an alternative source of legitimacy to the imperial state for a large section of the population.

Gradually, the range of socialist approaches – utopian schemes, and the ideas of Saint-Simon, Proudhon and the syndicalists – gave way to the socialist ideology that had emerged in what was taken to be the leading capitalist state in continental Europe: Germany. Socialist ideology moved away from conceptions linked to the varied experience of supposedly less developed capitalist nations: French socialism before the First World War never developed as a serious rival to that in Germany, in either organisational or ideological terms.[40] No substantive rivals to technocratic planning emerged – there were syndicalists, anarchists and groups emphasising schemes for worker-based control of enterprises, producer cooperatives and small independent producers.[41] But the identification of these doctrines with smaller enterprises evoked forms of production typical in the less advanced parts of the capitalist world, and they were politically tainted by Marxists with the claim of being linked to petty capitalist enterprise. The main analytical weakness these alternatives suffered, furthermore, was that no convincing mechanism of coordination between these enterprises, groupings or cooperatives was ever specified. Vague evocations of cooperation in place of capitalist competition and the marketplace only engendered in Marxists the suspicion that the latter mechanism – marketplace competition – was being let in through the back door.

The binding force radicalising the pre-First World War socialist movement was the presence in Marxism of 'the best available theory of exploitation and the best available theory of history',[42] an important consideration in an era in which radical intellectuals were committed to scientific explanations for the analysis of society. Marxism offered an advanced intellectual framework claiming that the existing economic system – capitalism – was based on worker exploitation, so that the needs of workers and capitalists were ultimately irreconcilable. In an exposition by Otto Bauer in 1908 of the fundamental principles of the SPD, we can see a fusion of the SPD's popular, or 'vulgar', Marxism with the principles of the technocratic planning paradigm:

The mode of production of material life determines the social, political and cultural process of life.

The history of all hitherto existing society is a history of class struggles.

The value of a commodity is determined by the labor socially necessary for its production.

The wealth of the propertied classes derives from the surplus value produced by the workers.

Capitalist society tends to increase more and more the misery of the workers.

Small business will be destroyed; the control over the means of production falls into the hands of a continuously decreasing number of big capitalists.

Monopoly capitalism has become a fetter on the mode of production which arose under it and with it. The centralization of the means of production and the socialization of labor will reach a point where they will be incompatible with the external capitalist form. The final hour of capitalist private property is approaching. The expropriators will be expropriated.[43]

Socialism in a technocratic form overtook its potential rivals within the working-class movement at the end of the nineteenth century because of its suitability to the needs of a working class functioning in the emerging large enterprises and their respective labour union organisations. It is especially in the last two points of the platform above that the convergence between the first principle of the technocratic planning paradigm and the character of economic development in, especially, Germany can be seen. The gravitational movement of socialism in the direction of Germany contributed to the bringing of Marxism to centre stage in socialist ideological discourse. The powerful vision of economic progress presented by Marx – 'The country that is more developed [industrially] only shows, to the less developed, the image of its own future' – promoted the focus in socialist thought on Germany, and even on events in the US. With Marxism, socialist ideology was seen to be firmly linked to modernity.

The socialist ideology that emerged in Germany went under the rubric of Marxism. In a formal sense, this ideology preserved the anti-state and internationalist rhetoric associated with Marx, but gradually the SPD found itself linked politically to the German state, with its ultimate 'betrayal' (Lenin's word) being its support for the German war effort in 1914. Ideologically as well, the fabrication of a form of Marxism that synthesised it with bureaucratic-administrative forms resulted in an infidelity to its anti-state origins. When this synthesis was linked in the Soviet Union with the concept of the state as a vehicle for economic development, socialism was represented to the world in a form that had surrendered its internationalist origins and became identified with an all-pervasive national state.

The support for war credits in 1914 by the SPD was, without doubt, a betrayal of the internationalist principles of Marxism. But the movement away from Marx's anti-state orientation by the SPD (which had been advancing in a statist direction since the tenure of Ferdinand Lassalle, who died in 1864) and later by the Bolsheviks was the only way to bring coherence to their shared vision of a form of socialism that was linked to central planning. Marx's own vision was notoriously incomplete, with a Hegelian inhibition against utopian constructivism: the new society would emerge 'out of the womb' of the old one – the tendencies in the already existent capitalist society. In the present day, the opinion that central planning has proved to be a failure is so ubiquitous that pejorative opinions of Marx's economics invariably focus on identifying his views of post-capitalist society with central planning, with defenders distancing Marx from this approach. Less important here than an exegesis of Marx's views is the historical fact that socialism, and especially Marxism, the most fully developed form of socialist critique of capitalism in the early twentieth century, became wholly identified with a centrally planned alternative based on the principles of the technocratic planning paradigm.

The first principle suggesting an inexorable growth in the efficient scale of enterprises and of units of production in modern capitalism had been first postulated by Marx himself as early as the 1860s: his critique of the economics of his own day emphasised its failure to capture the dynamic, evolving character of capitalism. There are several statements in Marx concerning an inexorable concentration of capital in a few hands, and even suggestions of the emergence of a separation of ownership and control in the management of great enterprises. Unlike his followers from the middle of the twentieth century onwards, whom we will meet in Chapter 5, there is little in Marx's writings to suggest that this growing predominance of large firms implies a decline or collapse of the competitive mechanism as a regulatory device in capitalism. This is just as well for the coherence of Marx's analysis of capitalism, since economic analysis using the labour theory of value (even without its associated problems of transforming labour values into market prices) would be inoperative if monopolies were ubiquitously present.

But one important aspect of the first principle of technocratic planning that is legitimately linked to Marx's ideas is the notion that the petty producer is an atavistic remnant, to be destroyed by capitalist evolution, a principle maintained in the catechism of vulgar Marxism above. Politically, such a notion proved to be an obstacle to the forming of alliances between workers and these small producers, with its implication that socialists might wish to expedite small capitalists on their path to oblivion: in a leading element of dissent from SPD orthodoxy, the revisionist Eduard Bernstein points to the persistence of small and medium-size enterprises in the midst of the emergence of giant entities in the leading capitalist economies.[44]

The second principle of technocratic planning was an explicit adoption of planning as a mode of regulation for the economy. Was Marx a central planner? In one sense, he and his followers clearly were not. Marxists deviated from technocratic planning as a broad intellectual movement in their rejection of the notion that meaningful planning could take place under capitalism: the Marxian heritage reinforced the notion that capitalism possessed inherent contradictions that could not be rectified without the whole system being replaced. A Marxian account of the perturbations in employment and business activity in capitalism was in terms of class conflict, in which crises played a necessary and efficacious role for capitalists in the restoration of profitability and accumulation by reducing the bargaining power of labour through the creation of an industrial reserve army – unemployment.

Capitalism thus inherently generated fluctuations in economic activity and employment, as well as possessing long-term tendencies in the direction of stagnation or collapse. Marxist political economy was then able to account for the widespread growth of militarist and imperialist sentiment in the great capitalist powers in terms of the imperatives of capitalist expansion (for Lenin, imperialism was capitalism at its 'highest stage'), and the need for ruling groups to distract the working classes from the blatantly dysfunctional and exploitative nature of capitalism. Bernstein's hints of incipient economy-wide planning in the midst of late capitalism were rejected as heresy by orthodox Marxists.

A clear and continuing aspect of Marx's thought was his distaste for the market exchange, most especially the exchange of labour power, as a means of regulation and allocation for an economy. There are statements about the anarchy of production under capitalism and of the conscious coordination of production in the post-revolutionary era, but these notions are not elaborated upon. The usual explanation is that Marx was following Hegelian practice in not being overly speculative about the future, and that prominent exemplifications of capitalist planning were only beginning to emerge in his lifetime (Marx died in 1883, but his substantive work ended in the 1870s). Marx, on occasion, hints that the conscious coordination of the factory serves as an exemplification of the future post-capitalist society, but these are passing references. Statements in this regard are clearer in the writings of Friedrich Engels:

> The contradiction between socialised production and capitalistic appropriation now presents itself as an antagonism between the organisation of production in the individual workshop, and the anarchy of production in society generally... the production of society at large was ruled by absence of plan, by accident, by anarchy; and this anarchy grew to greater and greater height... the social anarchy of production gives place to a social regulation of production upon a definite plan, according to the needs of the community and of each individual. Then the capitalist mode of appropriation... is replaced by the mode of appropriation of the products that is based upon the nature of the modern means of production. With the seizing of the means of production by society production of commodities is done away with, and, simultaneously, the mastery of the product over the producer. Anarchy in social production is replaced by systematic, definite organisation.[45]

Even more starkly, Lenin makes it clear in 1917 that the regulation and coordination of the post-capitalist economy is not a problematic issue:

> The whole of society will have become a single office and a single factory, with equality of labour and equality of pay... it is quite possible, after the overthrow of the capitalists and the bureaucrats, to proceed immediately, overnight, to supersede them in the control of production and distribution, in the work of keeping account of labour and products by the armed workers, by the whole of the armed population.[46]

If for Marx, and even Engels, the concepts of a general plan were still vague, for Lenin, all these difficulties had been swept away by the example of Henry Ford: operating like 'a single factory' will permit the new system to function autonomously, without any central direction. In Lenin's enthusiasm for Taylor's notions of scientific management, concepts of plan rationality and efficiency converged with strict control of workforce activity: with the embrace of the Plan, socialism in its Soviet manifestation found little room for workers' control.

The third principle viewed peripheral activities such as administration, marketing and, especially, finance as waste, all to be eliminated in a rational approach to the organisation of economic activity. The economics of Marx suggests a denigration of activities taken to be peripheral, based on the distinction between productive and unproductive labour. The latter category would clearly include middlemen in the inter-industry sector – scrap iron merchants and wholesalers – as well as those engaged in marketing, advertising and related activities for the firm. Whether the productive–unproductive distinction in Marx was meant to be applied in so literal a manner is unlikely, since workers in the arts and culture, individuals whose work Marx greatly valued, would, for Marx, fall into the unproductive category. While this exegetical issue is out of bounds here, the impact of the productive–unproductive distinction on both left-wing critiques of capitalism and the practice of socialist economies is undeniable: both Marxism and technocracy emerged as opponents of the Weberian notion that the burgeoning state and capitalist bureaucracies were aspects of an emergent rationality in the regulation of social and economic affairs. The most deleterious aspect of the Marxian productive–unproductive distinction (one inherited from classical economists Smith and Ricardo) was that it created obstacles for progressive and working-class groupings accepting the Marxian framework to conceptualise and formulate a coherent critique of modern 'industrial' economies emerging after the Second World War, since four-fifths of the working population they claimed to represent were employed 'unproductively' outside of the manufacturing sector.

In technocratic approaches, as epitomised by Veblen, bureaucracy is viewed as wasteful, gratuitous and dysfunctional; Marx's critique of the proto-Weberian sentiments in Hegel's *Philosophy of Right* led to a Marxist perception of bureaucracy as having a functional role only in the sense of being the agent and executor of the interests of the dominant class in society. In addition, because of the Marxian distinction between productive and unproductive labour (a distinction absent in the orthodox economics of the early twentieth century), the engineering prejudice against peripheral activities was reinforced. We thus see in Lenin the notion that the execution of bureaucratic functions is a trivial matter, and that they could be performed by any literate citizen: 'Accounting and control – that is the main thing required for "arranging" the smooth working, the correct functioning of the first phase of communist society ... The accounting and control necessary for this have been simplified by capitalism to the extreme and reduced to the extraordinarily simple operations – which any literate person can perform – of supervising and recording, knowledge of the four rules of arithmetic, and issuing appropriate receipts.'[47] As a curious by-product of these tendencies, which were then reinforced by a prejudice in favour of 'Red' over 'expert' decision making (the latter taking a particularly manic form in the Stalin era), and contrary to broad perception, Soviet ideology was always very anti-bureaucratic.[48]

More ambiguous is the Marxian approach to finance. Marx's most fully developed formal model of a capitalist economy is embodied in the schema for production and growth in Volume 2 of *Capital* (published posthumously in an edition by Engels) in which finance plays no role; otherwise, in his extensive written observations on finance, there are hints of its role in the process of investment and innovation. Whatever Marx's true views, the heritage of orthodox Marxism is one in which fiduciary money in capitalism is linked in a fairly orthodox manner to its exchange value in a commodity money such as gold, and finance facilitates a realisation of the value of physical output in monetary terms, thereby permitting interactions between different sectors of the economy. This functional role for money only comes about accompanied by speculation, financial crises and business fluctuations.

Marx is more explicit about his rejection of a role for finance in post-capitalist society in his *Critique of the Gotha Programme* of 1875, in which the introduction of labour credits in the lower stage of communism (what was later to be called socialism) was clearly a mechanism to incorporate the mundane transactional roles of money without its playing a significant role in investment decisions or in intra-firm relations. Thus, the heritage from Marx, whether or not representative of his true views, is of finance playing a gratuitous and even destructive role in capitalism, a perspective developed in Rudolf Hilferding's *Finance Capital* of 1910. This book generalised from the close bank–industry relations typical in Germany during this period to suggest a new development in capitalism, in which finance played a key role as a control device, coordinating the great monopolies. The latter notion became a major theme in radical and Marxist writings throughout the twentieth century, and will be discussed in the next chapter.

It was the fourth principle of the technocratic planning paradigm that proved to be most problematic in a Marxist context: for all Marxists, including Lenin, the role of the state was the most troublesome aspect of the planning process. It was the repressive, class nature of the capitalist state and the inherent contradictions of capitalism that were used by Marxists Karl Kautsky and Rosa Luxemburg to contest the arguments of Eduard Bernstein in prewar debates. While Bernstein could not deny the overtly repressive nature of the state in Imperial Germany, he distanced himself from the orthodox Marxist notion of the continuing immiseration of the working class by pointing to a long-term rise in the income of German workers. His position resembled that of the English Fabian socialists, albeit embellished with the use of Marxist categories in his socialist rhetoric. But to orthodox Marxists, Bernstein's doctrine was without even a hint of coherence: he had surrendered the Marxist critique of capitalism based on its inherent contradictions. Most significant, however, was Bernstein's position suggesting a rejection of Marxist internationalism in favour of a socialism emerging in the context of a national state.

As we have seen above, Marx had been hostile to Friedrich List and his notions about using the state as a fulcrum of economic development, because of both the 'national' and the 'state' components in Listian rhetoric. There is thus a major difficulty with the view that the logic of Marx's thinking led ineluctably in the direction of central planning. The capitalist state was viewed by Marx (and Engels) as an agent, or the embodiment of the dominant classes in society, an analysis that did not change with the spread of the franchise in the latter part of the nineteenth century to encompass adult male suffrage, and did not, apparently, differ between the liberal French Third Republic and authoritarian Imperial Germany.

Marx's post-capitalist society was self-administered – there was no place for the state either as the coordinator of an economic plan or as an entity to delineate national boundaries – a view impossible for us to reconcile with the substantive history of central planning in the twentieth century or, in truth, even to make sense of. But this appears to be Marx's position. For Engels, 'State interference in social relations becomes, in one domain after another, superfluous, and then dies out of itself; the government of persons is replaced by the administration of things, and by the conduct of processes of production. The state is not "abolished". *It dies out.*'[49] And Lenin's pamphlet, *The State and Revolution*, is laced with anti-state quotations from Marx and Engels.

Evidence for the centrality of an anti-state position in Marx can be seen in his taking an 'un-Marxist' position on the transition to communism by late-developing economies. The orthodox Marxist position, put forth by the Russian Marxist Georgi Plekhanov, was that since Marx conceived of communism as a society emerging first in the most developed capitalist societies, those less developed had to pass through the appropriate stages to reach a level appropriate to transition. But Marx's anti-state predilections were so powerful that, in the 1880s, instead of following what would become the orthodox Marxist line of Plekhanov, he indicated the possibility of leaping over stages. The Russian commune, the *mir*, he speculated, might form the basis of a direct move to a communist society, without the intermediate stages of market capitalism and its associated state apparatus.[50] It would appear that any socialist adaptation of the technocratic planning vision of the state as an agent of development would have been an anathema to Marx.

By the beginning of the twentieth century, socialism was identified with the first three principles of the technocratic planning vision; with the emergence of Soviet planning, it became linked to the principle of the developmental state. The First World War played the important role of placing the state alongside the giant firm as an exemplar of planning, as can be seen in the glowing account of the German war economy from Yuri Larin (who was to be the father-in-law of the Bolshevik Nikolai Bukharin) in articles written during the war, but reprinted in the Soviet Union in 1928 as an official publication.[51] The perspective here, one that became an integral part of Bolshevik orthodoxy, unites the technocratic planning principles of the inexorable growth of concentration and planning and their links to rational coordination of the economy, even in capitalism, with the role of the state as the central coordination mechanism:

> The centre's activity has consisted in uniting in one branch the outstanding enterprises of an industry...We see that this central regulation of the procurement of materials is supplemented by the central distribution of orders for the industry in question...with, furthermore, planned regulation of sales...Thousands of mutually hostile small and medium-sized competing enterprises were united in an a single network. (pp. 19–20)
>
> Clearly the economic reorganization we are observing today is by no mean a 'socialism of the state'...On the contrary, it is only the highest stage, the most developed form of the organization of private appropriation – a 'capitalist collectivism'...*Industrial cartels, trade syndicates, trusts in all industries, bank consortia – all of these engender and proclaim the new direction, ever more rapidly growing in magnitude and significance.* (pp. 29–30)
>
> Capitalism...has already outgrown the fetters of private competition while still remaining capitalism – but on an 'intensive' path of internal reorganization. The special interest of the observations being made here is that Germany is a prototype of the path destined for all. Insofar as the war especially accelerates the new phase in the development of capitalism, the cessation of the war will perhaps waken these changes. But further developments, so long as capitalism continues to exist, must move it along in this direction. (p. 32)

In the Bolshevik interpretation, Imperial Germany, with the most feeble of allies, found itself at war with a group of nations that, even before the entry of the US into the conflict, greatly outmatched it in terms of ownership and access to economic resources, including raw materials, of all kinds. Germany's economic deficiencies vis-à-vis its enemies became a critical issue when it was evident that this was to be a war of extended duration. The economy that emerged was unmatched as a model for central planning, with the setting of priorities for the economy as a whole. There was conscious coordination of relations between individual sectors and the breaking of bottlenecks, including the securing of raw materials and/or the finding and innovation of substitutes. Large units proceeded with rationalisation and coordination of their sectors to eliminate inefficiency and redundant capacity. There were active programmes to promote the conservation and efficient use of economic resources, including raw materials and labour. The latter was a particularly scarce commodity in the war context, one that had to be efficiently allocated and directed.

Many of these notions were flights of fantasy.[52] The Raw Materials Section created by Germany during the war saved it from disaster, with the other great success of state planning being the building of nitrate plants needed for munitions and agricultural production. But state control could not avert continuing crises in resource management: the major reason for the shutting down and consolidation of industries during the last two years of the war was not a visionary view of rationalisation and planning, but the need to conserve resources devoted to transport and coal. It is sometimes claimed that Britain was, in fact, more successful than Germany in channelling industrial and labour resources to the war effort.[53]

And here we have to disentangle the bewildering series of political events that unfolded along with the war. In 1914, the SPD, including the orthodox Kautsky and the wayward Bernstein, both deviated from Marxist internationalism by supporting war credits; Kautsky's 'renegade' behaviour was denounced by his disillusioned former acolyte Lenin. After the First World War, the SPD re-created itself as a nationally oriented party in favour of an evolutionary move to socialism in the Bernstein mould, accompanied by Kautsky and the majority of the prewar party. By contrast, in 1917, the Bolsheviks made a revolution in the name of Marxist internationalism and an orthodox adherence to the technocratic planning perspective. What then emerges, even more definitively than in the prewar era, is that *an adherence to economic planning orthodoxy came to be identified with political and social radicalism, with any deviation from this orthodoxy a sign of betrayal.* These tendencies were exacerbated when traditional Marxist anti-state principles were dismissed by the Bolsheviks soon after their seizure of power. With the emergence of the doctrine of socialism in one country in the mid-1920s, Marxism for the first time was explicitly linked to the fourth principle of technocratic planning, the developmental state, so that the state's role in socialism was heightened even further: internationalism became merely a regime-serving slogan. In the Soviet Union and for those abroad under its influence, internationalism and antagonism to the existence of the national state were no longer seen as principles of Marxist legitimacy. It was, rather, adherence to technocratic planning orthodoxy that emerged as the standard and test of true socialism, with everything else being a deviation.

The ever-closer identification of Marxism, and even socialism in general, with the principles of technocratic planning from the beginning of the twentieth century served greatly to facilitate the notion that history was pointing the way to the future. Marxism itself had secured the notion that capitalism had inherent contradictions, while the technocratic planning perspective indicated the ease of transition to socialism: the socialist future is prefigured in present-day capitalist development. The first principle of technocratic planning indicated that capitalism was already consolidating and in the process of introducing planning within enterprises, albeit in an unsystematic manner. The fulfilment of this process would take place under socialism, where capitalist achievements in accounting and scientific management would be brought to consummation through the treatment of the economy as one big enterprise (a notion that, in its literal form, as we shall see in the next chapter, was soon abandoned by the Bolsheviks).

The admiration of the Bolsheviks for Taylor's techniques for the control of labour indicates a view of workers in the labour process that, in a socialist context, is passive and prefigures the advocacy (and de facto practice) in the Soviet context of the use of coercion in the form of labour armies.[54] The second and third principles lent themselves to the creation of a planned economy based on a purely technocratic approach, with little worth preserving in the old system – finance and marketing were treated as purely gratuitous elements. The principle of the state as the key actor in the process of economic development had already been present in Russia before the Revolution. When, however, in an agricultural context, murderous coercion was combined with the notion of an inexorable growth in the efficient scale of enterprises, de facto state ownership and a belief in the inherent efficacy of top-down planning, it had disastrous consequences.

In the late 1920s, the Soviet Union introduced an economic system that was a radical departure from anything functioning in the modern world. In part, this new system reflected an adherence by the leadership to Marx's rejection of both private property and market mechanisms.[55] But this attitude and its maintenance for over 60 years were powerfully reinforced by views held from the beginning of the twentieth century on the nature and trajectory of real existing capitalism in the form of the principles of technocratic planning, views that also continued to be held through most of the twentieth century even by non-Stalinist Marxists, non-Marxist socialists, and non-socialist critics of economic orthodoxy.

* * *

To this day, democratic socialists have found it difficult to extricate themselves from an identification with notions of centralised state control of the economy embodied in the technocratic planning paradigm. In reaction, many professed progressives have absorbed neoliberal views of economic regulation and the role of the state in the absence of a viable socialist alternative. A partial list of the deleterious aspects for socialism of its long identification with the technocratic planning paradigm and central planning is as follows:

1. The association of this perspective with the murderous totalitarianism of the Soviet and associated regimes and their failure as economic systems.

2. The inadequacy of this paradigm both in its role as an analysis of capitalist development and as a prototype (in the Soviet and similar contexts) of how a socialist economy might operate. The by-products of these failures have been that progressive theorists and practitioners have been diverted into misguided and irrelevant critiques of contemporary capitalism, or have retreated into pragmatic tinkering with the existing structures of the capitalist economy. The latter directionless approach to public policy implicitly concedes the argument to Hayek that societal evolution is inevitably dominated by the exigencies of a spontaneous capitalist order, one not subject to rational, democratic control by the members of that society.

3. The focus on top-down planning of the productive forces in the economy tends to relegate to a secondary consideration the role of *human* development and agency in economic progress. In an associated political aspect, the planning paradigm leaves little room for the traditional socialist notion of workers' control.

The next chapter will be largely concerned with the first of these deleterious effects of the planning paradigm, and Chapter 5 with the second. The rest of the book, Parts II and III, engages with the third element of the critique of central planning and offers a socialist alternative centred on human development and democratic control of society.

4
Socialist Theory and Practice

Decades of debate and discussion on the nature of socialism reach a moment of truth in the period after 1917. The Bolshevik Revolution took place in what was, in terms of both area and population, decisively the largest nation in Europe. But it was a distant land for the bulk of West Europeans, and was too poor and backward to be an appropriate venue for a Marxian transition to communism. Nevertheless, the existence of this gigantic 'workers' state', in the context of the troubled postwar economic and political situation, profoundly affected the political and intellectual atmosphere in the West: a socialist transformation of the society and economy was no longer an abstract consideration.

The argument made in Chapter 3 was that socialists' perception of the trajectory of capitalism informed their view of the nature of the new society. This chapter begins by examining how, in fact, the socialist analysis of modern capitalism influenced the construction and direction of the Soviet economy. What follows is an exposition of the debate on the nature of socialist calculation that took place in Western capitalist countries: strangely, the debate proceeded almost as if the Revolution had never taken place. All sides in the discussion attempted to override or evade a whole set of troublesome issues affecting both capitalism and socialism, including the relationship between the centre and the base and, most especially, the role of intertemporal decision making in economic outcomes. Serious engagement with these issues would, of necessity, involve consideration of the role of finance in economic allocation, a question barely touched on by these groups and one that eludes simple solutions to this day.

Central planning and real existing socialism

Central planning was a system of economic management that presided over a large part of the world for much of the twentieth century. Arguments persist over its success or failure as an economic system. An attempt will be made here to wade through the extraordinary history emerging in the wake of the Bolshevik Revolution, separate the contingent from the systemic aspects of these events, and extract any useful conclusions for dealing with the issues surrounding the general efficacy of planning. An encapsulated version of Soviet economic history is presented below, followed by more general considerations.

> The pre-revolutionary Russian empire was undergoing a steady, but not spectacular, level of economic and social development, with an emergent but still relatively small industrial sector that in some areas was approaching world-class standards. Culturally, and despite mass illiteracy, Russia was already a world centre, having produced many of the great writers, musicians and mathematicians of the age. The political regime of the Romanovs was primitive and its bureaucracy backward, but was not, until its intervention in the events leading to the First World War, wholly dysfunctional, and had not acted as a complete brake on Russian economic and cultural development.

> Radical Marxists such as Rosa Luxemburg, Vladimir Lenin and Leon Trotsky wrote perspicaciously about militarism, imperialism, international tension and war. But in the period surrounding the Bolshevik Revolution, much of the intellectual focus of the Bolshevik Party was, from a twenty-first-century perspective, simply odd – a continuation of an esoteric prewar dispute over whether Russia, in a post-revolutionary situation, would have an interim capitalist phase or pass directly to socialism; Lenin's exegetical discussion, on the eve of the October Revolution, of the correct Marxist view of the nature and even the existence of the state in post-revolutionary society in *State and Revolution*; the utopian musings of 1920 in the *ABC of Communism*, at the height of the carnage, famine and chaos of the Russian Civil War, by Nikolai Bukharin and Evgenii Preobrazhensky, who would emerge as leading theoretical protagonists (on opposing sides) in the new state.

> In fact, the new regime was confronted almost immediately after the October Revolution with profound threats to its own survival in the form of civil conflict and foreign intervention. The Bolsheviks were ultimately victorious in the civil war, but the policies of this first period of Soviet power, dubbed in retrospect 'war communism', are generally conceded to have been a disaster, extending the duration of the civil war and exacerbating the suffering of the population. The Marxian inhibition on the fleshing out of details of the post-revolutionary situation manifested itself as improvisation: the Bolshevik state, far from disappearing, fought the civil war through grain confiscation, seizure and direction of industrial property, and terror against civilians perceived to be hostile to the new regime. But strikingly, the Bolshevik state, so bloated in a security context, did not succeed in constructing a state apparatus for the allocation of economic resources.

Much of this failure may be excused by the conditions of civil war, but the lack of any kind of intellectual preparation for this task seems linked to the Leninist notion that the post-revolutionary economic transition would be a trivial matter. Relatively late in this period, the concept of *khozrachët* – an obscure term indicating the need for the maintenance of the integrity of the accounts of individual enterprises – had to be introduced. The absence of such a concept in the economics of war communism can be explained in two ways. It might be an indication that little thought had been given earlier to notions of economic organisation. Alternatively, it may be seen as a demonstration of how dogmatic, in this early phase of Soviet rule, had been adherence to an extreme version of the engineering perspective of the technocratic planning paradigm: individual enterprises were to be mere cogs in the centralised, direct, natural (tonnes of coal) allocation of resources. No need had been anticipated for the maintenance of financial coherence in the operation of individual enterprises through a concept such as *khozrachët*.[1]

This abjuring of any coherent financial planning mechanism was made worse by the inevitably high inflation accompanying a civil war of this magnitude and the state's attempt to use this inflation to confiscate resources to fight the war. But the transition to hyperinflation may well have been exacerbated by the new regime's conscious attempts to eliminate the use of money.[2] In addition, a central doctrine of the new regime was the millennial proposition that the events in Russia were only a prelude to a worldwide revolution that would somehow obviate or even eliminate all of these problems.

Adventurism is the mother and father of the *Thermidor*. The key economic policies ending war communism were a reversal of the government's anti-money policy in the most orthodox of ways, with the introduction of the gold-backed *chervonets* currency and by a de facto recognition of a private market in agriculture and the replacement of grain requisitions with a tax in kind. The New Economic Policy (NEP) was successful in reviving the economy, but was persistently thought of as a retreat. Such an attitude is an indication of how powerfully the technocratic planning paradigm had taken hold as a model of true socialism, despite the catastrophic results of experimenting in this direction during the war communism period.

With the technologies surrounding the mechanisation of agriculture existent by the 1920s, even in the absence of the as yet unexploited development of mass production of chemical fertiliser, the agricultural problem was on the verge of being solved in the developed nations of the world for the remainder of the twentieth century. Agricultural output was also increasing in this period in the USSR, but, in the eyes of the government, not quickly enough: at one point, the claim was made that shortfalls in grain deliveries to the market were caused by a collective strike by peasants refusing to deliver grain at prices they considered to be too low. In fact, more rapid increases in production were inhibited by interference in the agricultural sector, including attempts to hold down state purchase prices for grain below market levels.[3]

A growing movement developed within the Party for 'something' to be done. The motives for a change in direction emerged from a combination of impatience (linked to what were perceived to be imminent military threats from the capitalist world, most especially the British Empire, but not Germany, with whom there was clandestine military cooperation); a general disdain for the peasantry, especially of the more prosperous kind (the so-called *kulaks*); and an ideological distaste for the use of material incentives to peasants to increase agricultural production. A prime example was the proposal by Trotsky's associate Preobrazhensky for the extraction of 'tribute' from the agricultural sector by way of taxes to finance industrialisation. Opposition to aggressive policies towards the peasantry gradually grew weaker, perhaps because supporters of the NEP were seen to be defending a retreat from true socialism by citing the efficacy of market incentives – 'enrichissez-vous', said Bukharin to the peasantry. Preobrazhensky's notion of agricultural extraction as a vehicle for financing industrialisation (most especially in the form of the purchase abroad of capital goods) was taken over by Stalin and combined with his ingrained faith in the inherent potential for efficiency gains from large units of production[4] and a willingness to go to war with the *kulaks*. We see the initiation of a new civil war by the Communist Party against a large percentage of the population, as well as the almost simultaneous initiation of the first five year plan: the beginnings of the Soviet centrally planned economy.

The Stalinist economic system, in the form of collectivisation and the first five year plan, thus erupted in 1928 and 1929. It departed from the NEP and returned to the true path of socialism as dictated by the technocratic planning perspective and its fourth principle, the developmental state. This economic strategy was fused with a politics embodying Stalin's nationalistic slogan of 'socialism in one country' and his notion that the coming of socialism would bring about an intensification of the class struggle in society. The system had aspects of irrationality that verged on the suicidal: the new civil war of choice with the peasantry by the Party was undertaken under the presumption that the shelling of Ukrainian villages with artillery would be an efficacious procedure for increasing the amount of grain extracted from peasants; a dismemberment of the Red Army officer corps was conducted on the verge of a world war, with the elimination (for no good reason) of thousands of officers. These and other bizarre events were without parallel in the even more sinister National Socialist Germany.

The peculiar aspects of Stalinism should not distract us from analysing and evaluating policies that are explicable as part of an extended intellectual tradition: they were not simply an improvisation by a group of revolutionaries. The overall economic strategy of the Stalinist state was based on intellectual foundations that had been built up over decades, and these policies, emerging from the application of the principles of the technocratic planning paradigm, were broadly replicated in the post-Stalinist Soviet Union and other communist states after the Second World War.

As noted in Chapter 3, the Stalinist economic system often received a favourable reception in much of the Western world in the 1930s (as did German fascism) due to its apparent capacity, in contrast to capitalism in parliamentary democracies, to avoid mass unemployment and generate impressive rises in a range of economic indices. Information on the mass starvation from collectivisation and the enormous numbers in labour camps could not be completely repressed, but, for various reasons, was often wilfully ignored. When the war came, the predominant role that the Soviet Union played in the defeat of National Socialist Germany proved to be its greatest achievement, not only politically but also economically. It managed to evacuate over 1500 factories to the east at the height of the invasion, perhaps the quintessential example of the efficacy of centralised control; its success in mobilising resources exceeded that of any major participant, out-producing Germany in armaments in a period in which it had lost half of its industrial capacity to occupation and with the Germans having access to the resources of most of Europe.[5] The quality of Soviet weaponry was, overall, very good.

The success of the Soviet war economy led to an overestimation (by all parties) of its capacity and achievements over the long term. Questions, for instance, of rational incentives for enterprise managers and others were obviated in the context of a war against extermination and enslavement; the ability to focus on the mass production of a small variety of models (the classic example being the T-34 tank) for the achievement of a finite and well-defined goal – victory – ideally suited the centrally planned economy. By contrast, Hitler's determination to let spontaneous forces and rivalry continue to function during the war helps to account for the failure of National Socialist Germany's war economy.[6]

The Soviet Union's most unambiguously positive achievements as a civilian economy took place in the 1950s and 1960s. Starting from low levels, both consumption and overall economic output grew at rates (whether using official Soviet or CIA calculations) that exceeded those in, especially, the slower-growing parts of the capitalist West, such as the US and the UK: in the 1960s, Paul Samuelson's famous economics textbook had a graph showing the Soviet Union surpassing the US as an economic power by the end of the twentieth century if contemporaneous trends continued.[7] Even for many who disapproved of its politics and social system, the Soviet Union was seen by many to be setting the pattern for future development, an opinion reinforced by the launching of Sputnik in 1957.

It now seems curious to note that by the 1970s, the Soviet Union had largely fulfilled the long-term goals it had set in the first five year plans, emerging as a world leader in the production of steel, cement and energy products. All this took place at a time when capitalism, with the collapse of the Bretton Woods international currency system in 1971 and the oil price shock of the mid-1970s, was facing a permanent slowdown from the postwar golden age of capitalist growth. Yet in this period it became clear to observers, both Soviet and foreign, that the Soviet economy was entering a period of stagnation, masked temporarily by the rise in international oil prices. It was in this period of crisis and slowdown for capitalism that the latter's superiority over central planning in terms of innovation and flexibility became clear. In the early 1980s, Mikhail Gorbachëv had witnessed a shocking gap between the living standards in Canada and those in the Soviet Union, one that, if anything, seemed to be widening. This continuing contrast with the rich West was reinforced by the success of, first, Japan, and then South Korea and other capitalist economies, in doing what the Soviets had promised for decades – transforming poor nations swiftly into modernity. These economic realities were central aspects of the downfall of the Soviet system.

The Soviet economy as the embodiment of centrally planned socialism

1. *The Soviet economic system never evolved into an alternative system to capitalism for developed countries*, either in the Soviet Union itself or in its most economically advanced offshoots, the German Democratic Republic and Czechoslovakia. The strongest case for suggesting that the system implemented in the Soviet Union was an economic success has been made in the book *Farm to Factory* by Robert C. Allen, which views the overall record of economic growth of the Soviet Union between 1928 and its demise, and especially until 1970, in a favourable manner. The striking comparison in Allen's book, however, is not with advanced capitalism, but with developing countries: 'in the absence of the communist revolution and the Five-Year Plans – Russia's fate would have been somewhere between India's and Argentina's'.[8] This argument has particular force in the context of the depressed world conditions after 1928, a period in which the export-led strategies that Japan and the Asian tigers had pursued in the postwar world were not an option. The key aspect of Soviet planning success, according to Allen, was the use of output as opposed to profit indicators (linked to so-called soft budget constraints) in the context of the notorious problem of idle or excess labour in the countryside, typical

of developing countries: 'Output [was] expanded by breaking the link that capitalism imposes between the wage and the marginal product of labor. Giving firms high output targets and a soft budget constraint broke that link and was a source of growth in the Soviet Union in the 1930s.'[9] Allen suggests that this industrial strategy would have resulted in exceptional growth even without the additional investment resources generated by forced collectivisation.[10]

Even if we accept Allen's conclusions concerning Soviet success in the context of viewing it as a developing country facing the worldwide stagnation of the 1930s, it tells us little about central planning as a general economic system, one that would be relevant to economic regulation in countries at all levels of economic development. The failures of the Soviet economy after 1970 cannot simply be accounted for, as Allen suggests, by proximate and contingent events – an incorrect decision to invest in the reclamation of existing facilities rather than in the construction of greenfield sites in industries such as steel and the diversion of resources for new technology from civilian to military use.[11] The latter conclusions are implausible. The centrally planned system never appeared to be on the verge of a breakthrough to advanced capitalist standards, one that was merely thwarted by a series of managerial errors and the pressures of the Cold War. By the 1970s and 1980s, Japan and, later, other Asian countries were challenging established capitalist economies with the inherent quality, and the quality control, of their products in areas of advanced manufacture, such as cars and electronics goods, while a visitor to Moscow would find little besides the metro that was modern (and Soviet) and was worthy of approbation. Visiting Vladivostok in 1989, away from the dazzling relics of the Tsarist regime in the capital, I found the universal shoddiness of material life – and not merely its backwardness in a technological sense – to be breathtaking. By the time the Soviet system collapsed two years later, there had emerged, unlike in Japan, very few products or other aspects of material existence that were thought worthy of emulation in the rich capitalist West.

From one perspective, Soviet failure can be seen as an inability of the economic system to generate technological innovations, despite the fact that, through to the 1980s, mathematicians and theoretical physicists in the West were still learning to read Russian to keep up with developments in specialities in which the Soviet Union excelled. In broader terms, however, it was not simply a question of a failure in technological innovation, but a generalised inability to produce goods (and services) of decent quality. These deep inadequacies were present in a society not bereft of a capacity for excellence, as evidenced by the eminence of its best scientific and mathematical work and its capacity for cultural achievement, which is palpable in the world's concert halls to this day. The Soviet bloc was producing very few finished goods outside of the military sector that would have been envied (or purchased) for their quality or distinctive aspects by Western consumers or industrial buyers. The failure in 'the attainment ... of the material requisites of wellbeing' (to use Alfred Marshall's phrase) was not an aspect of a universal societal dysfunction, but one specific to the economic system as narrowly conceived.

The nature of this stagnation was not only a slowdown in the growth of existing products but, more significantly, an inability to respond to the dramatic changes taking place in Western economies. The initial postwar years – the Golden Age of Capitalism from about 1947 to 1971 – took place in the context of technologies that had all been up and running in the interwar period. During this capitalist golden age, Soviet growth rates in established industries, such as energy products, the production of raw steel and the generation of electricity, were at high levels. But even in this apparently successful period of growth, the centrally planned system lacked the capacity for the kinds of continuous improvement characteristic of capitalism in established areas such as consumer electronics (radio and television receivers) or efficiency in the use of energy and materials.[12] It was, however, in the post-1971 period – a period of slowdown in the growth rate of capitalist economies – that Western capitalism demonstrated its superiority vis-à-vis the centrally planned alternative as a vehicle for technological progress, most strikingly in the context of the electronics revolution. A further, seemingly paradoxical aspect of these triumphs of Western capitalism was that they took place accompanied by substantial intervention by the state, whether in the form of expenditure and direction by the US Department of Defense (see Chapter 9) or the state-directed industrial policies of Japan and other nations.

It would be inappropriate to have expected the economically retrograde Soviet bloc to replicate the technological achievements of the whole capitalist world; the alternative strategy of borrowing and imitating the technologies of more advanced countries has taken place throughout the history of capitalism. For societies such as those in the Soviet bloc, with their high levels of general and technical education and therefore presumed capacity for understanding and adapting these new procedures, such borrowing and imitation should, in principle, have yielded the kind of success that this policy yielded for Japan and the Asian tigers. And yet it did not. The usual range of proximate excuses contains elements of truth: the Cold War undoubtedly played a role in inhibiting trade expansion with the West and the importation of new technology through legal means (most strikingly in contrast to Japan).[13] But even within the Soviet bloc, trade was of a limited, bilateral variety due to the lack of acceptance of the rouble as a common currency and the autarchic orientation of the constituent centrally planned national economies.[14]

Furthermore, the suggestion by Allen, mentioned above, that the drain on resources from military expenditure diverted resources from civilian development is undoubtedly correct. But in the capitalist West, the very electronics revolution that produced such an insuperable chasm with the socialist bloc encompassed spillovers to the civilian sector from innovations that, in their crucial phases, had emerged from military programmes in the US. Perhaps the real question is why there was so little spillover from the military sphere, not only of advanced technology, but of quality and quality control, in the civilian industries of the USSR. Where were the civilian equivalents of the AK-47 rifle in the form of washing machines or vacuum cleaners?

As we shall see below, much of the answer to these questions is embedded in Hayekian notions of competition as a process of continuous struggle and the market as a purveyor of information. Soviet approaches to technological change in the civilian sector seemed to embody a presumption that discontinuous leaps would permit them to forge their way to equality with their Western rivals, often verging on a Mr Micawber-like presumption that 'something will turn up'. On occasion, such a path is possible: today we see many developing economies that have never had viable land-line telephone networks simply bypassing this technology with cell phone infrastructure. But such instances, though striking, tell us little about the typical process of development in economic systems. The South Koreans from the 1960s onwards, with their highly cartelised domestic economy, faced markets at home in key sectors almost as monopolistically captive as those in Soviet-type economies, but their export-led strategy meant that they continually had to match or surpass the technological, quality and efficiency standards of their international rivals, and could have no illusions about their own inadequacies. (In my experience, Soviet producers and consumers, lacking substantive ground for comparison, often sincerely believed in the world-class standard of specific procedures and products that to foreigners came across as quite ordinary.) If the Soviet military sector was, for an extended period, immune to these problems, it was due not only to the resources devoted to this sector overall, but specifically to the monitoring of military developments abroad in a highly rivalrous context, so that the delusionary propensities of an insular society were largely mitigated.

2. *The Soviet Union was an administered rather than a planned economy* (in the words of a famous article),[15] so that the notion that it was offering an alternative to capitalism of an economy rationally organised by an overarching plan is a dubious proposition. Centralised targets emerged from a bargaining process with individual enterprises based on an extrapolation from existing levels and trends, rather than being part of an integrated overall plan. Planning of all sectors of the economy in material terms was rejected as a serious proposition by many eminent Soviet economists, who proposed instead the integrated, planned development of a few key sectors, in a manner not very different from that found in a

range of capitalist economies. In fact, true planning in physical terms was never really a serious proposition, since as late as 1951, the five year plan consisted of only 127 products, with rouble investment expenditure remaining the dominant control mechanism over these highly aggregative plans.[16] It has been suggested that a continued adherence to administrative control of all sectors of the economy was more a reflection of an ideological distaste, coming from Marx, for market mechanisms than any serious notion that all aspects of a modern economy could be 'planned'.[17]

Soviet success in the Second World War with planning is the exception that proves the rule, because of the unique situation of a small number of prioritised tasks that had to be fulfilled for a limited period of time. Even here, it can be argued that it was, rather, 'the informal system of high-level improvisation and individual initiative, coupled with mobilisation from below, which carried the Soviet Union through its greatest emergency'.[18] The perpetual presence of taut, unrealistic goals in the first five year plans was the school in which the art of improvisation was mastered by planners and enterprise managers, and permitted them to survive in the chaos of the 1941 invasion. As we shall see below, these impossible planning targets had been used as a substitute for the kinds of Hayekian competition that propel capitalist economies.

3. *Very few authorities on the Soviet economy have ever argued that it failed because it was too egalitarian.*[19] Soviet incomes were low enough at all levels for rouble-based and other material incentives to generate changes in behaviour. Critics of the system suggest, rather, that the incentives were perverse, either in the positive sense of encouraging anti-social or rent-seeking behaviour (such as the hoarding of resources by enterprises), or in the negative sense of discouraging innovation and enterprise: the prime incentives remained focused on the fulfilment of output targets. Furthermore, the ability of Soviet-type economies to generate sufficient saving for high levels of economic growth, even in the absence of a capitalist class, was never in question.

The notion, however, has been advanced on occasion that the lack of fear of unemployment in Soviet-type economies reduced the level of work intensity and resulted in excessive turnover among workers.[20] But this supposed lack of worker efficiency due to some want of insecurity in employment is hard to separate from the peculiar rhythm of the worker's life in this perpetual shortage-ridden, war-type economy. Very much like the proverbial soldier, the Soviet worker's existence was, in the famous phrase, 'an existence defined by long periods of boredom interspersed with occasional moments of terror': annual plans were furiously fulfilled in storming activities at the end of the year, and discontinuous commands came down from the centre in the form of campaigns, reallocating resources to priority sectors and to shock workers with little regard to the costs of these changes: a perpetual war economy.[21] And yet, a potential advantage of job security for the national economy – a lack of concern on the part of the workforce about displacement by new technology – was relatively unexploited, because installation of new equipment often interfered with the planners' single-minded obsession with output targets and, therefore, workers' bonuses.

4. *The Soviet conceptualisation of socialism had no place for workers' control.* The tensions between a workers' control and a technocratic planning conception of socialism can be found in the anti-syndicalist writings of Kautsky and Lenin, and in the latter's actions in the earliest days of the Bolshevik Revolution: they are not the product of Stalinist 'deformation'.[22] Lenin's notion of workers' control, from the very inception of Bolshevik power, 'meant a sort of political supervision of the activity of managerial staff, rather than workers' management'.[23] Such an approach is congruent with a technocratic planning view of socialism as a coordinated activity integrated through centralised direction; workers' control would, as well, impede Lenin's desire to implement the management principles of F. W. Taylor and Henry Ford in Soviet industry.[24]

The general pattern of subordination of labour in subsequent Soviet history is well known. But an important phenomenon of the Stalin era, the development of the Stakhanovite movement, illustrates issues that would be present in any economy dominated by a central plan. In August 1935, in a carefully prepared demonstration and with help from his fellow workers, the miner Aleksei Stakhanov hewed 102 tons of coal on his shift, or 14 times his quota.[25] The distortions of priorities and resources brought about by the subsequent cult of the exemplary Stakhanovite worker were soon evident to Soviet planners and others, but the movement persisted until Stalin's death.

The Stalinist regime went down the potentially perilous path of acceding to the semi-spontaneous emergence of Stakhanovite enthusiasm because it was in a bind. A central problem for both capitalist and socialist managers is how to make their enterprises, including the workforce, function efficiently. Lenin had claimed that his interest in Taylorist scientific management was in its objective aspects, such as the rational distribution of machines and tools in the workplace. But, as Lenin and every Marxist was aware, Taylorism as a programme of scientific management was notorious not so much for its contributions to firm efficiency, but for its association with methods for the intensification and increased control of the work process – a reduction in shirking by ordinary workers and the overriding of the autonomy of skilled workers in their planning and pace of work. Soviet leaders were defensive about identifying too closely with such managerialist approaches, not merely for the obvious reason that they were supposedly in control of a workers' state, but because of the Stalinist prejudice in favour of 'Red' over 'expert' decision making, noted in Chapter 3, and the dangers to the planning conception of giving too much initiative to directors at the enterprise level.[26]

Soviet leaders were also as wary of skilled worker (often old craft) autonomy as the Taylorists. Stakhanovism represented an attempt to generate enthusiasm and higher productivity from below without relinquishing control over the overall planning process or over the direction of individual enterprises.[27] In the broader context of the planning regime, neither worker nor enterprise initiatives were welcome as mechanisms for generating efficiency: 'Stakhanovism represented a way of intensifying production but without succumbing to the managerialist or autonomist implications of this emphasis. In the absence of any automatically operating means of compelling management to lower costs or otherwise "sell" products at competitive prices, Stakhanovism provided such compulsion.'[28] This desperate attempt at controlled voluntarism illustrates the unresolved tensions between a conception of socialism centred on planning and one linked to workers' control and initiative. It probably only functioned in an efficacious manner in the war for survival between 1941 and 1945.

5. *The greatest and most lasting economic successes of the socialist countries were in the context of human development indicators – health (including medical provision, sanitation and egalitarian nutritional sufficiency) and, especially, education.* All of these accomplishments have to be seen in the historical context of the imposition of famine and mass murder, most especially during the Stalinist period, during which, by one calculation, between gulags and restrictions on peasants, four out of five of the working population of the Soviet Union at the apogee of repression lived in the dismal and highly inefficient conditions of forced, or unfree, labour.[29] But the failures of socialism extended long after Stalin's death, and the relationship of this system to education, human and economic development will continue to raise important issues in the following chapters about the use and misuse of human assets. Education in the social sciences and the arts was despoiled by censorship and repression; biology was subject to the perversions of Lysenkoism through the Khrushchëv era; most other pure sciences were left untouched, though applied sciences suffered greatly from limited access to journals and world-class equipment.

The genuine accomplishments in human development of the Soviet-type systems were never ranked by them as major achievements in an *economic* context, because these regimes had for so long put an emphasis on physical output indicators and had made such poor use of their human assets. When the system collapsed, its world-class assets were embodied almost solely in human beings, rather than in its largely obsolescent capital stock.

The collapse of Soviet power in 1991 was coincident with the substantive abandonment of radical socialist movements and intellectual discourse in the rich countries of the Western world. In one sense, this is a curious development, since much of the space taken up by radicalism was occupied by followers of Leon Trotsky who, subjectively at least, were as anti-communist (or, as they would say, anti-Stalinist) as any committed right-winger (or, in the case of Henry Kissinger and Edward Heath, much more so). Trotskyism was a radical current of thought that continued to have a significant voice in the capitalist world in discussions about the Soviet Union throughout the latter's history. For followers of Leon Trotsky (and the British Conservative historian Edward Hallett Carr in an 'objective', less politically committed way), the Soviet Union was on the correct path, but had taken a wrong turning.

Trotskyists and almost all other left-wing groups (including even many reformist communists and social democrats) were in essence adherents to a version of the technocratic planning perspective, believing that the Soviet Union was a progressive, post-capitalist development – a workers' state that became the victim of bureaucratic deformation. This deformation had been partially caused by historically contingent events, including, it was claimed, the destruction of the most progressive sections of the working class during the civil war, leading to bureaucratic (Stalinist) takeover of the reins of power and the lack of a genuine popular participation in the process of planning. Trotsky's follower Isaac Deutscher put special emphasis (as did the left-wing economist Paul Baran) on Russian backwardness. According to them, bureaucratic deformation and lack of democratic participation in and control of decision making meant that even objectively progressive measures, such as the collectivisation of Soviet agriculture (initially supported by Trotsky), would be carried out in a brutal, dysfunctional manner. This view of the Soviet Union refracted itself back in the form of debates about socialism in the capitalist world: the most significant group of radical critics of capitalism were those who, no matter how censorious they were of the Soviet Union and other representations of real existing socialism, were seeing them as perversions of a fundamentally progressive, correct path to a new society (the Russian title of Trotsky's famous critique of Stalin's Soviet Union, *The Revolution Betrayed*, is *What Is the Soviet Union and Where Is It Going?*). This process continued for much of the twentieth century, with a test in the Western capitalist world of the purity of one's radical socialist credentials being a capacity to offer a critique of real existing socialism that did as little damage as possible to the inherent logic of a centrally planned organisation of the economy.

Chapter 5 will explore further the demise of the technocratic planning tradition in its radical and more moderate guises in the West in the 1980s. But a quite different debate on the nature of socialism and its rationality had emerged earlier in the academic community – one that was curiously tangential to the considerations so far explored, but highly revealing about the dilemmas facing all economic systems, both capitalist and socialist.

Socialist calculation

As we have seen in Chapter 3, Lenin viewed the running of a socialist economy to be a trivial matter of administration. Perhaps as a result, the formal problems of directing a socialist economy were largely left unexplored in the pre-revolutionary writings of those who would subsequently confront these issues.[30] The key debate on the possibility of a rationally constructed socialist economy took place elsewhere, and with only peripheral consideration of the substantive development of the emerging Soviet state. It is the reaction to this debate, as much as the original debate itself, that has proved to be of continuing relevance to an understanding of the economics of both capitalism and socialism. A stylised and abbreviated summary of the original debates is as follows:[31]

In the early twentieth century, the Austrian philosopher and economist Otto Neurath produced a vision of a socialist economy whose distinguishing characteristic was an allocation of resources using a natural – physical and engineering – perspective, a reflection and strong version of the emergent technocratic planning view described in Chapter 3. The Austrian economist Ludwig von Mises, responding to this and similar views after the First World War, focused on the issue of the efficient allocation of capital goods in an economy to substantiate his claim that the construction of a socialist economy on a rational basis was impossible. Capital goods had to be priced if firms were to make rational decisions on their use – the pursuit of efficiency could not be based on a simple engineering criterion of the best way to make something, since a range of techniques for a given production decision invariably exists. The choice of the most efficient one for society as a whole would have to incorporate a calculation of the relative scarcities of the range of capital goods, raw materials and labour associated with each of these techniques, a calculation that would have to be made in value, rather than physical or engineering terms. According to Mises, the value parameters necessary for such efficiency calculations could only emerge from the prices generated by a market for capital goods in which the enterprises participating in this market were privately owned.

In the 1930s, the economist Oskar Lange took up the challenge of Mises' claim of the impossibility of constructing a socialist economy. He readily acceded to the need for efficiency calculations to be made in value terms rather than using purely natural or engineering criteria, but claimed that these values could emerge without a market for capital goods, and without private ownership. In Lange's model, there was a free market in labour and complete consumer choice. The Central Planning Board, beginning with an array of prices (the rueful joke in socialist countries decades later was that one capitalist country would have to be preserved to obtain these prices), would instruct each enterprise to set its levels of output so that price was equal to marginal cost and to minimum average cost, conditions for efficiency familiar from a competitive free-market (capitalist) equilibrium. Any surpluses or shortages would be eliminated through iterative trial-and-error price movements: these adjustments towards market clearing equilibrium would mimic those found in Léon Walras's model of the general equilibrium of supply and demand in a market economy. In Lange's only critical reference in this article to the contemporaneous situation in the Soviet Union, the continuing presence of shortages there was an important sign of misallocation of resources.[32] Lange had thus refuted the argument that socialism was incapable of achieving static efficiency.

As Paul Craig Roberts has commented, a curious aspect of Lange's model is that it did not resemble or correspond to any substantive proposal for the operation of a socialist economy, either before or after its dissemination;[33] Lange himself rejected the market socialist solution in socialist Poland two decades later in favour of central planning using the newly emerging computer technology (the latter technology wholly the creation of the capitalist West). Lange's own claims for the efficacy of the system outlined above were modest, being limited to the assertion that its superiority over capitalism was that it could yield competitive price outcomes in sectors where scale economy considerations would dictate the need for the dominance of a monopoly producer (an echo of the technocratic planning perspective), and some muted notions of income equality, presumably linked to an uncompensated nationalisation of property formerly in private hands.

The central importance of Lange's article, however, is not as a practical model for socialism but as an existence proof – rational valuation and decision making, the Alpha and Omega of economic orthodoxy, can exist in an economy without capital markets or private property. And this was how the article was received: the mainstream of economic orthodoxy declared the socialist Lange the victor over the defender of capitalism, Mises. The advantages of this Lange-type market socialist economy are that 'it may be possible to achieve price-taking behaviour on the part of economic agents, even when the number of buyers and sellers is small ... [and] that governmental control of the distribution of resources [would] obviate the need to leave society's Pareto-efficient welfare frontier in order to reach an acceptable income distribution'.[34] Thus, according to the consensus of orthodox opinion in economics, the socialist Lange had 'won' the debate with the defender of capitalism, Mises: Lange had demonstrated that socialism as specified by him could match the desirable efficiency properties of a free-market competitive equilibrium. Nothing in Lange's model from the 1930s, however, yielded a ready mechanism for alleviating the mass unemployment that was raging across the capitalist world at the time.

Dissent from this consensus has emerged in recent decades. From the mainstream of economics, there has been growing interest in the role of information in economic allocation, and most especially how asymmetries in the distribution of information might distort economic outcomes. Hayek is often considered the great progenitor of this idea. The notion has been attributed to him that the great failure of Lange's scheme is that the Central Planning Board could never gather all the relevant information about enterprise potential and behaviour, thus leaving substantial leeway for opportunistic and socially dysfunctional behaviour on the part of individual enterprises.[35]

In a rewriting of the history of the debate, Don Lavoie made more radical assertions.[36] Hayek and Mises were perfectly aware, according to Lavoie, that a *formal* solution to the problem of static efficiency for an economy – the existence of a rational price structure – could emerge in a socialist economy, one without markets and private property. The Austrians were suggesting, however, that this orthodox, static justification for capitalism – that it was working appropriately when prices were linked to costs in a formal competitive equilibrium – missed the true efficacy of markets, competition and capitalism: Lange's defence of socialism on the basis that it could, in a formal model, replicate the static efficiency characteristics of capitalism was beside the point.

For Lavoie and the Austrians, capitalist competition is a dynamic process, and it is only through the attempt of individual entrepreneurs to survive in this environment that more efficient solutions, technical and organisational, are discovered and emerge: through the process of competition, new information is *created*. The import of Hayek's view is not, as in its adaptation in the mainstream literature, merely that there are costs and asymmetries to the acquisition and use of information. The true position is more stark: information in the form of a freestanding set of blueprints embodying efficient solutions simply *does not exist*, and is therefore not available either to a putative socialist planning board or to individual enterprises. What is present in the real world is an envelope of potentialities, one that capitalist competition impels enterprises to reach for. Thus, real markets and real competition are needed to *generate* the information that will then permit the efficiency gains possible only under capitalism. These efficiency gains cannot be simulated by socialism merely by instituting an admonition from a Central Planning Board that socialist enterprises must follow a pricing rule.

Lavoie's argument continues: the dynamic form of competition present in capitalism is not merely concerned with finding better solutions for the production of the existing range of output. The competitive process impels enterprises to engage in the innovation of new products and services involving risky investment in new technologies and ways of doing business. In capitalism, these risks are borne by the owners of the enterprise, either in person or by their surrogates making the decision, who must weigh the uncertain benefits against the costs of proceeding. The state-owned enterprise has no basis, *even in principle*, upon which to make rational investment decisions, since the risks involved in these decisions are taken neither by an owner-entrepreneur, nor by a share-owning public in the form of financial market evaluation of the success or failure of these decisions. Thus, the Lange pseudo-market socialist economy replicates the efficiency properties of the competitive equilibrium model of (capitalist) economic orthodoxy, but produces few of the substantive virtues of real existing capitalism with its dynamism and innovative qualities. Lavoie's intervention in the 1980s, with his emphasis on the dynamic virtues of capitalism vis-à-vis socialism, proved to be particularly apposite in the context of the decaying Soviet economy of the period.

Let us step back from the claims and counterclaims surrounding the winner of this debate and put it in historical context. Otto Neurath is, in the English-speaking world at least, a shadowy figure in the context of the economic calculation drama. His scheme for an economy based on in-kind, barter calculations first emerged in 1910[37] and was repeated in subsequent writings. It is usually treated as a foil for the Mises critique, one that emerged in the wake of Austrian defeat, dismemberment, and economic and political chaos at the end of the First World War.[38] Mises accepted with alacrity the identification of socialism with in-kind calculation, but such a position in its strong form was perhaps uniquely linked with Neurath; it was criticised by other Austrian socialists and Marxist writers using arguments not dissimilar to those used by Mises.[39]

Neurath's ideas reflect a strict adherence to the tenets of the technocratic planning paradigm – a belief in scientific management and in the ability of engineers to decide on appropriate methods of production using criteria of technical efficiency (paralleling the contemporaneous ideas of Veblen).[40] The Neurath article cited by Mises deals with the economics of a war economy and discusses, with disconcerting objectivity, the beneficent aspects of war: the full use of productive capacity attendant upon the release from the restrictions of money, credit and cartels that are present in a peacetime capitalist economy. Because of the presence of unemployed resources, the cost of war is low:

The whole institution of the money economy is *only one of the possible ways* to bring about the circulation of goods. It might prove not to be the best way, even in times of peace ... *in our economic order a permanent advance without crises is not possible* ... [The] obstructions are caused by production and consumption, not by the political order or the distribution of income, but by the market economy and the credit system ... war forces a nation to pay more attention to the amount of goods which are at its disposal, less to the available amounts of money than it usually does ... Money reveals itself more clearly as only one of the many means to provide goods. The state usually fashions this tool with more energy in times of emergency than otherwise, and utilises it for its needs. If it proves useless, the state does not hesitate to make changes in the economic order. If productive capacity is intact but not money affairs, one last possibility remains – *economy in kind*.[41]

The ability of the state to manage an economy on this basis is inextricably bound up with Neurath's perception of the evolution of capitalism in an article written somewhat later: '[it is] the emergence of large organizations [that make] possible the unification and cooperation of different branches of production, as shown by the example of trusts. Within [large] economic organisations money calculation can be reduced to a minimum and the possibility cannot be excluded that here too state cartels and state trusts prepare the ground for new developments.'[42]

Despite the modern-day English-speaking focus on abstract considerations in the economic calculation debate, both these participants were deeply involved in the politics of the day. Neurath, at one point associated with revolutionary events in Bavaria, was primarily a participant in the debates within the Austrian Social Democratic Party, a non-revolutionary grouping that was notable for its pioneering achievements in municipal housing;[43] Mises would serve as economic advisor to the extreme right-wing Austrian chancellor Engelbert Dollfuss. The Mises critique of Otto Neurath's engineering solution to economic allocation in postwar Austria was taking place in the context of a nation that had been laggard economically in its prewar incarnation as an empire and which now, in its dismembered form, was experiencing significant macroeconomic and financial instability, including very high and then hyperinflation.[44] A generous reading of Neurath's schemes for in-kind calculation and, by implication, central planning is that they are attempts at dealing with macroeconomic instability and mass unemployment in a period before a Keynesian alternative existed. By contrast, the Lange model, with the relatively limited role suggested for the Central Planning Board, cannot claim to be able to enforce full employment and has, as we have seen, only marginal advantages over a parallel capitalist system: it functions purely as a formal solution to the possibility of operating a socialist economy.

What emerged with John Maynard Keynes's recasting of economic thought in the 1930s[45] was a delineation between micro- and macroeconomics. In the pre-Keynesian period, critics of orthodoxy, as we have seen in Chapter 3, often traced the macroeconomic fluctuations that destabilised whole economies to the malfunctioning of individual markets at the microeconomic level. By contrast, the dominant view emerging from orthodox theory was from the law of markets of the early-nineteenth-century economist Jean-Baptiste Say. This law suggested that fluctuations in individual markets moved in a direction that generated stability overall in the economy: to doubt the ability of individual markets to stabilise themselves was to question the possibility of overall stability in the economy, and vice versa. Keynes's intervention limited his critique of capitalism to its tendency to generate inappropriate fluctuations in prices and output in the overall economy: he did not link these broad-based fluctuations to price and output instability in individual markets, but noted the special issues surrounding the financial sector and labour markets.

The great success of Keynes as a liberal theorist in the 1930s was, thus, to offer an explanation for fluctuations in capitalism that cordoned off the problem in specific, manageable directions. In the technocratic planning approach of Neurath and others, the Gordian knot is cut by controlling output in each individual sector, thereby stabilising the economy as a whole. Keynes's approach, by contrast, incorporated the liberal, orthodox view that ordinary markets were stable and rational, and in no need of central direction. Financial markets, however, were a special case: their volatility was linked to an inherent uncertainty concerning the future, a problem not likely to be unique to capitalism. Government planning could be limited to keeping a watchful eye on financial markets and occasional interventions using fiscal policy as a corrective to oscillations in overall economic activity. In the period after the Second World War, the economic rivalry that emerged was between two world systems – a socialist one based on a technocratic planning, and a capitalist one that relied predominantly upon Keynesian regulation to contain the macroeconomic fluctuations endemic to capitalism; in some quarters, a pre-Keynesian faith in the capacity of capitalism to equilibrate itself remained undiminished.

Keynes's system preserved the efficiency virtues of the liberal capitalist economy in which microeconomic investment decisions are taken at a decentralised level by firms. At the same time, the Keynesian system promised to seize for capitalism the greatest claim to legitimacy of the centrally planned regime – the maintenance of full employment – but to do this without the need for crude sector-by-sector direction. In the 1970s, the Keynesian regulatory regime, seemingly so successful in the postwar period, began to crack at the seams: the virtues of decentralisation inherent in a capitalist economy were becoming difficult to disentangle from capitalism's capacity for becoming, or tendency to become, unstable.

Competitive dynamics in capitalism and socialism

An understanding of the operation of real existing socialism and its failures is important, not only for an evaluation in a substantive historical context of the efficacy of planning, a major issue in Part I, but also for the themes that will emerge in Chapter 6 and subsequently. If the socialist economies were ultimately a failure, this fact reflects poorly not only on the efficacy of central planning, but potentially upon the notion that the raising of levels of human development, including education, is highly conducive to economic development, since achievements in socialist countries in this area appear to be their one indubitable success.

Arguments attempting to excuse the failures of central planning as an economic system can claim that the egregious misuses and decimation of society's human assets in Soviet history noted above were historically contingent events linked to a lack of democratic tradition in Russia and Stalin's psychopathic personality. But the failures of centrally planned socialism extended long after Stalin's death and were replicated in other countries. The relationship of this system to education, human and economic development will continue to raise important issues in the following chapters about the use and misuse of human assets. If the Soviet system was ultimately bested by capitalism, it was a form of capitalism, as in the case of Japan and South Korea, in which state planning played a central role, and in which technological achievements emerged in various Western countries, especially the US, using various forms of non-market financing and organisation. In Part II, it will become evident that an essential aspect of these accomplishments involved commitments by the state to education and human development in these capitalist countries, vital to their economic development but largely outside the logic of the employment of labour in a capitalist context.

Hayek's emphasis (as interpreted through the exegesis of Lavoie) of the dynamic efficacy of capitalism has proved more convincing than anything emerging from economic orthodoxy as a critique of the operation of a socialist economy, whether it be of a centrally planned or a Lange market socialist variety. An unintended consequence of replacing the orthodox static efficiency defence of capitalism with Lavoie's dynamic justification, however, is to undermine the notion of the invariant superiority of capitalism as an arena for rational allocation of economic resources. Once the focus on the efficacy of capitalism turns to its dynamic characteristics, questions surrounding intertemporal decision making are brought to centre stage, including the role of the financial sector in this process. These notions may be illustrated in the context of orthodox and Austrian attempts to confront Soviet and modern capitalist history.

Central planning and economic theory

1. *The limitations of orthodox analysis of central planning.* The most egregious economic failure of centrally planned economies was in collectivised or semi-collectivised agriculture, which seems readily traceable to the aspect of coercion in its origins and, in an orthodox textbook manner, a failure to provide adequate or appropriate material incentives. In this

area, there is unanimity: no serious defence of the Witches' Sabbath of the Soviet collectivisation of agriculture is forthcoming in the contemporary literature. But even in Eastern Europe, where the transition to state control of agriculture after the Second World War was, on the whole, less horrific than in the Soviet case, the 'gradual abolition of all the distinction between town and country', one of the demands of the *Communist Manifesto*, took place at a slower pace than in Western Europe. For other branches of the centrally planned economy as well, much of the existing literature has exploited orthodox principles of microeconomic static efficiency, with journalists focusing on queues and the hideous sight of empty shelves for common household items and basic foodstuffs.

While this system of allocation through queuing was a major source of discomfort and inefficiency in the lives of consumers, the filling of these empty shelves with the demise of socialism had the immediate effect of rationing these goods by income instead of by queue: the deeper problem had been the inherent poverty of these economies. In this context, the weaknesses of the centrally planned system are better understood by focusing, as did Mises, on the less visible reality of prices in the inter-industry sector. In the centrally planned system, these prices functioned as accounting points, but had no obvious links to any microeconomic rationality criteria: they were 'a consequence of historical development and ... influenced by ad hoc social and economic considerations'.[46] The piecemeal Soviet reforms of the 1960s were doomed: the economist Evsei Liberman attempted to promote enterprise autonomy by interpreting the notion of *khozrachët* (by then a sanctified Leninist concept) to mean that enterprises should be profitable – the value of the enterprise's output should be greater than its inputs. But, echoing the Mises critique of the 1920s, what meaningful interpretation could be imposed upon these value calculations when the weights used to generate them were arbitrary?

It would be convenient if analysis of the operation of the actual Soviet economy could be matched up with the a priori static efficiency critiques made by economic orthodoxy and Mises. In some situations, this can be done quite easily: the Soviet successes in steel, cement and energy products correspond to products whose output could be readily communicated in natural units (weight, energy) in the statistics published in the USSR, in contrast to the meaningless rouble calculations of the 'output' of machine tools. Even here, however, difficulties abound – a steel measure in tonnes precludes considerations of different quality grades of steel, timely delivery and so on, calling into question how to compare the value of a Soviet tonne of steel with its Japanese equivalent.

But a generalised orthodox critique of a natural economy will be insufficient even for an evaluation of the static efficiency characteristics of central planning, which took a specific path in its historical development: it became a perpetual shortage economy, a fact observed by Lange. The economist Alec Nove notes that the balance between sectors achieved in the original formulation of the first five year plan was destroyed by political intervention in 1929 and 1930 that resulted in substantial, unrealistic increases in all targets that 'were far beyond practical possibility'.[47] What emerged were institutionalised shortages, as elaborated upon by János Kornai.[48] The enterprise's perpetual deficit of the inputs necessary for production caused a hoarding of inventories and added to the inherent pressures on the enterprise to function in an autarchic manner (to make as much as possible of the necessary inputs itself rather than relying on suppliers) because of the absence of the possibility in the planned economy of purchasing necessary inputs through (legal) monetary exchange. Was this failure to produce a balanced plan a mistake, or a policy? If it was a mistake, it was one perpetuated by all centrally planned economies, at all times.

There are two reasons why central planning became identified with perpetual shortages, even in the inter-industry sector. First, running an overheated economy was a mechanism for the maintenance of full employment and the elimination of (especially rural) unemployment, one that became a key aspect of the legitimation of central planning from the 1930s on. The control of official prices resulted in a system endemically plagued with repressed inflation and shortages.

Second, the setting of unrealistic plan targets that resulted in shortages was an attempt to find substitutes for the Hayekian imperatives to efficiency that emerge from capitalist competition. For Hayek, efficacious ways of doing things for an enterprise emerge in the context of competitive processes – this knowledge cannot simply be read in a universally available blueprint of best practice, as presumed by economic orthodoxy and implicitly by the architects of the technocratic planning perspective. The latter group advocated the formulation of plans based upon the constraints of the 'law of value' – using available cost parameters to formulate realistic plans, as opposed to those emerging (as did the revision to the first five year plan) under the heroic slogan that 'there are no heights that the Bolsheviks cannot reach'. Stalin, though identified with this slogan at the time of formulation, late in life rebuked the economists who were suggesting that the law of value was not operative under socialism.[49]

Western observers, viewing this discussion through the prism of orthodox economics, have invariably sided with defenders of the 'law of value under socialism' approach, even when it emanated from Stalin: clearly, an adherence to any such principle introduces a modicum of rationality to the adventurism that characterised socialist economies, especially in the context of campaigns (for instance, the onetime Cuban target of ten million tons of sugar per year), which distort priorities throughout the economy. But if a centrally planned economy is to simulate the dynamism of capitalist enterprises, in which 'the bourgeoisie cannot exist without constantly revolutionising the instruments of production', in the words of the *Communist Manifesto*, and not simply accede to existing cost parameters as binding constraints, a substitute for the role of capitalist competition as an impetus to this process of change had to be found: the roles played by overheated plans, campaigns and Stakhanovism were therefore systematic, and not accidental.[50] The procedures found in centrally planned economies can thus not be modelled in an orthodox manner as maximisation of output subject to objective technological constraints; they are better perceived as an attempt to simulate capitalist behaviour in its Hayekian conception as a process of constant struggle.

The Hayek–Lavoie critique of central planning in terms of its lack of an autonomous mechanism through capitalist competition for the lowering of costs in the short term is complemented by the longer-term inability of the Soviet economic system to produce a significant body of commercially useful civilian innovations, despite its substantial scientific and technical base. This failure is unsurprising, given the lack of incentive to innovate on the part of socialist enterprises, all of which had output targets to meet. But innovation, in the conceptualisation of Joseph Schumpeter, is a substantial, discontinuous event, as we shall see in later discussions. In the final flourish of the technocratic planning paradigm in Chapter 5, the provenance of technological change in capitalism is taken to be the large, monopolistic firm: there would appear to be no reason why, under socialism, such innovations could not issue from an industry-wide central planning authority. That the Soviet Union and other Soviet-type economies were so manifestly unsuccessful as innovators gives support, rather, to a Hayekian perspective on innovation,[51] making it a continuous aspect of the habits and procedures of competitive behaviour in all its activities, rather than a discontinuous, largely technological transformation, emanating from a centralised authority or a monopoly.[52] In fact, the historical record seems to suggest that the reality is more complex than is indicated by either the Hayekian or the Schumpeterian approach, so that the very military expenditure that was such a burden to the USSR probably ended up being beneficial – having essentially a negative cost – to the US economy, and most certainly to the capitalist system as a whole, in the same period.

2. *The ambiguities of ground-level decision making in the Austrian context.* Lavoie's interpretation of Hayek suggests that both orthodox neoclassical theory and Lange's socialist adaptation assume that the most efficient way to produce different levels of output for each enterprise can be based on knowledge freely available to every enterprise (and to the Central Planning Board as well, in Lange's case). Decades earlier, Hayek outlined the market dynamics through which knowledge is dispersed:

> Assume that somewhere in the world a new opportunity for the use of some raw material say, tin has arisen... All that the users of tin need

to know is that some of the tin they used to consume is now more profitably employed elsewhere and that, in consequence, they must economise on tin ... The whole acts as one market, not because any of its members survey the whole field, but because their limited fields of vision sufficiently overlap so that through many intermediaries the relevant information is communicated to all.[53]

Hayek's powerful rhetoric, however, asserts as an analytical principle an issue that needs to be resolved empirically. Is it necessarily true, in all times and places, for all conditions of exchange, that the information received at the ground level by an individual trader in the form of prices will always be richer, and exploited more successfully, than that gathered and then distributed by a central source? Contrary evidence comes from the economic transformation of poor countries such as Japan and, later, South Korea after the Second World War, some of the most remarkable events in the history of capitalism, which were partially facilitated by state monitoring and dispersion of worldwide best-practice techniques in steel, cars and other industries: these practices fulfilled the Gerschenkron prediction cited earlier that late-developing economies will often employ centralised mechanisms, including those of the state, in order to compensate for, and make best use of, their limited resources in individuals with the skills necessary to organise and direct economic affairs.

The other notable development in this period was the veritable explosion in new technologies emanating from the US, especially in the electronics sector, substantially as a result of state finance and direction. The knowledge-rich nature of these innovations and the incumbent informational externalities attached to them suggest that the role of the state in these developments is a likely and not an accidental aspect of this history: the Market and the Plan both played important roles in these great successes of capitalism, as we shall see in subsequent chapters. Thus, Lavoie's emphasis on the dynamic aspects of Hayek's critique of central planning can paradoxically generate a focus on ways in which the processes of development and innovation might be facilitated by departures from a pure laissez-faire liberalism.

Even if it were to be conceded, as Hayek suggests, that economic decisions are best made at the ground level, we still have to face the realities registered by the technocratic planning paradigm: at the beginning of the twentieth century, the key players emerging in capitalism were no longer the individual traders and entrepreneurs that were part of the Austrian recitation, but giant entities. These great firms, far from being modern representations of ground-level traders making use of local information, had the advantage over their smaller competitors that their scale permitted them to devote specialised resources to monitor developments worldwide in technology and best-practice management. The subsequent lowering of the costs of such monitoring over the last century has largely dissipated this source of competitive superiority accruing to large firms. The resultant evolution in the balance of advantage between large, established entities and smaller firms and new competitors has been a component in the emergence of a more competitive capitalist environment in the latter part of the twentieth century, a development obscured by the Hayekian presumption of the *invariant* superiority of ground-level knowledge.

And the technocratic planning presumption that these giant firms gained advantage from being vast islands of planning caused difficulties for both the Austrians and economic orthodoxy. For Hayek, 'the dispute about "economic planning" ... is not [one over whether] planning is to be done or not [but] whether planning is to be done centrally, by one authority for the whole economic system, or is to be divided among many individuals',[54] a dichotomy that raises more questions than it answers in the period since the Great Transformation, when the 'individual' in question (or 'person', as the US Supreme Court would have it) may be the corporation Exxon. The main responses from economic orthodoxy have been either the notion from Coase, encountered in Chapter 2, that firms will increase the extent of their activities as long as the costs of using the market exceed the benefits, or the Panglossian presumption (never as popular in academic writing as the Coasian approach, but implicit in much public policy writing about firms and competition) that even giant firms can be accepted as ground-level entities emerging from a market-determined environment because their existence and survival are the result of a Darwinian process of capitalist competition. The Hayekian notion of the invariant superiority of ground-level and market-generated information is in need of refinement if it is to function as an empirical hypothesis and not degenerate into dogma or tautology.

3. *The Austrian emphasis on the dynamics of capitalist development leads to a focus on the roles of the state and of finance in this process.* The grand socioeconomic paradigms under consideration here have traditionally dealt with the roles of the state in the economy as an embarrassment. Hayek's vision of capitalism as a spontaneous order as presented in Chapter 1 is an extreme example: he avoids a role for the state in the assignment and regulation of property rights, a role present even in economic orthodoxy, since for Hayek a legal system will emerge through a natural process of free exchange in a quasi-common law process. By contrast, technocratic socialists such as Lenin were, at some moments, convinced that it would be possible to abolish the state altogether, with the economy operating autonomously by way of a scientific, managerially based plan. In the case of both Lenin and Hayek, the contempt for the legitimate role of democratic decision making in economic regulation is a likely contributor to their willingness to be linked to authoritarian regimes (Lenin's

leadership of the Soviet dictatorship and Hayek's support for the post-1973 regime in Chile). For the mainstream of economic orthodoxy, a mechanism for the overriding of democratic decision making on social issues has been the use of the imperatives of economic efficiency and growth to dictate how the state 'must' behave. The centrality of the latter approach has been apparent in recent years in economic orthodoxy's support for the wresting of a nation's monetary regulation from democratic control and handing it to unelected bankers in the name of central bank independence.

The financial sector raises the greatest difficulties for all schools of economic analysis under consideration. The Hayek–Lavoie argument makes an eloquent case for the efficacy of capitalism over socialist alternatives in terms of its superior dynamism in the context of decisions taken about change, risk taking and innovation. In capitalism, these intertemporal decisions take place in the context of interaction with the financial sector. With the coming of the Great Transformation, finance, the most universally unpopular aspect of the economic order, had new-found visibility because of the enormous need for financing of the investment projects of the great firms and public works by the state.

Economic orthodoxy, as it matured in the latter part of the nineteenth century, tended to treat finance as either an invisible aspect of capitalist relations or a nuisance. Even though the development of capitalism has always been accompanied by a concomitant evolution in the depth and sophistication of financial relations, economic thought dating from Adam Smith and David Ricardo has been designed to see through the veil of finance to the real factors working underneath. This money-as-a-veil presumption is complemented by the orthodox and market socialist focus on the pricing decisions of firms, a static approach that obviates the need to consider decision making – investment and innovation – that invariably involves the financial sector.

The financial sector is not only the facilitator of innovation and innovation in capitalism, but its Achilles' heel – the focal point and, in many interpretations, the source of the fluctuations in output and employment that, by general consent, are its most egregious aspect. The reader will not need reminding that the crisis of capitalism of recent years had its origins in the financial sectors of those very countries – the US and the UK – that are so proud of the sophistication of their financial structures and institutions.

Economic orthodoxy proved weak in its ability to defend free-market capitalism: its static formal conceptualisation of the competitive process was readily replicated by Lange in a model without private property. What emerges as significant in the socialist calculation debate is the limited relevance of orthodox conceptions of efficiency in both their capitalist and socialist (Lange) manifestations for consideration of the relative merits of these two systems, and an irony: key aspects of capitalist dynamism – the facilitation of trade and, most especially, efficiency in investment and innovation – are tied, perhaps inextricably, to the very domain identified with, and in some narratives the source, of macroeconomic instability – the financial sector. The irony comes full circle when we remember that the mitigation or elimination of this instability was a prime motivation for the invention of schemes for technocratic planning of the whole economy by socialists and others in the first place.

For adherents to the technocratic planning paradigm, most especially in its Marxist manifestation, there is no ambivalence about the role of the financial sector – it plays a parasitic, dysfunctional role. The quintessential exposition is to be found in Rudolf Hilferding's *Finance Capital* of 1910, a work of major influence on Marxists throughout the twentieth century. For Hilferding, the first principle of the technocratic planning paradigm is axiomatic:

> Free competition promotes a constant expansion of production as a result of the introduction of improved techniques...The ultimate outcome of this process would be the formation of a general cartel.

The role of finance is to exacerbate this process:

> The tendencies towards the establishment of a general cartel and towards the formation of a central bank are converging, and from their combination emerges the enormous concentrated power of finance capital, in which all the partial forms of capital are brought together into a totality.

Money ceases to play a role even under capitalism, and its elimination facilitates the accession to a planned economy:

> The whole of capitalist production would then be consciously regulated by a single body which would determine the volume of production in all branches of industry. Price determination would become a purely nominal matter, involving only the distribution of the total product between the cartel magnates on one side and all the other members of society on the other. Price would then cease to be the outcome of factual relationships into which people have entered, and would become a mere accounting device by which things were allocated among people. Money would have no role. In fact, it could well disappear completely, since the task to be accomplished would be the allocation of things, not the distribution of values. The illusion of the objective value of the commodity would disappear along with the anarchy of production, and money itself would cease to exist.[55]

What the orthodox defenders of capitalism have in common with socialists in the garb of the technocratic planning paradigm is their common devolution to the ideal of an economy in which money and finance play no active role: for the former group, finance emerges as merely a veil, a superficial appendage or convenience in capitalism, so that real outcomes remain unaffected by the presence of money and finance; for technocratic socialists, finance, with its dysfunctional and destabilising role in capitalism, is to be replaced by a natural economy in which, as Hilferding says, 'Money is to have no role.'

But there is one great difference between the orthodox and technocratic socialist cases. The claim by capitalism's defenders that money is merely a veil does not affect the day-to-day functioning of capitalism. Such an approach may well represent a failure of analysis, but its deleterious influence on economic policy and the real-world functioning of capitalism has largely been limited to generating two dysfunctional kinds of public policies. First, it has led to an inadequate public regulation of financial institutions and activities, thereby exacerbating any inherent instability in the financial system; second, this 'money is a veil' notion is often associated with deflationist sentiment (money is only a veil, but it should be 'sound'), such as the bullionism of the early nineteenth century, which included David Ricardo as an advocate, and the broad-based desire and intention to reintroduce the gold standard in the interwar period of the twentieth. Both of these corollaries of the doctrine of money neutrality, emanating from capitalism's defenders, contributed to policies that have threatened to destroy that very system. But capitalism has, so far, survived. By contrast, the technocratic socialists' advocacy of a natural economy was directly implemented in the form of a passive role for the financial sector in the centrally planned economy,[56] with deleterious consequences for its functioning as an efficient and innovative system on a day-to-day basis, eventually generating a stagnation that led to its ultimate demise.

Socialism's identification with the technocratic planning paradigm had catastrophic consequences. The technocratic planning paradigm, as we have seen, put forth at various times acute and perspicacious analyses of trends in capitalism. But when a serious representative of this perspective, such as Hilferding, posits a socialist path to economic development in which 'money is to have no role', it underlines how sterile and utopian such an approach can be. Over the course of the twentieth century, furthermore, the paradigm's dismissal of finance as a purely wasteful activity, even in capitalism, resulted in it making no substantive contribution to an understanding of the role of finance in capitalism comparable to that of Keynes and his followers, such as Hyman Minsky.

The technocratic planning paradigm's focus on the obsolescence of competition and a one-sided emphasis on planning and large-scale enterprises lent itself to the generation of a centrally planned system in which all impetus and innovation were expected to come from the top, a tendency reinforced by the paradigm's dismissal of a role for the financial sector in economic decision making. In its analysis of capitalism, the technocratic planning paradigm proved to be politically expeditious for socialists, facilitating the denunciation of 'the big monopolies' and the 'big banks' in their populist rhetoric; at the same time, the emphasis in this approach on the inevitability of bigness and planning, even in capitalism, suggested that the path to the new society would be a straightforward one. When, as we shall see in Chapter 5, the path of capitalist development turned out to be more complex, and in some ways in direct contradiction to the paradigm's notion of the extinction of competition in capitalism, socialist analysis and its identification with this paradigm were seen to be largely irrelevant to the problems emerging in the twenty-first century.

The ultimate failure of centrally planned economic systems was not simply a contingent or accidental matter. It was, rather, an inherent aspect of the weaknesses of central planning vis-à-vis capitalism in areas of dynamism and innovation. Capitalism's dynamic advantages are inseparable from decentralised decision making by firms that are mediated by the financial sector. Capitalism's defenders (both orthodox and Austrian), as well as proponents of market socialism, have tended to push the role of the financial sector to one side: it was, after all, the overriding of the financial sector and its association with general instability in the economy that was a central motivation for the construction of the technocratic school of central planning in the first place. Any programme of socialist development that is not tied to central planning must, of necessity, confront the question of the role of finance in the rational allocation of resources and develop mechanisms for mitigating its deleterious effects on, especially, economic stabilisation: these issues will be returned to in Chapter 12.

*   *   *

A last note on planning. It appears to be a unanimous conclusion in the twenty-first century that there is no place for central planning in the domain of rational economic allocation. But if the world continues to dither and bicker about climate change, and if the moderate-to-pessimistic forecasts prove to be accurate, might it not come to pass that a central text on economic allocation that we feel the need to consult is Nikolai Voznesensky's *The Economy of the USSR during World War II*,[57] written to reflect the experience of implementing a war economy to cope with an invasion by four million soldiers? We may yet be forced to choose between the unpleasant prospects of living in a rigidly centrally planned economy and extermination.

5

Ironies of History: Markets, Planning and Competition

After the Second World War, planning – in gradations from Keynesian macroeconomic policies to Soviet central planning – emerged as a functioning alternative and rival, in both the political and the intellectual sphere, to free-market regulation. Political and economic radicalism in the Western capitalist world became identified with those who, even when they were critical of real existing socialism, did so in a manner that did as little damage as possible to the inherent logic and efficacy of a centrally planned organisation of the economy. These radical critics included communists, but also others who were actively hostile to the political regimes in countries dominated by the Communist Party, such as Trotskyists. The intellectual ballast for these critics of capitalism came first from the perceived economic achievements of the centrally planned economies; this line gradually faded, most especially in the rich world, with postwar capitalism's success in maintaining relatively full employment and growth. An indication, however, of the continuing importance of the demonstration effect of these substantive examples of central planning is the collapse of this radical critique incumbent on the events of 1989 to 1991.

A second line of reinforcement for a radical critique was derived from an updated version of the technocratic planning paradigm, the New Economy, to be discussed in detail below. Its outstanding achievement was its focus on the dynamics of capitalist development, in contrast to an economics mainstream that was centred, more than ever, on the unchanging aspects of capitalist market allocation as an emanation from axioms of rationality. The new manifestation of the technocratic paradigm observed, sometimes with alarm and sometimes with sanguinity, the continued growth in the predominance of giant firms, entities that appeared to possess an ever-increasing control over their domains. For socialists schooled in the technocratic paradigm, these developments augured the growing predominance, even under capitalism, of the plan over the market as a means for the allocation of resources. This trajectory in the evolution of capitalism signalled that following The Plan was, in historical terms, the correct path, and that any transition to socialism would be straightforward: capitalism had already completed much of the task.

This new version of the technocratic planning paradigm failed, and took with it any remaining notion of centrally planned socialism as an intellectually respectable doctrine. In the East, communist central planning collapsed, not of its own weight, but vis-à-vis the demonstrably more dynamic and innovative capitalist system. In the capitalist West, the giant firms supposedly exercising ever greater monopoly control were seen to be functioning in a world that was becoming increasingly competitive. These great events induced a heralding of the victory of the market over the plan, with the logic of the marketplace dictating a limited role for state behaviour of any kind, much less planning. In this competitive, survival-of-the-fittest world, state action was seen to be a gratuitous luxury.

No coherent narrative based on these postwar developments could emerge from partisans on either side of the market versus plan debate, because the dichotomy never made sense in the first place. As we have seen, the firms that were the greatest exemplars of the technocratic planning paradigm at the beginning of the twentieth century existed in the context of a capitalist environment of competitors and finance: their success cannot be readily extrapolated to a situation in which these elements cease to exist – The Plan of socialist dream. Furthermore, the expanded ability on the part of individual enterprises to control, manage and monitor their internal and external environment did not, over the long term, lead to increasing control over their respective domains: rather than engendering a world of monopoly capital, this expanded facility, and its ever wider dissemination worldwide, generated an increasingly competitive environment.

This long-term trajectory in capitalism of accelerating competition in no way lent itself to an easy transformation into 'one big factory'. In the capitalist West, as we shall see here, the technocratic planning paradigm failed as a template for the economic transformation of society, just as it had proved unsuccessful as a model of development for centrally planned economies. Socialism, if solely identified with schemes for a Plan, will find itself relegated, in Trotsky's phrase, to the dustbin of history – precisely the fate of Trotsky and others who forged an identification of socialism with technocratic planning.

Postwar debates

Where is capitalism going?

The period after the Second World War in the capitalist world was characterised by unparalleled economic growth up until the early 1970s. But even during this golden age of growth, there were widespread doubts concerning the future of capitalism derived from the history of interwar stagnation and mass unemployment. And after the inauguration of the People's Republic of China in 1949, anti-capitalist forces had dominion over one-third of the world's population. The latter rivalry was compounded by a pervasive fearfulness linked to the presence of thermonuclear weapons.

In general, support for national planning was inversely related to satisfaction with the functioning of a capitalist economy in an autonomous manner: planning and competitive capitalism were the great rivals of the day. Liberal economists such as Mises, Hayek and Milton Friedman maintained faith in a self-regulatory capitalism, but they were a group with limited political and intellectual influence. The emergent body of economic opinion with direct access to political decision making was identified with Keynesian macroeconomic regulation, even if some of the dramatic interventions in the early postwar period, such as the West German currency reform of 1948, were inspired by traditional, pre-Keynesian free-market policies. The Keynesian consensus dominant in the Western world reflected, in the context of the emerging postwar boom, a willingness to accept, with only limited modifications, capitalist microeconomic allocation, but memories of interwar stagnation compelled explicit attention to macroeconomic regulation.

The encapsulation of the desire to put macroeconomic planning of a Keynesian kind on a rational basis can be seen in Jan Tinbergen's *On the Theory of Economic Policy* of 1952:[1] macroeconomic targets such as the levels of inflation and employment would be regulated by manipulating fiscal and monetary policy instruments. To achieve society's desired targets, the optimal levels of these instruments would emerge not, as traditionally, from subjective judgements made by monetary and fiscal authorities, but from statistical estimation of the effects of manipulating these variables in the context of the structural relations and boundary conditions of the economy. There would then be a precise, empirically based mechanism for smoothing out and controlling cyclical movements in the economy: planning at the macroeconomic level would become consistent with what would remain a capitalist, free-market economy. By the 1960s, with the diffusion of mainframe computer technology, we see the first attempts, such as those at the Brookings Institution in the US, at performing large-scale empirical simulations of economic models. Comparisons with the contemporaneous flight to the moon would not be absurd in terms of scope and ambition.

The ultimate failure of Tinbergen's grand vision was due to the emergence of a broad-based realisation that the macroeconomic system of an economy is too complex to yield easily to statistical estimation of its underlying structure; attempts at manipulation of policy variables are likely to induce an alteration in the expectations and behaviour of consumers and other economic actors, thereby causing the parameters of that very structure to change. There were thus seen to be limitations to treating the economy as a straightforward problem in control systems engineering: consumers and others are not elements in an inanimate engineering mechanism, but a collection of living, volitional individuals who form opinions and expectations on the state of the world that will be affected by governmental action. A tax cut, far from generating a predictable, parametric response from consumers, might recast patterns of consumption altogether. Thus, macroeconomic planning, the most modest and potentially the most viable form of economic regulation of a whole economy, was seen to fail in principle by the 1970s.

This pioneering work in macroeconomic planning, having inspired a generation of development and elaboration, lost out in the 1970s to a resurgent free-market ideology. One version of this free-market critique postulated a particular pattern to, for instance, the response of consumers to a tax cut – consumers will consider the fact that they will be liable for the future interest payments on the resultant increase in the deficit, so that the presumed expansionary effects of the tax cut will never emerge. Under such conditions, the state is powerless to influence macroeconomic demand using Keynesian-style fiscal policy measures, such as a tax cut. Even for those economists who found this kind of super-rationality unlikely, the underlying message has had its impact: the response of consumers and of the economy in general to changes in governmental policy is likely to be complex and unpredictable.

While Keynesians in the US limited their notions of planning (itself a suspicious term in a Cold War context) to macroeconomic regulation, the nations of postwar Western Europe often used planning mechanisms in order to emulate the US economic model. The image that the US possessed of itself was one of free enterprise and entrepreneurial capitalism. But Europeans saw something quite different: a modernity linked to giant firms, contemporary technologies and professionalised techniques of management. It was this vision of the US that was to serve as a template. Various forms of state intervention were undertaken, such as the consolidation and reorganisation of enterprises considered to be overly small and inefficient; resources were directed towards prioritised sectors – those singled out either because of their identification with the typical activity of an industrial power, such as the car industry, or those linked to contemporary technologies, such as nuclear power or electronics. These activities in France, under the rubric of *dirigisme* and often accompanied by elaborate indicative plans, were more the fruit of a technocratic ideology than of any left-wing movement.[2] In France, as in many other European countries, emulation of US economic prowess involved conscious direction and intervention by the state to create a modern industrial society.

In the US itself, there remained a powerful resistance to the notion that its modernity, wealth and technological achievement were linked to the presence of giant firms and a professionalised managerial class. Despite the self-evident reality of this pervasive corporatism, there persisted in popular ideology a notion of American capitalism that was identified with the entrepreneurial behaviour of, especially, small enterprises, with great innovations the product of the lone heroic inventor. The Thomas Edison of US iconography was the craggy figure depicted by Spencer Tracy in the film 'Edison the Man' of 1940, and not the industrialist-planner of genius so admired by the German industrialist Emil Rathenau. One reason for opposition to the European view that the US was the embodiment of corporatist modernity was the Cold War. It was felt necessary to resist the emerging notion, to be found in James Burnham, William Whyte,[3] the George Orwell of *1984* and Billy Wilder's 1960 film 'The Apartment', that 'we' – that is, the capitalist West – were becoming regimented, conformist societies, epitomised by the culture of the modern corporation, a view that tended to narrow the distinction between Soviet totalitarianism and the free capitalist West.

Furthermore, the largest firms were averse to an excessive focus on themselves: the US was a nation, with its supreme economic and political power, that could not claim the need for national champions. In addition, US corporate plans for a postwar world of free trade and international investment might be disrupted if a corporatist, *dirigiste* ideology were to lead to Listian state policies of tariff protection and economic nationalism in Western Europe. Academic economics, as we shall see below, remained wedded to a prospective in which Keynesian macroeconomic regulation took place alongside an orthodox microeconomics of free markets and competition for its analysis of business activity.

By the 1960s, there emerged in the US an alternative to this free enterprise orthodoxy in the form of a revised version of the technocratic paradigm of the earlier part of the century. This new paradigm, to be dubbed here the New Economy, reached its culmination with the publication of Paul Baran and Paul Sweezy's *Monopoly Capital* in 1966 and John Kenneth Galbraith's *The New Industrial State* in 1967.[4] It was arrived at by three overlapping paths: the modern corporation approach, monopoly capital theory, and analyses of the corporate economy by mainstream economics. Left-wing, radical and socialist ideologies became wedded to and identified with strong versions of the views embodied in the New Economy paradigm on the future direction of capitalism. The substantive failure of this ideology to account for the trajectory of capitalist development, along with the collapse of the centrally planned economic system, promoted the descent of the technocratic planning view of socialism into irrelevance.

The modern corporation approach has its origins in *The Modern Corporation and Private Property* of 1932 by Adolf Berle and Gardiner Means, a lawyer and an economist, respectively.[5] Written before the reforms of the New Deal, the book traced a crisis in private property relations due to the emergence of a separation of ownership and control in large firms in the US that was documented in detail in this book for the first time. In a manner largely unheralded by economists (an early exception being the always perspicacious Karl

Marx), the introduction of laws on limited liability and the sale of equity to the public in the latter part of the nineteenth century had often resulted in the passing of control of the great firms from the entrepreneur of economic mythology to professional managers. There was a clear danger, according to Berle and Means, that these managers might pursue goals that were in conflict with the desires of shareholders, and in the extreme case, walk away with the wealth of the firm.

By contrast, the academic economics profession (as opposed to a burgeoning business literature from Peter Drucker and others), even well into the postwar era, was still devoted to an analysis of firm behaviour in which its internal structure of decision making was treated as a black box. Alterations in firm behaviour were to be accounted for predominantly by a firm's passive response to changes in the external environment – changes in the factors affecting the firm's cost and demand curves. Mainstream economists eventually modified some aspects of this approach after the Second World War, but in a rather anodyne way, as we shall see below.

It was inevitable, however, that the prominence of giant firms since the beginning of the century would eventually generate attempts to alter this methodology, since these giants clearly had, and actively exploited, a capability for shaping this external environment to their needs and desires. It was to this very capacity for control on the part of the giant firm that Galbraith directed his attention in *The New Industrial State*. Galbraith suggested that he was proposing a conceptual revolution for the analysis of industry comparable with that executed by Keynes for the issues surrounding macroeconomic stabilisation. The vision of the new industrial state, most especially in its application to the great US corporations of the 1960s, was intended to replace competitive analysis based on supply and demand.[6] Yet his view of the industrial system now seems more of a generalisation of contemporaneous and transitory aspects of the US industrial system than an analysis of its operation that might indicate its future trajectory.

In Galbraith's exposition, the giant corporation, of which GM was the quintessence, was characterised by an ability to control its environment. For Galbraith, as in the traditional theory of monopoly, the large share of the US car market held by GM gave it freedom from the constraints of competition. Galbraith also acceded to the widely held view that consumers, and therefore the demand for the giant corporation's products, were subject to control through manipulation by advertising. The giant corporation was thus freed both from the constraints of competition from rival producers as well as from the whims of consumers. Furthermore, through integration of its production facilities, it could also override the market and exercise control over the conditions of supply for its inputs, while the use of internal sources of funding, such as retained earnings, permitted the giant firm to proceed with its investment plans without reference to perturbations in financial markets. The latter notion complemented the common postwar

Keynesian view that interest rate manipulation by the monetary authorities would be ineffectual in regulating spending in the economy at all times, and not only in exceptional periods of crisis, because large firms are indifferent to interest rate movements.

Galbraith's concept of the technostructure was an agglomeration of well-established elements. The widespread recognition of the separation of ownership and control was interpreted by Galbraith as meaning that a decisive change had taken place in the internal regulation of giant firms. They were no longer run by entrepreneurial buccaneers, but by professional managers, who, freed from the binding constraints of competition and financial markets, were driven by a series of long-term goals. These goals were underpinned by the central imperative to retain control over the environment in which the firm functioned and by the need to respond to the imperatives of modern technology. These imperatives dictated that those who had control and understanding of the direction of technological change possessed significant influence within the firm. Technological imperatives, however, could never completely override the traditional firm focus on profitability: we thus hear an echo of Veblen's notion of a conflict, actual or potential, between the 'logic of the machine' and the 'logic of profit' within the firm.

Galbraith's notion of the imperatives of modern technology embodied two distinct aspects that were amalgamated in exposition. First, it was asserted, modern production techniques tended invariably to generate lower unit costs at large scales of production, a static conception of economies of scale familiar from the technocratic paradigm of the earlier part of the century. Second, and more importantly, Galbraith borrowed from his former Harvard colleague Joseph Schumpeter the notion that the source of technological dynamism and innovation in business was large, monopolistic firms rather than the lone inventor or entrepreneur of legend. In Galbraith's exposition, the two aspects – the static and the dynamic technological advantages possessed by these giants – were conflated, so that the cost advantages accruing to GM due to its large volume of production were combined with the notion that new products or falling costs in the future would emerge from innovations originating from large firms. And Galbraith was happy to speak about 'large, monopolistic firms', as if the questioning of the conflation of these two distinct concepts – bigness and monopoly – were an act of academic pedantry.[7]

The key element that unified these elements of the Galbraithian system – monopoly power, the manipulation of consumers through advertising, the control of inputs and finance, the internal control of the firm by a technostructure, the economics of large-scale production and the technological dynamism of the giants – was the concept of *planning*. Because the large firm had *control*, it could *plan*. This vision of planning as the mode of regulation in modern capitalism, replacing and overriding marketplace relations, is familiar to us from the technocratic planning paradigm: as early as the 1890s, Friedrich Engels perceived that the future socialist society could be seen in microcosm in the conscious coordination to be observed within the firm. Though Galbraith had no particular sympathy with the state socialist economies of the day, it comes as no surprise that a Soviet edition of *The New Industrial State* was forthcoming upon the book's publication in the US.[8] Once again, vindication of a socialist path to development, in this case the actual one being undertaken in the Soviet Union, was supported by showing it to be a fulfilment of trends in contemporaneous capitalist society in the direction of planning and centralisation.

In the political discourse of the day in the US, the Galbraithian system was congruent with the policies advocated by mainstream economists of the liberal Democratic persuasion, such as Paul Samuelson and Robert Solow. Even as they criticised the lack of analytical rigour in his analysis, these left-of-centre economists were admirers of Galbraith's eloquence in the *Affluent Society* of 1958,[9] with its contention that rich nations (most especially the US) were neglecting the public sector: 'private affluence and public squalor' were pervasive, the existence of poverty in this context was a disgrace, and resolute public action should be undertaken to eliminate it. They were also comfortable with the practical implications of Galbraith's presumption that the market power of the great corporations had grown, leading these figures to advocate a watchful eye by the antitrust division of the US Department of Justice.

Other versions of this moderate-left New Economy paradigm emerged in this period from David Lilienthal and Adolf Berle, centring on the inevitability of the predominance of these corporate giants and the need for the elites running these firms to behave in a socially responsible manner. This doctrine of 'corporate social responsibility' was denounced on the right by Milton Friedman.[10] He replied that in a competitive free-market economy, the 'responsibility' of those in control of enterprises is to maximise profits for shareholders: the freedom of action for a firm to act in a socially responsible manner (by, for instance, making financial contributions to charitable institutions or the arts) could only exist in those (exceptional) cases in which competitive forces are not properly constraining and disciplining the firm's activities. In such circumstances, the appropriate response would be antitrust procedures to bring about competition in that industry, rather than exhortations to the firm to do good.

The fashion for the doctrine of corporate social responsibility subsequently faded, only to resurface in various forms, most especially through the public relations departments of multinational corporations. The particularly glutinous forms taken by these doctrines of benign corporatism, with their pretension that, in a modern context, the corporate executive could play the role of the Confucian mandarin or the Roman aristocrat, leave one almost sympathetic to the intellectual coherence of Milton Friedman's defence of the free market in this period. One last indication of the spirit of the age on the moderate left was the emergence of a literature suggesting a convergence between the capitalist West and the socialist East, with planning and managerialism becoming progressively more characteristic of capitalism, and the green shoots of political liberalism and economic reform in the East after 1956 taken as indications of a movement in a westward direction by the socialist states.[11]

There was thus a range of views among economists on the state and the direction of change of competitive forces in capitalism. In general, economists left of centre were dubious about the binding force of competition in modern industrial society, suggesting, mostly in implicit terms, that it had declined from a former age dominated by markets and competitive rivalry; the right saw the capitalist economy as one constrained by competitive forces. In this spectrum of ideas, a version of the New Economy paradigm, monopoly capital, emerged on the 'extreme' left in the interwar period. It was committed to an analysis of the economy as one dominated by monopolistic forces, a domination that then had consequences, both economic and political, for the trajectory of society. Such an approach was, however, problematic. Despite the heritage of the technocratic planning paradigm in left-wing ideology, the transition to an intellectually respectable theory of capitalism that had a notion of monopoly at its centre was a difficult one, especially for Marxists. Classical Marxian economic theory was rooted in notions of a market economy in which competitive pressure induced firms to reduce their costs through labour-saving technological innovation. This new technology, while reducing costs for every individual firm that adopts it, lowers the rate of profit for the economy as a whole, since labour is the source of the surplus value that generates profits. The demise of capitalism due to the tendency of the rate of profit to fall is thus inextricably linked to competitive processes. Traditional Marxist doctrine is thus not easily reconciled with the ubiquitous presence of monopoly.

But the forces directing left-wing thinking towards monopoly were powerful as well. First was the pervasive influence of the technocratic planning paradigm, a doctrine that retained its popularity on the left because of its reassurance that the socialist 'one big factory' notion was consistent with the movement of history. Purveyors of the monopoly capital doctrine shared with Bernstein, Hilferding and other left-wing thinkers discussed in Chapter 3 the notion that capitalist trends in the direction of centralisation were facilitating a straightforward transition to a planned economy. Second, the notion of monopoly capital was congruent with the embrace on the left since the interwar period of a Popular Front strategy in its Trotskyist, Stalinist and other forms. This political movement united all anti-fascist forces, including the previously despised petty bourgeoisie and their representatives, against the big monopolies. Third, in the most ambitious formulations of the theory of monopoly capital, there was a desire to take advanced forms of mainstream empirical research and theory in economics and turn them on their head by demonstrating the radical implications they implicitly embody, just as Marx had done with David Ricardo: the attempt was to demonstrate that the emergence and ubiquity of monopoly in modern capitalism not only created problems for the regulatory authorities, as suggested by Galbraith and many mainstream economists, but posed a threat to the viability of the capitalist system.

The theory of monopoly capital represents the most influential development in economic theory from a radical perspective in the postwar era. Beginning with the Polish economist Michał Kalecki in the interwar period, the doctrine evinced a new rationale for a belief in the inevitable decline of capitalism. While traditional Marxist theory was, as described above, rooted in a competitive dynamics leading to a decline in the rate of profit, the new doctrine was centred on the growth of monopoly leading to an increase in the share of profits compared with wages in national income. This squeeze on workers' income generates a crisis of underconsumption in capitalism – insufficient spending by workers – and a tendency towards stagnation. The title of a book published in 1952, *Maturity and Stagnation in American Capitalism*,[12] by a leading disciple of Kalecki, Josef Steindl, encapsulates the problem faced by the theory: capitalism was not stagnating but booming in the 1950s and 1960s.

The suggestion made by Paul Baran and Paul Sweezy in their *Monopoly Capital* of 1966 was that these tendencies towards stagnation were present, but were compensated for by expenditures undertaken by the capitalist class designated collectively as the 'surplus'. This surplus consisted of a host of gratuitous outlays, most notably on the sales effort, including advertising, and that undertaken by the military. In these cases and others, the Baran and Sweezy critique was consistent with moderate-left distaste for advertising and with President Eisenhower's farewell address condemning the military-industrial complex. As in the Kalecki–Steindl analysis, monopoly is generating an underlying tendency towards stagnation in capitalism, but its manifestation was now to be seen in the attempt by capitalists to compensate for this trend – the new 'law', according to Baran and Sweezy, was the tendency for the level of surplus to rise over time. While the particular interpretation of the monopoly capital thesis put forth by Baran and Sweezy was famous in its day, it is the term itself that has continued to have traction – as a focus of anti-capitalist critique during the Soviet period, and as part of an extensive neo-Kaleckian literature offering a unified micro- and macroeconomic alternative to mainstream economics.[13] This literature was often supplemented by a re-evocation of Hilferding's *Finance Capital*, in which ever-growing monopoly control of business was complemented by webs of financial connections, which sometimes reinforced and sometimes controlled the great monopolies.

Left-wing literature had never accepted a perspective that the state was an impartial executor of democratic will; the monopoly capital thesis in its variants gave a central role to the state as an underwriter of monopoly control and a countervailing force against stagnation.[14] But such a view has an air of redundancy about it – if monopoly control of civil society by the great corporate vested interests is really so complete, why should it be necessary to bring in the state to underwrite this power? After all, an expanded state whose control has been wrested away from business interests by populist or radical forces is the greatest nightmare that monopoly capital can face, short of revolution. In the period under consideration, business interests in the US, even in this golden age of capitalism, were developing an obsessive preoccupation with the role of the state and the dangers it posed that would culminate in the election of Ronald Reagan.[15] Only occasionally in this period were radical writers, such as Gabriel Kolko, willing to remind their audiences of Marx's vision of a dynamic, Promethean capitalism that disrupted and transformed everything before it, a regime in which capitalists invoked regulation and control by the state to tame competitive forces that they were incapable of controlling on their own.[16]

The corporatist and monopoly capital approaches erred in their view of the direction of change of competitive forces in the capitalist economy. But these schools were at least sensitive to the fact that dramatic changes had taken place, both within capitalist enterprises and in the environment in which they functioned, and that such changes had profound implications for capitalism and the way we conceptualise it. By contrast, to borrow the ferocious words of the physicist Wolfgang Pauli, the mainstream of economics was 'not even wrong' – the transformation in the conduct of business since the Victorian period was barely reflected in economic analysis. Even worse, the methodological principles of mainstream economics left the discipline unprepared to consider the underlying forces that were generating these profound changes.

As we have seen in Chapter 3, by the 1930s there were some stirrings away from a Marshallian orthodoxy that analysed capitalism as consisting solely of firms in competitive markets, punctuated by the irregular presence of monopolies. The new approaches introduced a range of models to deal with markets that were less than competitive as a normal case: they were reflecting in an implicit way a widespread feeling that the emergence, and now ubiquity, of giant firms indicated the presence of a change from a world of competitive markets to one that was less competitive. Models were developed that were 'in between' those of (perfect) competition and monopoly: some embodied a traditional competitive view in which excess profits were eliminated, but introduced the possibility of advertising and product differentiation being undertaken by firms.[17] In models of oligopoly, competition 'among the few' replaced the unitary monopolist. These ingenious constructions, long considered the major achievement of the microeconomics of the interwar period, faded in influence in the postwar era and were largely relegated to textbook chapters and research topics concerned with exceptional issues.[18]

The surprising development of a retreat from realism in favour of a resurrected version of competitive theory resulted from a desire in academic economics, as in several other disciplines in the postwar world, such as mathematics, philosophy and music theory, to recast the subject on more rigorous analytical foundations. In economics, this tendency took the form of an increased centrality of general equilibrium theory, in which the influence of supply and demand in all markets is dealt with simultaneously rather than, so to speak, on a case-by-case basis: for such models to be viable, individual markets that deviate from competition can be present, at best, in what remains a sea of competition. A second motivation for the rise of general equilibrium theory had a more political-economic dimension: when all markets are fully competitive, it is possible to demonstrate with mathematical rigour that an equilibrium derived for a whole economy was (Pareto) optimal. Under such conditions, as noted in Chapter 1, no individual's condition could improve without making someone else worse off – a legitimation of capitalism in a Cold War context that some found convincing. Overall, the mainstream of economics had little to say about trends in the competitive environment in capitalism at a conceptual level. It was happy to excoriate Galbraith for his grand generalisations and to make a virtue of treating deviations from competition as purely pragmatic issues, to be dealt with by the appropriate anti-monopolies authorities. To the extent that any trend was detected, it was among antitrust specialists, who saw in the growth of giant firms a retrograde movement away from a former age of competition.[19]

On the issue of the internal governance of the firm, the mainstream response to the changes emerging in the postwar world consisted of attempts to recast in traditional terms the issues raised by the new situation. Thus, the separation of ownership and control that had emerged in large companies, one that had signalled for Berle and Means in 1932 a crisis in property relations, was reconsidered by the mainstream in the 1960s in a much more narrowly defined manner: if those in control of the great corporations are not wholly responsible to their owners (the shareholders), will the traditional presumption still hold that the primary goal of the firm is to maximise profits? A class of alternative goals for manager-dominated firms was offered – the firm might choose to maximise sales, for instance, because executive remuneration seemed to be tied to the magnitude of the firm's overall activities, rather than its profits.[20] Such solutions hinted at some empirically relevant hypotheses, for instance, that managers might be willing to indulge in even unprofitable takeovers of other firms using cash that otherwise would have been paid out to shareholders as dividends. But, so presented, the separation of ownership and control was not a crisis in property relations – it was merely a change in the large firm's maximand.

Even this departure from orthodoxy was marginalised by a growing literature suggesting that managers would be forced to return to the straight and narrow of profit maximisation by the discipline of actual or potential stock market takeovers, which at the same time served the purpose of legitimating the superiority of Anglo-Saxon-style stock market-based financial arrangements over bank-based alternatives prominent in continental Europe, especially in West Germany. Overall, the mainstream literature on separation of ownership from control had little to conclude about the effect of this phenomenon on the overall environment of modern capitalism. It postulated merely that this separation might have resulted in a weakening of the imperative to maximise profits in favour of 'something else', be it an alternative goal or, as Schumpeter had earlier suggested, a bureaucratised sapping of entrepreneurial zeal.

A figure who addressed the issues surrounding corporate governance in more detail and with more imagination than Schumpeter, Galbraith or mainstream economists was the business historian Alfred DuPont Chandler, seen earlier in Chapter 2. His grand narrative had first appeared in the 1950s, but his major impact was made with the publication of *The Visible Hand* in 1977. The book was issued in the context of an incongruous set of public attitudes towards the economic events leading up to the First World War. On the one hand, it was a period in which the US was seen to emerge as the supreme economic and industrial power in the world and the epitome of all aspects of modernity in material life. But, oddly, historians typically pictured it as the age of the Robber Barons; the dominant economic perspective on the changes in this period was that the emergence of giant firms represented a transition from a competitive economy to one dominated by monopolies and self-serving professional managers – a wholly negative view. A broad public in the US was ripe for an account of the emergence of these giant firms that legitimated them in terms of their efficiency and modernity.

In Chandler's exposition, the firms concerned are never monopolies: they are subject to substantial competitive pressure from rivals and from financial markets to yield adequate returns. Furthermore, and in sharp contrast to Schumpeter, there was no mystification of the entrepreneur. On the contrary, the emergence of the separation of ownership from control was viewed as an aspect of the professionalisation of management – the supersession of GM over Ford in the 1920s is viewed as the victory of the professional manager Alfred Sloan over the inspired amateur Henry Ford. Professionalisation of management, the very creation of a profession called management, is a key theme for Chandler: the development of specialisms in finance and, especially, cost accounting were key factors that prevented large, multidivisional companies from collapsing under the weight of diseconomies of scale. A crucial reason why the great firms had an advantage over their smaller rivals was the very presence of these specialised divisions, populated by individuals trained in new disciplines such as marketing and purchasing, as well as in traditional ones devoted to engineering and scientific research.

Lastly, in Chandler's exposition, the development of the firm actually benefited from the separation of ownership and control: its professional managers, who typically in this period had a long-term commitment to the company because of lifetime tenure there, fended off greedy, myopic shareholders who, if in full control, would have taken out the bulk of the company's profits in dividends. The firm, far from being faced with a static decision to maximise either profits or sales, has to choose from a range of different courses of action to deal with uncertain streams of returns in the future. Chandler documents how the managers of the great firms, in a manner analogous to those in Galbraith's technostructure, took long-term decisions to mitigate this uncertainty through the maintenance of control over production, marketing and finance.

Chandler had thus managed to generate a major redirection of thought on the events of the early twentieth century in the US. First, he had come up with an account of the emergence of giant firms in which they were the epitome of modernity and efficiency. Second, he had given historical support for the account of events that had been given contemporaneously in the technocratic planning paradigm, with the visible hand of management having demonstrated its superiority over the invisible hand of the market. But by the time of the publication of *The Visible Hand* in 1977, the public argument was shifting dramatically in the opposite direction. The centrally planned economies were visibly faltering and, more significantly, there were important aspects of world capitalism that were exhibiting a powerful dynamism and generating an acceleration of competition. These latter developments were mistakenly seen as a fulfilment of Hayek's spontaneous order rather than something even more complex – the working out of the logic of Chandler's managerial system in the direction of ever more intricate and sophisticated planning, leading to a world economic system that was more competitive than ever before.

The acceleration of competition

Galbraith's vision was, indeed, a reflection of important aspects of the US industrial system of the 1960s, with the US maintaining overwhelming dominance in the world capitalist economy. In areas of high technology, its hegemony was as yet unchallenged, and in traditional industries such as steel and cars, giant firms in the US and in many other industrial nations were insulated from significant international competition. With large shares of the domestic market, the giants of these US industries had substantial control of their environment and had settled down into quiescent habits of behaviour, so that Galbraith's paradigmatic GM did seem to be the master of all it surveyed in the domestic economy. Even its critics did not question its role in generating low unit costs – it was seen as the epitome of large-scale manufacture, making optimal use of contemporary technology and modern management techniques. In Western Europe, there was a fear of being overwhelmed by US industrial power and modernity, as evidenced by the publication in 1968 of Jean-Jacques Servan-Schreiber's book *The American Challenge.*[21]

And yet, these books by Galbraith and Servan-Schreiber were not sign-posts for the future development of capitalism, but indications of the end of an era. The hegemony of the US car industry by the Big Three (GM, Ford and Chrysler) took definitive form with the substantive demise of peripheral firms during the Great Depression and then the self-immolation of potential competitors during the Second World War; it was only in the 1960s that the first hints of competition in the US domestic market from imports could be noted. With his US-centred perspective, the rise in business concentration in the US car market over the twentieth century was taken by Galbraith as characteristic of a long-term downward trend in the intensity of competition, a position shared with almost all those expressing an opinion on this matter. By the 1980s, however, it was becoming clear that a new, more competitive world was emerging, one threatening the dominant position of New Industrial State behemoths such as GM.[22]

The unwinding of this giant-firm hegemony had been delayed by the world wars, interwar stagnation, and the consequent protection and subsidies given to giant firms by national governments worldwide. All of these factors inhibited the emergence of new domestic competition and the expansion of international trade and investment that would increase levels of competition worldwide. In the Golden Age of Capitalism after the Second World War, all of these conditions were reversed: the maintenance of high levels of macroeconomic growth permitted the emergence of new firms to challenge existing ones in the context of a general expansion of economic activity within and between nations, enhanced by reductions in tariffs and other governmental restrictions. The first challengers under the umbrella of the postwar boom were the nations of continental Europe. By the mid-1950s, West Germany had joined the US and the UK as an industrial power, and in the 1960s we see the first serious incursions into the US car market by Volkswagen.

But Germany was merely re-establishing its prewar stature as an industrial power. More significant are the emergence of first France and then Italy as major industrial players: even in the case of France, we are dealing with an economic system that contained a substantial rural and agricultural sector before the war, while Italy's transformation from a semi-developed to an advanced economy (albeit with extreme differences between regions) achieved in reality what had been claimed for the Soviet Union in its propaganda. It was not, however, the European resurgence that shook the *New Industrial State* perspective on the nature of the industrial economy. For good or ill, the dominant perspective on the world economy comes largely from US sources, and it was not until the US economy felt the force of the industrial transformation in other countries that the picture presented of the world industrial economy began to change.

And the nation that signalled this change was Japan. The Japanese intervention into the car industry, with its just-in-time inventory monitoring and raising of standards of quality control, proceeded to dismember the national oligopolies existing in the US and other nations. These successes were, furthermore, a demonstration that challenges to the leading nations of the industrial world could take place from supposedly peripheral countries on the basis of the superiority of their management techniques. Starting in the 1970s, Japanese exports, especially to the US, became serious threats to the US domestic car, steel and electronics industries, and to the role of American companies as standards of excellence worldwide. At first, Japan's competitive advantage was attributed to cheap labour. It soon became obvious, however, that Japanese industrial success in, for instance, the car industry was to a large extent a function of superior management: the vaunted GM of *The New Industrial State*, far from being the epitome of efficiency and modernity, was holding several months' worth of inventories of many components, whereas Japanese firms succeeded in functioning with inventories measured in hours. For a substantial period, the focus of attention was on the special characteristics of Japan that permitted it to join the White Man's Club. The subsequent emergence of South Korea and other Asian tigers led to a search for Confucian characteristics, and then to a *reductio ad absurdum* of this whole attempt at cultural exegesis, most especially as new players emerged from other parts of the world.

The acceleration of competition is the product of what is, from a static perspective, a widening of the domain of markets with improvements in transport and communications coupled with an expansion in the facility and ambition of management. From a dynamic perspective, the advance of competitive pressure is linked to the increased dispersion and formalisation of managerial technique, so that the cost-accounting and inventory control methods originally associated with a select group of mostly very large firms had become widely available. This tendency is part of a typical process in capitalism by which there is an increase in the supply of a scarce, highly rewarded resource, in this case management facility, both within nations and worldwide. But there is good reason to believe that this process of dispersion will be accelerated under contemporary conditions. As we shall see in Chapter 8, an important consequence of investment by multinationals has been the accelerated dissemination worldwide of the managerial and worker knowledge embodied in these organisations.

An even more powerful force for dispersion of this knowledge, however, is its tendency to cease to be implicit – key aspects of best-practice managerial technique become routinised, mechanical and subject to study in textbooks worldwide, as a set of Chandler-type protocols. In this sense, managerial technique is similar to other forms of knowledge: in its early manifestations, it contains procedures and implicit forms of knowledge that are difficult for outsiders to imitate, but there is an inherent desire and tendency in capitalism to reduce these procedures to the learned routines discussed in Chapter 2. Thus, the making of steel was, until the nineteenth century, an art with low yields whose secrets were embodied in a handful of individuals and organisations. The substitution of scientifically based, routinised procedures – over centuries in the case of steel, or decades in the case of semi-conductors – increased the potential for imitation and replication, in the absence of legal protection for these procedures in the form of patents. As a result, battles over intellectual property rights are likely to become increasingly central to the political economy of the twenty-first century. In a similar way, the very openness and transparency of managerial innovations such as the assembly line have lent themselves to replication on a worldwide basis. Individual cultures, such as that of Japan, may then bring their own ingenuity to improving upon the technological and managerial aspects of steel production, but their first task has been to master the existing formalised procedures, an undertaking greatly facilitated, as we shall see, by their commitment to educational development.

Thus, rational, planned activities of established firms in a particular sector are often conducive not to the emergence of a *New Industrial State* regime of control in that sector, but to the acceleration of competition in that sphere. In the case of the car industry in the US, this process was long delayed. The immediate consequence of the exploitation of standardisation in parts, processes and products was the generation of economies of scale and the growth of a US industry characterised by a few large producers dominating the sector. But, in a development that unfolded over more than half a century, the standardised nature of the final product, the car, and the uniform nature of the protocols of the assembly line were readily replicable by other nations and permitted worldwide competition in the mass-produced vehicle.

The elaborate forms of product differentiation in modern capitalism, first commented upon by economic theorists in the 1930s, were, paradoxically, an attempt to assert an individuality for products that, at base, were more uniform in character than ever before, a process epitomised by the GM practice of offering up a range of different brands, all using the output of the Fisher Body plant. The promotion of uniformity in production techniques and of goods sold was linked to a desire to create volume effects in production and marketing through the creation of a mass market. This desire helps to explain the alacrity with which IBM permitted Microsoft to offer its operating system for the personal computer to IBM's rivals; for the same reason, the launch of the CD player by Philips and Sony was accompanied by the publication of a Red Book of specifications that was available to potential competitors. In both these cases, efforts in the direction of creating a mass market through product uniformity soon resulted in the emergence of highly competitive sectors in which the initiators ceased to dominate: assiduous corporate planning created high levels of market competition.

These attempts by great firms to exercise control over their environment from the beginning of the twentieth century contributed to the unravelling of this strategy by the dawn of the new millennium. Within the organisation, aspects of this control involved the replacement, wherever possible, of craft-based techniques of production with scientific, objectively replicable protocols, and of formalised, even academically inspired, procedures for firm accounting, the structuring and training of management, and the direction of labour. Within sectors, the great firms needed standardised specifications to facilitate mass production – for electrical equipment at the beginning of the twentieth century, and for personal computers and related operating systems at a later date. And here is the irony: in processes that were long delayed over the twentieth century by war and economic depression, these attempts by the giant firms to exercise control over their own organisations and the sectors in which they functioned facilitated imitation, emulation and rivalry in nations far from the heartland of the Second Industrial Revolution. These giant firms had created the prerequisites for competition for their products and the very lack of control of their destiny that they had been attempting to avoid.

We have thus seen that economic planning in its most elaborate form – that to be found in the Soviet Union – was a failure, for reasons grounded in the economic logic of the system created. Western socialists after the First World War found themselves with the task of attempting to formulate an alternative to capitalism, but along with other adherents to the technocratic planning paradigm, their analyses were deeply flawed. In many countries, this alternative took the form of schemes for economic planning: the collapse of socialism can be substantively linked to the incoherence of such schemes, rather than to any proximate excuse. Socialism was being looked for in the wrong place.

The demise of technocratic planning: the Alternative Economic Strategy

The deleterious effects of the technocratic planning paradigm on the development of a coherent socialist alternative in the twentieth century are exemplified by events in Britain. Left-wing political economy focused attention away from policies addressing the existing class structure, such as radical reforms to the school and university system, that might have permanently transformed society in an egalitarian direction. Changes of this kind, unlike the highly desirable but alleviationist National Health Service created after the Second World War, would also have served as a component of a strategy of economic development for an advanced economy such as Britain.

Instead, the theory and practice in Britain of moderate socialism may be characterised as aimless, with an unfocused attachment to planning of some sort. When radical socialist tendencies were able to influence the policies of the Labour Party in Britain in the 1970s and 1980s with the Alternative Economic Strategy (AES), the focus was upon working through a thorough-going version of the technocratic planning paradigm. The AES remains the most radical programme to become the official policy of a major political party in a leading capitalist country in the postwar world. The irrelevance of this programme in the worldwide economic conditions emerging in this period signalled the demise of the planning paradigm and the rise to predominance in Britain and in other countries of the reconstituted liberal alternative. It is this sad history that is reviewed here.

Planning in the interwar period in Britain, for a broad spectrum of opinion, functioned as a central focus of economic debate, though it was often little more than a catchphrase expressing a generalised state of disaffection with the economy.[23] There emerged a range of anti-laissez-faire positions that paralleled those to be found in continental Europe: socialism as workers' control or in the form of centralised state management, with a particular admiration for the successes of planning in the First World War; techno-cratic approaches; forms of corporatism, emphasising cartels and combina-tion in order to avoid the 'anarchy' of competition;[24] pre-Keynesian schemes for macroeconomic pump-priming of the economy; and, following on from Joseph Chamberlain in the prewar period, an emphasis on protectionism within the context of the Empire. All of these developments, with the excep-tion of Keynesian theories of macroeconomic regulation (which were of no influence on substantive economic policies in the interwar period) and the creation, along with the US, of the national income accounts, remained weaker and less developed than their continental European equivalents, partly because of the continuing resonance of laissez-faire ideology in the land of its birth.

The history of the Labour Party passed from a commitment in 1918 to 'a systematic and comprehensive ... planned cooperation in production and distribution'[25] to a profoundly unsatisfactory interwar period in which the Labour Party emerged first as complicit with the deflationist poli-cies on offer in the 1920s and then, through its own disunity and lack of coherence, as a counterpart to the directionless Conservative regime of Stanley Baldwin in the 1930s. The disparate range of opinions emerging from the Labour Party in the interwar period is also a reflection of the weakness of the links between socialist intellectual opinion in Britain and the working-class movement. The whimsicality of the former is indicated by the fact that before the Great War, the Fabian Society held positions indistinguishable from those of the more progressive members of the Liberal Party, and yet later, without renouncing earlier positions, such prominent Fabians as Sidney and Beatrice Webb and George Bernard Shaw could offer uncritical support for Stalin's regime at the height of the Terror in the 1930s.

The lack of a coherent position within the Labour Party on planning and the organisation of the economy was not due primarily to this sociological division between intellectuals and workers, but emerged as a product of intellectual differences on the appropriate modes of economic regulation for an economy. Within the Labour Party, the logic of marketplace efficiency still played an important role, so that only a specific faction around the economist and prolific writer G. D. H. Cole was committed to systematic central planning. Nationalisation, as it emerged as Labour Party policy, was characterised by a technocratic tendency, identified with Herbert Morrison, that wished to see key sectors, like the Central Electricity Board and the BBC, governed by competent individuals with a disinterested, long-term perspective on the sector at hand.[26] There was no clear indication, however, that such proposals were part of an attempt to plan the economy overall or to revolutionise its mode or direction of operation. Furthermore, since all proposed nationalisations involved full compensation of the owners, nationalisation was not self-evidently part of any programme of redistribution of income or wealth, and issues of workers' control of these nationalised enterprises were never seriously broached.

The 1945 Attlee government remains at the centre of controversy to this day, despite a range of achievements that has remained unchallenged, such as the nationalisation of the Bank of England and the creation of the National Health Service. From a right-wing perspective, emerging from the last years of the Thatcher–Major era, the 1945 Labour government was said to have wasted resources on social programmes that should have been committed to industrial revival, with housing better represented in the Cabinet than industry.[27] This class of views will be contested in Part II: it implicitly dismisses the role played in economic development of improvements accruing to the stock of human assets incumbent upon social programmes. The provision of housing, most especially for those on lower incomes, is not a gratuitous luxury but a complement to other aspects (including education) of a strategy of human and economic development.

In fact, much of the new government's functioning seemed to be consumed with day-to-day survival considerations, including the need to raise the level of exports: the latter problem was exacerbated by the high level of the initial postwar value of the pound. Britain's acquiescence to pressure from the US to act as a junior partner in the Bretton Woods exchange rate system by becoming fully convertible, and its continuing focus on soft Commonwealth and Empire markets for exports, indicate a more likely source of postwar sluggishness in Britain relative to other West European nations – its desire to retain a role for itself as a great power.[28]

From another perspective, as quoted earlier in the Introduction to Part I, 'Much of the Left's energy has been dissipated by industrial experiments in planning...it seems indisputable now that had the 1945 Labour government concentrated on rewriting the 1944 Education Act and reconstructing the university system, a genuine and lasting transformation of the society may well have been possible.' In retrospect, this judgement seems overly stark. Without doubt, the Attlee government's approach to education at all levels was inadequate even to serve the needs of economic modernisation, much less those of socialist transformation. But much of the nationalisation, such as that for gas, electricity and other utilities, now seems unexceptional, as does the taking into public ownership of the poorly run coal industry.

Most controversial in the long run was the nationalisation of the steel industry, a sector that, along with the nationalised car industry of future Labour governments, became emblematic of Labour policy failure in economic intervention. Steel nationalisation was never part of an attempt at coherent central planning. Its rationale was muddled, since there were no redistributive effects (as the nationalisation was compensated), nor was it an attempt to control Pigovian-style negative externalities (since pollution was not a major policy consideration at the time). Nationalisation appeared to have a dual motivation: first, nationalised firms could play a role in maintaining full employment; second, there was a belief, emerging from technocratic planning concepts, that nationalisation would eliminate the uncertainty generated by competition and would thereby yield more rational long-term investment decisions for publicly owned monopolies.[29] The latter presumption – a false one – was that steel and other comparable industries would continue to operate in an international context that would leave scope for idiosyncratic direction at a national level. This failure of analysis ultimately doomed any attempts to assert the dominance of plan over market.

The lasting memory – from both the left and right – of subsequent Labour governments until the Thatcher accession of 1979 is the presence of perpetual loss making in sectors such as steel, cars and coal, alongside peripheral achievements such as the creation of the Open University and failed attempts at reform in the creation of comprehensive schools. The Labour Party's association with the trade union movement was long perceived as a political asset, not only because of the large number of voters within the latter's catchment, but because of the implicit Labour Party claim that they could exercise influence over this powerful group: the Labour Party could 'deal' with the unions, thereby limiting strike activity and excessive wage demands.[30] In the longer term, the Labour Party's trade union link was perceived by many to be a sordid association with a special interest, with the deals made being concessions to blackmail.

These Labour governments are striking examples of the role that intellectual coherence, or its absence, can play in public policy: the willingness of so much of society to move in the direction of right-wing adventurism under Margaret Thatcher can be partially explained in these terms. By the 1970s, the failure of real existing socialism in Eastern Europe and the Soviet Union was almost universally accepted. Socialism in the form of the loss-making nationalised car and steel industries was not only unpopular but, equally importantly, lacking even a putative rationale, and this heritage of pointless nationalisation did the Labour Party enormous damage from the 1960s onward. In the early 1970s, two radical economists, Andrew Glyn and Bob Sutcliffe, suggested that Britain had emerged from the Second World War in the unique position among large nations in Europe of having a working class undecimated by the war and postwar reconstruction: their pioneering analysis of declining profitability in British industry was thus linked to the power of its working class. In the atmosphere of the time, however, the doctrine was successfully taken up by the right, rather than being, as intended, an argument for a radical rejection of a failed capitalism.[31] It was under these conditions that the free-market alternative of Mrs Thatcher was able to gain broad support.

When the Labour Party came together with its own logically coherent, if unviable, alternative, it was only through harkening back to an era in British history – a period now long past, if it had ever existed – in which Britain could perceive its leading sectors as sufficiently dominant and secure from foreign competition to permit the setting up of a centrally planned alternative to capitalism, a return to the 'real' Labour Party of the 1918 platform. The Labour Party took a dramatic turn to the left in 1973 with the adoption of its AES (the name was given in 1975), rejecting the moderate revisionist political economy epitomised by the Anthony Crosland-inspired 1957 party document *Industry and Society*. The AES was eventually put to one side by the Labour Party in 1983. The six key elements of the AES were commitments to reflation, public ownership, planning, price controls, industrial democracy and import restrictions.[32]

The first four of these aspects of the programme were meant to be part of a coordinated effort to deal with deficiencies of the economy at both a macro- and a microeconomic level. Thus, policies of reflation (increases in aggregate demand to promote investment, employment and economic growth), in the absence of changes in the microeconomy, would continue to fail: they would inevitably become part of the notorious stop–go cycles that had brought other periods of expansion to a halt. Structural changes in the microeconomy were needed so that upswings in business activity were not constrained by bottlenecks in the supply of capital goods resulting from deficient investment, and by inflation resulting from monopolies taking advantage of favourable demand conditions to raise their prices inordinately.

Firms were to be brought under public ownership ('a significant public stake in each sector of the economy'), involving at least two dozen leading companies. It was unclear, and perhaps intentionally so, whether this nationalisation would include foreign-owned firms. Nationalised firms would set standards for the rest of the business sector. First, they would undertake high levels of investment, using funds that these firms, prior to nationalisation, might have devoted to dividend payouts and to taking over other firms. Second, they would have to show restraint in the setting of prices, most especially since the firms nationalised were likely to be near-monopolies or dominant firms in one or more sectors of the economy. Price restraint by the nationalised firms would help create a competitive atmosphere for the remaining firms in the sector. Furthermore, this restraint in the setting of prices would be coupled with the pursuit of employment policies designed to give a favourable trade-off between employment and inflation.

Planning agreements and price controls would reinforce these standards for the top 100 companies left in private ownership. Targets would be negotiated with the firms concerning employment, investment, and production over a five year period, covering pricing policy, product development, marketing, and export and import levels. Generalised price controls were not so much an inherent part of the overall economic strategy as an explicitly political gesture: they had been the centrepiece of the famous social contract by which the government would control price increases and the trade unions would, in turn, restrain wage demands.

Import restrictions were perhaps the most controversial element in the AES package. These 'temporary' measures were meant to satisfy two goals simultaneously. On the one hand, it was hoped that they would help mitigate the stop–go cycle – reflationary policies would no longer be brought to a halt by a rapid deterioration in the balance of payments due to the sucking in of imports. The other justification for import controls, however, brings into question a key premise on which the whole AES had been constructed – the growing pervasiveness of monopoly in the economy. If the monopoly power of British firms was growing in this period, why was it necessary to use import controls as part of a long-term strategy for the recovery of British industry to give it breathing space from ever more destructive international competition?

Industrial democracy, in the form of worker participation in firm decision making, was to be introduced for its own sake, but it was also hoped that democracy, by reducing worker alienation, would reinforce the other reforms designed to re-energise British industry. The introduction of elements of worker participation in the AES programme was the only aspect that could be described as intrinsically left-wing or progressive, since nationalisation was only proposed to take place in the context of full compensation to owners. (AES supporters and radical commentators were generally in favour of wealth redistribution, but not by way of nationalisation per se.) Thus, the AES, for all its left-wing rhetoric, was largely concerned with the claim that it could improve the management of the business sector in Britain through extensive government participation and direction.

The economic context in which the AES was originally enunciated was one in which the British economy had experienced relative economic decline compared with other nations, but was not obviously in a situation of crisis. In the period following the Second World War, Britain's rate of economic growth was consistently at the bottom of league tables of major industrial nations, and by the 1970s, standards of per capita income were being equalled or exceeded in a range of countries in the Common Market.

But in this golden age of world capitalism ending in about 1971, even these apparently low rates of growth were higher for Britain than for any other comparable period in the twentieth century. In absolute terms, material standards had vastly improved. With no clear trends present in either direction in the gap between rich and poor, living standards even for the poorest sections of society were rising. Unemployment was low by international and historical standards; inflation, until the oil price rises that emerged in the wake of the Arab–Israeli war of 1973, was low enough to be considered more of an obstacle to macroeconomic expansion than a serious threat to economic stability. Crises in the balance of payments leading to devaluation, though present in other nations, most notably the US in 1971, tended to be treated in Britain as national traumas and symbols of decline.

Lastly, British industry, which in the years immediately after the Second World War had appeared to be the only significant rival in the capitalist world to the US in a range of key traditional industries and high-technology sectors such as computers, was now finding itself pushed aside by new entrants such as Japan. The 'natural' process of deindustrialisation inevitable in advanced economies as the relative shares of the economy shifted from manufacturing to the tertiary (services) sector (or, in Britain's case, partially into the primary sector, with oil being extracted from the North Sea in large amounts in the late 1970s) was taking place at an inordinate rate.[33] The feeling in Britain that it was undergoing a period of decline was pervasive.[34]

Thus, the context in which the AES emerged might have appeared propitious, since the notion that Britain was in a state of decline was widespread. Also pervasive was a national consciousness of Britain's former greatness, so that the AES's implicit assertion of the possibility of economic renewal thorough unilateral national action might well have come across as plausible, while in most other nations of Western Europe, a multilateral context and a sense of the constraints of the international economy were emerging as the norm. Furthermore, the measures proposed, with the exception of the proposal for the introduction of elements of workers' control, were not inherently left-wing.

Why, then, was the AES unable to generate broad-based political support? The failure of the Labour Party AES in political terms is partly linked to the specific historical conditions that emerged in the mid-1970s. The rise in the price of oil had helped precipitate an inflation so severe that a key element of the AES – the need for reflation – was seen to be inoperative, and a policy of price controls as part of a social contract simply broke down. Equally inoperative was the notion that the profits of the monopolists could be directed to better ends: a general acceptance (based on the work of the two economists cited above) that there had been a long-term decline in the profitability of British industry obviated the question of the redistribution of these profits.

The AES also failed because of the public perception that nationalisation in sectors such as steel and cars had been, in a host of ways, unsuccessful. From a political perspective, Anthony Crosland and the right wing of the Labour Party demonstrated political astuteness compared with the proponents of the AES. For Crosland, Keynesian macroeconomic management was within the domain of politicians, but he generally opposed the notion that political involvement, through either nationalisation or planning agreements, could be a vehicle for the improvement of the performance of the business sector. His opponents on the Labour left suggested that his opposition to AES-style micro-management of the economy by government was due to his old-fashioned views on the nature of the contemporary British economy. There can be little doubt, however, that Crosland's primary reason for opposing such policies was that government involvement in the business sector evoked little public sympathy.

The weaknesses embodied in the AES do not undermine the fact that it represented an attempt to put forth a programme for the regeneration of the British economy that was underpinned by a coherent intellectual argument. Not until several years into the Thatcher era could it be claimed that political actors were motivated by a set of doctrines of such intellectual clarity. By contrast, the programme of the mainstream Labour right represented by Crosland's *Future of Socialism* of 1956 seemed to be little more than an eloquently worded version of *on s'engage et puis on voit*. The AES largely emerged from the tireless advocacy and theoretical work of Stuart Holland. His analysis, as set out in *The Socialist Challenge* of 1975, dwarfs in theoretical ambition and detail any comparable work in the postwar world from the Crosland revisionist group or any other assemblage within the Labour Party.[35] The theoretical skeleton may be put forth in the following propositions, some only implicit in Holland's work:

There is a growing tendency towards monopoly in the British economy.

The management of privately owned large firms can be readily replaced by state ownership, or supplemented with governmental directives.

'Socialism in one country' is a viable proposition.

I will address each of these propositions in turn:

There is a growing tendency towards monopoly in the British economy. This notion is a central aspect of the technocratic planning paradigm that dominated the left-wing literature of the economics of the twentieth century. What is distinctive in Holland is that he focuses only briefly on the traditional critique of monopoly power – that powerful firms that dominate individual markets can exploit consumers. Rather, for him, the word 'monopoly' is used in a more metaphorical, populist sense to connote very large, most commonly multinational, firms. He measures this phenomenon by looking not at levels of concentration in individual markets, but at aggregate concentration – the share of the 100 largest firms in the British manufacturing sector, which grew substantially over the twentieth century. This process of the growing predominance of large firms is, however, as in John Kenneth Galbraith's *The New Industrial State*, viewed as inevitable and emerging from the exigencies of modern technology: survival of the fittest dictates the prevalence of these giants in the contemporary world. As in Galbraith, management and decision making in these large firms have become separated from ownership. These managers, substantially freed both from the constraints of traditional competitive forces and from the demands of shareholders, can exercise significant freedom of action in their decisions.

For Holland, there are two main reasons to be concerned with the emergence of these giant, multinational firms. First, their presence and behaviour limits national sovereignty: governments, especially socialist governments, lose control over fiscal and monetary policy, as well as foreign exchange, when large, multinational firms pursue tactics to avoid the effects of governmental direction and taxation. The second reason to be concerned with the growth of the predominance of these large firms is that their monopoly power worsens the trade-off between unemployment and inflation: governmental attempts to lower unemployment through additional expenditure will be thwarted by the ability of the monopolies to use their market power to put up prices. This first proposition contains the essence of Holland's worldview. It also embodies his critique of Crosland's notion that it is possible to limit government involvement in economic activity to the realm of macroeconomic (monetary and fiscal) policy, and let the private sector take care of business affairs: for Holland, the emergent 'mesoeconomic' economy dominated by large, multinational firms makes such an approach impracticable, if not impossible.

The very premise of the first proposition above was false. The problems being experienced by British industry were not those of growing monopoly predominance, but of increasing international competition and relative decline. In the immediate postwar world, key elements of British industry had cultivated habits of monopolistic sluggishness because of their substantial control over domestic and Commonwealth markets and the scarcity of international rivals. Progressively, British firms had to face unprecedented competition first from continental rivals, and then from Japan, Asia and other nations. The high levels and rapid rise in aggregate concentration in the UK were largely a manifestation and reflection of its stagnation in the context of increasing international competition and a shrinking industrial base. Mergers in the UK accounted for much of the rise in concentration: managers, with poor prospects for the investment of funds in their own companies, chose to take over other firms rather than pay dividends to shareholders. For a host of national economies that grew far more rapidly than the UK, such as Italy, the small-firm sector was a key element in their rapid economic growth, giving the lie to the notion that gigantism was an inherent and inexorable part of all modern forms of capitalist development.

It is indubitably true that the emergence of giant multinational firms, and other changes in the international economic and financial arena, may impose limits on national sovereignty: governments, especially potentially socialist governments, can lose control over fiscal and monetary policy, as well as foreign exchange, when, for instance, large, multinational firms pursue tactics to avoid direction and taxation from national governments. Monopoly, however, had nothing to do with these developments. It was the growing preponderance of the international dimension in every nation's economy – the dramatic rises in the flows of direct and portfolio investment, international trade and finance – that was critical to the thwarting of national sovereignty, rather than monopoly power: very large firms in a *competitive* environment (in, for instance, an international context) would be at least as eager as any monopolist to avoid governmental controls and taxation. To the extent that the emergence of the multinational is, as we shall see below, an aspect of a more generalised internationalisation of the economic environment, it is a fact to be faced by all nations and has little to do with monopoly per se. As Holland correctly points out, the British economy has an exceptionally large component of multinational activity. Any realistic view of Britain's place in the world economy at the time would have resulted in demands for regulation at the supra-national level, such as the European Union (or the European Economic Community (EEC), as it was then known), rather than relying on the limited resources of a nation state. But the Labour left of the 1980s was adamantly opposed to the EEC.

The second reason for concern about the role of giant and multinational forms (mesoeconomic power, in Holland's terms) is that it can exacerbate the trade-off between unemployment and inflation. It is true that monopoly power can sometimes cause the price system to act perversely – in a notorious case in the US, the American Tobacco Company was able to raise cigarette prices in the context of general deflation during the Great Depression of the 1930s. But in general, the notion does not even make logical sense: why should a monopolist's pricing policy exacerbate inflation, which is the *rate of change* of prices?

The management of privately owned large firms can be readily replaced by state ownership, or supplemented with governmental directives. The transition from capitalist to socialist direction is a smooth one in Holland's Galbraithian world, echoing the presumptions of the technocratic paradigm in its socialist manifestations. In such a world, where technology dictates that it is the big firms that are the harbingers of the emergent new industrial state, it is sufficient to focus on this small number of large entities rather than the sea of enterprises in the economy as a whole. Furthermore, since the managers of these large capitalist firms have substantial freedom of action due to monopoly power and their independence from shareholder demands, the redirection of the large firm's activities in a socialist direction will be a straightforward process. Company managers as specialists can be left to deal with day-to-day decisions, but now the overall directives will be set by socialist planners.

Typical of the forms of intervention in the AES would be price restraint by the nationalised firm in order to create a competitive atmosphere for the rest of the firms in the sector. This identification of pricing policy with competitive behaviour is familiar from standard economics textbooks and corresponds to the ideas of the socialist economist Oskar Lange in the 1930s, discussed in Chapter 4. As we have seen, he suggested that the question of ownership is irrelevant in determining whether or not an economy is efficient: a publicly owned, socialist economy could simulate the efficiency of a competitive capitalist economy by being instructed to set its prices in a competitive manner. Neoclassical orthodoxy had been convinced by Lange's argument and conceded that competitive prices could just as well be simulated in a socialist context.

For Hayek, by contrast, competition under capitalism was about much more than pricing policy. It involved (as in Marx) a continual renewal of the forces of production, risk taking and the introduction of new technology. Thus, while it is reasonable to think that telephone services, like those for water, can be straightforwardly provided by a single nationalised producer, the issue takes on a new light once the telephone sector is transformed into telecommunications. As a nationalised industry, we would have to answer the question: *how much* of the public's money should be invested (risked) in the new goods and services being offered by the telecommunications industry, and *in what* new sectors should it be invested? The presumption is, of course, that under capitalism, these questions are simply answered: in a privately owned firm, by virtue of holding the firm's shares, the owners have acquiesced to partaking in the risks embodied in new ventures. Investments on the part of the firm will proceed as long as they are perceived to add to the value of the firm and therefore the net worth of the shareholder.

This capitalist decision rule on investment is perfectly coherent. There is no equivalent rule in a nationalised context. Let it be conceded that when the AES speaks of the need for 'more' investment in industry, it is implicitly invoking a Keynesian criterion whereby aggregate investment must be at a sufficient level to underpin full employment. The question still remains: investment in *what*? Would massive expenditure on capacity in the 1970s and 1980s in the car and steel industries (likely key sectors for expansion under the AES) have been of long-run benefit to the British economy? The spectre of massive, Soviet-style investment in obsolescent spheres of activity must be coupled with the extraordinarily detailed planning agreements discussed above, covering all aspects of firm behaviour. Besides the obvious costs of administering any such agreements, the multiplicity of goals to be met promised to generate for the economy as a whole the kind of incoherence and lack of direction characteristic of existing nationalised industries.

Furthermore, the viability of the AES programme of planning agreements is linked to a particular view of the modern, large firm, also derived from Galbraith, in which large companies are already self-sufficient islands of planning. For the AES, then, it would be relatively unproblematic to introduce government-directed planning agreements with dozens of large firms as a replacement for existing firm-based planning procedures. But in reality, for even the largest firms, trade with other firms appears to account for about 75 per cent of sales.[36] Meaningful planning agreements would then involve not only a firm-by-firm determination, but also a morass of calculations concerning the *interactions between* firms.

The above few paragraphs could have been written by any paid-up member of Mrs Thatcher's favourite think tank, the Institute of Economic Affairs (IEA). But to observers in the early twenty-first century, the AES programme for the regeneration of British industry, involving nationalisation and dozens of detailed planning agreements with firms, evokes not so much a right-wing hostility as a form of incredulity – how could anyone have believed in such a thing?

It would be a shame if the incredulity evoked in response to the AES programme were to generate an uncritical attitude to the rationality of investment in a capitalist economy. That problems exist in a Keynesian, macroeconomic context are well known. But even in the area of microeconomic decision making, where it was suggested above that capitalist investment appraisal sets a standard for rationality, there are major difficulties to be faced: as we have seen, in the postwar US, the free-enterprise steel and car industries failed egregiously to respond to new competition, while many of the successful sectors of the supposed free-enterprise US economy were created by having government money 'thrown at them' during the Cold War. There are thus good reasons to question the unadorned efficacy of the free market as a vehicle for long-term investment and development, even in the context of that supposed bastion of capitalism, the US. But considered criticisms of free enterprise investment lose their force when the alternative in front of the public is AES-directed nationalisation and its morass of planning agreements.

'Socialism in one country' is a viable proposition. It is perhaps unsurprising that nations with a great imperial history will view the growing internationalisation of the economy mainly as an imposition upon national sovereignty and a threat, rather than as an emerging, inevitable aspect of world economic evolution and a new set of opportunities for its own development. For Holland, the multinational appears out of nowhere – like the monolith in '2001 – A Space Odyssey', and serves little purpose but to thwart socialist management of the economy. In fact, the multinational is not a peculiar imposition upon the world economy but an aspect of a more general series of changes in the direction of what would now be called globalisation, involving trade, finance and international dealings of all kinds, that continue to evolve to this day. Western Europe and the EEC are treated as problems to be coped with rather than as potential allies in trying to tame international capital. This strikingly national perspective is certainly curious in the context of the non-Stalinist socialist intellectual tradition, but what is more apposite is the gross underestimation of the momentum behind this process of globalisation. Within a few years of the publication of Holland's book, attempts to control exchange rate levels and currency movements would substantially disappear within major capitalist economies.

Britain did have peculiar problems in an international context: historically, Britain's own economic development may well have been disadvantaged by the Empire-oriented emphasis on overseas investment, so that in Britain in the 1970s there was a net outflow of foreign direct investment funds. Part of the AES strategy was a set of governmental measures to control outflows, but given the likely disincentive effects of this and other aspects of the AES on potential inflows, its prospects for improving net inflow were clearly dubious. The British state was simply not powerful enough to cause international capital flows to bend to its will. Proceeding more logically, Mrs Thatcher made brilliant use of bellicose patriotic rhetoric as a cover for policies that implicitly conceded Britain's ordinary status in the world economy. At enormous cost to the domestic economy, her administration created an environment of sound money and broken trade unions that acceded to the needs of international capital and made Britain a first port of call for foreign direct investment in Europe by the late 1980s.[37]

For left-wing critics, the AES was deemed to be insufficiently radical.[38] Overall, however, the 1980s signalled not only the demise of socialism in the politics of both Eastern and Western Europe, but also a shift in intellectual focus to free-market economists and social thinkers. In the twenty-first century, socialism as an intellectual movement has become a peripheral activity, preoccupied with a range of schemata for running a hypothetical economy on a planned basis: the irrelevance of such activities to substantive present-day realities has led socialism to be perceived as a peculiar special interest. Among progressive movements, socialism now has far less influence than the ecological movement and feminism on the politics of the contemporary world and on social and economic thinking. Socialism, having found itself identified with schemata for economic planning, has been cast into irrelevance.

In recent years, there has been a revival of critical views of the functioning of the capitalist economy, in terms of its worrisome tendency to manifest instability and generate high levels of unemployment, as well as concerns about growing inequalities of income and wealth. But these tendencies have not generated any substantial call for a revival of AES-type technocratic planning solutions to these problems. The top-down technocratic planning paradigm, now defunct, had defined what it meant to be socialist in the twentieth century. It has, as a by-product, marginalised strategies for confronting capitalism that begin from the ground up – focusing on human development, equality and democratic control. This class of approaches will be developed in what follows.

Part II
Human and Economic Development

Introduction

Part II links the failed socialist strategy of central planning of Part I and an alternative path to be discussed in Part III, a socialism focused on policies to promote human development and democracy. The discussion in Part II supports the proposition that approaches of this kind are not merely speculative ventures, but are well-grounded in the historical record: a programme of human development centred on education and equality has a substantive basis in how economies have developed successfully in the past, and are likely to do so in the future.

The earlier planning approach became a central aspect of the socialist programme of transformation because it appeared to emerge as an inherent aspect of Enlightenment rationality and linked socialism to the trajectory of progressive historical developments: capitalism in its most advanced aspects was seen to be re-creating itself in a planned direction, so that the planning model was objectively the correct goal for socialists to be pursuing. Furthermore, given this trajectory, the path to socialism would be facilitated both strategically and tactically by going with the grain of history and modernity. The strategy failed universally because this perspicacious analysis of capitalist development was flawed.

Socialism emerged overwhelmingly as the dominant rival to capitalism precisely because it represented an alternative vision of modernity. Rather than rejecting the transformation of material and social existence brought about by capitalism, as did some reactionary, religious and marginal socialist groups calling for a return to a pre-capitalist golden age, the *Communist Manifesto* heralded these developments: 'The bourgeoisie, during its rule of scarce one hundred years, has created more massive and more colossal productive forces than have all preceding generations together.' The dominant strain of the socialist movement was thereby pursing goals in harmony with the desire of the great mass of individuals in society to improve their material existence. But as capitalism persisted in the twentieth century, socialists of the most radical stripe often became identified with strategies – labour stoppages and militant demands for wage increases even in inflationary conditions – that, at least in the short run, seemed to make life more difficult for ordinary people and harkened back to Lenin's horrific doctrine of *chem khuzhe, tem lushche* – the worse, the better. A persistent stain on socialism has been the suspicion that its purveyors have manipulated the needs and aspirations of ordinary people in order to pursue their own vision of the future.

This history is important because the methodology being pursued in Part II parallels that in Part I: the path to socialism pursued here is seen to be congruent with the trajectory of history and modernity. The current version of apologia for capitalism links it to perpetual innovation, with incentives for wealth creators and risk takers used as a justification for inequality; associated doctrines are creative destruction (the destruction of existing sectors and jobs as a concomitant of innovation) and the postulation of an inevitable trade-off between equity and efficiency. The alternative view presented here suggests that economic development, including innovation and technological progress, is not a beneficent gift of wealth creators: the boundaries between innovation, adaptation and diffusion of new methods and ideas are more fluid than is generally suggested, a fact necessitating a broad base of skills across the population. A healthy ecology of development implies that economic equality will be complementary to the cultivation of these widely dispersed skills, so that there is no trade-off between equity and efficiency. Furthermore, the focus on risk taking in capitalist ideology ignores the need for security for the planning of the enhancement of skills by household members. And creative displacement – building on existing skills and sectors – is more characteristic historically of successful innovation than is creative destruction.

A key to economic success in the modern world is the human, and especially the educational, development of the population, a social process that only reflects itself in standard measures of economic growth with substantial lags. Under capitalism, advances in human development that promote economic growth have taken place only in an imperfect, inadequate manner. There is no claim here, however, for the superiority of a programme centred on equality and broad-based education because of its role in promoting economic growth. On the contrary, the socialist motivation for pursing an intensive programme of human development is not to enhance a nation's growth rate, but to expand the possibilities for human freedom, personal flourishing and democracy. The nature and substance of a socialist educational programme will, therefore, differ significantly from one emerging from a growth-oriented political and economic discourse.

The danger can be, however, that the socialist programme is seen to be fulfilling its own ends rather than the desires of a broad-based public. Successful socialist policy will not succeed by attempting to fool a public into accepting a half-hidden agenda. On the contrary, a programme with socialist goals must be seen as congruent with the needs and aspirations of the population if it is to succeed politically and embed itself socially. A broad public has rejected both central planning and free-market fundamentalism on the common-sense basis that these grand schemes didn't deliver the goods: the extent to which a socialist programme facilitates material improvements overall can act as a reality check on its efficacy and militate against adventurist experimentation with people's lives.

In order to be successful, educational programmes must take place in an economic and social environment that gives individuals and households an opportunity to make long-term, rational plans to fulfil their goals. Such an environment must embody high levels of household security, social mobility and equality. Education then appears not as an elixir but as a powerful facilitator of economic growth and social equality in the context of a broader set of elements that promote human development. A highly unequal society may find that even a well-conceived educational programme is of little efficacy in facilitating growth. Educational opportunity, economic security, mobility and equality emerge not as gratuitous luxuries that rich countries might choose to indulge in, but as the very sources of material development itself.

Human development is, thus, a much broader process than that encompassed by school education, and socialist policies must pursue social equality and solidarity in tandem with an educational programme. In place of a free-market vision of individuals responding to material rewards and punishments, including insecurity, a socialist vision focuses on the ability of individuals and households to plan for the future and control their own lives in a secure environment, and to exercise this control collectively in a democratic context. Such a programme is, as a by-product, likely to be at least as successful in terms of long-term material growth as one emerging from a hard-headed capitalist strategy of inequality and insecurity.

The precise nature of this material growth and how we measure it remains, however, a problematic issue: far from being an objective indicator of material improvement, the conventional economic growth calculation warps our decisions concerning economic success and failure with a host of dubious empirical presumptions and implicit value judgements. Part II thus begins with a discussion about the relationship between education and economic growth, one that inevitably leads to questions about its components – education and economic growth; along the way, key issues that emerge are exemplified in the context of the history and institutions of the US.

6
Education and Economic Growth: The Statistical and Historical Record

A vast statistical literature lays claim to the notion that enhanced education can boost the incomes of individuals and of whole economies. A straightforward argument could be developed here using this received wisdom: the positive relationship between education (and not, as previously, planning and centralisation) and economic success in modern capitalist societies can be redirected for socialist purposes. But no such simple story is readily available. The lines of causation between education and economic advance at the social level are murkier and more complex than any confident reporting of significant statistical results might indicate: aggregative statistical procedures may not be an appropriate vehicle for reporting on this relationship in other than a generalised way. The reasons for these difficulties should not surprise us – education is deeply embedded in the fundamental structures of society; its nature and role raise issues of a basic kind concerning human development and even personality formation.

Even if a simple link between education and economic growth were to emerge in a decisive way statistically, it cannot be argued in a socialist context that an enhanced programme of educational development and social equality is desirable *because* it promotes economic growth. On the contrary, and most especially in the context of rich countries, socialism focuses on the enhanced ability of all individuals to function freely and to exercise democratic control in society – this is the relevant form that 'growth' takes.

It would be inconvenient and troublesome, however, if education had proved to be a gratuitous luxury, one that had actually posed an obstacle to the achievement of higher material standards for median-income earners. The evidence to be reviewed below shows that no such dilemma exists; here, and in subsequent chapters, a narrative with more intricate lines of causation will supplement, reinforce and complicate this conclusion.

Education and growth: the statistical nexus

Economic growth, the growth rate in per capita GDP (a deceptive identification, as will be seen in Chapter 10), is the central parameter conditioning economic, social and political events of the last half millennium. It elevated the residents of Christendom from respectable participants in a world culture and polity to the Lords of Human Kind by the nineteenth century;[1] it has transformed material and social life across the planet. The growth calculation is now ubiquitous and pervasive in public discussions and academic research concerned with national economic success and failure: it is curious to note, therefore, that its emergence at the centre of economic debate is little more than a half century old. Economic growth, at least in an implicit form, had been central to the concerns of classical economists such as Adam Smith and David Ricardo or even earlier in their focus on the production, extraction and accumulation of economic surplus,[2] a tradition that led to Marx's ambitious attempt at modelling economic growth in a capitalist economy, all the while suggesting why this process embodies elements that could lead to its destruction. But this perspective gave way in the latter part of the nineteenth century to a neoclassical school whose key considerations were not growth, but the efficient allocation of given resources among alternative ends: why, for instance, nations with given endowments of land, labour and capital will find it mutually beneficial to engage in free trade. It is these issues that dominate the development of formal economic theory until the middle of the twentieth century, with the sole exception of the questions surrounding business cycles and unemployment in the wake of the Great Depression of the 1930s. The fact that two of the pioneers of growth modelling in the first half of the twentieth century, Frank Ramsey and John von Neumann, were formidable mathematicians hints at the analytical obstacles to its development.

But even as mainstream economic theory in the late nineteenth century was moving its focus away from the process of economic growth – this in a period of some of the most tumultuous changes in material existence in human history – there was a literature before 1920 from List, Weber, Schumpeter, Marxists and others who had been attempting to confront issues surrounding the growth process. The views of these figures, many of whom we have already met in the context of the technocratic planning paradigm, went beyond a strictly economistic view of growth to consider it in the context of a broader range of historical and institutional factors. Much of the formal development of the theory of economic growth in the contemporary period can be seen as a gradual (albeit grudging) concession to the need for the incorporation of a range of these non-economic considerations, including education.

After several pioneering developments, economic growth became a central concern of formal economic modelling and empirical testing in the latter part of the 1950s. One prerequisite for the development of growth modelling was the emergence in the interwar period of a rigorous conception of national income (which in accounting terms is identical with national output), so that the complexities of economic development could be reduced down to a simple maximand, 'economic growth', or the growth rate in national income. The trend in academic economics towards a focus on economic growth in the US was inseparable from the atmosphere of the Cold War: Nikita Khrushchëv's slogan 'catch up and overtake the West', the influential, if misleading, notion of a decisive link between economic power and military capacity, and the contest over models of development for the non-aligned world. Growth models by Roy Harrod and Evsey Domar[3] had postulated a fixed relationship between the amount of capital in an economy and its level of output, so that the higher the level of investment (an increase in the stock of capital), the more rapid the rate of increase in output – economic growth. In this famous Harrod–Domar model, the path to higher economic growth was simple – increase the level of investment: high-saving economies (such as the postwar Soviet Union, and unlike the US) will, therefore, be high-growth economies.[4]

The literature on economic growth in its contemporary form emerged with the subsequent development of a neoclassical theory of economic growth, one congruent with the assumptions of standard microeconomics; it is now almost wholly identified with the work of the MIT economist Robert Solow, in part because he complemented his theoretical construction with empirical estimates for the US economy. Solow's theoretical model (published at the same time as an equivalent conception from Trevor Swan), like the Harrod–Domar, postulates the existence of an aggregate production function, a generalised relationship between the economy's output and its inputs.[5] Unlike the simple fixed relationship between output and capital (and implicitly labour) in the Harrod–Domar case, the Solow model makes the typical neoclassical assumption that additional inputs of capital can be substituted for labour (which in Solow's model is explicitly introduced) to yield greater output, but at an ever diminishing rate, and definitively postulates the presence of full employment in the economy. In such a model, there is no secret path to economic growth – high rates of investment will, in the long run, be neutralised by the effect of diminishing returns to capital. A nation's long-term growth rate (per capita) cannot be increased by its choice of a higher rate of investment; in fact, there is a tendency for the per capita incomes of different nations to converge to the same level. It is these predictions of the model – that per capita growth is (in the long run) unaffected by the rate of investment, and that there is a tendency for per capita incomes to converge – that have emerged as the distinctive and characteristic aspects of this neoclassical perspective.

The neoclassical theory of economic growth was problematic on several counts. First, many economists seemed uneasy with the neoclassical prediction that increased investment could only increase (once and for all) the level, but not the rate, of growth of output per head. This presumption violated their intuition on the matter, and limited their opportunity to offer policy prescriptions that would promote growth. Second, technical change is accounted for, but not really embodied in, an explanatory framework in the neoclassical model: it is an exogenously determined parameter in Solow's construction because, according to him, we cannot even begin to analyse its provenance in terms of economic processes. In the adaptation of the neoclassical theory of economic growth to empirical estimation in the form of a growth accounting exercise, Solow's statistical estimates for the US economy from 1909 to 1949 yielded what seemed to be disappointing conclusions, namely, that increases in capital per labour hour could explain less than 15 per cent of the increase in output per head over this period. The subsequent headline result, that more than 85 per cent of the observed increase had been due to technical change, emerged when the statistical residual was so identified. Ensuing research into this form of growth accounting engaged in a process of 'whittling away at the residual':[6] we see emerging a range of studies suggesting that when labour is differentiated by 'quality' (commonly years of schooling), a substantial percentage of that residual can be accounted for by increased levels of education, which, in a neoclassical context, are interpreted as causing a once-and-for-all increase in income. This conclusion complemented the unprecedented intervention by the US federal government into the educational sector in the context of the Soviet launching of the Sputnik satellite and a subsequent panic in the US about its educational inadequacies – 'What Ivan Knows But Johnny Doesn't', in the words of a famous book of the day.

These postwar growth theories were thus permitting an empirical calculation of the effect of education on economic growth, but one that had a rather ad hoc quality, bolted on to theoretical structures emerging from the nineteenth century in which labour is treated merely as a commodity. It was only in the 1980s that more plausible approaches emerged in variants of 'new growth theories'. In the most popular form of new growth theory, education was directly linked to economic growth: here firms characteristically compete in markets by offering new products and improving their quality (as opposed to the neoclassical growth models, with their homogeneous products embedded in perfectly competitive markets). In this context, higher levels of investment by private firms, complemented by enhanced human capital, can generate new technology, some of which spills over to other firms: this process then causes the overall growth rate in the economy to increase.[7] The ingenious constructions of endogenous growth theory thus give an economic rationale for enhanced education that is linked to an explanation for technical change – the latter becomes an endogenous aspect of the functioning of the economic system and not merely manna from heaven, as in the neoclassical approach.

Research embodying a range of approaches to economic growth has generally, although not unanimously, found a linkage between increased education, as measured by years of schooling, and economic success.[8] The studies have had a host of obstacles to overcome, including the possibility of reverse causation – that more schooling is merely a luxury indulged in by richer societies, that schooling merely acts as a credential for individuals, gaining them higher income even in the absence of becoming more productive, and that more able individuals will seek more education. Other problems have proved even less tractable in the context of these broad-based statistical tests – the problems of differentiating between the substantive quality of a given number of years of schooling in different countries,[9] and the absence or inadequate representation of non-school forms of training such as apprenticeships in available statistics. Symptomatic of the limitations of the education–growth studies is the fact that it has proved difficult to distinguish statistically between the neoclassical and the new growth presumption – whether the influence of education is on the level or the growth rate of GDP.[10] Furthermore, while the effect of education is usually statistically significant, the strength of the education variable varies significantly among these studies. These and other limitations point to the difficulties of generating decisive conclusions from this research, which, however, generally finds a significant economic role for enhanced education.

Much of this literature has been reframed, especially with regard to richer (Organisation for Economic Co-operation and Development (OECD)) countries, in a series of studies by Eric Hanushek and Ludger Woessmann.[11] Their research uses a range of international studies testing achievement in mathematics, science and reading across countries, the most well known of which is the Programme for International Student Assessment (PISA).[12] Many, but not all, of the problematic issues mentioned above can be neutralised by replacing years of schooling as an indication of levels of education with measures of scholastic attainment emerging from these tests; as a representation of the explanatory variable 'education', these tests perform more robustly and decisively than years of schooling in demonstrating a linkage between education and economic success.

All kinds of questions can be raised about this methodology – are we concerned about the alacrity with which the full range of human capabilities is identified with results on a particular class of diagnostic tests simply because of their easy availability across nations? And do we fear that the tail can begin to wag the dog – if these test results are taken to represent school achievement in elevating cognitive capacity, is there not a danger that the school curriculum will begin to reflect the content of these tests?[13] Having raised these caveats, it must be admitted that the results emerging from these studies, with statistical verification of the notion that economic achievement among nations in the modern world is linked to cognitive capacity, will strike most of us as intuitively plausible and can be supplemented by the historical narratives below.

A good deal is lost in the way of easy explanation, however, in the process of replacing 'years of schooling' with measures of cognitive development from test scores.[14] These scores necessarily emerge from a complex social process, so that a simple policy admonition of the kind 'in order to improve economic performance, increase the years of schooling in the population' is no longer possible. Thus, even if it were to be generally conceded that education is the key to explaining differences in economic achievement between nations, using a measure derived from these test scores means, as we shall see in the following chapters, that the task at hand has merely begun.[15]

Once test results are the measure of education used to explain economic performance, as in the studies by Hanushek and Woessmann, a veritable Pandora's Box of complications emerges as we try to link these results to the factors that might have generated them. In addition to the quantitative measures above – years of schooling, expenditure per pupil or teacher–pupil ratios – the range of other considerations that might impinge upon cognitive capacity is immense. We may wish to consider the constituents of school quality: how will the efficiency and equity of educational processes be affected by streaming by ability, and by differences in the age at which school begins, and by differences linked to traditional versus progressive approaches in the classroom? These choices are major components of present-day public policy debates, with broad implications for the economy and society. As we shall see in Chapter 7, other policy disputes are widespread surrounding efficiency in education – the question of the use of market mechanisms such as vouchers to promote consumer choice, and issues concerned with teacher evaluation and tenure.

An even more fundamental obstacle to the telling of a simple 'education–growth' story is the range of non-school factors that may affect cognitive development. Family resources and the education of parents are central considerations when tracking achievement at the level of the individual child. At the national level, the social environment, most especially the distribution of income, is likely to have a complex relationship with educational achievement, as both cause and effect. One perspective, centred on the IQ literature, largely dismisses the role of the social environment as a causal factor explaining educational achievement, suggesting, for instance, that the distribution of income emerging naturally in capitalist society – with an absence of conscious efforts to promote redistribution on the part of the state – will accurately reflect the dispersal of inherent abilities and intellectual capacities (see Chapter 11). In such a case, efforts to promote equalisation of income in society merely deprive the most able members of society of both the means and the incentive to expend their own resources on the acquisition of education. An alternative view posits that economic and social inequality inhibits the cognitive development of deprived groups in society, and that this is not easily compensated for by even a well-designed and resourced programme of schooling for children. Central questions in this context, to be confronted in subsequent chapters, involve childhood intervention – at what age will it be necessary to intervene, and at what level of resource commitment, to compensate for deficits in the social and economic environment?

Major controversies thus surround the question of the role of social environment, most especially the distribution of income, in educational achievement. In the opposite direction, the role played by cognitive achievement in determining the distribution of income in society is an ambivalent and controversial one. The presumption that such a line of causation exists is often associated with justifications for inequality: some individuals are more highly paid because they are more able and are, as a result, more productive. Alternatively, the notion that cognitive achievement plays a causal role in determining the distribution of income in society has also been used to underline the central role of educational policy in the promotion of social equality, and will be considered in Chapter 10. Among non-school factors that are likely to advance learning are a range of child-care, vocational and firm-based activities, as well as the presence of opportunities and sources of encouragement to learn that are 'in the air', such as educational components of BBC programmes or general societal attitudes towards education. These latter factors, along with lag effects, can easily be consigned to the glutinous category of culture, but may play an important role in explaining differential societal success in cognitive achievement.

Above and beyond these questions, however, are a whole further set of considerations surrounding the nature of education and its effects upon the economic and social environment:

1. *The breadth of the education required for economic growth.* In conceptualising the impact of education on economic growth, some approaches lend themselves to the need for education diffused across the population, raising the quality of the labour input and its productivity; other theoretical approaches make a claim for widely dispersed education on the more specific grounds that the adaptation and implementation of new technology demand a widespread and increasingly literate public.[16] The alternative view is that 'we' only need a few highly educated individuals to be concerned with the innovation of new technology and its consequences,[17] a view also in conformity with notions of the economic efficacy of education through its engendering of an elite capable of producing Schumpeterian thunderbolts of new technology.

It is education widely dispersed across the population that is relevant to the exigencies of socialist democracy; it would be convenient if it were also in conformity with economic tendencies.

2. *The nature of the education required for economic growth.* Is it of a focused, vocational kind, or is it centred round broad-based academic and cultural knowledge? Narrowly based educational experience must not, however, be arbitrarily identified with vocational settings. For many individuals, cognitive skills are most readily acquired in a non-school, vocational context: the workplace as a venue for learning should be promoted as a key social goal.

Once again, it is the acquisition of broad-based knowledge that most fulfils the demands of socialist democracy, and if it also facilitated successful economic development, potential policy conflicts and dilemmas would be minimised.

3. *Education and external effects.* Do the economic returns to personal investment in education accrue substantively to the individuals acquiring that education? If, by contrast, there are significant positive external effects on society from the enhanced education of individuals, it would reinforce the strictly empirical consideration that the economic effects of an educational programme are likely to yield their economic effects with a long lag. Delays in the impact of education on economic activity will occur for many well-established reasons, including the time it takes to educate individuals and integrate them into the workforce, and intergenerational effects within a family – the impact of better-educated parents upon their children's learning. The presence of external effects in education, however, is an additional source of lags, as heightened educational levels of individuals will cascade onto others over time and only register in economic terms through an extended process of diffusion.

If the benefits to education were to accrue wholly or largely to individuals, it becomes more difficult to justify, strictly from the perspective of economic efficacy, a socialist orientation on education. The most radical educational programme that would be relevant in such a context would be some form of egalitarian meritocracy: individuals would simply be left to make market-based decisions concerning the pursuit of education, with perhaps interventions to compensate for inequalities in income and access to information about educational opportunities, and to correct possible capital market imperfections that limit the ability of individuals to borrow to pay for education. The presence of pervasive external effects, by contrast, gives economic support for a socialist approach to education that pursues a long-term, collective strategy of economic and social development, and not one that merely compensates, in an egalitarian manner, for deficits at the individual level.

In the literature considered above, the efficacy of education is judged in terms of its economic benefits as a social investment – the extent to which enhanced performance on diagnostic tests in mathematics, science and reading produces improvements in the level or growth rate in national income. There are several objections to such a procedure:

1. Even in the context of dealing solely with the *economic* benefits of improvements in educational systems, it is peculiar and inappropriate to assign a zero value to the consumption benefits accruing to children of improved educational facilities. At the individual level, rich people (and sometimes others, such as families with a desire to segregate their children on a religious or racial basis, or to see them mix in the right circles) often pay for private tuition so that their children are provided with music lessons, sports facilities, lower levels of bullying and manifold other advantages. The school commitment of resources and the costs to parents of these benefits, profound as they are in the life of the child, cannot easily be categorised as investment activity that is likely to lead directly to higher income for the child in the future; these aspects of consumption in the educational process are considerations that rich people (and others, if they could afford it) think are worth paying for, and are as economic as any gains to children in their human capital. There are, in addition, other possible economic benefits that might accrue to society as a result of a successful educational programme, such as improved monitoring of children's mental and physical health and a reduction in crime rates.

2. This last consideration – how an improved educational system could be of economic benefit because of crime reduction – points to how desiccated a strictly economic approach to education can become, and how far it can take us away from notions of education as a vehicle for the improvement of the human condition. An improved educational system that moves a child away from a life of crime is not desirable purely because of its economic benefits – the savings to society accrued from reduced incarceration and the enhanced contribution to GDP because of greater participation in legal economic activities. On the contrary, the role of education in promoting cognitive skills has always existed alongside a parallel set of considerations surrounding character formation and the inculcation of social norms: an exclusive focus on the economic benefits of directing children away from a life of crime would have appeared bizarre to Enlightenment figures concerned with education, such as Wilhelm von Humboldt. Economic analyses that proceed to evaluate the efficacy of educational programmes, without mentioning considerations of moral formation even parenthetically, are in danger of giving these aspects an implicit weight of zero, or of making the silent value judgement that these are matters only appropriate for family or church, and not for schools.

Substantial resources have always been devoted in state educational systems to processes of socialisation, a fact that becomes incomprehensible from the perspective of a narrowly economistic analysis of education and of Hayekian notions of societal values emerging from a spontaneous order. In approaches to these non-cognitive considerations, we frequently observe a dichotomous strategy: an emphasis on the acceptance of discipline, deference to authority, fitting in socially and resignation to one's role in life for the great majority; an inculcation of characteristics of leadership, self-confidence and class identification for the well-born.

By contrast, a socialist approach to education, following on from Enlightenment traditions, must attempt to prepare all children with not only the intellectual capacity, but also the self-confidence, to be able to participate as citizens actively and equally in democratic processes, both political and economic. Contrary to traditional approaches, this citizenship not only has a local and national component, but gives children an international perspective that permits them to make disinterested evaluations of their own nation's history, politics and place in the world.

Consideration of the role of education in society thus takes us far beyond the bounds of the education–economic growth literature; these issues will be pursued in subsequent chapters. Below, the education–growth nexus is re-engaged.

How seriously do we take the results? I

While the conclusions of the education–economic growth literature are largely consistent with the notion postulated here that enhanced levels of education are congruent with economic success, it would be facile to cite these results as authority without noting their problematic aspects. In the process of making this critique, important aspects of the interaction between human development and economic growth are brought to the surface that remain submerged in the theoretical and statistical models reviewed above.

All of the mainstream models of economic growth and their associated empirical tests share a range of ambitious and even reckless presumptions, including the notion that increased saving is always transmuted into higher investment, and that the economy always functions at a level of full employment. This is a critical issue in the understanding and evaluation of the functioning of capitalist economies, with the presumption of full employment fundamental to disputes between mainstream economic orthodoxy and dissenters from this orthodoxy, including Keynesian economists. Here, however, central attention will be given to a further presupposition embodied in these growth models: that inputs of capital, labour and available technologies are always used to maximum effect at every level of output. This notion is an invariant one in both the theoretical and statistical versions of these growth models, and is linked to the orthodox approach of viewing the economy as being in a perfectly competitive equilibrium. It is of particular interest here for several reasons. First, as we shall see, the presence of a fully efficient competitive equilibrium reinforces the tendency in the standard economics literature to treat technology as a Schumpeterian *deus ex machina* and to segregate it from other aspects of human intelligence and creativity. As a result, there is a propensity to understate the efficacy of broad-based enhancements of cognitive capacity and to consign the role of technical progress solely to an elite.

Hayek's dynamic approach to competition, seen in Chapter 4, can serve as a basis of a critique of approaches that presume the presence of a globally efficient competitive equilibrium. For Hayek, if we use the model of perfect competition as our standard, one in which '[producers] are assumed to know the lowest cost at which the commodity can be produced', there could be no objections to the pseudo-competition offered up by Lange's market socialism. But 'this knowledge which is assumed to be given to begin with [in the model of perfect competition] is one of the main points where it is only through the process of competition that the facts will be discovered'.[18] In real capitalist competition, according to Hayek, what we observe at any moment are firms, industries and whole economies functioning with greater or lesser success within a frontier dictated by technological possibilities. It cannot be axiomatically presumed, as in orthodoxy, that all activities are taking place on this frontier.

Confirmation of the efficacy of Hayek's approach to competition is present in some of the most dramatic instances of recent economic history: the steel industry worldwide was revolutionised in the 1960s and 1970s by Japanese producers, not through any grand Schumpeterian technical innovation, but by imaginative managerial practices and creative use of available, but widely neglected or under-exploited, technologies. In other industries, Japanese success was characterised by managerial practices that often had little to do with new technologies: a key innovation of 'the machine that changed the world' – the Japanese car factory – was the *kanban*, a simple card system for controlling inventories that was only later adopted for the emerging computerised technologies.[19] These great changes were not the result of a Schumpeterian thunderbolt of new technology from an elite, but the implementation by the management and workforce of Japan of a panoply of alterations to production and distribution systems; central to underpinning these developments had been the proceeding and on-going educational advancement of the whole population. Hayekian methodology proves useful here as a device for mounting a critique of the elite view of technical change, despite, as noted above, Hayek's own elite propensities.

What accounts for the adherence to this implausible and empirically unsustainable presumption of universal efficiency? Given that exception to this presumption of efficiency is sometimes made for the governmental sector,[20] there may exist a temptation to attribute the adoption of this methodology to ideological prejudice in favour of private enterprise. More likely, however, it results from a bold, even desperate, attempt to extract mean-ingful economic results from broad swathes of economic data. In the absence of the presumption of generalised competitive efficiency, little meaning and few lessons can be gleaned from the outcomes in such an economy, since the price weights necessary for any such calculation of outcomes would no longer be a reflection of real costs and alternative uses. We might wish, for instance, to perform a statistical test that measures the inherent efficacy of different forms of expenditure, one that tells us, for instance, whether additional outlay on education will yield more economic growth than equivalent amounts spent on physical capital. We will not get far along this road if, to an uncertain degree, the resources devoted to these alternatives are dissipated because of racial or caste discrimination in the case of educa-tion, or corrupt practices in the case of physical capital: what may appear statistically to be the inherent inefficacy of education for economic growth in a given society may merely be due to the inefficient use of these resources due to discrimination. These instances of inefficient use of inputs can be dealt with on a case-by-case basis, but impose severe and perhaps irredu-cible limitations on the substantive meaning we can extract from the grand narratives of theoretical and statistical models of economic growth based on assumptions of universal competitive efficiency.

There is a second reason for questioning an empirical methodology that simply presumes that all inputs are being used efficiently: the education and socialisation of the workforce – activities that often yield economic benefits only with a long lag – may become invisible. An illustration of this point can be seen in the context of the debate surrounding the Asian growth miracle. In a well-known study of the spectacular successes achieved in economic growth by a set of newly industrialising countries (Hong Kong, Singapore, South Korea and Taiwan) from 1966 to 1991, Alwyn Young[21] accounts stat-istically for these levels of growth by increases in participation rates (most especially by women), investment-to-GDP ratios, improving levels of educa-tion, and inter-sectoral transfers of labour from agriculture to, largely, manufacturing. Once these factors are accounted for, it is claimed, there is nothing exceptional in the performance of these economies in terms of the growth rates in productivity, either in the whole economy or in manufac-turing. Neoclassical growth theory, according to Young, can well explain most of the difference between the performance of these and other postwar economies.[22] And predominant opinion among economists has agreed: 'The only overwhelming lesson I see in Asian growth is that one way to get a lot of output is to use a lot of inputs',[23] a conclusion comfortably in line with Solow-type neoclassical growth theory, and excluding the necessity of presuming any Asian secret linked to a government-directed deviation from free-market incentives.

Has anything of interest really been explained here? We are told that improving educational attainment in these economies contributed 1 per

cent per annum additional growth in labour input in each of these economies, the implication being that, even in the absence of enhanced education, Asian growth, due to its high levels of investment, would have still been
exceptional, but perhaps 1 per cent less. Unfortunately, however, the results
emerging from Young's exercise in growth accounting are no more than just
that – an ex post accounting of results, rather than an explanation of the
factors affecting growth: would the vast investment programmes pursued in
these countries ever have been undertaken in the first place in the absence
of the social and educational prerequisites necessary to bring them to fruition? These prerequisites were crucial at all levels of human capital development. In the larger economies of Taiwan and South Korea most especially,
a social transformation of the population had taken place beginning in the
1950s – from rural to urban, from agriculture to manufacturing, and from
levels of educational attainment that were modest (even if already high by
the standards of very poor countries) to a world-class standard.

Can we simply take for granted that the economy and society would have
absorbed and reallocated this enormous movement of people successfully?
Could the efficacious geographical transfer of the population from rural
to urban environments, and the transition from agricultural or traditional
labour activities to manufacturing work, have taken place without the major
investment in human assets represented by public policies promoting income
redistribution and, especially, the substantial investment in schooling? And
in a world in which we cannot simply assume that nations can effortlessly
assimilate best-practice technology on the outer reaches of a production
function, the great achievements of these Asian societies in sophisticated
forms of education proved crucial:

An emphasis solely on investment assumes that the state of technological
knowledge at any time is largely embodied in machinery and codified in
blueprints and associated documents ... However, only a small portion of
what one needs to know to employ a technology is codified in machine
manuals, textbooks, and blueprints; much of it is tacit and learning is as
much by doing and using as by reading and studying ... What makes the
Asian miracle miraculous is that these countries did these things so well,
while other countries were much less successful ... [T]o say that [high rates
of investment] were all that was required offers too limited a perspective on the magnitude of the achievement ... Rising human capital can
be viewed simply as an increase in the quality or effectiveness of labour,
adding a third factor to the conventional production function. An alternative view perceives the effects of sharply rising educational attainments, in particular the creation by these countries of a growing cadre
of reasonably well trained managers, engineers and applied scientists as
providing a comparative advantage in identifying new opportunities and
effectively learning new things.[24]

The link between industrial policy and skills enhancement is an intimate one:

> industrial policy is the parent of skills policy in East Asian economies. The remarkable transitions from underdevelopment to mass production and thence to high-value-added production systems [in] Singapore, South Korea, Taiwan and Hong Kong were fostered through an awareness of their implications for skills demand, and through substantial institutional transformations in vocational education and training to meet the growing needs. It was largely because of their success at foreseeing linkages with the demand side that these governments were able to match their economic miracles with equally radical structural transformations in their skill formation systems.[25]

The commitment to high levels of educational standards was complemented by the maintenance of distinctly low levels of inequality in these economies. Public policy acts, affecting both education and the level of inequality, permitted these economies to operate closer to the frontier of their possibilities and made viable the high rates of investment that were necessary prerequisites of the exceptional growth rates attained.[26] The theoretical and statistical presumption (implicit in Young's estimation technique) that we are always on the frontier of a production function obscures, rather than enlightens, one of the most remarkable social and economic transformations of modern times.

The Asian miracle critics are correct, however, in suggesting that there is no recipe, no easy lesson for economic development to be culled from these events. All of the nations of the Asian miracle have found their growth rates slowing down to less than miraculous levels in the years beyond those covered in Young's study, most especially in the wake of the financial crisis of 1997, a slowdown that in no way obviates the historic achievement of these nations. The group, in any case, never shared a common strategy of economic development – the successes of the administered and centralised export promotion approach found in South Korea were matched by comparable growth achievements in, at the other extreme, a relatively open, free-market city-state such as Hong Kong; the forms of political governance in these societies were equally diverse. More significantly, a range of other developing countries in the postwar world have strenuously attempted, with far more limited success, to follow the import substitution–export promotion strategies of the east Asian economies, and it beggars belief to suggest that the exceptional growth rates of the east Asians compared with these other economies were simply due to high levels of expenditure of investment capital.

What the Asian tigers succeeded in achieving was a social transformation, in a brief period, from very-low-wage to middle-income entities, with these rises in per capita income complemented by the emergence of statistical indicators of levels of health and education that now bear comparison with the richest nations in the world. From the perspective of orthodox economics, the task confronting nations was how to deal with their given endowments of land, labour and capital in the context of mutually beneficial free trade. By contrast, a key aspect of the success of, first, Japan and then the Asian tigers in the transition from low-wage to middle-income economies has been the creation of a population capable of confronting the challenges of modernity.

A clear requisite of this development has been the explicit cultivation of a population with high levels of formal education. No less important for economic growth, as we shall see in Chapter 8, are the skills and acculturation acquired by the workforce of these nations from the very act of being involved in contemporary forms of economic activity – forms of implicit and *in situ* learning. For many of these nations, this process of 'learning by doing' on the part of the workforce only came about because of jobs created in manufacturing through the violation of the canons of free trade, specialisation and comparative advantage. In this sense, movement away from the presumption of labour as a mere commodity poses several challenges to economic orthodoxy: the state not only plays a role in the provision of formal education, but must often channel investment resources to avoid the dangers of an exclusive specialisation in the kinds of tasks, such as the harvesting of tropical fruit, that may well emerge from strict adherence to laissez-faire policies.

And just as the impetus for the search in the academic literature of the 1950s for the sources of economic growth lay in the Cold War conflict between the Soviet Union and the US, so the education–economic growth literature, including the discussion of endogenous growth, has burgeoned into a new orthodoxy, in all likelihood in response to the startling Asian example – the phrase 'education, education, education' is on the lips of the most philistine politicians. For the richest countries, it is commonly presumed, the gains from monitoring and adapting existing world best-practice technology and administration are minimal. Therefore, the nature of the improvements to be culled from education emerge either from new technologies or, more passively, from being able to win 'the race between education and technology', by equipping the labour force with the skills necessary for adapting to new technologies. In both cases, the central justification for enhanced education in a society is its link to technological development – either it is a concomitant to the production of this new technology, or it facilitates a society's adaptation and accommodation to these waves of creative destruction. Technology – the facilitator of higher levels of economic growth – is the new elixir.

Interlude: technology as an elixir

The theory of production in mainstream economics is usually presented in the context of the availability of a wide range of alternative techniques, each using varying amounts of factors such as labour and capital. These alternatives, as Nathan Rosenberg has suggested,

> constitute a spectrum of what Schumpeter called 'eligible choices' ... [I]n what precise sense is it likely to be the case that a wide range of technological alternatives will ever be 'known'? Since ... the production of knowledge is itself a costly activity, why should technological alternatives representing factor combinations far from those justified by present prices be known?

If we proceed in this way, suggests Rosenberg, 'we are really allowing factor substitution to swallow up much of technological change'. In fact, most technological change does not take the form of a Schumpeterian thunderbolt – the setting up of a new production function – but is a mere substitution of one factor for another.[27] The supposition of a wide range of choices of techniques that are readily available to potential users is concomitant with the orthodox presumption that the economy is operating on the frontier of the production function. These presumptions in economic theory leave exogenous technical change in the form of discontinuous, observable technological innovations as the source of efficiency gains.

This approach is reinforced by statistical methodologies commonly used in academic studies that need to find concrete measures, such as levels of R&D expenditure or numbers of patents, as statistical surrogates for innovative activity. These procedures find common ground with Schumpeter's notion of innovation as taking the form of discontinuous thunderbolts of creative destruction. The latter approach invariably generates a focus on the small group of creators, who, it seems, must be properly remunerated if they are to bestow their technological bounty upon us. Dilemmas in public policy are thereby posed between equity and technological progress, and (given the supposedly severe constraints on resources available) between broad-based science education of school children and a focus on those who are gifted.

But drawing a line between the successful modification or adaptation of an older technology and the introduction of a new one is often difficult. The present-day enthusiasm in academia for Schumpeter's seemingly radical focus on discontinuous technical change is one that preserves the standard dichotomy between an existent technology, for which a full set of blueprints is available, and an utterly new one. The awkward possibility of shades of grey – that economic outcomes are critically affected by the extent to which firms and societies successfully adapt to existent technologies – poses the possibility that the links between education and economic growth might not simply flow through the creation of new technologies (by, invariably, a small subset of the population), but are a function of the efficaciousness and creativity with which the society as a whole responds to these changes, or even to the more mundane challenges of maintaining and supervising existing technologies, tasks which apparently consume the great majority of even academically trained engineers.[28]

At a popular level, the innovative entrepreneur – James Dyson in the UK or Steve Jobs in the US – functions symbolically as the economy's saviour, returning the nation to its former unchallenged position. This cult of techno-nationalism 'assumes that the key unit of analysis for the study of technology is the nation: nations are the units that invent, have R&D budgets, cultures of innovation, that diffuse, that use technology. The success of nations, it is believed by techno-nationalists, is dependent on how well we do this.'[29] This is an odd fixation in the age of the multinational.

Simplistic notions of technical change as the source of material progress founder on the historical reality that, at both the national and the individual level, the appropriation of these gains is a highly contingent matter. Thus, the post-Second World War electronics revolution had its provenance in the US (to a minor extent in Britain and the Soviet Union; see Chapter 9), but the successful adaptation of some aspects of these developments in Japan, and then other nations in the Far East, resulted in the virtual elimination of the production of mass consumer electronics in the US and the UK, with Asian nations cornering the bulk of world manufacture.

This example reminds us that an excessive focus on gains from new technology may distract attention from other forms of national economic advantage gained from human intelligence, such as facility in design, or complementary forms of creativity, such as the managerial successes in quality control of Japanese manufacture. These manifestations of creative intelligence, unless associated with a specific patent or copyright, are likely to be precluded from consideration when there is a presumption of universal best practice in the use of existing technologies.[30] In the 'technological change causes economic growth' story, other forms of creativity play little part: one notes, for instance, the (substantively unremunerated) musical innovations of Mississippi Delta blues players that resulted in billions of dollars of revenues, domestic and foreign, accruing to the popular music industry in the US and the UK over eight decades.

In an academic setting, but in a way that has pervaded the public consciousness, it has been suggested that, when improvements in quality are fully considered, the historical gains to new technology have been even greater than those emerging from standard national income deflator price calculations.[31] In the popular literature emanating from the US, there is no doubt that technology will solve social conundrums ranging from slow economic growth to obesity, with the technology fairy coming along just in time to sort out climate change issues.[32] For Michael Mandel, at the time editor of *Business Week*, 'our economic future is inextricably linked to our ability to come up with more technological breakthroughs that equal the internet in magnitude. Such large scale innovations drive growth, create new jobs and industries, push up living standards for both rich and poor, and open up whole new vistas of possibilities.'[33] For others, technology policy, generating the new 'weightless economy' (an economy based on brains, and not the messy business of making things) is the key to prosperity, economic growth and US competitiveness.

The mainstream of academic economics has gone from ignoring technical change and economic growth until the mid-twentieth century to suggesting subsequently that all other social decisions were of a secondary nature. This perspective has reached beyond economics and the academy to pervade and even dominate discussions of public policy issues. In the 1960s and 1970s, some consideration was given in public discussions of alternatives to economic growth as a focus of public policy. The subsequent slowdown in growth and a sense in nations such as the US that their leading positions were fragile in an increasingly competitive world have made a search for alternatives to economic growth look like a gratuitous luxury. And the word from the academy is that the creation of new technology is the key to economic growth. Since this formal economics literature emerges largely from the US, where much of this new technology had been created, such a development is unsurprising; for the great majority of nations, however, the task at hand is, rather, the monitoring and adaptation of these new technologies.[34]

A policy of focusing on R&D and taking economic growth as the criterion of success may be misguided, even for advanced economies: R&D itself supports relatively few jobs, and innovation and production are often closely tied, so that R&D will tend to migrate abroad with production, the dominant element of value added.[35] Under these conditions, the ultimate distribution of benefits from new technologies is unclear. On a national basis, while the US was the fount of new technologies in the 1950s and 1960s that were to prove crucial to its subsequent development, perhaps the greatest beneficiaries were Japan and the nations of east Asia, with their successful adaptations of these technologies. The easy presumption that continuous innovation is the key to broad-based national economic success in leading economies in this new weightless, knowledge economy is questionable. One may take issue with the presumption in the popular and academic literature that innovation of new technology is the uniquely appropriate focus of economic and social policy.

Education and industrial revolutions

The broad consensus in the statistical literature that education plays an important role in economic development needs to be complemented by a historical narrative if the precise nature of the education–growth linkage is to be demonstrated in a convincing manner. It is difficult, however, to ignore the sheer complexity of the historical processes being described:

there are periods of economic development – the early Industrial Revolution in Britain, among other cases – that appear to be retrograde in the cultivation of both formal education and skills; furthermore, the very fact that the stock of skills and know-how embodied in the workforce can cumulate by virtue of economic development can threaten to reverse, or at least confuse, the line of causation presumed in the education–growth linkage (see Chapter 8). Perhaps most significantly, the social returns to education, even in first approximation, are so saturated with external effects that they become hard to trace, much less measure, as they diffuse through society, and these effects are likely to register with, possibly, very long lags. An easy confidence displayed in measures of the cost–benefit of educational expenditure is thus likely to be misplaced.[36]

The processes by which mass literacy and then more advanced compulsory education became an inherent part of modernity are only beginning to be integrated into the history of capitalist development, with its traditional focus, from the First Industrial Revolution (and the juridical changes incumbent upon the French Revolution), on labour being transformed from its medieval role of serf to a commodity in the form of free labour. Britain, having entered the Industrial Revolution with levels of literacy well above the European norm, seems to have been characterised by a stagnant or even contrary movement in educational standards in this period.[37]

But it is the British experience that now appears to have been exceptional, or misunderstood: 'In England, the first phase of the industrial revolution was associated with stagnant education. In the continental countries, on the contrary, the industrial "take off" was always associated with educational progress.'[38] As we shall see in Chapter 8, the dissemination of formal education was relevant to, at most, an elite group of innovators in the British Industrial Revolution. With the British experience functioning as the template for capitalist development, the expansion of compulsory education in the Western world in the nineteenth century was long considered not as a factor generating economic growth but, rather, a luxury indulged in for other reasons by nations growing richer. Even into the twentieth century in advanced economies, industrial development continued to be linked by orthodox economic theorists to the expansion of markets, by Marxist economists to physical capital accumulation, and by theorists of management to the successful manipulation of the behaviour of an undifferentiated proletariat through Taylorist and other procedures. The educational revolution taking place at the time, a central aspect of the Great Transformation, passed unnoticed as an economic phenomenon.

By the latter part of the nineteenth century, the Second Industrial Revolution evidenced a dramatic rise in the use of high-level science in industry. For a transitional period, many of the great technological heroes in the public's mind, such as Edison, were from a craft tradition, though even he had to rely increasingly on a panoply of scientifically trained personnel.

These individuals, however, were still drawn from an elite group within society. Why, then, do we observe generally, and most especially among populations in the forefront of economic development, such as the US and Germany, such a dramatic expansion in schooling throughout the general population, culminating in the US by the early twentieth century in broadbased, localised support for state-financed high school education?[39]

The growth of white collar clerical, secretarial and other activities in the most advanced capitalist economies helps to account for much of the concomitant emergence and expansion of mass education in the leading countries of the Great Transformation. A good deal of the development of elective forms of higher (as well as professional) education is readily explained by its role in the creation of a managerial class. This is especially true in the US, where a largely vocational motivation for higher education was displayed less diffidently than in other countries with the creation of a range of academic degrees directed at business, such as the MBA. Alfred Chandler's 'visible hand' presupposes that the giant enterprises in the US at the heart of the Great Transformation were able to enjoy the virtues of scale and scope emerging from large absolute size, vertical integration and diversified breadth with a minimal loss of administrative flexibility, and even a level of decentralisation. Central to these developments was not simply the creation of a set of administrative structures that conformed to these firms' respective strategies, but a rich array of personnel to administer and carry out these tasks successfully: Chandler's 'visible hand' revolution is only comprehensible in this context. By contrast, as suggested by the Gerschenkron hypothesis described earlier, late-developing countries such as Russia had to rely upon rigid centralisation and protocols to deal with a paucity of administrative personnel.

A growing and ever more sophisticated government civil service bureaucracy played an important role in coordinating and regulating this expansion of the private sector. The philippics against the growth of bureaucracy, both within free enterprise and in government, notwithstanding, an educated white collar workforce to fulfil these manifestly necessary bureaucratic functions emerged during the Second Industrial Revolution and continued to expand throughout the twentieth century. Thus, in a fairly uncontentious way, the growing share of white collar labour needed to carry out clerical, secretarial and other activities within the largest, most modern industrial firms in advanced capitalist economies explains much of the concomitant emergence and expansion of mass education in the leading countries of the Great Transformation.[40] This change is linked to the introduction and augmentation of marketing, purchasing, research, legal and financial activities within these firms, and the multiplication of separate entities devoted to these activities, such as insurance companies.

For both Europe and the US in this period, the relative importance of formal (including vocational) education in society indubitably increased in comparison with that in the First Industrial Revolution, though the extent of this shift is a matter of contention. For Europe, Germany's success has long been linked to a knowledge- and skill-based approach to economic and industrial development, in contrast to Britain, which had been seen as laggard in mass education, and especially vocational and industrial training. Discontent with vocational training and, especially, technical education has registered for a century as a key problem by those concerned in Britain about putative economic decline vis-à-vis Germany;[41] the issue, as we shall see, continues to emerge in different forms to this day.

There has been some dispute over the role of formal education and training in the US during the Second Industrial Revolution compared with *in situ* skill development. The emphasis in one approach is that, at least in its earlier phases, education and training played a secondary role in the accretion of knowledge: both technical and administrative facility emerged through a slow process of *in situ* learning in the context of what was, in relative terms, already an advanced economy. Technical specialists and managers developed their skills less through formal education than through practical, shop floor experience and by moving between technologically related sectors.[42] The expansion of industrial capacity in the US is seen as fuelled by a massive infusion of labour from immigrant and rural areas, which, in the former case, was barely literate in English, with a successful elimination of craft worker control of labour processes and a relative absence of skill formation on the shop floor.[43] Taylor's approach to scientific management, explored in Chapter 2, had indicated to management the desirability of reducing work to strict protocols and routines – in the manner apparently realised in the assembly line – with minimal need for autonomy and decision making from a relatively unskilled labour force.

Is, however, the historical evolution of the educational levels of the workforce simply to be explained by the unfolding needs of an autonomous and objective process of technological change? The intervention by Harry Braverman considers whether the forms of technology that become available to society are dictated solely by the limitations and imperatives of the state of technological knowledge. Do they, in Taylor's words, reflect the 'one best way' of pursuing a task?

Braverman, reflecting a Marxian tradition, postulates that the forms of technology that emerge in a capitalist society reflect not only the constraints of nature and the existing state of knowledge, but a range of factors linked to social and power relations, especially the conflicts between labour and capital inherent in that mode of production.[44] Most specifically, he claims that a process of de-skilling was pursued and substantively realised by employers in the US in the twentieth century. For Taylor, the motivation for this process of the reduction of work to protocols and routines was the promotion of efficiency, in keeping with, and analogous to, the rational organisation of space on the factory floor. Braverman and others, however, contended that Taylorism was a political act by employers to reduce workers' autonomy and control over the nature and intensity of the work process. Traditionally, the characteristics and pace of this process emerged from a resolution of the conflict between owners (by way of their hired foreman on the shop floor) and workers, most significantly the residual guild-like groupings among skilled labour. For Braverman, the Taylorist process of de-skilling was seen as an inherent, rather than deviant, aspect of capitalist development. In the battle between owners and craft workers, Taylorism was a weapon to seize control of the work process by the capitalist class:

> the new conditions of employment that were to become characteristic of the automobile industry, and thereafter of an increasing number of industries, were established first at the Ford Motor Company. Craftsmanship gave way to a repeated detail operation, and wage rates were standardized at uniform levels... *only as the capitalist mode of production conquers and destroys all other forms of the organization of labor, and with them, all alternatives for the working population.*[45]

Braverman's thesis has been debated in an extensive literature surrounding the 'labor process'.[46] He clearly delineated the desires and intentions of management: the question remains – did Taylorism succeed in reducing work to protocols, controls and monitored behaviour, eliminating worker autonomy and de-skilling the labourers themselves? The answer is a complex one. Throughout the nineteenth and early twentieth centuries in the US, there was an expansion of jobs occupied by white collar, non-production workers and so-called low skill labourers at the expense of artisan occupations, giving credence to Braverman's de-skilling hypothesis in the context of manufacturing work.[47] But substantial pay differentials for educated blue collar workers persisted throughout the Second Industrial Revolution period, and these workers had a disproportionate presence in the US in the new, high-technology industries of the day (the car industry being an exception), with employers showing a preference for those workers with an academic preparation in science, algebra and mechanical drawing.[48]

The expansion of public education played a central role, furthermore, in the sustained increases in agricultural productivity from the latter part of the nineteenth century in the US, with farmers there having an exceptional capacity, both in cognitive terms and in breadth of attitude, to use the latest methods being diffused by the Department of Agriculture and innovations emerging from suppliers of machinery and other inputs.[49] The vast increase in educational resources accompanying the Second Industrial Revolution, especially notable in the US, can thus be seen to have a material basis and economic justification, not only in white collar work but in both industry and agriculture, promoting economic gains to individuals and to the economy as a whole. The expansion in resources devoted to education was a necessary accompaniment to the Second Industrial Revolution.

Even more overtly, the post-Second World War development of a rich educational infrastructure at the university level in the US was a formative influence, source and impetus to the economic and technological achievements of this period, keeping in mind that this infrastructure was filled almost exclusively by graduates of US public schools. As will be seen in Chapter 9, the links in the US between university departments and business in science and technology have been the source of much admiration worldwide, as well as generating disquiet about the potential compromises of objectivity, integrity and long-term research goals resulting from these links.

But the most striking fact about tertiary education in the US in the period after the Second World War was how much there was of it – with almost half the school-age population participating in it. This exceptionally high proportion of the population going into higher education, compared with any other country, was servicing not only the needs of the burgeoning scientific and technical industries, but administration, the arts and the educational sector itself. The historically unprecedented level of participation in higher education taking place in the US after the Second World War became a key aspect of its role as a focal point of modernity for other countries. As we move to the end of the twentieth century, we see other rich countries making strenuous efforts to emulate these rates of participation, which they have often succeeded in surpassing in the twenty-first.

As early as the 1970s, the focus of capitalist success had partially shifted away from the US and in the direction of other nations, most especially Japan. Arguments emerged, on a regular basis, that shop floor flexibility and autonomy of its workforce played a key role in that nation's revolutionary lean production manufacturing, critical components of which were high levels of worker literacy, numeracy and in-house training.[50] These issues in recent years have intensified and taken a different form with the rapid loss of so-called unskilled work in manufacturing in many rich countries and mediocre results in the US and the UK on international comparisons for school children in tests of literacy and numeracy.

In the end, the precise mechanisms behind the education–growth linkage, or measurement of the economic returns to education in a time series, have been hard to pin down: 'since increases in educational levels have been associated with increases in other investment, urbanization, and industrialization ... it is impossible to disentangle their individual effects'.[51] This range of interacting factors, as well as the complications that emerge from consideration of the external effects incumbent upon educational development, are to be considered in subsequent chapters.

How seriously do we take the results? II

We find ourselves with a popular narrative, converging with an academic one, in which improved education is conducive to economic growth through the mechanism of technological change fostered exclusively through free enterprise. The popular role of technological change as offering something for nothing – a path to good health or a cure to environmental difficulties without the need for undue exertion or a curb on appetite – is universally tempting. In the US, the fount of much postwar innovation, this enthusiasm has been reinforced by the perceived role of new technology in the victory of free enterprise in the Cold War and the promise that high technology is central to the maintenance of US dominance as an economic power. The widespread enthusiasm for new technology as an elixir is underwritten, as we have seen, by theoretical and statistical procedures in academic work that presume that existing resources are already being used efficiently, leaving little but technological change to do the heavy lifting as a source of economic growth. If a nation's technological achievement were the product solely of a relatively small body of world-class researchers, it would be unsurprising if some concluded that expenditure on higher education beyond this elite group is wasteful.

The empirical results confirming the education–economic growth nexus appear to be robust and reinforced by the broad historical narrative: the rich nations of today are the well-educated ones of a century ago, and the anomalies of the past – of nations that were relatively well-educated but poor – are hard to find today. There are reasons, however, to question not so much the link between education and economic improvement, but the particular formulations of this relationship in the economics literature.

For the capitalist system treated as a worldwide entity, it is simply untrue that periods of rapid economic growth are readily linked to high levels of discontinuous technological change. Economic growth as a focus of economic debate surfaced during the Cold War, with education emerging as a key component. The central role of discontinuously created new technologies as the fuel for this growth gained centrality in academic economic discussions at about the time of an important alteration in the nature of technical change in the real world that only became clear in retrospect. For most of the twentieth century, through to the end of the Golden Age of Capitalism in the early 1970s, technological improvements, and the concomitant economic growth, took the form of adaptations of a range of technologies seeing the light of day in the late nineteenth and early twentieth centuries. These technologies – from their conception through to the marketing of the products consequent upon these new technologies – were financed and developed by profit-making, predominantly very large companies. Thus, postwar economic growth took place overwhelmingly in the context of a range of technologies in the industrial and agricultural sectors – electrification and electric motors, the internal combustion engine, chemical processes (including chemical fertiliser) and even the electronics of radio and television – that were already well established in the stagnant interwar years.[52]

Events, as we have seen, then took a strange turn. In the midst of the golden age, a dominant concern in the capitalist world had been that Khrushchëv's desire to catch up with the West was going to become a reality – the Soviet steel industry may not have implemented the latest innovations in this sector (though neither had the US), but its high level of output and rate of growth were – just as earlier in the century – the standard by which a great economic power was judged.[53] Using the calculations made by the CIA, the Soviet Union's overall rates of economic growth were causing it to close the gap with the US. With the end of the golden age in the 1970s, capitalism struggled to maintain itself, with levels of unemployment unprecedented since the interwar period, high inflation and decisively slower economic growth. Yet, it was precisely in this period that the inadequacies of the Soviet economic system became evident, as, for the first time since the beginning of the century, a host of products based on qualitatively new technologies began to emanate from the capitalist world, most especially from the electronics sector: with Cold War restrictions and the systemic failures of the centrally planned system to adapt or innovate these technologies independently, an unbreachable gap opened with the capitalist West.

In light of these developments, there emerged in the 1980s a defence of capitalism and a critique of central planning based on the dynamic properties of capitalism rather than its superiority in terms of static efficiency. An important reason for this change in perspective was the granting of a key role to entrepreneurial finance for the astonishingly rapid advance of the electronics sector, one that, more in general than in explicit terms, has been used to justify financial deregulation. In academic circles, this switch in emphasis began in the 1980s, but took place slowly, with a gradual change in focus from the importance of static efficiency to the dynamic properties of capitalism as described in the models of endogenous growth. In this literature, unlike that emerging from Lavoie and the neo-Austrian acolytes, the efficacy of capitalism was linked not to a somewhat generalised conception of the risk-taking, innovative properties of capitalism, but to a well-defined process by which capitalist competition generated technological change (supposedly a concrete, measurable variable), which then raised the growth rate of the economy. These developments were accompanied by an ever-increasing lionisation of Joseph Schumpeter as the prophet of innovation, despite the failure of his technology-driven theory of business cycles and the Delphic nature of his pronouncements on the provenance of this innovation.

But while Schumpeter's approach to technological innovation may approximate events from the beginning of the twentieth century, most especially in the US, in which the source of new innovations were profit-making, often giant firms, it is far less suited to deal with the outburst of new technology and products derived from them in the post-Second World War period. Here we see a complex interaction of profit-making pursuits by individual firms, often guided, goaded, subsidised and constrained by the visible hand of the state, usually in the form of the US Department of Defense, and interacting with a range of non-profit-making institutions, including government laboratories and universities. At the time, much of the expenditure on military equipment and its associated research was seen as a drain on the civilian economy and, through the processes by which these projects were pursued and financed, wasteful in its own terms.

Thus, as we shall see in Chapter 9, the invention of the transistor by AT&T in 1947, perhaps the quintessence of Schumpeterian long-term planning by a capitalist monopoly, albeit one abetted by the largesse of the government in the form of wartime profits, was perhaps the crucial invention in the emergence of the modern electronics industry. But the subsequent development of this invention and the complementary progress in computers and other branches of electronics took place in the context of aggressive intervention by the state. Extensive fundamental research was carried out under government contracts by universities, and AT&T itself was subject to overwhelming pressure to license its invention to potential competitors – often relatively new firms that were the product of entrepreneurial finance initiatives.

What accounts for the difference between these outbursts of new technology and invention? In two interconnected ways, technological progress without state intervention appeared to function better in the earlier of our two periods. First, the level of competitive rivalry was less severe at the turn of the century: the theory and the substantive development relevant to the internal combustion engine and to electrical equipment emerged over decades – at a leisurely pace, by contemporary standards. Furthermore, the diffusion of techniques and technologies – in this world substantively without multinational enterprises – took place slowly between nations. With a very limited number of actual or potential rivals, and a slow rate of diffusion of the new technologies among them, the potential for the acquisition of monopolistic quasi-rents from these new technologies exceeded that in later periods, so that these technologies emerged almost wholly through the activities of profit-making entities.

Second, an aspect of the increasingly competitive environment in the later period is, as we have seen in Chapter 5, the more rapid diffusion of new technologies due to their progressively more abstract, scientific nature. This is a seemingly inexorable development that has continued on to the present day: the process by which craft and implicit knowledge embodied in an individual person or group of people is transformed into explicit, replicable empirical generalities is inherent in the development of science. This process is paralleled in the logic of modern manufacturing technique, with its constant desire to reduce craft mysteries (such as the ancient art of steel manufacture, or the early techniques used in the production of semiconductors) to replicable protocols.

The process of formalisation tends to accelerate the rate of potential diffusion and potential competition: the more an innovation is linked to abstract formulae rather than to craft embodied in the innovator, and the more the manufacture and the replication of this innovation are linked to concrete, written protocols, the more potentially competitive is the environment. The nature of this competition, however, changes, as these replicators, imitators and potential competitors need to have, or have access to, individuals with formalised education and training capable of understanding the science behind the innovation and the protocols of manufacture. These developments enhance the importance of formalised training and lower the value of traditional, informal and *in situ* knowledge.

A central factor thus determining the trajectory of the future technological environment and its influence upon the economy will be not only the size and characteristics of the pool of individuals capable of innovating new technologies, but the number of those with formalised knowledge adequate for monitoring and replicating new developments. The harvesting of the fruits of technological change increasingly centres on the role of intellectual property rights (IPRs), a mechanism for entrenched entities (both nations and firms) to construct barriers to new competition. It is the balance of political and power relations, most especially in the international domain, rather than any Hayekian spontaneous order, that will dictate the evolution of laws and regulations governing IPRs, regarding which fierce conflicts have emerged both within nations and, most especially, between rich and poor countries over the role of the patent system and other intellectual property rights as, on the one hand, an incentive to new invention and, on the other, a barrier to new competition.

The interconnected evolution of competitive pressures and the role of formalised knowledge lay behind the distinctive post-Second World War patterns in technological change. A range of capitalist heroes emerge from the period, from AT&T as the paradigmatic Schumpeterian monopolistic enterprise that gave us fundamental innovation, to the Hayekian entrepreneurial firms that ferociously competed and disseminated the new technologies. The venture capital that often financed new firms in this sector became part of a narrative on the virtues of unfettered finance that led to the beginnings of the deregulation of the financial sector in the US in the 1980s. But all these developments differed fundamentally from the earlier transformation that had taken place at the beginning of the twentieth century because of the central role played by the state.

It does not appear to be fortuitous that state financing and intervention played a central role in the take-off phase of the electronics revolution of the 1950s and 1960s in the US: this key technological development of the postwar period might not have taken place, or might have been delayed for an indefinite period of time, in the absence of state involvement. In the context of the technological and economic conditions of the postwar world, unencumbered free enterprise and its associated capital markets were unlikely to be able to realise commercial gains in the context of a host of obstacles: the high level of spillovers in these science-based innovations, the long period of gestation taking place before the development of commercially successful products, and the substantial uncertainty present concerning the commercial potential of these endeavours.

These key sectors of postwar economic development were thus potentially experiencing what can be seen in retrospect as forms of product and, especially, capital market failure. The role of independent venture and start-up capital in this process thus appears to be an important, but secondary one – it facilitated the rate of development and dissemination of early-stage innovations that had been financed by the state, but these decentralised, uncoordinated private sources of capital could not, on their own, have brought about these innovations. The heuristic justification for financial deregulation and unencumbered capital markets emerging in the 1980s in the wake of the triumphs of Silicon Valley is thus somewhat diluted.

The triumph of capitalism over the centrally planned economic system was engendered by two phenomena – this new wave of technological dynamism in the West, and the rapid emergence from poverty to affluence of nations such as Japan and South Korea – in which state action played a central role in the financing and even the direction of these developments. This reporting of historical facts is not intended as a surreptitious defence of central planning, or even of state action, but it does bring into question any simplistic narratives, whether they be of a Schumpeterian, Hayekian or endogenous growth kind, by which an unencumbered free enterprise triumphed over inherently dysfunctional state direction of economic activity.

Underlying both these success stories – the American and the east Asian – is a distinctive commitment to education, one whose development, in great measure, is beyond the logic of the marketplace and, substantively, has taken place through state action, whether at school or university level. For the US in the post-Second World War era, the role of the state has been conspicuous both indirectly, through funding for the training of scientists, and directly, through procurement of, and payment for, university science and technology resources, most especially, though not exclusively, through the US Department of Defense. These substantial state commitments raise important economic and political issues concerning how this funding might have shaped the trajectory of these new scientific developments and technologies, and how they might have developed in the absence of state involvement, assuming that they would have emerged at all. It is sobering, moreover, to note that this remarkable mobilisation and coordination of entrepreneurial and intellectual resources was largely directed to the creation and procurement of weapons for mass killing.

* * *

If we proceed from the above validation of the education–growth narrative with appropriate caveats, we are then confronted with the need to insert an additional link in the chain: in the context of the perspective offered by Hanushek and Woessmann above, education, in the form of years of formal schooling, has only an imperfect relationship to output in the form of cognitive capacity as measured by standardised tests. In the chapters to follow, the provenance of cognitive capacity is to be explored in the context of formal schooling and the use of inputs such as class size, teacher quality and school choice. A further important consideration will be the desired output – is it to be a heightened cognitive capacity that suits the needs of employers, or one more broadly based? And which of these alternatives is more conducive to the cultivation of that universally lauded result – labour flexibility?

The predominant focus in the chapters to follow upon formal education is not due to any presumption that the magnitude of its effects is invariably greater in some absolute sense than other influences on human development. It is, rather, that in the context of rich countries, where education through to late adolescence is compulsory, schooling is overwhelmingly the most readily available and powerful public policy instrument for direct intervention in the lives and consciousness of individuals and, potentially, for the effecting of fundamental social change. For this reason, schooling has always been an arena of contestation between right- and left-wing political views. Both perspectives evince ambivalence about the educational process – the right wing conscious of its potentially disruptive aspects, the left fearing its repressive characteristics and its role in the assignment and reinforcement of preordained social roles to children of different classes. But a key difference is that, ambivalent or not, right-wing analysts rarely question the key role that education plays in the assignment of children to their proper roles in society. By contrast, much energy on the left has been diverted away from a focus on education by the notion that that it is merely a secondary consideration – an aspect of society's superstructure that will invariably reflect and reinforce the norms of the existent capitalist society. Perhaps for this reason, no coherent left-wing alternative view of the educational process is available to oppose the powerful human capital conception and its concomitant policy emphasis on reforms based on market mechanisms. Without an alternative programme, opposition to these market reforms is often seen merely as support for the status quo.

The leading candidate for the social determination of cognitive achievement outside of schooling is the household. This is a favourite consideration for right-wing writers, who are eager to moralise about social breakdown and individual responsibility (that is, when they are not hinting that some groups in society suffer from a lack of economic or cognitive success because it is not 'in the blood'). It is indubitably true that households play a key role in the development of children's cognitive capacity and overall repertoire of competencies. It would also appear that public policy is less central to learning in a household context than it is in formal school learning.

But the public policy role in learning linked to the household, while indirect, is not negligible. We are regularly reminded by right-wing commentators that entrepreneurs need an atmosphere of certainty in order to plan and invest. This logic, however, applies no less to the plans and investments that a family makes in relation to the maintenance and enhancement of the human assets of its constituents, most especially those of its children: deprivation and insecurity are obstacles to the formation of coherent strategies by a family for investing in itself. For this reason, it is not only true that formal educational programmes play a role in the promotion of reduced inequality and enhanced mobility; the obverse is also true – these educational programmes will be more effective in enhancing intellectual capability if the societies in which these programmes are being pursued evince minimal levels of income and class inequality. Giving all households the capability of developing and executing such plans is a key socialist goal.

In the chapters of Part II that follow, the outline of the argument presented here concerning education and growth is filled in. In Chapter 7, the individualistic approach to education embodied in the mainstream human capital literature is contrasted with a historical perspective examining the societal genesis and impact of educational advance; Chapter 8 focuses on learning that takes place at work and in the process of living in society. Chapter 9 uses the history of the US to exemplify the key roles played by public policy in economic development in the contexts of education, technological advance and industrial enterprise: technological advance, far from being an elixir offered up by an elite, emerges as part of a complex, socially embedded process. Chapter 10 calls into question the very meaning of the phrase 'economic growth', so that the initial 'education → economic growth' argument migrates into a broader range of considerations of the 'human development → economic development' kind. The discussion is then advanced to suggest that human development is not merely a means to the achievement of economic goals, but an end in itself.

7
Education as a Social Process

The individual components of the link between education and economic growth will be considered – and deconstructed – here and in the following chapters. This chapter deals with formal education, which poses difficulties for analysts of capitalism because labour has traditionally been viewed as a relatively undifferentiated (and presumably uneducated) entity whose services can be bought and sold on the marketplace. For defenders of capitalism, the ending of the supposedly mutual obligations of lord and serf of the medieval era initiated an era of freedom for labour, while for Marxists, a period of continued exploitation under a new guise emerged.

In both orthodox and Marxist economic analysis, this way of dealing with labour maintained its popularity long after any period of empirical relevance because it proved malleable for constructing models of how capitalism worked. When departure from the notion of labour services as a commodity became unavoidable, this challenge was met in economic orthodoxy through a concept – human capital – that preserved the notion of capitalism as an arena of individual decision making and free choice. This identification of the enhancement of human capital with free choice came about by directing attention to the acquisition of formal, elective education by young adults. But individuals are overwhelmingly shaped and transformed, at a much earlier stage, by systems of compulsory schooling that are the product of societal decisions: the forms this schooling should take are at present the focus of intense controversy. Any attempt to understand the educational process must reflect its socially embedded nature and long-term influence on societal and economic formation.

Human capital theory

In his critique of the capitalist system, the most famous apologist for slavery in the *ante bellum* US, John C. Calhoun of South Carolina, focused on the relationship between capitalist and labourer: while the slave owner could realise any demonstrable improvements in the value of the labour he or she owned by making use of the slave's elevated productivity or by selling the slave at an enhanced price in the marketplace, the capitalist, by contrast, had little material interest in improving the living conditions or the skills of the labourer.[1] Under capitalism, as Alfred Marshall noted, the very freedom of the labourer to move to a new employer made it unwise for any individual capitalist to invest unduly in either the health or the general education of his or her workers.[2] Calhoun's perception of the employment relation under capitalism lies at the centre of the doctrine later developed independently, and from a very different perspective, by Karl Marx, whose theory of exploitation flows directly from the fact that the capitalist does not purchase the labourer but merely hires his or her labour power.

The intervention of Gary Becker has been central to the emergence of a view on these questions on the part of contemporary capitalist ideology. In earlier work, the issues surrounding human capital had been developed largely from an empirical perspective.[3] But it was Becker who successfully reoriented the whole question of the augmentation of the skills of labour away from the capitalist employment relation: the latter was, as we have seen, fraught with difficulties for the defence of capitalism because of the capitalist's inherent lack of interest in investing in the improvement of the skills of potentially mobile workers. Instead, the predominant emphasis in academic and public discourse concerning the development of human skills and knowledge has followed Becker in focusing upon the economic returns to education and the calculations that would be made by isolated individuals about investing in themselves. The core of the analysis of educational enhancement in society thus shifts away from the social, political and ethical issues surrounding the generation of an educated population in a democratic society and towards one emphasising investment decisions on the part of individuals. The decision to become educated becomes merely a type of investment decision and an exercise in free choice.

The investment process, as conceived by the early-twentieth-century US economist Irving Fisher, had linked the possibility for high rates of investment in physical capital to individuals and societies (largely of white, European origin) who had saved at high levels by constraining their impatience to consume in the present.[4] The later theory of investment in human capital parallels that for physical capital: in analytically well-behaved situations, the individual must defer present consumption because of the explicit costs of education and the indirect costs of foregoing income from employment, all for the sake of higher income in the future.[5] Those individuals who successfully constrain their impatience to consume in the present will earn more in the future, as will individuals and societies with a greater taste for risk; the latter groups will also have higher variance of income. These considerations give an exegesis for Milton Friedman's notorious declaration that inequality of income in a society is 'at least in part and perhaps a major part – a reflection of deliberate choice in accordance with the tastes and preferences of the members of the society'.[6] And for Becker, the link between the theory of investment in human capital and personal income distribution is that abler persons can expect a higher rate of return from investing in themselves, and therefore will do so to a greater extent than others: a meritocratic theory of income distribution.[7]

Human capital theory's greatest successes have been in these polemical directions – as justifications, for instance, for increased fees, and for loans rather than grants, in higher education. But as a mode of more generalised justification for the rationality of capitalist investment processes in a human context, the analogy with investment in physical capital is of limited use. One problematic aspect of the human capital literature is that it deals poorly with issues surrounding class. A concrete aspect of the class dimension in the enhancement of human capital is the complementary role played by the possession of property and financial assets acting as collateral in the financing of elective education.[8] Government loan schemes act as only a partial mitigation for less-than-affluent students facing the prospect of large debts in an uncertain world.[9] These uncertainties are all the more baffling and terrifying for those (I include myself here) with no precedent in their family and immediate surroundings of individuals who have successfully followed the trajectory of higher education and professional development. These are aspects of a more general point: 'Since skill acquisition and identity formation are so inextricably linked, precisely the most important, "formative" learning in a person's life cannot possibly be conceived or motivated in terms of rational investment in the longer-term pursuit of individual interests. The decision what kind of work skills one wants to acquire in order later to sell them in the labour market is inseparable from the decision what kind of person one wants to be.'[10] The bonds constraining young people (and their parents) because of limited perception of alternative possibilities are no less real for being subjective, and are an important element of class distinction not easily captured in income distribution statistics.[11]

Human capital theory ignores the social formation of the individual whose choices are being analysed by the theory. The absence of a social dimension also causes attention to be focused on the acquisition of skills and capabilities by individuals, distracting attention from the inherently societal aspects of the educational process itself. Below, one insufficiently considered societal aspect will be explored – the fact that educational development is invariably saturated with external effects. Intimately linked to the question of external effects is the reality that educational improvement in the modern world has not been predominantly concerned with individual choice at all, as in the case of higher and elective vocational education, but remains tied to the compulsory, largely state-financed activities that take place in schools. In our own time, when more than half the population in rich countries pursue forms of elective education beyond that which is compulsory, it is still the nature of the experience during the obligatory years of schooling that is of overwhelming significance to individual and societal development. This latter process takes place, and is crucially conditioned by, the context of the family and social conditions under which children develop in these years. There is a link between external effects and the historical reality of compulsory school education: in areas of its greatest efflorescence from the latter part of the nineteenth and early twentieth centuries to the present, governments and communities in the most dynamic economies have been responding to the fact that the economic and social efficacy of enhanced education extends far beyond the pecuniary gains to individuals.

Nothing better delineates a right-wing from a progressive, socialist view of society than their respective attitudes to human development, including education: for the former, there is an emphasis on the quasi-biological notion of those who are intrinsically able choosing elective, including higher, education because they will benefit from it, as well as the older moralistic conception that higher education is chosen by those willing to constrain their desire to consume in the present. An alternative socialist approach views human and educational development through a critical examination of school and preschool institutions not only in their own terms, but also in the context of the range of influences impinging upon the lives of children from birth, including forms of material and psychological deprivation and lack of opportunity linked to social and economic inequality. The socialist presumption is that the great majority of individuals, even in rich societies, have been deprived from birth of the opportunity to fulfil their potential in the narrow terms of their economic productivity and, more importantly, in their role as free citizens in control of their destiny. The great bulk of the population is in little need of lectures from the well-off informing them that their status in society and that of their children is due to the fact that they are insufficiently able or overly impatient.

Educational development and external effects

As we have seen in Chapter 6, a distinction is made in the economics literature between two approaches to education. First, microeconomic studies show substantial monetary returns to the pursuit of elective education by individuals, in which increases in educational attainment can be treated as an investment that individuals undertake. The costs are the explicit funds put forth to pay for education, and the opportunity cost of the income foregone by undergoing the educational process. The benefits for the individual may be measured by the future stream of enhanced earnings incumbent on this investment in education. Another approach in academic studies, however, has been to assign the calculation of the social returns to education to a macroeconomic literature that attempts to measure the returns to education to society as a whole. These returns embody any external or spillover effects, which are presumed to be largely of a positive kind – benefits from educational investment that accrue to society, over and beyond those (especially enhanced income) that accrue to the individual receiving the education.

The discussion of these spillovers in the economics literature is a curious one. The prominent free-market economist George Stigler notes that the presence of such educational externalities could be an issue of major significance, but passes on to other issues.[12] In general surveys of the education–economic growth literature, the question is discussed in a brief and perfunctory manner.[13] Statistical studies have often noted the presence of external effects to educational improvement, but have usually found them to be of a small order of magnitude.[14] The human capital perspective maintains its central place – the economics of education remains a literature dominated by the individual's decision to invest in education.

The argument here, by contrast, is that externalities associated with elevated levels of education are pervasive. When they are properly considered in the context of an evaluation of the effects of educational improvement on society as a whole, they reduce significantly the centrality of the individualistic human capital perspective on education, most especially in a long-term context. A social approach to education and its effects will quite naturally focus more, for instance, on the education and training system for artists emerging in Renaissance Italy over an extended period rather than on the biographies of individual giants such as Michelangelo or Titian. It is this perspective that motivates the replacement here of the term 'human capital' with 'human assets'. Why, then, do these pervasive external effects show up in statistical tests only in a limited way? A key reason is that these tests, on the whole, implicitly posit a well-nigh instantaneous effect of enhanced education on, for instance, economic growth: if formal education, and most especially its external effects, influences economic growth only with a long lag, the growth effects of education are likely to be substantially underestimated in most statistical tests.[15]

Education is likely to make its impact with a lag that is long and variable. As we shall see in Chapter 10, the most remarkable cultural transformation of the last half millennium took place in Japan in the 50 years after the Meiji Restoration of 1868, but its world-changing economic effects only manifested themselves well into the post-Second World War period. By contrast, the growth effects of the Asian tiger strategy of integrating human development with industrial policy described in Chapter 6 emerged with a much shorter lag than in the case of Japan, both for a range of historical and externally determined economic reasons, and also because of the advantages the Asian tigers had in the precedent-setting example of Japanese development.

Is it appropriate to treat the presence of external effects to cognitive improvement as a peripheral aspect of the process of economic development? The approach taken by mainstream economists is peculiar in light of the general focus in recent decades on language as the decisive 'invention' of human beings (probably *Homo sapiens*), an innovation whose efficacy emerges, most indubitably, at the level of social interaction. Below, however, in response to the economists' persistent, usually implicit presumption that spillover effects to cognitive development are of a marginal kind, I list a host of ways in which the economic gains to society as a whole of an individual's cognitive improvement are greater than the gains (specifically income gains) that accrue to that individual, most especially in the context of long-term societal development.[16] There are, as noted above, substantial difficulties in empirically verifying and measuring the external effects of these improvements. But some attempt to enumerate the external effects emerging from cognitive improvement is imperative to give plausibility to the notion of their pervasive presence and to highlight the reasons why, as will be outlined in Chapter 10, the effects of educational improvement are likely to be registered economically only with long lags. A narrow listing of external effects, emphasising those most likely to impinge on economic growth, is as follows:[17]

Improvements in communication skills. Improvements in individuals' communication skills, such as language literacy, especially when manifested outside the sphere of employment, yield unremunerated gains to society as a whole. Such gains are analogous to the positive externalities inherent in purchasing a telephone in 1930: the value of everybody else's telephone is increased. For instance, the more literate and numerate consumers are, the more articulate they will be in communicating, in verbal and written form, their wants to producers. An enhancement of communication skills thus lowers the costs of search on the part of all consumers, which promotes market efficiency. Improvements in knowledge by consumers in particular areas can enhance the monitoring of product quality.[18]

Emulation. Much new learning is communicated by imitating a master of an art, and these 'lessons' may take place even when they are involuntary on the part of the master.[19] Noam Chomsky points out that language acquisition on the part of children occurs even in societies in which communication with adults is discouraged or forbidden. As economies develop, the number of individuals whose skills are worthy of imitation is likely to increase, as does the number of firms and other institutions whose superior organisational capability can be observed at first hand.

Spillover effects from accretions to knowledge which are general or which have fuzzy boundaries. The more basic and fundamental (general) any accretions to knowledge by an individual or institution (for instance, a firm) are, the more difficult it is for that individual or institution to capture the full value of that knowledge (examples being Newton's laws or Maxwell's equations). In a more modest context, improvements to knowledge and skill in one sector of economic activity may yield positive benefits in another when the boundaries between these activities are unclear: it proved difficult for Xerox to appropriate the full value of their innovations in software (much of which was harvested by Apple and Microsoft), perhaps because their perspective was delimited to the domain of office copiers. This phenomenon may help to account for the continued presence of industrial clusters such as Silicon Valley, in which closely related products are produced in the context of the conviviality and interpersonal relations present within a restricted region and community (see Chapter 9). Technological spillovers of this kind have been singularly emphasised in the new economic growth literature. As, over time, the ratio of science to craft-based knowledge rises and the cohort of individuals capable of monitoring these increments to knowledge increases, possible spillover effects become more likely. Appropriate levels of education in a society are thus crucial not only for the development of new ideas, but for the assimilation and appropriation of already existing knowledge on a worldwide basis, a role perhaps of especial importance for developing countries.

In addition to these educational externalities, in which societal gains exceed those to individuals, there is a further aspect to much skill acquisition: many kinds of accretion to knowledge in specific sectors, such as semiconductor manufacture, only realise their full economic value in the context of skill development in other sectors, such as ceramics. Such complementarities do not, strictly speaking, indicate the presence of external effects, but they give learning an additional societal component, and increase the likelihood of the clustering of firms in given localities.[20] As we shall see in Chapter 9, the famous Silicon Valley cluster was the result of the presence, both planned and serendipitous, of a range of complementary skills in a context that promoted the realisation of the economic value of those skills. The difficulties and the time involved in the integration of skills from diverse sectors are further reasons to expect to see lags in the beneficial effects of cognitive improvement on economic development.

Raising society's 'productivity' as a parent. The exceptional efforts made in Japan from the late nineteenth century to educate the whole of their population, including women, were motivated by the presumption of the spillover effects attendant on the upbringing of children by educated mothers. In the context of intergenerational transfers of knowledge, 'human capital accumulation is a *social* activity, involving *groups* of people in a way that has no counterpart in the accumulation of physical capital'.[21]

Public good effects. The enhanced knowledge of individuals in society may well spill over to others due to non-exclusionary aspects in the consumption of culture. For instance, the well-educated adult population of New York City in the 1960s supported a range of commercial and listener-sponsored talk and music radio outlets.[22] The cognitive and cultural benefits of the presence of these high-quality outlets, designed to service the well-educated, also accrued to others, such as young people: the latter were free riders who were not the immediate targets of the commercial advertising and appeals for funds that sustained these stations. Publicly displayed art and architecture and other amenities can function in a similar way.

There are, in addition, a range of non-market effects that are sometimes linked to higher levels of education but remain of a somewhat speculative nature: personal characteristics with interactive attributes that may be cultivated by societal (especially educational) institutions and are not likely to be fully remunerated at the personal level.[23] Some of these effects, such as the inculcation of notions of honesty and fair dealing, may well, in the long term, promote higher levels of economic growth; other effects of this kind – the promotion of tolerance of racial, ethnic and religious differences or an appreciation of democratic procedures – may be desirable, but their relationship to economic growth is less clear.

Cognitive development, therefore, has a substantial societal component: 'the generation of skills can be and has to be conceived as the production of a collective good'.[24] It is not merely the product of individualistic Becker-type decisions to invest in oneself, but is the by-product of actions taken by others, often in earlier generations: this fact largely accounts for the predominant role of the state in education in societies oriented in the direction of economic improvement. An additional component to the educational process that distances it from Becker's model of individualistic, market-based decision making is the fact that, historically, much of what is interpreted by economists as improvement in the quality of human capital consists of 'spandrels'[25] – accidental by-products of the elevation of levels of literacy and general education that were undertaken by individuals or societies for reasons unconnected with attempts to increase either personal income or society's rate of economic development. Thus, one early-nineteenth-century European visitor to the US, expecting to be presented with a rough-hewn frontier society, was amazed (disappointed?) to be confronted with a literate culture among ordinary people, more extensive than what he had left behind in Europe: bibliolatry in the US had generated these exceptional levels of literacy.[26]

The nineteenth-century US example exemplifies the point that even if there is a long-term link between education and economic development, there have been historically diverse motivations that have engendered these literacy and educational programmes in societies; opposition, in various forms, has come from those who have feared that the poor would learn to despise their lot in life, leading to incendiary and revolutionary sentiments on the part of the rabble.[27] The question then arises – one relevant from the perspective of both economic development and socialism – does a society's rationale for pursing educational activity make a long-term difference in the qualitative aspects of that education? For example, in the early modern period, not only were there fewer resources devoted to schooling in general in Catholic countries than in Protestant countries, but this schooling was more likely to be concerned with the inculcation of faith and discipline than with literacy or anything resembling Enlightenment or scientific approaches to knowledge;[28] a king's counsel in eighteenth-century France worried about the overproduction of priests and lawyers – unproductive labourers – in the system of education existing at the time.[29] A modern critique, to be considered below, questions whether the protocols of discipline and silence in mass schooling are merely a by-product of endeavouring to educate children, or whether the inculcation of this discipline in schools – the discipline of the factory – has historically been an end in itself, so that it is the socialisation of the masses, rather than education, that has been the prime learning outcome aimed for by school administrators.[30] Under these conditions, failures in educational achievement for the great mass of students are only to be expected.

In other cases, a strong input of non-economic motivation in educational programmes has resulted in curricula and social interactions that significantly deviate from what would have been expected if education were simply being mapped onto enhanced productivity. At the upper end of the ruling spectrum, tuition in elite institutions such as British public (that is, private, fee-paying) schools or even in leading US engineering schools has included the cultivation of a sense of class solidarity and socialisation into the ruling group.[31] In some contexts we see the reverse pattern, so that educational developments that may appear to have non-economic motives are rooted in a strategy for individual or societal economic development: in nineteenth-century Europe, middle-class children (mostly girls) were educated in 'the arts', proverbially in the service of family strategies for upward mobility; as noted above, the relatively advanced level of literacy among Japanese women at the beginning of the twentieth century was not part of a feminist policy initiative, but linked to the highly plausible notion that better-educated women were more productive in their role as mothers.

Is education that is *intended* to increase individual productivity the most successful in so doing? From business pressure groups and others concerned with practical affairs, it is a truism that education for the masses should be concerned with preparing them for employment. The question then arises of the time horizon involved – are we thinking about an education that makes an individual suitable for a first job, or for a lifetime of employment? We thus return to the fundamental contradiction of a free labour market as posed by John C. Calhoun: it will rarely be worthwhile for individual capitalists to educate their workers in generalised skills that they can transfer to other employers.[32] A widespread consensus has therefore developed that the most important skills to be developed outside of the workplace are mastery of fundamental literacy and numeracy, with much task-specific vocational training administered in a non-workplace context a waste of time.[33] Such narrowly focused training, from the perspective both of the individual worker and of society, is likely to be less productive than a broader, seemingly less practical education that equips individuals with the literacy and numeracy that are essential for a lifetime of work in changing circumstances. But in the case of literacy especially, the notion that it involves a particular 'skill' to be mastered is wide of the mark: reading with comprehension, as we shall see below, takes place alongside the assimilation of the cultural context and the factual information relevant to the text at hand. Literacy, numeracy and broad-based knowledge therefore emerge as the underpinning of modern civilisation, culture and democracy as well as key prerequisites for economic development.

There appears to be a more or less universal aspiration to higher education, with one survey in the UK for the year 2004 showing 97 per cent of all mothers wanting their children to go to university.[34] But the limitations on knowledge of employment possibilities incumbent on being a child, exacerbated both by an inability to finance long-term study and by a lack of guidance and example available to children of working-class backgrounds, will often propel even the most diligent child from such a background into a set of decisions that may prove to be overly myopic from the misleading perspective of neoclassical economics, with its common presumption of a universal capacity across classes for rational intertemporal optimisation.[35] Practical, applied and supposedly relevant education for supposedly ordinary children merely exacerbates the aspects of irreversibility in the accretion of knowledge by individuals: young people become locked into a limited skill base and become less flexible in response to changing economic and social conditions. The acquisition of basic education is more valuable for a lifetime of work than the ability to manipulate a soon-to-be-obsolete piece of computer software demanded by an employer.

The attitude and strategy adopted by parents of children from elite backgrounds are very far from this short-term, practical approach. It may appear that the additional resources devoted to the children of the affluent are solely forms of consumption expenditure that give these young people pleasure and integrate them with like-minded members of the same social class. But this explanation is not sufficient to explain the demanding academic standards typically maintained in elite contexts. We find in these schools an emphasis on traditional disciplines – not just mathematics and the sciences, but even supposedly impractical ones such as history and philosophy. These subjects offer good mechanisms for the cultivation of the ability to pursue independent research, the capacity for literate and articulate expression, and the logical development of ideas. This broad-based learning, reminiscent of classical education, is intended to engender the flexibility and self-confidence to pursue a lifetime of cognitive and managerial tasks. The well-off who have set out this agenda wish their own children to be endowed with a capacity for flexibility and self-confidence that comes from the mastery of a curriculum emerging over millennia.

Such an education poses the danger that at least some children subject to this environment will be endowed with a capacity for critical thinking about society, and the even greater threat exists that these habits will spill over to the masses. Is a challenge of this kind to the established order likely? A century after the decrying of business influence in academic life in Thorstein Veblen's *The Higher Learning in America*, his worst fears, it would appear, have been realised: under the pressure of rising fees, there has indeed been an expansion of business-related pursuits, including the establishment worldwide of degrees in business studies. But what is really striking is less the expansion of these activities than the presence of substantial deviations from this practical ideal, and the persistence at the university level of purely academic subjects such as philosophy, even in the US. We see the continued presence of these subjects, and even their permeation into the curricula of the most prestigious law schools and MBA programmes. For a century, business people and right-wing publicists have been grinding their teeth about an anti-business atmosphere, real or imagined, in elite institutions, most especially universities.[36] Whether this radical reputation is justified is questionable, but in broader terms the breadth and character of the activities that take place within the university clearly depart from the role of merely preparing an elite in a vocational way to fulfil its role in society.

It is perhaps fantastic to speculate that a new 'contradiction' will emerge in present-day capitalism in the form of an economic, competitive need for thoroughgoing basic education and critical thinking to become pervasive across classes. But analogous unintended consequences have emerged before in history, with a scientific revolution centred on the movement of heavenly bodies eventually leading to the questioning of the origins and legitimacy of existing political structures. More directly, the uneven, contradictory but indubitable development of democratic participation in the twentieth century took place in the context of a pervasive expansion of schooling and literacy, often alongside disquiet among conservatives that the latter development was exciting, and giving power to, the vulgar mob. If economic and educational development are concomitant, and it has proved impossible to reconfigure this education in a manner that preserves its economic efficacy but eviscerates the necessity for critical thinking, then the expansion of academic learning may yet play a role in the creation of thoroughgoing democratic participation in society.

Education wars

Those with power in rich countries have responded to an increasingly competitive environment and economic crisis by putting pressure on their working populations, accompanied by continuing 'blame the victim' lectures suggesting that the plight of workers is their own fault – if not laziness, then their limited acquisition of appropriate skills and education. In the US and the UK, perceived deficits in the educational system, most especially in its supposed failure to produce a sufficient quantity and quality of graduates in so-called STEM subjects – Science, Technology, Engineering and Mathematics – are offered in the press as explanations for the decline in manufacturing employment, the size of the trade deficit[37] and, as we shall see in Chapter 10, the growth in income inequality.

This drama has now been playing itself out for decades.[38] Reforms designed to correct failures in the educational system have taken various forms, with the lines of dispute between left and right concerning these issues often confused: conflicts include those over progressive and traditional education, the introduction of market mechanisms and choice into school systems, the monitoring of the performance of teachers, schools and pupils on the basis of standardised tests, narrow versus broad curricula, and the importance of class size.

A way of bringing order to this mass of considerations is to focus on the continuing conflict between traditional and progressive education. In recent times, reforms have been directed against school regimes identified with progressive education: there has been a gravitation towards more traditional educational regimes with fact-based curricula and structured learning. These traditional regimes are often perceived to be more egalitarian in the transmission of knowledge and to have a greater suitability for the great mass of children than progressive educational programmes. But progressive forms of education, with their emphasis on humane, creative, critical and interactive learning focused on the individual child, are often better suited to the needs of elite children and closer to what these children are likely to receive in their own homes. They also embody an upbringing for children that would be appropriate for individual autonomy and self-realisation in all children and for the construction of a truly democratic polity. From a socialist perspective, it is the reconciliation of this potential conflict between equality and human freedom that is the central issue to be engaged in the education wars, a focus often obscured in present-day controversies.

The great education wars of the present day are to be welcomed: in the English-speaking world a least, at no time since the post-Sputnik period has education been so much at the centre of attention and debate. As we have seen in Chapter 6, however, discussions concerning the efficacy of this most vital of human activities have centred almost exclusively round its facilitation of economic growth. Left commentary and policy has been, if anything, even more dysfunctional and inappropriate. Marxist tradition is burdened with a history of consigning education to a secondary consideration, an aspect of the superstructure of society or, more egregiously, viewing this activity, which is central to human liberation and equality, with suspicion because of its inevitable embeddedness in the existent capitalist culture. Horrifically, left approaches to education have also become identified with anti-schooling schemes and anti-intellectual ideologies that do little to serve the needs of the great majority of the population and often violate canons of Enlightenment rationality.

Many of these issues have been most thoroughly engaged in the US, which emerged as a world leader in the development of mass education in the latter part of the nineteenth century in the context of the burgeoning Second Industrial Revolution economy. The US had, further, to confront questions of assimilation and integration of a population with an exceptionally high level of cultural heterogeneity, including a large proportion of residents whose first language was other than English. To critics of twentieth-century education in the US, there had been a nineteenth-century system that remains a model of democratic pedagogy, with a curriculum embracing a common core of knowledge and skills necessary for all citizens, a 'community-centered' conceptualisation of education that played a crucial role in the 'making of Americans'.[39] By the early twentieth century, alternatives to the academic curriculum for non-college-bound students had been developed by progressive educators: 'Curricular differentiation meant an academic education for some, a non-academic education for others; this approach affected those children – mainly the poor, immigrants, and racial minorities – who were pushed into undemanding vocational, industrial, or general programs by bureaucrats and guidance counselors who thought they were incapable of learning much more.'[40] We thus have a situation in which what is labelled 'the progressive education movement' is identified by its critics with policies encouraging social and racial stratification in American schools.

The writings of the philosopher and educational theorist John Dewey (1859–1952), the intellectual fount of the progressive education movement in the US, function as focal points for these culture wars. Dewey's approach to learning is linked to his leading role in the distinctively American school of pragmatism, in which even the traditionally abstract discipline of philosophy is recast with a methodology that focuses on problem solving: the way we get to truth – child or adult – is by coping with substantive problems. From a twenty-first-century perspective, pragmatic philosophy, manifesting itself as an activity-based approach to learning, has had some notable successes in the imparting of foreign language and musical skills, such as the Suzuki method for the violin and, as will be noted below, in aspects of science learning; contrarily, it has yet to demonstrate efficacy in the passing on of higher-level historical or mathematical knowledge. Mathematics learning was barely addressed by Dewey (at a time when the world of mathematics was exploding with abstraction), and the philosopher and mathematician Bertrand Russell reserved particular scorn for the philosophy of pragmatism in his *History of Western Philosophy*.

Dewey's ideas have been of worldwide influence, with some of his ideas paralleled by roughly contemporaneous and apparently independent developments emerging in the post-revolutionary Soviet state. This is not a coincidence: both societies – the early-twentieth-century US and the new Soviet state – were concerned with re-examining the educational process, with the aim of educating large, ethnically heterogeneous populations and inculcating a sense of nationhood linked to the respective notions of democracy in the two states.[41]

At the heart of Dewey's reforms was the institution of 'child-centered' as opposed to subject-based learning: 'the typical points of the old education [were] its passivity of attitude, its mechanical massing of children, its uniformity of curriculum and method. It may be summed up by stating that the center of gravity is outside the child. It is in the teacher, the textbook, anywhere and everywhere you please except in the immediate instincts and activities of the child himself.' His approach to learning was, he suggested, nothing less than a Copernican revolution: 'the child becomes the sun about which the appliances of education revolve; he is the centre about which they are organized'.[42]

The typical classroom 'with its rows of ugly desks placed in geometrical order ... is all made "for listening" ',[43] a passive form of learning by which the material 'is not translated into life-terms, but is directly offered as a substitute for, or an external annex to, the child's present life'. Three evils result from this mode of instruction. First, 'the lack of any organic connection with what the child has already seen and felt and loved makes the material purely formal and symbolic. The second evil of this external presentation is lack of motivation ... The third evil is that even the most scientific matter, arranged in most logical fashion, loses this quality, when presented in external, ready-made fashion'.[44] Note that in this critique of what is characterised as a passive educational process, the first and third of these evils relate to cognition, which the new activity-based learning is meant to alleviate: 'No number of object-lessons, got up *as* object-lessons for the sake of giving information, can afford even the shadow of a substitute for acquaintance with the plants and animals of the farm and garden acquired through actual living among them and caring for them ... Verbal memory can be trained in committing tasks, a certain discipline of the reasoning powers can be acquired through lessons in science and mathematics; but, after all, this is somewhat remote and shadowy compared with the training of attention and of judgment that is acquired having to do things with a real motive behind and a real outcome ahead.'[45]

Dewey's central focus was not ultimately upon these first and third evils linked to cognition, but the second evil of the traditional mode of instruction, which was concerned with lack of student motivation. For the child, 'There are not only no facts or truths which have been previously felt as such with which to appropriate and assimilate the new, but there is no craving, no need, no demand.' What is needed is 'an end which is the child's own' to motivate the process of learning.[46] Buried within Dewey's concern with the motivation of the child are issues surrounding class and inequality, an issue which, here and elsewhere, he is only willing to approach elliptically:

> by far the larger number of pupils leave school as soon as they have acquired the rudiments of learning, as soon as they have enough of the symbols of reading, writing, and calculating to be of practical use to them in getting a living. While our educational leaders are talking of culture, the development of personality, etc., as the end and aim of education, the great majority of those who pass under the tuition of the school regard it only as a narrowly practical tool with which to get bread and butter enough to eke out a restricted life.[47]

Dewey signals, again indirectly, that his educational methods are designed to compensate for inequalities in home background:

> If we take an example from an ideal home, where the parent is intelligent enough to recognize what is best for the child, and is able to supply what is needed, we find the child learning through the social converse and constitution of the family. There are certain points of interest and value to him in the conversation carried on: statements are made, inquiries arise, topics are discussed, and the child continually learns... Participation in these household tasks becomes an opportunity for gaining knowledge... if we organize and generalize all of this, we have the ideal school.[48]

Critics of progressive education counterpoise a community-centred view of education with the child-centred, progressive view emanating from Dewey's writings, and yet Dewey asserts that 'the school itself [should] be made a genuine form of active community life, instead of a place set apart in which to learn lessons'.[49] The sharing of so much in terms of the goals of education between Dewey and his critics (especially those left of centre) has not prevented intense hostility breaking out between them. Critics have claimed that Dewey's emancipatory ideas have been perverted by corporate capitalism:[50] what began as Dewey's notion that education should follow the needs and motivation of the individual child became, in the context of pressure from local business interests, a restriction of an academic curriculum to a select, college-bound stream, with vocational and 'practical' courses for others.[51]

Thus, much like the infamous system instituted in Great Britain in the wake of the 1944 Education Act, which invidiously separated out those capable of academic work at the age of 11 from 'the others', a similar separation took place in the US, but under the rubric of Dewey's admonition to fulfil the needs and desires of the individual child, and of democracy: 'Requiring all to take college preparatory studies, said the experts, was elitist; providing an "appropriate" education for every child was democratic.'[52] To critics of the progressive reform movement, its failure 'stems from the contradictory nature of the objectives of its integrative, egalitarian and developmental functions in a society whose economic life is governed by the institutions of corporate capitalism',[53] one in which Dewey's ideas were channelled through the prism of a business community's desire for a workforce suitable to its needs and an educational infrastructure anxious to appear accommodating in this context.[54] For an elite, the new education 'was child-centered, meaning that children's interests and activities were the basis of the curriculum. In big public school systems, however, the "new education" meant vocational and industrial education to train the children of the masses for work in farms, shops, factories, and homes.'[55]

Progressive education, as it emerged in the US, achieved many of its intended goals. For college-bound children in the US, elements of this child-centred elite education permeated the public school system and helped to alleviate the gratuitous burden of rote learning in education: it contributed to the creation of a well-educated, efficacious professional class appropriate to the dominant role of the US in the twentieth century. It is for the children of the masses that the new system failed. As Dewey suggested, school education was invariably regarded by them as 'a narrowly practical tool with which to get bread and butter enough to eke out a restricted life'.[56] His thoughts on education were largely directed at responding to this continuing fact of social existence – that for the great majority of school children, the standard academic curriculum does not motivate them to learn. But the reforms supposedly inspired by Dewey were, for this group, a failure. Dewey's intention to meet the needs of the vast majority of students with their 'practical impulse and disposition' was interpreted in progressive reform as a policy to stream students according to their school grades and the newly emerging IQ tests. Progressive education, its critics contended,

> turned the academic curriculum into elite knowledge for the college-bound, while excluding the large majority of students from gaining deep knowledge of scientific, social, and economic principles, from preparing for higher education or the professions, and from developing the ability to make an original contribution to the advancement of knowledge. At the very moment when science and technology were about to transform modern life, and at the very time [the late 1930s] when the world was

entering a prolonged period of political and military crisis, expert educators were insisting that most students needed a curriculum that limited their access to knowledge and narrowed their understanding to the practical problems of daily life.[57]

The new system could thus be faulted for depriving the great majority of students – future citizens – of the opportunity to gain the knowledge to permit them to engage seriously with the great social and political issues of the day, and for its insidious use of IQ tests to label students in terms of their ability (see Chapter 11). When successful, vocational programmes can provide young people with employment-relevant skills. But, as noted above, an emphasis on practical, vocational training poses real dangers to students in terms of their future employment security: in a world of rapid economic and technological change, many practical skills learned in a vocational context will become obsolescent in the period of a student's future employment, while a more academic education, one linked to literacy, numeracy and broad-based knowledge, can often engender flexibility in a changing environment.

For critics, the Dewey-inspired education movement has been deleterious for the great majority of students in its cognitive aspect – the adaptation to the classroom environment of Dewey's notions on how children learn. For its defenders, 'This model of education supplanted an older one in which children sat still at desks all day and simply absorbed, and then regurgitated, the material that was brought their way. This idea of active learning, which usually includes a large commitment to critical thinking and argument that traces its roots back to Socrates, has helped shape American primary and to some extent secondary education, and this influence has not yet ceased, despite increasing pressures on schools to produce the sort of student who can do well on a standardized test.'[58] For the more extreme proponents of progressive education, 'the particular topics or courses do not matter so much as the ways of thinking that are taught (or not taught) in [courses of study]'.[59] To opponents, progressive education has exacerbated educational inequalities. A leading protagonist in these curriculum wars is Eric Donald Hirsch, Jr:

> The strength of the progressive movement – its lasting contribution – was its empathy with childhood. Its fatal flaw was its faith that the knowledge Americans need would naturally develop when the child became fully engaged in concrete experiences without the encumbrance of a defined academic curriculum... It does not seem to occur to the intellectual descendants of Rousseau that the four-year old children of rich, highly educated parents might be gaining academic knowledge at home that is unfairly being withheld at school (albeit with noble intentions) from the children of the poor.[60]

Thus, according to Hirsch, reading with comprehension can only take place in the context of a substantial amount of implicit background knowledge, a cultural literacy best provided, for other than privileged children, by a school curriculum rich in content, delivered in a more or less traditional manner of lectures and review. This cultural literacy 'constitutes the only sure avenue of opportunity for disadvantaged children'.[61]

There has thus emerged a deep division concerning the substance of an educational programme to be labelled progressive, with both sides representing important and legitimate aspects of this notion. For the followers of Dewey, progressive education involves an emphasis on individual autonomy, active learning and critical thinking; educational systems cannot be expected to reverse shortfalls in levels of achievement by children from low-income or ethnic-minority families, which can only be rectified by reforms (or, as some would argue, as we shall see below, radical change) in the social and economic structure of society. Critics of the Dewey tradition claim that an educational programme focusing on the progressive goals of egalitarianism and social solidarity will need to embody a relatively strict, content-based curriculum and procedures of a traditional kind: only such an educational programme, it is argued, can narrow the achievement gap between different groups in society, a narrowing that plays a crucial role in the raising of a society's average attainment levels.[62]

Those promoting a content-based curriculum complain of the lack of an adequate knowledge base in American students' education,[63] but Hirsch concedes above that progressive education, with its focus on active learning and critical thinking, may well be suitable for 'the four-year old children of rich, highly educated parents'; Diane Ravitch, another prominent critic of progressive education, makes it clear that, in the US, elements of a flexible, progressive approach combined with rich content works well in elite contexts.[64] And those very Asian societies held up as the standard-bearers of traditional approaches regularly look to the education of the children of Western elites for what they take to be its superior flexibility and creativity.[65] If, at their best, progressive approaches have the capacity to create an environment for children that is less oppressive and unpleasant than traditional education, as well as having a greater capacity for releasing a child's creative potential, should such approaches be restricted to an society's elite? In nominally rich societies, these are not speculative questions. They are issues that fall within the practical domain of how such societies wish to allocate their scarce, but abundant, resources, and will be explored in depth in Chapter 11.

The complications of sorting through these controversies and giving them a simple left–right assignation may be seen by considering the reforms proposed in the UK by the secretary of state for education, Michael Gove, in 2013:[66] we have the unusual circumstance of a Conservative minister citing the Italian communist Antonio Gramsci as an intellectual hero.[67] Gove's intention had been to provide a core academic curriculum – English, mathematics, science, history, geography and foreign language – for all pupils. In each of these subjects, the focus would be upon substantive over conceptual skills, with an emphasis, for instance, on chronology and narrative in the teaching of history.

The plan ran into universal disapprobation. It was criticised for having too narrow a focus by preventing 14-year-olds from pursuing vocational subjects and the creative arts.[68] A second complaint, from the historian Richard Evans, directly echoes Dewey: 'A return to narrative in the classroom – to passive consumption instead of active critical engagement – is more likely to be a recipe for boredom and disaffection' and does not engender the cultivation of critical thinking.[69] Evans was also concerned with the overly national focus embodied in the Gove curriculum: right-wing politicians often link calls for a more fact-based curriculum with demands for a patriotic approach to the teaching of history. As a result, children in the UK acquire detailed knowledge of the royal succession, while in the US, children study the teachings of the Founding Fathers (who rebelled against that succession): a national focus is perhaps not the best way to engender mutual understanding between nations. As we have seen, however, others find virtues in factual approaches, suggesting they are more egalitarian than those that focus on broad conceptual issues. They give ordinary children the raw material that elite children imbibe as a matter of course – material that is a prerequisite for more creative approaches.

By far the most widespread criticism of the Gove reforms, however, is that, whatever their intentions, they are pushing children past the age of 14 into an elite mould rather than fulfilling their need and desire to follow a vocational path:

> Of course Gove is right that there is no greater educational crime than writing off a child because of his or her class. But it is perhaps just as unforgivable to judge all children by an elite academic standard under which many will thrive, but which for others will be a millstone of educational failure that will forever hang round their necks ... It is bizarre to insist that the school system must assess children and young people in a way that bears no relation to how they will go on to be appraised in the labour market.[70]

We thus have a situation in which the presence of class division manifesting itself in the context of the school means that society is faced with a range of unacceptable alternatives, all purporting to be progressive and to promote the welfare of children. Either we follow the Gove path and offer an academic curriculum to all pupils, in which case we confront the spectre of a large percentage of 15-year-olds in school faced with demands upon them for an exegesis of *Hamlet* – a waste of time, a humiliation and a mild form of torture for all concerned, both teachers and pupils. The alternative path is to consign a large percentage of the student population to a category – already at the age of 14 – in which their education is linked, not to their future status as citizens in a democratic polity and participants in a world culture, but to how they will be appraised in the labour market. Are these two alternatives the best that can be offered to children in the twenty-first century?

But what is even more bizarre is that the Gove initiative was taking place in the midst of his own Conservative government's focus on academies and free schools,[71] whose claim to superiority was based on their ability to function free of governmental (especially local government) interference. The overwhelming tendency in contemporary educational reform is away from uniformity of curriculum for all students and in the direction of choice and specialisation. In both the US and the UK, a whole set of initiatives have been proceeding in the direction of the marketisation or fragmentation of the publicly funded school system.[72] One example in the US is the implementation of voucher schemes designed to engender parental choice and competition between schools. While symbolically important as a free-market initiative and a major subject of controversy, these schemes have encompassed very small numbers of students, with indifferent results.[73] Of far greater significance in the US and UK has been the development of, respectively, charter schools and academies, with about 4 and 14 per cent, respectively, of total school enrolment in recent years.[74] In both cases, their independence from local government control and the superior governance provided by outsiders[75] (often from the business world) are offered as the keys to their success; this very independence can lead to situations in which children's learning can be put at risk by sponsors' idiosyncrasies, such as a desire to promote creationism in the school curriculum.[76]

Charter and academy schools, however, are responding to a genuine need, even if the driving force behind these ventures are often rich donors and business interests of various kinds. Many low-income parents are desperate to alleviate the low levels of achievement that their children experience in existing institutions: it does little good for defenders of present-day educational structures who are themselves of elite background to opine how well the local school serves *their* children.[77] Charter schools in the US, despite indifferent results overall, have shown gains for children from the poorest backgrounds;[78] in the UK, the academies promoted under the Labour government, largely in deprived areas, registered improvements in performance over the schools they had replaced.[79] It remains unclear, however, to what extent the achievements of successful charters and academies are linked to diversion of resources from mainstream state schools[80] rather than the vaunted independence of these schools.

What emerges is an educational strategy that has abandoned any concept of a community-centred view of education designed to integrate children into a common citizenship. The development of charter schools and academies is a method for dealing with the supposed problem of finding a proper vocational role in society for children from poorer families: academies in the UK emerged from technology colleges. For *The Economist*, charter schools have been successful because of their exceptional freedom to 'shape the school to the pupils' by, for instance, changing the length of the school day. In one exemplary school, for instance, the school year is continuous, with short and relatively frequent bursts of holiday, 'because that keeps learning on track and kids out of trouble'.[81] In such a context, monitoring teachers 'by results' (almost invariably children's scores on centrally administered tests) is a natural concomitant. Thus, in the US, when Eric Hanushek points to the centrality of teacher quality, his means of effecting improvements in this outcome for the US involves the capacity for a school to fire the bottom 5 to 10 per cent of teachers each year.[82] Unsurprisingly, recommendations of this kind have been unpopular with the teaching unions in both the US and the UK.

Charter schools and academies in the US and the UK have been introduced to deal with the dire standards of academic achievement at the poorer end of society and to keep these kids 'out of trouble'. The concept of teacher quality, with its narrow focus on students' test scores, privileges a facility for administering drill and discipline in schools with low intellectual aspirations, in which the pedagogue's intellectual capacity and qualifications are of minimal consideration: the designers and executors of such schemes would find the educational experience emerging from this situation to be unacceptable for their own children. The charter school–academy path seems to be an implicit ratification in the school system of the existence, and permanent presence, of social stratification.

The contemporary debates on the nature of education are to be welcomed. But the fact that they are conducted in the twenty-first century, almost universally, in such a dreary and negative manner even in the richest countries is shocking. If the reader will forgive the semi-tautology, the future of humankind is embodied in its children, and education plays a central role in their development. But what is largely on offer are strategies for rectifying the supposed inefficacy of existing educational structures in order to facilitate higher economic growth: little effort is made in current debates on education to integrate educational reforms with a strategy for producing a more enlightened, freer society. After more than a decade of postwar growth, John Kenneth Galbraith's *Affluent Society* of 1958 was emblematic of a widespread popular discourse in the US indicating the need to look beyond bald measures of national income in considering how best to organise society. Galbraith's focus was the underprovision of resources in the public sphere, including those for poverty alleviation; for others, it became fashionable to write about an emergent crisis in the use of leisure time, under the presumption that the typical work week was set to plunge substantially below the norm of 40 hours a week. The discourse surrounding education in this post-Sputnik era remained, as we have seen, largely concerned with its contribution to economic growth and, implicitly, military power. By the mid-1960s and 1970s, however, and in the wake of the civil rights movement in the US and the war in Vietnam, there was an intensification of critical analysis of the goals and direction of society in general, and of the substance and goals of education in particular. But from the 1980s to the present, the public discourse on education has returned, almost wholly, to its practical efficacy in an economic context.

How did such a state of affairs come to pass? Why, then, has education, this central aspect of human and societal development, returned to being an independent variable in an economic growth equation? Underlying this reversal of fortune are the events described in Chapter 5: if the rich countries, especially the US, viewed their economic status in the postwar world as unchallenged, the precariousness engendered by the more competitive environment evident by the 1980s has now consigned a humanistic perspective to education to the margins of public discourse. As a result, contemporary discussions almost exclusively focus on questions of how education can be used to promote a nation's economic growth rate or, at the extremes of socially aware debate, on the effects of education on income distribution and social mobility.

Radical prescriptions

The emergence of a more competitive, less secure economic environment does not sufficiently explain the fact that the momentum of argument over education has in recent decades been dominated by right-wing opinion and purely economistic concerns: left-wing failures have contributed as well. As argued in Part I, the failure of socialist doctrine in the twentieth century was, to a great extent, to be laid at its own door – an incorrect analysis of the movement and direction of the capitalist economy contributed to the enunciation and implementation of an inappropriate and dysfunctional prescription for a new society.

In the context of education, something comparable, or at least analogous, took place: on the whole spectrum of the left, we see a set of developments that helped engender a reaction on the right – the predominantly pragmatic, economistic approach to education of the twenty-first century. From Marxist thinking, we see a powerful and articulate view emerging in which the arena of education is to be viewed with hostility and distance – as part of the superstructure of capitalist oppression. The most prominent radical writers of the 1970s stood apart from the education wars, having replicated the early-twentieth-century socialist view that treated school activities as part of society's superstructure, whose faults could be rectified only after a general transformation in the structure of society. This tendency was accompanied by the activities of a cultural left whose educational experiments, conceptual and actualised, were dysfunctional and adventurist: there were tiny but very visible and vocal movements for de-schooling and free schools, as well as sectarian and advocacy-based tendencies in education that often took anti-intellectual and anti-rational stances.

What has resulted from the adventurous and whimsical policies associated with the left is something that is both horrifying and ironic – in the US especially, where anti-intellectualism and hostility to scientific thought are peculiarly pervasive in right-wing circles, the latter have been able to pose as defenders of traditional intellectual values and educational standards. The left of this period can thus take partial blame for the present dismal state of the educational debate, having reproduced both the rigid substructure–superstructure dichotomy and the adventurism characterising socialist practice and thought evidenced in Part I.

Karl Marx cannot, however, always be held accountable for the failures of Marxism. In one of his few interventions on education, he condemns those who would advocate that

> Workers should [not] desire ... as happens in the United States of America, [that] the state whose budget is swollen by what is taken from the working class should be obliged to give primary education to the workers' children; for primary education is not complete education. It is better that working men and working women should not be able to read or write or do sums than that they should receive education from a teacher in a school run by the state. It is far better that ignorance and a working day of sixteen hours should debase the working classes than that eternal principles should be violated.[83]

Marx suggests that 'if the apostles of political indifferentism were to express themselves with such clarity, the working class would make short shrift of them and would resent being insulted by these doctrinaire bourgeois and displaced gentlemen, who are so stupid or so naive as to attempt to deny to the working class any real means of struggle'.

And yet a century later, the most prominent Marxist commentary on education in the Anglophone world, from Samuel Bowles and Herbert Gintis, came close to supporting the kind of quietism on this issue that Marx is condemning: 'The politics of education are better understood in terms of the need for social control in an unequal and rapidly changing economic order.' There is 'a close correspondence between the social relationships which govern personal interaction in the work place and the social relationships of the educational system. Specifically, the relationships of authority and control between administrators and teachers, teachers and students, students and students, and students and their work replicate the hierarchical division of labor which dominates the work place.'[84]

The origins of the vast and unprecedented commitment of resources made to public education in the US in the nineteenth and twentieth centuries is thus seen not as an accession to 'the demands of common people', but as part of a process by which 'progressive elements in capitalist class were not so much giving workers what they wanted as giving what would minimize the erosion of their power and privilege the structure of production'. The historical role of educational change is perceived not as a complement to a strategy for economic reform, but as a substitute for it: 'The main impetus for educational change was not...the occupational skills demanded by the increasingly complex and growing industrial sector... [Rather,] schools were promoted first and foremost as agents for...social control'.[85] It makes perfect sense that the genesis of the schooling movement in the US is not to be found in demands for a more highly schooled population, because there is little indication, according to Bowles and Gintis, that the emergent demands of the modern economy needed individuals with this extra schooling. Furthermore, the impetus for more schooling did not come from below, because, it is claimed, additional years in school for individuals are not well linked with better jobs and higher remuneration: 'the mental-skill demands of work are sufficiently limited, the skills produced by our educational system sufficiently varied, and the possibilities for acquiring additional skills on the job sufficiently great so that skill differences among individuals who are acceptable for a given job on the basis of other criteria including race, sex, personality, and credentials are of little economic import'.[86] Bowles and Gintis conclude that school reform, if it is to contribute to a better social order, 'must be part of a more general revolutionary movement – a movement which is not confined to schooling, but embraces all spheres of social life'.[87]

In more recent writings, Bowles and Gintis modify the analysis above. They take a more subdued attitude towards social transformation: 'We took it as obvious that a system of democratic, employee-owned enterprises, coordinated by both markets and governmental policies, was both politically and economically viable as an alternative to capitalism. We remain convinced of the attractiveness of such a system, but are less sanguine about its feasibility and more convinced that reforms of capitalism may be the most likely way to pursue the objectives that we embraced at the outset.' They also note that previously there had been an under-emphasis on 'the value of schooling in contributing to productive employment' and on the pressures operating on schools 'from the democratic polity'. A more important shortcoming, they suggest, is that they 'neglected to devote much attention to how economic systems other than capitalism might better facilitate the achievement of the enlightened objectives of schooling'.[88]

What has remained unchanged in the Bowles–Gintis analysis is the passivity towards the role of education in society that emerges from their methodology: if in 1976, educational transformation 'must be part of a more general revolutionary movement', in 2002, it will emerge from speculation on how non-existent 'economic systems other than capitalism' might better facilitate the achievement of the enlightened objectives of schooling. We have seen this approach to social transformation before in Part I, as socialists veered between a 'nothing less than revolution' political approach and a quietist attitude towards social change. For the Bolsheviks, a real revolution involved a complete transformation of the capitalist base of productive relations in society in accordance with the dictates of the technocratic planning paradigm, a strategy that resulted in the revolutionary adventurism of collectivisation and the first five year plan. In Britain, on the other hand, this very base–superstructure dichotomy generated a curious passivity: focused on the base of productive relations and the issues surrounding nationalisation, only half-hearted reforms were effected in the educational and social structure by the post-1945 Labour government in Britain. For Bowles and Gintis, the most prominent socialist intellectuals in the US to have focused on education, the traditions and methodology of socialism led them to stand on the sidelines as the most ferocious of culture wars was fought out between left and right, and within the left, on the substantive nature of educational activity.

By contrast, intervention into the education wars by the cultural left produced not passivity, as in Bowles and Gintis, but adventurism. An emblematic example was the famous book *Deschooling Society* of 1971 by the radical Catholic theologian Ivan Illich. In ringing and uncompromising terms, we read that 'We cannot begin a reform of education unless we first understand that neither individual learning nor social equality can be enhanced by the ritual of schooling. We cannot go beyond the consumer society unless we first understand that obligatory public schools inevitably reproduce such a society, no matter what is taught in them.'[89] Illich suggests that the goals of schooling are conceived, at least for the children of ordinary people, as preparation for 'the world of work': 'From the beginning of [the twentieth] century, the schools have been protagonists of social control on the one hand and free cooperation on the other, both placed at the service of the "good society", conceived as a highly organized and smoothly working corporate structure. Under the impact of intense urbanization, children became a natural resource to be moulded by the schools and fed into the industrial machine. Progressive politics and the cult of efficiency converged in the growth of the US public school.'[90]

Illich's libertarian design for de-schooling society superficially appears to have affinities with Hayek's abjuration of planning: 'The contemporary ideal is a pan-hygienic world: a world in which all contacts between men, and between men and their world, are the result of foresight and manipulation. School has become the planned process which tools man for a planned world.' His solution, however, is a spontaneous coordination based, not as in Hayek, on self-interest, but upon good will, in a world 'that has lost its humane dimension and reacquired the factual necessity and fatefulness which were characteristic of primitive times'.[91] Illich's scheme centres on the abolition of compulsion: 'To deschool means to abolish the power of one person to oblige another person to attend a meeting ... [Schools would be replaced by] educational networks, [which] would require some designers and administrators, but not in the numbers or of the type required by the administration of schools. Student discipline, public relations, hiring, supervising and firing teachers would have neither place nor counterpart in the networks I have been describing.'[92]

Illich is advocating a system in which access to classes would be free or purchased with educational vouchers. The advantage of 'a system of tuition grants such as that proposed by Milton Friedman and others' over traditional schools is that '[e]ven if they attend equal schools and begin at the same age, poor children lack most of the educational opportunities which are casually available to the middle-class child. These advantages range from conversation and books in the home to vacation travel and a different sense of oneself, and apply, for the child who enjoys them, both in and out of school. So the poorer student will generally fall behind so long as he depends on school for advancement or learning. The poor need funds to enable them to learn, not to get certified for the treatment of their alleged disproportionate deficiencies.'[93] In this new arrangement, by contrast with traditional schools, students learn what they need to know: 'Fundamentally, the freedom of a universal skill exchange must be guaranteed by laws which permit discrimination only on the basis of tested skills and not the basis of educational pedigree.'[94]

Illich's system is naïve and absurd. For adults desirous of mastering the kinds of skills mentioned by him, such as learning to become a chef, such networks already exist, and the problems of credentialism are, relatively speaking, minimal: adult students, especially if they are fee-paying, will not be satisfied with a diploma that does not endow them with the skills to prepare a restaurant meal. None of these examples, however, begins to address or rectify the issues surrounding objective standards versus decentralised, flexible learning approaches in childhood learning, nor the role of credentials in so-called higher-level disciplines, such as Illich's own PhD in history. Nothing in this voucher scheme really helps to alleviate a central issue of concern for Illich – how can we rectify the low levels of achievement that schools generate for children from poor backgrounds? Voucher systems, in the period since the publication of his book, have been sometimes supported by poor families, and by those advocating for the poor, as a mechanism for dislodging the entrenched patterns of failure in the schools frequented by poor children. Overwhelmingly, however, voucher systems have proved to be applications of a right-wing faith that the market would generate improvements in school performance without the need for additional resources, the poor locked in an unequal battle with middle-class parents in terms of their ability to monitor and evaluate school performance and their potential flexibility and physical mobility in dealing with alternative choices.

Illich, like the contemporaneous radical libertarian philosopher Robert Nozick (to be discussed in Chapter 10), wakes up to find himself in bed with right-wing acolytes. For all of Illich's complaints about the poor pay of teachers,[95] his scheme for teachers to be paid according to the number of pupils they can attract for any full two-hour period[96] poses the possibility of returning the status of teachers to the low level of supplicant common in the Middle Ages, or in the *shtetl*. Illich's central problem is that his assertion of the need for free choice in education is not relevant to children; his prose seems to show no recognition of the fact that the needs and the capacity for free choice and rational decision making are different between children and adults. Perhaps because of his own elite background, Illich fails to understand the central role that educational and related institutions can play in the first years of life in the formation of a personality equipped with sufficient knowledge about the range of personal opportunities, and about the world in general, to make free choice meaningful.

His own work remains important, not because of his fruitless pursuit of a substitute for schooling, but because of his vision of what education should be – a process of 'engendering a life-style which will enable us to be spontaneous, independent, yet related to each other'[97] – in other words, equipping us with those very capacities for free choice and decision making that would be prerequisites of Illich's convivial society.

Also representative of the radical tendencies of the 1970s was the British free school Summerhill, a private school famous for its absence of curriculum and compulsion, and with a salacious notoriety for its laissez-faire attitude towards students' personal, including sexual, activities. The school itself, founded in 1921 and functioning up to the present day (having received a satisfactory OFSTED[98] report in 2007), serves a self-selected elite and is of no great significance. The public perception that Summerhill was a radical extrapolation from progressive, Deweyist tendencies has done the latter no favours. Attempts at radical anti-curriculum reforms among the broader population, however, with a special focus upon deprived children, have had unfortunate consequences:

> an educational philosophy of 'do your own thing' was the worst possible prescription for poor children, because it left to their own devices the very children who were most in need of purposeful instruction. Poor children in classrooms where teachers "facilitated" instead of teaching were at a terrific disadvantage as compared to privileged children who came from homes where educated parents read to them, took them to museums, surrounded them with books, and supplied whatever the school was not teaching. There were no such protections for poor kids.

If the school did not make the effort to educate them, no one else was likely to. The radical idea that poor kids should be left free to learn or not was a large gamble with their lives (the gamblers were upper-middle-class graduates of prestigious universities). This laissez-faire approach to education was an abandonment of the fundamental promise of public education to provide social equality.[99]

We thus observe a range of left responses to challenges posed by mass education in the twentieth century, many of which proved to be highly dysfunctional – either a passivity rooted in a traditional base–superstructure view of society, in which educational reform awaits changes in the fundamental power relations of society, or an adventurist approach little connected with the needs of the great mass of the population. The influence of the base–superstructure configuration pervaded socialist regimes of all kinds, most blatantly in the context of the post-Second World War Labour government of Clement Attlee, with its sidelining of educational reform. But even when socialist regimes engaged in extensive initiatives in the field of education, as in the case of the communist regimes of the Soviet Union and Eastern Europe, they were subsidiary aspects of strategies for industrial development and the inculcation of Stalinist worldviews; for a range of social democratic regimes, education was largely conceived of as an aspect of general social welfare provision, along with housing and health provision, to ameliorate deprivation.[100] In all of these cases, the combination of the necessity to alleviate the desperate material needs of the population with the presence, explicit or implicit, of a perception of society linked to a base–superstructure configuration meant that education was never a focal point of social transformation for left-wing regimes.

In the twenty-first century, this pattern may have changed. Critical, largely left-of-centre engagement in the education wars has had three components. First has been an emphasis on the role of economic and social equality as a complement and concomitant to successful educational programmes, to be discussed in Chapter 10; second has been a focus on the importance of early childhood development, to be considered in Chapter 11. Third, dissenters from the market-based consensus have been using substantive examples of successful, largely social democratic educational systems to counter the reforms that dominate present-day public policy: Finland has served as a particular focal point.

Finland has caught the world's attention due to its placement since 2000 at or near the top of the world PISA rankings (see Chapter 6); in recent years, its rankings have declined somewhat vis-à-vis a group of mostly Asian countries, though they remain well ahead of those for the US and the UK.[101] The focus on the Finnish model because of test results is tinged with irony, since it is a system that downplays the centrality of testing and ranking: for Pasi Sahlberg, a key figure in the Finnish Ministry of Education and Culture,

Finland's approach is in contrast with that of the Global Educational Reform Movement (GERM), which involves '[m]aking schools and teachers compete for students and resources and then holding them accountable for the results (student test scores)... [which has led to education becoming] a commodity where the efficiency of service delivery ultimately determines performance'.[102] The irony is more apparent than real, since most observers agree that the PISA tests serve the useful purpose of giving a rough picture of the worldwide distribution of educational standards and achievement, with similar tests playing a comparable, and necessary, role in large, heterogeneous national educational systems, such as that in the US. By contrast, Sahlberg's critique of the GERM is less against centralised testing per se than the role that testing plays in transferring models from the corporate world by making teachers redundant and closing down schools that fail to achieve prescribed targets, in simulation of a competitive market economy.[103]

Sahlberg's objections to the GERM are both on humanistic grounds ('The current culture of accountability in the public sector as it is employed in England, North America, and many other parts of the world often threatens school and community social capital; it damages trust rather than support it'),[104] and more pragmatic ones: using the counterexample of the Finnish system and its international test results, it is evident to him that GERM is not the best way to proceed with educational reform ('None of the best-performing education systems currently rely primarily on... education policies that advocate choice, competition, and privatization as the key drivers of sustained educational improvement').[105]

Finland's success has nothing to do with disproportionate inputs into education – indeed, it is below the US and UK in terms of expenditure on education per pupil and the length of the school year.[106] And despite the indubitably justified protestations made by Sahlberg that Finland makes important interventions into early childhood development, formal education there, as in much of continental Europe, does not begin until the age of seven. In Finland, the world outside the schoolroom appears not to be so lethal, even for poorer children, as to force a lengthening of the school day and year merely, as suggested above by *The Economist* in the case of academies in the UK, to 'keep kids out of trouble'. In the next chapter, forms of learning outside of the classroom – *in situ* – will be examined as they take place in the general society in which individuals from their earliest years absorb and emulate the norms, skills and habits of the general culture and, at a later stage, engage with the work process. Without deep pockets of exclusion dictated by poverty, economic equality thus helps to promote *in situ* learning through the presence in the general society of a common culture that is absorbed outside of the classroom.

Two aspects of the Finnish educational system are of especial interest. The first of these is the exceptionally high standing given to the teaching profession. In contrast to the GERM tendencies to make teacher remuneration and employment insecure and contingent on student test results, Sahlberg suggests that 'Many Finnish teachers have told me that if they encountered similar external pressure regarding standardized testing and high-stakes accountability as do their peers in England or the United States, they would seek other jobs.'[107] He reports polls placing teachers higher in status than medical doctors, architects and lawyers. With secure tenure, teaching hours well below the OECD average and systematic classroom training, the Finnish teaching profession can choose from among the highest-quality graduates and can demand MA degrees in upper-level subject specialisms, even though salaries are ordinary by OECD standards. The popularity and prestige of the teaching profession in Finland should not be surprising: elite private schools in other countries can also attract highly qualified staff with ordinary levels of remuneration in the presence of good working conditions, as will be seen in Chapter 11. The treatment in Finland of teaching as a profession and its apparent success contrasts markedly with Taylorist tendencies that dominate market-based reforms in many countries.[108] This contrast, and the apparent success of the 'Finnish way' in these matters, is of significance both for education and for the discussion in Chapter 12 of working life in the twenty-first century.

A second notable aspect of the Finnish system is the absence of streaming ('tracking') as a key aspect of the reforms: 'The central idea...was to merge existing grammar schools, civic schools, and primary schools into a comprehensive 9-year municipal school.... All students, regardless of their domicile, socioeconomic background, or interests would enroll in the same 9-year basic schools governed by local education authorities.'[109] Education after this period is optional, with students choosing between academic and vocational high schools. As we shall see in Chapter 11, academic research indicates that delays in, or absence of, streaming contribute to successful educational outcomes overall, promoting equality of educational outcomes and the reduction of the role of family background in student performance; in addition, relatively late subject specialisation and breadth of initial training help to maximise the acquisition of transferable skills and contribute to individual mobility and flexibility in the workforce.[110]

Finland thus appears as a leader and successful representative of an educational strategy embodying the absence of streaming, freedom of choice, and late subject specialisation – all components of any socialist educational strategy for the cultivation of social equality, individual freedom, flexibility and security. The Finnish case is of particular interest because its present success is apparently linked to specific policies initiated since the 1970s rather than the presence of deep-seated cultural advantages. For Sahlberg, present-day Finnish eminence in the educational domain can be accounted for by the successful channelling, in the context of specific policy initiatives since the 1970s, of societal resources so that 'by the end of the 1990s, [Finland] became a world leader in reading, science, and math...[a] shift from an elitist and socially divided system of education onto the most equitable public education system in the world'.[111]

But, however encouraging the success of a system giving high status to the teaching profession and promoting equality in education, questions remain concerning the lessons to be learned from the Finnish experience for other nations and for a socialist approach to educational issues. A lack of streaming and differentiation may well have promoted, in the Finnish context, equality of educational outcomes, but for societies starting out with greater levels of inequality than had existed in Finland in their period of reform, such strategies may not be readily available. As we have seen above, when an attempt was made to impose a uniform academic curriculum on state schools in the UK, the programme ran into broad opposition because of its lack of suitability for many students (children from deprived backgrounds could not cope with, or were alienated from, a thoroughgoing academic curriculum) and what was perceived to be the necessity of focusing on a narrow band of subjects to make it viable. Can it be, then, that the causation from lack of streaming to greater equalisation of outcomes may, in part, have a reverse component, whereby a more equal society (such as Finland), with less variance in the life experience of children upon entering school, makes a lack of streaming a plausible and even economical strategy, while it is non-viable in the UK or the US?

And if the socialist goals of education are to be an equal opportunity for self-realisation and full development of personal capacities and not a mere equalisation of opportunities, it is impossible to ignore the reservations from the business class in Finland, and even more so from middle-class parents in the UK, about the lack of streaming in the Finnish system: how do you permit the full realisation of individual excellence in such a context, most especially in subjects such as mathematics, dance and music, where early exposure and intensive development may be critical? Will not affluent parents be tempted to find private tuition to satisfy a child's intensive focus in some such area? If the goal of a socialist educational programme is not equality of outcomes per se but the realisation of each child's potential, then Finland's educational system is likely to be only a very partial realisation of this aspiration.

Sahlberg suggests that the system emphasises individual attention and student counselling, but the resources available for such activities are clearly limited in a system that proudly boasts that its expenditure per student is below the OECD average: if 40 per cent of students in Finland opt for non-academic study when given the opportunity (after nine years of schooling), can we be certain that such decisions represent genuine free choice on their part, rather than resulting from insufficient attention being devoted to children who stumbled or found themselves alienated from their academic studies, perhaps because of the residual aspects of class background acting upon children's aspirations and achievement in the school environment?

Finland has become a focal point for the opposition to market-based reforms, its Dewey-inspired model finding support even among critics of this philosopher's influence on educational systems: 'from an American perspective, Finland is an alternative universe. It rejects all the "reforms" currently popular in the United States, such as testing, charter schools, vouchers, merit pay competition, and evaluating teachers in relation to the test scores of their students.'[112] The danger exists, however, that in the process of battling against these market-based strategies, attention is distracted from the goal, one realisable in the context of rich countries, of an educational system in which children have the opportunity to develop their personal capacities fully. The setting of Finland as a left-wing standard, with its rejection of testing as a means to judge, discipline and sift schools and teachers, may distract attention from the construction of more radical strategies for educational excellence, which go further, and also forego the use of testing to judge, discipline and sift students. Finland's path is suggestive of how to proceed, and of how social and economic equality acts as a facilitator of successful educational development. But however salutary its example, Finland is a small country buffeted by an international context generating economic instability and increasing inequality, and it would be inappropriate to impose upon this nation the burden of solving all aspects of this most fundamental question concerning the future of human civilisation.

And since attention was originally devoted to Finland because of its success on international test scores, it is upon the latter, pragmatic objection to the GERM that other critiques will dwell, to fade if Finland's international testing success should ever recede. There has recently been a focus on problems with Finland's test score results: its success in minimising between-school variation is matched by the highest within-school variation with respect to students' mathematics (PISA 2003), science (PISA 2006) and reading (PISA 2009); second, Finnish grade 8 students have performed modestly on the two TIMSS (Trends in International Mathematics and Science Study) rounds in which Finland has participated. One study suggests that Finnish performance on PISA 'is an enigma', with classroom observations 'more likely to explain Finland's modest grade 8 TIMSS performance than its well-publicised and repeated PISA successes'. Furthermore, Finland's achievements in minimising levels of between-school variation in PISA tests 'may not be a consequence of the quality of classroom interactions but a complex and partially understood interaction of curriculum and culture'.[113]

A key reason why the debates over the Finnish educational system have taken on the character of a left–right conflict is the long-term role of Nordic countries as standard-bearers for economic equality, most especially in contrast to the US and the UK. Since Finland's high average test results emerge from the low level of variance in these results across schools, regions and students, it is plausible to associate this success with its low levels of poverty, an issue to be engaged in Chapter 10.[114] But egalitarian Norway has not registered the kind of success that Finland has had in the PISA races, and Finland's own emergence as an exceptional performer only took place in the 1990s as a result of a series of reforms instituted in the 1970s: there are no simple stories to be obtained showing a mechanical relationship between national educational success and income equality. Above-average levels of economic equality, as in the Finnish context, prove to be a facilitator, but far from a sufficient condition for the creation of a successful educational system.

A missing element

Marx's most visionary writings emphasise that emancipation from capitalism involves movement away from labour power as a commodity to a situation in which human beings exist as ends in themselves. The concept of human capital does nothing to address Marx's concern that the overwhelming mass of human beings in capitalist society function in their working existence as objects to be used in the process of capitalist production. But even if we put such considerations to one side, concentration on individual decision making in human capital theory is a distraction from the fact that the most important forces shaping human development take place in a social context. Thus, the compulsory school environment that a child confronts is linked to a range of political and social decisions made long before the child was born, decisions whose impetus came from both economic and non-economic motivations. Furthermore, non-formal varieties of learning exist in society, including the work environment, as well as those cultural aspects that have cumulated over generations, partially through the external effects of learning. The integration of these influences, as well as the class and family background of the individual under consideration, are decisive aspects of one's educational formulation and take place in a context far removed from individual decision making and, in many cases, long before any personal decisions about elective education.

Individuals not only plan, but are shaped as individuals by an environment that is, to a substantial extent, the product of societal decisions. Households make crucial decisions about the development of human assets, and we must offer them an analogous set of considerations to those conventionally given to capitalists as planners. Thus, at the heart of mainstream analyses of the origins of capitalism is an examination of the role of property rights in capitalist development. As noted in Chapter 1, Douglass North and others, following on from a well-developed literature from Marxist historians, have emphasised the role of the presence of secure property rights and a constrained role for the state to create the kind of environment conducive to the investment and risk taking necessary for capitalist development. But if working people are to be viewed not as commodities but as planners, with a forward-looking perspective for themselves and their children, it makes little sense, either for the individual or for society as a whole, to impose upon them a form of unlimited liability that makes household planning impossible.

And yet such demands are increasingly being made upon working people, when they are called upon, in the name of flexibility, to abandon accumulated skills and life plans in response to transitory economic conditions, or to accommodate themselves to unemployment in their sector of work in the name of creative destruction. Pressure from employers for practical, applied and 'relevant' education for the great mass of the population is likely to continue, despite the tendency of such forms of education to create a workforce that is inflexible – unable to respond to changing economic and social conditions and to plan working careers in a reasonable way because of a limited and overly focused skill base. For a broad range of free-market theorists, just as business cycle downturns are part of the process of creative destruction that can play a productive role in reallocating physical capital to its most productive use, unemployment is viewed from the perspective of labour as a commodity, with disappointed expectations merely part of the market process of incentives, rewards and creative destruction. The notion of individuals and households as planning entities leaves open the possibility that such forms of disruption to the continuity of material life may be not only inhumane, but inefficacious for long-term economic development.

Once humans are taken seriously as capital assets, albeit assets that attempt to plan their own destinies, a disinhibited approach to laying off workers in downturns can have long-term negative effects on labour productivity. These negative long-term consequences can emerge through the absence of work-based learning for young workers and the deterioration of accumulated skills for older ones,[115] with worker insecurity about employment interfering with life planning. From the perspective of human beings as capital assets, cutbacks in consumption by the poor can be very different in their developmental effects on society from a reduction in consumption by the affluent: in the former case, life planning and the household security that underpins it can be put into disarray by any such constriction.

Considerations surrounding income distribution cannot, therefore, be framed simply as a trade-off between equity and efficiency, because high levels of inequality, rather than invariably promoting efficiency through the creation of material incentives, may inhibit wealth creation by deranging attempts at household planning. Thus, a missing element to be explored in the following chapters is the interaction between the social environment and the household in its capacity as a planning entity.

8

The Working and Living Environment

In Chapters 6 and 7, we found ourselves with a narrative in which formal education facilitates economic development. In Part III, it simultaneously acts as a vehicle for personal realisation, the expansion of democratic participation and control of decisions in the modern world. But a narrative based exclusively on formal education would be overly simplistic, with an implicit acceptance of a hierarchy of learning 'between the mode of transmission [of knowledge] in a technical society, with its schools, and an indigenous one, where cultural transmission is in the context of action'.[1]

The economic and social history of the Western world has continued to belie this simple dichotomy between higher forms of knowledge taught in schools and more practical forms of learning. Formal education has, indeed, grown in the prominence it occupies in both the personal and the working lives of individuals and society. In absolute terms, however, individual psychological and intellectual formation continues to be subject to predominant influence from the family, with the working environment and societal influences playing a significant role in learning. The influence of family, the working environment and the broader society is invariably conditioned by class background.

A socialist strategy for human liberation, one that is congruent with the exigencies of the functioning of a modern economy, cannot merely consist of policies entailing universal and equal access to formal education from the earliest years. Associated, concomitant and complementary aspects involve opportunities in the working and living environment for all as participant and decision maker: the socialist future of humankind involves not only formal education but equality and democratic control in society, with the work environment embodying rich opportunities for learning.

Contemporary trends, however, appear to be moving in the opposite direction. Increasing gaps in income and wealth are dictating a fragmented assimilation of the *in situ* knowledge that can be gained simply by living in an advanced economy, and learning in the workplace has been inhibited by the emergence of high levels of unemployment, especially among young people. The growth in inequality in the present day, and the concomitant rise in household insecurity, have inhibited or even derailed long-term household planning of human assets and processes of democratic control. It is in such a context that new socialist strategies must emerge.

This chapter highlights the centrality of learning outside the context of formal education for both individual and national economic development. Most specifically, it focuses upon the role of the workplace as a context for learning and the household as a focal point for planning and skill development. These forward-looking activities are facilitated by the presence of household security rather than an environment of creative destruction.

Learning in the working and living environment

Formal education accounts for only part of the process of the acquisition and dispersion of economically relevant knowledge and skills. The terminological distinction between unskilled and skilled labour has a strong element of social evaluation by embodying the invidious distinction between hand and brain work.[2] In reality, the productivity of even supposedly unskilled labour is contingent upon the human resources that workers bring to tasks as a result of their background, so that much factory work in the past and at present has been dependent on the strength and dexterity of former peasants. In the contemporary world, the advantages accruing to the inhabitants of rich nations extend beyond their acquisition of high levels of formal education; they also embrace a set of implicit or *in situ* advantages simply as a result of growing up, working and living in a leading economy.

In the present day, one-sided policy approaches to human development are common, most especially the doctrine 'if you educate they will come'[3] – a (formally) educated workforce is often held to be the key to attracting investment, both domestic and foreign, with educational policy playing a central role in regulating long-term economic growth and income distribution. But if the working environment itself plays a key role in the learning process, should we rely on whether 'they' (as domestic or international actors) decide it is worthwhile to invest and make jobs available to the population? In reaction, we observe from Ha-Joon Chang a 'just do it' philosophy:

> What really distinguishes the rich countries from the poorer ones is much less how well educated their individual citizens are than how well their citizens are organized into collective entities with high productivity ... Education is valuable, but its main value is not in raising productivity. It lies in its ability to help us develop our potentials and live a more fulfilling and independent life.[4]

Chang's reaction against the widespread education-as-panacea doctrine is salutary, but unreflective of the experience of his home country South

Korea, whose world-historic emergence from poverty emanated, as we have seen in Chapter 6, from a powerful fusion of formal education with industrial policy acting in a complementary manner. In the worst manifestations of an exclusive focus on the industrial aspect of such a strategy, as we shall see below, already developed countries may rely upon their possession of advanced enterprises and sectors to presume an inherent and unshakeable superiority of their 'know-how' that obviates the need for the cultivation of abstract and formalised knowledge.

Overall, however, Chang's emphasis on active engagement in underwriting employment and industrial development rather than waiting for 'them' to invest is supported in the discussions in the chapters to follow. A key (largely implicit) presumption driving Chang's approach is the importance given to the role of *in situ* learning in economic development, in this case learning that emerges from working in the context of 'entities with high productivity', as opposed to formal education. The general notion that there exist whole other domains of learning outside of formal education – here dubbed *in situ* – represents, in truth, a bigger challenge to the education–growth story than any claim dismissing the economic role of formal education in the modern world.

When *in situ* learning becomes an important part of the narrative of economic development, a whole host of important issues needs to be reconsidered. In evaluating the role of the great inventors and innovators of the Industrial Revolution in Britain, opinion among economic historians has moved on from the notion that these practitioners were mere tinkerers, the inheritors of a practical tradition of mechanical engineering from the late Middle Ages. In fact, many of the inventor heroes of the First Industrial Revolution, such as James Watt and George Stephenson, had links to the artisan tradition, but felt the need to supplement this practical knowledge with self-acquired scientific literacy.[5] A widespread recognition has emerged of the importance of these innovators' absorption and adaptation of elements of the abstract achievements of the scientific revolution beginning in the seventeenth century, in which Britain had played, and was continuing to play in the nineteenth century, a central role. Thus, even if the executors of the First Industrial Revolution were not themselves individuals with scientific training in the modern sense, it is hard to dissent from the notion that 'The mechanics, ironmongers, and chemists who are responsible for the technological advances of the age ... moved in a milieu in which the effects of the Enlightenment were pervasive ... the Enlightenment was the reason why the Industrial Revolution was the beginning of modern economic growth and not another technological flash in the pan.'[6]

The social basis of the ability of these practical innovators to absorb aspects of the new science was the fact that, as we have seen in Chapter 6, Britain emerged into the early modern period with levels of literacy and general educational achievement that were exceptionally high by European standards, even if they appeared to stagnate during the Industrial Revolution itself. There is a convincing flavour to recent research suggesting that, in general, achievements in literacy in Britain and other Protestant countries account better for their relative success as vehicles for capitalist development than do Max Weber's claims of an exceptional work ethic among Protestants.[7]

Are, then, great industrial revolutions simply the fulfilment of a top-down strategy? In such a view, the First Industrial Revolution was engendered by the creations of an elite group of enlightened practitioners, which were complemented by an accelerated exploitation of a homogeneous, unskilled workforce, as in Marx's notion of the original accumulation of capital in Britain. More generally, this approach would suggest that industrial revolutions take place when an innovative elite imposes a regime of creative destruction that obliterates existing sectors and replaces them with new ones, in the process making workforce skills obsolescent.

The record, on the contrary, shows that these great revolutions entail a process of building on initial advantages that are broad-based in the economy and society. The economic historian Robert C. Allen concedes that the industrial enlightenment described above – intellectual developments involving a dispersion of earlier scientific achievements in Western Europe[8] – may well have been a prerequisite for the First Industrial Revolution. But this revolution's substantive provenance in Britain, as opposed to, for instance, France, was due to the fact that Britain was, in contemporaneous terms, an already highly developed economy. In the presence of a rich array of technical specialists, the exceptionally high wages (and abundant energy sources) already in place induced the innovation of the range of labour-saving (and energy-using) devices associated with that revolution. Even strong advocates of the top-down industrial enlightenment view suggest that 'Britain was…fortunate to possess a class of able and skilled people, larger and more effective than anywhere else…the high quality of workmanship available to support innovation, local and imported, helped to create the Industrial Revolution.'[9]

Thus, the notion that newly emerging capitalist countries were faced with the straightforward task of creating a malleable, homogeneous proletariat suitable for capitalist development has been questioned in recent years. This tendency has been reinforced by a reconsideration of the role of guilds in the maintenance and transmission of skills in early capitalism. Clearly such a review is overdue, since this stylised view of capitalist development never accorded well with what was known to economic historians, where even the vanguard industries – the cotton mills, and later the railways and shipyards – had their machines maintained and repaired and had key inputs supplied to them by groups of skilled workers organised in groups resembling, and often with residual ties to, traditional guilds: 'Given the frequent assertion that skilled craftsmen and innovators played a crucial role in initiating the Industrial Revolution, there is surely some value in enquiring how this pool of skilled labour was created. This is all the more the case because according to one estimate, in the late sixteenth and seventeenth centuries roughly two-thirds of the English male labour force had at one time or another been apprenticed in one of the greater cities, primarily London.'[10] The tenacity with which craft unions and guild-like groups were able to maintain their influence well into the twentieth century, despite intense employer opposition, is testament in part to the importance, even in conditions of mass production, of this supposedly atavistic phenomenon. This issue has continued resonance today in discussions over vocational education.

In the nineteenth century, continental European nations, still overwhelmingly rural, that wished to match the British industrial achievement found the need to compensate for the *in situ* advantages of a British population already imbedded in the employment fluidity and money-based economy of urban life, as well as the discipline and time keeping of the factory. The great thrust to predominance of the US in the late nineteenth and early twentieth centuries was also reliant in its early phases on the skills acquired by technical specialists and managers from working in an already (relatively) developed economy; this high level of *in situ* skill development was then reinforced by the great advances in formal education that took place. In Chapter 9, we will see that even the great electronics revolution of the postwar US was less a matter of Schumpeterian destruction of existing sectors than a building on the *in situ* skills embodied in these sectors.

These *in situ* skills play a central role in economic development, a fact that can dramatically affect our conception of what it means for an economic activity to be successful or viable. Thus, in a book notable in the literature of modern economic history, Robert Fogel calculated the social rates of return on railroad construction in the nineteenth-century US and concluded that this construction had been excessive, given the range of alternatives, including canals, that were available; railroad building had been fuelled by the substantial government subsidies offered to this sector.[11]

But somewhat over a decade later, the no less prominent intervention by Alfred Chandler[12] highlighted the pioneering role that the railroads played in the Second Industrial Revolution in the US. As we have seen in Chapter 2, the railroads had to solve not only unprecedented engineering issues, but management challenges as well, in dealing, for instance, with timetabling and coordination. The US railroads responded by creating new forms of management involving a delineation between staff and line responsibilities – the fundamentals of the new management structures of the Second Industrial Revolution. The railroads also appear to be the source for modern cost accounting techniques, engendered by the complexity of the affairs being managed. These developments in the US railroad sector necessitated the cultivation of new skills for both workers and executives that were eventually embedded *in situ* and became especially relevant to the even more sophisticated Second Industrial Revolution sectors that were emerging.

In other words, the supposedly overbuilt railroad sector proved to be the seed pool for a range of *in situ* skills and techniques that were central to the Second Industrial Revolution in the US. When we consider these accretions to human assets and to the concomitant institutional development into our calculations, is it still true, as Fogel suggested, that the US railroads were overbuilt? The more general issue here is that a focus on *in situ* learning can reinforce a Chang 'just do it' approach as a strategy for economic development. Calculating the value of such *in situ* effects is, of course, difficult, and their supposed presence could be an excuse for an undisciplined approach, in which any project can be justified by its correlative benefits to skill development: such a criticism has frequently been directed at countries pursuing strategies for growth of import substitution. The alternative, however, of presuming that these *in situ* effects have a zero value is also unviable.

Below, the implications of the presence of *in situ* learning are investigated first for real economies, past and present.[13] The nature of these *in situ* advantages encompasses the whole process of economic development, so that the examples offered here can only be suggestive. First, there are important, if elusive, advantages to 'being in the world' in an advanced economy. Thus, Britain's exceptional lead in urbanisation by the nineteenth century compared with most of its competitors gave it a population that had adjusted or was inured to factory life and other aspects of modernity. In contrast to the overwhelmingly rural populations of continental Europe, urban dwellers in Britain were accustomed to a world in which money changed hands for daily bread and a range of the necessities of life. The expectation of most workers in Britain, that they were not bound either morally or legally to a particular job or employer, meant that a labour force appropriate to the needs of early capitalist development was in place. It was thought unnecessary, therefore, to devote undue resources to formal education, as the Germans were doing, to teach British workers things that came 'naturally'.[14] In the interwar US, ordinary inhabitants had more experience than Europeans with the physical paraphernalia of modern life, such as cars – both driving and disassembling them – a fact contributing to the exceptional mobility of the US labour force over a vast expanse. In addition, there was a greater familiarity in the US with the more superstructural aspects of contemporary existence such as finance – home mortgages, buying on credit and bank accounts – all of which prepared the population for the explosion of white collar work in these areas in the postwar world. In more recent times, the entrepreneurial imagination that created eBay in the US emerged from an environment in which internet use was complemented by a culture, already in place, of the aggressive retailing of goods and of consumers accustomed to searching for bargains.

A second, more palpable element engendering *in situ* learning for the residents of an advanced economy has been the greater likelihood, compared with less developed economies, that the individual in question would be working in an up-to-date enterprise. During the Industrial Revolution, the factory played a crucial role in the creation of contemporary working life, with its reinforcement of habits and work routines in the factory – from the machine and the timepiece[15] to the inculcation of work discipline. Modern enterprises have, furthermore, offered opportunities for learning even in low-level activities, so that a receptive high-school graduate working for Wal-Mart in the US received a far better education in the functioning of highly efficacious (if ruthless) retailing and inventory control than his or her counterpart with an equivalent school background working in the traditional retail sectors still existent in many other countries. It was these managerial factors – supply procurement, inventory and cost regulation – rather than the quality of the cuisine, that so impressed Soviet observers when McDonald's opened restaurants during the Gorbachëv reform period. By contrast, workers received, by general consent, good formal education in the school systems of Eastern Europe and the Soviet Union during the central planning period. But when they went out to work in the centrally planned system they received additional 'learning' by working in notoriously inefficient enterprises using obsolescent technologies that were idle much of the time, which then stormed furiously at target points at the end of the month and year.[16] Thus, in centrally planned economies, workers' (and managers') lack of familiarity with and absorption of the habits and discipline of the modern enterprise were likely to make them less productive than their counterparts in the US, even in cases where their school qualifications demonstrated a comparable or higher level of academic achievement.

Advanced economies will also gain disproportionate advantages over their rivals by the very fact of their intimate knowledge of not only the largest, but the most sophisticated markets for consumer and inter-industry goods and services. In the contemporary world, there has remained, contrary to widespread predictions, a significant demand in rich countries for locally based writers of computer software who possess the design skill and business knowledge to service the specific needs of their clients. In addition, the goods and services offered up in rich nations will, in many cases, be harbingers of what will be demanded in lesser economies in the future. In the US in the first half of the twentieth century, 'the mass consumer as target mightily concentrated the collective entrepreneurial mind to turn out more and more inventions of a second order of ingenuity. These were the hallmarks of the United States' fabulous consumer market',[17] with the status of several leading companies such as Coca Cola, even in the twenty-first century, due to little more than the cumulative impact of image building.

Participants in established economies thus possess a range of *in situ* advantages – the learning that comes about simply from living and working in an advanced-level economy and its associated enterprises, and the gains associated with a large internal market. Perhaps the most formidable obstacles for any potential challengers to established economies are *in situ* advantages embodied within institutions – firms, the financial infrastructure and government bureaucracy. The advantages that emerge in these contexts build on prior human asset and institutional development: the high-level functioning of these institutions further cultivates *in situ* learning for both workers and management, as we have seen above. This co-determination and development of human assets and institutions suggests that, in the present context, one can put to one side the literature posing a dichotomy and rivalry between these two factors for explaining economic development.[18]

Some of the *in situ* advantages of advanced economies will have, however, an inherent tendency to evaporate. Being close to the market in advanced economies reverses itself as less developed economies grow: the emergence of mass cinema production in India and China, for instance, symbolises the ability of emergent economies to satisfy their specific cultural and material needs. In addition, there are several new factors accelerating the deterioration of *in situ* advantages in the present period, and they are of two kinds: those related to the more rapid dissemination of knowledge, and those linked to the ubiquitous presence of the multinational enterprise.

Dissemination of knowledge improved dramatically over the twentieth century, and has eroded the tendency for modernity to be identified solely with the largest enterprises. As we have seen, at the beginning of the twentieth century, a key competitive advantage of giant firms in the US had been their ability to act as monitoring stations for new developments in science, technology and business practice throughout the world. In more recent times, this privileged ability on the part of large, established enterprises in advanced countries to monitor state-of-the-art technology and business affairs has been reduced by developments in the electronic dispersion and storage of knowledge, all factors militating in favour of an increasingly competitive environment both within economies and internationally. These difficulties for large, established firms are exacerbated by the tendency, described earlier, for the rate of diffusion of new ideas to accelerate as the ratio of science- to craft-based knowledge rises, so that it has become easier for newcomers with the appropriate formal education to overcome the obstacles to entry into even (and perhaps especially) high-technology sectors. In such an environment, the role of intellectual property rights in the protection of the wealth of advanced countries takes on an ever greater centrality, as technological advantage is ever more connected with replicable science rather than craft-based mysteries.

A further factor accelerating the deterioration of *in situ* advantages in the present period is linked to multinational activity and the increasingly international orientation of established firms. When Wal-Mart sets up abroad, foreign workers performing day-by-day tasks for their supply chains or retailing outlets will gain the skills that had formerly accrued only to US domestic workers; the speed of locally based employees' mastery of the techniques of Wal-Mart's software programs for inventory control is likely to be more rapid now than in the days when even sophisticated inventory control in retailing was linked to a craft-based feel for the market.

The increasingly international orientation of established firms also threatens the ability of national economies to retain *in situ* advantages. In earlier periods, the marketing of new products worldwide by the great enterprises in the US was part of a life cycle: they were first offered to the home market, and only in their maturing phases were they marketed abroad.[19] But in the contemporary practice of large firms, it is much more typical, as in the case of the great software producers such as Microsoft, to make a global launch of new products, so that competitive advantages to the home country, and the incumbent *in situ* advantages of its workforce in using this software, are diminished by this process. Such tendencies are both a response to, and a cause of, an increasingly competitive environment. They are reinforced by the contemporary corporate fashion in favour of offering even proprietary items for sale on the market rather than retaining these items for exclusive use (as had been the former practice of IBM with its in-house semiconductor production), a complementary aspect of the practice of vertical dis-integration (out-sourcing). Thus, current corporate practice – the worldwide marketing of goods, including inter-sectoral products such as business software, and the increasing tendency for proprietary products to be marketed – promotes the dissemination of world-class working environments globally, the elimination of advantages linked to the possession of nationally based technologies, and the dissipation of on-the-job learning advantages to employees of advanced economies.

Historically, a common pattern of response to the erosion of *in situ* advantages, from Imperial China in the early modern period to Britain and the US more recently, has been one of denial, only at a later stage evincing alarm at decline, as evidenced in Chapter 7. In early-twentieth-century Britain, dominant groups manifested a disdain for industry as opposed to more gentlemanly pursuits.[20] In the British engineering sector, faced with a decline vis-à-vis the German industry, we find a conviction that learning which results merely from working in a British context (*in situ* learning) will be perfectly adequate, and that technical training is for foreigners: 'interest...in gaining university technological qualifications...remained sluggish [before the First World War]...when the war came, it still grew painfully slowly, in the face of a scarcely diminished confidence in the value of experience'.[21] At both school and university level, Britain was correspondingly laggard in this period in matching the achievements of its chief economic rivals, Germany and the US.

The presence of *in situ* advantages may now be a consideration working in reverse for rich nations. Countries such as the US and the UK have permitted a rapid rundown of their industrial sectors, with a concomitant loss of well-remunerated jobs that has contributed to a widening of the income distribution within these societies.[22] All this has taken place in the name of free trade and the efficacy of creative destruction; what has also been lost or dissipated is a range of *in situ* skills used in networks of complementary activities in these industrial clusters. It is highly implausible that advanced countries can successfully respond to these losses by the creation of planning zones and production networks in imitation of the export-led development strategies of a range of Asian economies; US manufacturers such as Apple no longer even pretend that domestic production is a serious consideration.[23] For nations that have lost manufacturing capacity, undoing these declines will be a long process, and is perhaps irreversible: as we have seen in Chapter 6, even a residual specialisation in the innovative aspects of manufacturing becomes difficult in the absence of a successful interaction between skills in the manufacturing sector and those linked to research and development.[24]

An implication of the discussion above is that the creative destruction strategies pursued by the Thatcher and Reagan administrations and their successors from the 1980s to the dawn of the new century were dysfunctional. In both countries, these policies were initiated with high levels of unemployment and characterised by a pronounced rise in inequality that weakened living-in-the-world *in situ* development for large sections of the population, with the decimation of whole industries writing down the value of work-based learning in these sectors; the insecurities engendered by these policies upset the ability of many households to formulate long-term plans and develop their human assets. This general perspective will be defended below and in subsequent chapters.

There is, however, an alternative view of these developments. For both the US and the UK, the period under consideration, especially the 1990s, was one of indubitable success in GDP growth,[25] with the US maintaining the elevated economic position of its multinational enterprises, most especially in areas of high technology.[26] A key role was played by financial markets in the US: their size and sophistication, and their proximity to productive and technological capacity in the US and to consumer markets, made them a magnet for capital worldwide. The financial sector was crucial 'not only in pushing so-called "inefficient" firms out of business, but also in supporting risky but innovative startups through the US's unique venture capital markets, whose disbursements grew tenfold in the 1980s alone'.[27] The package of policies embodying creative destruction, union busting and financial deregulation in both the US and the UK thus appears to have been a great success.

The question arises: a great success for whom? As we shall see in Chapter 10, the rises in inequality in both countries over this period bring into question whether the putative gains have reached more than a small section of the population; more generally, we may question whether growth in GDP is an appropriate metric for judging economic success. For the US in particular, real hourly earnings have been stagnant for large sections of workers.[28] Furthermore, the policies of financial deregulation pursued in both the US and the UK are widely regarded as having been central to the generation of the economic crisis of 2007–8 and the subsequent stagnation in the US and worldwide. Whether the above strategy can serve as a model for other nations is contingent on the extent to which the attraction of resources from the rest of the world – financial capital from Europe to the US (at least partly because of the greater malleability of labour markets there), as well as foreign-born graduate students in science and engineering – are part of a zero sum game that not all nations can emulate simultaneously.

This economic strategy and the economic policies associated with it also generated winners – vested interests in favour of a neoliberal strategy for economic development. They are likely to use every intellectual and rhetorical weapon at hand to defend such policies. One class of such devices involves a focus on national competition for survival: it may take the form of the need for competitiveness with other nations (an issue discussed in Chapter 10), or, more primitively, it may use the device of focusing blame on other nations, as in the case of conflicts between countries over the (mal)functioning of the European single currency, which is commonly approached by attributing the difficulties experienced to the feckless Southern Europeans. Other common devices direct attention to domestic residents as the cause of all problems – the unemployed, those on public assistance and immigrants. But in the context of a rising share of top-end incomes, it is becoming more difficult for those with power to make demands for financial probity in the form of cutbacks to public services under the rubric of equal sacrifice.

The dominant neoliberal strategies have thus tended to be of benefit to, at most, a highly restricted group within society. Such strategies may, in fact, not be viable in the longer term because of the instabilities they inherently generate; they may also provoke social and political conflict both between and within nations. In the discussion below and in subsequent chapters, however, the focus will not be upon a critique of how these policies exacerbate economic instability. Rather, starting from a positive focus on broad-based human development linked to household security and equality of opportunity, neoliberal policies are, rather, seen as factors interfering with the ability of households and the individuals within them to make long-term plans for the development of their human assets. The mortgage debts linked to the economic crisis of 2007–8 are thus seen as symptomatic of this economic insecurity, with the looming crisis of student indebtedness in various countries even more directly an indication of the blockages to human development in the present-day economy.

Employment and training

The significant rises in levels of unemployment since the economic crisis of 2007–8 have generated a renewed urgency for the pursuit of policy approaches to deal with this problem. The issue to be addressed here, however, is of a more long-term nature. In Chapter 7, a key component of economic development is seen to be the expansion of formal education. The consideration here, by contrast, concerns the role of work experience in the *in situ* learning process,[29] so that rises in unemployment, and especially youth unemployment, incumbent on the crisis of 2007–8 pose a threat not only to social stability and well-being but to the human component of long–term economic development.

In the OECD, unemployment rates have been around 7 per cent, with rates in the US and UK at about 5.5 per cent; only Japan, among large OECD countries, has maintained a rate well below 4 per cent. The European Union and the euro area generate the highest registered unemployment rates among rich countries, with rates of almost 10 and over 11 per cent, respectively; Germany is the exception among large European economies, with unemployment falling to under 5.0 per cent.[30] In most OECD countries (Germany being an exception among large countries), these trends have been accompanied by significant rises since 2007 in the share of those unemployed for 12 months or more. Long-term unemployment especially creates the risk that the skills of the unemployed population – their stock of human assets – will be run down and that employers will treat workers as damaged goods. The recognition of this possibility in the economics literature concerning the hysteresis effect is a rare instance of the treatment of labour as other than a commodity, and has profound implications for the costs of unemployment to society.[31]

Present-day labour market conditions are especially unfavourable to young and low-skilled workers, who face severe difficulties in entering employment and finding stable and decently paid jobs.[32] It is often claimed that such problems are exacerbated by established, unionised workers whose presence and interests will be dominant in collective bargaining,[33] so that 'unions may have helped to prevent increased earnings inequality, but...largely at the cost of greater unemployment'.[34] In a related issue, it appeared to be orthodox doctrine as of a few years ago that deregulation of labour market institutions and wage flexibility were 'the keys to economic success',[35] with the latter identified with economic growth. Policies to weaken unions and introduce labour market flexibility are easy to dismiss in the context of the role they play in the exacerbation of inequality, but it is useful to pursue this question further.

It is difficult to make a straightforward comparison of relative success in mitigating unemployment in the market-driven US labour system compared with the EU, with its stronger employment protection legislation and greater union influence. US success in unemployment vis-à-vis Europe only emerged after 1990, with the problems surrounding German unification: prior to this date, European protection of existing jobs proved to be of greater weight than any weaknesses in job creation.[36] In the last decade, the issues surrounding the European single currency and the widespread financial crisis of 2007–8 have further exacerbated the difficulties in isolating the role of labour market institutions in generating or mitigating unemployment. The relative success of some countries in the European Union with high levels of unionisation and centralised bargaining in containing unemployment, including youth unemployment, complicates the drawing of any simple empirical conclusions.

In addition to the intrinsically deleterious effects of increasing unemployment, the latter's significant rise in recent years may be exacerbating other long-term trends that have reduced the bargaining power of workers and have generated increasing inequality. Overall, the pressures mounting on the working population of the OECD, especially the young, are unprecedented since the early post-Second World War period. The US, in the period leading up to the crisis (1984–2008), evidenced a decline in long-term employment not accounted for by job loss statistics, likely due to employer-initiated terminations, with the concern that 'employers are moving toward greater reliance on temporary workers, on subcontractors, and on part-time workers'.[37] The dramatic rise in job loss in the subsequent recession period has exacerbated these tendencies.[38] In Britain and other European countries, there appeared to be no decisive tendency in workers' perception of job risk in the pre-recession period, but overall well-being at work was already declining due to work intensification and increasing perception of a lack of autonomy in job tasks,[39] developments likely to have accelerated in the subsequent period of job loss and recession.

It is in this context that rises in youth unemployment consequent on the 2007–8 crisis emerge as particularly pernicious, impinging upon *in situ* learning, long-term economic development and social participation. In the period since the crisis, the youth unemployment rate in rich countries has increased to over 18 per cent (over 20 per cent, if we include discouraged workers – those who have given up looking for work), with 16 per cent neither in employment nor in education or training. The job market for young people has been characterised by longer job search periods and lower job quality than heretofore, with more than one-third of the cohort unemployed for at least six months. There are significant variations across countries, with youth unemployment rates below 10 per cent in Switzerland, Norway, Germany, Japan, Austria and the Netherlands, with the euro area and European Union at 23 per cent, the UK at 21 per cent and the US at 16 per cent.[40] This period has evidenced, as well, substantial increases in part-time and temporary work and 'overeducation': youth with higher levels of education are increasingly taking up jobs that they are overqualified to do, in some cases displacing young people only capable of working in the limited number of unskilled jobs available. The long-term scarring associated with high youth unemployment entails a loss of work experience and an erosion of skills already acquired. Increasing numbers of young people face a transition to working life that involves more and longer periods of unemployment and spells of temporary or suboptimal employment. It appears that the effects of this scarring upon long-term employment and wages can persist for decades.[41]

These are issues of the utmost consequence for the maintenance of societal cohesion in rich countries. Few, if any, of these longer-term problems would be alleviated by free-market solutions that downgrade remuneration, working conditions and unemployment benefits.[42] Some of the most politically effective right-wing critiques of employment protection legislation for young workers suggest that it may generate unemployment, with employers fearing that it will be difficult to dismiss workers once hired. But even if right-wing policies were successful in yielding an increase in youth employment in marginal, transitory work by removing employment protection legislation, such forms of work are likely to offer little in the way of dealing with the necessity, indeed the obligation, to give all young people an opportunity to integrate and participate fully in society. In most cases, the latter involves a path to a career that includes the acquisition of broad-based skills in the context of full-time employment. An adequate resolution of the issues surrounding full participation is a prerequisite for the generation of democracy in the workplace and society.

In general, mechanisms have emerged in the form of Active Labour Market Policies (ALMP), the most important of which are training and vocational programmes, and those intended to assist in job search by making links between employers and employees.[43] The intention of ALMP is to lower the level of unemployment for any given level of job vacancies in the economy (in formal economic terms, to move the Beveridge curve relationship inward). Critics of this skills mismatch approach to unemployment suggest that the onus of unemployment is then shifted onto workers who supposedly lack the requisite skills: 'The point of the argument is to then say: "We don't need to ramp up demand or infrastructure investment. We need to fix people" ', all reinforcing the desire of firms to shift the costs of training to the public sector.[44]

To the extent that full participation in society has a professional identity as a prerequisite, then the issue of training is critical, most especially for the majority of the population who do not complete degrees in higher education. What is the relationship between present-day trends in ALMP, most especially training, and broader democratic goals? Two broad generalisations can be made. One decisive contemporary opinion, as noted earlier, is that much task-specific vocational training administered in a non-workplace context is a waste of time: the most important skills to be developed outside of the workplace are a mastery of fundamental literacy and numeracy. Thus, the sinister notion that the non-college-educated working class could simply be taught the practical skills needed for work, with the higher learning left to others, turns out to be an inoperative strategy: narrowly focused training outside of the workplace, from both the perspective of the individual worker and that of society, is likely to be less productive than a broader, seemingly less practical education that equips individuals with literacy and numeracy and other broadly based skills that are essential for a lifetime of work in changing circumstances.[45] In such conditions, basic academic knowledge emerges not so much as the underpinning of modern civilisation, culture and democracy but as a necessary aspect of the functioning of contemporary capitalism.

The second broadly held opinion about training in contemporary capitalist society somewhat contradicts the first; it also has more ambivalent ramifications for individual autonomy and democratic control. From an employer's perspective, the skills learned at work should be relevant – as narrow and focused as would be consistent with fulfilling the job at hand, and not necessarily those that would contribute to the worker's autonomous functioning across a range of employment in a lifetime of work. Such an approach cuts across the needs of the majority of young people, for whom participation in working life is a crucial aspect of the learning process, one that will take place under the aegis of capitalist enterprise: 'The formation of skills through work, through training, and through everyday activities...is hard or impossible to substitute through other channels'. But 'it is not merely the amount of work experience that counts: the extent of training, its utilization, and the quality of the learning environment are crucial'.[46] It is for this reason that workplace learning and, inevitably, German approaches to these problems have received special attention among the range of ALMP, most especially its dual system integrating classroom learning with training in the form of work-based apprenticeships. The latter emerge out of consensual agreements between employers (and employer associations), labour unions and the state. This system involves a degree of voluntary commitment to training provision on the part of employers in the presence of a detailed regulatory framework; monitoring institutions for these agreements exist in Germany but are absent in Anglo-Saxon countries.[47]

Most especially in the wake of the crisis of 2007–8, the pressing need to lower levels of youth unemployment, and the apparent efficacy of the German dual system in facilitating this result, may mask the fact that in pre-crisis times, German apprentices occupied roughly the same place relative to unskilled workers and college graduates as is held by high-school graduates in the US:[48] these apprenticeships do not appear to be mechanisms for the construction, or reconstruction, of a middle class from working-class occupations and backgrounds. On the contrary, the German vocational training system has been linked to policies of early streaming that exacerbate divergence in academic performance in school based on class background.[49]

The collective and corporatist nature of the dual system in Germany embodies a range of on-going conflicts between labour and capital. The first issue concerns who pays for the costs of these apprenticeships, which are commonly linked to 'compressed wages and limits on mobility, rather than [to] an emphasis on training for firm-specific skills'.[50] German labour unions' acceptance of wage compression for apprentices to the level of one-third that of a skilled labourer is usually contingent upon, among other factors, firms' willingness to create an adequate number of apprenticeships and the quality of training. The state plays a role, sometimes with business-friendly approaches to training regulations that lower the costs of training to firms, and at other times by posing the threat of a training levy in order to, for instance, encourage firms to create subsidised apprentice places for disabled or difficult-to-place young people.[51]

This second issue surrounding the German system exemplifies the fundamental tension over worker training described above: 'while trade unions prefer to have the broadest possible training to foster the trainee's occupational autonomy, employers advocate a narrower and directly operational training'.[52] The interests of the young worker, and of the broader society, can be identified with the labour union position on this issue. It is preferable, if for no other reason than the sacrosanct notion of labour flexibility, that young people be trained broadly and equipped with a capacity to learn a range of new skills to adapt successfully to a lifetime of work. The transfer of a version of the German worker training system to the UK or the US, with their weaker labour union presence, is in danger of taking the form of indenture of young workers to serve the immediate needs of cooperating enterprises – with a fine tuning of workers' skills to suit the demands of the employer.

A third issue underlying potential conflict between labour and capital in the arena of training is concerned with the use of associated technology. It has recently been suggested, in the spirit of Braverman and Noble (see Chapter 6), that the technologies (and concomitant skills) adopted in a particular work context are not purely dictated by the state of technological knowledge, but have an important level of mediation contingent on class and power relations: 'What are relatively low-skilled and poorly paid jobs as cleaners and nursing assistants [in hospitals] in the United States have been transformed into more-skilled, better-paid jobs, with broader tasks and in less Taylorized work organizations, in Denmark, the Netherlands, and, to a lesser extent, France' as a result of conscious public policies in the latter cases.[53] In more general terms, the characteristics of worker training and the technological conditions associated with this work are not mere technocratic questions to be sorted out by experts, but are linked to broad issues of class power and the resultant social decisions and outcomes. In the context here of so-called low-skilled work in rich countries, it is inappropriate for the working conditions and the technologies used (in, for instance, hospitals) to be determined by levels of minimum costs that can be attained with transitory labour.

Socialist strategies must have a long-term focus on bringing about, wherever possible, a professionalisation of so-called menial tasks, with the intention of giving such jobs a personal dignity and higher remuneration than would be dictated by so-called free-market outcomes. With the increasing centrality of tasks such as care for the elderly in the economy of the twenty-first century, the political economy of socialism must redirect some of the attention traditionally given to enterprise and especially production-level work practices and concern itself with the raising of the status of the labour force involved in these services.

The forms of *in situ* learning that take place in the enterprise are thus irreplaceable, but have precarious aspects in the context of broader social needs. Most especially in periods of economic crisis, including mass unemployment, with bargaining power shifted in the direction of the employer, worker training and the work processes adopted are likely to move in a narrow, employer-focused direction that is not in the longer-term economic interests either of the young worker or of society in general. Furthermore, in such strained economic conditions, there is likely to be increasing impatience, from young workers no less than others, with attempts to include in the learning process elements of non-vocational, academic education, such as study relevant to general citizenship. The alacrity with which many young people, especially those from working-class backgrounds, pursue vocationally oriented formal education or apprenticeships and abandon academically oriented studies should not be accepted sanguinely as a fact of life.

This is in no way to denigrate non-academic education, with many of the luminaries of our civilisation, from athletics to music, notable for intense mastery of a craft and not themselves intellectuals or people of culture.[54] But given the importance of academic study of, for instance, history and civic affairs for critical thinking and democratic control of society, any tendency for it to be given a secondary role must be considered a retrograde development. In the current climate, 'the European model [of skill formation] identifies employability, not citizenship, as the central goal of education and training':[55] the education of 'the others' most especially – the majority of the population who do not complete university – is less likely than ever to equip them intellectually to assert themselves individually and collectively in the social and political environment in which they function. In the workplace, young workers especially find themselves as supplicants in depressed labour conditions, and are less likely than ever to assert control over their conditions of employment.

Present labour market conditions are thus conducive to the generation of a generalised passivity on the part of the workforce vis-à-vis its immediate conditions of employment, with little assertion of worker demands through either substantive labour union activity or spontaneous action. Perhaps as a result, practically all discussion in the popular and academic literature has taken the form of what 'we' (the decision makers) can do for 'them' (the passive and likely insufficiently skilled working class) to make them more attractive to domestic employers, rather than emerging as a response to emphatic demands from workers for change. A further level of passivity is evidenced at the level of the nation state, where the necessity to make the economy attractive to foreign investors is often seen as a key task of national economic policy. For decision makers in contemporary society, little attention is directed at how to integrate this working-class grouping (indubitably a majority of the population) into a democratic polity in which it has significant influence over its own destiny. A complementary goal would be the transformation of the workplace into a venue that offers continuous opportunities for skill enhancement and broad-based learning to the workforce. These characteristics – democratic participation and opportunities for learning – would be central in distinguishing a capitalist from a socialist enterprise, and will be re-engaged with in Chapter 12.

Security and household planning

Once human beings are viewed as assets and not commodities, conventional conclusions concerning the nature of rational economic policy may well be upturned. A common aspect of right-wing ideology is to suggest that policies leading to higher levels of insecurity for the general population and a redistribution of income in favour of the well-off are not only a price worth paying, but inextricable aspects of capitalist dynamism and development. In pursuit of this Brave New World, individual households are to take personal responsibility for investing in themselves, whether in the form of making decisions about retirement or education for their children. Thus, it is claimed, the reduction of state compensation for the bad decisions of individuals, such as guaranteed pensions even for the feckless, reduces moral hazard and raises societal efficiency. In his prescient book, *The Great Risk Shift*, Jacob Hacker documented for the US, well before the crisis of 2007–8, that the squeeze in the incomes and rising indebtedness of ordinary families had been complemented by a dramatic rise in economic insecurity emerging from an increase in the volatility of family incomes and an erosion of state and private benefits linked to unemployment compensation, health care and retirement.[56] And for a range of countries across the OECD in this period, 'households have now become more directly responsible for the management of financial risks than before, with fewer layers in between'.[57] This process of individualised 'optimal investment policy',[58] as we shall see in Chapter 12, is, in the eyes of the visionaries of finance, only in its initial stages.

Ironically, a concomitant aspect of the ideology generating this insecurity has been that these measures have been necessitated by the need to create an environment of stability in which businesses could invest, innovate and make plans for the future – low taxes, stable prices and a malleable workforce with minimal recourse to collective rights. This new ideal of flexibility is well suited to an elite of workers, whose ability to create individualised flexible employment by moving between firms 'makes Silicon Valley an exciting place for high-tech professionals', even if for janitors, flexibility has meant a reduction in wages and working conditions.[59] In such an environment, typical households will have a deteriorating capacity to develop strategies and plans for their own long-term development: they are impelled, with increasing insecurity and flexibility, to accommodate employers' needs, functioning more like commodities than as fulcrums for long-term planning. With the presumptive excuse of the need for the creation of an environment in which capitalist planning and innovation can flourish, countries across the OECD since 1980 have adopted policies under which employers have increased their freedom to hire and fire at will and dictate terms and conditions of work.[60] It is not at all evident that these policies have been successful in improving economic performance, even in the myopic terms in which success is cast.[61]

In the context of long-term societal and economic development, it makes little sense to treat human beings in the twenty-first century as commodities who should passively accommodate themselves flexibly to the work conditions on offer. On the contrary, people have plans and aspirations for, among other things, the development of their skills and capacities and those of their offspring: the economic success of public policies will be substantially contingent on the extent to which these policies facilitate the ability of individuals and households to execute and fulfil these plans. In societies with high levels of economic insecurity, all but the highest-income groups will suffer material and cognitive distractions from rational planning due to insecurities surrounding the threats posed by unemployment and ill health. For those (the great majority of the population) with minimal stocks of wealth, shortfalls in income pose a substantive threat to the maintenance of normal life, so that the cost of disappointed expectations is not the same for all income groups.

In societies with wide class divisions, the upper layers of society benefit from social networks and personal contacts that, when combined with the advantages linked to formalised knowledge and financial resources, yield a sense of security and control over the future that facilitates rational planning by a household or an individual. Societies that have mitigated some of the damaging effects of inequality will experience higher levels of social mobility than more unequal ones (see Chapter 10), and are likely to enjoy long-term benefits in economic development from policies in which households have a capacity to plan their futures in a rational manner. From a slightly different perspective, it has been argued that

> the human capital of a nation is improved by a well-functioning system of social services. Such a system makes it possible for the workers to feel less insecure, and gives them a feeling of belonging to the system. Such a sense of belonging leads to stable societies with a strong sense of cohesion. In addition, a well-functioning system of social services may lead people to be willing to take more risk in starting new risky projects, knowing that failure will not condemn them to poverty. In short, a well-functioning social system creates a 'risk-taking social capital' that ultimately leads to an improvement of the productivity of a nation.[62]

Thus, many of the sacrifices demanded of the working class in recent years may well have been of minimal efficacy even if viewed from a purely economic (long-term GDP growth) perspective: if labour is viewed as a capital asset and not a commodity, improvements in 'efficiency' from higher rates of exploitation and insecurity have to be weighed against a deceleration in the growth, or even a depreciation, of the human capital stock.

The most straightforward reason to suggest that greater equality and household stability are conducive to growth is through the influence of income distribution on human capital formation – the ability of individuals to invest in education. It is still common for these issues to be considered as if questions of differential endowments of wealth and access to credit markets for children of different classes were of no significance,[63] despite the presence of such gaps even in societies thought to be relatively egalitarian.[64] As we have seen in Chapter 7, human capital theory views decisions on how much (and what kind of) education to acquire to be based on rational calculations of expected returns linked to the individual's intrinsic ability. There is also commonly an emphasis on different rates of time preference between individuals – impatient individuals will not be willing to defer consumption in the present in order to acquire more education.[65] But households have differential access to information. Under such conditions, notions of decisions made by a typical individual have to be abandoned. As we have seen, all parents may want the best education for their children, but the ability to evaluate the efficacy of different educational paths will vary significantly between households of different classes.

Even where in a formal sense the relevant information concerning schools and education is widely available, households will still vary by class in terms of their possession of the ability to interpret this information – the cognitive capacity and educational background needed to choose and monitor schools, and the ability to use a range of family and personal analogies to evaluate educational strategies (in the household in which I grew up, there were no individuals of professional capacity anywhere in the family, so that the term 'professional' was, by default, identified with a 'doctor').[66] In societies dominated by notions of place and with limited horizons dictated by class, even egalitarian schooling may make limited headway in generating economic mobility.[67] In the absence of deficiencies in physiological capacity (not being hungry or diseased), less-than-affluent households will still suffer from insufficient financial resources to purchase high-quality child care, a lack of domestic physical resources (the space in the home to study, as well as books and computers), and from the home psychological environment needed to undertake study in a fruitful way.[68]

At the level of elective or higher education, the risks in terms of life trajectory undertaken by the great majority of young people whose families do not possess a stock of wealth may prove to be substantially higher than the highly touted entrepreneurial risk undertaken by a capitalist. The combination of fees or explicit debts to pay for higher education and the deferment of income from employment may threaten penury if the time and financial resources committed to education are not readily compensated for by employment. Unlike the well-off, most young people do not have the option of living off a stock of family wealth for an extended period if employment prospects turn out poorly.[69] The imposition of these financial risks on young people may well damage economic development. Some will choose to avoid or defer such education, while others may choose educational studies that are perceived to be lower-risk in terms of immediate employment, but will also offer lower returns to the individual and to the economy in the long term: the individual undertakes training as an electrician rather than as an electrical engineer. Even Goldin and Katz, who trace rising inequality in the US to failures in student educational achievement in the race against technology (see Chapter 10), are willing to acknowledge the possibility of reverse causation – that rising inequality has created obstacles to the completion of secondary and tertiary education.[70]

The labouring household is thus, in contrast with much capitalist activity, subject to something close to unlimited liability on its investment: even free higher education embodies profound individual risk, including lack of success on the programme undertaken, its unsuitability perceived only after extensive commitment, and the failure to find employment upon completion. The imposition, in addition, of explicit financial costs on post-high-school education creates obstacles and risks to knowledge and skill acquisition that are not symmetrical between classes and are likely to distort society's investment in human assets. These insecurities also disrupt the ability of households to act as agencies of planning for their children. Furthermore, the transitory aspects of a relationship to the workplace engendered by flexibility militate against the exercise of democratic control in the workplace at a collective or individual level.

The adoption of an outlook in which human beings are assets that plan for their own future and not mere commodities to be allocated to some supposed optimal use has powerful implications for public policy. The conventional argument is that policies that promote household stability – subsidies and tariffs for industries at risk or employment protection for those at work – are often popular with those being protected, but at the cost of economic efficiency for the society as a whole: obsolescent technologies and whole industries impede the introduction of new developments. The maintenance of backward-looking practices not only inhibits economic growth, but is self-perpetuating through the political vested interests that support them.

These arguments are indubitably correct in their own terms. During the boom years in Japan after the Second World War, commentators were constantly noting the high costs of tariff supports to its inefficient agriculture,[71] with the burden of high food prices foisted upon the poorest elements in the society; a dramatic contrast has also been observed between the success of China's highly successful export-oriented sector and its largely state-owned and politically propped-up 'rustbelt' industries.[72]

These costs of inefficient allocation are real, and of a not insignificant order of magnitude. However, the usual presumption is that this is the end of the story – that great economic successes such as postwar Japan and China in recent decades would have done even better by, respectively, rapidly eliminating agricultural tariffs and running down the rustbelt sector. But are such acts of creative destruction necessarily efficacious, given the resultant dislocation and instability introduced into the households of those declining sectors? If we associate long-term development with the ability of individuals and households to make long-term plans about their future, policies that slow down disruption and contribute to stability and security at the level of the household may be more conducive to long-term development than those linked to creative destruction and the flexibility of the workforce. The latter heroic-sounding policies are likely to derange the capacity of households to make rational plans for the future.

The case in favour of the promotion of increased economic security for households is illustrated here by an instance commonly used to demonstrate the inefficacy of such policies – the notorious example of agricultural subsidies in the US since the Great Depression. With great unanimity, the economics textbook discussions of agricultural subsidies in the form of price supports have decried them as burdens on the general population in the form of a misallocation of resources, with unnecessarily high prices for consumers and the generation of unneeded surpluses. Even their nominal purpose, to give assistance to indigent farmers, is thwarted by the fact that richer farmers inevitably benefit disproportionately from these higher prices;[73] these acts of public policy also engender vast political lobbies for their perpetuation.

It is possible to accept all of these arguments but to note, as has the historian Sally Clarke, that these subsidies – even if irrational and wasteful – may well have averted deep social disruption: New Deal intervention had initiated a revolution in US farm productivity (see Chapter 9), but 'What is striking about this disappearance of farmers is not only that it proceeded so quickly but that it also took place so quietly.'[74] The high rate of increase of agricultural productivity was accompanied not by a rise, but by a dramatic decline in the rate of farm foreclosures: subsidies and price supports reduced to manageable decline what might well have been a social catastrophe.

Courses of action that treat labour as if it were an undifferentiated commodity would be highly dysfunctional for the economy as a whole if they were successfully implemented. Strictly from the perspective of long-term economic growth, would not an alternative policy of laissez-faire creative destruction have been dysfunctional, with the resultant negative effects on the stock of human assets of household bankruptcies, rural unemployment and mass migration to urban areas? Public policies that slow down an 'inevitable' change in the economic landscape to manageable proportions may well facilitate not only the realisation of humanitarian goals, but economic development as well.

The residual effects of the conception in economic theory of labour as an undifferentiated commodity have remained in place in our own day. In the early twentieth century, we have seen its manifestation in Taylorist notions of labour as a passive object to be moulded to the needs of modern production in both capitalist and, through Lenin, socialist schemes for societal organisation; in recent times, the call for labour to show flexibility – to abandon accumulated skills and accept work in an unrelated field at a lower wage – is part of the rhetoric of both right-wing politics and a broad range of free-market economics. For those voices, ordinary people must be willing to abandon their life plans to accommodate even transitory changes in labour market conditions if the economy is to operate appropriately, an adaptation to short-term events that the politicians and economists advocating such policies would consider a catastrophe in their own lives.

* * *

The perspective in this chapter views human beings and their households as fulcrums of planning rather than as mere commodities to be allocated to their optimal use in the capitalist marketplace. They develop their skills *in situ* by interacting in the world and by participating in the work process, as well as through formal education. Public policies promoting equality and household security reinforce the capacity of individuals to plan the development of their skills in all of these contexts, in the process fostering economic development for the society as a whole. There may well be no dilemma forcing us to choose between policies promoting equality and security, on the one hand, and policies of economic development, on the other. Socialist policies compatible with such a perspective will be considered in

Chapters 11 and 12. As an interregnum, Chapter 9 contrasts the mythology of the US as a quintessential example of unfettered free enterprise with the historical reality of its development, along the way exemplifying many of the issues already discussed. Chapter 10 examines the substantive meaning of the term 'economic growth' and, in this context, the implications of increasing inequality.

9
The US as Exemplar and Paradigm

For much of the twentieth century, the US was a standard of the good life, for perfectly explicable reasons. In a war-torn, class-ridden, poverty-stricken and undemocratic world, America was distinctive for peace, class mobility, wealth and the absence of mass terror. This transcendent position reached its height in the period immediately after the Second World War. The vibrant role of the US in the interwar period in the forms of culture characteristic of the twentieth century – cinema, popular music and jazz – was now supplemented by overwhelming military, political and economic predominance.

The most important source of its international prestige in economic affairs, however, has remained its singular superiority in levels of per capita income, which was double that of the nations of Western Europe in 1950. In the postwar period up until the early 1970s, the US experienced lower growth rates in national income and higher levels of unemployment than Western Europe and Japan. Even with this erosion, the US continued to maintain its leading place in the calculation of national income per capita. In 2014, it was richer than any state in the European Union (excluding Luxembourg) – by 16 per cent in comparison with the Netherlands, by 20 and 21 per cent compared with Germany and Sweden, respectively, and by 40 and 41 per cent compared with the UK and France, respectively.[1] As we shall see in the next chapter, much of this apparent predominance disappears for typical workers when these figures are modified to reflect the highly unequal distribution of income in the US and the exceptionally high number of hours worked per year.

The US is an old nation and invariably embodies idiosyncratic and peculiar aspects. It is, for instance, the centre of world science and simultaneously the location of a vast creationist movement. These are fascinating and troubling aspects of the culture, but will be dealt with only in passing. The focus here will, rather, be upon the persistence in the US of a distorted view of its own development that, in retrospect, made the revival of pre-New Deal pieties in the 1980s a plausible event. Thus, even in the late nineteenth century, as we have seen, the American view of Thomas Edison as the lone curmudgeonly genius contrasted with the more realistic perspective held abroad (see Chapter 2) that he and those like him in the US were grand systems builders.

By the end of the twentieth century, this gap in perception had become a chasm. It is epitomised by attitudes towards the postwar electronics revolution, a key aspect of US hegemony and, even more so, the gateway worldwide to the technology of the twenty-first century: the Edison myth has been re-created in the popular lionisation of the heroic entrepreneurs Steve Jobs and Bill Gates. The creations of these individuals, however, so visible to the consuming public, only emerged in the context of an electronics sector in the US that had its origins in important elements of state enterprise and planning; of no less fundamental significance was the pioneering role played by the state in the US in creating the educational infrastructure that made the electronics revolution possible.

The mythic history of the electronics sector as solely the triumph of entrepreneurial individualism has served as a totem for the renewed political economy of unfettered capitalism in the US from around 1980, reinforced by the disintegration of European centrally planned economies in the period from 1989 to 1991. The decades since 1980 have been characterised by such rapid rises in the levels of inequality and wealth in the US as to make it once again exceptional among major capitalist economies, but not in an altogether positive manner. While growing inequality is to be observed in other economies, its rapid ascent in the US (and the UK) is linked, at least in part, to explicit political decisions that have generated inequality and a willingness to accede to the judgement of the market.

In one sense, American hegemony has remained in place. At a cultural level, the mass marketing of films and television programmes in the US has been successfully transferred abroad and has often smothered local output. In a broad range of academic fields, the American accent has become, figuratively and literally, pervasive. In economics, the US brand offers a view of rationality linked to individual decision making that has only a distant connection with the decisive role played by collective and state action in the nation's rise to world dominance. Like Ancient Rome even after its demise, the US continues to structure worldwide the terms in which intellectual discourse can take place about the future of society.

US history – the peculiar and the explicable

The US emerged in the late eighteenth century with a singular history among large countries. It conducted its political affairs on the basis of a republican constitution emerging from Enlightenment discourse, abjuring an established church and approaching a separation of citizenship from nationality for white Europeans. The rhetoric of its politics moved decisively in a democratic direction in the first half of the nineteenth century. Yet the functioning of this democratic republic continued undisturbed, even in the midst of civil war, at a time when democracy was considered a volatile and subversive political form by the great sages of the era. Its population ranked in per capita terms among the richest in the world, and, as we have seen, was already notable for its exceptional levels of literacy.

Europe's past was tied to the collective institutions of the medieval manor, guild and church. Much of the tumult of the history of the early modern period was engendered by aspirations to extricate social affairs and personal life from the strictures of these institutions. The US, by contrast, had a primordial myth of the independent farmer: the free, unsupported and unconstrained individual was taken to be not so much an aspiration as a primary, natural state of existence. The state was not to be seen, in European, Hegelian terms, alongside a civil society, but as an encumbrance, perhaps a 'necessary evil'[2] upon a free and unfettered individual. This view merged with democratic politics and rhetoric in the election for president of Andrew Jackson in 1828, defeating the incumbent John Quincy Adams who had plans for federal expenditure on domestic improvements, including the building of a national astronomical observatory, dubbed by its enemies 'lighthouses of the skies'.[3] A history of anti-state and philistine rhetoric has somehow continued to co-exist in the US into the twenty-first century alongside periods of enormous expansion in state power and planning, as well as intellectual dynamism and educational development. And since 1828, all arguments on social and political affairs have been couched in the language of democracy.

Various aspects of the traditional story were dubious.[4] The myth of the independent farmer is to be seen in the context of the use of state power to subdue aboriginals and to add substantially to the territories of settlement through a war of aggression with Mexico; the prosperity of this independent farmer was also linked to coordinated state and quasi-state action for the financing of the railroads and, as we have seen in Chapter 1, the setting up of grain markets. For the conurbations already in place, from New York to Chicago, internal improvements, city planning and urban hygiene were central concerns.

The notion that social existence in the US distinguished itself from that in Europe by its unfettered and individualistic character may be further contrasted with a range of instances of collective action. In a positive direction, we observe a deeply rooted movement for public education; more negatively, we see an intolerance of non-conformity that drove religious minorities such as Catholics and Mormons to live in tightly clustered communities. The latter exceptions to what we would now consider to be the normal exercise of civil rights pale in comparison to the existence of slavery as the basis for the leading export of the US *ante bellum* economy – cotton. If a conceptualisation of citizenship and national identity that is not linked to ethnicity, race and religion remains the most significant contribution by the US to juridical procedure in republics, it was deeply compromised by the legacy of slavery: not until the passage of the Civil Rights Act of 1964 do we see the general revocation or striking down of a host of laws and ordinances at the state level that violate the principle of equality before the law with regard to ethnicity, race and religion, such as the anti-miscegenation statutes.

Already by the early twentieth century, the US was perceived by a range of observers to have engendered a new form of capitalism, a coherent system of planned production and continuous innovation. In this period, Europeans remained predominant in technical innovations in areas such as chemistry that were closely linked to the latest developments in high science. But it was the American Edison who fully implemented the practical implications of the great achievements of Faraday and Maxwell in the theory of electromagnetism with the electrification of a great city. In the implementation of the assembly line, attributed to Henry Ford, the US was seen to make a managerial innovation in manufacture comparable to any technological discovery.

By the beginning of the twentieth century, the US was not only notable for the exceptional characteristics of its industrial development, but was emerging as a focus of interest worldwide and a symbol, for good or ill, of modernity. Both its supporters and its detractors agreed that it displayed immense dynamism, with rapid rises in per capita income even in the context of massive immigration. The political system was unique among the great powers, with its century-long uninterrupted tenure of republican-democratic forms and practices (outside of the South), in the context of a political stability rivalling that found even in Great Britain. No society was more successful in inventing and exploiting new mechanisms of mass production and distribution for the transmission of traditional European culture, such as with the sale of the opera recordings of Enrico Caruso. But what made this the American Century as much in culture as in economics and politics – much to the dismay of many on both the left and the right of the political spectrum – was the capacity of this vast and diverse society to find indigenous aspects of its culture, such as the music of ragtime, that had a capacity for mass appeal. As the century wore on, Hollywood and rock 'n' roll played as great a role in the perception of American hegemony as did mass production and space exploration.

Why, Werner Sombart asked at the beginning of the twentieth century, was there no socialism in the US, with its enormous working class ranged against the most advanced form of capitalism in the world? There are proximate answers to this question: the Socialist Party in the US suffered repression due to its opposition to participation in the First World War;[5] labour union development in the US, as in Britain until 1906, was inhibited by judicial decisions ruling union actions as restraints of trade. These rulings, coupled with aggressive action, including violence, on the part of employers, constrained working-class organisation until the New Deal. But not even then was Franklin Roosevelt's Democratic Party transformed into a British-style labour party, much less into something more radical on continental European lines.[6]

The absence of a socialist movement in the US was partially linked to the presence of ethnic and racial tensions within the working class in the US. The potential for such conflict was undoubtedly high, with immigration from diverse national and religious backgrounds in Europe, as well as from Asia and Latin America, interacting and competing with the large population of former slaves and their descendants. These divisions were often successfully exploited and exacerbated by employers and by right-wing politicians, and not just in the former Confederacy. Unlike Europe, where socialism was linked to a secularist agenda, populist agitation, much as in seventeenth-century England, was diffused using the language of religious renewal, as in the presidential campaign of 1896 of William Jennings Bryan, a figure who later supported the creation story of Genesis in the Scopes trial of 1925.

Sombart's answer to his own question makes the original query sound almost rhetorical – there was no socialism in America because the living standards of the working class had been raised to a level of comfort that precluded the need for militant action or organisation. For Sombart, the primary impetus for these high living standards – the presence of free land and the possibility of becoming an independent farmer as an alternative to being a worker – was now disappearing. With the 'closing of the frontier' (famously decreed by the American historian Frederick Jackson Turner to have taken place in 1890), Sombart suggested that socialism was likely to experience 'the greatest possible expansion of its appeal' in the future in the US.[7]

And despite the failure of the Sombart thesis as a predictive model, the high wage story retains some explanatory power: there is little doubt that growing living standards in postwar Western Europe were an aspect of the gradual dissipation of working-class militancy and socialist political organisation in this period. But if we thus move to account for the absence of working-class, socialist politics on the basis of growth, rather than levels of income, it becomes difficult to explain the conservatism of politics and labour in the Great Britain of Sombart's day, since Britain was in this period (with the exception of the Netherlands) the slowest-growing country in Western Europe. Sombart's story also doesn't work too well if we take it literally – that a high absolute standard of living dampens militancy – since US workers in his time were poor in comparison to the standards achieved in postwar Western Europe, where militancy and socialist politics persisted for many decades. The notion that US workers in Sombart's day were well-off relative to foreigners – a variant hypothesis – would have presumably struck them as irrelevant; in any case, workers of recent immigrant stock – those capable of making such a comparison directly – were often more militant than other workers.

The high wage explanation is not sufficient to account for the absence of socialism in the US, as Sombart recognises at various points in his text. What was peculiar to America was the presence of a high and rising standard of living combined with its success in instilling a sense of legitimacy in the population towards the government and its associated institutions. The Civil War of 1861 to 1865, with its demand for a massive sacrifice of blood without external threat, was a successful test of this legitimacy matched in no other country.[8] For newcomers of European stock, the separation of citizenship from nationality inherent in the US constitution was key to instilling in them a sense of their rights as citizens, as opposed to a presumption that their presence in the country was due to the sufferance of the majority.

The Lincolnesque basis of legitimacy in the US ('of the people, by the people, for the people') was reinforced in the late nineteenth century by the presence of institutions as advanced in every particular as any in the capitalist world – electoral democracy (outside of the former Confederacy), a meritocratic civil service, an independent, often elected judiciary, a sophisticated legal and institutional framework for the setting up and operation of business, and the absence of de facto medieval residuals in rural areas (with the exception of analogous social structures in the former Confederacy).[9] In the context of the regulation of industry, the US government's antitrust framework was without parallel. In other respects, the US was unrivalled in the progressive nature of its institutions, fulfilling demands that in other countries would fall under the rubric of socialism. We observe the efflorescence of state-funded, secular school education and even universities, offering the prospect of income and class mobility, if not equality, and thus dampening the frustrations of those upwardly mobile groups that were an important aspect of radical political and intellectual life in Europe, and a separation of church and state that gave no basis for a radical politics rooted in militant secularism, as was to be found in France and Italy.

In addition, the US became in this period the epicentre of the myth of upward mobility from independent ambition and entrepreneurial activity, disseminated through the British writer Samuel Smiles (1812–1904) and later the American Horatio Alger (1832–99). Legitimacy in an economic context was thus reinforced in the US not with any claim to economic equality per se, but to an equality of opportunity, a notion long implicit in British liberal ideology, but having far greater pungency in the context of American republican institutions, practices and habits, as even a grumbling Sombart was willing to concede: 'One must accept that there is a grain of truth in all the nonsense spoken by the Carnegies and those parroting them who want to lull the "boorish rabble" to sleep by telling them miraculous stories about themselves or others who began as newsboys and finished as multimillionaires.'[10]

Indeed, there has long persisted in the US an image of the UK as a society more equal than the US in terms of claims on resources (as evidenced by the presence of the socialist National Health Service), but less mobile because of the residual effects of a class system, epitomised by the presence of a royal family. The role of class, blatantly and overtly present in the UK two generations ago, interacted subtly with the issue of mobility in terms of the differential access to economic and political power offered to an elite, as well as the limited aspirations embodied in 'knowing your place' for the lower end. Propagandists for American uniqueness highlighted these aspects of stratification in Europe, as if they were absent in the US, and coupled them with claims that the US was uniquely receptive to the emergence of the next Thomas Alva Edison: the US as the land of opportunity, most especially for entrepreneurial endeavour.

To the extent that this notion of the US as *der goldene Medina* (the Golden Medina) possessed a modicum of validity, it was a product of the sheer absolute superiority of the US in levels of per capita income and the provision of broad access to education of all kinds compared with Western Europe from the nineteenth and over much of the twentieth century, as we shall see below. Social mobility was due less to the US being a unique bastion of entrepreneurial freedom than to the more substantive presence of an elaborately funded state educational system that provided the possibility of individuals rising through the professions as employees, and only occasionally as independent business entrepreneurs.

In broader terms, America's dominance, far from being a manifestation solely of spontaneous action by lone entrepreneurs, was underwritten by its success, most especially compared with Britain, in the creation of industrial giants whose characteristic planned and coordinated nature was a key inspiration for the technocratic paradigm of technocrats and socialists. But the American myth remained that of the independent creative genius – Edison and the young Henry Ford – despite their reliance at every stage on a rich infrastructure of skills and intellect at least partially created by collective action, without whose presence their schemes would never have come to fruition.

The economy, culture and politics of the US had been a subject of intense study and curiosity by others in the first part of the twentieth century, but the period after the Second World War was one in which the commanding dominance of the US was underwritten by its moral prestige. The US emerged after the war associated with its role in the creation of the United Nations, the associated declarations on human rights, the Marshall Plan aid programmes for Europe, and an anti-colonial rhetoric. In material terms, the US was without rival for the first decades after the war, setting a standard that other nations felt to be dispiritingly distant. The lead in school education pioneered earlier in the century by the US was now reproduced in an expansion of higher education from both the state and private sectors that was unmatched anywhere in the world.

If in the first part of the century the US had already established a predominance in the practical implementation of technologies, from the electrification of cities to the invention of the safety razor, after the Second World War these accomplishments were now matched by supremacy in theoretical pursuits, such as pure mathematics and physics. The illustrious individuals who had fled totalitarian interwar Europe were instrumental in the maturation of scientific and technological activity in the US after the Second World War. But the human and institutional infrastructure already in place meant that the dispersion of mathematics and high science was unprecedented in breadth and depth, a fact reflected in subsequent decades both in the theoretical productions emanating from academic institutions and in the application of high science in nuclear power and electronics.

The presence of notable exiles from Europe was perhaps of even greater significance in high culture than in technology; the US became a centre for European classical music, with residency by composers Arnold Schoenberg and Igor Stravinsky and a host of eminent conductors and instrumentalists. But even here, the domestic soil was already rich, and the ferocious Schoenberg had to concede that he had never heard a better performance of his *Verklärte Nacht* of 1899 than that produced by the augmented Hollywood String Quartet. As if it were not sufficient that it had achieved parity with Europe in the replication of classical music, the period after the Second World War also saw the worldwide realisation that the US, most especially through its African-American citizens, had created in jazz a new and distinctive branch of the Western musical tradition that in its postwar manifestation as be-bop was self-consciously high art. An even more pervasive influence was the emergence of rock 'n' roll in the mid-1950s – a popularised synthesis of African-American electrified blues with a largely white country and western tradition. Thus, the US became emblematic of modernity worldwide, not merely because of the vision of a high material standard that it represented, but because of its striking influence on both high and popular culture: debates on modernity – almost wholly identified with the 'Americanisation' of life – already in progress since earlier in the century, continued at a new level of intensity.

The impact of this Americanisation worldwide, but especially in Western Europe, was profound: as postwar prosperity unfolded, this region found itself confronting American-style mass consumption, youth culture and the other consequences of affluence in its daily life. In a range of instances, European nations failed, as in access to higher education, and in others succeeded, as in the provision of universal health insurance, in finding solutions to the problems of affluence superior to those in the US.

But the US precedence in modernity was present not only in economic and social life, but also in political affairs. In the case of former fascist countries, there were issues surrounding the construction, or reconstruction, of liberal political democracy. More pervasively, mass immigration has forced Europeans to confront the quintessential American issue of the relationship between citizenship and national or ethnic identity: for example, Germany was reluctant until recent times to offer citizenship to long-standing guest workers from Turkey or their children, but gave a right of return and citizenship to foreigners claiming German ethnicity. Even European countries with long republican traditions, such as France, have often dealt with this question in an obtuse, unthinking manner (such as the infamous phrase found in French textbooks offered to francophone Africa – 'Nos ancêtres les Gaulois'), with others resorting to genocidal approaches, as in the former Yugoslavia. And few European nations besides France have embraced the relatively rigorous separation of church and state embodied in the US constitution, thus prohibiting the privileging by the state of any particular religious practice or institution.[11] If in daily life the US has not always dealt with issues concerning race, ethnicity, religion, gender and immigration with any greater justice or efficacy than other nations, its constitution, especially as amended after the Civil War, had set a standard for the juridical and political equality of all those living within its borders long before other rich nations.

Postwar Western Europe had to deal with unburdening itself of its past history, which it did sometimes eagerly and at other times with regret. The changes in daily life were palpable, with the transition from a predominantly rural to an urban economy and society having barely begun in many countries, and the necessity for the recasting of political procedures and institutions in formerly fascist and authoritarian states. In the US, the situation was very different. Postwar prosperity and full employment merely permitted a return to the dreams of material affluence put on hold by the interwar depression – cars and household appliances were not new in postwar US, just more freely available: only television was newly visible in the ordinary life of upper-middle-class families.

Politically, the eighteenth-century constitution continued its uninterrupted functioning, US citizens noting with amazement the movement in France from a third to a fourth, and eventually to a fifth republic, with not even McCarthyism and Cold War paranoia impinging seriously upon the stolid self-confidence with which the US viewed the world. In important ways, the US had become the oldest country in the world – an American child's breakfast of the mass-produced product of a great corporation, Kellogg's Corn Flakes, might well have been the same as that of her great-great-grandfather: in Europe, the introduction of such delectations for breakfast represented a profound disjunction with the past. Americans in this period were not forced to think about change to the same degree, because it took place with less discontinuity and did not have its origins in any other nation's culture.

In the present day, American culture may well prove less adaptable to changing relations with other nations, precisely because of its ownership of the twentieth – the 'American' – century. Past successes and the illusions attendant on them may generate an obduracy that makes it impossible to respond to present-day challenges. Already in the interwar period, Hollywood movies absurdly depicted foreigners, from Parisian policemen to Czech shopkeepers, speaking fluent if pleasantly accented English, a practice that continued well into the postwar period of US hegemony. But, like sleepwalkers, Americans have woken up in the twenty-first century, and this fantasy is an approximation of reality: hoteliers in Paris, as well as corporate executives and academics in Europe, will function in English. For many Americans, this relatively recent development is taken as a verification of continued hegemonic power and cultural superiority, and an excuse not to learn languages, or anything else, from foreigners. When coupled with a history that is perceived as defeating all challengers – the Axis powers in the Second World War, the Soviet Union in the Cold War, and even the later economic rivalry with Japan – there is, at worst, in the collective psychology of the US a notion of divine protection, one that makes it unnecessary to deal seriously with substantive realities such as climate change.

And the grand myth of the heroic entrepreneur continues to be of great assistance to right-wing political movements in the US seeking a return to former glories by pursuing a path of individual self-reliance and low taxes. The realities of American history are something quite different. Much of the earlier achievement of the US is located in collective action in various forms, most importantly in the commitment to education, as well as in acts of planning in the economic sphere, as will be seen below.

Economic development and government enterprise

A few years ago, I was asked to review a few chapters of a book proposal by American academics. The prospective book was well-constructed and distinctive: for a nation notorious for marinating in its own history and institutions, this book was a rare foray into comparative economic history, in which a European model of government involvement in industry was contrasted with the hands-off US approach. The analysis was admirably even-handed in weighing the merits of each system, but ultimately left me, in a proverbial sense, speechless. A key premise of the whole book – that US industrial affairs can be described from a fundamentally laissez-faire perspective – was based on an innocent blindness to the substantive and rich instances of state involvement in the US economy that have proved critical to its development.

The mythology of independent enterprise is compromised at its epicentre – the US agricultural sector. By 1890, 'the development of large-scale, government-financed agricultural research appears to have been primarily an American phenomenon not copied abroad'.[12] As a result of the passage since 1862 of acts of Congress creating the US Department of Agriculture (USDA), the land grant colleges and agricultural experiment stations, practically all agricultural scientists throughout the early twentieth century were full-time government employees.[13] Though the resulting agricultural research made little direct contribution to productivity for many decades,[14] the disproportionate electoral weight of the agricultural sector in US national politics continued to underwrite the development of these institutions and their expansion in the 1930s and subsequently.

There is a purely economic rationale for the exceptional level of government intervention in this sector, one perhaps implicit in the minds of the participants but not formalised until a century after the original acts of Congress:[15] even when the individual, atomised farmer has the intellectual capacity to pursue agricultural research and is not constrained financially from so doing, such research will rarely be undertaken, as any resulting benefits will quickly be dissipated to others. US farmers, realising these limitations, had formed thousands of voluntary associations by the early twentieth century, which were conduits, along with county agents, for the diffusion of research from the USDA, experiment stations and land grant colleges; attending meetings offered by the public extension service in order to become acquainted with the latest research and techniques became a regular and important activity.[16]

Starting in the 1920s, more dramatically in the 1930s, and continuing during and after the Second World War, the agricultural sector evidenced substantial rises in productivity that were sustained for many decades, reflecting the successful assimilation of the products of free enterprise, such as tractors and other machines powered by the internal combustion engine, as well as foreign innovations, such as the invention of chemical fertiliser. These developments were complemented by the activities of government and government-financed institutions in the creation of a broad range of scientific innovations and procedures, as well as the offering of assistance and guidance in the introduction and implementation of these transformative changes: the government played a central role in the creation and dispersion of a scientific-technological revolution in US agriculture.[17] From the perspective of dynamic efficiency, the American agricultural sector emerges as an exemplar not of disinhibited free enterprise, but of successful governmental–private sector collaboration.

The by-products of this revolution in the agricultural sector have been manifold. On the one hand, this scientific productivity revolution was of disproportionate benefit to well-off farmers and owners, with resulting pressures driving smallholders, sharecroppers and others off the land that were only partially mitigated by the New Deal interventions described in Chapter 8.[18] But the depletion of rural areas and escape to urban centres are a commonplace of capitalist development. What is striking is the extent to which the vast subcontinent embodying the US did not follow this cultural pattern of an educationally backward rural sector, as we shall see below: the origins of the high school movement are to be found in the Midwest, with respectable rates of college attendance engendered by the land grant colleges, largely, in the early decades, for non-agricultural pursuits.[19] The role of federal government in the creation of these institutions of higher education interacted with unprecedented action at the state level for public school enrolment, giving the US a uniformity and depth of education across its great expanse (outside the former Confederacy) that was to have profound consequences for its economic development during the twentieth century.

In industrial development, the US had a world presence even in the *ante bellum* period, with the 'American system of manufactures' notable for its distinctively high volumes, uniformity of output and use of interchangeable parts. These early triumphs of the system of free enterprise in the US had their origins in 'armory practice' – the demands from the early nineteenth century by the US Ordinance Department that weapons be produced using interchangeable parts. In what would now appear as a slow process of dispersion, the know-how embodied in armouries was diffused via the machine tool industry through a range of consumer products. This culture of interchangeable parts, especially new techniques in pressing and stamping steel introduced by bicycle manufacturers, was later to be central to the emergence of the mass manufacture of Henry Ford.[20]

Several elements of the development of mass manufacture in the nineteenth and early twentieth centuries thus parallel those to be found in the following discussion of the postwar electronics industry: the US government's role as a source of market demand and in directing development in the primary stages of the new technology; the reliance of the new sectors on the *in situ* skills embedded in the older, displaced ones (bicycles in the context of car manufacture, and vacuum tubes or valves in the case of electronics); the necessity for innovation in the context of a high-wage economy. An important difference in the case of electronics, as we shall see below, is the central role played by science and science-based education in the evolution and dispersion of technology in the postwar context. Both of these American success stories cause difficulties for primitive narratives built around laissez-faire and creative destruction.

But this myth of free enterprise and the heroic entrepreneur has proved persistent, partly because it contains important elements of truth. The US economy from the late nineteenth century until the Second World War had evidenced forms of government intervention in its development: distinctively high tariffs, a deep engagement in the technology and the dissemination of knowledge in agriculture, the financing of the railroads, government activity concerned with the setting of uniform standards in the electrical industry and other sectors, and, as we shall see below, First World War involvement in the reorganisation of the infant electronics industry with the creation of the Radio Corporation of America (RCA). All this is true, but overall, the Second Industrial Revolution of the late nineteenth and early twentieth centuries – the emergence of giant firms, mass production and the innovation of new technologies – took place under the aegis of private enterprise uncoordinated by any state agency, and was often directed and sometimes founded by an entrepreneur. This history may thus be summarised as follows:

1. Technological and institutional innovation in the US (and other countries) largely took place within firms, with leakages from these technological achievements to other firms sufficiently small to make investments in new technology profitable, largely as depicted in the literature of endogenous growth theory.
2. The direction of the development of these new technologies was almost exclusively initiated and directed by firms for the purpose of making a profit in the private sector.
3. Investment in new technologies was undertaken by firms using funds from internal sources and externally from financial institutions and private individuals.

By contrast, the high-technology industries emerging after the Second World War – electronics (semiconductors, computers, telecommunications), aircraft manufacture, atomic power and space exploration – took a very different path. Of these, the electronics sector has had perhaps the most powerful and permanent impact worldwide. In contrast to the Second Industrial Revolution, the innovations of the postwar period emerge in a very different way:

1. Technological innovation in the high-tech sector emanated from a complex web of firms, universities and governmental institutions.
2. High-tech research and development, especially in the crucial first two postwar decades, was largely, though not exclusively, initiated and guided by an interaction between private enterprises and governmental agencies, most especially the US Department of Defense (DOD).
3. As in earlier times, investment in new technologies was undertaken by firms using internal sources and a range of financial institutions and private individuals, with an important role for investment banks and equity-based entrepreneurial finance. But in the postwar period, the government (largely the US DOD) played a key, and in the early decades an overwhelming, role in the financing of research and development of new technologies, whether undertaken by companies, universities or a

governmental agency. Government financing of companies' innovation often took the indirect form of generous 'cost-plus' contracts and/or a guaranteed market for the purchase of the products of firms.

The role of defence expenditure in the postwar US was a subject of great controversy. To President Eisenhower (or his speechwriter) in 1961 we owe the phrase 'military-industrial complex', with its implication that much of this expenditure was unnecessary and due to a corrupting influence on political processes; Baran and Sweezy, as we have seen in Chapter 5, thought that defence expenditure was, like advertising (though even more sinister), part of the economic surplus – useless expenditure maintained to prop up a capitalist economy that would otherwise collapse.[21] Some economists were concerned with possible inefficiencies in weapons acquisition, with cost-plus agreements permitting cost overruns and possibly excessively high profits for contractors.[22] Others noted the high cost to society in terms of the drain on civilian resources.[23]

And yet, with all these negative characterisations of defence expenditure, a profound paradox emerges. In the early postwar years, US hegemony appeared to be linked to the great Second Industrial Revolution sectors such as cars and steel, which were engendered and sustained (albeit with some government contracts) by private enterprise. But the performance of these sectors, once so emblematic of US power, was ultimately undistinguished in comparison with that of their international rivals, and began a long contraction. What eventually emerged as the industrial basis of American economic and military power in the postwar world were sectors in which the financing and coordinating role of government was crucial. If earlier the list of sectors with a high level of government involvement included only agriculture, in the postwar world it embraced a whole new set of activities in which the state played a key role, not only in the financing of these sectors, but in the planning and the development of new technologies; in the case of the internet, the US government was central to its creation.[24]

The US that thus emerged in the twenty-first century was one that had suffered precipitous decline in a range of traditional free enterprise industries, in many of which, such as textiles, this was an inevitable product of the increasing competition from lower-wage countries. In other cases, however, such as the car industry, rapid decline was linked to the failure of this free enterprise sector to maintain its enormous historical advantages when faced with superior management, production techniques and products from others, most notably the Japanese. By contrast, many of the distinctive advantages that the US has retained are embodied in a series of high-technology sectors that are the product of state financing, planning and coordination[25] combined with intense competition between enterprises and entrepreneurial financial activity.

Most importantly, all of these sectors were underwritten by several generations of state investment in public and university education, complementing a rich *in situ* base of practical skills with the intellectual infrastructure to make these developments possible. Other elements of US advantage in the tertiary sector, such as the sophistication of its financial institutions, were also made possible by this exceptional commitment to education. An distinctively practical and business focus in American universities may have facilitated this extraordinary outburst of new technologies, but the key characteristic that differentiated the postwar US from any other contemporaneous society, and any other society in history, was the sheer size of its intellectual establishment, either on a per capita basis or in absolute terms.

And yet, the myth of the entrepreneur has been the impetus in recent decades for a neoliberal reconstruction of society in the US in order to recapture past glories linked to this mythology. Its most recent ideological incarnation in business school circles in the US has been an updated version of the Schumpeterian doctrine of creative destruction – the notion of innovation as invariably disruptive, but inexorable and inevitable in the contemporary world: we can do little but fatalistically accede to its power.[26]

The postwar electronics revolution in the US fits poorly with these notions of innovation being acts of creative destruction and disruption. The semiconductor was central to the early history of this revolution, with its invention and development prerequisites for progress in almost all other aspects of electronics: the Japanese later dubbed the semiconductor the 'rice' of the industry. The semiconductor also plays a special role in capitalist mythology. In its genesis, it appears as the quintessence of Schumpeter's thunderbolt from a great monopoly: the overturning of the well-established vacuum tube (valve) industry appears to be a prime example of creative destruction of an older sector, with the newer one rising from the ashes.[27] And, far more than the mainframe computer with its identification with the Goliath IBM, many of the subsequent semiconductor and microchip developments were the products of firms beginning as entrepreneurial Davids, leading us to a giddy 'overthrow of matter'[28] with the aid of heroic, risk-taking venture capitalists.[29] All of these entrepreneurial elements are relevant to the overall story, but must be seen in the context of a sector that emerges from a complex web of relationships between firms, government contractors and universities, whose different aspects are not easily disentangled.

Bell Labs announced the invention of the transistor in 1947, but this discovery had not been made serendipitously. The notion of solid state amplification had emerged as early as 1936, with the research arm of the great private US telephone monopoly AT&T, Bell Labs, seeking a replacement for mechanical relays by electronic connection.[30] Bell's development of the transistor proceeded independently of government funding, though Second World War research and expenditure on radar gave it an important impetus.[31] An exceptional aspect of the emergence and development of this sector was the crucial role played by the absorption and integration of the latest achievements in solid state physics,[32] a fact that underlines the importance of the existence in the US of a sophisticated intellectual infrastructure from the universities in the genesis of the electronics revolution. The centrality of pure science also plays, as we shall see below, a key role in explaining why the role of government in the innovation process, so peripheral at the beginning of the twentieth century, emerged so prominently here and in subsequent developments.

An important contribution to early research efforts was also made at a less abstract level in materials research by chemists and metallurgists, some of it linked to wartime work: 'the "linear model" of technological development – wherein scientific research precedes technological development, from which useful products emerge – does not encompass very well what happened in the case of the transistor'.[33] In addition, the new industry was dependent upon the prior existence of skills and the institutional infrastructure from sectors it was later to replace. The emergence of the famous Silicon Valley area of California is linked to the presence, from the early years of the twentieth century, of an extensive electronics sector to serve the needs of the US Navy, shipping companies and then ham (amateur) radio enthusiasts;[34] Charles Litton and other tube manufacturers from the interwar era built up a sector whose familiarity with a range of materials and vacuum techniques, cleanliness and precise protocols in manufacturing made them competitive in quality control with the great East Coast manufacturers. Many of these *in situ* skills and institutions were important for the postwar semiconductor sector, as was the entrepreneurial model of a new firm emerging with little capital on the basis of contracts with the US DOD; some of the older manufacturers became suppliers of equipment to the newer industry.[35]

Even in this apparently most striking example of Schumpeter's creative destruction, the notion appears to be deeply inadequate. It is vague enough to permit various readings, but the language he uses – comparing this process to a gale, or even a bombardment[36] – seems to suggest a sanguine attitude towards the destruction of now obsolescent sectors for the sake of creating anew. But this Wagnerian linkage between destruction and new creation comes up against the historical reality that new developments, be they the cotton industry of the Industrial Revolution, the car industry, or the revolution in miniature of the semiconductor, rely upon the existence of embedded activities, whose associated skills and ways of life can then be transferred to the new activity. In addition, as noted in Chapter 6, older technologies tend to remain in place longer than is generally recognised because of the persistence of bugs and difficulties in implementation of the new techniques and machines.[37] Thus, creative displacement, rather than creative destruction, is the norm for socially beneficial developments: the notion that laying waste to a region or sector is a prerequisite for progress is false.

The invention of the transistor by Bell Labs generated enormous interest and excitement in the scientific and engineering community. But for Bell, the device was largely conceived merely as a replacement for the vacuum tube; diffusion in the civilian sector was slow, with some applications in telecommunications and hearing aids. In consumer products more broadly, there was little more than the furtive (and premature) issuance of a transistor radio by Texas Instruments in 1954. Broadly speaking, 'The *ad hoc* manufacturing technology of the early fifties, while sufficient to sustain at least – with military help – a minor industry, would have been unable to support the sort of growth the industry was experiencing by the early sixties.'[38]

A decisive factor engendering the rapid transformation of this sector was the role of the US government, largely through the US DOD. The state played a central role in the funding and directing of research and development by firms and universities, and, more importantly and unambiguously, the DOD created a large and lucrative market for these untested products that permitted firms to undertake long-term development by shifting much of the risk of failure to the tax-paying public through the use, in the 1950s especially, of cost-plus contracts.[39] It not only provided an open chequebook for the provision and engendering of unprecedented new products and their replication in massive numbers, but was constantly prodding and monitoring companies to meet the demands of military technology.[40]

The role of the DOD in providing a market for these new technologies was decisive. One key enterprise, the Silicon Valley startup Fairchild Semiconductor (in fact, the subdivision of a more conventional firm), played a central role in the emergence of reliable and cheap transistor production with the planar process (based on research at Bell Labs). This development was critical to the economic viability of the integrated circuit,[41] and was perhaps the most important innovation since the invention of the transistor itself. Fairchild, along with Texas Instruments, also produced the first integrated circuits about the same time, around 1960. Yet even Fairchild, which generally avoided military financing of R&D in order to prevent the DOD from controlling its research and product development, agreed that 'only the military and the large weapon system contractors... would have the necessary financial resources to buy the complex and expensive products'.[42] US government purchases of integrated circuits as a percentage of total production were 100 per cent in 1962, 94 per cent in 1963 and 85 per cent in 1965;[43] as late as 1959, 85 per cent of total electronics research and development was financed by the federal government.[44]

With the invention of the integrated circuit, a technological revolution beginning in 1947 that might have lasted for the rest of the century if governed by the demands of the free market was consummated in less than a decade and a half with government financing. The increased reliability, and the doubling of the number of transistors on a microchip every 18 to 24 months that followed the emergence of the integrated circuit ('Moore's

Law'), made the semiconductor a viable, and then a necessary, commercial product, symbolised by the creation by Intel in 1971 of the microprocessor – a so-called computer on a chip.

The decisive role of the government as a market for these devices in the early phases of its development is indisputable; its other functions were also of significance, if more contentious. Efforts to spread knowledge by Bell Labs were complemented by government sponsorship of conferences and symposia starting in the early 1950s.[45] In the wake of the invention of the transistor, the US government's aggressive antitrust stance thwarted any temptation on the part of AT&T to preserve control over its development, with a consent decree of 1956 forbidding it to sell semiconductors or computers commercially and demanding that it give royalty-free licences on all transistor patents up to the year 1956, and at 'reasonable royalties' thereafter.[46] As noted above, the invention of the planar process, a key element in the development of the integrated circuit, took place at Fairchild in 1959 without explicit government support. But the shaping of silicon technology, and later the development of the planar process and the integrated circuit, 'were closely coupled with military procurement and the establishment of reliability and performance standards by the Department of Defense',[47] with a more rapid dispersion of these new technologies than would otherwise have taken place because of governmental demands for multiple sourcing of products.[48] Overall, it is hard to avoid the conclusion that 'By creating, supporting, and disseminating diverse approaches to technical innovation in semiconductor microelectronics, government agencies were extremely important in the overall development of micro electronic technology and thus also in the development of the microelectronics industry.'[49]

Early innovations emerged from the AT&T monopoly and from the established receiving tube firms, such as General Electric and RCA, with their extensive research facilities and rich experience in the production of electronic devices. But with older firms hesitant to abandon the lucrative tube market, by the mid- to late 1950s the impetus was shifting to firms that were either new (Fairchild Semiconductor) or new to the sector (Texas Instruments),[50] generating intense competition among the contracting firms, as they often span off into new enterprises. There was a broad, fluid range of supplementary finance available from other companies (as in the creation of Fairchild Semiconductor by Fairchild) and from established investment banks; by the late 1960s, managers and engineers were leaving Fairchild to start new ventures, facilitated by the emergence of a range of venture capital enterprises and an independent semiconductor equipment industry.[51]

The firestorm of energy leading to the introduction of the microprocessor in 1971 and beyond is thus seen to be the product of a complex interaction of forces. In its genesis and early development, the sector was characterised by planning with a long-term time horizon from AT&T and the US government;

further impetus then emerged from intense competition engendered by the fluid entry of new firms, often financed by equity-based venture capital with a much shorter, typically five-year, time horizon. Venture capital here – in sharp contradistinction to some later forms of financial innovation (such as the bundling of subprime mortgages; see Chapter 12) – was characterised by a hands-on, intimate knowledge of the sector, with investors often being engineers and/or entrepreneurs themselves.[52] The resultant intense competition engendered rapid imitation of Fairchild's silicon transistor planar process and manufacturing techniques for integrated circuits in the 1960s.[53] As will be discussed below, this shift to shorter time horizons in the semiconductor industry may reflect the gradual predominance of engineering over fundamental scientific achievements as the product matured.[54]

Other important participants in these developments were universities such as MIT and Stanford, key players in the 'military-industrial-academic complex',[55] whose intensity of integration with these practical high-technology projects – mostly state-financed and with a military connection – was perhaps without precedent in the history of capitalist development.[56] These tendencies were enhanced in the Cold War context: as late as 1968, 73 per cent of university and college research and development was funded by federal government, with 58 per cent of the total going for defence and space-related research.[57]

Educational establishments in the US thus played an important role in the formal development of these technologies, a practical orientation to which they had been directed since the late nineteenth century, generating Veblen's deep sarcasm about the nature of these university–business links. US higher education has aspects that still distinguish it from universities in other countries in the context of research and development and patents, including the possible compromises to its integrity from business, the military and (among private universities) rich alumni. In these aspects, as well as the presence of athletic scholarships, sororities and fraternities, the US university system remains singular, most especially when compared with its European counterparts.

But in the period after the Second World War, the most important characteristic of the US educational system that permitted it to contribute to this monumental, world-transformative technology was not so much a business orientation that lent itself to involvement in projects for the practical development of these technologies, but, rather, the sheer size and coherence of the university sector in the US, in both its state and private incarnations. The offerings of US universities dwarfed what existed, and ever had existed, in any country, with scientific and technical subjects ranging from pure mathematics and theoretical physics to the full spectrum of engineering disciplines, as well as provision of specific programmes relevant to semiconductor research.[58] The richness of the university infrastructure undoubtedly promoted mastery of a range of other skills – administrative, entrepreneurial and even legal – that were significant in, for instance, Silicon Valley development.[59]

This high level of human infrastructure, the product of an incomparably rich and elaborate university system emanating from state and private sources, had been underwritten by the development of its predominantly state school system. In the pre-Civil War period, US school participation was surpassed only by Prussia; by the early twentieth century, the US was a world leader in participation rates in secondary school with, strikingly, many of the highest rates for the smallest towns.[60] The notion of the US as a uniquely mobile society was significantly reinforced by these developments.[61]

It was the existence of these educational prerequisites that provided both a human infrastructure for the engendering of the entrepreneurs and the personnel for the extraordinary, and extraordinarily rapid, emergence of the electronics sector. When coupled with the *in situ* advantages embodied in individuals inheriting the already advanced development of this sector (such as the key role of amateur ham radio operators in the post-First World War electronics industry), the superiority possessed by the US must have seemed insurmountable. Yet, within a few decades, the US was to be challenged at the very highest levels in electronics, not exclusively, or even particularly, by its European peers, but by nations such as Japan and, later, other Asian nations that, in the immediate postwar context, had appeared to be among the poorest nations in the world. The very sophistication of this sector, with its high component of pure science and its constant desire to put in place strict protocols of manufacture to replace black art,[62] meant that the rapid emergence of the new technology in its early phases could only take place with extensive state subsidy. But somewhat later, this high scientific component helped promote a rapid diffusion of this revolutionary technology to potential international competitors with the appropriate educational prerequisites.

The period of development in the electronics sector up to 1971 (with direct control of the internet by the US military stretching into the 1980s)[63] is thus to be characterised by an admixture of elements with long-term considerations, such as the development of *in situ* skills and institutions, government and big firm (such as AT&T) planning, and advances in formal education, combined with shorter-term, entrepreneurial behaviour in a fiercely competitive environment. But since that time, the seemingly inexorable unfolding of Moore's law has lowered the price of computing power so far as to push the public's focus almost wholly onto applications of this power and its use with the internet – this being the weightless world of entrepreneurial startups and competition, with the Lourdes of this new faith being the garage in Los Altos, California where the electronics hobbyists Steve Wozniak and Steve Jobs started the Apple Computer Company in 1976. Apple's success, however, presupposes not only the range of long-term elements that made cheap computing power and the internet available, but also those 'networks of engineers, entrepreneurs, and financiers in Silicon Valley ... [that] gave them access to the region's unique expertise in manufacturing, product engineering, sales and marketing'.[64] A one-sided focus on these proximate entrepreneurial accomplishments is often accompanied (echoing views of Thomas Edison from a century earlier)[65] by a denigration of the centrality of formal schooling in this process, noting that our heroes Wozniak, Jobs and others failed to complete their university degrees.[66]

There are elements of validity in this entrepreneurial story. From the earliest days of semiconductor development, initiatives and innovations from the new semiconductor startups were instrumental to the rapid pace of development and, especially in the context of products for consumers, the market-driven nature of capitalism guided priorities in user-friendly (but computationally wasteful) directions that might never have entered the consciousness of engineers. It was a capitalist form of competition: cooperative ventures in Silicon Valley, such as Varian Associates, sometimes with a left-wing orientation (and subject to McCarthyist scrutiny), were on occasion successful, and their forms of worker participation were mimicked by capitalist firms; their cooperative structures invariably degenerated in the context of the need to engage venture capital funds for expansion and the desire of employees to cash in their share of the rise in the value of the enterprise.[67] Without question, and most especially given the contributions of Soviet scientists to solid state and semiconductor theory and practice in its early phases,[68] the deficit of the Soviet bloc in later stages of the elaboration of the electronics revolution reflects not only Cold War isolation, but the failure of the centrally planned system to find a substitute for the decentralised entrepreneurial initiative seen in the US. But a challenging alternative to the latter did emerge in the form of the directed system found in Japan and, with even greater contrast, from the highly centralised, corporatist South Korean system,[69] even if the latter was ultimately propelled by the need to respond to the exigencies of international capitalist competition.

We are thus confronted with the paradox that the most striking exemplification of capitalist dynamism in the postwar world, the electronics revolution, developed in its critical initial phases, as did other science-based industries, with substantial participation from non-profit-making entities – research from the universities, and finance and direction from the US government. These developments were in sharp contrast to the emergence of great industries and technologies in the late nineteenth and the beginning of the twentieth century, which were engendered almost exclusively by capitalist firms intending to make a profit on their investments.

Was this dramatic change in the provenance of innovation in the postwar world merely an aberration – an artefact of Cold War politics? More likely, it is a reflection, as suggested in earlier chapters, of the fact that these technologies, especially in their inception, have a much higher component of pure science than those at the beginning of the twentieth century. Furthermore, in their manufacture, the exceptional demands for purity and uniformity of electronics components lent themselves strongly to the elimination of craft-like procedures and towards rigid (and hence replicable) protocols in production. But both the science component and the rigid protocols in manufacture necessary in this sector will discourage profit-pursuing capitalist enterprises from undertaking research leading to these innovations: in contrast to craft-like skills, the permeable nature of the objective knowledge necessary to replicate these innovations means that they will be easily dissipated to rivals, including foreign producers with the appropriate intellectual preparation, in the absence of successful patent and copyright protection. The explosion of innovation that took place in the US emerged in the context of lucrative gains from government contracts coupled with a strong regulatory and antitrust atmosphere that inhibited monopolisation and appropriation by individual firms of technological breakthroughs. Of more fundamental significance, the technological achievements in this and other sectors emerged in the US from its unprecedented success in educating its population in schools and universities, almost exclusively in the context of state and non-profit-making entities.

And yet, in the twenty-first century, the US remains the epicentre of a popular and academic discourse supporting the ideal of a pure and unadorned form of capitalism, with more progressive voices apologetically and defensively requesting that its harshest consequences be curtailed. One prominent group of dissenters from this dialogue, almost invariably identifying themselves with progressive political views, have accepted a version of the narrative above concerning the importance of the role of the state in contemporary economic and technological development.[70] In the desire to seem hard-headed and relevant in contemporary discussions, the progressive aspects of their programmes – equality and democratic participation – are invariably muted in favour of an emphasis on the efficacy of state participation for generating successful outcomes in the international race for economic and technological superiority. But there is nothing intrinsically progressive about an anti-laissez-faire position on economic development, and the retreat to such a stance is testimony to the continuing ability of neoliberal argument, emanating most powerfully from the US, to shape and constrain the domain of acceptable political discourse.

Late Rome

As we shall see in Chapter 10, the US in the twenty-first century is distinctive for having the widest distribution of income and wealth among rich countries. This extreme disparity has emerged as a result of developments in this direction since about 1980 in the US and Britain that, up to the present, have appeared in a less pronounced form in comparable countries. Even before the great movement of these decades, the US appeared somewhat above average, but not exceptionally so, in income shares at the top end.[71] This fact appeared to be mostly of academic interest, however, because in the early postwar period, average incomes in the US were so much higher than in other countries.

Furthermore, the relatively wide dispersion in income and wealth in the US in the postwar years was compensated for by the widespread perception, since at least the nineteenth century, that the US was a land of opportunity, a nation with exceptionally high levels of income and even class mobility for residents of European descent. The nation was distinctive for its absence of residual feudal aspects such as class deference and the recognition of aristocratic lineages, characteristics that had persisted even in republican France. The constitutional separation of citizenship and nationality and of church and state gave immigrants from a range of ethnicities and religious groups the notion that their juridical status was on a par with that of the settled population, and that the hurdles to be faced in their personal elevation were largely of an economic nature. When coupled with an unparalleled commitment to public education, the US emerged with an image, and a perception of itself, as uniquely egalitarian because of its mobility. Unfortunately, in the telling and retelling of the story to itself, the focus of the US on its uniqueness has been almost exclusively on its role as an arena for the heroic entrepreneur, rather than as a nation that has succeeded, in an unprecedented way, in creating a literate society through state activity.

In the present day, any claims of US superiority concerning the standard of material welfare of its population over other nations are substantively restricted to its higher levels of per capita income when corrected for purchasing power parity. Unlike in the immediate postwar period, these differences are now relatively modest; the residents of the richest nations are now well enough off that considerations other than average income invariably impinge upon any evaluation of an economy's success or failure. But the central issue remains – even with this exceptionally wide dispersion of income and wealth, can the US maintain its historical claim to being a land of opportunity? The consensus of studies on income mobility is clear – the US appears to be unexceptional among rich nations in income mobility, and inferior to several. Such a result is unsurprising, given the lower levels of income inequality evidenced in America's rivals and the intuitive notion, to be confirmed in Chapter 10, that inequalities of income and wealth work against mobility, other things being equal. Across rich nations, the progressive characteristics that were pioneered in the US and engendered these high levels of mobility, most especially the commitment to school and higher education, have now been matched in other rich countries. In recent years, the rapid rises in tuition cost for post-high-school education have reversed the century-long identification of the US with exceptionally fluid access to education for all classes in society.

Inequality now emerges as the characteristic aspect of the US economy and society in the twenty-first century. Perhaps even more distinctive are the high levels of personal insecurity and poverty in the US, with, in general, a less generous social safety net, including unemployment benefit, compared with other countries and continuing issues surrounding health insurance. With a long-term stagnation of wages for a large section of the population, the middle class (an elastic term in the US context) have become disillusioned with their prospects for material improvement. Whether or not we fully accept the presence of a structural relationship between inequality and bad things in society, such as poor health and crime, it is hard to avoid the even more intuitive notion that inequality is associated with social fragmentation and immobility. Groups at the lower end of the social spectrum – culturally isolated and economically insecure – find it difficult to plan and organise a strategy for themselves and their children for social and economic elevation, most especially one that involves the long, indirect and perhaps culturally alien process of advanced education.

And possibly linked to social inequality, as both cause and effect, are a further range of aspects of US society that have emerged as peculiar in recent years, such as the overt and blatant influence of the interests of the well-off in political processes, underlined by Supreme Court decisions progressively declaring that legal limits on contributions to political campaigns by the rich are restrictions on First Amendment rights of free speech. In the context of a society with weak countervailing forces in the form of labour union organisation, and the exceptionally overt role, compared with other countries, of special interests in political processes, politics in the US often has more resemblance to that in countries with an unsteady tradition of political democracy than to that of a nation in serious contention for being ranked as the oldest democratic republic in the world.

While the US was once, as we have seen, a focus of progressive developments, it is now a centre of anti-progressive and even anti-Enlightenment ideas and movements among rich countries. In cultural terms, the US has mystified the rest of the world by maintaining an overwhelming hegemony of academic scientific learning while possessing a substantial political movement that promotes a synthesis of human anthropology from the creation story of Genesis and the children's television cartoon 'The Flintstones'. There is an old left-wing tradition of seeing such views as a cry of despair or alienation from oppressed groups or even, in the context of its earlier manifestation in William Jennings Bryan, a reaction to the social Darwinism of its day. But even putting to one side the imperfect correlation between these primitive views and the class status of the individuals holding them, the more substantive problem is that a virulent, well-developed ideology of ignorance is in itself an obstacle to social progress. The aggressive and even institutionalised presence of this ideology in many areas of the US not only inhibits social mobility for many individuals from lower incomes, for whom the cultivation of a scientific worldview becomes difficult, but also threatens the cultivation of rational discourse in the broader political and social context.

In the name of a laudable reluctance to accept the word of experts, the US has generated an anti-intellectual culture unparalleled in the developed world that somehow exists alongside the US maintaining itself as the world centre of scientific, and in many cases general, intellectual discourse. Such a happenstance, in earlier times, might have evoked amusement or even derision, as it did for political and literary commentator H. L. Mencken. But the combination of the influence of corporate propaganda and a situation in which a section of the US population has been inculcated with pre-modern notions of how the world works means that, for instance, much of the collective reaction to the issue of climate change in the US is distinctively infantile – a combination of denial, apocalyptic religious fatalism and a faith that a technological fix will solve the problem in a costless manner.[72] This reaction, potentially disastrous in itself, also does not bode well for rational responses on the part of the public to future challenges, environmental or otherwise.

The past successes of the US, however, still weigh heavily in contemporary discourse. The meaning of that history is subject to intense intellectual struggle, with one perspective embodying the persistent myth of the heroic entrepreneur. An alternative, more progressive narrative for the twentieth century would focus upon the overwhelming success of the US in assimilating and raising the cultural and skill level of a vast, heterogeneous population, including the deluge of largely European immigrants and what remained, in absolute terms, a very large rural population in the early twentieth century. Central to this success was the aggressive role of the state in the creation of a system of school and higher education, without precedent or parallel in the world, and a juridical structure in its constitution in which citizenship and its incumbent rights were separated from nationality. These powerful mechanisms served the non-white population of the US far less well, with often (especially in the old Confederacy) little protection of citizenship rights and scant opportunity to benefit from the singular abundance of state-financed educational institutions in the US.

Its continued lead in the postwar world in formal education, combined with the cumulative aspects of *in situ* human development, were key aspects of the retention of US predominance. In this period, in contrast to the beginning of the twentieth century, many of the leading sectors of the economy, such as electronics, that absorbed these skilled individuals were not the products of unadulterated entrepreneurial free enterprise, but of a deep admixture between the latter and financing, coordination and direction by the state. The identification of this most successful economy and polity worldwide with the assimilation and (albeit imperfect) integration of this heterogeneous collection of peoples has been a powerful progressive symbol, in sharp contrast to the anti-immigrant and nativist sentiment that is gaining a new prominence and respectability in the present-day US and other countries.

Given this well-known and attested history, it may seem surprising that the US remains the fount of laissez-faire ideology. Academic economics is dominated worldwide by journals and university departments centred in the US. The dominant conception of society emerging from the US academic world would have been familiar to orthodox practitioners of the early twentieth century: individual consumers, workers and entrepreneurs interacting with market institutions in the free exchange of goods and labour, with the state playing a residual and passive role. Imaginative attempts to modify this orthodoxy, most notably of a Keynesian variety, have a tendency to founder because of the intense individualism of the central doctrine: leading contemporary left-of-centre economists succeed in putting small punctures in the orthodoxy found in their own textbooks, but leave the overall vision undisturbed.

More than ever before, the US determines the framework – efficiency, productivity, economic growth – in which discussions of the good society are to take place. The US is not only the predominant source of scholarly articles and textbooks on economics, but sets the terms for popular discussion by way of an army of allies, such as the anonymous figures (both the authors of its articles and even its book reviews) who produce *The Economist*. This British publication, with two-thirds of its circulation in North America, offers its readers an 'economic orthodoxy lite', with a focus on the heroic entrepreneur (as symbolised by the presence of a column called simply 'Schumpeter'): its broad reach is indicative of the extraordinarily wide influence of this market ideology, embracing as it does not only the formal writings of the academy, but a respectable middle-brow audience as well. The widespread and fatalistic acceptance of the dictates of the marketplace on the part of much of the public, from high unemployment to levels of inequality without precedent in living memory, is linked to the dissemination of this right-wing ideology as scientific veracity in both an academic and a popular context.

The US no longer functions as a standard for the good society, arguably not even in material terms. But in so many ways it continues to set the agenda for discourse worldwide on the standards for societal success. The US offers to the rest of the world a model of capitalism well suited to elites – an unequal society in which the bulk of the population is regulated by market forces, while innovation (including financial innovation) from an elite is the source of wealth creation. US intellectual power, in both its academic and more popular manifestations, continues to play a central role in controlling the terms in which this discourse takes place worldwide, partially, and ironically, because of the continued power and coherence of the university system, much of which was constructed through collective social action and governmental expenditure. Ideologies, and the political decisions that spring from this intellectual basis, cannot merely be put to one side by the rest of the world, given the weight the US has in macroeconomic and financial events, and the looming crisis over climate change.

The influence of the US may be taking on a trajectory resembling that of Rome: long after its demise in the West at the school textbook date of 476 A.D., Rome played a dominant role in intellectual culture for the subsequent millennium, with Latin language and literature and the sixth-century legal code of Justinian. Many individuals may find the social democratic choices made in Western Europe about how to organise society more attractive than those to be found in the US, but as long as the intellectual discourse is conducted in American terms, these choices will be perceived to be subjective and arbitrary. It is not merely the presence of long lags in the maintenance of influence of great powers that is in operation here, but the failure of the forces of social democracy to offer a coherent alternative.

The inability of European social democracy to mount a coherent defence of its policies will ultimately leave it vulnerable to dismantlement. Compared with the well-developed notions associated with free-market economics, social democracy has become notorious for the absence of a unified conception that gives an overall shape and coherence to individual policies: it is almost as if social democratic policy makers have internalised the Hayekian notion that the imposition of direction and unification on individual policies would smack of a totalitarian constructivism. In the context of this failure, the policies associated with social democracy are therefore characterised by critics as improvisations, a response to political pressure groups, a sentimental and unrealistic attachment to fairness, or luxuries that can be dispensed with in a crisis. Perhaps even more egregiously, if a coherent alternative to the free-market model of society cannot be formulated, individuals and groups who find themselves repelled by the consequences of unrestrained capitalism will accept the latter's claim to be coextensive with rational approaches to social affairs, and may embrace post-modern, religious or other critiques of rationality itself.

The search for a coherent alternative to what remains the pervasive free-market ideology is thus not merely an academic indulgence but a practical necessity. There may be a temptation to appear tough-minded about the problems confronting us. We may thus decide to accept the terms in which the current debate is posed, for instance the notion that we are engaged in an eternal battle with 'the others', but suggest that a deviation from free-market principles, in the form, for instance, of state intervention in industry, will do the job better: such an approach is unlikely to threaten the hegemony of free-market discourse on the trajectory of the economy and society. A true alternative must dare to be utopian – to base a view of society on principles of human development, equality and solidarity, leading to a control of social decision making in which democracy is not merely an empty phrase.

With contemporary developments, in fact, leading in the direction of increasing inequality, as we shall see in the following chapter, the obstacles to the creation of an alternative path seem ever greater, and at the same time its creation seems ever more necessary.

10
Economic Growth and Inequality

Economic growth emerged in the second half of the twentieth century as the dominant justification for economic policy and, to a great extent, for social action in general. Growth, it was claimed, would obviate, or at least mitigate, sources of conflict in society and generate the resources for doing good things such as alleviating inequality. But does economic growth, as conventionally measured, truly reflect the increased capacity of a society to pursue its desired tasks? There are good reasons to believe that it does not. True economic development is an extended process, one that is only reflected in growth statistics with a long lag, if at all. Inequality, furthermore, is not a problem that we can put off dealing with until we can afford to do so, since it impinges upon the very process of economic development that is the source of increased economic capacity. Lastly, we may ask whether we have let the tail wag the dog – growth was supposed to expand the range of societal choices, but are the exigencies of growth now being used as excuses to dictate social outcomes?

Why is growth desirable?

The very phrase 'economic growth' is problematic. It poses an analogy with a natural function, such as the growth of a tree, when in fact, as commonly employed, the phrase merely indicates the rate of increase in an accounting relationship: gross national income is defined as part of an accounting identity in which current income is equal to expenditure on current goods and services – gross domestic product, or GDP. In the exposition below, the terms 'national income' and 'GDP' will be used interchangeably. The modern form of these accounts shows the influence of Keynesian theory in the way that expenditure is divided between consumption (which largely responds to changes in income and wealth), investment (whose inherent volatility was seen as the central cause of business cycles), and governmental functions, which in traditional Keynesian theory can be manipulated to compensate for the volatility of investment.[1]

I will introduce the central aspects of a critique of the national income measure with what I hope is a colourful personal anecdote, true in all details if my memory holds, even if slightly out of focus in terms of chronology. I spent my earliest years growing up in Manhattan Beach, Brooklyn, in housing created from Second World War US Army barracks, in which the four of us (my sister not yet born) were all crowded into a single room, conditions more pleasant than my description might indicate. At some point my father placed a bet on the Irish Sweepstakes, in the US a famous but illegal form of off-track betting; we managed to win $400 simply because our horse had succeeded in entering a race. With that princely sum, we were just about the first family on the block to purchase a TV set, a magnificent instrument with a seven-inch screen that managed to work upon occasion. One day, while watching a precursor of the notorious infomercials now to be found on US television, I, as a child, was fascinated by an all-purpose machine that could slice and dice vegetables as well as knead dough and do other things – all for only $9.95! I asked my father why we didn't purchase such a wonderful device, and it was here that I had my epiphany: he explained to me that any machine that performed so many *different* functions probably couldn't do any *one* of them very well. This is the essence of the critique of national income offered here: it is regularly used for highly diverse purposes – as a measure of aggregate demand, of (in per capita terms) economic welfare and, third, of a nation's overall economic capacity – and fulfils none of these tasks adequately.

Of these three purposes, GDP is best suited as a measure of aggregate demand. The national income accounts in their present form have their origins in the interwar period as a tool in the implementation of Keynesian policies to regulate business cycles. The Keynesian theory replaced an older metaphoric image of unemployment as being due to the presence of sludge in the water pipes (such as a labour union) that prevented the clearing of the labour market. Instead, unemployment from a Keynesian perspective was seen to be a question of too little steam pressure (in the form of aggregate demand) being produced to get the engine going at full capacity. National income served as the Keynesian measure of this steam pressure. At present, a focus on GDP for this reason – for the purpose of regulating the overall level of economic activity and mitigating unemployment and business cycle fluctuations – is its least problematic role, at least among Keynesian economists. The high growth rates and low levels of unemployment that characterised the capitalist world of the 1950s and 1960s were attributed to successful Keynesian regulation and brought forth an early version of the 'end of history' argument, by which economic growth in rich countries, taking place in the context of little change in the distribution of income, obviated class conflict – 'a rising tide lifts all boats'.

In the midst of this period of collective celebration, disquiet remained about the inherent untidiness of the Keynesian synthesis. At the microeconomic level, Keynesian economists generally presumed that the invisible hand of competition between capitalist firms was a suitable mechanism for the allocation and distribution of resources in society, in the absence of specific forms of market failure such as air pollution. In general, the academic consensus was that any redistribution would be best effected by progressive income and wealth taxes: forms of direct interference in free-market allocation from the activities of labour unions or minimum wage legislation were never convincingly integrated into Keynesian orthodoxy by those who argued in their favour. The panoply of legislation created in the US in the 1930s, such as the Glass–Steagall Act regulating the banking sector, were generally passed over unnoticed as merely part of the institutional backdrop to the functioning of the economy. Any notions that these regulations were putting a leash on a financial sector that would otherwise be dangerously unstable were proffered in a muted way. The consensus of an inherent stability and efficacy of the capitalist allocation of resources at a microeconomic level rested uneasily with the macroeconomic arm of the Keynesian synthesis. The Keynesian model was, after all, a mechanism for regulating, rather than reforming or reconstructing, a capitalism that was perceived to be inherently volatile at the macroeconomic level, a system driven by the animal spirits of capitalist psychology; Keynesianism never even pretended to offer a mechanism for structural reform of this instability.

The period of the 1970s saw the cessation of this golden age of growth, with higher levels of unemployment than had been seen since the early years of the postwar recovery, and concerns about the level of inflation; these events vitiated confidence in the Keynesian model of managed capitalism. But the 1970s were also characterised by the loss of any residual belief in the developed capitalist world that the centrally planned economic system of Soviet-type economies offered an alternative mode for the regulation of an economy in which, perhaps, stability and full employment could be exchanged at a reasonable cost for the obvious inadequacies of the centrally planned system.

This perceived lack of an alternative to capitalism, in the context of an economic crisis in nations evincing, at least nominally, a Keynesian-style ideology, contributed to a revival in the popularity (most especially among individuals and groups not likely to be victims of these doctrines) of nineteenth-century liberal ideas. The Keynesian identification of unemployment with a deficiency of aggregate demand was rejected in favour of a reconstituted version of the liberal view, taking the form of a postulated natural rate of unemployment. From this perspective, the only sustainable way to deal with unemployment is to increase labour market flexibility and remove institutional barriers to the adjustment of wages. Since the crisis of 2007–8 and the renewal of the spectre of mass unemployment in many countries, there has been some revival of Keynesian ideas and an increased emphasis on the need for the maintenance of a sufficiency of levels of aggregate demand to mitigate economic collapse: GDP and its associated statistics have once again become the focus of urgent public concern. It is this largely technocratic role of national income in the regulation of aggregate demand that has led to it being adopted as a measure for other purposes.

The role of national income as an indication (in per capita terms) of economic welfare is more ideologically tinged. Despite the emergence of other measures in popular discourse, especially in the context of poorer countries, such as the Human Development Index of the United Nations,[2] growth in national income remains ubiquitous as an indication of improvements in material welfare in a given society, and for making comparisons between societies. Thus, as a riposte to left-wing or elite critiques of consumerism, we are told that economic growth is essential because people 'want to better their lives ... and only with more economic output can more people live a more enjoyable and more satisfying existence'.[3]

There can be no doubt that rises in national income in the early postwar world reflected increases in living standards. Economies across the Western world (and in the Eastern bloc as well) experienced consequential improvements in their material standard of living, with the great bulk of the population having the opportunity to make significant additions to the quantity of domestic housing space, and to improve the quality of domestic life with devices for the alleviation of work in the home, such as vacuum cleaners, and for entertainment, such as television. For some groups, even in Western Europe and North America, rising income permitted the purchase of minimum sufficiency in food and clothing for the first time. Medical care underwent a revolution with the introduction of antibiotics. Perhaps the most decisive improvement in the quality of life came about through the emptying of factories, mines and farms – the offering to a large portion of the population the possibility of earning their living in the less arduous and dangerous context of white collar work.

In the wake of these dramatic changes in material life, there emerged in this period a large literature critical of this mass consumerism – the supposedly gratuitous expenditure on the part of a public that had been manipulated by advertisers to purchase goods they really didn't need. One of the earliest and most prominent examples, Galbraith's *Affluent Society* of 1958, combined this critique with a call for a focus on the eradication of poverty in the context of an increase in public sector expenditure, as embodied in the book's famous phrase, 'private wealth amidst public squalor'. From our present perspective, however, Galbraith's concentration on gratuitous expenditure by consumers was dysfunctional and distracted attention from the real gains for the great mass of the population in this period. Much of this literature, down to the present day, takes the form of patronising lectures from well-heeled authors on the presence of a popular addiction to consumption goods, one that serves little purpose but to alienate a public exercising its free choice in the context of available possibilities for living and consuming; its focus on how adults can be manipulated by advertising, furthermore, focuses attention away from its egregious and sinister use in the manipulation of children. While earlier critiques of consumption by the masses were often from elite, right-wing sources,[4] the great body of anti-consumerist critiques, from the 1950s to the present, have largely emanated from individuals who would identify themselves politically as being left of centre (or, in the case of Baran and Sweezy, a more definitively left-radical viewpoint). The baleful result is the established presence of a right-wing populist defence of the freedom for consumers to spend as they choose against left-wing elitists. Any reform programme based on socialist or environmental principles must put forth a convincing vision of an alternative path that does not simply admonish the population to behave better.

There are good reasons for hesitating to identify improvements in well-being simply with the rises in per capita income that have taken place in rich countries in the past few decades. First, increases in welfare result not only from rises in per capita income, but, in principle, from reductions in the number of hours worked per year, under the presumption that these cutbacks are voluntary; the latter tendency has had markedly divergent trajectories in advanced economies, with modest declines of 1.4 per cent in the US and 5.5 per cent in the UK from 1980 to 2013, in contrast to an 18.3 per cent decline in France and an 11 per cent decline in the Netherlands, so that hours worked in France and Netherlands in 2013 are 83 per cent and 77 per cent of those in the US, respectively, and 89 per cent and 83 per cent of those in the UK.[5]

Second, in the context of negative externalities in consumption (such as traffic jams from more cars on the road), an increase in the production and sale of cars may generate little or no improvement in welfare if there is no decrease in the average journey times of households. It would thus be difficult to contend that the share of rises in per capita income in recent decades that is accounted for by the purchase and use of cars (and paying for roads and maintenance) is matched by comparable improvements in personal mobility.

The growth rate in GDP may also underestimate improvements in the population's consumption of goods. As noted in Chapter 6, hedonic calculations suggest that improvements in the quality of many goods, such as quieter engines and improved safety features in cars, are not fully represented in real income calculations. Perhaps more significantly, a declining rate of purchase of durable consumer goods such as cars or television sets may be consistent with a rise in the number of vehicles or televisions per household. In general, declines or slow growth in income among, for instance, poor people do not necessarily signal greater deprivation in the consumption of durable consumer goods.

But it is no repetition of the misplaced anti-consumerist critiques of the past to suggest that, in the present day, the correspondence between economic growth in rich countries and any reasonable concept of improvements in human welfare has deteriorated. The most straightforward reason for this disconnect is that for the last three decades, as will be seen below, there has been a rapid widening of the gap between rich and poor, most exceptionally in the Anglo-Saxon economies. While, for several decades after the Second World War, the distribution of income in most rich countries was relatively stable, so that that the rising tide of rapid economic growth did indeed 'lift all boats', more recent economic growth has often been of little benefit to the less well-off, or even middling, groups in the economy.

Economists, however, are still in the habit of treating an economy's overall growth rate as the central parameter for judging its success, with rises in inequality as a peripheral consideration. Increases in inequality, however, can cause us to re-evaluate our perceptions of this success: from 1975 to 2006, average family income grew in the US at a rate of 32 per cent, compared with 27 per cent in France. But the rise in inequality in the US was so great in this period that, if we exclude the top 1 per cent in the US and in France (where inequality also increased, though more modestly), growth was 18 per cent in the US and 26 per cent in France.[6] This widening of the income distribution is an important issue not only for considerations of economic welfare but, as we shall see below, because of its longer-term effects on economic capacity.

Economic capacity and lags in economic development

The third use of national income, as a measure of a nation's overall economic capacity, plays a pervasive role in public discourse, but one that is rarely subject to critical evaluation. The notion that GDP growth – economic growth – can measure the expansion of a nation's economic capacity with a simple scalar measure parallels tendencies in other disciplines in the twentieth century, such as the search in psychology for 'g', an overall measure of the limits of an individual's cognitive power in terms of biological capacity, to be examined in Chapter 11. The argument here will be focused on this aspect of the limitations of the GDP measure – as an indicator of a nation's capacity to pursue various tasks – and on the commonly encountered notion that expenditure on physical infrastructure and education, or public action to mitigate inequality, are luxuries that await sufficient economic growth to make them affordable.

The idea that national income measures the gross economic capacity of a nation is a pervasive, if hidden, presumption of contemporary political discourse, with Margaret Thatcher and others suggesting that, for instance, tax cuts for the rich are necessary to generate the growth in national income necessary for society to be able to afford the good things in life, such as aid to the poor. For the economist Joseph Stiglitz, 'growth increases supply ... [and] should in theory, make [choices between alternatives] less painful'.[7] But growth in national income (economic growth) is an imprecise or even inaccurate measure of changes in a nation's capacity to make economic choices in the future. Standard measures of national income violate meaningful conceptions of economic capacity, which should in principle be linked to notions of sustainable consumption. In strict analogy with good accounting practice for firms, a society whose rapid growth in consumption takes place alongside a neglect of its physical infrastructure is living in a fool's paradise, and is falsely measuring its income; in an ecological context, the national accounts fail by not incorporating the depreciation of the natural environment into the income calculation. The additional element introduced into the discussion here will emphasise that changes in national income poorly represent increases or decreases in the flow of services available from the stock of human assets. Growth in national income, therefore, does not give an accurate notion of the trajectory of a nation's economic capacity.

A relatively trivial aspect of measuring a nation's economic capacity concerns the continuing focus in public discussions on aggregate, as opposed to per capita, levels of GDP, as when in 2010 it was widely reported that China had surpassed Japan as number two in the world GDP stakes. What possible significance can be attached to this 'event'? Clearly, it tells us nothing about the present-day possibilities for material consumption in Japan compared with China, a country that remains poor on a per capita basis. What, then, is the purpose of such a comparison? A search through some of the common recitations of the importance of economic growth may give a clue, such as the notorious failure of the late-nineteenth-century French economy to expand in comparison with Imperial Germany. But France's slow growth in national income, as noted in Chapter 2, is substantially accounted for by stagnation in the growth of its population numbers, so that in per capita income terms, improvements in French living standards were closer to those in Germany than to the laggard gains in Britain. In this and other cases, the true reason for concern about rankings of GDP and its growth in absolute terms is as a measure of a nation's capacity to make war (either in a literal sense or in the context of economic warfare) – today an indication of the lingering influence of US Cold War obsessions in popular, and even academic, discourse.

GDP as a measure of economic capacity, however, is about more than war making. As suggested above, it is often employed as an indicator of the limits to the ranges of economic choices available to a given society: growth in GDP supposedly alleviates the need to choose between good things – consuming more, and also helping the poor. The critique here focuses on two elements: first, the inappropriate use of the growth rate in national income as an indicator of a nation's enhancement in its overall economic capacity – its long-term economic development; second, the fact that the inappropriateness of this measure shows itself in a particular way: many activities that generate increases in an economy's (long-term) economic capacity, such as education, will register in the GDP accounts only with a long lag.

GDP growth rates are a deceptive indicator of increases in a nation's economic capacity, which are better measured by considering the growth of economic income. In a well-known definition, economic income is the maximum amount that an individual can consume in a given time period and still expect to be as well-off at the end as at the beginning.[8] The literature in this area deals with a range of issues,[9] but converges on notions linked with capital maintenance – economic income is not simply net cash inflow, but *sustainable* net cash inflow. There is, thus, a tension between a conception of income simply as money flowing in (which the national income measure comes close to doing) and economic income. This tension is most visible in the context of a firm, where an attempt is made in company accounts to keep a record of the change in the value of its assets, which must then be reconciled with the income statement. The motivation for so doing is that an accounting system that identified income purely with net cash flow would not signal to a firm the dangers of running its machines 24 hours a day – it would be blind to their accelerated depreciation under these conditions. In principle, if not in practice, an appropriate deduction for this accelerated depreciation should bring the firm's calculation of its income closer in line with this economic income than it otherwise would be.

In the case of firms with publicly traded shares, the value of the firm's assets is calculated not only in the formalised accounts of the firm (which often take the form of historic cost valuation of assets and mechanical, tax-driven rules for their depreciation), but on the stock market. Let us presume that the firm suddenly makes a discovery that is expected to be economically lucrative in the future (but not immediately), and this fact becomes public knowledge. How is this information – a perceived increase in the firm's long-term sustainable cash flow – likely to appear in measures of firm performance? In the firm's capital account, whether this discovery will register as an increase in the value of the assets of the firm will be contingent on accounting conventions and firm strategies, especially with regard to the registration of patents on this discovery. In the company's annual income statement, however, the impact on the profits registered is likely to be minimal or non-existent – the reconciliation in the income statement with any increase in firm value recorded in the capital account will take place 'below the line'. The one immediate manifestation of this discovery is a likely jump in the share value of the company, a reflection of an expected increase in the firm's economic income – its sustainable net cash flow over time – one not likely to be immediately visible in standard calculations of a firm's profit.

For the firm, thus, there are mechanisms, most especially in the imperfect form of stock market evaluation, for registering changes in its long-term, sustainable cash flow – its economic capacity. There is no equivalent mechanism in the national accounts. Four ways will be highlighted below in which the economic income perspective sheds light on the inadequacies of standard approaches to economic growth as an indicator of the growth of economic capacity:

1. The issues surrounding infrastructure and the ecological critique concerned with common property resources.
2. The problem of economic irreversibilities.
3. Human assets and external effects. We have seen in Chapter 7 that there are significant positive external effects to educational improvement that are put to one side by the individualistic focus of the human capital literature. As a result, many of the benefits to society of improved education will register in conventional national income calculations only with a substantial lag; lags may also exist because of the residual *in situ* advantages of established economic powers. A key empirical proposition here is that educational development will emerge in conventional national income indicators with long and variable lags.
4. The relationship between economic growth and income distribution. Much of what appears as consumption by poor people in the national accounts is, in fact, expenditure to maintain human assets. Furthermore, both poverty and income distribution will have reciprocal relationships with educational attainment and economic mobility in a society. Income distribution considerations are thus key components, along with formal education, in the development of the human assets of a society and, therefore, of its economic capacity.

These considerations are considered in turn.

Problems of economic measurement associated with the infrastructure and the natural environment each exist for distinct reasons. In the case of infrastructure, neglect of the upkeep of roads, bridges and ports takes place in the context of the likely invisibility of their deterioration in the short term; politicians focusing on the next election can claim to make savings in the public finances, with the costs to be borne by later generations. This problem is only exacerbated by a one-sided emphasis on the conventional economic growth measure. Thus, an article in *The Times* of London[10] in 2004 lamented the fact that supposed achievements from high economic growth whose foundations were built during the Thatcher era were being threatened by a relentless rise in public spending and government employment by a Labour government. But much of this enhanced spending was to compensate for shortfalls in spending provision in the pre-Labour era for the National Health Service. If we accept that this expenditure was necessary maintenance in the context of the nation's health, than the growth rates in national income registered in the supposed golden age of the Thatcher era had been, to use my former president's syntax, over exaggerated when considered from the perspective of economic income. Environmental campaigners, by contrast, have an additional burden. Unlike the physical infrastructure, over which, as a rule, governments have stewardship, environmental issues are often concerned with the running down of key elements of a collective capital stock that are common property, such as the atmosphere and the oceans in the context of climate change. With the special complication that these forms of deterioration cross national boundaries, modifications to national income growth calculations to incorporate deductions for this deterioration are unlikely to take place.[11] Nevertheless, this line of argumentation plays an important role in counteracting a continuing tendency to treat GDP as a good measure of overall economic capacity: it is still common to suggest that the best way to deal with environmental problems is, first, to generate sufficient economic growth (rise in GDP) to be able to deal with these problems.[12] Such an argument is inherently unpersuasive if the growth in the economic capacity to cope with this environmental deterioration is poorly measured by these GDP rises in the first place. It would be as if a firm had a strategy for earning the cash to renew its obsolescent capital stock by running its existing machines 24 hours a day: the firm had better take care that the resultant increase in revenues does not mask an accelerated collapse of existing equipment that makes their replacement impossible.

The problem of irreversibilities means that decisions made today restrict choices in the future, so that growth rates emanating from those decisions do not necessarily correspond to greater economic capacity in the form of enhanced choice. Issues surrounding public transport illustrate that decisions made in one generation may well exclude alternatives forever, a story told most vividly in the case of Los Angeles in the film 'Who Framed Roger Rabbit?' The group conspiring to frame our eponymous hero were involved in a conspiracy to rid Los Angeles of trams (this is all taking place in the 1940s) for the sake of the oil companies. The wry subtext of the film is that, of course, the villains succeeded. In fact, the story told in the film closely paralleled what really happened in a host of US cities, in which a social decision was made to remove trams, buy up rights of way for highways, and zone residential living conditions to low-density, car-oriented living.[13] Decisions on public transport have little to do with the textbook picture of the individual consumer choosing between goods. In many of these cases, there is not much room for marginal decisions – either the environment is optimised for the car or it remains suitable for public transport. Many European cities are fortunate in the fact that they are too old and too cramped to be completely destroyed to accommodate the car; in the US, New York City partially survived the schemes of the city planner Robert Moses for this reason (see Chapter 1). But in newer cities, the development of car-oriented, low-density environments is well-nigh irreversible, and it is hard to feel anything but *Schadenfreude* for the feeble attempts of present-day Los Angeles to introduce public transport.

The presence of significant positive external effects resulting from cognitive development, discussed in Chapter 7, gives an additional reason to believe that the path of the growth rate of economic income will deviate from that of the conventional national income measure. Figure 10.1 shows economic growth in Japan from 1870 to 1998 using a conventional national income measure denoted by y, its trajectory indicating the growth rate in different time periods of real (corrected for inflation) income per capita in each sub-period (1870–1913 (1.5 per cent); 1913–40 (2.8 per cent); 1955–73 (8.2 per cent); and 1973–90 (3.0 per cent)).[14] The slow growth of 0.8 per cent from 1990 to 1998 signals the beginning of a period of stagnation in the growth of y, but in no way mitigates the world historical significance of the transformation of this society over the previous decades. In 1870, Japan's per capita income was 23 per cent of that in the UK and 37 per cent of the

g_y = growth rate in real national income per capita

Figure 10.1   Japanese growth history: y

West European average, slowly advancing by 1913 to 28 per cent of the UK and 40 per cent of Western Europe. It is only in the postwar boom that we observe the Japanese miracle: following recovery to pre-Second World War levels in 1955, a stupendous growth then takes place that propels Japan to rough parity with the UK and Western Europe by 1973.

These statistics document an elevation of material life in Japanese society from deprivation to affluence and are undoubtedly indicative of a significant rise in the material well-being of the population. From the perspective of economic capacity, many of the caveats about the use of the national income growth measure discussed above, such as environmental pollution, are probably of secondary interest for much of this history. It is, rather, the large proportion of the increases in business investment and governmental expenditure devoted to war making and to war-making capacity before 1945 that vitiate the use of the growth rate in y as an indicator of the expansion in the capacity of Japanese society to provide consumer and other material benefits to its population.

There is, however, something important missing in the narrative implied by looking solely at the trajectory of y. It would appear from this trajectory that the period 1870–1913 was one of only moderate success, with the post-Second World War period the locus of Japan's transformation into one of the richest states in the world. But such a recitation of events masks the fact that the pre-First World War period contains perhaps the most extraordinary economic and cultural transformation of the past half millennium of global history. Japan emerged from the 250-year Tokugawa period before the Meiji restoration of 1868 with a sophisticated bureaucracy and the highest rates of literacy in Asia: primary school enrolment rates in 1882, early in the reform process, were already 47 per cent of those in Germany and 52 per cent of the rates in France.[15] But self-imposed isolation from the west of the Tokugawa period had dictated that Japan had been overwhelmingly a traditional society both in material and intellectual terms.

The subsequent transformation involved the construction of physical (including war-making) capacity, but was dominated by a modernisation in cultural and intellectual formation: rises in literacy and school enrolment only partially capture a transition from a traditional Confucian cultural orientation to a focus on German bureaucracy, the biology of Charles Darwin and the physics of James Clerk Maxwell. Is there any historical parallel for the speed and thoroughness with which this reorientation of Japanese culture took place?[16] There may well have been negative aspects to this rapid transition, including a disruption of cultural norms that led some sections of the society in the direction of a deranged militarism in subsequent decades.[17] From a strictly economic perspective, however, the period from 1870 to 1913 is one of world historical significance and the truly miraculous phase of Japanese development, one that transformed the economic potential of the society.

An alternative perspective on Japanese growth would be embodied in a conjectural history of the growth of ei (economic income), tracing the evolution of Japan's economic potential over this period, with economic income represented by consumption plus the net rate of accumulation of natural, physical and human assets. Unlike the growth rates in y, however, they cannot be readily calculated, for several reasons. First, growth in ei is an indication of the rate of expansion of economic capacity – the increased *potential* to pursue a range of activities – but this growth may never be realised and observed. One reason for a gap between growth in economic capacity and its actualisation will be the influence of macroeconomic conditions. For example, in Figure 10.1, for the whole sub-period 1955 to 1990, Japanese growth in y is very high (5.6 per cent), but from 1955 to 1973, it is at the stupendous level of 8.2 per cent, partially reflecting buoyant world markets and therefore the ease of using existing potential to full capacity in the midst of this golden age of capitalism. A portion of the decline in the growth of y to 3 per cent from 1973 to 1990 probably reflects weaker worldwide and domestic macroeconomic conditions, with concomitant lower levels of utilisation of physical and human capacity, rather than any substantial decrease in the growth rate of economic potential ei in this period.[18]

A second reason for a failure to realise economic potential may be particularly relevant for dealing with communist and former communist countries. In the case of China, the exceptional growth rates in y since the market-based reforms commencing in 1978 may have had as prerequisites the great achievements in literacy and general education since 1949 (in contrast with the weaker performance of India since independence),[19] despite the murderous brutality and irrational policies that accompanied the communist revolutions in China and other countries. Whether these increases in economic potential would ever have been realised under the pre-reform, centrally planned regime in China is conjectural and problematic. But the ei perspective underlines this important question: was China's economic emergence purely a matter of market reform per se, or was it linked to this prior expansion in its economic potential, especially with regard to its human assets?

The perspective taken here is that the trajectory of national economic potential is centrally determined by the development of its human assets. In the perspicacious, if premature, words of Dr Lyon Playfair, 'Raw material...is being made available to all...and Industry must in future be supported, not by a competition of local advantages, but by a competition of intellects.'[20] A century after this prognostication, Japan began its rise from abject poverty – for the first time in history, we observe a great industrial power emerge that is almost completely bereft of raw materials. Unfortunately, the very complexity of the role played by human assets in the development of economic potential generates further obstacles to the measurement of the latter in any precise way: even concrete indicators, such as increases in school enrolment, are likely to disguise the extent to which these increases are also accompanied, in the Japanese and other cases, by a reorientation from traditional to modern, scientific disciplines.

These difficulties, however, do not justify an approach that simply abandons any attempt to chart the trajectory of growth of a nation's natural, physical and human assets. It may well be foolish for a country to pursue a strategy of economic growth that results in excessive amounts of pollution (with the excuse that they will deal with it when rich enough to afford to do so): the modified national accounts incorporating the resultant deterioration in the value of the natural capital stock illustrate that such a strategy may well be dysfunctional. By analogy, accelerated growth in national income may emerge from egregious forms of labour, long hours and dangerous conditions for children and adults. But such forms of growth, resulting in a depreciation of the human capital stock and derangement of household life, may not be conducive to long-term development, as will be seen below. In the opposite direction, societies that have made exceptional efforts to educate their population, often underpinned by stability and security in household existence, will see much of this appreciation in the value of the human capital stock register as increases in national income, but almost invariably with a long lag.

A correct understanding of these issues is vital not only for an understanding of the economics of the historical past, but for economic policy. If policy makers naïvely use growth rates in per capita income as an indication of the rate of increase of a nation's economic capacity, some awkward judgements can easily emerge: the gains in national income accruing to Japan in the decades after 1868, if such accounts had existed, might have been taken as an indication of only modest achievement, instead of the remarkable transformation that actually occurred. If our contemporary obsessions with 'the' growth rate had then been in place, would not an imaginary pre-First World War IMF have called for less investment in school facilities in Japan and more in silk production?

For the reasons indicated in Chapter 7, rapid growth in economic capacity associated with accretions to human assets is likely to appear in growth rates in national income only with long lags; in the case of Japan, this general tendency may have been reinforced by its specific circumstances – militarism and defeat in war delaying the realisation of economic potential in terms of goods and services, followed by the Golden Age of Capitalism after the Second World War, a period uniquely conducive to the realisation of economic potential. But the presence of these lags from educational improvement is a more general proposition. A study by Lars Sandberg shows only a weak association between literacy and income for 20 European countries in 1850, but a much higher one between literacy in 1850 and income in 1970.[21] In the case of Sweden, there is some controversy surrounding the traditional view that it was an exceptionally poor European country in the mid-nineteenth century,[22] and Sandberg's resulting use of Sweden in this context as 'poor but educated'. Perhaps the most striking European example, one not used by him, is Finland, demonstrably poor in 1870 (a per capita income 69 per cent that of Sweden, and 58 per cent of the West European average) but with relatively high levels of literacy,[23] which reached West European average incomes in the 1970s and then surpassed them. We now find it difficult to encounter poor, educated countries. And while overeducation – the failure of societies to make good use of an increasingly educated population – may come about for a range of reasons to be discussed in Chapter 12, the apparent overproduction of, especially, highly skilled graduates may simply result from the lags inherent in the processes by which this increase in skills is absorbed into the economy and registers as higher current income.

Education, in the raw sense of an increase in formal schooling, is no royal road to economic growth. Substantial lags will be observed because of the time needed for the effects of newly educated workers entering the workforce, intergenerational effects, and the working through of the multiplier of the dispersion of the spillovers from cognitive development discussed in Chapter 7. For instance, the process of emulation of those individuals with newly acquired skills may well be an extended process. But this cognitive dispersion has several other socially embedded aspects that may also result in lags before substantive improvements in material life can be observed: it is possible, for instance, that concomitant improvements in the physical infrastructure (most obvious in the case of computer facilities, libraries and scientific equipment) may need to take place before we can observe significant rises in material conditions resulting from improved cognitive functioning.

If aspects of the physical infrastructure are complementary to educational advance, then human infrastructure plays an even more central role. Broad-based societal development of cognitive capacity involves the presence of households whose members have achieved sufficient levels of security in health, nutrition and general material existence to be able to proceed with planning and organising the augmentation of their skills and cognitive capacity; these households must also have the financial resources to pursue learning activities. The more substantial the barriers linked to class and ethnicity, the greater the obstacles to the use of formal education as a transformative device: in unequal societies, many children are unlikely to receive from their home environment a range of habits, attitudes, cognitive and social skills that those from privileged groups take for granted. In societies with limited upward mobility, incentives to pursue cognitive development may be reduced because of the perception that the potential material rewards from this pursuit are of a restricted nature. Thus, if cognitive development is a key requisite of economic advance, then the complementary role played by social equality may dictate that it is not a luxury indulged in once a country becomes rich, but an essential aspect of this process.

Inequality and national income

In the rich nations of Western Europe and North America, the Golden Age of Capitalism after the Second World War largely took place with no obvious trend in the distribution of income within nations, so that the rapid growth of this period was coincident with widespread material gains across these societies. The general deceleration of economic growth beginning in the 1970s witnessed the emergence to prominence in both academic and popular discourse in the Anglo-Saxon world of a range of economic arguments under the general rubric of neoliberalism. On the whole, these doctrines did not address the question of economic equality directly, but were broadly consistent with the pursuit of a range of public policies concerning governmental expenditure and taxation, the regulation of labour union activity and the privatisation or deregulation of formerly public services, that, in fact, engendered inequality. Thus, the neoliberal notion that the economy would operate more efficiently with a reduction in the burden of taxation is superficially one without any inherent class bias, but its most prominent realisation in subsequent decades was the lowering of tax rates for high earners justified by the supply side claim, put forth in an academic context by Martin Feldstein, that lower tax rates would generate incentives for those on high incomes to be more entrepreneurial.[24] Alongside these academic arguments, there was a more popular rhetoric from Arthur Laffer and others, to be discussed below, that opined the virtues of inequality.

The growth of inequality since the 1980s has shown some of its earliest and most explicit manifestations in the Anglo-Saxon world. For a range of other rich countries, this tendency towards growing inequality has been emerging, though less decisively, with those defying this trend not obviously less successful in terms of overall economic growth.[25] The trend towards growing inequality has been robust for a range of different measures and measurement techniques, reflected in overall growth in both income and wealth inequality, most distinctively in the increasing shares of the top layers and often declining shares for the bottom groups.[26] And especially since the crisis of 2007–8, the presence and persistence of low-wage work and poverty are widespread, though important differences exist between countries.[27]

One element generating this process of growing inequality within rich nations has simply been the dispersion of national economic policies first undertaken in the UK since the accession of Margaret Thatcher in 1979 and of Ronald Reagan in the US in 1981, most especially the decline in tax rates for higher earners: between 1970 and 2004 in the US, average tax rates for the highest income group fell from 75 per cent to 35 per cent (in the UK, the fall was from 92 to 43 per cent (for the year 2000)).[28] But an explanation based on ideology and national economic policies, though important, is only part of the story, one that does not account for the ease with which these policies have been foisted upon the constituencies of these nations and the plausibility that the neoliberal doctrines have acquired in public discourse.

The leading candidates to explain this growing inequality are technological change and increasing international competition. The former story has been told for the US by Claudia Goldin and Lawrence Katz: growth in inequality in the past three decades is accounted for by a process through which less educated workers have suffered in 'the race between education and technology' – a race, it is claimed, that the US has lost not so much because of any discontinuous surge in technological change, but by a stagnation in the production of individuals with improved educational qualifications – a process that has transformed the US from being a world leader in the education field to being a mediocre performer in the OECD;[29] as we shall see, there are reasons to posit a reverse system of causation for these developments, with greater inequality being primarily a cause, rather than the effect, of educational failure. Other studies have reinforced the familiar image of robotics displacing well-paid car production workers, with rich nations experiencing 'reduced labor input of routine manual and routine cognitive tasks and increased labor input of nonroutine cognitive tasks' due to technological change, thus explaining a substantial portion of the demand shift 'favoring college labor' in the US since 1970 and the resultant broadening of the distribution of income.[30]

One hesitates to attribute rising inequality solely to the elusive technological genie: some wheel it out whenever labour is displaced, even in the context of depression, with the ameliorating suggestion that any pain caused is for the sake of progress and creative destruction.[31] Hints in the data are present suggesting that an explanation for growing inequality based exclusively on technology is insufficient: growing inequality in the personal distribution of income has been paralleled by another trend – a comparable increase in many countries in the ratio of profits and property income to wages. Such a development suggests a weakening in the bargaining power of labour vis-à-vis capital, perhaps partially attributable to technological change, but the latter's effect on the relationship between profits and wages on its own would, in a priori terms, be unclear.[32]

In some countries, most especially the US, the increase in the profits share has been partially masked by rises in the remuneration of CEOs and other executives (registered in national accounts as wages), with CEO-to-worker compensation ratios rising from about 20 to 1 in the early 1970s to over 200 to 1 in 2011, having peaked at over 350 to 1 at the turn of the new century. These extraordinary changes in the remuneration of upper layers appear to be nothing more than rents siphoned off from firms' increased possibilities for profits at the expense of workers; gains have been particularly pronounced in the financial sector.[33] The reasons why these developments have taken place most definitively in the US appear to be the incentive to do so because of the low average tax rates on upper incomes, and a long-standing idea, once only an arcane academic notion, of binding executive pay to 'performance'.[34] In contrast to similar schemes for workers, this elevated form of piece work takes place in a context in which CEOs and other executives, unlike workers, often control the terms and conditions under which this remuneration is paid: institutional structures and power relations have played a key role in these changes.[35]

A growing weakness in labour's bargaining power is readily accounted for by the gradual evolution of a more competitive environment in the postwar world, with a consequent decline of the power of organised labour both in wage negotiation and in political influence: the intensification of competition and enhanced mobility of capital described in Chapter 5 have been to the disadvantage of those at the lowest levels of education through a hollowing-out process by which well-paid working-class jobs either have disappeared or have seen their pay and working conditions deteriorate. Increasing inequality overall is, thus, a consequence of the increased power of capital vis-à-vis labour: the expanding purview of firms has induced a search for the cheapest sources for labour worldwide and has been complemented by improvements in transport and communications that have facilitated this process. The growing international fluidity of corporate capital is evidenced not only in seeking out low-cost labour on a worldwide basis, but in a seemingly ever-expanding facility for the avoidance of corporate taxation in host countries and the seeking out of a range of subsidies and forms of tax relief there. For rich individuals, the expansion of tax haven facilities in recent decades has eased the shifting of financial wealth for the avoidance of tax, as we shall see in Chapter 12.

These longer-term developments have converged with a discontinuous expansion in the labour available from developing countries, symbolised and exemplified by the entry of China and India as participants in world capitalism in the 1980s, and the former Soviet bloc in the 1990s – the 'great doubling' of the pool of world labour:[36] 'It is almost impossible that globalization of the magnitudes observed in the 1990s and 2000s would not impact the distribution of earnings and incomes in the USA and elsewhere.'[37] It is thus appropriate to take an ecumenical view of the question of rising inequality, incorporating many of the elements specified above: 'The combination of digitalization and globalization partially moots the debate over whether trade or skill-biased technical change drives inequality more: offshoring and digitalization go together. The rapid expansion of mass higher education in developing countries has allowed low-wage countries to compete in high-tech sectors, weakening the comparative advantage of advanced countries in these sectors.'[38]

The emphasis placed by different groups regarding the provenance of this growth in inequality has proved to be of importance in a political context. Explanations centred on changes in taxes and public policy (such as the policies pursued under Reagan and Thatcher) often have a country-level focus and straightforwardly seek alleviation through changes in national economic policy, most especially a revocation of many of the tax reductions on upper incomes that have taken place in recent decades: the advocacy of such policies is often identified with politics of a moderate left persuasion.[39] By contrast, the more internationally based explanations for growing inequality have a broader range and complexity of political agendas for the alleviation of growing inequality. We thus see the advocacy of public policies to inhibit free trade and the free movement of capital: these policies are associated with those who trace the cause of growing inequality in rich countries to the elimination (or the threat thereof) of well-paid jobs in, especially, manufacturing due to the relocation of these jobs abroad. Those promoting these invariably modest forms of national economic planning (commonly, but not invariably, associated with left-wing political views, often labour union-based) are often fiercely opposed not only by right-wing free-market advocates, but by many members of the moderate left who reject restrictions on international economic activity as a form of public policy.[40]

Explanations for growing international inequality linked with technological change can have about them an air of inevitability: the resultant policies emerging to deal with workers supposedly displaced by technological change are invariably concerned with accommodating and acceding to these developments. Thus, for Goldin and Katz, the persistent displacement of workers with lower levels of skills is used to focus on what they perceive to be present-day failures in public policy in the context of education. But others, as we will see in Chapter 11, structure discussions of inequality in terms of what individuals deserve based on their intrinsic intelligence and character, and how these personal traits affect the level of education they acquire: the winners have a right to their income gains, and the losers are merely the victims of their own inadequacies. If growing inequality is linked to the rapidity of technological change, it is argued, those individuals who have invested in the skills required to prosper in such an environment will need material rewards sufficient to motivate them to undertake that investment.

Ultimately, however, the provenance of growing inequality – whether it is due to increasing international competition or to technological change – is a secondary consideration here. Of greater importance are the deleterious effects of growing inequality and insecurity on the society and economy, and whether policies to halt or reverse such tendencies should be promoted even in the face of claims that they are in violation of conventional canons of economic rationality or, heaven forbid, the imperatives of economic growth.

Can inequality be justified by the presence of a trade-off between equality and efficiency? A prominent intervention from the economist Arthur Okun in an older literature takes such a relationship for granted: 'We can't have our cake of market efficiency and share it equally.' Inequality in capitalism was, according to him, something '*intended* to encourage effort and channel it into socially productive activity'.[41] We might well ask: intended by whom? The whispered implication from the American liberal Okun is that inequality, while a necessary evil, has been sanctioned, with conscious intention, by society through a democratic process of public policy formation because of its efficiency properties. Note that, by contrast, for a true free-market liberal such as Hayek, inequality is an inherent part of the naturally evolving spontaneous order and not to be tampered with by public policy initiatives. We thus observe contrasting attitudes towards inequality among leading protagonists in the modern era – it receives principled support as part of the natural order of things from liberals such as Hayek and Milton Friedman as well as, with a somewhat different orientation, from social Darwinists (see Chapter 11). For American liberals such as Okun and European social democrats, by contrast, acquiescence to inequality is a contingent, empirical question: it is acceptable only to the extent that it is consistent with efficient operation of the economy. Rising inequality in recent decades is causing a renewed intensification of discussions on the nature of this trade-off.

The economist Simon Kuznets had cautiously detected widening inequality in early phases of growth as an empirical regularity.[42] The predominant prejudice in mainstream economics had been to complement the incentives argument above with stories of the form

inequality $\rightarrow$ saving $\rightarrow$ economic growth

Despite the fact that, in a strict neoclassical growth model (see Chapter 6), long-term growth is unrelated to the rate of saving, this notion from classical economics – that upper income earners (the 'wealth creators') will be the source of saving that will serve to finance growth – has continued to have sway, in both academic and political discourse. The Kuznets results showing a trajectory of economic growth that, in its early stages, is correlated with rises in inequality has been contested as an empirical generalisation, since, as we have seen, Japan, South Korea and Taiwan maintained high levels of economic equality in the context of great success in their early growth phases. But the powerful example of mainland China since the late 1970s, with its spectacular growth rates accompanied by sharp rises in inequality, has been of influence in debates over economic development, most especially among the elites of poor countries, who can find it easy to convince themselves that their own self-aggrandisement is to the general good.

In the wake of the economic crisis of 2007–8, this positive link between economic growth and inequality has been contested from Keynesian and other economic perspectives: inequality tends to reduce aggregate demand, with possible adverse effects on the level and growth of income; it can also be a source of economic crises, as lower-income groups pile up debts that eventually become unsustainable, while those on upper incomes save too much, resulting in deficiencies in aggregate demand. The argument against inequality below, however, will advance the discussion developed earlier: inequality poses dangers to the long-term development of a society's human assets and therefore its economic potential. Socialist policies promoting equality, far from creating a dilemma because of the supposed deleterious effects of equality on economic development, are, on the contrary, in line with the grain of history in expanding society's economic capacity based on its human assets.[43]

The presumption that there is an unfortunate but necessary trade-off between good things like equality and efficiency is a deeply resonant one, and perhaps accounts for the ease with which politicians and others convince the public (and themselves) of the destructive notion that the path out of an economic downturn is for ordinary individuals to surrender to the necessity of cutbacks in public expenditure and to make material sacrifices for the sake of economic recovery. Ruling groups making these decisions, usually themselves immune to any substantive negative consequences from these cutbacks, may or may not be sincere in their protestations of the need for general sacrifice. But what is indubitable is how useful such a view is to them. In the 1980s, I was flabbergasted to hear from an elderly woman in Moscow (no apologist for the regime) that a compensatory aspect to the dreadful sacrifices suffered by Soviet society in the process of collectivisation in the late 1920s and 1930s was the fact that, in their absence, 'we couldn't have won the war': the notion that suffering can take place without purpose and without compensation is often difficult for individuals to bear.

Rising inequality continues to have its defenders. A durable political notion in the US, despite its lack of status in the economics literature, is the Laffer curve: so great is the increase in effort of the well-off as a result of reductions in their tax rates that the resultant increase in economic growth is of general benefit, including a rise in the total tax revenues collected from the rich. The element of truth in this notion relates to the blackmail proffered by the well-off in many countries, whose threats to move to more welcoming locations often play a role in encouraging governments (or giving them the excuse) to set low tax rates and permit schemes for legal tax avoidance. In practice, the question of withdrawal of labour by the highly remunerated is typically intermixed with the different question of whether high tax rates discourage private sector investment,[44] with nations some-times pursuing a race to the bottom by undertaking measures to create a pleasing environment for international investment.

In its strict labour effort formulation, the Laffer curve has had little traction in academic economics in the land of its origin, even in right-wing circles: highly paid CEOs in the US have, on the whole, no other nation to flee to, and the notion that even greater remuneration would generate significantly more effort from them beggars belief. In mainstream economics, after all, the well-established textbook notion of the backward-bending supply curve of labour suggests that higher levels of income might well be taken in the form of a lessening of effort, most especially by those who are more affluent: this would appear to be an aspect of the reduction in hours worked per year in rich countries noted above. I once made the mistake of offering the jocular suggestion to some prominent economists that the drastic reduction in quantity of output of composers between the eighteenth century (Handel, Haydn) and the nineteenth (Verdi, Brahms) might be due to the more successful enforcement of property rights in the latter period, making Verdi and Brahms comfortably well-off without the need to churn out compositions at the extraordinary rate of their predecessors.[45] This thesis about incentives for musical composition was never meant to be taken overly seriously, but is at least as plausible as the Laffer notion that the rich will make Promethean efforts in return for lower tax rates.

Even if the Laffer curve in its literal form has been rejected by mainstream economics, the underlying dogma of the discipline remains that 'incentives [are all that] matter' – that effort will invariably be encouraged by higher material rewards, and that negative incentives such as taxation will discourage effort. When left-of-centre economists support policies for the redistribution of income that appear to interfere with prices and allocation in a market economy – the strengthening of union power, minimum wage legislation and taxes on luxury goods – they do so in a defensive manner.

Current arguments in favour of greater equality thus typically embody the commonly presumed trade-off between equity and efficiency, but emphasise the consumption benefits that might then accrue to the less well-off.[46] Such approaches are insufficient for dealing with the questions surrounding economic equality: they tend to have an apologetic tone about them, as if support for equality were the ethical thing but fraught with negative economic consequences. Thus, the best-known argument in recent decades in favour of income equalisation as an aspect of justice is that of the philosopher John Rawls. For present purposes, the key element of his programme, dubbed the 'Difference Principle', is that 'unless there is a distribution that makes both persons better off... an equal distribution is to be preferred', with social and economic inequalities 'to be to the greatest benefit of the least advantaged members of society'.[47] Such a principle is consistent with a substantial deviation from a generalised equalisation of income if inequality generates better material conditions for the least advantaged than would a more equal society. The *Stanford Encyclopedia of Philosophy* assures us that this is likely to be the case: 'The overwhelming opinion... is that in the foreseeable future the possibility of earning greater income will bring forth greater productive effort. This will increase the total wealth of the economy and, under the Difference Principle, the wealth of the least advantaged.'[48] Rawls's 'strongly egalitarian conception'[49] is thus a highly contingent matter, a focus on notions of justice and fairness in the distribution of resources that leaves little room for considerations of the role of inequality in class dynamics, democratic participation and societal evolution.

But even Rawls's modest intervention in favour of equality was not to pass muster in the newly emergent Gilded Age of the 1970s. Rawls performs a rarefied thought experiment – what kind of income distribution would result in a 'veil of ignorance',[50] in which individuals didn't know where in the income spectrum they would find themselves? The emergent society would possess characteristics of fairness, at least in some lights, but to others it would be in violation of natural liberty: let us postulate, says Robert Nozick,[51] that into some such egalitarian Elysium comes Wilt Chamberlain, a real-life figure, famous for being the first basketball player over seven feet tall to make effective use of his height in the professional game. Everybody,[52] according to Nozick, is happy to offer him extra remuneration to encourage him to play, even if the resulting income distribution then becomes more unfair according to the previously postulated Rawls criterion or any comparable one. What objection could there be to this exercise of freedom and consumer choice, and, by implication, any new income distribution that emerges under such conditions? Arguments of this kind have a familiar ring to economists – free choice results in Pareto optimal improvements, in which some members of the society are better off, and none made worse. The story has to be structured very carefully to make it part of a general parable about income distribution: in the real world, a newly rich individual emerging from Nozick's parable may well choose to buy up great swathes of land and dispossess existing residents, making it unlikely that 'everybody' is in favour of the new situation. But in its own terms, and in the context of the time it was written, the argument had a devastating impact – why should we not be, in Milton Friedman's phrase, 'free to choose'?

The essentially timeless, static framework in which Rawls's problem is originally posed means that, no matter how cleverly it is done, egalitarian rules of the kind postulated by him will degenerate, with outcomes gravitating in Nozick's direction – in favour of an income distribution dictated by autonomous individuals having free choice. But real societies have to reproduce themselves over time. The individuals in this parable, indulging in their free choice to widen the income distribution, are presumably adults (with the interested parties in this case likely to be predominantly male), with few four-year-olds actively participating in the decision. For a living, on-going society, a key question surrounding the transformation taking place in the distribution of income embodied in this parable is how the very personal identity of members of society, both current participants and future generations – their mentality, repertoire of skills, knowledge and social attitudes – might be affected by these changes: what kinds of people and what kind of society will emerge from this process? The issues involved in dealing with income distribution thus move far beyond any simple disputations over fairness among contemporaneous individuals and onto issues surrounding the whole future trajectory of society.

In reaction to the rise in inequality in income and wealth in the past three decades in rich countries, a literature has emerged rejecting the anti-redistributive notions above, including Richard Wilkinson and Kate Pickett's *The Spirit Level*, in which they purport to find a positive relationship between inequality and other bad things, such as murder rates, mental illness and obesity, in a range of countries in the twenty-first century. In its strongest form, *The Spirit Level* suggests that it is inequality per se, rather than poverty, that is the fundamental problem in the rich countries under consideration. The book and its associated literature have had the salutary effect of signalling the complex and socially embedded nature of inequality: it can shape aspects of physical and psychological well-being in society that extend far beyond unequal access to resources for consumption.[53] But this largely statistically driven hypothesis (that the correlation with bad things across countries is better with inequality than with poverty) is neither convincingly confirmed nor very plausible: in rich countries 'The Wealthy Kids Are All Right',[54] and are not typically handicapped by even high levels of inequality in the society at large. More importantly, *The Spirit Level* fails to integrate the observed empirical relationships between, for instance, inequality and health outcomes into a plausible conceptual framework concerned with human and societal development.

The questions surrounding the conceptual basis for viewing national income and its distribution converge here. The predominant view in economics is, as we have seen, that national income is a good representation of society's capacity to pursue various activities. The distribution of this income within society is treated as a distinct and separable matter, with the relevant economic issue being whether an overly equal distribution might weaken material incentives and, therefore, growth in GDP. A dual critique of this separability notion will be presented here. First are its pernicious political consequences. Public services and policies directed towards economic redistribution will tend to be seen as luxuries only affordable in a state of affluence. In conditions of economic slowdown, they are perceived to be no longer affordable. The second and more significant reason for rejecting the notion of dealing with national income as a good measure of economic capacity, one that can be readily separated from the distribution of that national income, is that it is untrue. When rises in economic capacity are seen solely from the perspective of short-term GDP growth, the debilitating effects of inequality on long-term economic development are invisible: hard-headed policies for squeezing the poor are seen as perhaps unpleasant, but economically sound. In a longer-term context especially, we need to reconceptualise the relationship between GDP and its distribution.[55]

More comprehensive than either the distribution of income or wealth for judging the fairness of a society is the capabilities notion, from the economist and philosopher Amartya Sen, of the range of substantive freedoms with which individuals are endowed. It is, unfortunately, elusive and hard to measure. Sen rejects the dichotomy from the political philosopher Isaiah Berlin (subsequently adopted as Cold War dogma) between a primary (or negative) freedom – 'not being interfered with by others' – and a secondary or positive form, as found in Spinoza or Marx, linked to self-realisation. For Berlin, 'The "positive" sense of the word "liberty" derives from the wish on the part of the individual to be his own master ... Socialized forms of [this notion] ... are at the heart of many of the nationalist, communist, authoritarian, and totalitarian creeds of our day.'[56] Instead, Sen offers a reconfiguration that encompasses both of these categories, with a seamless link between the negative aspects of freedom (such as the absence of censorship) and its positive form (the endowment of literacy): a just society offers all individuals the opportunity to acquire a range of substantive capabilities in order to function freely in society – 'the freedom that we actually have to choose between different styles and ways of living'. Consideration is thus given both to the freedom with which choices are undertaken (analogous to concerns about negative freedom) as well as to the positive freedoms associated with the opportunities that individuals actually have.[57] The approach taken in this book is similar, but with a special focus on rich societies, the formation and transformation of children's lives and its consequent effects on societal development, collective interaction and democratic control, and not solely upon individual functioning.

An important supplement to inequality measures that captures some of the outcomes embodied in the social dynamics of a capabilities approach are statistical measurements of intergenerational economic mobility. As a matter of logic and arithmetic, it is possible to construct examples in which greater income mobility enhances inequality, leading to a possible conflict between egalitarian goals.[58] In the twenty-first century, however, the literature on economic mobility decisively supports the intuitively plausible proposition that, in general, more unequal societies will be more immobile in relative terms, with those who are poor more likely to persist in that state, and with family background playing a more important role in subsequent economic success than in more equal societies.[59]

In general, the empirical literature overwhelmingly sanctions, with relatively few anomalous cases, a classification of rich countries into those of lesser and greater equality, with the more unequal ones having greater inequality not only in income, but in wealth, and experiencing higher levels of both poverty (usually measured by the percentage of households below 50 per cent of median income) and household insecurity, and lower intergenerational mobility, at least partially because of the lower provision of a range of social welfare benefits typical of such societies.[60] The US and the

UK, with high levels of income inequality, appear to do poorly compared with other nations regarding levels of intergenerational mobility, poverty and child poverty. In the case of the US, these widely confirmed conclusions put to rest the nation's long-standing self-image as a land of opportunity.[61]

As we have seen in Chapter 7, school children across the OECD have been subjected to a panoply of uniform examinations on mathematics, science and literacy in recent decades. In studies considering the family and socio-economic background of the children involved, the less than exceptional achievement in reading and mathematics scores for the UK and the US is substantially accounted for by the high 'socio-economic gradient' (most specifically, the presence of poverty).[62] US school children go from mediocre performers in science and mathematics to the upper range of achievement internationally when only those from the public schools with the lowest level of poverty (fewer than 10 per cent of students eligible for free or reduced-price lunch) are included.[63]

Furthermore, there is little indication of an efficiency–equity trade-off in education, in which more equal education systems would systematically show a lower mean performance for their students. On the contrary, one major study claims that in countries with better test results, epitomised in Europe by Finland, students' individual performance tends to be less influenced by family background or the school they attend than in countries doing less well on these tests.[64] In general, the evidence here is that children's educational outcomes are strongly influenced by family and socioeconomic background, but that the nature and forms that schooling takes in different countries may play a role in mitigating these family background effects, with longer preschool education and delays in tracking being decisive.[65]

The emergence and widespread dissemination of the above literature surrounding the empirical reality of a dramatic rise in inequality have not succeeded in bringing this issue to the centre of debates concerning economic and social policy. With economic growth and a supposed trade-off between equity and efficiency still at the centre of policy discussions, considerations of economic equality are treated as luxuries, to be put aside until whatever on-going economic crisis is alleviated. This view complements the widespread notion discussed earlier, from Galbraith's *Affluent Society* of 1958 to Margaret Thatcher, that dealing with poverty is merely another good thing that we do when we are rich enough to do so. An alternative perspective can be developed by viewing the effects of inequality on personal and social reproduction. The core of the argument here was anticipated many years ago by one of the founders of modern growth theory:

> In many countries, a part of expenditures on food, education, public health, and so forth, serves to increase productive capacity. (And wouldn't we also have to allow for depreciation or replacement of human beings?) ... economists usually settle for a less satisfying but more practical

division of total output into consumption and investment along more or less practical lines.[66]

Thus, once our central concern is with the construction of an indicator of overall productive capacity, we must abandon the standard delineation used in the GDP accounts between consumption and investment – a division that was constructed for the purposes of regulating aggregate demand. The distinction is an inappropriate one in the context of long-term economic development and the presence of class divisions in society: the meaning of the word 'consumption' needs to be reconceptualised. For the well-off, most of the consumption registered as such in GDP accounts is just what it appears to be – goods electively consumed to satisfy desire. For the poor, by contrast, much of the expenditure registered in GDP accounts as consumption is for depreciation or replacement: it is capital expenditure in a human context – what Marx called the 'reproduction of labour power'. The resources devoted by a poor person to basic foodstuffs, or to the heating of her dwelling, or to the health and education of her children, contribute to the maintenance of the human assets of her and her family. In the context of poverty-level wages, life consists of a 'constant struggle to juggle household finances, just trying to get by ... one paycheck away from homelessness'. The effects upon children are predictable: 'Because they cannot afford day care, their children sometimes move from house to house, between different relatives or neighbors, watching too much TV and sometimes not doing their homework. Older children grow up too fast because they become caretakers for their younger siblings.'[67]

For individuals at the lower end of the income spectrum, deprivation can thus mean not just reduced consumption, but the wasting away of their human assets and those of their children: given these elemental facts of human existence, it is no wonder that tabloids and other forms of media owned by right-wing millionaires find the need to focus on feckless and wasteful expenditure by poor people.[68] But policies that overlook the realities of inequality may have consequences that affect not only the happiness of members of society, but its whole future development, most especially in the context of the close convergence in international comparisons between inequality, the incidence of poverty and child poverty, and broader-based notions of social justice.[69]

It will come as no surprise that the free-market economist George Stigler viewed this matter with alarm and attempted to demonstrate that, for rich countries at least, the question of subsistence was a trivial matter: in a pioneering use of the mathematical technique of linear programming, he calculated that food sufficiency could be achieved at 1950 prices for less than $100 a year.[70] While these estimates have been questioned, there is little doubt that billions of people since that time have survived on a food allocation of less than $100 a year at 1950 prices; it is also clear that subsistence in all cultures has always been at a level above biological sufficiency. Is subsistence, then, an irrelevant economic category? Non-economists seem to be unaware that economics, with its utilitarian, subjective theoretical core, makes no principled distinction between a necessity and a luxury,[71] with little exception made even in development economics – the economics of poor countries.[72] A pioneering attempt at developing a concept of subsistence relevant to rich nations had focused on the minimally sufficient resources necessary to function as a normal person in society.[73] Perhaps more relevant to the perspective taken here are the ideas emerging from the writings of Amartya Sen discussed above, which emphasise, more ambitiously, the minimal resources necessary for the full development of the potentialities of individuals within the household.

There is little explicit mention in the literature (an exception being the Domar comment above) that inadequate consideration of the accretion of human assets can also lead to an incorrect calculation of the trajectory of economic capacity. Thus, existing national income accounting methodology can make no adjustments for the accelerated depreciation of the stock of human assets, both in physical and in educational terms, that can take place in periods of intense development in industry and agriculture. As a result, GDP growth will overestimate increases in economic capacity if there has been an accompanying deterioration in the human capital stock. This point may now appear self-evident when confronting the abuse of children in a labouring context, or the Soviet one-sided obsessions with technological achievement in the process of development and the consequent brutal treatment of workers and, especially, peasants.

But even in the most striking examples of economic success – for instance, the US in the late nineteenth and early twentieth centuries – is it not possible that levels of misery have been generated that are unnecessary, if not dysfunctional? Thus, horrific conditions for, especially, the lowest grades of work appear to have persisted in the steel industry in the US into the early twentieth century. These conditions are often noted in discussions, but commonly with the mitigation that individuals chose this sector over other work.[74] It is suggested, furthermore, that these conditions were an aspect of the extraordinary accumulation of physical capital and overall growth rates that were bringing the US to world predominance: with the inevitable trade-off between equity and efficiency, humanitarians naïvely wishing for an enforced reduction of the work week from 70 hours should weigh their desire for a reduced burden on workers with the loss of present and future productive capacity accompanying any such politically imposed move. But such a supposedly hard-headed calculation presumes that there is no long-term cost to society, purely from a productive perspective, of the deterioration in human assets incumbent upon working under such debilitating conditions. If a correct evaluation were made, might the decimation of individual workers and their household and social existence, including that of their children and subsequent generations, mean that the misery imposed upon these workers was largely gratuitous from the perspective of long-term development?

Socialism vs. 'economic realities'

Two claims on public attention that constantly derail attempts to evaluate policy from a longer-term perspective are 'the embattled state' and the exigencies of economic growth. National economic survival continues to be the *leitmotif* of the daily press, filled invariably with the familiar rhetoric of efficiency and competitiveness. Even before the outbreak of the financial and euro crises, the dominant ideology has centred on competitiveness and economic growth as the means for the avoidance of mass unemployment, but also an aspect of a worldwide battle for supremacy through economic power: the efficacy of education has been viewed in the context of a contest between nations, in Cold War times in terms of rivalry with the Soviet Union and subsequently linked to the Yellow Peril threat emanating first from Japan and then from China. The onset of economic crises only helps to institutionalise an atmosphere of generalised agitation and is used as an excuse to treat expenditure on basic public services as unaffordable luxuries that must be cut, policies often accompanied by handouts and giveaways to the well-off as part of a strategy of recovery. This is a turnabout from the way events are ordered in the natural world, where when an animal is faced with starvation or deprivation, evolutionary survival places a priority on the protection of vital organs, including the brain; peculiarly, orthodox policy prescriptions often cancel, or even reverse, this priority.

The notion that economies are engaged in an economic war with other nations is a pervasive one. The journalist Thomas Friedman contrasted the olive tree, representing 'the warmth of family, the joy of individuality, the intimacy of personal rituals, the depth of private relationships' with the Lexus, 'the drive for sustenance, improvement, prosperity and moderniza- tion – as it is played out in today's globalization system.'[75] The latter was the dominant and constraining force, requiring all nations to pursue a strategy of low taxation, deregulation and reduction of union rights: globalisation and increasing competition constrain the ability of national governments to pursue egalitarian strategies and to indulge in the luxury of excessive social spending.[76] In earlier literature, this notion of a nation's competitiveness was typically linked to changes in its unit labour costs relative to its trading partners, with the latter negatively related to changes in its exchange rate and to wages and social costs for its workers, and positively related to the growth rate in productivity. More recent empirical work has avoided this kind of explicit calculation of competitiveness, but a popular perception has remained that 'the forces of globalization put the systems of social secu- rity in rich countries at risk ... [with] a race-to-the-bottom scenario ... as rich countries are forced to adopt low labour standards and lower wages ... and to scale back on well developed social security systems in order to remain competitive'.[77]

This perception appears to be incorrect: it is not evident that international competitiveness has acted as a significant constraining force on nations' economic activity.[78] This fact should not prove surprising, given that the major nations of the world are only to a limited degree in economic competition with each other.[79] But there is an element of veracity buried in the competitiveness rhetoric: small countries on a social democratic path do appear to have been constrained in their behaviour due to the influence of international economic forces. While, contrary to right-wing myth, there is no evidence historically that relatively egalitarian countries, such as those in Scandinavia, have experienced lower GDP growth over the long term as a result of their relatively high rates of taxation and social spending, these countries have consistently pursued policies involving relatively light taxes on capital by international standards, with higher rates on labour incomes and consumption (the latter likely to be regressive).[80] One interpretation is that such policies are pursued because of their pro-growth character;[81] an alternative is to suggest that small nations of this type feel under a particular constraint to retain and attract mobile international capital, even if it means creating taxation regimes that may seem inconsistent with their social democratic policy goals.[82] If the international economy is imposing ever more severe constraints on the progressive policies of, particularly, smaller, relatively open economies, future developments in social equality may require coordination across larger agglomerations such as the European Union, Japan or the US.

Other discussions of global competitiveness avoid the crude race-to-the-bottom rhetoric of earlier times, with the World Economic Forum (WEF) defining competitiveness as 'the set of institutions, policies, and factors that determine the level of productivity of a country. The level of productivity, in turn, sets the level of prosperity that can be earned by an economy.'[83] Despite the abandonment of the overt Hobbesian 'war against all' rhetoric of earlier notions of competitiveness, the analysis retains the short-term focus of former approaches. Its distinctive recommendations take the form of free-market solutions, imprecating against restrictive and discriminatory rules on foreign direct investment and limitations on foreign ownership, and on the virtues of openness in international trade: it is only then conceded that the 'vast empirical evidence' in favour of the latter is highly contested. Furthermore, labour is to be flexible so that it can be shifted 'from one economic activity to another rapidly and at low cost [we may ask: low cost to whom?], and to allow for wage fluctuations without much social disruption [once again, to whom?], with the promotion of meritocracy [and not, for instance, solidarity or cooperation] at the workplace.'[84] The standard of success for Europe in recent years in this battle for competitiveness remains Germany, where significant wage restraint has been present since the mid-1990s.[85] But recitations of German economic performance rarely put this success in the context of the general declines in labour's share of national output in Germany and elsewhere discussed above, or indicate how this story generalises to other nations: is German success at competitiveness merely part of a zero sum game that disadvantages other nations, most especially those within the eurozone?

And, despite gestures in the direction of the longer-term notion of 'sustainable competitiveness' with the inclusion of a range of ecological and social considerations, the US and the UK remain unshaken in their top ten competitiveness rankings despite their egregious performance, noted above but not mentioned in the WEF study, in levels of poverty and child poverty.[86] It is as if there were a division of labour between organisations such as the WEF, that deal with masculine, practical issues such as economic competitiveness, and feminine organisations such as UNICEF, that discuss child poverty. In fact, these so-called practical approaches merely make a virtue of myopia.

Economic growth remains, however, an even more central concern of public policy than competitiveness, especially for rich countries. In the economics literature, it is usually presumed that rises in per capita GDP will be closely linked to increases in a nation's productivity, the latter often approximated by rises in output per employed worker. In Baumol et al. (2007), quoted above, three prominent economists, whose guiding figure is William Baumol, a leading American liberal academic, are quoted as dismissing considerations of income distribution in evaluations of national income on the basis that such questions involve subjective value judgements while, presumably, ignoring the issue does not: 'As for income equality or inequality, the value one places on this is inherently subjective, and thus measures of GDP "adjusted" for differences in the distribution of income should not be given undue weight'; on the same page, these economists, with some dismay, note that when modifications for inequality and the value of leisure were made, income per capita in some countries in Europe in 2006 was calculated to be higher than in the US in a study for the OECD.[87] The Baumol et al. philippic against the lack of a work ethic in Western Europe that follows comes across as unintentionally hilarious, and is not even sound in the context of orthodox economics, in which the substitution of leisure for work can be perfectly rational.

For these authors, however, in the long run, 'only one economic statistic really matters: the *growth of productivity*', the main reason being that it is the appropriate measure of the growth of economic capacity – the growth in the ability to deal with, for instance, an ageing population. It would be difficult to contest the centrality of productivity increases to economic achievement – the success of postwar Japan in, for instance, the car industry was driven by brilliant managerial innovations that reduced costs below those of its competitors. Clearly, important lessons can be learned by careful examination of these innovations.

But the search for policy recommendations for the economy based on facts about productivity at the economy-wide level can be much more problematic. In national accounts, government output is calculated by measuring its inputs, which consist mostly of labour hours: the governmental sector will not register rises in productivity for the economy as a whole, even when services are improving, so that if this sector's share of the economy increases, this automatically lowers the measured labour productivity growth of the whole economy, regardless of its performance.[88] And in the context of a societal focus on economic growth and, therefore, the growth rate in productivity, such notions will soon fall foul of Baumol's disease: just as a broad-based policy to promote the proliferation of string quartets will do little for the level, much less the growth rate, of productivity in society,[89] programmes to transform education – if they are undertaken seriously – will be labour-intensive and wreak havoc on measured increases in productivity. When attempts are made to measure rises in the efficiency of governmental expenditure explicitly, the danger exists that productivity-increasing solutions will be foisted on the weaker members of the community: on-line higher education may have a range of efficacious possibilities for improving student learning,[90] but its likely implementation will be not in elite universities, but in state institutions eager to save money, despite the exceptional need of many of their students, especially those from poor backgrounds, for guidance and personalised instruction. The important role of the universities as centres of diversity of opinion and approaches to knowledge will also be compromised by this one-sided approach to efficiency.

Economic and productivity growth can thus be presented as a neutral, technocratic tool when, in fact, it can be all-encompassing in its demands, dictating social outcomes and constraining the range of meaningful choices. We thus read the following typical discussion in *The Economist*: 'Diana Farrell, of the McKinsey Global Institute, argues that the real problem holding back innovation in many developed countries is too much government in the form of red tape and market barriers. She points out that planning restrictions have prevented the expansion of Ahold and other efficient retailers in France.'[91] Increases in the measured productivity of the retailing and construction sectors can easily be generated by lifting planning restrictions constraining the emergence of car-oriented, low-density living environments. But would such changes represent social, or even economic, improvement? Being productive in this context means building American-style out-of-town shopping centres, the enervation of urban and town centre pedestrian-friendly environments, and the marginalisation of a range of smaller retail outlets and their associated wholesalers; the supposed efficiency gains rarely include consideration of the necessary road building undertaken at taxpayers' expense, the invisible congestion costs of greater car use, and the erosion of the public good characteristics associated with a vibrant city centre. (Whether such projects will continue to be commercially viable in the age of internet shopping remains to be seen.) In a world in which the views of management consultants commonly guide decisions on social issues, arguments surrounding the flourishing of families and the upbringing of children in the context of an integrated approach to community development and transport planning – notions that might interfere with schemes to raise productivity growth – come across as just so much noise.

A focus on the exigencies of economic growth and its corollary, the growth rate of productivity, can thus preclude other – any other – considerations in the making of social decisions. This privileging of economic considerations above all others is not simply the province of economists. We live in an age when, for instance, public bodies perform benefit–cost calculations on the regulation of mercury pollution in which benefits are calculated in terms of the reduced loss in future wages for children whose IQs are lowered (in straightforward terms, whose brains are damaged) by eating fish caught by freshwater anglers.[92] How is it that, in societies putatively richer than ever before, the economic calculus has become the *lingua franca* of social discourse to an extent that would have surprised even Herbert Spencer? One reason appears to be the desire to ape the achievements of the exact sciences, with numbers, parameters and decisive conclusions, even if the social judgement arrived at takes the form of a pseudo-scientific exactitude in which it is presumed that brain damage to children can meaningfully be translated into shortfalls in IQ and then into income lost to society.

The blatant long-term inefficacy of such a state of affairs helps to clarify why an attempt here to cultivate an alternative vision and direction is not a fanciful or feckless undertaking, but a necessity. The creation of a society under truly democratic control, and perceived as such by its constituents, will be the subject of the remaining chapters. The discussion, introduced here and continued in Chapter 11, starts with childhood, because that is where we all begin. Most contemporary discussions of the social role of education focus on its role in enhancing productivity. We now find that even the most eloquent defences of the importance of education feel the need to make arguments for its role in facilitating growth:

> As with critical thinking, so too with the arts. We discover that they are essential for the goal of economic growth and the maintenance of a healthy business culture... If our only concern were national economic growth, then we should still protect humanistic liberal arts education.[93]

It must be confessed that this somewhat defensive approach has, on occasion, been echoed in this book, with the caveat that 'liberal arts' is perceived here to embody not only subjects such as literature, but universal preparation in science, mathematics and a host of putatively impractical and unnecessary forms of knowledge as well. Do we, then, have to return to the Victorians to find unabashed resolutions in favour of education for its own sake?

> we shall find, as a matter of experience, if we know the best that has been thought and uttered in the world, we shall find that the art and poetry and eloquence of men who lived, perhaps, long ago, who had the most limited natural knowledge, who had the most erroneous conceptions about many important matters, we shall find that this art, and poetry, and eloquence, have in fact not only the power of refreshing and delighting us, they have also the power [of] fortifying, and elevating, and quickening, and suggestive power, capable of wonderfully helping us to relate the results of modern science to our need for conduct, our need for beauty.[94]

Unfortunately, Matthew Arnold's argument for education in terms of the cultivation of 'sweetness and light' will not go down well in today's *macho* discourse. A greater obstacle, even than his obtuse identification of knowledge with a mastery of Latin and classical Greek, is his attitude towards 'the masses', with their growing tendency towards anarchy: the latter is to be weaned out of them by 'culture', or, if necessary, in 'the old Roman way...flog the rank and file and fling the ringleaders from the Tarpeian Rock'.[95] This class of attitudes is not only offensive to (most) modern sensibilities, but a peculiar one in retrospect, given that it was not the docile masses, but the members of Arnold's own class across Europe, who at the time were bringing violence and destruction to Africa and Asia and, in 1914, to Europe itself.[96] Education for its own sake has been deeply scarred by its entanglement with such elitist notions. But more modern and acceptable versions of this doctrine exist. The philosopher Harry Brighouse writes:

> Students need the kind of education that will enable them to be effective participants in the economy, but there is no reason for states in developed countries to steer the education system towards the specific demands of employers...children have a right to learn about a range of ways of living and to the kind of education that will enable them to reflect on their own way of life in the light of these alternatives...[they] should be educated so that they can have rich and flourishing lives independently of their participation in the economy...schools should educate children so that they can be effective, and reasonable, participants in public decisionmaking and execution.[97]

Arguments of this kind are not unprecedented. They can be found in an extensive literature already emerging in the twentieth century (to be revisited in Chapter 11) suggesting that rich societies have attained sufficient freedom of action to move beyond narrow economic criteria for evaluating the role of education in society. Are these progressive goals to be dismissed as utopian, unrealistic and too expensive as a societal project? They have implicitly been brushed aside: contemporary debates about education for the masses are largely preoccupied with carefully weighing, for instance, the economic efficacy of smaller classroom size compared with higher qualifications for teachers, with the success of these alternatives measured by improvements in PISA scores or their equivalent. The form that such an education takes, dedicated as it is to the efficient replication of cogs for the economic machine, remains narrowly utilitarian, authoritarian and ultimately sterile.

An approach to child development for the masses of the kind proposed by Brighouse will immediately be dubbed utopian. In the context of a societal focus on economic growth and therefore the growth rate in productivity, such notions will, as suggested above, be subject to Baumol's disease: programmes to transform education – if they are undertaken seriously – will ruin attempts to generate measured increases in productivity for the overall economy. Real education is extravagant in its use of – most especially – human resources, in both a quantitative and a qualitative sense.

For an upper range of the population, this fact is simply taken for granted. The necessity for well-planned schemata for endowing the next generation with a capacity for controlling their own lives and mastery over the social environment takes the form of careful monitoring of the child's physical and psychological well-being beginning from – or before – birth. The human and physical resources present in the home environment dictate that even before entering a select group of, typically but not invariably, private schools, the forms that upbringing and education take have only limited resemblance to the experience of ordinary children. In school, core material is usually mastered in a manner that shows only modest gains in PISA-type tests over the best state institutions with an academic orientation.[98] But education for mastery implies the replication in modern terms of the 'sweetness and light' of well-rounded individuals idealised by Matthew Arnold, with children receiving individual attention in a stimulating physical and psychological environment that exists in another world from the prison-like atmosphere of schools for the masses. Mastery subsumes aspects of down-to-earth attainment, including physical culture and sports training and hands-on command of how things work in the world of mechanical and electronic devices, as well as in the natural environment.

And despite Arnold's self-absorbed depiction of himself as being engaged in a losing war with the Philistines,[99] we shall see in Chapter 11 that elite institutions have continued to offer students in the twenty-first century the opportunity for deep engagement with the world heritage of music and drama. When gaps appear in this idealised depiction of elite education, the parents of these children have the material resources and the intellectual capacity to compensate for these shortfalls explicitly, as well as passing on through travel and general worldliness a familiarity with how things work in the world of economic and political power. Schooling only reinforces the home side advantage.

Few interventions by Stalin have received universal approbation from Western scholars, but the curious episode towards the end of his life when he intervened in a controversy concerning the nature of language is an exception. Some Soviet linguists, perhaps over-zealous to demonstrate their ideological rectitude, had declared language to be part of society's super-structure. As a consequence, it would evolve with the productive forces and, even more strangely, under capitalism, different classes would speak essentially different languages. No, said Stalin in an article published in *Pravda*, language is not part of the superstructure. Not surprisingly, the controversy came to an end.[100] It is necessary here, however, to take issue with Iosif Vissarionovich. In the twenty-first century, widening inequality within countries worldwide, combined with improved communication and mobility emanating from technological and political changes in countries such as China and Russia, has produced an international elite in direct and regular contact, and fluent in its own language, English. What had been an aberration even in the plutocracies before the First World War (such as a German-speaking elite in Hungary) is now an international norm. With economic inequality reaching, on occasion, stupendous magnitudes, as in the US, this elite is well aware that its central concerns and self-interest are more closely linked to its counterparts in other countries than its compa-triots at home.

Is it, then, 'socialism or barbarism?', as the famous slogan suggests, with even rich societies taking the form of plutocracies in which the ruling elites are ever more distanced economically and culturally from the mass of the population? Neoliberal policies over past decades have damaged or disman-tled the economic and social accomplishments of previous generations, with little gained in compensation. Dreams of a maturing democratic polity with advancing wealth, technology and education seem to have dissipated. Does the elite's endowing of its own next generation with a capacity for control-ling their own lives and mastery over the social environment offer any hints on how to construct a socialist, democratically controlled society built on real, existing non-utopian foundations?

The strategy for societal transformation that emerges in the next chapters is concerned with giving an opportunity for self-realisation and develop-ment of personal capacities to all individuals from their earliest years, one that is not contingent on, and compensates for, limitations in household circumstances; a complementary aspect of the programme is to promote a capacity to exercise democratic control on a regular basis in the working and living environment and in the context of the broader society. The goals of such a programme are plausible because they are congruent with the central role played by human assets in the economic and social development of contemporary societies. Furthermore, the realisation of this strategy takes place largely through the use of off-the-shelf public policy tools such as taxation, expenditure and regulation, rather than through a discontinuous construction *de novo* of societal institutions. The present unpropitious economic conditions, rather than generating a reconsideration of the policies that led to this predicament in the first place, have tended to engender a focus on short-term, mostly free-market bromides under the guise of coping with economic realities. By contrast, the strategy to be pursued here has a long-term time horizon, one designed to find a path for survival, and even flourishing, in this dangerous twenty-first century.

* * *

In recent years, widespread discussion – and disquiet – has emerged from the suggestion by Robert J. Gordon that productivity growth in the US is likely to fall to a fraction of 1 per cent in the future: the large gains in labour productivity (2.33 per cent per annum) from the late nineteenth century until the early 1970s will not be repeated.[101] His claims have had a wide reception, since he was practically a lone voice suggesting that the productivity surge of the mid-1990s observed in US statistics was less likely a reflection of the widely heralded new economy based on computer technology than a transitory phase reflecting largely economy-wide cyclical factors and rapid increases in the productivity of the computer industry itself.[102] According to him, the low-hanging fruit have been picked: the electronics revolution has not yielded, and will not yield, gains to productivity and to consumer welfare comparable to the Second Industrial Revolution benefits from electrification, the internal combustion engine, indoor plumbing and running water.

The question arises why this prospective decline in productivity growth has been treated as a source of such alarm. One reason is that Gordon's pessimism merely reinforces other present-day economic tendencies: much of what is increasingly desired in countries as they grow rich includes services such as personalised care for the elderly and infirm, activities that are unlikely to experience rapid increases in productivity, and cannot do so, by definition, if these increases emerge from the government consumption sector, as noted above. The approach taken by Gordon appears to maintain a fatalistic association between an absence of new technological bounty and a stagnation in productive advance, which then results in slow economic growth that makes the maintenance of full employment impossible. The resignation associated with this long-term narrative then spills over to the headwind of recent decades associated with increasing competition from poor countries and the resultant downward pressure on wages: these events contain, he suggests, 'a sense of inevitability'.[103]

Gordon's remedies are limited to poaching skilled labour from poor economies,[104] a short-sighted strategy for a nation with pretences to global moral leadership and a bad example in an ecological context of a rich country gratuitously generating population growth to fulfil proximate economic objectives. Further explanations for the widespread alarm expressed by the prospect of a productivity growth decline might be a historical association of periods of slow productivity growth with macroeconomic stagnation and mass unemployment, and one other factor, perhaps the most significant one: perpetual growth is the key mechanism used by economic orthodoxy and those with the reins of economic and political power to avoid confronting the central questions surrounding economic and social equality.[105]

Extraordinarily, a sense of helplessness has also been present in an opposite direction. A report from the McKinsey Global Institute has outlined a range of a dozen 'disruptive' technologies soon to be upon us, linked to continuing developments in the electronics sector, energy and gene sequencing.[106] If hosannas can be expected from techno-optimists and others, the response from the moderate left was disquieting:

> Even a quick scan of the report's list suggests that some of the victims of disruption will be workers who are currently considered highly skilled, and who invested a lot of time and money in acquiring those skills. So should workers simply be prepared to acquire new skills? [They] might well ask ... what will happen to us if, like so many students, we go deep into debt to acquire the skills we're told we need, only to learn that the economy no longer wants those skills? Education, then, is no longer the answer to rising inequality, if it ever was (which I doubt).
>
> So what is the answer? If the picture I've drawn is at all right, the only way we could have anything resembling a middle-class society — a society in which ordinary citizens have a reasonable assurance of maintaining a decent life as long as they work hard and play by the rules — would be by having a strong social safety net, one that guarantees not just health care but a minimum income, too. And with an ever-rising share of income going to capital rather than labor, that safety net would have to be paid for to an important extent via taxes on profits and/or investment income.[107]

What capitalism thus seems to offer us, in light of recent discussions, is stagnation if the technology fairy doesn't come, and if he or she does appear, the prospects are, if anything, worse. Either we are then subject to the tender mercies of the Schumpeterian ghouls of creative destruction, or we follow

Krugman's path: in a defensive way, still acceding to the 'dictates of the market', we create a supplicant underclass that is reliant on state munificence.[108] Clearly, Krugman's call for a strong social safety net and redistributive taxation would be part of any socialist programme, but where is the sense of forward movement? Is this the best we can do?

Part III
Socialism and Human Possibilities

Introduction

The narrative presented up to now has attempted to demonstrate that socialist conceptions of human development are congruent with broad-based practical strategies for effecting economic growth and achievement. In this sense, it conforms to the dominant socialist programme of the twentieth century. As we have seen in Part I, 'Socialism and Central Planning', the earlier approach presumed that the vision of a rational organisation of society could be observed in incipient form in the structures and protocols of the great capitalist firms, and that a practical, non-utopian socialism would follow along these lines. Despite perceptive insights into the workings of capitalism and perspicacious critiques of economic orthodoxy, the planning approach was deeply flawed. Socialism became identified, simultaneously, with dysfunctional and authoritarian approaches to the organisation of society.

In Part II, a renewed endeavour was made to link a strategy of socialist development to tendencies in contemporary capitalism: education is widely regarded as a key requisite of economic growth, and also acts to promote income equality and mobility. In the broader context of human development, low levels of inequality and high levels of security in society facilitate educational programmes and complement them by permitting individuals and households to plan their lives in a coherent manner. A vigorous programme focusing on the human development of all tiers of society will conform both to the exigencies of the modern economy and to the traditional socialist focus on social equality,

As we shall see in the following chapters, it would be disingenuous to imagine that a true socialist programme could be implemented in contemporary society without confronting a host of problematic issues. What is the nature of this new educational programme? Does it simply involve more resources, or do we have to reconsider the structure and organisation of the educational system, and, indeed, the very content and goals of that education? How does a transformed approach to education and human development impinge upon the daily life of individuals as they work, vote and function as free citizens, and can such a focus on individual realisation and personal development be reconciled with traditional socialist concerns with solidarity and democratic control at work and in society? And, having surrendered the possibility of directing an economy by way of a central plan, what mechanisms are available in a socialist context to promote, if not guarantee, full employment of human capabilities, and not just full employment in its crudest sense?

These questions will be posed here rather than answered definitively. But at a time when politicians and social thinkers have resigned themselves fatalistically to coping on a day-to-day basis with each emergent crisis, or have adopted the attitude that an aimless pragmatism is the height of worldly wisdom, it is worthwhile to address these considerations. In the absence of a belief that society should unfold autonomously from a Hayekian spontaneous order or a social Darwinist survival-of-the-fittest mechanism, is there any choice but to confront these issues?

11
Education in a Free Society

Education is not an independent variable in an economic growth equation. In its broadest sense, it is a fundamental aspect of, and prerequisite for, human existence. Even if we are not blank slates, our functioning as human beings is deeply conditioned by what is consciously and unconsciously passed on to us: we are shaped by the actions, attitudes and behaviour of others and the environmental context in which these interactions take place, most especially in the first years of life. No more fundamental question about society can be asked than how we are to be educated.

Hayek's dilemma

> The demand for equality of opportunity or equal starting conditions (*Startgerechtigkeit*) appeals to, and has been supported by, many who in general favour the free market order.[1]

Hayek's dilemma was to articulate his objections – in the name of liberty – to a free society that embodied equal opportunity for all classes in society: the danger was always present for Hayek that, like John Stuart Mill (see Chapter 12), some of his fellow liberals would gravitate to support of workers' control and a range of socialist policies. As we have seen in Chapter 1, Hayek had constructed a capitalist utopia that is the most complete of its kind in a liberal mould, one in which economic and social outcomes emerge through voluntary processes of market exchange. In mainstream economic orthodoxy, by contrast, such 'invisible hand' outcomes only take place in the context of an initial disposition of property rights. A common means of legitimating this distribution of income and wealth in society is to claim that it has been ratified by a democratic decision-making process (as hinted at by Arthur Okun in Chapter 10). But political democracy was often opposed, or held in suspicion, by the nineteenth-century liberals Hayek so admires, and by Hayek himself. The great *coup* of Hayek's spontaneous order, as we have seen in Chapter 1, was that property rights themselves are the product of this evolutionary process of market exchange. These property rights are not imposed or arbitrary, and cannot be easily altered without upsetting the whole of the dialectical interaction between different aspects of this spontaneous order.

But why and how, in more specific terms, will even well-meaning attempts at creating equal opportunity limit or distort the functioning of the spontaneous order? At one juncture, Hayek suggests that the process of individual decision making and risk taking that is an essential part of the spontaneous order must be 'borne not only by those who decide but also by their descendents':[2] attempts to give all children in society an opportunity to develop their capacities as human beings would pervert the spontaneous order, because the profligacy and irresponsibility of individuals would no longer be constrained by the effects their decisions would have on their offspring. Hayek does not pursue this outburst of Old Testament and Victorian sensibility in any detail, and it seems to be of little influence (except in magazine advertisements for luxury watches) in contemporary debates.

Hayek is opaque, but on firmer ground, in opposing any attempt to eliminate the disadvantages accruing to some groups in society by imposing, in the style of Plato or Sparta, a uniform upbringing upon all children: 'utilization of dispersed knowledge is...made possible by the fact that the opportunities for...different individuals are different, and because many of these particular circumstances are known only to them...in the absence of a unified body of knowledge of all the particulars to be taken into account, the overall order depends on the use of knowledge possessed by [the] individuals and used for their purposes'.[3] Thus, there would be dangers, purely from the point of view of efficacy, in attempting to impose even a well-constructed barracks-style educational system. The family environment, by preserving the range and variety of experience to which individual children are exposed, is superior in the 'utilization of dispersed knowledge' that is of such importance in the efficient functioning of society.

Yet Hayek's use of the term 'different' in addressing the opportunities open to individuals resembles the disingenuousness of the US Supreme Court in 1896 in its upholding of the legality of racial segregation with the phrase 'separate but equal' in the Plessy vs. Ferguson decision: it is simply a fine phrase occluding the presence of inequality. At present, a generalised barracks-like Spartan solution to the problems of inequalities in education is nowhere being proposed. There is, however, a genuine threat, as opposed to a fantasised one, to political democracy and, therefore, the use of dispersed knowledge in the making of social decisions: in the context of a widening of income and wealth in the nations of the rich world, most exceptionally the US, even the limited gains made in the direction of popular control of public affairs may be eroding, with decisions increasingly being made by a small, like-minded group with a common outlook on the world.

Hayek's argument against public policies promoting equality reinforces one earlier found in *The Road to Serfdom* of 1944 – the 'slippery slope' notion that movement in the direction of equality, most especially in the context of government policy, leads down the totalitarian road:

> There is...much to be said in favour of the government providing on an equal basis the means for the schooling of minors who are not yet fully responsible citizens, even though there are grave doubts whether we ought to allow government to administer them. But *all this would still be very far from creating real equality of opportunity, even for persons possessing the same abilities*. To achieve this government would have to control the whole physical and human environment of all persons, and have to endeavour to provide at least equivalent chances for each; and the more government succeeded in these endeavours, the stronger would become the legitimate demand that, on the same principle, any still remaining handicaps must be removed – or compensated for by putting extra burden on the still relatively favoured. This would have to go on until government literally controlled every circumstance which could affect any person's well-being.[4]

There is an element of truth in Hayek's declaration here, as we shall see below: the cultivation of equal opportunities for human development across society will, of necessity, extend far beyond *pro forma* equality in access to classroom education. But his famous prediction that such developments necessarily entail, even if inadvertently, movement along the road to serfdom has that rare honour in the social sciences of having been decisively refuted. All across the Western world, the extension of provisions of the welfare state and of access to state education at school and higher levels in the decades after the publication of Hayek's *Road to Serfdom* were coincident with an extension of civil rights, civil liberties and democratic participation in the public sphere; countries with strong social welfare regimes have consistently stood at the highest levels in rankings of press freedom and absence of censorship.[5] At a fundamental level, these interconnections reflect the indissoluble links between the negative and positive liberties discussed in Chapter 10 and, substantively, a tendency for populations in societies with heightened levels of economic security to be more tolerant than others. The problem posed by Hayek seems to have existed largely in his imagination.

Hayek's reasons for opposition to the pursuit of equal opportunity have never achieved popularity among defenders of the free market. Few go down his path of opposing it *even for persons possessing the same abilities*, as he says above, thereby leaving outcomes, including the inheritance of property, to the unfolding of the spontaneous order. For him, it is this order, emerging out of processes of free exchange, which is to be defended by those with a belief in liberty, rather than any notion that this process yields a fair distribution of rewards: while it is important for the maintenance of the market order that individuals believe that their well-being depends primarily on their own efforts and decisions, for Hayek there is invariably a substantial component of luck in the determination of market outcomes.[6]

The very richness of Hayek's conceptualisation of capitalism as the unfolding of a spontaneous order leads him into difficulties. We have already seen an example of this problem in his critique of central planning in Chapter 4: he develops a notion of capitalist competition as a dynamic intertemporal process, but then fails to confront successfully the consequent issue of the role of the financial sector both as a facilitator of this dynamism and as a source of destabilisation. Similarly, when dealing with the question of the distribution of rewards in capitalism, Hayek's intertemporal and intergenerational spontaneous order can make no promise of just outcomes for members of society, even for children. Few have followed him down this path, with libertarians like Robert Nozick finding it far easier to defend capitalist income distribution in the context of a timeless (and presumably childless) world in which intergenerational effects are precluded from consideration (see Chapter 10).

The most influential defences of the market order are to be found not, however, in Nozick's libertarianism, but, as Hayek notes, in Catholic and quasi-Calvinist teaching: he ruefully concedes that the legitimation of capitalism (especially, he says, in the US) has invariably been linked to the notion that it 'regularly rewards the deserving'.[7] Since the late nineteenth century, this notion of capitalism as a system of just deserts has been embodied in mainstream static microeconomics, both as a prediction (loosely speaking, those who are more productive will tend to be paid more) and often as a normative rule (they *should* be paid more).[8] We thus have a concoction of various elements from Catholic and Calvinist teaching: the Augustinian heritage of a (far from innocent) child with an immortal soul whose subsequent success in worldly activities, including presumably any inherited wealth, is (especially in the Calvinist context) a sign of grace, combined with an economic theory that links remuneration to productivity.

In political terms, these two principles can be used to bind together all those citizens who view themselves as 'working hard and playing by the rules' against scroungers, reprobates and the undeserving poor. But when these two elements combine with nineteenth-century social Darwinism and twentieth-century psychology and biology, we have a unified theory of remuneration in capitalist society linked to the exigencies of biology and capitalist competitive processes. The IQ wars of the twentieth and twenty-first centuries speak to fundamental perceptions of the future of humankind.

Is it all a waste of time?

The path charted by Hayek has rarely been followed by others who wish to defend the distribution of economic resources emerging under free-market conditions. If his phrase 'same abilities' is taken to refer to inherent, biological potential, the overwhelming majority of those who abjure the pursuit of equal opportunity do so because they – implicitly or explicitly – reject the same abilities premise on class or racial terms, so that the pursuit of this goal is a waste of time. Many such individuals believe that capitalism already distributes resources on a meritocratic basis and that inequalities in income and wealth reflect the distribution of individual qualities dictated by natural endowment. This doctrine is pervasive, but elusive and difficult to confront directly because it is so often expressed in a muted form with the use of words such as 'able' and 'capable'. These central questions concerning human capacity take their most explicit forms within the covers of journals of psychology, neurobiology and child development.

In earlier times, the qualities that were in the blood were linked to character and even diction: it has often been noted that the well-born nature of the eponymous hero of Charles Dickens's *Oliver Twist* was reflected in his elevated language, distinctly different from those among whom he had been raised. In our time, however, it is not nobility of character or diction that is inherited, but overall mental capacity: some people are just born more capable than others, facts then reflected in the distribution of economic resources. The academic and intellectual underpinning for this supposedly common-sense view of the world is the concept of overall mental capacity, 'g', as measured through a statistical surrogate, the intelligence quotient, or IQ. In the words of one of the pioneers of research in this area, ' [intelligence] denotes, first of all, a quality that is intellectual and not emotional or moral: in measuring it we try to rule out the effects of the child's zeal, interest, industry, and the like. [It] denotes a general capacity, a capacity that enters into everything the child says or does or thinks; [it is] by definition an innate capacity: hence a lack of it is not necessarily proved by a lack of educational knowledge or skill.'[9]

In modern times, this capacity is no longer thought to be passed from one generation to another through the blood, but genetically. The development of the concept of IQ at the beginning of the twentieth century by Alfred Binet had a pragmatic motivation – to construct a measure to isolate those children in need of special assistance because of their low scores. Binet in 1909 had already inveighed against those who assert 'that an individual's intelligence is a fixed quantity, a quantity which cannot be increased. We must protest and react against this brutal pessimism.'[10] But even for Binet's relatively straightforward diagnostic purposes, an IQ test cannot locate mental deficiency in children performing poorly, since weak results may reflect a whole range of causes other than inherent cognitive inadequacy, including the individual's cultural background, attitudes, health and physiology. Thus, if a child's level of motivation were to play an important role in IQ test score results,[11] then these tests could serve neither as a decisive mechanism for locating those who were deficient in intelligence, nor as a statistical surrogate for g. The inherent limitations in the use of the IQ measure at its point of origin are only exacerbated as we proceed through the twentieth and into the twenty-first century, when performance on these tests is seen as a quasi-biological measure of overall mental potential and capacity.

The IQ measure soon moved on from its unpretentious beginnings with Binet to play a central role in twentieth-century attempts by the human sciences to emulate the stupendous achievements of the physical sciences and the more slowly emerging accomplishments of the life sciences. In economics, the unified conceptualisation of a nation's economic activity with the creation of the national income measure released a flood of theoretical and empirical literature related to its regulation and growth; for psychology, the emergence of an empirical surrogate for g in the form of IQ gave both a unified focus to measures of mental activity and a scalar variable for use in empirical testing. In contrast to psychoanalytic approaches, psychology was now possessed of a parameter that could be used to test scientific, objectively verifiable hypotheses. And compared with the equally empiricist behaviourist school, there was a unity and directionality to IQ research, with the ready possibility for integration with evolutionary theory, genetics and neurological investigations. So powerful has been the pressure to find objective measures of this kind that, even among the critics of the IQ measure, one of the most popular alternatives in recent times has involved replacing the g concept with a broader set of competencies, as well as a notion of 'emotional intelligence'.[12]

The prestige of the science-is-measurement ideology has been as powerful in psychology as in economics. Unlike the national income measure in economics, however, the centrality of IQ in public discourse had been somewhat neutralised in the postwar period because of the association of this statistic and its quasi-biologistic interpretation with interwar fascism and eugenics; this politically controversial role of the IQ measure is most strongly evident when it is seen to be correlated not only with income, wealth and social status, but with race. The reconstitution of investigation in this area in recent decades has been linked to the increasing prestige of biological approaches to human behaviour, most especially with the mapping of the human genome. The most widely noted research in this area, the Minnesota twins studies, has involved children reared either in the same family or apart, including a range of biological relationships, from identical twins to adopted children; attempts to parse the roles of biology (genetic endowment) and the broader social environment in IQ have often claimed to find an important, even predominant, role for the biological component.[13]

Historically, the influence of IQ studies (without, however, attributing these conclusions and motives to all researchers involved), with its notion of a substantial, innate and (as usually interpreted) fixed biological component to general intelligence, has followed well-defined patterns. It was used as far back as the 1920s in the US to separate students into academic and non-academic streams, and formed the philosophical and intellectual basis for academic segregation at age 11 in Britain under the 1944 Education Act.[14] The IQ measure has been used in research purporting to demonstrate that present-day capitalism is already substantively meritocratic, with obstacles to social mobility linked to the presence not of class hierarchies but of inherent, relatively unchangeable differences in intellectual capacity between individuals.[15] Others have used biologistic approaches to explain the emergence of the Industrial Revolution in Britain (primogeniture forced genetically well-endowed aristocratic offspring to seek their fortunes away from agriculture) or to claim IQ as the decisive explanatory variable in differences in per capita GDP between nations.[16]

The most important policy conclusion emerging from those committed to a fundamentalist approach to these IQ studies is a quietism about the possibilities of the alleviation of inequality by way of various forms of social engineering by the state, most especially through the educational system.[17] Thus, Arthur Jensen in 1973 famously answered 'Very little, if at all' to his own question 'How Much Can We Boost IQ and Scholastic Achievement?' through, for instance, compensatory education.[18] Others have proceeded along similar lines, though some research in this tradition has found a distinctive role for the environment (socioeconomic status) in IQ determination among impoverished families.[19] The predominant emphasis, however, has been to focus on 'nature' rather than 'nurture' in the formation of intellectual capacity and associated forms of economic and social attainment.

The most prominent figure in public discourse in recent decades in dealing with these issues has been Charles Murray. The singular characteristic of his large output is his elaboration of the social implications of what he takes to be the conclusions emerging from IQ research.[20] There are inherent, hard-wired constraints on intellectual capacity that are binding on a large percentage of the population:

> Many children are just not gifted enough to learn to read and write at more than a rudimentary level...and the schools can only tweak their performance at the margins...The problem is not that [they] have not been taught enough, but that [they] are not smart enough.[21]

The writings of Charles Murray have the characteristic of focusing on key issues affecting the trajectory of education for all children in the twenty-first century and, perhaps unintentionally, their link to class and hierarchy in society. His admonition to 'remove the ideological blinkers and stop pretending that all children can or should pursue the academic track'[22] follows directly from the inherent genetic limitations outlined above. But, Murray suggests, let us put to one side the demonstrable fact that 'Only a small minority of high-school graduates have the intelligence to succeed in college.' For the sake of argument, one can replace the inflammatory term 'intelligence' with that of 'academic ability', working 'from the simple and easily demonstrable proposition that what you see in the academic ability of high-school seniors is what you get.'[23] Murray's Modest Proposal is as follows:

> set up a single goal to represent educational success, which will take four years to achieve no matter what is being taught…attach a large economic reward to it that usually has nothing to do with what has been learned…urge large numbers of people who do not possess adequate ability to try to achieve the goal, wait until they have spent a lot of time and money, and then deny it to them…stigmatize everyone who doesn't meet the goal…call the goal a 'B.A.'[24]

It is impossible to argue against Murray's proposition that the goal of education is 'to bring children to adulthood having discovered things they enjoy doing and having learned how to do them well. The goal applies equally to every child, across the entire range of every ability.'[25] But since, according to Murray, only 10 to 15 per cent have the academic ability to succeed at university, the practice in the US, now present in the UK and other countries, of sending half the population in pursuit of a BA is dysfunctional and wasteful, and it would better to abolish it. Its replacement by certifications of professional qualification and the more widespread use of distance learning in lieu of campus study will better serve the needs of both employers and job seekers; these changes can unfold without the need for any government involvement or subsidy. 'Get rid of the four-year requirement, and many young people who are eager for careers in business, say, would do just fine in the eight or ten courses in marketing, management, and finance that they are highly motivated to take.'[26]

Many elements of Murray's programme are unfolding in the US and UK, with rising university fees beginning to make study on a university campus a luxury for the well-off. Whether market-based certifications of qualification can simultaneously serve the needs of employers 'and' job seekers is, however, dubious: as we have seen in Chapter 8, the fine-sounding notion that qualifications should be set to meet the needs of employers is flawed. From the employer's point of view, the ideal engineering or accountancy graduate will be able to 'hit the ground running'. But for young workers (whether they know it or not), and for society as a whole, the supposedly impractical aspects of study, those involving basic skills, prepare young people for a lifetime of work for different employers and under changing conditions, including the possibility of working, as most people do, far from their original field of study. That is why handing over the setting of qualifications to the needs of employers is so inefficacious for individual workers, and for society as a whole.

In the context of societies, such as the US, that have experienced dramatic increases in economic inequality in recent decades, Murray's vision of a streamed, vocational education for the overwhelming majority – 85 to 90 per cent of the population – is an influential one, and complements the notion that only a small portion of the population are capable of absorbing the knowledge that would be necessary for full participation in forms of political and economic democracy. It leads, however, to some peculiar notions:

> For the student who wants to become a good hotel manager, software designer, accountant, hospital administrator, farmer, high-school teacher, social worker, journalist, optometrist, interior designer, or football coach, four years of class work is ridiculous.[27]

The question arises here of what kind of world Murray lives in, or wishes to create. In the list above, perhaps he is referring to high-school teachers for other people's children – for the great mass who inevitably 'don't make the grade' – and not for those of his own class. The critical issue in the twenty-first century will not be how well societies educate the children of the elite – which all societies do according to their own lights – but their success at realising the human potential of those from marginal backgrounds. I studied high-school physics a half century ago with a friend from our housing project in Queens, who would go on to complete an MA in engineering and a PhD in physics (he was a year behind me in school because, like many other superlative achievers, he had not been deemed suitable at the age of 11 for the 'special progress' track) and go on to become a notable figure in the US high-tech industry. The daunting task of setting challenges for such a student in science class was met by our teacher, an aspirational actor on Broadway who had a BA in physics from one of New York City's free higher educational establishments. If, by contrast, my friend had progressed through a Murray-style educational system populated by mediocre, certificated teachers for the masses, would his highly productive career as engineer and physicist ever have emerged? Extraordinarily, this indifference to academic qualifications for teachers in school has now registered as a legitimate position to take in educational debates.

It is indubitable that Murray has successfully focused on fundamental tensions in present-day higher education, with its on-going conflict between meeting vocational as well as broader educational and cultural goals, all in the context of participation by half the population. He is also correct that university is far too late a stage to impart familiarity with history, science, and great works of art, music and literature,[28] tasks that should have been fulfilled at school. It is typical of the best right-wing thinkers that they alight on an accurate analysis of present-day social situations: much of what passes for higher education, in the context of the levels of academic achievement with which students enter, is wasteful and even farcical. For Murray, these failures are embedded in the intellectual limitations of the vast majority of the population and imply that social decision making will inevitably reside with an elite. An alternative approach would be to consider why social inequality and the present methods for educating children from the youngest ages have been generating these supposedly immutable chasms in educational outcomes, and then devise a strategy for alleviation: the goals of such a programme would be to realise the intellectual and overall human potential of individual children and use it to extend democratic participation and decision making in society.

It would be unfair to segregate Charles Murray from others who make their case for inequality surreptitiously: his frank social Darwinist legitimation of social segmentation is merely held more consistently, more explicitly and less disingenuously than it is by those who weakly claim that some people are inherently more able than others. By contrast, Hayek's liberal justification for class division, with its admonition that we accede to a spontaneous order that invariably embodies a substantial component of arbitrariness, has had no traction outside the bounds of academic discourse. In Chapter 4, in the famous debates between Oskar Lange and Ludwig von Mises, Lange at one point suggests that the future socialist republic will have to build a statue to Mises for his assistance in clarifying the nature of the problems of rational socialist organisation.[29] No such statue was ever built to Mises in the communist-led Poland to which Lange returned after the Second World War. It would, perhaps, be pushing irony too far to suggest here that a future socialist society should build a statue to Charles Murray for delineating with exceptional clarity the gap between the socialist worldview and that of both social Darwinists and professed liberals.

Does the existing state of knowledge dictate that the distribution and existing levels of academic achievement are a reflection of hard-wired biological constraints? On the contrary, it appears that there is more to say about this modern form of Augustinian predestination. Even researchers accepting the inherent validity of the IQ measure and its straightforward decomposition into genetic and environmental causes have reined in the more extravagant claims for a genetic fatalism. As noted above, one study claims that, in the context of impoverished families, a predominant role is played by the environment (socioeconomic status) in IQ determination;[30] more broadly, claims of exceptional correspondence in preferences for beer and religious practice among identical twins supposedly reared apart merely underline the lack of true environmental variance in all such studies.[31]

It is easy to make light of the cavalier approach sometimes taken in academic research to the relationship between a supposedly hard-wired intelligence and the social environment. One study[32] claims that individuals with high measured intelligence have views on economics that are highly correlated with those of the average economist, attitudes embodying a favourable view of marketplace allocation. Do such results evidence, as the researchers involved seem to think, a link between innate intelligence and the ability to grasp correct free-market principles, and therefore economic success? Perhaps a more straightforward explanation is that 'intelligent', upwardly aspirational individuals are better than the rest of us at internalising and expressing an unfeigned enthusiasm for the dominant ideology of the society in which they live: would not such individuals have waxed eloquent, in the context of the Soviet Union of 1950, about the virtues of a society planned in a rational, coherent manner?

In recent times, the greatest upheaval within the IQ literature has resulted from the realisation that IQ is far from being a fixed, biologically invariant constant. The gains in IQ scores across the world, dubbed the Flynn effect, were dramatic over the twentieth century, with some indication that this process may have reversed itself recently; IQ can also increase or decrease relative to peers in teenage years.[33] In general, IQ appears to be far more contingent and malleable than indicated in the traditional psychological literature, which is not consistent with it being an invariant measure of biological capacity.

In response to these issues, there have been efforts to salvage the traditional approach to IQ and the genes–environment dichotomy using the notion of a feedback loop between genes and the environment, so that 'Within a generation, genetic differences drive feedback processes – genes use individual multipliers to determine and magnify IQ differences between individuals. Between generations, environmental trends drive feedback processes – environment uses social multipliers to raise the average IQ over time. Twin studies, despite their evidence for feeble environmental factors, and IQ trends over time, despite revelation of potent environmental factors, present no paradox.'[34] Even for one untutored in psychology or genetics, the logic of this approach is easy to see: my brother's superior genetic endowment (including five inches in height) helped place him in a different 'environment' for playing basketball – high-school and college teams – and left me to play in the schoolyard: initial biological advantages were reinforced. Using the latter and related approaches, psychologists continue to use a discourse centred on IQ, but one stripped of the immutable and exogenous characteristics that originally gave it such explanatory power: a recent survey for the American Psychological Association of the state of research on IQ retains the central concept, but concedes so much scope for the mutability of IQ and the effects of the environment, most especially social class, on the IQ measure as to leave little of the original concept intact. For a recent president of the Association, 'Intelligence cannot be fully or even meaningfully understood outside its cultural context.'[35]

For many contemporary researchers, however, shifts in the 'nature–nurture' boundary do not deal sufficiently with the underlying problem: the dichotomy between characteristics in an organism that can be defined as genetic or innate and those acquired from an external environment is a 'folk understanding' of a process that, in fact, involves the continuous interplay of the organism (and its genes) with its environment. As a result, 'the underlying assumptions of contemporary psychological models reflect largely outdated ideas about what it means for something to be innate'.[36] The relationship between brain and behavioural development is, in fact, 'one of interdependence and reciprocity: Behaviors influence brain development and the brain mediates all behavior', engaging 'both inherited and environmental factors and…their continuous interaction'.[37] The focus in this literature is thus upon on the plasticity of the brain in its interaction with its external environment.[38]

And, in the spirit of this latter emphasis on brain plasticity, we have seen the emergence of a new discipline surrounding 'expert performance', claiming that the latter can be cultivated in a wide range of activities with a well-defined process of supervised practice, starting at very young ages and maintained at high daily levels for more than a decade. Researchers in this area have even suggested that 'With the exception of fixed genetic factors determining body size and height, we were unable to find evidence for innate constraints to the attainment of elite achievement for healthy individuals.'[39] While the efficacy of expert performance has been downplayed in a recent review of the literature,[40] this approach has served as a useful antidote to those who would crudely derive a genetic fatalism by extrapolating from Mozart's prodigious achievements, apparently unaware of the example of his great contemporary (and slow developer) Joseph Haydn. The case of Haydn underlines the role of the external effects associated with learning described in Chapter 7, and how in a rich environment (such as the musical culture of mid-eighteenth-century central Europe) a capacity for 'genius' might emerge from an individual endowed with what appears to be ordinary raw material. It is, thus, likely that the individualistic controlled experiments used by the advocates and opponents of expert performance may be an insufficient basis for deciding these issues.

Nor is it necessary to presume that human beings begin as a blank slate[41] and to take the extreme position on human malleability found in some earlier radical left-wing thinkers: 'The difference between the most dissimilar characters, between a philosopher and a common street porter, for example, seems to arise not so much from nature, as from habit, custom, and education.'[42] On the contrary, research is on-going on brain development and its links to genetic inheritance: there may well be lock-in effects in children's cognitive development observed as early as one year. These effects may be due, at least in part, to environmental factors, such as prenatal exposure to alcohol and malnutrition.[43] In general, however, the unfolding of human cognitive capacity from, and before, birth is a field in its infancy: 'we know nothing about the genetics of nonpathological variation in the cognitive capacities of the brain ... After more than a century of claims that high intellectual or artistic accomplishment is somehow rooted in heredity and, more specifically, in the possession of "genes for high intelligence" or "genes for creativity", there is no credible evidence for their existence.'[44]

One clear conclusion from recent research is that cognitive differences apparently set in very early,[45] with the infant mind interacting and 'testing hypotheses' concerning its environment: 'A new picture of childhood and human nature emerges from the research of the past decade. Far from being mere unfinished adults, babies and young children are exquisitely designed by evolution to change and create, to learn and explore. Those capacities, so intrinsic to what it means to be human, appear in their purest forms in the earliest years of our lives.'[46] The very nature of this plasticity in its early stages implies that the emergence of a child's cognitive facilities, attitudes and habits is a highly contingent matter: 'Experience is changing the brain from the very beginning. Everything a baby sees, hears, tastes, touches, and smells influences the way the brain gets hooked up.'[47] For the US, there is strong evidence that appropriate motivation, concentration and attitudes are formed in the context of social class at a very young age.[48]

Even looking purely at cognition, the influence of social class at very young ages appears to be potent. Much of our existing knowledge of children derives from their performance observed in laboratories.[49] By contrast, an influential study from the 1990s by Betty Hart and Todd Risley involved observing 42 families for an hour each month for two and a half years, from when the children were seven to nine months old until they turned three years old.[50] In terms of words heard, the average child living with recipients of welfare (state benefits) was having half as much experience per hour (616 words per hour) as the average working-class child (1251 words per hour) and less than one-third that of the average child in a professional family (2153 words per hour), cumulating by the age of four in deficits of millions of words for the poorer social groups; children in families in the upper end of the social spectrum also received a distinctively higher proportion of words of encouragement in contrast to prohibition.[51] In a more recent study, significant differences in language proficiency linked to the socio-economic status of the family have been found in children as young as 18 months.[52]

These latter studies deserve to be at the centre of debate about the future of the human race, rather than buried away in discussions among educational psychologists. It is disconcerting to see studies with congruent results concluding that early childhood intervention as public policy should be supported on the basis that such intervention would be beneficial from an economic cost–benefit perspective, both social (economic growth) and individual (earnings).[53] Most especially in rich countries, such a narrow economistic approach seems to trivialise and marginalise what could be a key component of a programme for human liberation, democratic participation and equality.

One reason for the marginalisation of this research is that it is invariably interpreted in terms of the cognitive deficits of children growing up in poorer environments,[54] rather than being framed in the broader context of the flourishing of all human beings and how this is contingent on social and environmental factors present at, or even before, birth. Partially as a result of the narrow perspective to which this kind of research has been consigned, the resources devoted to it have been minimal compared, for instance, with the pursuit of 'better' weapons of mass destruction. While dismissals of the work of Hart and Risley as registering the genetic inputs of the parents[55] seem merely cavalier, it is legitimate to claim that these central issues affecting the future of humankind cannot be resolved on such a slender reed of empirical verification.[56]

It would appear that there is a great deal to play for in the domain of human transformation. No one should be surprised that, in highly unequal societies, with dramatic contrasts in the life experience of young children from different classes,[57] increased inputs of formal education do not act as magic bullets. A sobering assessment emerges in a US context:

> current policy initiatives are misguided because they either deny or set to the side a basic body of evidence documenting that students from disadvantaged households on average perform less well in school than those from more advantaged families. Because they do not directly address the educational challenges experienced by disadvantaged students, these policy strategies have contributed little – and are not likely to contribute much in the future – to raising overall student achievement or to reducing achievement and educational attainment gaps between advantaged and disadvantaged students. Moreover, such policies have the potential to do serious harm.[58]

The Head Start programme in the US for three-year-olds, for instance, has had mixed results in terms of cognitive development;[59] by contrast, other studies, often beginning their interventions at birth, claim success in both the cognitive and non-cognitive domains.[60] But whatever the potency of the environmental forces shaping human development in the very earliest years of life – and they seem to be substantial and to give the lie to mechanistic formulations of IQ fatalism – human beings continue to be affected by, and respond to, the general and school environment in which they find themselves as they grow older. A milder form of fatalism that might easily emerge from the above research – 'it's all over by the age of three' – should give way to an understanding of the ways in which we all can continue to learn throughout our lives.[61]

A key aspect of a socialist education programme, to be discussed below, is how to endow individuals with an education that has a low centre of gravity – one that gives the basis for learning and adapting to changing circumstances in one's life and the general environment. Such a well-grounded education not only promotes the vaunted flexibility that is so commonly heralded as a key aspect of economic efficiency (but is often merely a euphemism for the imposition of economic insecurity upon workers), but also enriches human life with an enhanced capacity to learn new things on a life-long basis; it also contributes to an alleviation of the kind of material insecurity that is associated with individuals whose skills are precariously limited to a narrow repertoire.

Current fashions for biological reductionism, such as the claim that there are genes for religious belief, are clearly an aspect of the readiness of contemporary society to attribute facility, skill or capacity to natural ability. But it is also commonly a sign of a societal failure, and a willingness to use biology as an excuse – the Anglophone who announces to a Dutch person, in English, that she has no gift for foreign language, and the Dutch person replying in mildly accented English that he has the same problem. The common opinion that singing in tune and moving in a graceful or agile manner are deeply embedded natural gifts would seem odd notions in societies where these capacities emerge as part of a child's upbringing. Johann Sebastian Bach, when teaching music to his own or other people's offspring, took it for granted that all children, including those with learning difficulties, were capable of mastering the fundamentals of musical composition: it was a craft that could be mastered by dint of hard work. Bach, of course, recognised that some children evinced originality and taste[62] in this sphere, while others did not. But the ability to participate in music was, for him, a widely distributed characteristic of humankind in the context of proper instruction and individual application. It was not an esoteric, rare skill possessed only by a limited number of individuals having special gifts.[63]

Are, then, all individuals equally able? The very question implicitly presumes the existence of a scalar that can act as a summary measure of human capacity – something resembling the psychologists' g, from which the IQ statistic was derived as an empirical surrogate: only under such conditions would it be meaningful to rank how able people are. For national economies, as we have seen in Chapter 10, the presence of a unique measure of economic capacity and potentiality is a dubious proposition: the conceptual and substantive obstacles to the creation of such a metric in the context of individual human capability are likely to be even more formidable, if not insurmountable.

But even if we retreat from asserting a belief in the existence of a unique overall mental capacity that can be measured, and merely presume the presence in individuals of a range of such capacities, our understanding of the relationship between natural and acquired ability is a complex one. If I may use a slightly facetious example, let us presume that among the Mongol population of the thirteenth century there was a (normal?) distribution of natural facility in horse-riding ability (taking into consideration the possibility of special tuition for the children of the elite). Any such variance in ability among Mongols, however, would have been swamped by the differences between the standard of Mongol horsemanship and that of, say, the average European. It is the European unfulfilled potential in horsemanship that is of especial interest, and this is indicated in a substantive way by the standards set by the Mongols: what would have appeared as exceptional or even miraculous ability in Europe would have been part of normal social upbringing in a Mongol context.

This wasted potential and truncated development, emanating from childhood experience, and in the context of class divisions in society, must be a central focus of socialist analysis and activity. Academic research largely confirms what most of us have always taken for granted:

> social-class differences in the quality and quantity of children's activities do not largely stem from fundamental differences in parents' desires to help children develop or cultivate their skills and talents. Instead, these differences stem from parents' differential access to a wide range of resources, including money, the human capital to know how best to assess and improve children's skills, the cultural capital to know how best to cultivate children's talents, and the social capital to learn about and gain access to programs and activities.[64]

This chapter will conclude by outlining a long-term strategy of human development in the context of formal education. In order to remove the discussion from the realm of speculation, the resource commitment made by the well-off to the upbringing of their own children is used as a point of comparison. In no way is it suggested here that the present practices of elites dictate appropriate priorities for human development, or that the upbringing accorded to their children represents some sort of an ideal of the repertoire of attitudes and faculties that a child might acquire. The helplessness, passivity and immobility imposed upon affluent modern children when they grow up in a low-density, car-oriented suburb might be invidiously contrasted with earlier generations of working-class adolescents, many of whom were impelled, but perhaps also empowered, by circumstances to take responsibility for their own lives and those of other family members.[65]

In the cognitive domain, elite standards for the teaching of academic subjects may have to be combined with greater attention than is given at present to so-called practical skills, including an enhanced familiarity with how things work at a mechanical and biological level, if individuals are to be liberated from magical thinking or a feeling of helplessness in the face of the complexities of contemporary technological culture. In a host of ways, the present-day upbringing and education of elite children is not to be emulated. But the compendium of capabilities acquired by the children of this exclusive group in society, and the human and financial resources necessary to bring this process to fruition, take the question of upbringing and human transformation away from the realm of utopian speculation and into the domain of substantive goals and targets. The issue, however, is not simply one of providing a successful programme in the context of schooling, since children, like the rest of us, live in the world: it appears that even well-designed schoolroom exercise programmes for children are no substitute for children having outside environments that are usable for play.[66]

In the 1960s, the greatest technological power in the world devoted substantial resources to sending a member of the delicate species *Homo sapiens* to the moon, and is now planning a similar expedition to the planet Mars, partially fuelled by the adolescent presumption that this is all part of the greatest possible human adventure. Given the sinister purposes to which these technologies have also been devoted, these activities appear wasteful but innocent. But a far more interesting and challenging adventure, and a more productive use of resources, would be a serious exploration of the limits of human potential and development. Unless we accept the implicit notion of a genetic fatalism – that there is nothing much that can be done in this area – can we not proceed, using methods already well-established among certain classes of society, to explore not other worlds but our own potentialities as human beings?

Culture

The cultivation of formally acquired skills is central to economic and social development. But other factors, as we have seen, also play an important role in this process, such as the presence in society of a range of *in situ* skills. These capabilities, such as a facility for fixing things, bargaining, preparing food or making music, are often cultivated in the absence of any institutional tuition. Another factor that appears to play a critical role in development is the nature of a society's culture – the set of values, attitudes and habits that are inculcated into individuals from birth as they go about daily life.[67] Cultural attitudes embedded in the fabric of society can affect its ability to engender social and political cooperation; cultural values and capabilities can also condition whether a society can respond flexibly to economic, technological and social change. Societies embodying cultural values that lend themselves towards cooperation and permit them to respond flexibly in the presence of change are, it is argued, more likely to experience economic and social progress.

But the concept of culture can be a treacherous one. It has the potential for being used in an elastic manner that makes it incapable of being refuted, so that aspects of economically successful cultures become identified *ex post* with efficacious cultural characteristics: if formulated in this manner, we may find ourselves replacing the genetic fatalism outlined above with a softer, but equally consigning, version in which the dysfunctional characteristics of certain cultures act as binding constraints on development. At what point in history do these deep characteristics reveal themselves? And how do we disinter, and predict, the incipiently productive aspects of a culture when that population is mired in poverty – the lazy Japanese of the beginning of the twentieth century and the hopelessly superstitious and tradition-enslaved Ashkenazi Jews of the nineteenth?

Any attempt to make a facile linkage between development and culture can quickly devolve into a morass of cause and effect. The economic historian David Landes assures us that cultural factors in the Europe of 1500 made its subsequent global dominance a certainty;[68] the political scientist Samuel Huntington makes a similar assertion about the success of South Korea compared with Ghana in the decades after 1960.[69] But no contemporaneous figure isolated this factor to prognosticate the subsequent successes of, respectively, Europe in 1500 and South Korea in 1960. On the contrary, Ha-Joon Chang, in a chapter entitled 'Lazy Japanese and Thieving Germans', notes a tendency, at least as far back as the nineteenth century, to use cultural deficiency as an explanation for 'endemic' economic backwardness.[70]

And, conveniently, the interpretation of cultural factors can often reverse itself in the wake of economic success, with the so-called Confucian heritage now no longer a burden imposing conformity and lack of innovation on its population, but emblematic of the diligence and high educational standards of East Asia. For most of the post-independence period, the Hindu-centred culture of India had been the focus of highly pejorative analysis as a force constraining economic development in that country.[71] Recent achievements of the software industry in India and of individuals from this background living abroad have generated a more positive interpretation of that nation's ancient culture in relation to the possibilities for economic development: its mathematical learning, going back to the invention of the number zero, its history of entrepreneurial activity and its family structures. The use of culture as an explanatory variable for long-term economic success can thus easily devolve into journalistic chit-chat and, in a perhaps more sinister fashion, a fatalism – softer than a genetically based racial inferiority, but just as damning – that some societies are inevitably mired in a dysfunctional culture, one that acts as a binding constraint on progress.

Progressive analysts have, therefore, objected to the fatalism embodied in the presupposition of an autonomous role for culture, because it can be seen to preclude conscious efforts to transform and develop a society; in addition, analysis in terms of cultural backwardness can come across as condescending, or worse. Furthermore, an active role for culture is traditionally downplayed in traditional Marxist intellectual architecture because culture is seen to be merely part of the superstructure of society. Such an approach, however, can have the unfortunate effect of generating a passive attitude to this powerful force, as can be seen in the account given by Richard Lewontin of time spent by himself and Carl Sagan with creationist Christians in Arkansas:

> Sagan and I drew different conclusions from our experience. For me the confrontation between creationism and the science of evolution was an example of historical, regional, and class differences in culture that could only be understood in the context of American social history. For Carl it was a struggle between ignorance and knowledge.[72]

In Lewontin's view, there is little that can be done about ignorance that emerges from poverty. By contrast, it is Carl Sagan's forthright and sincere advocacy of science and rationality, in his books for a popular audience and his television series 'Cosmos', that have influenced the world in a progressive direction: a more passive approach that is content merely to ruminate over the cause–effect relationship between fundamentalist religion and scientific ignorance, and that presumes that history consigns certain groups to backwardness, is not conducive to bringing about social change. In another context, we can all be grateful that Jamie Oliver, far from being discouraged by the relatively low level of the culture of food preparation in his native Britain, has used this fact as a spur to become a great public educator in this domain, finding for himself an eager audience, even in France.

And cultural traditions can be 'created' from seemingly weak foundations,[73] the most dramatic examples in recent times being the transformation in decades of a number of East Asian cultures – Japan, Taiwan, Singapore – into masters of technological and social infrastructural aspects of Western capitalism that had been hundreds of years in development: the supposedly inherent characteristics of these cultures were rarely detected before the fact of their substantive economic achievement resulting from conscious and determined policy. More mundanely, we observe the success of small groups of determined individuals in British music education, in the form of the Associated Board and other organisations, in transforming what had been known as a land without music in the nineteenth century into a respectable musical culture in the twentieth.[74]

These developments can always be traced to deep cultural aspects, such as the so-called Confucian ethic in Asia, or the musical achievements of British culture in the fifteenth to the seventeenth centuries, but these are *ex post* conclusions: a nation's deep traditions may serve as focal points for subsequent developments, but cultural dispersion with any degree of depth in the modern world is usually the result of conscious acts of public policy. Thus, it is indubitably true that the luminous creative figures of late-eighteenth- and early-nineteenth-century Germany – Goethe, Kant and Beethoven – presaged the possibility of a widespread literate culture in an otherwise retrograde area of Western Europe, but this transformation was not inevitable or organic; it only came about through the interaction of rapid industrialisation and urbanisation with an intense programme of state-funded education.

And such acts of public policy, if sustained, may then enter into the fabric of the culture itself: the reason why Richard Hofstadter's *Anti-Intellectualism in American Life* of 1962 still reads so well today is, ironically, that he was wrong in his pessimistic trajectory of cultural development in the US. The picture he paints is of a society weighed down by evangelical religion and by a business sector that is 'in the vanguard of anti-intellectual culture',[75] and, furthermore, suffers the unintended consequences of the widespread introduction of John Dewey's ideas on progressive education into the schoolroom (see Chapter 7):

> Dogmatic, apocalyptic predictions about the collapse of liberal culture or the disappearance of high culture may be right or wrong; but one thing about them seems certain: they are more likely to instill self-pity and despair than the will to resist or the confidence to make the most of one's creative energies. It is possible, of course, that under modern conditions the avenues of choice are being closed … but in so far as the weight of one's will is thrown onto the scales of history, one lives in the belief that it is not to be so.[76]

Fifty years on, the issues posed by him are still being engaged with, not least because the constituency on the side of liberal culture and its 'will to resist' has remained a formidable force in society. Undoubtedly, the single most powerful factor that has shaped this constituency has been the cumulative effects of the expansion of publicly funded education. Various other public institutions have played an important, if subsidiary, role, emblematic of which in Britain would be the half century of wildlife programmes on the BBC by David Attenborough.

An example of the role of public policy in cultural affairs concerns the controversy surrounding the transmission of advertising to children. This issue comes into particularly sharp focus in the US, with a signal event being Ronald Reagan's vetoing in 1988 of a bill that would have limited advertising during children's programming and required broadcasters to provide educational programmes for children as a condition of licence renewal.[77] Would even Friedrich Hayek have supported Reagan here in the latter's defence of the spontaneous order – the blocking of any governmental interference in the natural process by which advertisers influence the opinions of children in a free market? Reactions from those concerned with children's welfare were furious: 'Every aspect of children's lives – their physical and mental health, their education, their creativity, and their values – is negatively affected by their involuntary status as consumers in the marketplace.'[78] Some have suggested that 'In the late twentieth and early twenty-first centuries corporate-produced children's culture has replaced schooling as the producer of the central curriculum of childhood' and that commercial dynamics are 'forces that impose themselves into all aspects of our own and our children's private lives'.[79]

The assertions in the latter quotations lack credulity. By failing to locate the problems discussed in class terms, they ignore the fact that the 'forces that impose themselves into all aspects of our own and our children's private lives' do not do so equally throughout society. The children of the elite and upper income levels in the US and elsewhere continue to reproduce, by any objective measure, credible levels of school achievement and replication of high culture. Their parents cope with a commercialism that is perhaps more intrusive than that in the past, but remains more of an annoyance than a threat. In addition, other groups in society are not merely passive recipients of commercialism: it would be a mistake to underestimate the presence of spontaneous creativity in society, sometimes taking the form of rebellion against, and sometimes a creative reshaping of, the commercial culture. It is indubitably true, however, that for much of the population, the high aspirations of parents for their young children run into ever greater obstacles, unknown to society's upper levels, in opposing commercial forces: the harassed single mother using the television or computer as a child minder is a familiar image.

With little apparent willingness to engage in any explicit class analysis of the question of cultural dissemination, we see in its place the *ersatz* radicalism of cultural studies: the problem of transmission of culture is implicitly surrendered as a hopeless task. Cultural studies refuses 'to equate "culture" with high culture [and] attempts to examine the diversity of a society's artistic, institutional, and communicative expressions and practices'.[80] It cultivates in children a media literacy that 'respects children's intellectual ability to deal with the complexities of power, oppression, and exploitation' rather than being placed in a 'contemporary right-wing, test-driven educational context'.[81]

The words are brave, and the sentiments are admirable, but 'arming' children by having them make a critical analysis of some aspect of commercial culture is ultimately a negative, defensive strategy. In the absence of substantive knowledge of the cultural heritage and standards of excellence as points of reference, children (or anyone else) are incapable of making anything but the most vapid and superficial of cultural critiques. By contrast, the elite of society attempts, and often succeeds, in giving its children an education in the household, school and broader environment that is 'progressive' – flexible and interactive, leaving room for the cultivation of creative impulses and yet demanding of achievement of substantive knowledge. Critiques of commercial culture emerging from such children, encouraged to appreciate Sophocles and Shakespeare, can have a richness unknown to those who have solely been subject to a cultural studies perspective.

Public policy thus plays a crucial role in cultural evolution, most powerfully in the context of public education. It also influences culture through creations such as Attenborough's BBC programmes and by decisions on whether or not to constrain, for instance, advertising to children on television. But it is indubitably true that cultural development, rather than being the product of conscious, or even self-conscious, acts of public policy, often emerges as an aspect of Hayek's spontaneous order, such as the appearance of video games (though somehow one suspects the good professor, born in nineteenth-century Vienna, would have been uncomfortable with this example). In such circumstances, the danger exists that well-meaning cultural guardians may impose a straightjacket on forms of cultural innovation emerging in unexpected places: there are endless examples paralleling that of the incipient genius of jazz, the young Bill Basie, inhibited by a music teacher accepting no deviation from the study of 'serious' (European classical) music.[82] The Count Basie problem points to the conflict between the passing on of a cultural heritage and permitting that culture to evolve, flourish and innovate in a spontaneous manner. In the case at hand, there is the additional tension – existing in many contemporary cultures but quintessentially in the US context – between a dominant (European) culture and an emergent (at the beginning of the twentieth century) African-American cultural (in this case musical) identity. An easy resolution would be to take a mediated, moderate view on this matter. But such an approach would be inappropriate. The fact that there is ambiguity in the nature of the cultural identity to be passed on to children can be used as an excuse to pass on a weakened, anodyne and superficial version of the cultural heritage, perhaps by an exclusive focus on a supposed core of reading, writing and arithmetic: any such attempt at a Scholastic differentiation between form (the skill of reading) and content (the substantive material being considered) is unlikely to be successful.

The myths surrounding cultural spontaneity, of culture emerging naturally from certain individuals and groups (often, in a US context, projected upon African-Americans by the majority population), militate against a focus on the need for early exposure and formalised training in many highly valued human skills, for instance, music. As seen in Chapter 7, this romanticised emphasis on spontaneity, often associated with progressive education and left-wing political views in general, can even impinge upon the teaching of standard English in schools. In the resulting circumstances, right-wing advocates can often pose as the defenders of education and culture (a particularly absurd happenstance in a US context, with the strong tendency of its right wing to manifest philistine and anti-science attitudes) and as educational reformers for children from poorer backgrounds. This peculiar situation emerges from the central dilemma surrounding progressive education: whatever its suitability for children from families of a cultural elite, it often appears to be inegalitarian and inappropriate for children from ordinary or lower-class backgrounds. Under present conditions, such children may well benefit from a more traditional education, with elements of rote learning. As noted in Chapter 7, one of the clichés of present-day educational debates is that Asian nations, often highly successful in international testing races, complain that their methods are not suitable for producing the kind of creativity emerging from the best Western elite education.

The key phrase in the paragraph above is 'under present conditions'. For rich countries, it should be possible to dissolve any such trade-off between the spontaneity and creativity of progressive approaches to education and the egalitarianism associated with traditional approaches: it is a question of applying the appropriate focus, energy, enthusiasm and, above all, resources – a replication for all children at birth of the kind of opportunities that are now provided only to the children of an elite. The major obstacle to moving in this direction is the will to do so.

The inevitable limitations of any such programme, however, must be noted. The great mass of children, even in rich societies, grow up bereft of the cognitive repertoire, self-confidence and capacity for self-realisation that the upper range of society helps to inculcate into its children even before they enter formal schooling. Any attempt to use the public school system as a vehicle for the installation of equal opportunity in society imposes upon the school system an insuperable task – it must eliminate cognitive gaps rooted in home background and instil in children a capacity for the formulation and execution of lifetime goals of the kind that elite children are trained to do (partially by emulation of parents' behaviour) at home. Schooling is the most powerful single social mechanism for the equalisation of opportunity within society, but even the best-constructed schooling and even preschooling programmes are unlikely to be a sufficient remedy: these programmes are likely to be more successful in societies that are not overly unequal in the first place.

Strategies utopian and practical

It is thus appropriate to re-engage with the socialist goals enunciated in the Introduction. With a focus on its individualistic aspects linked to self-realisation, socialism is here perceived as a form of social organisation that gives to all individuals an opportunity for self-realisation and development of personal capacities. Such an approach implies an access to upbringing and education from the earliest stages of life that is not contingent on, and compensates for, limitations in household circumstances, a mitigation of the forms of deprivation and insecurities to which households are subject, and opportunities for employment that involve full exercise and realisation of personal capacities.

Even when considering human liberation from this individualistic perspective, with its focus on upbringing and schooling, the issues surrounding living in the world cannot be ignored. Thus, an 'upbringing and education that is not contingent on limitations in household circumstances' not only serves as a path to individual self-realisation, but plays a key role in any strategy to mitigate or eliminate economic and social inequality and to promote democratic control in daily life and in the broader society. But causation also proceeds in the opposite direction: the presence of deprivation and differential circumstances in the first place greatly complicates the execution of an educational programme of any real ambition, since with pronounced social and economic inequality, the household may fail as a vehicle of support for a child's formal education.

Of at least equal significance, however, is the role of the household itself in the child's upbringing as a source of *in situ* learning – the attitudes, behaviour, habits, cognitive development and implicit knowledge that emerge from that source. The diversity of experience in households can, as we have seen above, be a source of enrichment for society as a whole. But in societies with severe forms of social and economic inequality, as well as geographical, ethnic and racial segregation, what children learn in their households may diverge substantially and dampen any equalising effects of a common formal education. In addition, the work environment functions as a further source of *in situ* learning that can rarely be duplicated by formalised schooling.

We thus have a large literature confirming the efficacy of early childhood intervention in various domains, most especially of preschool education from very young ages, with the most robust claims for long-term success in the non-cognitive domain.[83] It is worthwhile, however, proceeding with care in this matter: it has been suggested that indiscriminate use of preschool facilities can deprive infants of important interaction with parents.[84] Furthermore, one must not pretend that even the most efficacious programme starting from birth can fully compensate for what can be offered in terms of life experience to children from the upper strata of society, even in the relatively mundane sphere of summer vacation activities. The outside world impinges even on the domain of physical activity, with school programmes of far less importance than the nature of the built environment in which the child grows up and the opportunities it offers for spontaneous physical activity (play).[85] Social class plays a pervasive role in the structuring of 'being a self' in a broad range of social contexts, including the school, which serves, in many contexts, merely to reinforce existing class divisions.[86]

With all these caveats, formal education is, and has been, the single most powerful public policy vehicle for social transformation in rich countries over the past century. The purpose here is to investigate the extent to which an enhanced educational policy can be used as an instigator and conveyor of social change – one element, albeit a key one, in the promotion of individual self-realisation, social equality and democracy. The path to be pursued is a circuitous one, the first step being a review of the contemporary debate on the relative economic efficacy of smaller class sizes versus 'better' teachers. The discussion then proceeds to a consideration of the nature of private, and most especially elite private, educational institutions. The purpose here is not to praise or blame the latter, but to give a concrete form to the resources involved in creating 'palaces for children'[87] in a twenty-first-century manifestation.

The class size debate is peculiar, because it involves one group of economists arguing that additional expenditure of resources on this activity makes little or no difference to 'output'. The rationale for this claim – an unusual one in typical economists' discourse – of a 'presumed absence of a relationship between resources and student outcomes' was that 'bureaucracy, unions and perverse incentives cause public education to squander resources, severing the link between resources and student outcomes'.[88] The debate itself has taken a rather arid form, with one economist, Eric A. Hanushek, reviewing existing studies and finding little benefit to reductions in class size, and another, Alan B. Krueger, taking an opposing position, claiming to find a significant benefit to class size reductions when the studies reviewed are properly weighted.[89] Additional support for the latter position is claimed on the basis of Project Star, a large-scale experiment conducted in Tennessee in 1985–9, with children randomly assigned to classes of different sizes.[90]

The editors of a book devoted to this debate offer the anodyne conclusion of a convergence between the positions of Hanushek and Krueger, importuning that 'All should be able to agree that targeting the expenditure of new funds in ways that have proven to be effective is far preferable to "throwing money at schools" without regard to how it will be spent.'[91] The conclusion drawn is incorrect. There has not been a convergence between the two positions: the Hanushek faction has been decisively victorious in political terms.[92] In both the UK and the US, doubts sown about the inefficacy of additional school expenditure have merely served as support for those favouring the managerial, and relatively inexpensive, paths to reform in academies and charter schools discussed in Chapter 7.

The debate itself has a range of curious aspects. Both sides proceed to deal with this most fundamental of human activities from a self-consciously economic point of view, in the form of benefit–cost calculations on the efficacy to society of class size reduction (presumably, but not always clearly specified, as a surrogate for increased expenditure on education). Even within this economistic framework, the purview of the approaches pursued is narrow, being largely focused on possible increases in individual incomes that might accrue to children taught in smaller classrooms,[93] substantively ignoring cognitive and non-cognitive spillover effects and possible consumption benefits to children emerging from increased school expenditure. The attempt to structure these questions in strictly economic terms leads to some strange statements: 'Apart from the opportunity cost of students' time, the number of teachers hired per student is the main determinant of the economic cost of education.'[94] It is intriguing to contemplate the phrase 'the opportunity cost of students' time' in the context of ten-year-old children – does it refer to the wages foregone from working in factories? And while it is true that teacher numbers and remuneration predominate in school costs, to identify these costs solely with expenditure on teachers is to obscure the range of amenities – sports facilities, music lessons, school architecture – that can make the educational process less unpleasant for children and may be aspects of both cognitive and non-cognitive enrichment.

A second curious aspect of these debates is that the alternative to increased expenditure on education – teacher quality – is not measured in terms of objective parameters, because 'The extensive research addressing this has found little that consistently distinguishes among teachers in their classroom effectiveness... credentials, degrees, experience, and even teacher test scores are not consistently correlated with teaching skill.'[95] Furthermore, a controlled experiment is cited that finds no improvement in teacher performance when an enriched induction and mentoring programme is introduced.[96] With, in general, teacher quality thus left a mystery, the path is open for systems of performance-related pay (linked to student results on centrally administered examinations) with a range of incentives of a positive and negative kind.[97] The predominant tendency, as we have seen in Chapter 7, most especially in the US and the UK, is firmly in the direction of marketised solutions and the imposition of Taylorist managerial schemes on teachers and their 'performance'.[98]

The empirical studies upon which these managerial strategies are based have a weak foundation. The claim that academic qualifications are of no consequence in teacher quality emerges from data so generalised that they aggregate teachers working at all grade levels.[99] The resultant general dismissal of the importance of academic qualifications in teaching performance would be per se absurd if taken literally at the upper secondary level, where the essential role of such qualifications in, for instance, upper-level science teaching and mathematics teaching is indubitable (see Chapter 7); managerialist schemes are often modified to give targeted higher pay for teachers in these groups, at the expense of women, who are more likely to be qualified in equally important subjects such as English. The associated dismissal in this literature of enriched induction and mentoring, and, by implication, all forms of on-the-job training for teachers, is deeply counterintuitive, and contrasts with prominent counterexamples such as Finland, discussed in Chapter 7, and the recognition sometimes noted, even in managerial circles, of the efficacy of teacher mentoring and collaboration within and between schools.[100]

The conclusion commonly reached, verging on tautology, that the best available measure of quality is the teacher's value-added contribution to student achievement[101] is a convenient one for managerialist advocates of payment by results for teachers. The naïve, or perhaps disingenuous, use of statistical regression techniques suggests that good teachers can overcome even problems of child poverty, with individuals attracted into teaching and then motivated by appropriate rewards and punishments. Characteristic of the difficulties emerging from this approach is 'The Elephant in the Living Room' – the powerful tendency among teachers to avoid teaching in more deprived schools, with 'the desire to teach easier students … typically a stronger motivator than the desire to improve salary': differentials of up to 50 per cent in some US contexts are needed to attract teachers to deprived schools.[102] The author of this article, having noted these facts, still keeps faith with the managerialist approach, advocating generous financial rewards for those teachers who produce 'unusually big gains in student learning', with termination for those who cannot produce results.[103]

Do advocates of managerialist approaches seriously believe that the problems of teaching in deprived schools can be alleviated in this manner? The US profession is already arduous by world standards, working time required at school per year being between 14 to 20 per cent longer than the OECD average:[104] are Taylorist management procedures and scolding individuals for a 'desire to teach easier students' the appropriate way to attract individuals into teaching as a lifetime profession? Teachers wishing to avoid teaching in deprived schools, most especially if they enter with advanced academic qualifications, may feel that their ability to impart knowledge will be impossible in the context of the issues of student alienation and classroom discipline endemic in poorer areas.[105] And even if we could succeed in isolating a miraculous group of good teachers who fortuitously combine academic knowledge and pedagogic excellence with the very different talents associated with the control of masses of disaffected children, what can we say about the motivation of individuals who elect to teach in these deprived areas merely on the basis of enhanced remuneration? The search for a hard-headed, inexpensive solution to the problems associated with deprivation is a distraction from serious confrontation with this issue. It is, perhaps, the last gasp of the free-market magical thinking of the 1980s, with damaging consequences for the lives of children.

Opponents of this managerialist approach to education have maintained a defensive posture for a range of reasons. Most straightforwardly, those critical of charter and academy schools, and of the paying of teachers by performance, are seen to be supportive of the teaching unions and their 'restrictive' practices, and in general of the status quo: their positive recommendations are seen to involve nothing more than throwing money at the problem. Of even greater significance is the fact that opponents of managerialism offer little prospect of change that is beneficial to the whole community: their prescriptions are largely identified with studies supporting the benefits of increased expenditure and reduced class size for the alleviation of the cognitive and non-cognitive deficits of deprived children.[106]

More generally, there has been a recent focus on the fact that mediocre performance on PISA and other international tests in the US can largely be accounted for by failures at the low end; high levels of inequality and relative poverty are generating what would otherwise be good, if not exceptional, results on these tests (see Chapter 10). While this emphasis on inequality is salutary in its own terms, it can lead to a presumption that there is no issue involving resources and education for normal (non-deprived) children, at an extreme suggesting that achievement in school (or in future income) for such children is a reasonable reflection of the child's natural endowment in terms of, for instance, IQ.

For the elite of society, there is every indication that this kind of fatalism about the cognitive development of their children is absent. Education is aggressively pursued, even at the preschool education level, despite the advantages already accruing to the well-born prior to entry in preschool programmes.[107] At least for the US, therefore, it is no longer appropriate to focus on the educational deprivation of poor children as the sole negative outcome associated with inequality: in the last several decades a substantial increase in the association between family income and children's academic achievement for families above the median income level has emerged. These growing gaps in educational attainment between the middle and the top are linked to the effects of growing income inequality on the ability of house-holds to act as platforms for the educational attainment of their children. But there seems to be an additional component: an increasingly explicit focus, at the upper end of the income spectrum, on parental investment in children's cognitive development.[108]

It is thus instructive to pursue this question from a more positive point of view: what benefits are to be gained, and what are the limits, to child-hood development in cognitive and other domains when resources are unconstrained? A way of grounding this issue in contemporary experience is to examine the benefits accruing from elective private education. Even if one accepts for the moment the presumption that 'Nobody is going to pay between £10,000 and £30,000 a year for an education that is just a wee bit better than the free option',[109] the question of what is meant by 'better' is not self-evident; one indubitable motivation on the part of parents is the prospect of smaller class sizes than in the public sector, though the ques-tion of why parents put such a high priority on smaller classes, and their substantive efficacy in the context of private education, are far from trivial issues.

The very top private schools in the US and the UK are massively over-subscribed, despite rapidly rising fees. The median tuition figure for elite private schools in New York is almost $40,000 a year, with additional costs (covered by fund raising, etc.) bringing expenditure per pupil to about $50,000, roughly two and a half times the typical expenditure per public school pupil in New York State.[110] In the UK, expenditure per pupil in private day schools is two to three times that in state schools.[111] These figures are only rough approximations of the resources devoted to each student, with, for instance, no weight given to the rich endowments of land and buildings associated with the most venerable of these private schools.

In the US, the intensity and supposed neuroses of the parents of these children are often mocked in the press: 'a group of parents sent a seven-page e-mail detailing concerns: there were not enough snacks, not enough "worldly" snacks like seaweed, zucchini bread with quinoa flour and bean quesadillas (so long as the beans came from BPA-free tin cans)'.[112] It is, however, precisely this kind of parental engagement in the life of the school and its activities that results in a 'deliberate blurring of sharp, compart-mentalized distinctions between family and school [giving the latter a] continuity and congruence of institutional purpose... [The] school is like an extended family.'[113] Involvement of this kind is not unknown in publicly funded schools, but the relative class homogeneity and professional back-grounds of the parents involved in elite schools enhance the intensity of focus and the impact of parents' opinions on the life of the school, so that, for this exclusive subset of the population, it approximates the democratic ideal of a community-centred institution discussed in Chapter 7.

The rich physical resource endowment of elite institutions is an issue of major significance: 'a school building tells students who they are and how they should think about the world. It can help to manufacture rote obedience or independent activity; it can create high self-confidence or low self-esteem.' Even for children at the preschool level, the kinds of resources provided give 'a silent but dramatic message. Good, sturdy play equipment, bright, comfortable rooms, and lots of interesting toys not only make kids happy but also tell them they deserve the best. The treeless, nearly grassless backyard of the low-cost child-care facility... delivers the opposite message, one that even the kindest and most skilful teacher cannot totally contra-dict... the lessons learned in nursery school may be reinforced (or under-mined) years later.'[114]

The nature of the elite school's superiority in resource endowment and the priorities set may vary between institutions, reflecting both the phys-ical context and cultural priorities. Thus, the physical plant of the New York City-based Avenues school offers a mere 215,000 square feet for its 760 pupils.[115] By contrast, the British Wellington School, 'set in 400 acres of lush Berkshire countryside', 'has 16 rugby pitches, two floodlit astroturf pitches, a state-of-the-art sports hall, 22 hard tennis courts, 12 cricket pitches, an athletics track, two lacrosse pitches and six netball courts, a shooting range, an acclaimed nine-hole golf course', as well as 'six art studios, a professional recording studio, several concert venues, its own theatre and TV crew'.[116] A prep school in New Mexico of 900 students has six classroom buildings, two libraries, an arts centre containing a theatre, art gallery and auditorium, and a sports complex of three gymnasiums, two football fields, four soccer fields, three baseball diamonds, 16 tennis courts and a nine-lane, all-weather track.[117]

What can be lost in mockery and voyeuristic envy of elite upbringing of their children is a focus on what the well-off are trying to do: like all such groups through recorded history, modern elites are attempting, even if on occasion quixotically, to prepare their offspring to rule, or, in more demotic contemporary discourse, for 'leadership' in a multinational context. Thus, in the Avenues school 'Mandarin or Spanish immersion begins in nursery school; each kindergartner gets an iPad in class. Students will someday have the option of semesters in São Paulo, Beijing or any of the 20 other campuses the school plans to inaugurate around the world.'[118] Furthermore, elite groups often give their offspring an opportunity to assimilate culture at a high level (though levels of ruling group philistinism vary across history and geography), with elite New York City schools having a range of offerings including Zen Dance, Roman Travel Writing and a theatre class on 'The Nature of Revenge'.[119]

Of even greater significance than any exotic offering or eye-catching expenditure of facilities and resources is the striking extent to which these elite institutions claim to deviate from the supposedly tough-minded, results-driven ethos of the managerial approach imposed in the publicly funded sector. Clearly, these schools are expected to deliver results, and invariably succeed, with, in the UK, an extraordinary concentration of entrants to Oxford and Cambridge coming from such institutions, and then on to the upper-level professions. There is, however, at least some evidence that the lifetime advantages accruing to elite school children cannot be accounted for fully in academic terms.[120]

It would be tempting to attribute any residual in worldly success of private school graduates over others to the contacts and interactions accruing both inside and outside these schools, as well as to stocks of family wealth. In the contemporary world, however, these financial and social advantages are complemented by a strategy within elite schools that appears, astonishingly, to evoke the liberationist ethos of the 1960s. If the rhetoric of these institutions does not suggest an adherence to Summerhill's fundamental principle that 'children should not be compelled or pressured to learn or expected to meet "standards" of any sort',[121] it appears equally distant from contemporary managerialist approaches to learning. For the headmaster of a leading boarding school in Britain, Eton College, what a school fundamentally is about 'is to do with holistic development – the all-rounded person; enabling young people to develop that true sense of self-worth which is, in my view, absolutely essential if [they] are going to be able to stand up for a purpose other than themselves', so that at Eton 'there are no lessons after lunch three days a week – that is time for sports, drama, music; each pupil has personal tutor'.[122] A particularly piquant observation on the need for such an approach has been made in the context of an elite US prep school: 'It is sometimes fashionable to stereotype "sharing and caring" efforts as sentimental psychobabble, attempts to accommodate feel-good student and teacher preferences that have nothing to do with academic learning and are often undermining of it. But this critique needs tempering ... the desire for decent community is a practical judgment about good workplace conditions.'[123] Dealing with the whole person and the creation of a community of learning are substantive, practical aspects of the education of individuals expected to hold power and make decisions in contemporary society.

In this context, we may examine the Eton headmaster's guide to building character in teenagers:

1. Encourage them to aim high.
2. Celebrate their diverse individual achievements.
3. Give them genuine responsibility to take the lead.
4. Allow them to fail and learn from the experience.
5. Don't treat them all the same way, and show them understanding.[124]

If principles 1 and 3 evoke the traditions of empire, with the inculcation of the confidence and arrogance necessary for children to perceive themselves as leaders from the youngest age, the remaining ones speak to the intensity of the learning process pursued at Eton: the attention to individual needs underlines why small class sizes are the *sine qua non* of all private school education.[125] In lesser private schools, a perusal of websites indicates that small class sizes, with a concomitant promise of individual attention from teachers and an improved atmosphere for learning (often, apparently, a euphemism for a lack of bullying), sometimes exist in the context of modest formal qualifications for the teaching staff, reinforcing the recent claim by an educational researcher that 'The reason that class sizes in independent schools are so small is because they need to be, because the teaching is less good than in the state sector.'[126] On the whole, however, this claim, an attempt to defend state school teachers against attacks by managerial-style reformers, appears to be unjustified. With teachers' wages not significantly worse in the private sector, private schools are able to attract teachers with higher qualifications than those in the state sector because of superior working conditions – better facilities and fewer hours worked per year.[127] Perhaps most significantly, the students' class background, combined with the private school's offering of small classes and its detailed interaction with parents, transforms the problems of discipline and truancy endemic to the state sector into a minor and occasional irritant.

At the elite level, the presence of the dilemma posed above, in which a choice has to be made between class size and teacher quality, is irrelevant. Small classes and related expenditure in elite institutions are vehicles for the fulfilment – here in the real world – of the 'utopian' goals specified for all children in a socialist society in the Introduction. Thus, children from this limited group are offered the opportunity 'for self-realisation and development of personal capacities', as well as 'the ability to exercise control over their working and living environment' and 'in the context of the broader society'. As we have seen above, current research tends to emphasise the long-term efficacy of preschool tuition in terms of the accruing of non-cognitive benefits. As a recent popular study has suggested, 'What matters most in a child's development...is not how much information we can stuff into her brain in the first few years. What matters, instead, is whether we are able to help her develop a very different set of qualities, a list that includes persistence, self-control, curiosity, conscientiousness, grit, and self-confidence. Economists refer to these as non cognitive skills, psychologists call them personality traits, and the rest of us sometimes think of them as character.'[128] But making too sharp a distinction between the cognitive and non-cognitive domains may create false dichotomies. Most learning situations are intertwined with, and inextricable from, these non-cognitive aspects, with feelings of failure and inadequacy built into the systems of non-elite education that most children live with.[129]

Undoubtedly, obstacles will exist to the implementation of a socialist, child-centred educational environment, even in the context of appropriate resourcing. Do we not run a danger, for instance, of generating a mentality in which all children 'must have prizes', where the desire not to traumatise the child with feelings of failure also leaves her without a sense that some answers are, objectively speaking, correct, and others not? More generally, there is a potential tension between equality of treatment for all children and excellence: parents can have legitimate concerns about the need for the creation of an educational context for the channelling of a child's intense and focused efforts in the development of high-level skills.[130] Advocates who voice egalitarian issues sometimes fail to recognise these legitimate concerns, characterising these 'highly educated white parents' as fighting 'to preserve a tracking system that keeps virtually every child of color out of advanced classes'. The writer on education, Alfie Kohn, is perhaps being quoted unfairly here, because he goes on to focus on what seems to be the real issue:

it is hard to deny the superiority of the instruction in gifted-and-talented programs and some other honors or high-track classes, what with hands-on learning, student-designed projects, computers, field trips, and other enrichments. But research generally shows that it is precisely those enrichments that produce better results rather than the fact that they are accorded only to a select few. What happens in those classes is more decisive than the fact that they are homogeneous [footnote omitted].[131]

Education, education, education. Resources, resources, resources. A glance at figures on public and private expenditure on educational institutions (including tertiary) per unit GDP among OECD countries (for 2011) gives an average of 6.1 per cent, with figures of 6.4 per cent and 6.9 per cent for the UK and the US, respectively.[132] If calls for equal opportunity for all children are to be taken seriously, a radical programme for using education as part of a broader strategy of social transformation will involve a substantial increase in levels of educational expenditure. The arguments against such a strategy in the end rest on the biologically hard-wired notion that 'it is all a waste of time' and on the apparent inefficacy of throwing money at the problem, using the example of high levels of expenditure in the US and its mediocre international test results.

And yet it is the US, most dramatically, which demonstrates how inextricable education is from issues of class. While important debates on educational philosophies, strategies and approaches are on-going worldwide, it is clear, as we have seen, that much of the supposed failure of the US educational system is linked to its exceptionally high levels of inequality. Unfortunately, any attempt to use education, including intensive preschool tuition, as part of a broader strategy to alleviate social deprivation at the low end – much less a more generalised equalisation of educational opportunities across classes – is bound to appear to be particularly wasteful and extravagant in highly unequal societies such as the US. Other wealthy societies that have not permitted inequality to develop and fester in the manner of the US are likely to find such programmes more effective, and less onerous: interventions that have proved most fruitful have focused on the child's earliest years, both with preschool programmes and with aid to parents in children's upbringing and their ability to secure employment (often abetted by the presence of preschool programmes).[133]

At the opposite end of the inequality spectrum, the richest residents of the US appear to be taking a lead in a strategy of investing in the human capital of their children as a mechanism for guaranteeing their future status. The ever-developing links of these children to the English-speaking elites of other countries bind them together culturally, and reinforce the material interests they hold in common emerging from the fluidity of capital across national borders in this New International Capitalist Order.

The issue of class can be seen in a concrete form using the example of controversies surrounding homework. Typically, it is taken to be 'the quintessential job of childhood. Homework creates a situation ... where the child must complete assigned tasks under minimal supervision and after little initial training... As in the workplace, when children move from beginners to experts with homework, they demonstrate responsibility and become skilled at managing tasks.'[134] But homework, like getting a job, is not the same experience for individuals from different class backgrounds, a fact obtusely ignored by most commentators on the subject. Thus, we have the case of the French president François Hollande's pledge to eliminate homework in French schools, with work being done at school, rather than at home, in order to foster educational equality for those students who do not have support at home.[135] And yet we find Hollande's intervention, and his central motivation, airily ridiculed in one of the leading outlets for putatively progressive opinion in the US,[136] apparently oblivious to the realities underlining homework and class background.

Recent research confirms the common-sense and useful notion (if not interpreted moralistically) that parental involvement in school affairs is conducive to student success.[137] Homework is an activity, however, where even the most sincere and dedicated efforts of parents with limited education may be of little use. Growing up in a cramped flat, with no one capable of guiding or assisting me past the age of eight, I remember homework as a farcical, humiliating and wasteful experience. I write this not as an act of self-dramatisation, but to underline that this reality continues to be faced by the majority of children growing up even in present-day rich societies. Tony Little, the headmaster of Eton College, has suggested that 'boarding houses should be attached to schools across England to provide children with a "structured environment" in which they can complete homework and take part in a range of extra-curricular activities'. He thus underlines the notion that homework, this essential 'job of childhood', has such strenuous needs for a 'structured environment' as to justify substantial public expenditure to permit these tasks to be carried out away from the home. If Little's proposal for such state-supported schools to 'meet demand from busy parents'[138] suggests an empathy limited to the plight of the harried upper middle classes, the broad principles are clear: all student work should take place in the context of structure, guidance and assistance from educators, and liberated from the vagaries of individual household circumstances.

Earlier in this chapter, I proffered the suggestion that a future socialist society might build a statue to Charles Murray. In this concluding part, irony and the reader's patience are stretched again by considering how a programme of socialist education can be informed by the present-day practice of the elite school. The first issue is with regard to resources: throwing money at education is an important aspect of any reform strategy. Well-off parents are often willing to pay for their children's education even when a seemingly adequate free alternative is present, with the payoffs showing up in exam results and university admissions. Perhaps of equal significance is the role of the elite school in reinforcing the non-cognitive advantages accruing within the family to children's personal development. The elite school cultivates confidence in the child not only through the instilling of fluency of verbal and written expression, but by offering personalised guidance: children are encouraged to believe that the trajectories of their lives and careers are issues of importance, giving them a sense of direction and personal development. By contrast, ordinary schools inculcate in the great majority of children a sense of failure and a lack of purpose to their lives at school, feelings that do not necessarily dissipate after school hours, or when the school career ends. Suggestions in both the academic and popular literature that the advantages accruing to graduates of elite schools consist solely of the links made to social networks are well-meaning but deceptive.

In dealing with the wider world, elite schools succeed in reinforcing advantages accruing through family background by giving children the tools of self-mastery at the youngest age: in the context of issues such as politics and business, fluency of expression is combined with self-confidence as an aspect of power, so that speaking and putting forth an opinion about the great issues of the day is part of the birthright of elite children. For the great majority of children, however, the school merely reinforces their own families' sense of bewilderment and lack of control over the general environment, whether with regard to national politics or the world of employment and careers.

Though in recent times most official pronouncements quite bluntly focus on education as a mechanism for preparing the masses to be part of the workforce, it is still felt necessary on occasion to perpetuate the fatuous claim that ordinary children are being trained in school to function as participants in a democratic process. But large classes, authoritarian structures and the protocols of discipline in non-elite schools belie this claim in the daily lives of children, with these conditions inculcating in the great majority passivity, boredom and sometimes rebelliousness. There is a chasm between the authoritarian context of daily life in school and the pronouncements about democratic processes that children are expected to imbibe, and be enthusiastic about. The result is the generation in the child of something approaching cognitive dissonance, in which issues surrounding democracy emerge as abstract and irrelevant, in many cases reinforcing the notion that the grand issues of politics should be left to those born to rule.

The question of classroom discipline is a central issue to both learning and democracy. Clearly, learning cannot proceed outside the context of order and calm. But the inculcation of democratic habits, procedures and ways of thinking is badly served by the authoritarian atmosphere typical of normal schooling. Private schools make the absence of disciplinary issues a key selling point, putting particular emphasis on high teacher–student ratios, with the additional but unadvertised reinforcement of good decorum coming from the involvement and upper-class background of the parents of fellow students. By contrast, protocols of discipline are a way of life in mass education, and one of the vaunted advantages of the independence of charter schools and academies is their ability, in agreement with parents, to adopt stricter disciplinary codes than is common in other state-run institutions.

The question arises why the discipline question remains a central issue in the pedagogy of children of 13 and older, when the cognitive and emotional capacity to pursue purposeful activity is manifestly already present: this fact is evident in the capacity of children to participate in games and other sporting activities, at both the individual and the collective level, largely without coercion. Since so much of the previous discussion has focused on the deficits of children from less than elite backgrounds, it is worth repeating the suggestion made earlier that, in looking for a measure of what 13-year-olds are capable of, we can point to the behaviour of children from working-class backgrounds of an earlier time and sometimes today – even in rich societies – who have been expected to shoulder adult responsibilities for earning money and caring for siblings.

The discipline question, as much as any cognitive issue, should receive intense focus from the preschool level, the latter involving not mere rhetoric but creative approaches that indubitably will involve throwing money at the problem in the form of personalised attention at this early stage of life. The issues involved in this task will include intensive efforts to isolate problems and disabilities involving individual children, but also aspects in the interpersonal and physical environment of the school that impede children from functioning collectively in an active and purposeful manner. Serious efforts to solve these issues will involve failed attempts along the way. But only in the presence of a substantive elimination of the discipline issue will it be possible to complement intense learning at the individual level with aspects of collective self-organisation and democratic decision making by the student body that involve issues of consequence in the life of the school. The presence of democratic processes and a lack of coercion as the norm in all schools will play an important role in alleviating the gaps in aspiration and achievement between those from elite backgrounds and other children.

One aspect of the elite school experience that seems to have been transformed radically in recent decades has been a backing away from the harshest aspects of the English 'public' (private) school in its traditional manifestation, and the clear notion of education as a rigorous, but pleasurable, experience: modern elites wish their children to succeed academically, but do not view gratuitous suffering as an important contribution to the building of character. On the contrary, advertising for these schools gives a prominent place to the pleasantness of the child's experience there. By contrast, current rhetoric surrounding mass schooling focuses almost exclusively, as we have seen, around examination success, with the misery, unpleasantness and alienation of ordinary school life in classes of 30 or more given an implicit weight of zero.

The stinginess and small-mindedness of the latter approach may, in fact, embody an overly myopic view of what is needed to motivate human beings in a productive direction. We have seen in Chapter 7 that Ivan Illich's radical proposals involved giving extensive freedom of choice to individuals on what they chose to study. These proposals were naïve in the context of working-class children, with the manifest danger that they would elect to acquire a body of skills that were immediately attractive to an employer, but were too narrow in the context of a lifetime of employment. No less important are the demands of a democratic polity. Many children, and disproportionately those from working-class backgrounds, might opt to eliminate from their studies those subjects necessary for their functioning as active and knowledgeable participants in a democratic society.

By contrast, elite institutions in a host of ways give their students a low centre of gravity, typically demanding that their students pursue broad-based programmes of study. In recent years, this propensity has been exemplified by the taking up in the UK of the wide-ranging International Baccalaureate, and the renewed fashion for that most venerable strategy for broad learning, the study of the classics – Latin and Greek. At the same time, however, elite schools partially fulfil Illich's demand for freedom of choice in their offerings that are largely intended as pleasurable aspects of life at school – the opportunity to study music, theatre, and a range of artisan and mechanical skills to a high level of proficiency. These opportunities widen the skill and knowledge base of their students in ways that sometimes open up the possibility of vocational or professional career development in these directions. Institutions of mass education, and the teachers working in them, often make heroic gestures in the direction of offering such opportunities to their students, but the possibilities that are put before children from elite backgrounds at an early stage of life, both at home and at school, are incomparably greater.

Elite educational institutions often function on the frontier of creative and innovative policies, a fact not linked to any lack of talent, imagination or dedication of those involved in mass schooling. In recent times, the draconian constraints increasingly imposed in the mass education sector by payment-by-results regimes function to exacerbate the problems of pursuing innovative strategies in the mass sector. But in a fundamental sense, the gap in innovation between the elite and mass education sector is a question of resources. The mass school creates an environment that is brutal to grow up in as a child and to work in as a teacher. In its most fundamental form, the constrained resources available in the mass school create an insoluble tension between progressive, flexible policies that permit the flowering of well-motivated and prepared students, on the one hand, and a regime embodying more traditional, learning-by-rote procedures and tight disciplinary codes, on the other. The latter approach has historically proved to produce better academic results with students from deprived backgrounds, and is therefore less likely to exacerbate existing inequalities in society. Elite schools begin with a far narrower variance of parameters of family background than mass schools, but complement this administrative advantage with sufficient resources, epitomised by the teacher–student ratio, so that tuition and attention can be devoted to individual children. The Gordian Knot concerning the predicament of a choice between liberal, progressive education and egalitarian approaches is thus broken by a brute force, Alexandrian solution – sufficient resources are directed at the problem.

In Oskar Lange's model of a socialist economy, discussed in Chapter 4, the Central Planning Board begins with an array of prices and then instructs enterprises to set levels of output so that price is equal to marginal cost and to minimum average cost. The rueful joke, already noted, was that one capitalist country would need to be preserved to obtain these initial prices even after the world socialist revolution; similarly, there would be no reason or purpose in prohibiting elite schools in a socialist society. First, the use of the power of the state to ban any activity that individuals choose to undertake should only take place in the most extreme circumstances, and as a last resort. Second, the elite school, whatever its deformations as a social institution, is a substantive example of what might be attempted, and what can be done, with relatively unconstrained resources in a schooling context. It poses a challenge and, in some cases, a standard to be met in the wider society.

A focused programme of formal education thus plays a key role in the realisation of the goal of equal opportunities for self-realisation and development of personal capacities, as enunciated in the Introduction, by enhancing children's knowledge of how the world works intellectually and giving them a repertoire of substantive, broad-based skills with a low centre of gravity. Furthermore, such a programme, even if only partially fulfilled, might bring about useful changes in attitudes across the population, with the school closing the gap between the well-born and the rest of the population. Young people from deprived backgrounds attending schools provisioned and run as palaces for children might rethink in a productive manner their relationship to their home environment and personal life.

And, if such schools do succeed in closing the gap in educational accomplishment between children born into the higher reaches of society and the masses, such a development might give the latter group a sense of entitlement about the world based on substantive accomplishment rather than empty 'yes we can' rhetoric. For example, a century ago, as we have seen, a powerful movement took place in the most advanced societies such as the US for a free education to be available through secondary school to the age of 18 for all children. With ever-growing demands in the present day for educational qualifications for employment, one might have expected this earlier development to be extended to four years of additional training, with the implementation of universal and free, or even grant-aided, higher and post-secondary education. Extraordinarily, tendencies in the US (and the UK as well) are now in the opposite direction, with the ability to pay becoming a barrier to post-secondary education. If a successful school programme succeeds at narrowing gaps in substantive accomplishment of children at the school level, the imposition of increasing financial barriers to further study will come across even more transparently than at present as unfair to children who have narrowed gaps in educational accomplishment with elite children. If the reader will forgive me one more outburst of New York irony, I would hope that unhappiness and lack of contentment with their lot might galvanise such a generation of young people to push for genuine, and not rhetorical, equality of opportunity.

The considerations in this chapter concerned with formal education interact in an intimate way with the focus in Chapter 12 on equality and security at the level of the household: real long-term progress is contingent on changes to both these spheres of life. But reform has to start somewhere, and the formal institutions concerned with preschooling and schooling are the most powerful mechanisms of public policy available for promoting equal opportunity in personal development and the capacity to exercise democratic control. Progressives concerned about present-day attempts to use schooling as a panacea and as a mask for the manifest social and economic inequalities that distort human development must not adopt a passive approach to education, one that awaits a transformation 'out there' in society before any meaningful change can take place in children's learning.

Education, including preschooling, as an aspect of a strategy for creating genuine equality of opportunity, involves the monitoring and facilitation of a range of cognitive, physical and emotional competencies: an understanding of their development in children and, specifically their relationship to social class, appears to be just emerging in the literature discussed earlier. A complementary aspect of this question is the effect of the home environment on the aspirations, levels of self-esteem and life horizons of children, and most specifically how these latter parameters are distorted through the prism of social class. Anecdotal evidence points to the limited horizons of children from the poorer end of society even in rich countries, often in the literal sense of an ignorance of life beyond the physical boundaries of the local neighbourhood. More subtly, these limitations in horizon can interact with family deprivation and insecurity to exacerbate the tendency in all human beings to make irrational decisions.[139] In the more proximate economic context of preparation for work, properly designed formal education, by emphasising broad-based, lifetime preparation for the acquisition of skills, should help alleviate the difficulties facing young people in the twenty-first century by giving them genuine, as opposed to enforced, flexibility in a rapidly changing work environment.

Educational reform also plays an important role in strategies for democratic control of political life and daily affairs. A common view among elite groupings is that ordinary people must be manipulated for their own good because of their limited knowledge and grasp of issues surrounding public policy (see Chapter 12). The resultant elite claim of a right to exercise control over public affairs is, in some ways, under greater challenge than heretofore: while notions of an incipient internet democracy are wildly exaggerated,[140] an increasing flow and ease of access of factual information, coupled with long-term rises in educational attainment in the population, have made the task of elite manipulation more difficult.

But deficits in the public's familiarity with the details surrounding contemporary political and civic (including business) affairs continue to expedite elite control of decisions: the public, as a rule, monitors elite activities and decisions only on a discontinuous basis, and overall manifests a lack of confidence in its right to rule in the interim, often deferring to these groups or to 'experts', such as bankers. The elevation in educational achievement postulated here in a socialist context plays a role in promoting the exercise of democratic control by facilitating the public's ability to translate this increasing flow of information into usable knowledge and to resist elite media manipulation of these information flows. In addition, a reformed educational system can help instil in the general population the habits, capacity and confidence necessary for exercising democratic control on a regular basis in the work and broader societal context: what elite versions of the educational process already do so well.

The question at hand is not, therefore, merely one of pounding facts into the heads of recalcitrant children. The ability to read with comprehension and then discuss a text concerned with political and civic issues has a cognitive dimension linked to reading skills, but an important element in the latter facility, as we have seen, is a factual base upon which to proceed: an understanding of a text concerned with a filibuster in the US Senate demands more than a comprehension of the individual words and phrases – it also involves familiarity with the facts surrounding the constitutional role of the Senate in the passing of federal law and the accompanying substantive history of, for instance, post-Second World War disputes in the US over racial desegregation. But this kind of factual knowledge of politics and civic affairs is often thought to be boring by much of the population at all stages in life, an attitude invariably more acute at the lower end of the class and income distribution. The resultant deficits in civic knowledge are in sharp contrast with the public's rich assimilation of factual knowledge about popular culture and sport and the pervasive self-confidence with which opinions are voiced on these matters.

The contrast between the public's response to these alternative spheres of knowledge – politics and civics versus popular culture and sport – cannot be accounted for by the supposed difficulty of the former compared with the latter. An important part of the explanation derives from the fact that the lived experience of the great majority of children in school, and later in work, makes democratic processes and participation seem at best an abstraction, and even an irrelevancy. The school experience continues to be one of authoritarian discipline, codes of silence and passive learning. Heroic attempts in publicly funded educational institutions to move beyond these limitations run up against the objective fact of resource constraints – ratios of 30 or more children to one teacher preclude individualised learning of mathematics as well as the cultivation of collective habits of democracy: such habits can only emanate from normal human interaction between individuals, an impossibility if for no other reason than the din of noise created by large numbers. In the present school context, it is the tribal aspects of politics, at best, that are engendered in children – a collective feeling of 'us' against the autonomous lawgivers and executors of discipline.

The evocation in the elite schools discussed above of the spirit of Summerhill-type free school experiments gives credit to the notion that there is something deeply wrong with any school system that needs to proceed in a context of incarceration, even when children have reached the stage of early adolescence. The broad conceptual failure of these experiments is an unwillingness to admit the necessary constraints due to the myopia inherent in being a child. These constraints are of two kinds. First, the cultivation of habits of individual agency in choice of fields of study will be limited by the necessity of instilling in children a broad base of knowledge necessary to cultivate flexibility over a lifetime of work: children cannot merely pursue their interests and affinities in an unconstrained manner.

Of even greater significance, however, is a second imperative of schooling, that of engendering in individuals sufficient intellectual capacity to function as free individuals – participants and decision makers in a democratic society and in a world culture. In the twenty-first century, the prerequisites for consideration of the political and social issues to be confronted will not merely emerge from familiarity with the details of laws and constitutions. The range of knowledge necessary for making sense of the world will embrace broad-based history (including the development worldwide of art, music and literature), the biological and physical sciences, and logical and mathematical thinking. The alleviation of the oppressive circumstances of daily life in school, inherent in present-day levels of resourcing, is central to the creation of a learning environment in which the curiosity inherent in children is successfully channelled into a desire to understand the fundamentals of science, history and rational inquiry, as well as politics, civic life, art, literature and music. A goal of education in society is to give the opportunity to all children to function in the manner of the most productive and creative individuals in society, whose activities seem to obviate and make irrelevant the gap between productive work and playful, spontaneous activity, a potential embodied in all of us as *Homo ludens*.[141]

The single-minded focus in public discussions on formal education as a facilitator of economic growth has marginalised traditional considerations of education's role and responsibility – the cultivation of a democratic commonwealth through the promotion of civility in human interaction, a sense of collective responsibility and solidarity, and the inculcation of broad-based rationality and culture. The widespread influence of a managerialist approach to educational excellence has encouraged the monitoring of achievement at the level of the individual child, teacher and school. This approach is underwritten by the promotion of a competitive mechanism at each of these levels to generate desired outcomes. It is worthwhile exploring in detail the efficacy of this mechanism.

One aspect of the role of competition is its signalling or informational role. As the economist George Stigler once suggested, it becomes difficult to determine how well one is performing in a foot race in the absence of competitors: the isolation of Soviet-type economies from international competition meant that many sectors found it difficult to judge their own performance by world standards. Furthermore, in some areas of endeavour, such as tennis and boxing, high levels of competitive interaction are necessary for skill development – the acquisition of forms of implicit and explicit knowledge – that would not be possible in any other manner. In other activities, such as playing football or a musical instrument, both competitive and cooperative interaction play a role in the refinement of skills. This informational role for competition in the monitoring and development of skills remains unexceptionable.

The behavioural role of competition in the generation of excellence is more ambivalent. It would be absurd to deny its importance as an aspect of human and higher animal consciousness. Mozart was a highly competitive being, resentful of mediocrities displacing him in favour and financial reward with the Viennese public and court. But even in desperate circumstances, he showed little willingness to accommodate his art, consisting of, as the emperor had said, 'too many notes', to the demands of the marketplace. Human beings have a rich array of motivations for pursuing excellence, only one of which is financial remuneration. In modern capitalist society, more so than in earlier times, success in many fields of endeavour is often identified with the levels of remuneration that they yield, with an elevation, especially in the US, of billionaire entrepreneurs and highly paid CEOs to the level of culture heroes. One is sometimes led to the conclusion that continuing media focus on the centrality of education is due to its continuing statistical association with elevated incomes rather than to any traditional respect for learning per se or its importance in the functioning of a participatory democracy.

An atmosphere of competition and its reflection in individual attitudes can generate dysfunctional outcomes. A child who, for one reason or another, has a demonstrable superiority over others in, for instance, arithmetic may grow complacent and develop in a truncated way if the child's only motivation is a desire to do better than others; by contrast, an atmosphere of competition can turn transitory discouragement from a small initial weakness in arithmetic into a lifetime of failure. A narrow-minded focus on being 'the best', especially among children, can limit possibilities for personal development. A child with a career ahead as a historian may need to master several foreign languages, but need not be the best in the class in any one of them: such a criterion might even discourage the study of these languages. Albert Einstein was well aware that his mathematical facility did not place him at the level of his greatest contemporaries, such as Henri Poincaré and David Hilbert, but he was able to make striking and imaginative use of mathematics in his physical theories without matching their facility. If children are conditioned to focus only on competitive excellence, the health and other benefits of athletic participation and the pleasures of amateur music making will be denied to all but a small group of individuals with pretensions to professional-level attainment.

An intense commitment to formal education is, thus, a key aspect of any programme of human liberation and development. A dominant characteristic of contemporary discussions is to focus exclusively on the role of education in economic growth, and to discuss these matters as if the sole human motivation for the pursuit of excellence were financial remuneration in the context of interpersonal competition. Such attitudes demonstrate a desiccated imagination and a limited understanding of the range of factors that motivate children and adults to strive for excellence. They also fail to recognise the central role of an educated population in the development of a truly participatory democracy, one that is capable of making rational decisions about the complex range of issues before it in the twenty-first century.

The school is, thus, the most significant public policy intervention for generating equal opportunity for self-realisation and development of personal capacities for all individuals in society. The strategy pursued here involves a special focus on educational resources from preschool to the age of 13. The intention is the full development of the individual capacities of children, combined with a high level of social integration; a key goal is the alleviation of cognitive and non-cognitive deficits linked to social and economic inequality. Formal education can only overcome these deficits to a limited extent, and it is likely to remain a limited form of compensation for family deprivation and for deficiencies in the social environment in which the child grows up.

The intensive commitment of resources to education at this young age serves to promote a reconciliation of excellence and egalitarianism. Individual attention to students' needs permits a tailored response to children's development. No doubt in some contexts, such as the mastery of specific arithmetic and mathematical techniques, the privacy and the infinite patience offered by the computer in the learning process will prove useful. But such devices are no substitute for personalised attention, and they can make only a minor contribution to the collective discussion and interaction inside the classroom that are central to learning. Tracking or other forms of segregation of students on the basis of some notion of generalised ability is obviated in the context of students receiving sufficient individual attention to be able to pursue specific disciplines to the limits of their capacity. Problems will invariably arise in reconciling this personalised, individual development of students with collective discussion and interaction inside the classroom, but these issues do not appear impossible to resolve.

The social atmosphere inside the school is an essential aspect of learning. A solution to the discipline question is a *sine qua non* of educational reform, to be facilitated by the intensive levels of interaction between student and teacher, most likely in small groups, from the earliest years. By the age of 13, children should know why they are in school and their own central role and responsibility in maintaining an atmosphere conducive to learning. The abolition of homework, with such work integrated and monitored in an extended school day, and the elimination of vacation periods lasting a whole summer would not only be necessary for egalitarian reasons – not permitting students to 'fall under the table' – but would be symptomatic of the notion that the school is taking its tasks seriously. If the longer days necessitated by the elimination of homework and shortened vacation time seem a horrific imposition on the life of the child, this is more a comment on the unpleasant environment of the present-day school than on the problems associated with extending the time devoted to supervised learning. If such a programme is to succeed, it will demand the integration of parents and local community, with parents both having a voice in the running of the school and being held accountable for the behaviour of their children.

Student learning involves the pursuit of individual interests reconciled with education for democracy and citizenship, the latter cultivated both in academic learning and in group interaction. The ability to cultivate and pursue individual interests can be facilitated by broad-based exposure to, and availability of, a range of activities, including music, athletics and mechanical arts. Decisions to pursue a special interest, either as an avocation or as a lifetime occupation, should emerge on the basis of genuine affinity and not as a result of the limitations in familiarity and opportunity to pursue alternatives dictated by class distinction.

A range of tensions, not necessarily undesirable, emerge between the likely desire of the child to pursue a special interest and the school's demand for broad-based learning. First, there is the necessity for the child to embrace a broad range of skills in order to be prepared for a lifetime of work in what is likely to be a diverse range of occupations. Second, the school plays a central role in the preparation to function as a citizen, with a capability and confidence to deal with the issues of the day. A lived atmosphere within the school of genuine agency over decisions by students, at both individual and collective levels, and responsibility for these decisions, would complement academic learning by acting as preparation for democratic rule of society as adults.

With a sense of both the agency and the responsibilities associated with adulthood embedded at the age of 13, it is probable that the exceptional resource demands made up to this age will decrease, with the social and disciplinary atmosphere in subsequent years gradually approaching that of a university. In such conditions, the discontinuity between high-school education and the range of post-high-school alternatives might well gradually dissipate: it is taken for granted here that post-high-school education in the twenty-first century should be free. The distinctions between so-called vocational and university education are also likely to evaporate, with vocational training having, over time, a greater academic component and academic studies offering enhanced opportunities for work experience. Careful consideration should be given to tuition relevant to social citizenship in all qualifications: it must be presented in a manner that appears to students as a necessary part of their formation as adults, and not merely a gratuitous burden and an imposition upon their time and energy. Lastly, the promotion of low-cost access to lifetime learning facilitated by contemporary internet technology is a likely development in a learning society, though even for adults, such learning needs an important component of human interaction to make it a successful and satisfying experience.

A powerful and focused educational programme is far from sufficient to bring about a society in which all individuals have an opportunity for self-realisation and development of personal capacities. First, with present and growing levels of disparity between the resources that families can offer their children, it is inconceivable that an equalisation of opportunities to develop cognitive capabilities can take place purely in the context of a reform to formal education. Second, since a substantial part of what is involved in the cultivation of cognitive skills involves not only schooling but living in the world – involvement in the working and living environment – growing economic disparities and an inability to exercise democratic control over these spheres inhibit the fulfilment of purely individualistic goals as well.

In the present day, despite the presence of a more knowledgeable and better-educated population than in earlier times, we observe powerful retrograde tendencies from the prospective of democracy and socialism, with less control of workplace affairs than previously and, in a host of ways, diminishing democratic control at the national and international levels.

Are there, in this context, still grounds for optimism?

12
Equality and Democratic Control

An overview

The long-term socialist strategy proposed here is explicit in having a trajectory in the direction of human development, equality and democratic control that is not easily deflected by the vagaries of the marketplace. It is thus in stark contrast to the disingenuous claims of free-market liberals that, for instance, policies of privatisation of public services are mere responses to the demands of a spontaneous order. It is also at variance with the policy prescriptions of American-style liberals and social democrats, who, especially in recent years, at best offer an amelioration and mitigation of the worst effects of an increasingly competitive environment, and at worst pursue policies of accommodation to these realities that differ little from those of the free-marketers.

A primary aspect of the socialist programme outlined in the Introduction is the cultivation of an opportunity for self-realisation and development of personal capacities for all individuals in society. Perhaps the most distinctive characteristic of the programme is its focus on access to upbringing and education from the earliest stages of life that is not contingent on, and compensates for, limitations in household circumstances – the programme outlined in the previous chapter. This focus on resources devoted to early childhood development and to education underlines the emphasis here on public policy intervention that is transformative and developmental, and not merely alleviationist. The complementary aspects of this developmental strategy deal with the mitigation of deprivation and insecurity in the household, permitting it to function as a stable environment in which children's formal education can take place and also act as a vehicle for *in situ* learning in the world. The setting of a standard of full employment is essential for the mitigation of this insecurity.

These policy goals – full employment and the mitigation of household deprivation and insecurity – might seem to set up a conflict between approaches focusing on formal education, discussed in Chapter 11, and those here that are directing attention to how we live in the real world. But in substance, there is no such tension. The capacity for children to flourish in school is crucially contingent on the living and working environment in which households exist. A successful school programme can help to diminish the gaps in opportunities for personal development for children from diverse class backgrounds, but school systems functioning in more equal societies find that task greatly alleviated. Furthermore, for all individuals in the household, work and the broader environment are arenas for learning throughout their lives: public policies that promote *in situ* learning and opportunities for employment are crucial in themselves and complementary to programmes of formal schooling.

A further aspect of the socialist programme is the ability to exercise democratic control on a regular basis. Democracy in the context of the broader society necessarily entails a genuine voice for the mass of the population in politics, taking place in an environment embodying freedom of speech and conscience; an essential complement to this freedom is transparency in the operation of political and economic affairs. Democracy in the public sphere is enriched and complemented when the mass of the population also has a voice in the workplace and in daily life, with genuine opportunities to exercise control and decision making on a regular basis. This latter constituent of democracy demands that we address questions surrounding relations of power in these localised contexts.

These aspects – education and the development of personal capacities, on the one hand, and the exercise of democratic control, on the other – are intertwined. Thus, for instance, formal education can play a role in the promotion of the capabilities necessary for individuals to exercise democratic control, encouraging the formation of attitudes, expectations and habits conducive to future democratic participation in the working and living environment and in the context of society in general. Of no less importance are public policies that impinge directly on the workplace to promote democratic participation, as well as measures to engender democracy in the broader social and political context.

A unifying characteristic of this programme is the promotion of equality. Public policies promoting equality fall into three categories. The first concerns the public provision of a range of goods commonly characterised as necessities, such as education, health care, transport, housing, food and basic amenities, with transport and housing of special importance with regard to a range of environmental issues dealing with the planning of the urban and living environment. Public policies that promote equality through provision of these goods and services are of particular interest here in their developmental, as opposed to alleviationist, aspects. These policies are linked, in a complementary way, to formal education and can play a role in the enrichment of *in situ* learning in the world, in which household members can flourish and develop their capacities.

A second aspect of these public policies promoting equality is concerned with the resources devoted to, and the jobs created for, this expanded public provision. Activities created or financed by the government function to underwrite policies of full employment, offering to individuals a range of opportunities commensurate with the development of their skills. The discussions in earlier chapters make clear why central planning is to be rejected as a mechanism for achieving full employment; the key consequence of such a rejection, as suggested in Chapter 4, is that careful consideration must be given to the role of finance in economic allocation, a particularly troublesome question when the financial sector's role in the exacerbation of economic instability is acknowledged. Governmental provision of employment also promotes equality by acting as a standard for the compression of the egregious expansion of differentials in remuneration evidenced in recent decades. An important additional development, for the promotion of both equality and democracy, would be a reassertion of collective bargaining and the implementation of worker representation and real decision-making power within enterprises.

The third aspect of public policy driving equality is intimately connected with the exercise of democratic control in the broader society. Progressive taxation plays a central role in reconfiguring the distribution of income and wealth in contemporary societies in an egalitarian direction. Central aspects of such a policy approach include the implementation of genuinely progressive taxation regimes and the cultivation of openness in the conduct of business, financial and political affairs – a liquidation, for instance, of tax havens and the secrecy surrounding them. In the opposite direction, present-day gross inequalities in income and wealth are contributing to the degeneration of democratic processes to a farcical game in which decision making by a broad public plays at most a peripheral role: actions to reduce these inequalities are a necessary aspect of a programme for the promotion of a democratic polity.

The mechanisms employed here will borrow policies with demonstrable records of achievement from social democrats and from others – even central planners – whenever possible, at least as a starting point, rather than conjure up solutions on how to reorganise society *de novo*: 'imaginative' forms of social experimentation by both the left and right have often taken place at the cost of serious disruption to the lives of ordinary people. The programme here, focusing on human development in the context of security and the continuity of household and social existence, dictates an abhorrence of overly speculative, rapid and revolutionary transformations in society. In the spirit of Karl Polanyi, it recognises the often functional, even if inadequate, role of existing societal institutions and the necessity for maintaining a continuity of existence even in the midst of transformation. Above all, change in the context of human development has an unfortunate asymmetry: public policies with negative consequences can quickly do long-term damage, while an uplift in human capacities is more likely to be observed on a time scale measured in generations.

Economic policies for working and living in the world

Central to any socialist economic programme is a commitment to full employment. Most especially for larger, rich countries and groupings (such as the European Union), it is neither necessary nor desirable to wait until some imaginary spontaneous order brings it about, or until 'they' (domestic or foreign business interests) find it profitable to hire labour. This commitment is to be effected by government policies: first, the active pursuit of functional finance – fiscal expenditure and tax policies to maintain full employment through the maintenance of appropriate levels of aggregate demand. There is a rich literature in this area, one being rediscovered even by mainstream Keynesians in the present period;[1] second, a 'jobs worth doing' programme focuses this fiscal commitment to full employment in the direction of projects emerging from socialist priorities.

Much public policy is, at present, moving in the wrong direction, symbolised by the US Federal Reserve's *de facto* abandonment of its statutory obligation since 1978 to pursue full employment as part of a dual mandate with price stability; the latter is the sole objective of the European Central Bank.[2] In the wake of the crisis of 2007–8, a range of alleviationist policies has emerged. In general, they accept the presence of mass unemployment as a fact of life. Each of these approaches will be examined below: basic income, legislated reductions in maximum hours worked, tax credits and subsidies to employers for job creation, employment protection schemes and employment guarantee programmes. The 'jobs worth doing' alternative will then be considered in the context of an overall fiscal framework to maintain full employment.

Public policies dealing with the working environment can only be formulated after a position has been taken on a central question: what are jobs for? This is an issue of general significance in the context of the high levels of unemployment emerging almost everywhere in recent years, but of particular acuity in the face of exceptional levels of youth unemployment. From a socialist perspective, a job is about much more than remuneration. Those individuals without paid work and who lack other significant responsibilities, such as the running of a household, will not benefit from the accumulation of skills and knowledge associated with the working environment; they are also likely to suffer from loss of self-esteem and their sense of personal identity. Furthermore, the place of work, from a socialist perspective, should be a fulcrum of democracy in which individuals have a voice and exercise significant control over their immediate circumstances: the unemployed are largely bereft of social citizenship.

Many of these issues come into relief in the context of the advocacy in recent years, from across a broad political spectrum, of a basic (or guaranteed) income paid to all adult individuals. In most formulations, it is paid to everybody at the same rate but not taxed; it is not contingent on a willingness or decision to work. It has affinities and minor differences with earlier proposals for a negative income tax.[3] Much of the support for this approach has come from those who, viewing high levels of unemployment as something likely to persist, find it an efficacious way of helping individuals avoid deprivation.[4] To the extent that such a proposal would replace a broad array of means-tested welfare benefits, it promises administrative savings and, since it is not contingent on a willingness to work or good behaviour of any kind, is non-judgemental and minimises governmental invasion of private lives. If, advocates claim, the threshold above this minimum income at which income tax is paid is set appropriately, the problems of a poverty trap that give a disincentive to work are no worse than under present-day welfare arrangements.

The longer-term effects of the basic income scheme on the expectations and attitudes of generations of young people, especially those with unattractive employment prospects, can only be guessed at.[5] Perhaps some among this group, following historical examples among the youthful idle rich such as Charles Darwin and Marcel Proust, will make productive use of their free time. But this kind of whimsical speculation is most likely useless. Legislation of a guaranteed income has not emerged in any major economy, and does not seem likely to do so.[6] The sociologist Amitai Etzioni makes the claim that such a programme is likely to be popular because, like Social Security and Medicare in the US, it will not be means tested.[7] On the contrary, it seems likely that the latter programmes, like their equivalents in Sweden, have legitimacy with the public because they are seen as something they have paid for, having contributed premiums on these programmes while working.[8]

The implementation of a guaranteed income programme anytime soon is unlikely; it is used here, rather, as a focal point around which to consider the question of social citizenship. For Etzioni, the guaranteed income is a device for reinforcing community responsibilities and loyalties. In his conception, the guaranteed income would exist alongside other policies to alleviate poverty and to support community coherence. Charles Murray advocates the pursuit of a policy of guaranteed income for quite contrary reasons: in the context of a world in which he reluctantly concedes that 'large scale transfers are here to stay',[9] the guaranteed income will replace all such transfers with a more efficient system. Of greater significance, with the exclusion of other welfare programmes, feckless behaviour by the poor, such as having children out of wedlock, will receive no additional 'reward', so that 'those people' will have to fend for themselves:

the importance of the [guaranteed income] on human relationships and the vitality of communities is...that the government has withdrawn all the ways in which the apparatus of the welfare state tries to take the trouble out of people's lives, and by that withdrawal has made it easier for people to behave in ways that lead to satisfying lives...Without the apparatus of the welfare state, marriage once again becomes the locus within which a man and woman can make a future together, laden with responsibilities and obligations that cannot be put aside...Regarding the community, a [guaranteed income] that has replaced the welfare state makes the community once again the locus within which human needs must be met.[10]

As we have seen before, Charles Murray manages to articulate, from his own vantage point, the essence of a major contemporary dilemma: a persistence of long-term unemployment threatens to institutionalise a fragmentation of society into a productive group and a substantial minority of the population permanently existing on subsidies from a resentful majority. In such a context, however, guaranteed income schemes over the long term would be divisive and unsustainable politically and socially, even if they could be made economically viable.

Any alternative, progressive path must be more in keeping with the demands of both economic, ecological, social and political sustainability and human decency: the relegation of part of the population to the category of useless individuals is unacceptable. Viable solutions point in the direction of a generalisation to the whole population of the kind of economic demands that the well-off quite reasonably make for themselves – a range of options in the working and broader environment, a base of material security even when pursuing risky investment (such as long-term study in the pursuit of a career, with options to reinvent oneself if such ventures fail), and opportunities for children to fully develop their human and professional capacities. Such demands must, of necessity, contain as an endpoint something resembling full employment, underwritten by appropriate macroeconomic stabilisation policies and by making work available on the large number of projects in society that need doing. Guaranteed income schemes must be thought of as measures of last resort, and at least a partial admission of a failure in the organisation of social and economic affairs: such schemes implicitly concede that a significant section of the population will be excluded from full economic and social participation.

Each of the remaining alleviationist policies has problematic aspects. Proposals for limiting the maximum number of hours worked per week emerge in the context of reductions in hours worked per year over the past several decades in many countries, as noted in Chapter 10, which are clearly a response to widespread demands in the population. As a policy specifically directed at reducing unemployment, it appears, in the French example of legislated reduction to a 35-hour week over the past decade, to have been neither as disastrous as critics have portended nor demonstrably successful in alleviating unemployment.[11] It is salutary here to be reminded that even if, as suggested above, participation in working life is a key aspect of human development and democratic participation, such notions are easily capable of being appropriated by, for instance, 'hip Silicon Valley firms like Apple' to accelerate exploitation of the workforce,[12] most especially in the presence of weak labour market conditions. For the present and foreseeable future, notions of work being linked to personal identity and self-fulfilment must not be used to mask the fact that for the majority of the population, long working hours are simply drudgery and inhibit leisure and personal and household development: reductions in work time in the long term are likely to be an aspect of a progressive polity.

A more marginal and proximate range of policies for attacking unemployment involves giving employers a tax credit that covers the payroll costs of hiring new labour,[13] an approach that may have perverse incentive effects on the currently employed labour force and may function merely as a subsidy to employers. Another policy intervention in this sphere is employment protection legislation (EPL). The literature on EPL suggests that it slows rates of both hiring and firing, especially in small and marginally successful firms; its longer-term effects on, for instance, labour productivity at the firm and national levels are ambiguous.[14] EPL can function most effectively when it covers a wide catchment area (such as the European Union or the US) and establishes itself as a norm for employment practice in the private sector. By putting inhibitions on rapid disgorgement of those in employment, it can act as a complement to strategies for government-induced hiring discussed below.

Other attempts for dealing with unemployment are embodied in a range of 'employer of last resort' and employment guarantee programmes,[15] to be dubbed collectively ELR. These programmes, identified with the names of a range of eminent economists, including Hyman Minsky, have been designed to alleviate unemployment while doing as little as possible to upset the parameters offered up by the free market, including the existing structure of output and income as well as the underlying trade-off between employment and inflation. The government thus 'does not displace private sector jobs since it offers jobs which are undersupplied or not supplied at all by the private sector'[16] by establishing the equivalent of an infinitely elastic demand for labour at a wage likely to be below that prevailing in the sector under consideration. In such programmes, unfortunately, the government may well end up ratifying and reinforcing existing wage differentials in a manner corresponding to present-day best-practice procurement.[17]

ELR proposals often include discussions of training and retraining for prospective workers, but their emphasis is on providing a counter-cyclical, rapid-response buffer stock to labour market fluctuations: their primary role is, thus, to supply jobs for a relatively undifferentiated class of unskilled labour. ELR approaches, often emerging from an earlier era, offer a mechanism for dealing with the cyclical unemployment of undifferentiated labour, but do not form an integrated programme for dealing with the renewal of work skills or alleviation of the increasing dispersion of remuneration that has emerged in the past decades. Despite their modest ambitions, these largely academic, unexecuted proposals are what have passed as left-wing policies in much of the contemporary world.

The Swedish labour market model, by contrast, had with substantial success dealt with many of these issues through the insistence by powerful labour unions on programmes for the upgrading of worker skills and active compression of wage differentials through centralised wage bargaining. The erosion of these institutions and procedures in Sweden since 1990, and the resulting widening differentials, seem to be largely accounted for by the processes of globalisation and their effects upon the bargaining power of workers vis-à-vis capital in the political arena and in the labour market.[18] As suggested above, any reconstitution of these institutions and procedures in a broad-based socialist project is likely to involve initiatives from large nations or groups of nations, and then participation and cooperation on a transnational basis.

In the twenty-first century, most programmes for dealing with employment, including the ELR, presuppose an acceptance of the structure of economic activity and income distribution dictated by the free market. The alternative discussed below to this range of alleviationist proposals may be seen as an attempt to expand and develop the conditions for the flourishing of households existing during the golden age period after the Second World War, with its relatively full employment. The contemporary context, however, is a society and economy that are substantially richer, and, overall, are making greater demands than previously for the acquisition of formal skills. In the earlier period, completion of the educational requirements that were universally available without charge (a high-school diploma) and/ or the acquisition of a range of skills mastered in professional training or in a work context were reasonably well-defined prerequisites for long-term employment and economic security.

Clearly, it would be absurd to idealise this period, with the multiple exclusions to this path linked to racial and gender discrimination common in most countries. But for many young people in the present day, aspects of this earlier, nominally less rich economic environment appear attractive. To replicate the earlier prospect of long-term employment and economic security consequent upon a diploma, a longer period of study leading to a BA university degree or its vocational equivalent is likely to be needed, qualifications whose financial cost have been rising rapidly in the US and the UK. Without question, one aspect of a replication for the twenty-first century of these earlier golden age conditions would involve free and equal access to post-high-school education and training.

In Chapter 8, the argument was developed that the cultivation of household (including employment) security is not just a good thing: security is not simply a luxury that, unfortunately, has to be traded off against a loss of economic efficiency. On the contrary, once labour is viewed not as a commodity to be shifted about freely but as an economic asset, a whole other set of considerations enter into the question of efficient allocation of labour resources. These 'resources' make long-term plans and decisions about the trajectory of their own lives at work and in the general society, and the lives of their children. In such a context, the disruptive effects of extreme flexibility of the workforce, however useful for individual employers, may be inefficacious for the development of society as a whole.

What would be the nature of a positive approach to employment in a socialist context? Emerging strategies for security and full employment should reinforce long-term goals directed at human development, democracy and social cohesion. The central goal of such a programme would be to provide a universal opportunity to pursue a career of employed work with remuneration commensurate with skill attainment. Even at the lower bound of income, a 'good job'[19] is one that secures (in combination with provision underwritten by the state) medical and retirement provision and a capacity to purchase food, clothing and 'non-essential' goods consistent with social norms; either in the context of employment or outside of it, there would be easily accessible and inexpensive opportunities for skill development. For households in the lower income bounds, the housing stock would meet minimal standards of construction integrity, square metres per person and amenities. Most essentially for households with children, all neighbourhoods must permit young people to flourish in an environment characterised by low levels of violence and social disorder, with stimulation provided by physical amenities such as parks and communal and sports facilities.

Thus, a strategy for employment links in, inevitably, with income distribution, social provision, and the ability of all households, even the poorest, to act as vehicles for the full development of the human capacities of the next generation. A programme of jobs worth doing is also intimately connected with strategies of training and *in situ* learning, both for young people and for workers in mid-career, thus permitting a genuine capacity to adapt to changing circumstances rather than an *ersatz* flexibility based on insecurity and instability in the lives of workers.

But what kinds of jobs are to be created? Industrial policies in rich countries that are pursued only to re-create lost manufacturing capacity for the sake of job creation and an attempt to chase an ephemeral competitiveness in the international arena are likely to be ineffectual. A far better strategy for such countries would be policies that expand employment as a consequence of projects that make substantive improvements to people's lives by developing the human and physical infrastructure and the living environment. Such a strategy, besides focusing directly on the alleviation of concrete societal needs rather than the vain pursuit of status in the international competitive arena, is likely to yield as a by-product long-term improvements to the society's productive capacity, including the *in situ* skills associated with these projects.

A great many of the activities that are desirable to pursue, such as care for the elderly, are, in any case, labour-absorbing activities. Furthermore, the exigencies of the Baumol cost disease described in Chapter 8 suggest that such pursuits will inexorably become more expensive relative to other aspects of the economy due to their limited scope for growth in labour productivity. Such developments are not, in principle, problematic – well-off individuals seek out the provision of well-qualified and plentiful staff to care for themselves and their aged relatives, and appear to consider it a 'price worth paying'. The great majority of the population in rich countries, however, rely upon public provision for care when elderly, with resultant pressures to provide such care more 'efficiently', that is, with cheaper, less well-qualified staff, and fewer of them. Care for the elderly is, thus, an activity that is both labour-absorbing and desirable, and will necessarily expand with an ageing population: many political disputes in the future will be concerned with whether the great majority of the population are to be left with second-rate care from unqualified staff for the sake of efficiency. We appear to have here, at least superficially, a quintessential trade-off between equity and efficiency.

But care for the elderly is perhaps exceptional among the range of such desirable projects in not embodying an important developmental component. By contrast, the expansion and intensification of educational processes described in Chapter 11 play key roles in advancing the trajectory of societal development across generations; as a by-product, long-term employment for teachers, administrators and adjunct personnel will, of necessity, be created by increased governmental expenditure on education. Furthermore, the construction and maintenance of these palaces for children – building structures, recreational facilities and a natural environment suitable for human flourishing – will provide substantial long-term work for those involved in construction and environmental maintenance.

It is unfortunate that even powerful advocates of policies for greater equality tend to discuss increased expenditure for education, health care and pensions collectively, and in an undifferentiated manner – from an alleviationist perspective – as if they were all good things that society can do when it can afford to do so.[20] A more suitable approach would be to underline the role that much of this expenditure, most especially that on education, plays in economic and social development. In addition, however, public policy measures on health care and pensions can also have a developmental component: they offer households security in these areas, thus acting as a foundation for long-term planning and development of the human assets of household members.

There is a complementary need to provide children with a home and neighbourhood environment in which they can thrive away from the school. Children growing up in conditions where the housing stock is substandard in terms of construction integrity, space and amenities such as heating will suffer significant handicaps no matter how favourable the school environment: there is probably no substitute for the setting of old-fashioned, centrally planned targets for some parameters, such as minimal numbers of square metres per person. In addition, an 'overprovision' of rented accommodation (financed or subsidised by the state) may well be useful in the promotion of labour flexibility and mobility – the very virtues that are often inhibited by the thin markets in such accommodation in countries such as the UK and US that are focused on home ownership.

At least as important as the quality of the housing stock for child development is the local environment. If certain neighbourhoods are considered 'no go' by adults, are they places where children should be growing up?[21] Past failures at slum clearance do not serve as excuses to avoid explicit decisions on the nature of the built environment. There was an indubitable need to relieve postwar shortages in housing (my own family, as noted in Chapter 10, spending the early postwar years in converted army barracks). But few people at present would choose to defend the specific form taken by postwar programmes for urban construction of public housing in most countries, with their long-term negative consequences on the built environment and social cohesion, and a reinforcement of class and racial segregation. In the context of many urban areas, much of what we observe is the result of short-term decisions made after the Second World War: the rapid building of inexpensive housing (often of poor-quality construction, and given its frequently short life, perhaps not really so inexpensive after all) that, at worst, has consisted of rows of cavernous buildings, often of seven or more storeys. These hideous constructions, littered across the urban landscapes of the Western world to this day, are, as Jane Jacobs has underlined, antithetical to the cultivation of the rich level of social interaction inherent in the urban environment. Those concerned with the welfare of children brought up in 'the projects' have upon them the extra burdens of counteracting their sterility and the competing attractions of gangs and drugs.

Outside of urban cores, there has been a complementary postwar tendency for the creation of a built environment of low density in the suburbs to service an inordinately influential but, in most countries, initially minority car-owning population. This suburban development, in comparison with urban housing, was, as a rule, less explicitly state-driven, but often guided by governmental decision makers such as Robert Moses (see Chapter 1) in the context of political pressure from property developers and, in a US context, white flight from urban centres and racial delineation through 'redlining' of neighbourhoods. The car-oriented suburban existence appears to remain a desired mode of living for many households despite its evident absurdities, such as the need for a car to purchase basic amenities and the continued infantilisation of children past the age of ten until they possess a driving licence. But for both the urban housing project and the low-density, car-oriented suburb, is it necessary for us simply to accept as a fact of life for the rest of the twenty-first century the decisions that created these environments as they rapidly emerged in the post-Second World War era? With ever-pressing ecological and energy considerations, combined with a deeper focus than heretofore on the effect of the built environment on child development, many present-day living arrangements, when depicted in the cinema, may well look as incongruous as the pervasive smoking of cigarettes in 60-year-old films.

All of the above implies no absence of jobs worth doing, a core of activities directed at preservation and development of the human and physical infrastructure. Long-term demand for the cultivation of the relevant skills will be underwritten by government expenditure creating jobs in these areas. The activities to be undertaken demand the cultivation of a range of proficiencies both of an old-fashioned kind, such as music teaching in schools and landscape cultivation in an urban environment, as well as more high-technology pursuits, such as the innovation and implementation of medical advances relevant to an ageing population or energy-saving strategies in new construction. Government expenditure in these areas will displace spending and jobs now devoted to creating the luxuries associated with the exceptionally skewed income distribution of contemporary capitalism; this new expenditure has the fail-safe characteristic of being worthwhile in its own terms, whether or not achievements in, for instance, energy conservation lead to commercially realisable gains in the arena of foreign trade.

This securing of the human and physical infrastructure is to be viewed as part of a range of necessary activities for long-term social and economic development. A clear implication of such a perspective is that, in contrast to the present-day tendency to constrain spending on education and assistance to deprived sections of society and physical infrastructure in an economic crisis, a very different strategy would be pursued: the trajectory of expenditures described here would be relatively unaffected by short-term perturbations in overall economic activity, with accommodations necessary to respond to an economic crisis or inflationary pressures more likely taking the form of changes in tax rates and monetary policy. It is consumption by the well-off, rather than these developmental expenditures, that is to be seen as a luxury that can be readily varied on a short-term basis to offset fluctuations in overall economic activity.

Taxation thus plays a role in macroeconomic stabilisation. In addition, taxation policy is central to the formation of a distribution of income and wealth corresponding to the needs of economic equity and political democracy: this role for taxation will be discussed below. But limitations are present in the extent to which taxation policy alone can be used to correct the extreme variations in income and wealth in contemporary economies. The diminution of income and wealth differentials can also be effected by the very expansion of governmental activity and procurement described above. First, the activities pursued can underwrite universal access to fundamental aspects of social reproduction – necessities – including health care and education. Provision of inexpensive living accommodation can set a lower bound on the parameters of physical construction and quality of neighbourhood existence: a constant concern must be whether they create an environment suitable for the upbringing of children. Public transportation systems should be inexpensive and attractive alternatives to the necessity for car ownership, with long-term environmental planning focused on facilitating such a development. In general, social procurement policies will have a goal of minimising the extent to which those on low income are subject to social exclusion.

A second way in which governmental activity and procurement can narrow differentials in income and wealth is by acting as an exemplar in its own activities for other areas of the economy in the setting of standards for remuneration and conditions of employment. As noted above in the context of the US, government procurement procedures often simply replicate existing free-market levels of remuneration at the low end. But government payment of low wages to street cleaners in its employ has nothing to do with efficiency – it is merely a form of redistribution of income away from the poorest-paid groups in society. At upper levels of remuneration, the public sector has been progressively imitating the absurd levels of upper-level executive pay in the private sector. This tendency has emerged with the claimed need to compete in the bidding for top-quality managerial talent and because of the out-sourcing or privatisation of many public services (such as the running of prisons or water provision), coupled with limited regulation of these *de facto* monopolies. The government bureaucracy's own internal hierarchy of rewards can straightforwardly be restructured in the awarding of contracts for these services. The very rapidity with which these wide differentials have emerged in both the private and public sectors of many countries may indicate that rewinding them will not be an insuperable task.

At the top end of those working in government service, the revolving door of employment of politicians and regulators who then join the industries they have privatised or regulated is a threat both to economic probity and, as we shall see below, to the maintenance of a democratic polity: in many cases, the notion of a lifetime career in public service may have to be reconstituted after years of overly intimate relations between the public and private spheres. In the context of some sectors, such as the financial industry, the creation of a class of civil servants who possess a detailed understanding of the institutions they are regulating is likely to be facilitated by the much tighter and intimate regulation of these sectors that is, in any case, desirable.

The perspective presented here of extended government provision based on long-term human development has, indubitably, problematic and ambiguous aspects. Clearly, the range of jobs worth doing will vary greatly even within nations, with urban issues perhaps less central in Arizona and water provision more so than in New York City or London; the exigencies of climate change are likely to redirect many of these priorities. A further issue arising is whether the government should vary its expenditure in order to mitigate what appear to be cyclical fluctuations in employment and economic activity in the form of ELR-type programmes. The suggestion above was that substantial participation in such programmes would dilute the long-term focus of the jobs worth doing approach and the creation of a career trajectory for workers. Thus, the main accommodation to short-term macroeconomic instability is not likely to be changes in overall levels of government expenditure, which are linked to long-term societal goals, but variations in tax rates or, in classic approaches to functional finance, changes in monetary policy.[22] The difficulties in separating cyclical (short-term) from long-term fluctuations suggest that a clear wall of separation between the various policy instruments may be difficult to maintain.

There are also questions surrounding the role of competition in the procurement of services by the government and the setting of standards for work. In the context, for instance, of government funding of improvements in the housing stock and environment of lower-income groups in urban areas, it will be salutary to review the serious errors, as well as the successful interventions, made in the postwar era. Best practice will invariably involve wide consultation and the open dissemination of relevant information: new projects must be integrated into the existing urban environment, and decisions must be reached on the disposition and amenities to be present in the new structures. This process will involve eliciting ideas, information and experience from the ground up, as well as competitive bidding for the substantive execution of the tasks involved. But competitive bidding implies that building contracts (and therefore employment) will be gained by some and lost by others. Is it, then, acceptable to have a long-term strategy of governmental activity that implies secure employment for some groups, such as teachers, but not for others, such as workers in the construction industry?

None of these questions can be easily resolved. The programme specified above links governmental activity to a set of ambitious goals – the initiation of projects that simultaneously promote social cohesion and economic development, secure long-term work and act to narrow the spread of remuneration currently present in the private sector. Both the latter two issues must confront the reality of labour heterogeneity, reflecting primarily differences in individual qualifications, but also individual needs and aspirations. Thus, for some participants in the labour market (such as those with extensive work commitments in the household), employment embodying a long-term career path may not even be the desired option. Under such conditions, simply setting an aspiration of full employment as a fundamental goal of public policy is overly simplistic. It elides public policy initiatives whose goals differ: on the one hand, facilitating the execution of individuals' long-term plans for employment in the context of skill acquisition and enhancement, and on the other, more traditional notions of the availability of some sort of paid work for those desiring it.

The heterogeneous nature of labour also impinges on any attempt to set rates of governmental remuneration (embodying, as well, conditions of employment) at a narrower range than that present in the current labour market. At the lower end of remuneration, a substantial government presence, based on its in-house activities and procurement, can play a role in mitigating reliance on other policy tools, such as minimum wage legislation. Setting the appropriate spread of remuneration at the higher end poses more substantial difficulties concerning the use of academic qualifications from school or higher education as a badge guaranteeing a level of remuneration for initial employment in government service: any such rigid correspondence is likely to reinforce current tendencies to view education solely from a utilitarian and remunerative perspective. With all these difficulties, the differentials in remuneration that have been emerging from the private sector in recent decades have been so egregious that even a partial correction emerging from an expanded role of government in the setting of remuneration would be salutary.

Expanded government participation in intrinsically worthwhile activities, as proposed here, provides a path for long-term human and economic development and underwrites the securing of long-term employment. Furthermore, it militates against contemporary tendencies in the direction of the imposition of a supposed flexibility and insecurity on the workforce. For those imbued with the entrepreneurial spirit, for whom security of employment is neither necessary nor desirable, nothing presented here implies any limitations on the ability of individuals to function outside the aegis and strictures of governmental activity in their own labouring activities.

Financial conundrums

The long-term plans for jobs worth doing cannot serve as an instant solution to the present-day crisis of mass unemployment in, for instance, large parts of Europe, nor can they deal definitively with the general issues surrounding macroeconomic instability. Solutions to the latter problems will entail, in addition, a commitment to full employment from government expenditure and taxation, and a focus on directing and constraining the activities of the financial sector of the economy.

As we have seen in Part I, the centrally planned schemata and their substantive manifestations in the twentieth century were designed, above all, to deal with the 'anarchy' of capitalist economic relations, most dramatically manifest in economic crises. For the technocratic planning paradigm that underwrote models of central planning, it was finance above all that epitomised the gratuitously wasteful aspects of capitalist economic activity. By the latter part of the last century, the centrally planned economic system was seen to have failed vis-à-vis its capitalist rival: for Hayek, this supposed anarchy of capitalist economic activity – the presence of decentralised decision making and risk taking – was, in fact, the very source of its dynamism. In capitalism, the presence of a financial sector is an inherent aspect of these decentralised decision-making processes.

Finance in capitalism is thus linked both to its capacity for dynamism and to instability, with the crisis of 2007–8 generating an intensified focus in both mainstream and heterodox economics on the role of the financial sector in economic instability. Given, however, the intimate relationship between the financial sector and general economic activity, it may appear fruitless to attempt to allocate a defined share of 'blame' for economic crises past and present to financial activities, with the implicit presumption that somehow the financial aspect of economic endeavour can be segmented and compartmentalised in a capitalist economy.

In the context of the innovations that have taken place in the financial sector in recent decades, even defenders of these altered arrangements have been willing to consider whether they may have exacerbated instability.[23] An emerging contemporary mainstream literature reinforces older and heterodox views suggesting that the financial sector can play a distinctive role in economic perturbations, locating the presence of financial cycles that have a life and a logic of their own as 'credit booms gone wrong'.[24] And the very virtues that make for the celebrated vibrancy and fluidity of the contemporary financial world can create an excessive 'elasticity' of monetary and financial regimes,[25] with consequent instability linked to a range of developments highlighted below, most especially the increasing use by banks and other financial institutions of financial markets as a source of income and liquidity.[26]

A limited discussion has also emerged of the benefits and costs of an environment that is conducive to financial crises. For many discussants, there is an evocation of the role of finance, even, or perhaps especially, in its frenzied bubble phases, as playing a central role in productivity-boosting waves of innovation (technological and otherwise). The quashing or dampening of these bubbles could, it is suggested, be very costly to long-term growth, a sentiment expressed even by Hyman Minsky, an economist whose career was devoted to investigating the negative consequences of financial instability.[27]

In critical discussions of the present system, the looming spectre of an unacceptable Soviet-type central planning alternative appears to be present.[28]

The question arises whether it is appropriate to make a full identification of the benefits accruing from progress, technological and otherwise, with headline-grabbing (as they used to be called), share-price-enhancing innovations in, for instance, software provision or pharmaceutical products. Financial bubbles may accelerate the introduction of these innovations to consumer and inter-industry markets; the extraordinary harvest of new products in the US in the first quarter of the twentieth century was broadly coincident with financial and especially stock market development, often in what seems to have been an atmosphere of frenzied speculation.

In the twenty-first century, it is the latest innovation in mobile phone technology that immediately catches our attention. But fundamental innovation is largely the by-product of the long-term investment in physical, and especially human, capital that is the main artery of human progress. As we have seen in Chapter 9, innovations such as mobile phones are low-hanging fruit – the by-product of the decades-long theoretical and substantive development of electronics and semiconductor technology that transformed the world. These processes contained a role for entrepreneurial finance, but also embraced long-term planning and financing from government. The key prerequisite, however, was the rich and widely dispersed human infrastructure whose skills had been enriched by *in situ* involvement in existing activities and the extensive educational system that had largely been underwritten by government expenditure. The relative weight of governmental activities vis-à-vis entrepreneurship and entrepreneurial finance is likely to have increased in favour of the former in recent decades with, as noted earlier, the greater predominance of pure science in the development of modern technology. Entrepreneurial finance has played, and is likely to play, an important but secondary role in fundamental technological innovation. The benefits of bubble-induced innovation may thus be exaggerated by focusing solely on any resultant acceleration of the marketing of innovations, an activity that may be merely a short-term, overt and partial manifestation of society's material progress: constraining, directing and regulating the financial sector may well inhibit its activities, but the incumbent losses to society are likely to be of a limited kind.

By contrast, the social costs of financial bubbles will be high if the plans that guide long-term investments are derailed by a crisis that engenders mass unemployment of human and physical resources. The costs of financial bubbles and the consequent economic instability may be higher than would be indicated simply by considering the GDP foregone, as is typically done,[29] since such a measure is not likely to take full account of the long-term disruption to the planning and development of the stock of human assets consequent upon a crisis. A vast literature of an anecdotal and fictional kind has dealt with the disruption to the lives and aspirations of individuals and households because of crises, past and present,[30] but there is little focus in economics on how these personal and household catastrophes translate into deficits in economic development for society as a whole. On the contrary, the pervasive influence of an interpretation from Joseph Schumpeter perceives these disruptions to be unintended consequences of a creative destruction incumbent upon progress, technological and otherwise. Though Schumpeter, perhaps more than any other prominent economist, linked capitalist dynamism and innovation to the financial sector, he dismissed its link to business fluctuations by giving a real-factors explanation for the leading exemplar of such fluctuations, the Great Depression of the 1930s: these perturbations are seen to be the inevitable by-product of economic development, including waves of technological change – 'innovations are at the root of cyclical fluctuations' – and cannot be attributed to the malfunctioning of capitalism and its financial sector.[31]

This discourse helps to reinforce the tendency in orthodox economics to preclude consideration of the role of finance in the economy, including its effect upon fluctuations in general business activity.[32] The neoclassical and technocratic planning traditions inherit from David Ricardo a classical dichotomy, postulating that finance, if it is not to obscure the role of real factors in economic outcomes, is to be seen as a diaphanous veil through which economic outcomes may be viewed. Real outcomes in the economy – the microeconomic allocation of goods and services – are dictated by relative prices and will therefore be unaffected by changes in the stock of money; the latter will only affect the general price level – the monetary economy. The substantive implications of such an approach were manifest in the famous theorem of Franco Modigliani and Merton Miller of 1958: in the context of the classical dichotomy and its associated perfect capital market, the value of a firm will not be contingent on its debt-to-equity ratio or (as subsequently demonstrated) its dividend payout ratio. In general terms, finance and financial variables (including liquidity ratios and ratios of short- and long-term indebtedness to the term structure of assets) can have no effect upon real economic outcomes in the business world and on the fortunes of firms.[33]

With money and finance just a veil, the search for the causes of an economic crisis, even one apparently initiated in the financial sector, must inevitably lead to the real sector of the economy. In recent decades, the dominant academic approach to these issues has been that of real business cycle theory, in which cycles are conceived of as the equilibrium reaction of a modelled economy to some kind of exogenous random shock,[34] with perturbations in the rate of introduction of new technology especially popular. Keynesian notions of the possibility of economic fluctuations emanating from the financial sector have been commonly treated as old-fashioned and not rigorously grounded in microeconomic theory.

The approach of economic orthodoxy to these issues left the mainstream of academic economics largely unprepared to deal with the financial crisis of 2007–8 – nothing in presentations of firm behaviour in orthodox microeconomics would suggest that the seizing up of bank liquidity would threaten paralysis in the real sector of the production, purchase and sale of goods and services. A by-product of the orthodox adherence to the centrality of the real economy is that, within economics, finance is a niche sub-discipline, with few academic specialists outside the financial sector sufficiently cognisant of institutional detail to be able to challenge, from a public policy perspective, decisions made by bankers and financiers – the insiders who make decisions concerning these issues on a daily basis. When the financial crisis erupted, the foxes were called in to put out the fire they had ignited in the henhouse.

Somewhat surprisingly, a broad swathe of heterodox and critical approaches, perhaps reflecting the technocratic planning heritage, parallel neoclassical orthodox approaches in claiming to look beneath the surface: the financial innovations of recent decades are seen as attempts by capitalism to cope with or counteract more deep-seated tendencies (such as falling profitability in the real sector), or, more commonly, the financial sector is seen as parasitic – a fetter on capitalist development. The political slogans that emerge from such an approach often contrast 'Main Street vs. Wall Street'[35] and are reminiscent of popular front strategies of earlier times based on the theory of monopoly capitalism, with its call for a united front against the 'big monopolies'.

The argument below will suggest that finance is fundamental to the operation of capitalism and, in some form, to decentralised decision making in general. The dramatic changes in the financial environment of recent decades cannot be characterised as natural emanations from some Hayekian spontaneous order; on the other hand, they are neither aberrations nor dysfunctional in the context of capitalist development, and have emerged for well-defined reasons. As in the case of earlier market-based developments, the state has played, and continues to play, a fundamental role in these dramatic changes.

Furthermore, many of the issues surfacing in the context of finance and its evolution raise questions about the regulation of any economic system with substantial amounts of decentralised decision making and allocation: as we have seen in Chapter 4, Oskar Lange's fantastic scheme for a socialist economy simply by-passes these issues. Any attempt to construct a real-life alternative to central planning, most especially in a socialist context, must weigh the costs and benefits of taming finance. But any such effort should also ask, in a positive fashion, whether present-day financial arrangements can be modified to bring them more in line with the fulfilment of the socialist goals for the widening of opportunities for self-realisation and the development of personal capacities; on a collective basis, can we reform the operation of the financial sector to enhance the exercise of democratic control?

In spite of the obstacles presented above by the dichotomy between the real and the financial sector at the core of mainstream economics, the latter possesses an elaborate, if heuristic, justification for the role of finance and its associated institutions in capitalism. The traditional arguments for the positive role of financial institutions in economic development fall into three classes. First, finance and financial institutions increase the efficiency of the use of investment funds. Financial institutions are seen to contribute to raising the efficiency of investment through the evaluation of projects and the selection of the most promising ones. Evaluating projects is costly, and specialised financial institutions develop cumulative experience in the evaluation of projects. Second, financial institutions attract household savings and mobilise them to finance the most promising projects. Third, financial institutions diversify risks by the pooling of projects undertaken.

Developments in recent decades in financial markets often cast a peculiar light on these principles. Much of the public perception of the efficacy of the financial sector is of its role in the monitoring, evaluation and nurturing of new products, most especially in the context of Silicon Valley-type technological innovations. But the activities of financial institutions in the context of the housing sector leading up to the 2007–8 financial crisis involved, in many cases, a perfunctory evaluation of key financial variables of individual projects (in a manner reminiscent of the activities of conglomerates in the 1960s and 1970s),[36] with a reliance upon compiling a broad portfolio to control risk. Furthermore, the need for financial institutions to attract household savings by offering attractive returns in an increasingly competitive market may have constrained their ability to focus on, and cultivate an expertise in, the monitoring of projects in a particular sphere of activity such as housing, as in the case of savings and loan associations in the US and building societies in the UK, or in a defined geographical area. Many recent developments, in the context of an increased 'Americanisation' – securitisation – of finance, in which the weight of allocation rests upon anonymous markets, tend to break the traditional identification made above between the financial sector and the activities of a range of financial institutions acting as the vehicles through which investment funds are allocated.

The dramatic transformation in the financial landscape worldwide since the 1970s has been underpinned by an electronic revolution in the collection, storage and transmission of data and of business and financial information, and has interacted with changes in the institutional structures, attitudes, and economic and social environment of the financial sector.[37] These changes may be parsed into a breaking down of barriers between segments of the sector – a de-segmentation of formerly separable components – so that the formerly specialised activities of commercial (clearing) banks, investment banks, insurance companies and other institutions (including non-financial institutions) find themselves with overlapping and competing interests in the same domains.

A second change has been a vast extension of securitisation and marketisation in the financial sector, such as when a multinational firm replaces the negotiation of a loan with a bank with the issuance of its own marketable debt (invariably underwritten by financial institutions), or a more vulnerable firm offers its debt on the market in a low-grade junk form rather than having it placed privately with an investor by a financial institution. Subsumed here, but of enormous consequence in its own terms, is the expansion and marketisation of risk, as in the emergence of derivatives and their associated markets. The emergence of vast markets for these instruments, while having, especially in their OTC (over-the-counter) manifestations, the characteristics of an uncontrollable 'wild beast', is not simply the emanation of a spontaneous order. We have seen (Chapter 1) that the creation of markets for the sale of bushels of wheat in the nineteenth century was enabled and encouraged by state authorities in the US; in a similar way, the derivatives market emerges from state intervention in product design and the regulation of new contracts.[38] The third aspect of this financial revolution – its internationalised and globalised nature – was, in a seemingly paradoxical manner, promoted by the collapse of the Bretton Woods system of fixed exchange rates, with the resultant expanded needs for the facilitation of trade and the hedging of risk between fluctuating currencies; financial globalisation then received a substantial reinforcement with the final collapse of the centrally planned economic system in Europe in 1991.

The cumulative and concomitant aspects of this transformation are part of a generalised intensification of competition in all spheres of economic activity, of which finance is one aspect.[39] Thus, in the US, in a system that began to break down in the 1970s, a typical arrangement between banks and large firms as borrowers – one that complemented a comfortable and intimate relationship between them on the lending front – was that the latter held substantial compensating balances in the banks' coffers as part of a *quid pro quo* in which these firms would be given priority access in periods of liquidity tightening.[40] It was largely at the initiative of non-financial firms that bank loans were increasingly replaced with firms' issuance of their own marketable debt: banks had to accede to being the mere underwriters of debt for these firms rather than lenders to them. This loss by the banks in the sphere of lending – their key income-earning activity – was partially recompensed by the fact that, initially, regulators did not require banks to write up this underwriting activity in their accounts as liabilities.

The link between financial innovation and regulatory failure is central to an understanding of the genesis of the former, and an indication of the obstacles that innovation creates for democratic control of economic activity: the creation myth of the eurodollar as an attempt to avoid regulation is often told in the context of the legal limits on the interest rates that could be paid to depositors within US borders. From other perspectives, however, the question of regulation has proved crucial for contemporary developments. The state's role as an ultimate provider of liquidity facilitated the development of, and may even have been necessary for, the existence of extensive markets in derivatives, as will be seen below. And in a different sense of the word 'regulation', the elaboration and extension of financial markets internationally are linked with the collapse of the Bretton Woods system in the early 1970s, with vast resources and new mechanisms needed to facilitate trade in the absence of fixed rates between currencies: these new mechanisms imposed a form of regulation upon currencies and on the behaviour of national governments that were no longer subject to the constraints of the Bretton Woods fixed exchange rate system.

These dramatic changes in the financial sphere can be seen to have efficacious aspects for capitalism and, in some respects, for any regime for the allocation of investment funds that is not fully centralised. In mainstream economic theory, the perfect capital market offers a static ideal of how finance should function in a capitalist economy: a universal and uniform rate of discount is present for the evaluation of all investment projects, with the capital market disinterestedly ranking projects in terms of their contribution to net present value. The provenance of the project (whether it emerges, for instance, from a small or a large firm) is not a consideration in the ranking of projects. By contrast, a dynamic approach to finance emphasises the role of the financial sector in the development of new instruments for savers, new mechanisms for the financing of projects, and the extension of the geographical domain of finance, factors central to the heuristic justification for the role of finance discussed above.

From these perspectives, the changes of recent decades have reduced traditional asymmetries between firms and even countries, tending to compress the capital market down to a single, uniform layer. The development of a market for less-than-investment-grade securities, under the invidious sobriquet 'junk', epitomised these changes. The junk bond market has often been associated with marginal practices, but is also an aspect of a widening and deepening of the market for funds for a range of projects and firms in the context of a capital market that is more sophisticated and more competitive, from both a static and a dynamic perspective, than heretofore.[41]

A notable aspect of the evolution of finance has been the emergence of the market for derivatives, marketable instruments usually embodying the risk on the primary instrument (for instance a bond, or a currency in the context of international trade) from which it is 'derived': even supporters of derivatives concede their potential for exacerbating financial volatility. But to treat these developments as merely part of a casino capitalism and a fetter on capitalist development would be inappropriate: the rapid expansion of a broad range of these risk-based devices was strictly necessary for the expansion of the volume of international trade and investment that continued to take place with the breakdown of the Bretton Woods system. In general, the rise of derivatives markets is an aspect of an increasing sophistication in the conduct of business: it creates a publicly available and marketable price for risk for firms – in many contexts, an easier way of dealing with risk than the clumsier device of a firm diversifying its own activities, thereby facilitating an expansion of trade and investment, including with the very poorest countries.

The new marketised financial landscape has, furthermore, been associated with various meritocratic characteristics, including a breaking down of insider and class hierarchies linked to the personalised nature of most traditional banking.[42] In more general terms, there is often claimed to be a greater openness and production of information associated with market relations (such as the issuing of a security to the public) compared with transactional relations (a loan negotiated between a firm and a bank): periods when firms desire to raise money from the public in share or bond issuance, or in the context of merger activity, have often been associated with maximum disclosure of new information about the firm's affairs. Such disclosure can be inhibited by the possibility, or the excuse, that valuable information will be passed on to competitors, thereby justifying universal public disclosure of this information as a public good.

The putative gains associated with this financial revolution may come at a high cost, with a resultant exacerbation of instability, as even supporters of this revolution quoted above will suggest; in the most literal sense, this revolution has proved costly, with a substantial increase of the share of GDP taken by the financial sector in the US and the UK since 1980, a tendency not in general replicated in developed economies.[43]

And some of these gains may be elusive in the context of potential fallacies of composition: innovation in the domain of finance is not necessarily comparable to equivalent effects in the real sector of the economy, and may have drastically different consequences.[44] Savings in the real sector in the control of inventories (stocks and work in progress) reflect a net rise in the productivity, and therefore in the real income, of the society as a whole: the famous just-in-time system permitted Japanese car manufacturers to hold lower inventories of glass, rubber and steel, which were real savings in the resources devoted to these products. An equivalent financial innovation, which permits every enterprise in the economy to perform the same volume of transactions with only half of their present holdings of cash, generates no equivalent societal gain: the marginal cost to society of (fiduciary) money creation by the government is close to zero. On the contrary, an innovation that merely permits every firm to economise on its holdings of cash may merely reduce the liquidity of firms, so that this financial innovation has merely contributed to the fragility of the economy.[45]

This kind of liquidity paradox is likely to be exacerbated in the context of a marketised environment for finance, with a euphoria generated by hedging and with derivative instruments promoting a tendency to underestimate systemic risk and perpetuating the illusion at the level of the individual economic actor (including financial institutions) that risk has been dispersed.[46] The need for the rapid unwinding of illiquid positions may be impossible if and when markets freeze up, resulting in the ultimate reliance on the state as the underpinning of this financial innovation.[47]

Much financial innovation has been related to a desire to avoid regulation, as we have seen in the context of the origins of the eurodollar, and to avoid taxes. Those for whom regulation is an imposition on the unfolding of a natural, spontaneous order will treat such developments in a sanguine manner: the increasing elasticity of financial instruments – the increasing speed and volume of their response to changing opportunities – exacerbates situations in which the regulated object disappears from view just as it is being regulated, thereby permitting economic actors to arbitrage international differences in regulation and minimise the latter's effect at the national level.[48]

As a result, measures proposed to reduce financial elasticity, such as capital controls and the so-called Tobin tax (a tax on the volume of the transactions to discourage international capital movements on a very short-term basis), are likely to be ineffective in the context of a financial environment dominated by derivatives and by currency swap arrangements that circumvent restrictive policies by obviating the need for explicit capital flows to take place.[49] And one may question the notion introduced above that transparency and openness are invariably advanced as financial allocation becomes more of a market-based phenomenon. On the contrary, the very complexity of the instruments associated with financial innovation – most specifically derivatives – have resulted in difficulties in knowing where the dog is buried,[50] and may well make many financial processes less transparent than before.

What kinds of public policy approaches are relevant to socialists in the context of the financial revolution of recent decades? Is it simply a question of taming finance, and is a return to the institutions and structures of earlier times possible or even desirable? Mainstream analysts concerned with the destabilisation associated with this revolution advocate an adaptation and accommodation to the rapid changes that are still in the process of unfolding. Thus, it is suggested, it is fruitless to attempt to reconstruct institutionally the lines of separation that used to exist between, for instance, commercial banks and investment banks. Instead, it is the regulation of functions (such as traditional commercial banking activities – the making of short-term loans and the facilitation of liquidity), rather than the institutions themselves, that should take place. Commercial banking functions might continue to exist within a broader financial conglomerate, but be regulated with the intention that they should serve a quasi-public utility role in the financial system as a whole – reminiscent of older proposals from

Irving Fisher in the wake of the crisis of the 1930s.[51] The most common response to the explosion of securitised financial devices, including derivatives, has been the suggestion that the large share of this growth that has taken place in instruments traded OTC should be corralled into organised exchanges that can be monitored and regulated.

Pervading these proposals is the implicit understanding that much current financial innovation emerged in the context of avoiding regulation, and that these activities function as a constraint on discretionary government behaviour. Many analysts evidence an ambivalent attitude towards this avoidance of regulation: the lifting of the oppressive hand of the government from the spontaneous order of capitalist interaction is seen as a positive aspect of the financial revolution, one mitigated only by its tendency to generate a periodic spontaneous combustion in the financial sector and in the broader economy. An important aspect of the latter problem is the presence of external effects associated with financial activity, exacerbated by the broad array of complex derivative instruments present in the financial system: the potential instability of a given financial institution may necessitate its holding higher capital reserves than would be prudent if only its own financial integrity were under consideration. A range of commentators are thus willing to concede that the financial system may have to sacrifice some of its putative efficiency by devoting increased resources to sterile holdings in order to promote economic stability.[52]

For socialists, however, it is not merely the combustible elements of the financial system that may legitimate a deviation from notions of efficiency dictated by market criteria. Of equal significance is the extensive and growing capacity of contemporary financial arrangements, so lauded by many of the commentators above, not only to avoid governmental regulation – to neutralise democratic monitoring and direction of the allocation of resources – but to dictate a form of financial prudence to nation states that imposes a particular neoliberal vision of society.

Finance has always played a key role in the monitoring and constraining of the behaviour of all economic actors – the individual, the firm and the nation state – in capitalist economies. These financial forms of economic regulation invariably have an element of conscious construction, rather than merely being the by-product of the eruption of a spontaneous order. As noted above, in the wake of the collapse of the Bretton Woods fixed exchange rate system, the vast expansion of financial activity, including innovations in the field of derivatives, facilitated a continued growth in trade and investment activity internationally. At the same time, the financial system has enlarged its role as a monitor and arbiter of the economic behaviour of nations at all levels of income and economic development: critical words not only from quasi-official organs such as the International Monetary Fund, but even from the private ratings agency Standard and Poor's, are often sufficient to cause powerful nations to readjust their economic policies. In what may thus emerge as an embattled context, constraints from the financial sector internationally may be the most substantial obstacle to any national economic programme for redirecting economic priorities in a progressive direction.

The extent to which recent financial developments have imposed binding constraints on the economic policy options open to the larger rich states, the prime candidates for socialist reform, must not be exaggerated. In recent times, rich states falling victim to the 'gnomes of Zurich' (the paranoid and xenophobic phrase from the British Labour Party of the 1960s) have sometimes found themselves, as in the case of France in the 1990s with its *franc fort* policy, subjecting themselves to the self-imposed constraints of an overly high exchange rate.

More egregiously, a large section of Europe is now foundering over the rigidities and deflationary aspects – both inherent and resulting from the policies pursued – in the euro single currency zone. The initiation of the currency was naïvely lauded by many progressives as a step away from narrow nationalism and in the direction of European unity, an acceleration of an economic and political integration that was thought to be forthcoming too slowly. From this perspective, it is notable, even paradoxical, that financial innovations of recent decades, especially the emergence and elaboration of derivative instruments, had reduced the need for such a unified currency by successfully facilitating an expansion of trade and investment between nations with different currencies. But the other motive for the introduction of a single currency – to constrain the behaviour of wayward states in a modern equivalent of the gold standard – has its goals reinforced by the role these financial innovations play in the monitoring and redirection of the actions of individual nation states. The financial sphere already imposes restraints on the freedom of nation states to pursue independent social and economic policies, but for those nations functioning in the context of a single currency, especially one directed to function in a deflationary direction, the constraints imposed may become binding.[53]

Given the latter fact, many states may be subject to inordinately onerous standards of financial probity as they attempt to expand aggregate demand to achieve full employment. In present-day conditions most especially, the socialist commitment to full employment may well need to move beyond the Keynesian focus of the postwar period on the manipulation of aggregate demand as the sole lever for its realisation. We must start from a vantage point that takes the provision of full employment (with the latter being focused on occupations commensurate with levels of skills developed, and especially with a range of opportunities for newcomers to the labour force) as a central societal goal, one not to be contingent on market-based fluctuations in aggregate demand. In the past, activities to improve the trade-off between aggregate demand and employment have been centred on Active Labour Market Policies (ALMP), discussed earlier, but no claims have ever been made that such policies, by themselves, are a path to full employment.

The contrast between an orthodox and a socialist approach to, especially, long-term employment emerges from the jobs worth doing programme described above. Many of the activities in this programme will have, as a by-product, an improvement in the employment efficiency of expenditure, with much of it involving the expansion of labour-intensive sectors (urban and environmental renovation, housing and public transport) or the expansion of labour use within them (such as education). Such a redirection towards activities with a high efficiency of employment is likely to reduce, almost by definition, growth in productivity per head and therefore growth in per capita GDP: one obstacle to the pursuit of such a strategy may, therefore, be the single-minded obsession with economic growth that is conventionally encountered in public discussions. An alleviating aspect of this strategy of redirecting priorities in the direction of education, urban and environmental renovation, and improvements to public transport is that these activities are likely to use, for many nations, a higher share of domestic value added than, especially, the consumption resources that have been diverted away from upper-income expenditure, thereby, if anything, mitigating international pressures on the currency.

A less substantive, but conceivably more pungent, possibility for improving the employment efficiency of the economy lies in a revival of the notions of wage compression and social contract discussed above, policies that had extended periods of success in the postwar period in the context of nations such as Sweden and other countries with relatively high levels of economic equality. The broad thrust of such strategies was always that generalised wage constraint has a greater chance of sustained success in an egalitarian context – in an atmosphere perceived to approximate one of equal sacrifice. A socialist approach to wage setting places notions of equal sacrifice in the context of a long-term developmental strategy that *necessitates* equality rather than viewing policies to promote equalisation merely as attempts to ameliorate unfairness. In the conception presented here, the more equal society is, in the long term, the more robust and capable one.

Can present-day financial arrangements be modified to bring them more in line with the fulfilment of the socialist goals outlined above? The answer depends upon what we want from a financial system. In the wake of the financial crisis of 2007–8, all serious observers have been emphasising the need to mitigate the high costs of instability, if for no other reason than to protect the 'gains' of the financial revolution of recent decades. Will the raising of equity holdings by banks and the monitoring of the individual functions of financial institutions be sufficient to exercise control over the financial system as a whole in the context of the unprecedented fluidity across the system, both geographically and across functions? And will the corralling and monitoring of marketised elements such as OTC derivatives be sufficient to prevent a repetition of the extreme forms of disciplining exercised by financial markets on national governments during the Asian crisis of 1997?

If the kinds of measures now being proposed fail to avert a new financial crisis within memory of the last one, even defenders of the financial revolution of recent decades may be forced to consider more constraining measures than those currently on offer. Such measures will involve a determined functional finance initiative at the national or transnational level, in coordination with a centralised financial authority that controls the activities of individual financial institutions and their functions.

From a socialist standpoint, it is inappropriate to accede to a perspective that looks upon such a process of increased regulation and centralisation purely in negative terms, as a loss of efficiency that must come about for the sake of economic stability. On the contrary, if we take as our ideal of innovation and economic development the bourgeoning of the postwar US electronics industry, we see a balance being maintained between the financing of long-term goals and priorities from the centre (largely the US Department of Defense, but also embodying the long-term expansion of human assets through state-financed education) and intense competition for projects, including initiation, impetus and innovation from below, with finance acting as a monitor and local risk taker.

We thus find that the exigencies of the contemporary economy will necessitate, from a socialist perspective, an important degree of centralised control of the overall economy. From one vantage point, such a development is unfortunate, with most contemporary radical notions for restructuring society quite rightly putting a focus on local control, ground-up initiatives and decentralisation.[54] The main factor compelling developments in a centralised direction is a negative one: there is a need for the construction of institutions to effect the full employment programme in the context of the powerful forces buffeting it in the contemporary economy, most especially those emerging from the financial revolution described above. The key institutional mechanism of control will be an entity at the national level whose primary directive is the coordination of governmental fiscal and monetary policies (which function almost everywhere today in separate domains) to maintain full employment, integrated with strong regulatory powers over financial institutions and financial functions.

A second aspect of centralisation is a more positive one. The entity coordinating monetary, fiscal and financial activities overall will also be charged with the monitoring and facilitation of projects consistent with the jobs worth doing programme: an important element of centralised direction is necessitated by the externalities embedded in programmes associated with climate change, the provision of housing, public transport and education. This centralised aspect of project development is, however, also linked to the maintenance of full employment: the forces of the contemporary financial revolution and the interconnected aspects of the real economy may prove to be so powerful as to derail a full employment programme, as specified above, based purely on the regulation of aggregate demand. In a public policy stance committed to full employment, the centralised setting of priorities for the allocation of key investment activities may be a necessary supplement to aggregate demand and financial regulation.

Nothing in these processes precludes, as took place in the electronics sector, competition between firms for contracts, as well as innovations and new ventures initiated from below. Decentralised forms of finance, acting as monitor and risk taker, are likely to play an important role in project allocation. It remains to be seen, in the wake of the housing debacle of the first decade of the twenty-first century, whether financial markets will continue to judge that the pooling of a large number of projects, each of which is monitored by a perfunctory examination of financial data, is a satisfactory method for containing risk, or whether such procedures will largely go the way of the conglomerate era of the 1960s and 1970s, with a return to fashion of the intimate monitoring that has typically characterised risk-taking ventures in high-tech sectors.

The changes proposed here in the functioning of the financial sector are, in truth, of a conservative nature and do not involve the dismantling of existing structures. They are largely focused on a redirection in favour of a commitment to full employment, to the allocation of investment expenditure in the direction of the priorities of the jobs worth doing programme and, as we shall see below, to the exercise of democratic control over the processes undertaken and the decisions made by the institutions concerned.

But for those who consider the proposals above to be fantastic and unrealistic, it is worth contrasting them with mainstream visions for the future of the financial sector. Several authorities, taking for granted the great gains to society from the financial revolution of recent decades, are willing to concede, at least implicitly, its role in increasing the level of risk to households in a financial context, as discussed above, and also its role in aggravating the macroeconomic and, especially, the employment performance of the economy. In a demonstration of the typically constructivist nature of the creation of institutions in capitalism rather than their emergence from a mythical spontaneous order, Alfred Steinherr, Robert Shiller and others have offered up schemes for coping with the insecurities foisted upon households in recent years.[55] Thus 'At present, liquid markets exist only for a small share of household wealth, and easy hedges are not available for the largest part of household wealth (such as real estate, future earnings, business cycles).'[56] What are needed, it seems, are public policies to encourage the creation of competitive free markets in insurance policies that, presumably, risk-averse individuals could purchase to hedge against threats to their livelihood, with medical students selling part of future income as a physician on the futures market and students contemplating a career in cyclical industries such as aircraft engineering hedging away their risk.[57]

One notes here the touching faith in the efficacy of free enterprise to create and sustain such markets (presumably without government assistance, even in a crisis). Among the many questions occurring in this context is how such a system deals with the asymmetries in information invariably present, such as the differences in the ability of households (for instance, the Steinherr or Shiller household compared with the one I grew up in) to evaluate these contracts. The answer, according to Shiller, is the 'democratization' of the financial sector, with people given the ability 'to participate in the financial system as *equals*, with full access to information and with the resources, both human and electronic, to make active and intelligent use of their opportunities', facilitated by government incentives to banks to provide banking services to poor people. If such information had been available to low-income people, we are told (in a 'blame the victim' narrative), '[t]he [subprime] crisis might never have occurred'.[58]

These proposals are, at base, little more than attempts to alleviate some of the egregious insecurities and inequalities emerging in contemporary capitalism by the promotion of market-based solutions to individuals to help them plan their futures in a rational manner. These schemes are what are offered up as progressive solutions. Shiller reminds us that 'social barriers prevent *some* from realizing, and profiting from their talent' and, in a remarkable passage, chastises Marx for the unstated assumption at the heart of his theory of exploitation that 'a poor laborer could never start a business by getting credit from a bank or capital from wealthy investors'. This, according to Shiller, is a serious misunderstanding of the nature of capitalist development on Marx's part, since 'in an ideal capitalist system, people with good business ideas can, in principle at least, do just that'. The present system has not yet achieved this ideal, but help is on the way, because 'there has been a long trend toward the democratization of finance, the opening of financial opportunities to everyone. It is a trend we must hope will continue into the future.'[59]

The above notions are part of what passes for a progressive approach to financial reform, since among more adamantly free-market theorists, as will be noted below, the capitalist firm *already* functions as an arena of free exchange in which, indifferently, workers can hire capitalists for their services, and *vice versa*: there is little need for any government intervention, even of the limited kind specified above, to 'level the playing field'.

The levelling and democratisation proffered above by Robert Shiller, the Nobel Prize exemplification of a left-of-centre approach to finance, is of a very limited kind. According to him, the need for leadership, as embodied in CEOs, is a central fact of modern life- and the public must be reconciled to the dramatic rises in executive remuneration that have come about in recent decades as a consequence of 'improvements in our capitalist system';

if not, there is a danger that 'The political climate may well stifle innovation and prevent financial capitalism from progressing in ways that could benefit all citizens.' The best way to reform the financial sector is not to institute democratic control of its institutions and functions, but 'to build good moral behavior into the culture of Wall Street though the creation and observance of best practices in its various professions – CEOs, traders accountants, investment bankers, lawyers, philanthropists'.[60]

These mainstream notions of financial reform are wildly fanciful – hinting at an individualistic utopia in which individuals are encouraged, or perhaps compelled, to use financial markets to alleviate problems of economic insecurity that these markets have helped exacerbate in the first place. Democratic control of the financial sector, however, is not on offer in these proposals.

By contrast, public expenditure and finance in a socialist economy will involve projects being carried out by a range of state organs and non-governmental (private or cooperative) contractors, with competitive bidding processes to allocate these contracts.[61] The changes in the conduct of financial activity – a greater centralisation around an entity with a directive for the maintenance of full employment, one that sets priorities for the allocation of investment activities and is integrated with fiscal decisions on tax and expenditure – are inherent consequences of the economic priorities being pursued. Overall, these changes are, if anything, less radical than those the financial sector itself has undertaken in the last several decades, not to speak of the individualistic utopias proffered above by mainstream economists. It would be absurd for socialists to proceed more radically and to suggest that the financial sector and its personnel can be reconstructed *de novo* in a precipitous manner. We will be living with the underlying structures of this sector, including the changes of recent decades, for a long time, with strategies for stabilisation and modification emerging from the existing parameters of the sector.

An important emendation to present practice, however, is the introduction of democratic control at various stages in the process of financial decision making. A key element of democratisation concerns the personnel making the decisions. In present practice, financial affairs, even in the context of central banks with their public responsibilities, are invariably administered by insiders to the profession, with frequently a revolving door between the government and the private (especially the financial) sector; in the older Saint-Simonian vision discussed in earlier chapters, finance is similarly directed by experts from the existing financial sector.

Socialist changes to present practice at central banks and government treasuries will invariably involve the appointment of a range of individuals from outside of the financial sector. These appointees will include representation for the needs of labour, with a special focus on the promotion of full employment and the protection of working conditions, and political appointees representing the public interest. The latter are not to be merely broad overseers, but individuals capable of, and active in, the detailed regulation of the range of financial functions existing in the contemporary economy, including, for instance, rating agencies.

But even good regulators often find themselves trapped in the system they are regulating, and the ultimate question – far from a trivial one – is how to institute true democratic control over financial processes. The direction of movement in a socialist context is one in which financial affairs, far from possessing a vaunted independence from political, that is, democratic influence, must be politicised – with the public participating in decisions surrounding investment priorities as well as those surrounding the stabilisation of the general economy. Underlining the issue of question of democratic control is the presence of information that is publicly available – what is the appropriate boundary between private business affairs and the public interest? This important issue is addressed below.

Progressive taxation

In a socialist economy, the expanded role for government activity described above is thus meant to play multiple roles. It promotes human and economic development through focused efforts to secure long-term full employment, thus underlining that the latter is a prime directive of economic policy and not a mere by-product of some intermittently successful macroeconomic manipulation of the economy. In addition, the policies described above attack inequality with the public provision of necessities and the wage compression regimes instituted by this public provision. Minimum wage legislation and policies to engender a reassertion of union influence in bargaining (to be discussed below) can also be used to facilitate wage compression.

Progressive taxes on income and wealth will invariably play a key role in income equalisation in such a context. They are necessary, furthermore, simply because there is rarely such a thing as a free lunch, and if, for instance, the opportunities for personal development that the well-to-do provide for their own children are to be offered to all, the resources have to come from somewhere. Much of the literature dealing with taxes from this perspective from the US and the UK has tended to focus on the Laffer–Feldstein problematic described in Chapter 10 concerning the elasticity of taxable income, especially at higher levels – do high earners stop working when taxed too much? This elasticity would be central to determining the revenue-maximising top rate of tax (the highest rate at which gains in revenue exceed losses from any disincentive effect). Academic research in this area emphasises the conceptual and empirical limitations of attempting to make any such calculation; consensus results of the empirical literature find low values for this elasticity – ones that would easily ratify significantly higher rates of tax on upper incomes than those existing at present. Such a result is unsurprising in the broad context of economic history, with successfully developing countries exhibiting tax regimes that are highly varied in their levels of taxation and the devices used to collect it.[62]

Two caveats must be introduced here concerning the use of the problematic of elasticity of taxable income as the sole criterion for determining the upper level of tax. First, taxes on income and wealth do not only play a role in the financing of worthwhile projects, but are also, in most of the economies under consideration here, the central mechanism of public policy for the construction of a distribution of resources consistent with human and economic development, as well as economic and political democracy. If present-day levels of inequality are truly thought to be a threat to democratic functioning, one might well reject the single-minded focus in the literature of an optimal top rate as one that maximises potential revenue from current income: confiscatory taxes on large wealth holdings may well be important for the construction of a democratic polity. The present-day plutocratic distribution of wealth has distortionary and destructive effects on democratic processes: why should democratic rule necessarily take second place to an economic calculation?

Second, some of the studies cited above conflate the general question of the extent to which high earners will work less if their remuneration in constrained, and the different questions surrounding losses due to tax avoidance and evasion, including the flight of funds into tax havens abroad. Powerful states such the US and the UK, as we shall see below, can hardly be treated as helpless or innocent bystanders in the presence of such phenomena.

The research into the effects of taxation has taken place in the wake of the widening inequality of the last several decades, described in Chapter 10, over a range of OECD countries, and the widespread lowering of the top rate of tax. The US and the UK have been of interest in this regard because of the exceptional extent to which income gains have been concentrated in the top 1 per cent of income earners in the context of dramatic reductions in the top rate of tax.[63] In the US context, exemptions and other 'tax expenditures' (to be described below) to top earners have dictated that despite a nominal top rate of 91 per cent in 1960, those at the lower end of the top 1 per cent were paying federal taxes of 34 per cent, with an average rate of over 70 per cent for those in the top 0.01 per cent. These rates, however, appear highly progressive compared with those in 2004, with the lower end of the top 1 per cent paying 31 per cent and the top 0.01 per cent less than 35 per cent. The lessening of the tax burden of upper-income earners appears to be due less to reductions in income tax rates (which have been partially neutralised by elimination of many categories of tax expenditure) than to reductions in corporate income and estate taxes.[64] The rise in the pre-tax income share in the US of the top 1 per cent from 6 per cent in 1976 to 17 per cent in 2007, most especially in the context of a tax burden at the top that now never exceeds 35 per cent, suggests there is scope for raising significant amounts of revenue from this group.[65]

Progressive taxation undoubtedly played an important role in income equalisation over the twentieth century.[66] It is, however, only one of the mechanisms available for the promotion of equality, which, as we have seen above, also include the public provision of goods and services and wage compression. Peter Lindert claims that the latter two forms of equalisation in social welfare states such as Sweden, rather than progressive taxation, have been part of a 'pro-growth with equality' strategy in these countries;[67] others have claimed that taxes on capital income in Sweden played an important role in income equalisation over the twentieth century and that reductions in these taxes in recent years have exacerbated inequality.[68]

The role of wage compression in policies to promote income equalisation will be addressed below. Here, however, a curious fact emerges regarding the public provision of goods and services as a mechanism for equalisation: while gross social spending shows much higher levels (per unit GDP) in typical social welfare regimes such as Austria, Denmark and Sweden (27, 27 and 29 per cent, respectively) than in the UK and the US (21 and 16 per cent), net expenditure percentages in these countries (24, 22 and 25 per cent for Austria, Denmark and Sweden; 26 and 25 per cent for the UK and the US) are quite comparable.[69] The resolution of this seeming paradox is far from trivial, with a range of difficulties including how to treat, in this context, publicly mandated private provision of sickness benefits by employers.[70] The major reason, however, why net social expenditure appears comparable in the US and in social democratic countries is the very substantial role played by Tax Breaks with a Social Purpose (TBSB) in the US, with their virtual absence in, for instance, Austria, Denmark and Sweden. The incidence of these tax breaks is difficult to track down, but many of them, such as tax breaks for private health insurance and pensions, tend to be regressive.[71]

At the moment – and, it seems, in every country – there is a range of tax breaks, exemptions and other modifications to the tax code that, individually, often appear to encourage worthy expenditure; taxes have also been proffered, at various times, to fulfil specific policy goals – taxes on consumption in general (to encourage saving), or on a specific range of goods (such as luxury goods), or on particular sources of income (unearned income or land); complications to the tax system often emerge from attempts by tax authorities to prevent tax avoidance, especially by the wealthy.[72]

These complications come at a high cost. At present, our ignorance of the contemporary situation with regard to income and wealth is linked not only to conscious attempts to avoid or evade tax, but to the sheer complexity of the tax systems in place and the conceptual difficulties in evaluating tax incidence. Thus, while 'tax evasion and tax avoidance need to be taken seriously and can quantitatively affect the conclusions drawn [here] ... legally tax-exempt capital income poses more serious problems than tax evasion and tax avoidance per se':[73] revenue losses in the US in recent years from a range of individual and corporate deferrals, exclusions, deductions, special rates and tax credits to gross income reach the magnitude of 6 to 9 per cent of GDP.[74]

While many of these tax expenditures (exemptions) are not necessarily regressive in their effects on post-tax income, in aggregate they add immensely to the complexity of the tax system, and probably account for the exceptionally wide gap to be found in estimates of the effective tax rates paid by those on the highest incomes,[75] or on the overall redistributive consequences of the tax expenditures themselves. Thus, the main conclusion of one study for the US was that tax expenditures on average raise after-tax incomes more for upper-income than for lower-income taxpayers,[76] a finding that does not necessarily contradict, but may be contrasted with, another stating that 'the single most effective program at reducing poverty in 2010 was the EITC (a tax credit to those working on low or moderate incomes)'. To exemplify these complications, until recently, the US government's standard measure of poverty did not include non-cash transfers and tax credits.[77]

Even when the effect of exemptions is to reduce inequality or to promote the public good in some other fashion, such exemptions by their very nature introduce complications to the tax system and add to the difficulty of discerning the incidence of tax, or even the true distribution of resources in the economy.[78] In the interests of democratic monitoring of public affairs and general coherence, an obvious concomitant of transparency in a tax system is a reliance primarily on income and wealth taxes, which are to be kept as simple as possible; a progressive tax system in such a context is no less transparent than a flat tax. Tax complexity is, on the whole, the enemy of economic and political democracy and is to be avoided even when, in any individual case, the introduction of exceptions and special cases seems desirable; when appropriate, explicit subsidies from the state are a preferable, and more transparent, method for reallocating resources.

The introduction of tax simplicity is a straightforward concomitant of Thomas Piketty's suggestions for global taxes on income and wealth.[79] The latter will invariably embody a surrender of the notion that a company (corporation) is a 'person', a pretence that reinforces, and helps to perpetuate, a series of absurd practices: the tendency to tax company owners' equity and the income flowing from it differently from any other form of wealth or income that the owners possess; the frequent avoidance of personal liability by managers for misdemeanours and crimes committed by an entity called 'the company'. Most egregious in this context is the right, as decreed by the US Supreme Court, of this 'person' to participate in politics through financial expenditure, at this point merely a minor reinforcement of the capacity of the wealthy to dictate political outcomes in putatively democratic societies. In the long term, it will be desirable to see through taxes at the corporate level and tax individual income and wealth; in the interim, the role played by corporations in facilitating tax avoidance necessitates the maintenance and enforcement of taxes on corporations. Such taxes will have to be supported by far greater public disclosure of corporate information than at present and, as we shall see below, an expanded role for workers and the public in corporate decision making.[80]

But progressive taxes on income and wealth do not merely serve the purpose of redistribution of economic resources. They are important for the facilitation of political democracy, because present-day wealth distributions permit small groups of people living in their own world to exercise absurdly disproportionate influence over political and economic processes that affect everybody; some aspects of this question will be addressed below.

Political economy: public affairs

What, then, are the elements of a real, functioning democracy? As noted in the Introduction, this term in recent times has been used with little connotation of rule by the people, and debased to signify merely the absence of overt terror exercised by the state. If, however, we take the original meaning of the term seriously, then equality functions as a unifying characteristic not only of the economic programme described above, but also of its political aspect – the ability to exercise democratic control. In its most modest aspect, it is a reasonable democratic demand that the actions taken by public policy decision makers (usually politicians, but ever more frequently billionaire 'philanthropists') – should also impinge upon their own lives. Democracy, in this minimal sense, is only a catchphrase when these individuals are the arbiters of the fate of the public school system and of public transport while they and their children frequent private schools and move around the city in taxis.

Equality in its political aspect, furthermore, demands the free flow of information. When little or no detail is forthcoming about important public policy processes, these governmental actions have a way of disappearing off the public's radar and no longer seem to exist. In a public policy context, the well-nigh infinite flow of information potentially forthcoming at any moment is inevitably sieved and interpreted by a range of intermediaries we usually think of as 'the media'. But other sources are also of significance, including academic and independent researchers as well as governmental output, both overtly political and bureaucratic (such as agencies dealing with health or the environment). The cognitive particularities and limitations we all possess mean that this flow of information is transformed into a different body of knowledge by each one of us.

A free flow of information is, thus, a necessary but far from sufficient condition for securing knowledge in the hands of the public that is adequate for democratic decision making. Even beyond the issues surrounding the securing of knowledge, however, we have to consider the mechanisms available for democratic expression of current concerns. In the US and other countries, the declining role of civic groups, most especially labour unions, has weakened the public's capacity to undertake collective action to hold politicians accountable; what is left for members of the public is the relatively passive role of supporting professionalised advocacy groups in the context of specific issues, so-called pressure groups.[81] The diminution of union power has, as we shall see below, been roughly coincident with rising inequality of income and wealth, thus forging a link between secrecy, failures of collective action and rising inequality.

These issues – secrecy, failures of collective action and rising inequality – converge (and sometimes clash) in confronting the influence of the rich on political processes and the question of tax havens. The political role of wealth and income inequalities in the distortion of democratic polity will be discussed below, but one aspect of this question – the role of secrecy – has manifested itself in a peculiar manner in recent times.[82] In the context of a 5000 per cent increase in the undisclosed financing of political advertising in the US between 2003–4 and 2011–12, Thomas Edsall asked donors to justify their anonymity. The response from the spokesperson for the billionaire (and right-wing) Koch brothers emphasised the role of anonymity in the defence of free speech, especially for dissenters to protect themselves against the threat of retaliation. The citation of a civil rights case from the 1950s involving the National Association for the Advancement of Colored People (NAACP) by the Koch representative left Edsall sputtering with indignation.

But the Koch position is, in the abstract, an impeccable one – the secret ballot has long functioned as an outlet for free expression in the context of elections. Edsall's anger is rightly linked to this tool of the powerless – anonymity – being used as a weapon by those whose power is already absurdly disproportionate and inconsistent with the functioning of a democratic polity. In such a context, openness functions alongside measures promoting equality for the furtherance of democracy.

Many of these issues are exemplified in the interaction of questions surrounding the free flow of information and those concerned with the growth of inequality, tax avoidance and tax evasion. The orders of magnitude are staggering, with a recent estimate that a third of all private financial wealth, and nearly half of all offshore wealth, is now owned by 0.001 per cent of the world's population, and that 'Almost all of it has managed to avoid all income and estate taxes, either by the countries where it has been invested and or where it come from.'[83]

The ignorance surrounding these data is, however, almost as unfathomable as the numbers themselves, a fact to which all of the researchers quoted here will testify: studies for the US report the 'paradox' of a doubling of the share of the income of the top 1 per cent from 1980 to 2010 but – absurdly – a rise in the wealth share of the top 1 per cent by less than 6 per cent. Such problems are perhaps predictable, given the survey origins of the wealth statistics in the studies above compared with the income data taken from tax returns.[84] Even in the latter case, however, distortions are likely to be present, as affluent individuals act to minimise tax liabilities; in general, these data were collected for purposes other than demonstrating the level and change of income distribution in society.

We are thus faced with multiple forms of ignorance: with fewer nations taxing wealth in comparison to income, trends in the former become difficult to measure with any precision, or even to detect. In some cases, such as that of the (legal) use of tax havens by the 2012 Republican US presidential candidate Mitt Romney, the facts were known to the tax authorities but not willingly disclosed to the public. Most especially in the farcical context of these acts being perpetrated by an individual aspiring to a nation's highest office in government, there is much to applaud in Norway's publication of all tax returns on the internet in 2005, an intervention that appears to have served as an inhibition to tax avoidance.[85]

In general, however, there is only a murky distinction between tax avoidance and evasion, and in the gap in our ignorance between levels and trends in income, on the one hand, and wealth, on the other. Tax havens are 'now at the heart of the global economy',[86] but 'The subterranean system that we are trying to measure is the economic equivalent of an astrophysical black hole', with a significant fraction of global private financial wealth, at least $21 to $32 trillion as of 2010, being invested virtually tax-free in more than 80 offshore secrecy jurisdictions. This calculation embodies only financial wealth, and 'excludes real estate, yachts, racehorses, gold bricks... [that] are also owned via offshore structures'.[87]

Unsurprisingly, these considerations might well cause significant alterations in our perception of the levels and rates of change of inequality worldwide, if only full information were available. The self-righteous complaints emanating from the rich about the devastating effects of corruption on the development of poor countries should be put in the following context: the looted funds invariably land for safe keeping and investment in financial institutions under the ownership and potential control of those very rich nations that are offering their sage advice on the virtues of good governance. Ignorance and confusion on the part of the public and regulatory authorities concerning liability for tax and the very existence of various income streams are exacerbated further at the level of the multinational company. These problems emerge not only due to the existence of tax havens as a repository for profits made abroad, but because of the common exercise by companies of a range of transfer pricing abuses that effect the movement of profits to low-tax jurisdictions.[88]

The political economy of the mitigation or elimination of these abuses has many aspects. Dealing with tax havens involves piercing the veil of secrecy with fairly straightforward administrative devices, such as automatic information exchange among tax authorities and public registries showing the true owners beneath the maze of beneficial ownership, trusts and foundations:[89] there do not appear to be any deep conceptual problems involved in dealing with this issue.[90] The case of correcting transfer pricing abuses on the part of multinational firms is more complex. The institution of unitary taxation[91] – treating the multinational as an entity and then apportioning tax appropriately to the countries involved – will involve dealing with an appropriate allocation of a multinational's profits to each geographical location, a problematic issue because of the interconnections between regional centres in generating the firm's profits, and because these regional centres might not invariably correspond to national boundaries. But, while this is difficult, we are not very far from the classic accounting problem encountered in Chapter 3 of the correct allocation of profits within a diversified firm, in this case to their appropriate geographical location, which invariably has to be solved by multinational managers: starting with a consolidated balance sheet, the provenance of profits must be traced so that the performance of subdivisions within the company can be evaluated. The conceptual issues involved in the taxation and regulation of multinational firms are no more complex than those that have to be solved by the managers of these firms themselves.

The major obstacles to regulation and control of both tax havens and the transfer pricing activities of multinational companies are not the objective complexities involved, but the political economy of blockage – the need to battle against 'the army of bankers, law firms, lobbyists, and public relations firms working at the behest of the beneficiaries of tax havens'[92] and the broad array of opposition to unitary regulation and taxation that has been mounted by multinational firms.[93] Thus, a 2009 agreement of the G20 compelled tax havens to sign bilateral treaties providing for exchange of bank information, but tax evaders appear to have simply shifted deposits to havens not covered by a treaty with their home country;[94] the Tax Justice Network, commenting on a 2013 OECD report of a new global standard for countries and tax havens to exchange information with each other, has expressed concern 'that powerful tax haven interests have inserted themselves into positions of influence in the OECD and forthcoming Global Forum Process'.[95]

From a socialist perspective, the leading impediment to the regulation and control of these abuses is a continued adherence to a capitalist ideology of the sacrosanct nature of private property. But there are ambiguities – perhaps even an ambivalence – in mainstream approaches to this question. As noted in Chapter 10, the apologia offered by American liberals for an acquiescence to inequality is its perceived role in the creation of wealth (the 'trade-off between equity and efficiency').

With, thus, even American liberals, those mildest of social democrats, making their support for inequality contingent on its delivering the goods, can we not have some sympathy with those right-wing analysts who view social democrats and American liberals, despite their protestations, as fundamentally socialist in outlook – individuals whose support even for private property itself is no more solid than its delivery of successful economic outcomes? By contrast, the justification for private property for the right-wing economist Milton Friedman is on the far more secure basis, following John Locke, of 'the ethical proposition that an individual deserves what is produced by the resources he owns... In my judgment, this proposition is... part of the reason why society has accepted the market system and its associated methods of reward.'[96]

This principled, Lockean justification for private property, that 'an individual deserves what is produced by the resources he owns', plays a subtle but pervasive role – a kind of cosmic background radiation – that helps to perpetuate abuses such as the tax haven and multinational manipulation to avoid taxes. The most impeccable official sources can tell us that 'Private-sector transparency is indispensable to business, and can be brought about through the use of standards as well as auditing and accounting practices that ensure access to information in a timely manner.'[97] But, as we have seen above, public disclosure (and therefore disclosure even to its owners, the shareholders) can be inhibited by the possibility, or the excuse, that valuable information will be passed on to competitors, revealing information to others.[98] This is the same excuse used by politicians for withholding information from the public – it will also fall into the hands of the enemy. It remains to be seen whether recent action in the European Parliament endorsing the creation of public registers for companies that give details on beneficial owners and trusts will succeed in piercing the anonymity and secrecy that currently is part of the ordinary way of doing business.[99]

There is good reason to think that these reforms, and others like them, will ultimately go nowhere. This is not so much because the fungibility and fluidity of wealth in the modern world make it impossible to trace, nor, in the end, is it merely a question of the overt corruption of the officials monitoring and executing these reforming directives. It is, rather, that tax havens and their equivalents will continue to have durability and a robustness as long as the dominant ideology among those making decisions is the Friedmanite position that 'an individual deserves what is produced by the resources he owns', with these decision makers, as wealth holders themselves, the personal beneficiaries of this ideology.

The inviolability of an individual's ownership of private property underwrites the legitimacy of the secrecy attached to beneficial owners and trusts. The long-held notion of the personhood of a company was perhaps most definitively established in the US, with a Supreme Court ruling as far back as 1819 giving it, by implication, the rights of a private citizen, including rights to privacy in the conduct of business affairs. The public (as well as the company's workforce) are residual claimants and may interfere in the conduct of a company's 'personal' affairs, such as its transfer pricing practices, only under exceptional circumstances. In recent years, as noted above, the idea of the company as a person has been imaginatively extended by a range of US Supreme Court rulings to include the freedom to make donations to political campaigns.

Tax havens and secrecy surrounding the ownership of world-spanning companies ultimately gain ballast from the continuing centrality of the seventeenth-century ideology of the inviolability of private property, the ludicrous notion that what a great multinational does is its private business, and from the powerful vested interests supporting these ideas. At the same time, however, as we shall see below, business and company spokespeople pose in the media as disinterested representatives of the public welfare when discussing the economy or even their own businesses. Firms pursuing military contracts gained from authoritarian regimes will not only be applauded for boosting employment in the national economy, but (except in those embarrassing instances when the recipients turn into foes) will receive support from the political leaders of their own countries in acquiring these contracts: this is in contrast to labour unions, which are presented in the media as representing merely a sectarian interest.

Are we, then, to view the working population and the public interest as mere residual claimants in the conduct of economic affairs? A contrary perspective is that 'Without real accounting and financial transparency and sharing of information, there can be no economic democracy. Conversely, without a real right to intervene in corporate decision making (including seats for workers on the company's board of directors), transparency is of little use.'[100] A variant of the latter perspective will be defended below.

The conflict between the public welfare and a privileging of the rights of private property can be seen with particular acuity in the context of patent protection. A broad consensus in the empirical literature of economics has emerged that strong patent systems tend to be dysfunctional and inefficacious,[101] with the benefits in the form of weak incentive effects easily neutralised and even reversed by the barriers to entry created by established firms.[102] In a manner consistent with the narrative concerning the emergence of the semiconductor industry in Chapter 9, competition and first-mover advantages, rather than patents, seem to be the prime impetus to innovation from privately owned firms. Academic specialists concerned with innovation are not averse to considering a general abolition of the patent system.[103]

But even if every economist in the US were to support abolition, it would be safe to make the prediction that Elijah will come down in his fiery chariot before the US voluntarily dismantles its patent system. On the contrary, recent times in the US have evidenced 'an enormous increase in the number of patents and in the strength of their legal protection'.[104] The US government, both directly (usually in complicity with other rich nations) and through its surrogate influence on the World Trade Organization and other organs, promotes stern regimes of Intellectual Property Rights (IPRs).[105] It does so because of the lobbying power of established firms whose economic value is tied to the monopoly rents gained on these IPRs. But there is a second reason: with much of these rents extracted from other countries (often poor ones),[106] strict IPR regulation is seen in the US (and many other rich countries) to serve the national interest. This fusion of the capitalist ideology of the inviolability of private property with nationalism is a common one, and is the antithesis of a socialist focus on the public interest and international solidarity.

These considerations – the free flow of information, the ideology of the inviolability of private property, and nationalism – bear on the question posed above concerning the requisites of a real, functioning democracy. Why have democratic institutions and procedures in the US and the UK done so little to halt the 'slow, steady slide towards economic oligarchy' in the US',[107] most especially in the context of a public in the US and elsewhere that apparently supports more egalitarian distributions of income and wealth than those presently existing?[108] Note that from a socialist perspective, democratic decision making is a good thing in itself, and not merely because it might lead to efficacious outcomes. Thus, a disproportionate influence by an economic elite is undesirable even when it emerges in an 'enlightened' form.[109]

The presence of economic crisis exacerbates the problems of democratic polity, as the great mass of the population may view themselves as mere spectators in a contestation between different elite groupings.[110] A public feeling not only bewildered, dispirited and insecure, but powerless, is then viewed by opinion makers as unpredictable, unstable and irresponsible. Elites commonly view practical politics as the art of manipulating a mass public bereft of the knowledge base for rational decisions.[111] In the absence of real agency on the part of the public – a functioning democracy – politics is perceived as a conflict between elite groupings and special interests, all vying for government favour.

With an implicit acceptance of such a context, contemporary political and economic debate is consumed with minimising the rent seeking that accrues to special interests from government favour. Much of the intellectual ballast for free-market developments, including deregulation, in the last quarter of the twentieth century was the claim by right-wing theorists that the deleterious effects of state–market interaction could be remedied by relying wholly on a market-based spontaneous order through deregulation and privatisation. By contrast, more recent left-of-centre critiques by Joseph Stiglitz and others of the economic order that has emerged after decades of these right-wing reforms focus on the need for explicit public policy intervention to minimise the rent seeking engendered by the persistent, and perhaps increasingly intimate, relations between the state and private interests.[112] In most of these conceptualisations, the public is a passive spectator witnessing the unfolding of these conflicts.

The US is a dramatic, well-documented case of special interest – overwhelmingly, private sector business influence – on state policy. Expenditure by registered lobbyists in Washington has doubled in nominal terms since the beginning of the century, with the leading three sectors being miscellaneous business, health, and finance/insurance/real estate.[113] Real estate has been subject to special scrutiny, most especially in the wake of the financial crisis of 2007–8, for the employment of revolving door lobbyists – those who previously worked for the federal government in sectors for which they are now lobbying.[114] The question of special interest campaign finance is a particularly serious matter in the context of US politics. The Democratic Party is by no means immune to reliance on donations from big business: the role of the latter in the making of substantive policy in the Obama administration would appear to be only marginally less than in an equivalent Republican government.[115] The personal economic status of politicians in the US (and the UK as well) also creates a distance between their lives and those of ordinary Americans.[116]

It would be deceptive, however, to paint a picture of capitalist economies so far under the control of special interests that public policy is completely dysfunctional. Among lobbyists in the US, health is ranked second only to miscellaneous business, and the lobbyists' money seems to be well spent: pharmaceutical companies are able to extract prices from health providers that are two to ten times greater in the US than in a range of other countries.[117] The obverse of these statistics is that the power of the great drug companies is not insurmountable: intervention by national governments substantially weaker than the federal government of the US permits them to reduce the costs of often life-giving drugs to their citizens. Even in the US, however, the free flow of information can inhibit the largest pharmaceutical companies, with the latter feeling the need to reduce payments to health professionals for promotional speeches in the context of a range of federal lawsuits over improper marketing of drugs; the coming on stream of the Physician Payment Sunshine Act, a part of the 2010 health reform law, requires all pharmaceutical and medical device companies to publicly report payments to physicians.[118]

Voter ignorance is often seen as reinforcing an alienation from the political processes in generating the public's passive role in public affairs. The suggestion is made that many voters, especially in the US, are confused or even deluded about current affairs, including the present state of inequality,[119] a situation that permits manipulation and often leads to demagogic and dysfunctional political behaviour. It is possible, however, to change the emphasis in this analysis and find something positive to say about the possibilities for public policy intervention on the basis of an important study comparing knowledge of public affairs among the general population in various countries.[120] It appears that knowledge of substantive issues in the news is consistently higher in countries with a high (Finland, Denmark) or intermediate (Great Britain) level of public service broadcasting compared with the US, whose commercially driven, marketised model is growing in predominance worldwide. Perhaps even more striking, however, is that the gap in knowledge on the basis of income and education is much wider in the US than in countries with an important public service component.

An important corollary of these results is that a fatalistic approach to the public's supposed ignorance of public affairs and its deleterious effects on public life is uncalled for: there appear to be substantive public policy interventions that can affect the level of the public's *in situ* knowledge that are literally in the air. The key result of this study, however, is that 'being interested is the single most important correlate of hard news knowledge in all four countries',[121] a less than shocking result for those of us who have spent our lives teaching classrooms of students. Two questions arise, the first of which was addressed earlier: what are the processes in school that cause such a large percentage of children to perceive that public affairs are not their concern? The second question deals with adults: can full participation in a democratic polity be possible unless involvement and influence are part of the lived experience of individuals in their daily lives, most especially at work? In the absence of an inculcation of democratic habits in daily life, is it surprising that, for much of the population, the conduct of political affairs is somebody else's business?

The political economy of work

As we have seen in Chapter 2, a key aspect of modernity in the functioning of capitalist enterprise was the emergence in the late nineteenth and early twentieth centuries of clear lines of control and delineation of tasks between staff, line and workers. Developments of this kind were indubitably necessary for rational organisation of the giant entities that were emerging. But these changes took place in the context of existing class divisions, and, especially in the US, there was a determined and explicit effort by management to give detailed direction to the work process in the form of Taylorism. These issues – the control of the firm in the form of staff and line delineation, and conflicts over the work process – are thus fundamental to questions surrounding democratic control of the workplace and the work process, and therefore the fabric of daily life.

Unions (trade unions in British terminology) have historically played a key role in determining outcomes in both economic and political spheres. Unions influence economic outcomes, even in the context of worldwide developments favouring capital vis-à-vis labour, by mitigating the effects of this changing balance: a strong relationship appears to exist between union organisation and wage compression across countries, with declining union representation linked to widening wage inequalities.[122] These effects tend to spill over to non-union workers even when the latter are not formally covered under collective bargaining agreements, so that the spread of the distribution of wages nationwide is tied to levels of union organisation.[123]

The changing balance favouring capital vis-à-vis labour also appears to be present in the deteriorating environment within the firm for workers, as we have seen in Chapter 8, with reductions in autonomy, intensified employee supervision and stronger Taylorist-type pay and performance systems. Unions appear to play a role in mitigating the worst effects of these developments, with evidence across Europe of a direct relationship between union power and the extent of task discretion afforded to workers within enterprises.[124] In many European settings, unions supplement works councils and institutionalised co-determination as forms of worker representation for dealing with worker grievances, as well as conducting negotiations over such issues as the nature of apprenticeships.[125] By contrast, with the US typically functioning under an employment-at-will doctrine in which the firm 'owns the job', US workers typically find themselves exercising complaints in the form of litigation, often at the individual level. Worker discontent, however, is most commonly expressed by exit from the job, resulting in the distinctively high level of job mobility in the US.[126]

There can be little doubt that, in both the economic and the political domain, unions have been 'very much on the defensive'[127] in rich countries since 1980, despite no obvious trend in numbers covered by collective bargaining agreements.[128] In the US and the UK as well as some other countries, however, there have been sharp reductions in union membership and coverage in the private sector, and only a small percentage of this decline can be accounted for by economy-wide movements away from traditionally unionised blue collar work.[129] In the US at least, the exceptionally high and even intensified level of employer opposition to union organising appears to have played an important role in these developments.

The rationale and the welcome for these developments in many quarters are often linked to a conception of human labour found in orthodox economic theory, in which it functions like any other commodity and is subject to laws of supply and demand. It is hard to imagine any set of facts that would modify this orthodoxy for its adherents, or its corollary – that the key to dealing with unemployment is for labour to become more attractive to employers. The typical mechanisms put forth for promoting this enhanced attractiveness are the removal of inhibitions on management for the setting of low remuneration for marginal workers and, in general, permitting management to use its workers as it sees fit – making it easier to fire workers and place them on flexible contracts, with a minimisation of worker autonomy. In all of these aspects, unions function as obstacles to management exercising freedom of action.

But if this orthodoxy has a modicum of validity, and the only path to full employment is one that validates present-day income inequalities and puts workers' working careers solely at the whim of employers, then so much the worse for capitalism. Present-day developments are offering a range of unattractive economic prospects for much of the workforce, with a decline in union power internationally linked to an exacerbation of inequality and a reduction of autonomy and voice in the workplace. In political terms, the effect of this decline, perhaps most striking in the US, has been to weaken the only significant countervailing force to an ever more blatant and explicit intervention from the interests of capital in the financing of political contests and the conduct of affairs of state.[130] This declining power of unions has also enervated their ability to support progressive politics in general, and specifically measures, such as the minimum wage, that in the past have mitigated rises in inequality. More profoundly, this decline has constrained the ability of unions to participate in the construction of broadly based alternatives to the neoliberal order. The building of a political economy for workplace affairs will invariably begin with a consideration of the best present-day examples of intervention in capitalist society and then attempt to advance upon them.

Management–employee relations in many rich countries appear to be moving in a direction typically found in the US:

> the basic thrust of developments in the industrial relations systems of advanced capitalism, involving the generalized weakening of unions or even the substitutions of unions with other collective actors, the erosion of bargaining coverage and the transfer of ever more regulatory matters to the firm level, and the increase in the heterogeneity of negotiated provisions to match a similar heterogeneity in market conditions, is unequivocally neoliberal in character despite differences in institutional form.[131]

How far other countries will move in the direction of US labour relations remains to be seen. As of 2009, one study for the US dealing with union organising reports that 'employers threatened to close the plant in 57% of elections, discharged workers in 34%, and threatened to cut wages and benefits in 47% of elections. Workers were forced to attend anti-union one-on-one sessions with a supervisor at least weekly in two-thirds of elections. In 63% of elections employers used supervisor one-on-one meetings to interrogate workers about who they or other workers supported, and in 54% used such sessions to threaten workers.'[132] The absence of union power, as in the US, thus appears to impinge not only on economic outcomes in the workplace such as wage inequality, but also on the fabric of life – the human rights connected with the workplace. In sections of the US, with its relatively weak unions, those rights, including the right to organise, are frequently violated.[133] By contrast, union power has continued to inform and shape politics and legislation in many countries.[134]

The economic and political roles of unions are thus intertwined. It is useful in this context to follow a typology outlined by Jonas Pontusson to represent a range of regimes focusing on the role of labour.[135] First, liberal market economies, epitomised by the UK and, especially, the US, are characterised by weak union membership and coverage (30 and 35 per cent, respectively, in the UK and 12 and 13 per cent in the US), with these unions being seen to have minimal impact on political processes and legislation; labour relations are typically dominated by the employment-at-will doctrine specified above.

At least some of the present-day weaknesses of unions in the UK and the US can be attributed to past failures in the strategies undertaken by organised labour in these countries. In Britain, a seemingly powerful labour movement in the postwar period interacted with the Labour Party to produce a political economy singularly lacking in vision, direction and purpose (see Chapter 5). One conclusion that emerges from the cases of both the UK and the US is the long-term failure of their respective economistic approaches, in which unions functioned almost exclusively to improve the pay and conditions of their workers. In contrast with the political approach of unions in Scandinavia, Anglo-Saxon unions often gave relatively little consideration to the broader economic and political context in which they were functioning and showed a lack of consideration for the effects of their actions on the rest of the working public: in the context of a precipitous decline in membership in recent decades, these unions have now been attempting to do what they should have been doing decades ago – to extend representation to women, workers in the public sector and in service industries, the low paid, and ethnic and racial minorities.

Unions everywhere have had to cope with the weakening labour market conditions emerging with the end of the postwar capitalist boom in the 1970s, but the deterioration of union power in these Anglo-Saxon economies has been exceptional. In the UK, the pursuit of an economistic strategy played a role in the rise of Thatcherism, with trade union activity seen by a broad section of the public to be opportunistic and merely of benefit to a sectional interest. With an implicit concession of 'the right of management to manage', trade unions were perceived to be irresponsible – resistant to the imperatives of technological change and modernisation, but offering up little in the way of alternatives for dealing with these realities. The maintenance in Britain of an archaic 'trade union' structure meant that, on occasion, the public was confronted with stoppages emanating from disputes over jurisdiction between trade unions, rather than with management.

US unions have followed a similar path, with an economistic strategy for unions declared at the beginning of the twentieth century by Samuel L. Gompers; there followed a more politicised interwar period involving

New Deal legislation and the emergence of the Congress of Industrial Organizations (CIO). In the postwar US, however, the Gompers approach triumphed, with unions hardly participating at all in the formation of economic and social policy, devoting themselves exclusively to the interests of 'their' workers – a category that often excluded, among others, female, non-white and public service workers. The main union body, the American Federation of Labor-Congress of Industrial Organizations (AFL-CIO), was linked to the state in its role as an appendage to US Cold War foreign policy.

The liberal market labour regime is a stylised version of the political economy of unions as it has emerged in the UK and the US since the 1980s, and is viewed unfavourably both in this book and by Pontusson. It is to be contrasted with two kinds of regimes characterised by substantially greater union influence. The second regime, the Nordic (Denmark, Finland, Norway and Sweden), has levels of union membership ranging from 50 to 70 per cent, and coverage from 74 to over 90 per cent.[136] The third regime considered is a continental model focused around France and Germany, but embracing a range of other countries – Austria, Belgium, Switzerland and the Netherlands – among which the rate of union membership can fall below 10 per cent (France), but where union coverage ranges from 63 to 99 per cent.[137]

In the synthetic representation here, Nordic social democracy is characterised by high levels of commitment to education. Its most characteristic aspect in this regard is an emphasis on late streaming and broadly based learning, with an important academic component present even in courses with a vocational orientation. This broadly based training cultivates flexibility in the workforce, with Nordic-style regimes having relatively limited inhibitions about job shedding by employers and a minimal gap between established (insider) workers and marginal, peripheral workers (outsiders), who are more likely to be young. Complementing these approaches are a range of ALMP to re-equip workers for new jobs and wage compression, most especially as stylised in the Rehn–Meidner model of postwar Sweden:[138] wage compression supports successful firms by dampening wage gains at the top and by squeezing inefficient firms with relatively high wages at the low end. The efficiency characteristics of this system are reinforced by the provision of universal benefits that obviate the problems surrounding poverty traps on means-tested benefits. The direct public provision of social services financed out of general taxes (rather than earmarked payroll contributions) further facilitates labour mobility in the Nordic model; high levels of female participation in the labour force are promoted by the generous provision of child care and elderly facilities.

By contrast, the continental variant is a more firm-based notion, with worker protection of jobs across cycles, strong laws against worker dismissal and the promotion of safety standards and hours reduction. Job training and skills development take place inside the firm or are sectorally based, with the specific skills regimes developed closely linked to the specific firm or sector. Such programmes support low job turnover and are reinforced by a political economy of employer support for generous unemployment benefits and job protection schemes. Many of these schemes are occupationally (and sometimes sectorally) based. The close link between workers' remuneration and skills development with the firm or sector in question lends itself to strong on-going union representation and the latter's emphasis on job security within the firm. As a consequence, these regimes put special emphasis on worker voice and democratic control through programmes of worker participation and co-determination.

Versions of the Nordic model often receive support from commentators, including Pontusson and Lindert, because of their presumed relative success in adapting to capitalism in the present difficult period. In Pontusson's case, the Nordic model facilitates economic restructuring by the promotion of labour flexibility. This is in contrast with a continental model that is more tied to security and skills development for workers within established firms and sectors. But, most especially in the period since the eruption of the financial and eurozone crises, all regimes have proved inadequate from the perspective of working people. Both the Nordic emphasis on the need for the creation of opportunities for individual development, especially for young people, and the continental focus on the establishment of adequate levels of job security and continuity of existence are reasonable demands to make of a well-functioning advanced economy that, as we have seen, are not being met.

The perspective here is that both of these stylised variants represent convergent and conflicting aspects in a workplace context of socialist aspirations described in the Introduction. In a crude sense, the Nordic model appeals to the former of the two fundamental aspects of socialism, emphasising individual opportunities for self-realisation and full development of personal capacities. Thus, 'access to upbringing and education from the earliest stages of life that is not contingent on, and compensates for, limitations in household circumstances' is reflected by educational systems of the Nordic variant that emphasise late streaming and broadly based learning, and possess an important academic component even in courses with a vocational orientation. The direct public provision of social services financed out of general taxes in the Nordic model, and the generous provision of child care and elderly facilities, promotes 'a mitigation of the forms of deprivation and insecurities to which households are subject', while ALMP and, in addition, adult education are consistent with attempts to promote 'opportunities for employment that involve full exercise and realisation of personal capacities'.

But a single-minded focus on personal achievement and development can easily turn the Nordic variant into a form of capitalist individualism flavoured by egalitarianism. The continental model, by contrast, is linked to the perception that, for a large portion of the population, continuity of employment in a particular skill or profession, and in a particular enterprise, is likely to play a key role in the maintenance of household security, most especially for those in mid- to late career. The notions of managerial theorists that we are all going to spend our lives functioning as entrepreneurs, changing jobs and careers every few years, are fanciful and, for many individuals, highly undesirable. The continental variant emphasises the role of collective solidarity within the workforce, with ordinary workers having opportunities to exercise control over the enterprise and also take responsibility for its destiny. These firm-based continental approaches lend themselves to the fulfilment of the notion that democracy must embody 'substantial levels of participation in decision making'.[139]

Extensions of the continental variant, from cooperatives to other forms of worker-controlled organisations, have thus been put forth as theoretical and practical alternatives to capitalism from its earliest days to the present.[140] For John Stuart Mill in the nineteenth century, worker control of enterprises was intimately linked to the progress of democracy:

> The poor [a term conflated by Mill with manual labourers] have come out of leading-strings, and cannot any longer be governed or treated like children...Modern nations will have to learn the lesson, that the well-being of a people must exist by means of the justice and self-government...of the individual citizen...The form of association...which if mankind continue to improve, must be expected in the end to predominate, is not that which can exist between a capitalist as chief, and work-people without a voice in the management, but the association of the labourers themselves on terms of equality, collectively owning the capital with which they carry on their operations, and working under managers elected and removable by themselves.[141]

Thus, alongside a pervasive narrative that has associated capitalism with democratic political institutions, there has been a countervailing one: democratic polity cannot readily be associated with capitalism because the latter is dominated by a work relation that contains the 'capitalist as chief, and work-people without a voice in the management'.[142]

Can organisations owned and controlled by their workers be operated efficiently? The analytical literature yields ambiguous results. It is at the level of the work process itself that the greatest claims are made for the efficiency benefits of worker involvement. Workers' monitoring of fellow employees is likely to be an efficacious way of guarding against shirking by individual employees.[143] More ambitiously, it has been suggested that 'A large body of evidence shows...the importance of worker involvement in the productivity improvements that contribute to making their own jobs, and the companies for which they work, competitive on a global scale.'[144] If true, this is an issue of importance, given the emphasis placed in earlier chapters on the role of dispersion and adaptation of new technology, as opposed to its creation *de novo*.

In dealings with the wider world, an early theoretical contribution suggested that worker-controlled enterprises, even in a competitive context, might behave in a perverse manner: a rise in the market price will cause firms to reduce output and workers employed (perhaps an implausible assumption in a worker-managed enterprise) in order to maximise profits per head for the remaining members.[145] Of greater substantive interest than this anomalous response in a static context are the divergent ways in which worker-managed enterprises might deviate from capitalist firms in their investment behaviour. A common conclusion is that enterprises with a cooperative or worker-managed orientation will, compared with equivalent capitalist firms, choose capital-intensive technologies when investing in new projects.[146] Such a capital bias was often seen as an obstacle to the generation of employment in the pre-1989 Yugoslav economy, with its widespread presence of worker-managed enterprises. Note, however, that the Rehn–Meidner plan in Sweden, discussed above, intentionally used high wages at the low end of the payments spectrum to eliminate low-wage, labour-intensive employment and as part of a strategy to encourage technological upgrading in the economy.

But the very notion that the worker-managed enterprise might over-invest in capital-intensive projects has been questioned. There are several reasons to suggest that, on the contrary, such enterprises might suffer from a shortfall of capital investment compared with a typical profit-maximising capitalist firm.[147] First, long-term investments by the firm might be constrained by the time horizon of typical members: they may be unwilling to make present-day sacrifices to invest in long-term projects that will be largely of benefit to future members. Second, firms managed and owned by workers may suffer restrictions on the capital that can be raised compared with a typical capitalist enterprise. Worker-run firms are likely to find it more difficult to make creditable guarantees to outsiders that they will constrain remuneration to workers, or that they will not make overly risky investments, leaving outside creditors holding the bag. Contrarily, risk-averse workers who feel committed, or locked in, to a lifetime of employment with a given firm may absent themselves from innovation and choose overly safe, low-return projects.

In general terms, only the capitalist firm has a well-defined objective: to maximise the value of the firm (including taking on the appropriate amount of risk) consistent with the needs and desires of the owner: there is no other constituency. It is in the context of investment, most especially in risky projects, that the well-defined nature of this capitalist constituency comes into prominence: as we have seen in Chapter 5, in the 1980s, as the telephone industry morphed into the multi-branched telecommunications sector, the formerly nationalised industries in most countries gave way to a range of projects in which the question of how much to invest in these new ventures was largely undertaken by individuals risking their own wealth.[148]

The problem of whether a worker-managed enterprise invests 'too much' or 'too little' compared with a capitalist firm is symptomatic of the complex constituency it has to satisfy. Like the capitalist firm, it has a social role to play in the efficient production of goods and services that it needs to fulfil if it is to survive. For perhaps a majority of its own workers, however, the enterprise is key to continuity of employment in a particular skill or profession and the maintenance of household security. These factors will invariably impinge upon firm decision making when workers have opportunities to exert control over the enterprise and take responsibility for its destiny. Other workers within the enterprise, however, will have desires and aspirations to develop careers and change employment, and these intentions will pull the firm in other directions.

This conflict between workers' aspirations that go both in a continental and in a Nordic direction, when combined with the exigencies of fulfilling the demands of the market, have tended to constrain the development of worker-managed enterprises. Unlike capitalist firms, whose growth and development are inhibited by failure, worker and cooperative management of an enterprise can also be shattered by its very success. The prominent electronics firm Varian Associates, discussed in Chapter 9, functioned as a workers' cooperative in the early postwar world, but by the late 1950s this structure began to fall apart, incumbent upon its growth and profitability. As a commercial entity, it experienced difficulties in securing outside finance for expansion because of its ownership structure; the cooperative form also inhibited individual members of the enterprise, some of whom were approaching retirement age, from reaping the full value of their share of the enterprise in an open market because they were required to sell their ownership rights back to the cooperative.[149]

The notion of the worker-controlled organisation has played the role of a theoretical antipode and alternative to the capitalist enterprise since the latter's earliest days. But workers' cooperatives have remained 'a peripheral form of organization that prospers only in narrow niches'.[150] Supporters of the worker-owned and controlled organisation as an 'alternative to capitalism' often point to the Mondragón cooperative centred in the Basque region of Spain as a prime example of the form's economic viability.[151] Functioning since the 1950s, it is by far the largest such organisation in the world, entering the twenty-first century with the participation of 80,000 workers, 110 federated cooperatives and 147 subsidiary companies. In 2013, Mondragón announced that its historically most important unit, the Fagor Electrodomésticos Group, was filing for bankruptcy protection.[152]

The Mondragón cooperative continues to be a source of controversy because of its symbolic role in the cooperative movement. In recent years, claims to success include a sharp compression, relative to comparable capitalist firms, of the ratio of top executive remuneration to that of its lowest-paid workers,[153] and its efforts to protect the employment of its members in the severe conditions of the contemporary Spanish labour market. In other ways, however, Mondragón does not serve as a model that could be widely replicated across the capitalist world. The long-term practices in Mondragón – the screening of applicants and the payment of an up-front entrance fee that cannot be refunded until retirement – signal an extreme version of the continental variant that is relevant only to those workers who are content to make a lifetime commitment to a particular enterprise. Furthermore, Mondragón offers only restricted employment protection and benefits to workers in its subsidiary companies, especially those located overseas, and there has been increasing centralisation of the top management structure since the 1990s. These developments reinforce concerns that, in general, the potential scale of viable, democratically controlled cooperative enterprises is severely limited.[154]

Mondragón makes no claims to innovation in the work process: at one point, its workers protested against the replacement of assembly line production with Swedish-style work teams, suggesting that they have no greater preference for forms of workplace experimentation that might threaten their remuneration than workers in capitalist firms.[155] Lastly, the question of how firms would interact in an economy dominated by worker-controlled enterprises has never been seriously addressed, even conceptually, so there can be no pretence that this form of organisation offers a solution to the pressing issues of macroeconomic stabilisation and full employment in the contemporary world: worker-controlled enterprises are, therefore, no 'cure for capitalism'.

More modest, but far more pervasive, forms of worker influence in the enterprise have involved elements of worker control without any important component of ownership.[156] In large firms across a range of European countries, worker or employee councils (almost always in the context of strong union influence) have rights to consultation on changes to working practices, dismissals and information about the general direction of the firm. In Germany, Austria, Sweden, Denmark and Luxemburg, these councils appoint representatives to a supervisory board of directors (a tier of control that supposedly supervises the activities of the executive management board). The consensus of research indicates that worker councils and representation on supervisory boards yield little in the way of influence on the fundamental decisions taken by the companies concerned; in recent years, there has been pressure in Germany to weaken the role of worker councils by shifting bargaining to the enterprise level and to weaken worker representation at the supervisory board level.

The establishment in law, however, of the right of workers to information and consultation about the company's future contrasts with the 'employment at will' and 'right of management to manage' of the liberal market regime characterised above. In a practical context, worker consultation probably plays its biggest role in negotiations concerning day-to-day practices, such as the installation of check-in clocks at work, and through its influence on government directives.[157] In recent times, a German job-share model, in which the government compensates workers for much of the lost wages when working hours are cut by employers, has been given credit for preserving employment in the downturn of 2007–8.[158]

In a world of rapid change, with workers having a wide range of needs and aspirations, it is inevitable that the political economy of work will have a strong component in the Nordic direction: the enterprise and its surrounding institutions must inevitably be a vehicle for individual development, one that conforms to the need for the cultivation of flexibility necessary for adapting to a range of tasks over a lifetime of work. But such an approach in its pure form could easily degenerate into a liberal market regime, albeit of a relatively egalitarian kind. For many workers, the continental emphasis on the cultivation of a focused range of skills, often within a specific enterprise, and continuous employment are central to their security and well-being. The notions of managerial theorists that demand an entrepreneurial flexibility across the population to accommodate perturbations in the market are unrealistic and, even if possible to fulfil, not necessarily desirable. For much of the population, the key aspiration is likely to be mitigation of what is perceived to be instability and insecurity at work.

Workplace democracy is an essential aspect of democratic polity: the incongruity between notions of democracy for society as a whole and a daily routine of command within the enterprise is manifestly obvious. An important component of worker control over the enterprise in the form of a substantive and not symbolic role in the enterprise's decision making will most probably need to be underpinned by worker holdings of shares in the company by which they are employed. Past successes by workers in improving life through political action, workplace activity and general solidarity are not to be underestimated. But only limited progress overall has been made in getting workplace activities to conform to the needs of those performing the work rather than to the desires of employers or the supposedly anonymous and inexorable forces of technology and the marketplace. Key roles in the cultivation of a new conception of work, one not based on authoritarian principles, will be played by diminutions in present-day class hierarchies, in the first instance by reductions in income and wealth inequalities. An important reinforcement of this *pro forma* equality will be the emergence of a new generation of young people who, as a result of their upbringing and experience in school, have learned to regard as normal a life of motivated work, democratic decision making and human solidarity.

But enterprises invariably have a broad constituency to which they are responsible. The parables above concerning worker control point to the difficulties of presuming that all the issues surrounding the day-by-day running and long-term development of the enterprise can simply be solved by a regime in which management is subject to the will of its workers: there are groups outside the enterprise that need representation in its decisions. In larger enterprises especially, the great majority of shares, in an economy far more egalitarian than the present one, are likely to be owned by the diversified holdings of workers outside the enterprise, most likely in pension funds. Any developing tension between these latter-day capitalists and workers in a worker-controlled enterprise is not necessarily undesirable, and may lead to productive resolutions – impelling equity and debt holders to be responsive to the needs of the workforce, but also reminding workers of the competitive exigencies of the outside world that may force change and adaptation for the sake of survival.

This latter force – that of competition – is often presumed to be sufficient to protect consumers, but a role for the state is widely granted in protecting them from bad business practices (adulteration of food), asymmetric information (the small print on terms and conditions of a bank loan) and monopolistic exploitation. The state, it is generally conceded, also has a role in regulating and disciplining the activities of the enterprise that adversely affect third parties. It is most probable that, in conventional sectors of the economy (that is to say, other than those in which the state will invariably play a leading role, such as in the development of technologies to cope with climate change), the state can best represent consumers and the public in an adversarial relationship to the enterprise, promoting, for instance, consumer protection and anti-monopolies legislation.

A last major issue returns us to the questions confronted in Chapter 8 concerning workplace learning, after which the future of work itself will be considered. For many individuals, the place of work is the main vehicle for the elevation of skills after leaving school. In a socialist context, it is an inherent and essential activity of the enterprise, not, as in a capitalist enterprise, bolted on to, and constraining, its value-maximising imperatives.

The notion of the enterprise as a venue for learning contains, however, a host of troublesome and difficult issues. First is the issue engaged with in Chapter 8: while the interests of the young worker and of the broader society are best served by the enterprise offering the broadest possible training, employers advocate a narrower, directly operational training. But enterprises may choose to satisfy such demands, if they are imposed from the outside, in a perfunctory manner: 'It is far easier to send people on formal training courses than to re-organize production processes or re-design jobs in order to expand opportunities for on-the-job and incidental learning.'[159] Even broad-based knowledge, if it is not to be received by workers merely as adding to their personal stock of credentials, must make a concrete contribution to the work process that is taking place within the enterprise.

A second consideration complicates the issue even further. In Chapter 8, doubts were raised about the common distinction between hand and brain work, and most especially any hierarchical ranking that privileges the latter. In the contemporary training literature, this critique frequently takes the form of questioning the superiority of abstract learning by individuals over context-dependent learning, the latter often being linked to group interaction in the work environment;[160] it is even suggested that the dichotomy between informal and formal learning is not meaningfully distinct, and that these forms of learning are mutually overlapping.[161] These discussions echo Dewey's distinction between activity-based and passive learning, seen in Chapter 7, and, like Dewey, much of this literature points to the efficacy of learning that takes place in a substantive, operational, goal-oriented process. The problem, however, is the ease with which activity-based learning within the firm can elide into narrowly focused task learning that is of only limited use to, especially, young workers confronting a long-term career and the likely need to acquire a broad-based repertoire of skills. The challenges in negotiating a balance between the acquisition of relevant, activity-based learning by workers and the acquisition of purely firm-specific knowledge would exist even within a worker-controlled enterprise, all the more in one engaged with the conflicting interests of capitalists and workers. The task is to construct institutions, and institutional arrangements, to ensure that regimes of broad-based learning for workers are sustainable and in workers' long-term interests.

Perhaps of even greater significance is the intimate relationship between high levels of training for workers and task discretion in the work process – the continuation of the century-old battle between skilled workers and Taylorist tendencies in management practice. As we have seen in Chapter 8, despite significant long-term rises in worker skills in recent decades, there is a clear and widespread perception of decreasing autonomy in job tasks.[162] These tendencies move in the opposite direction from the desired, socialist direction outlined for working life in Chapter 8 – an uplifting of skills accompanied by individual and collective task discretion by the workforce (the latter in itself conducive to learning in a work context), with a redesigning of the jobs themselves in the direction of professional identity, personal dignity and appropriate remuneration. In areas such as care for the elderly, which will inevitably expand in the future, the conflicts are likely to be particularly acute. The well-off will see to it that their own care is intensive, personalised and professional; for the great majority, however, under the banner of efficiency and affordability, a mass-produced service using the cheapest available labour is likely to be the norm. A professionalised service, with skill upgrading and task discretion, will be available only for those able to afford it.

We thus confront the spectre of a renewed form of Taylorism, with lack of task discretion linked to an underlying imperative of standardisation of delivery, and its natural concomitant – little need for high-level training for those workers executing these tasks. Note that a management strategy focused on standardised output and production protocols (such as the preparation of food in fast food outlets) may well take place even in the absence of any decisive forms of technological change that displace skilled workers. But the creation of such protocols sets the stage for the replacement by robots of unskilled workers who do repetitive tasks. Thus, in the recent book by Martin Ford, it is suggested that

> It's becoming increasingly clear...that robots, machine learning algo-rithms, and other forms of automation are gradually going to consume much of the base of the job skills pyramid. And because artificial intel-ligence applications are poised to increasingly encroach on more skilled occupations, even the safe area at the top of the pyramid is likely to contract over time. The conventional wisdom is that, by investing in still more education and training, we are going to somehow cram everyone into that shrinking region at the very top...[But] the numbers simply don't work.[163]

What is striking about this literature is how such a prospect is now greeted with such universal dread: many in the past would have treated the promise of the elimination of repetitive tasks at work as the dawn of an Athenian utopia of cultural efflorescence and democracy – one based on inanimate rather than human slaves. But Ford, like Paul Krugman (see Chapter 10), sees before him only the prospect of a sea of unemployment, to be allevi-ated by basic income schemes.[164] Ford and others are willing to indulge in wide-ranging speculation about the future:[165] it is just that their visions do not embody any confidence in the possibility of creative responses to the challenge of technological change that are linked to a comparable elevation in human capabilities.

At present, typical uses for new technology in services, such as on-line higher education or fast food, involve the creation of second-rate offerings that the well-off would not conceive of consuming themselves. But an alter-native path is conceivable. Human resources released from tasks that are now done by machines can, in the jobs worth doing programme described above, be redirected to offer to the general population the kinds of serv-ices the well-off take for granted in education, health care and care for the elderly. High-level services of this kind are not only labour-intensive in a quantitative sense, but call upon human judgement and task discretion. A focus on the development of these services will involve an elevation of the skills and an upgrading of the job descriptions for these tasks. In principle, such upgrading should be accompanied by a perceived enhancement of the dignity and status attached to these forms of employment. There appears, in addition, to be no lack of other jobs worth doing, even in rich countries, with a pressing need, for instance, for the reconstruction of the built environment. Such a focus is necessary to deal with the exigencies of climate change and other pressures that human beings are imposing upon nature; a focus on the built environment would also be desirable for the advancement of neighbourhoods suitable for the upbringing of children and the promotion of convivial interaction between households.

Perhaps, at some distant point in this century or the next, the seemingly inexorable development of technology will have so encroached on even the delivery of high-quality human-oriented services as to necessitate a substantial reliance on enforced hours reduction in order to keep the population at work, or to guaranteed incomes schemes. But such a happenstance seems far in the future: at present, there is a great deal of work to do.

The argument presented in Part III offers a path for human development in the form of education, social and economic equality, economic security and full employment. Democratic control of public affairs is facilitated by this human development, by policies to promote transparency in government and business, and by democracy in the workplace. In the last part of the discussion especially, concerned with the control of the enterprise, there is not a great deal to upset any but the most ardent advocates of free enterprise.

* * *

Is it socialism?

Conclusion

What is in a name? Some may argue with the use of the word 'socialism' to describe the ideas and policies adopted in the past chapters. From one perspective, there is little here of true socialism, with the notions presented here lacking many of its essential requisites: the abolition of private property – nationalisation or cooperative ownership of the means of production; a central plan for the coordination of economic activities; the elimination of money, finance and financial instruments as key allocative and distributive mechanisms in the economy.

More generalised objections from a true socialism perspective will observe that, in the programme proposed here, for perhaps the majority of human beings, their labour power will still be bought and sold on the market as a commodity. The alienation characteristic of capitalist life will still be present, with the great mass of the population exercising only limited control and influence over the work process. Furthermore, there is no mechanism comparable to central planning that claims to guarantee full employment. The latter remains here an aspiration rather than a structural characteristic of the economic system, and much of the ownership of the means of production, even if more widely dispersed than is typically found in contemporary capitalism, remains in private hands.

In the present day, the great majority of individuals objecting to the use of the term socialism here, even if they remain sympathetic to the policies presented, approach the question from a different point of view. For them, socialism carries with it a heritage of authoritarianism, adventurism and failure – the use of the term is an unnecessary burden for a programme that, in their view, reduces to little more than an intensive application of social democratic principles.

Why, then, call it socialism?

Let us review the nature of the programme that has been presented here. It is non-revolutionary, and abjures discontinuous change and quick fixes. On the contrary, it focuses on long-term developments and goals. Most worthwhile improvements in human life, whether external or internal to human beings themselves, take time to construct and for their beneficial effects to be realised. It is destruction that can take place quickly.

The creation of opportunities for the full development of human capacity across the population is to be realised by the intensive programme of child upbringing outlined earlier, most especially up to the age of 13. Tuition after 13 years will also be different from what exists at present, being modified in the context of what happened in the early years of schooling: there will be minimal streaming and segregation of groups by ability and between vocational and academic subjects. Opportunities to pursue interests and affinities in an intensive way will be present, but not to the exclusion of study relevant to citizenship. The ideal of tuition after age 13 is to be seen in the best examples of present-day elite university education, with guidance supplemented by substantial opportunities to pursue self-motivated and self-directed study, one major difference being a role for collective decision making by staff and students in the learning process, in place of present-day top-down directives. Free post-high-school tuition will be available to all, along with a lifetime of opportunities for education and personal development.

Equalisation of opportunities must also take place outside the domain of formal schooling – in the world and at work. Long-term full employment, an essential aspect of human development, is underwritten by macroeconomic stabilisation policies and reinforced by the jobs worth doing programme. And through the priorities and tasks pursued, the jobs worth doing programme, along with progressive taxation, makes a contribution to an equalisation of the economic environment in which households function and in which children grow up.

In addition to these aspects of socialism associated with personal realisation, democracy must be pervasive in the work context. Participants in the labour process are to be involved in decisions concerning the long-term trajectory of the enterprise and its detailed modes of operation, both as individuals and through collective representation. In a socialist context, the irreplaceable forms of learning that take place at work are an inherent aspect of its functioning and not, as in a capitalist environment, a concession that is, upon occasion, grudgingly conceded to the workforce. In the broader society, a necessary requisite of democracy is transparency – openness in governmental operations and political financing, and also concerning the activities of private entities such as multinational companies. Taxation systems, in order to be transparent, must not only preclude forms of tax avoidance, but must be intrinsically simple. Control of monetary and fiscal policies, as well as the financial sector in its detailed operations, is to be vested in individuals responsive to democratic control.

The binding of this programme under the rubric of socialism gives it a unity, focus and direction it otherwise would not have. Ideas and ideologies play a central role in the shaping of historical events, and are not merely reflections of underlying and supposedly deeper factors such as contemporaneous social structures and material conditions. The events incumbent upon the French Revolution of 1789, for both good and ill, emerged from a 'revolution of the mind' that had taken place in previous generations, rather than any decisive change in the material conditions of the population.[1] And socialism in the twentieth century was channelled, as we have seen, along a path of planning and centralisation to conform to a particular, and flawed, view of the trajectory of capitalist development.

A passive approach to the role of ideas is not only inadequate as historical analysis, but lets intellectuals off the hook. Principles, creeds and dogmas are often decisive determinants of real-world events. The demonstration of a link between belief systems and outcomes, when possible, not only yields a particularly coherent form of historical analysis, but may also be an appropriate guide to contemporary and future decisions. The abstract notions and schemes that shape concrete events are not purely the products of imagination or whimsy, but often reflect attempts to conceptualise and understand a complex and changing reality.

It is important here to underline the need for a break with present ways of doing things. The failures of contemporary capitalism, most especially the growth of inequality, have not come about because of some easily corrected aberration in capitalist development, such as a market failure or a policy approach gone wrong. They have emerged, as we have seen in earlier chapters, from the unfolding of the logic of the invisible hand, with an increasingly competitive economy greatly enhancing the power of capital over labour. The adoption of the name of an alternative path to capitalism – socialism – signals a movement away from present-day practices and reinforces resistance to the ever-present temptation to offer pragmatic reforms that start with capitalism but promise to 'do it better'.

Contemporary progressive approaches, accepting the realities of present-day capitalism, end up pursuing alleviationist strategies to social reform that are unfocused, defensive and reactive, and involve 'muddling through'. Without a well-defined alternative set of goals, progressive programmes are easily derailed by the practicalities of everyday life and the need to respond in a short-term manner to the crises emanating from capitalism itself. In the absence of a clear alternative strategy for development, capitalism, its attendant Hayekian spontaneous order and even its crises come across as natural, in which case responses typically involve an acceptance and passivity with regard to unfolding events (economic crises or growing inequality) or, at best, attempts at a short term alleviation of these problems. Even more directly, this abstract Hayekian notion that unfolding events in capitalism are spontaneous, natural and, perhaps, inevitable can be used to support market-friendly economic policies: anti-labour and anti-union measures receive rhetorical ballast when high levels of unemployment are perceived to represent not any intrinsic failure of capitalism, but wage levels that have been permitted to rise above their 'natural' level. And an acceptance of the inherently natural quality of capitalist institutions and relations means that even active, constructivist attempts to create a neoclassical utopia – market-style incentives and Taylorist forms of control imposed upon institutions and professions of all kinds – are seen as simply reinforcing an inherently natural way of doing things.[2]

At the rhetorical level, capitalism is often supported by a powerful individualism, a confluence of Darwinian survival-of-the-fittest ideas and a moralistic notion of rewarding individuals for hard work and achievement. Without a principled alternative path – which here is called socialism – the capitalist logic is easily internalised, with critiques of the existing order often reduced to slogans such as 'rewards based on work, not rent', or some other version of a fair form of capitalist distribution. An extreme form of this defensiveness and confusion can be found in the American liberal (progressive) tradition. Does, for instance, the catchphrase calling for defending the 'middle class' include single mothers, running two jobs, changing bed sheets in hotels? And once progressives have accepted and internalised the capitalist, Lockean principle of the inviolability of private property, public policies such as the control of cross-border financial flows by multinationals and the monitoring and control of tax havens can only be done apologetically and pragmatically, since the free disposal of one's property is a natural right – a part of the spontaneous order. Within the logic of capitalism, the assertion of the public good in these matters is a peripheral consideration.

The alternative, developmental approach presented here attests to the need for society to have goals, standards and directions. It offers a positive vision of the future, one based, first, on opportunities for self-realisation and full development of personal capacities and, second, on social citizenship, with individuals having the ability to exercise democratic control over public affairs on a regular basis, in both the working and the living environment.

The socialist framework centres progressive strategies around human development, social justice and democratic control: this framework then conditions the approach taken to substantive issues. Thus, enhanced education is not, as in the dominant contemporary view, to be promoted in order to accelerate the rate of economic growth, but, rather, serves the goals of self-realisation and democracy. The human focus of the socialist framework, furthermore, militates against the temptation to dub any strategy, such as state ownership and control of enterprises, as progressive simply because it is seen to contain an anti-laissez-faire aspect. Equality, furthermore, is seen in an intergenerational and societal context, rooted in self-realisation and democratic rule. The central question is: how, through time, do we create a society with broad-based opportunities for personal development and with democratic control? Such an approach is less likely than typical static, individualistic conceptions of equality to degenerate into sterile debates about whether the rewards to a particular individual are fair: the overriding issue is the creation of a good society.

The placing of equality as a central societal goal militates against it being displaced by other considerations in a crisis because it is a mere luxury, one that may well have to be traded off for the sake of greater efficiency. The underlying principle here – equality – gives a human focus to the notion of socialism, one that is absent in conceptions built around central planning. In contrast to a capitalist ideology often linked to a survival-of-the-fittest, social Darwinist individualism, socialism offers an alternative view of society that is rooted in classical (ancient Greek) concepts of personal realisation combined with citizenship and civic participation. Socialism rejects a fatalistic view of the human personality that is hard-wired at birth. In a socialist perspective, the development of the personality and skills of individuals is seen to be highly contingent on societal institutions and the nature of collective interaction, so that, for instance, the question of musical creation is less a matter of gawping at individual genius than of actively cultivating over time a vibrant musical culture from which individual creators can emerge. Broad-based household security can then be seen as a complementary aspect of equality in an intergenerational context, and especially in the earliest years of life, rather than a factor that discourages initiative and activity.

The view of democracy here is deeper than in typical contemporary conceptions. Democracy is seen as an active, on-going activity, and not just a form of negative liberty centred on the absence of state oppression. It is a process from the ground up, inculcated in a school environment that encourages active participation and carries on robustly in the workplace; it discourages a paternalistic notion of what *we* (those responsible for the conduct of public affairs) can do for *them* (the great mass of the population). The conduct of public affairs in a socialist democratic context, furthermore, implies a level of transparency for the monitoring and control of those in power that, by present standards, will appear to invade the privacy of the wealthy and corporations.

The association of the programme here with socialism links it to traditions of international brotherhood and solidarity and an abjuration of nationalism. Rich countries are not in a race or contest with China or anyone else. All nations need to pursue cooperative ventures on a range of common problems, most obviously with regard to pressing ecological issues such as climate change and the control of weapons systems. Such cooperation does not imply, in a socialist context, an accession to the brutal authoritarianism and repression of human (including workers') rights present in, for instance, China, or any other country: ruling groups in capitalist countries are often only too eager to look the other way in these matters under the guise of practicality, if there is good money to be made. Socialist ideology focuses on the support of oppressed people worldwide, rather than seeing international relations as a battle between 'us' and 'them'.

More positively, the socialist tradition of solidarity, cultivated within one's own country across broad groups in society, is the school from which rich countries can learn to cultivate a new relationship to the poorest ones. Within countries, socialist solidarity suggests that problems encountered domestically, such as poor levels of educational achievement or high rates of violent crime, are to be dealt with as issues that 'we' – the whole nation – must confront, rather than by way of vilification of specific ethnic, religious or immigrant groups: the socialist solidarity approach corresponds to that which would be used by most families having to deal with such issues. And solidarity also inculcates mutual respect between sections of the community, rather than simply imposing the dominant norms on 'lesser' groups. In an international context, for instance, residents of rich countries may wish to learn from a range of traditional methods of food preparation around the world on how to eat well without consuming large amounts of beef, given the negative ecological consequences of this practice.

In a more material context, socialist policies *within* rich countries are likely to be a necessary prerequisite for any new relationship *between* rich and poor countries. Such a new relationship will invariably involve, using various mechanisms, substantial transfers of resources to poor countries, whose resources and the fruits of whose labour rich countries purchase so cheaply. Whether a broad public in rich countries will support such policies is likely to be contingent on both economic and political considerations existing within these countries. Necessary, if not sufficient, economic conditions for the creation of a broad base of support in rich countries for economic transfers are, first, a wide perception that the burdens borne are to be shared in an equitable manner and, second, that the population functions in a context of sufficient material security to be able to contemplate the sacrifices necessary. Politically, broad-based accession to such a programme is more likely if the relevant decisions are seen as having been made in an open and democratic context, rather than having been imposed or executed by stealth. Thus, the economic and political considerations relevant to the creation of a new relationship between rich and poor countries correspond to those which lie at the centre of the construction of socialist democracy. The restricted focus in this book on the cultivation of socialism in the richest countries is by no means because rich countries' problems are of greater urgency or importance than those of poorer countries. Quite the contrary: a central purpose here has been to forge a strategy that is compatible with worldwide development and improvement in a concrete, realistic manner.

There are major obstacles to be confronted in the process of making the link between national or supra-national (e.g., the European Union) economic policies promoting equality, full employment and economic security, on the one hand, and international solidarity, on the other. Economic poli-cies to secure these national goals might well involve, at the very least on a short-term basis, restrictions on the free movement of labour across borders and, directly or indirectly (for instance, a bias in government procurement favouring national producers), limitations on free trade. Such policies in a broad sense militate against efforts to promote international economic solidarity, and will, in some cases, be seen to harm the interests of poor countries.

These difficulties are real, but most likely not insuperable. Longer-term solutions reconciling the desire of rich nations to maintain equality, full employment and economic security and those of poorer ones to pursue economic development through trade are conceivable. They can be seen in incipient form in the directives of the International Labour Organization covering remuneration and working conditions, stipulations most particu-larly relevant in the poorest countries. If carefully designed and successfully enforced, such directives permit trade expansion but inhibit a race to the bottom in wages and conditions, so that increased trade can take the form of genuine economic development in poor countries. But any reconciliation of this kind will only come about in the presence of a desire on the part of rich and powerful countries to bring it about, a development more likely to take place when the domestic environment of these countries is already committed to equality, full employment and economic security for their own residents.

If the state of affairs described above appears to be unsystematic and imprecise, and if it seems to demand, on the part of rich countries, a form of forethought, long-sightedness and even altruism that rarely occurs in the real world, the alternatives to a reconciliation of this kind border on the unthinkable. One possibility, a generalised submission by nations to the dictates of the market, might promote economic growth for some poor countries, but could well take place in the context of high exploita-tion of the workforce and an increasing inequality that promotes little true economic development. For many rich countries, such a regime is likely to engender, under present-day conditions, such powerful tendencies in the direction of inequality, unemployment and economic insecurity as to make the domestic political economy of such a situation increasingly unstable and unsustainable. An alternative strategy of generalised economic nationalism, often taking the form of the generation of sustained economic surpluses in the international arena by some nations, even when successful for the few, is likely to be a zero sum game for the system as a whole and, once again, to be unsustainable and unstable.

Most contemporary national economic strategies appear to be a combi-nation of the two approaches above. There is a widely accepted notion of the necessity of submitting to the dictates of the market, in the sense that the forces of international competition are seen to be inexorable and to constrain the pursuit of domestic policies promoting equality, full employment and economic security. But, far from adopting the classic, and optimistic, Ricardian position that free trade is universally beneficial, this market-based orientation is commonly accompanied by the assertion that 'we' are in a race or an embattled state with other nations, in which successful nations 'win' the battle. The notions suggested above concerning the need for a harmonised international reconciliation of the domestic needs of individual nations invite condescension from those for whom the international arena is, of necessity, perpetually embattled. But there is nothing realistic or hard-headed about the institutionalisation of such a state of conflict. It is, as suggested above, not likely to be sustainable from an economic perspective. Furthermore, such a state of rivalry and non-convergent, conflicting objectives takes place in the context of an imperative need for cooperation on ecological problems and weapons control, developments not likely to emerge from a psychology of 'war against all' between nations in the economic arena.

There is, thus, nothing in the programme discussed here that poses a solution to the gaps in income and wealth between rich and poor nations, international economic instability, weapons control, or a range of problems associated with the natural environment, most especially climate change. But a necessary precondition to dealing with these issues would involve, in rich and powerful nations especially, a population that responds to these problems in a flexible and rational manner, prerequisites that would appear to be coincident with a socialist programme: the cultivation of cognitive facility across the population, permitting rational evaluation of these problems, high levels of economic equality and economic security (including full employment) in order for the population to feel that burdens are being shared in an equitable manner, and democratic decision making, giving legitimacy to what may often prove to be difficult decisions. The perception and the reality of the presence of socialist democracy may thus be necessary components of a long-term strategy for survival.

We must take a positive approach to a socialist future. In *The Sane Society*,[3] the psychoanalyst Erich Fromm follows Marx in developing a picture of truly human, unalienated work as a manifestation and enjoyment of creative capacity – the satisfaction of a human need. This is a concept with which the elite of society are familiar: many of their peers will not rush to retire upon reaching pensionable age, as their work is part of, not a subtraction from, life. A well-functioning school system will attempt to give assistance to young individuals in finding and pursuing their interests, recognising that, as a by-product, such a procedure, rather than the pursuit of narrowly defined vocational goals, is likely to release the maximum level of creative and productive energy in an individual. And if such an approach is complemented by free and life-long learning, it will permit these interests to evolve and mature.

Marx and, even more explicitly, Fromm conclude that a concomitant of alienation is that life satisfaction is sought away from the work environment. By the time Fromm was writing, in the postwar US, this search for satisfaction typically took the form of a focus on consumption, often perceived by Fromm and others to be at an obsessive level, even for ordinary workers. It is probable that these circumstances will not disappear in the foreseeable future by making all employment intrinsically satisfying: Fromm was naïve in suggesting, for instance, that many people would look forward to a working life extracting the jewels of the earth in coal mining.[4] Indeed, a great number of professions, even common ones, are unlikely to be chosen for the intrinsic satisfaction they yield and would, ideally, be eliminated in their present form. The profession of urban bus driver yields no praise for successful negotiation of the host of obstacles offered up by traffic and passengers, but substantial liability for failure. In the context of contemporary technologies, however, only a limited kind of alleviation of these difficulties can be offered, in the form of rational organisation of traffic in cities, including restriction of private vehicles in urban centres. For workers in professions of this kind, perhaps the most attractive development likely to take place is a reduction in the norm of hours worked per year for a fully employed person.

These problems intrude into nominally more prestigious forms of employment. The role of school teacher in the contemporary world (other than elite contexts) is a debilitating one. For the sake of both pupils and teachers, the wasteful and brutal ritual of schooling as it commonly exists, and has existed, for the great majority of the population will have to be reconsidered and restructured at every level in a socialist context, with resource provisioning commensurate to its centrality to human civilisation. In the long-term reconstruction of education, the profession of teacher emerging from this process would have only a tangential resemblance to anything presently observed in education for the masses. But other aspects of alienation – the feeling that decisions at work and in society are in the hands of others who will not be paying the price of hard decisions – are more readily dealt with. Democratic control and the perception of equal sacrifice (the latter, especially, has proved important in all countries in wartime conditions) are prerequisites for public acceptance of the kinds of policies that might well be necessitated by society's laggard response to climate change.

From a socialist perspective, consumption is to be seen in the broader context of the enjoyment of life, with individuals in their early years given the skills and capacity to cultivate affinities for athletics, the mechanical and visual arts, music, food growing and preparation, as well as more stereotyped intellectual pursuits such as reading. In, especially, urban areas, conviviality can be encouraged with the cultivation of public spaces, recreational facilities and high density, the latter permitting an adequate provision of public transport, so that car ownership turns from a necessity to a luxury. The optimistic perspective is that possible slowdowns, or even reversals, in the rate of growth of consumption necessitated by ecological constraints will not be perceived as a catastrophe by the population in a socialist polity.

The socialist programme of human development and democratic control presented here is, thus, congruent with the exigencies of long-term global survival. The approach is optimistic in two senses. First, many of the paths have already been mapped out: they can be seen in the substantive achievements of past and present societies, and then built upon. There is little need for speculative ventures in the programmes to be pursued. Second, there is an unashamed optimism about the productive and creative possibilities latent, and often manifest, in human nature. Jürgen Habermas points to the need to struggle against 'the cynical defeatism of the so-called realist who fails to realize that the most pessimistic diagnosis does not excuse us from trying to do better':[5] a cynicism with regard to improvement in the conditions of life for the great mass of humankind is a typical contemporary stance, but is little more than a self-fulfilling prophecy that acts as an impediment to confronting the issues before us. 'A radical approach to social transformation is...neither utopian nor fanciful. The programme is realizable in terms of substantive, concrete proposals in the domain of public policy, and is linked to the highest aspirations of civilization. Perhaps only a pervasive and fashionable pessimism stands in our way.'[6]

Notes

Introduction

1. Summers (2014).
2. Einstein (1949).

Part I   Socialism and Central Planning

1. Auerbach (1992), p.10; footnote omitted.

1   Planning and Spontaneous Order

1. Marx (1867), pp. 283–4.
2. Descartes (1637), pp.7–8.
3. See Israel (2011), part II.
4. Kula (1986), chapters 21–3.
5. Acemoglu et al. (2011).
6. Carlisle (1974), p. 451.
7. Gide and Rist (1948), p. 232.
8. Such banks represented 'the realization of Saint-Simonian plans' Hayek (1952), p. 316, footnote omitted.
9. Gerschenkron (1962a), pp. 11–14.
10. The terms 'liberal' and 'liberalism' will be used throughout this book in their British, free-market sense, as when Friedrich Hayek and Milton Friedman referred to themselves as liberals. When the term is used, as in American English, to denote a mild form of social democracy, it will be qualified – 'American liberal'.
11. Gerschenkron (1962a), pp. 22–3; Gide and Rist (1948), pp. 236–8.
12. Carlisle (1968), p. 434.
13. Kunstler (2001), p. X.
14. Kunstler (2001) p. 32; Shapiro (1982), p. 486; Gandy (1999), pp. 23–4, 27.
15. Porter (1999), p. 416.
16. Simon, as quoted in Halliday (2007), p. 119; Halliday's insertions.
17. Spencer (1843), pp. 244–5, 247.
18. Porter (1999), p. 412; Halliday (2007), pp. 26–7.
19. Spencer (1857), p. 290; Spencer (1853), pp. 279–80, 304.
20. See Evans (2005).
21. Fogel (2004), p. 37.
22. Bauman (1976), pp. 13, 15; see as well Hayek (1982), volume 1, pp. 64–5.
23. Hayek (1944).
24. Hayek (1982), volume 1, p. 118.
25. Hayek (1982), volume 3, p. 167; emphasis in original.
26. Hayek (1960a), pp. 397–8, 399.
27. Hayek (1982), volume 2, p. 136; footnote omitted.
28. Hayek (1952), pp. 49–50.
29. Hayek (1982), volume 2, p. 5.

30. Hayek (1952), p. 154.
31. Hayek (1960), pp. 24–5.
32. Hayek (1982), volume 2, p. 5.
33. Hayek (1982), volume 1, pp. 84–5.
34. Hayek (1982), volume 1, p. 82.
35. Hayek (1982), volume 2, pp. 9, 109 (footnote omitted); Hayek (1952), p. 249.
36. Hayek (1952), p. 179.
37. Hayek (1982), volume 1, p. 22.
38. Hayek (1982), volume 1, p. 25 and note 37.
39. Hayek (1982), volume 1, pp. 11–12.
40. Hayek (1952), p. 392.
41. Hayek (1952), pp. 173–4; see also pp. 221–2.
42. Hayek (1977).
43. See, for instance, Graaff (1967).
44. In 1951, Kenneth J. Arrow elaborated upon the possibility, pointed out in the eighteenth century by the Marquis de Condorcet, that majority voting procedures might not converge with a consistent ordering of preferences on the part of the public (Arrow, 1963).
45. See Hayek (2011), pp. 35–7.
46. Scott (1998), pp. 59–61, 82.
47. Shapiro (1982), p. 487; on dispossessions, see as well Caro (1998).
48. Josephson (2002).
49. Scott (1998), p. 5.
50. Kunstler (2001), pp. 45–6.
51. Scott (1998), p. 104.
52. Jacobs (1961), pp. 238, 241, quoted in Scott (1998), p. 142.
53. Jacobs (1961), pp. 158–9, 167, 241–3.
54. Hayek cites Jacobs' *Death and Life of Great American Cities* in Hayek (1982), volume 1, p. 15.
55. Gans (1968), p. 33.
56. Hayek (1960), pp. 340–1.
57. Hayek (1960), pp. 349–50.
58. Coase (1960).
59. Stigler (1966), pp. 110–14; Chung (1996).
60. Jacobs (1961), p. 241.
61. Acemoglu et al. (2005).
62. Horwitz (1977) substantiates this argument for the evolution of the law in the pre-Civil War US, as does Skowronek (1982), chapter 1.
63. Polanyi (1944), pp. 181–2.
64. Polanyi (1944), pp.141–2.
65. See Simons (1948).
66. Pareto improvements: Hayek (1982), volume 2, p. 139; equality and stagnation: Hayek (1982), volume 2, pp. 6, 122, 188, note 24; Hayek (1960), pp. 42, 49, 430, notes 9 and 12.
67. Cronon (1991), pp. 109–19.
68. Hayek (1982), volume 2, pp. 33, 142.
69. Jacobs (1961), p. 241.
70. Hayek (1944), pp. 72–6; see also Sowell (1980), pp. 213–14.

2   The Giant Firm and the Plan

1. De Vries (1994). This notion had been anticipated by the 'aspirational principle' of Sir James Steuart in the eighteenth century: see Allen (2009), pp. 12–13.

2. Voth (2003).
3. Chandler (1992). This article is perhaps the clearest expression of his distance from mainstream theorising on the nature of the giant firm. Chandler reiterated these themes many times, most notably in Chandler (1977) and Chandler (1990).
4. Chandler (1992), p. 81, quoting Chandler (1990), p. 24.
5. The modern notion of perfect competition, in which advertising and marketing are an impossibility, only emerged with the publication of Frank Knight's *Risk, Uncertainty and Profit* of 1921: see Stigler (1957).
6. Hughes (2007), p. 1.
7. Leonard (2009).
8. Maddison (2006), pp. 184–7. Tooze (2007), chapter 5, casts an even more negative view of the progress of living standards of German workers in this and later periods.
9. Japanese per capita income approximately doubled over this period (Maddison, 2006, p. 206).
10. Chandler (1977), part II.
11. Landes (1983), pp. 285–7.
12. See Alexander (1929), chapter III 'Company Standardization'. The authorship of this book is ambiguous: 'The present investigation was made, and this volume was prepared, under the supervision of the Conference Board's Staff Economic Council, by Mr. Robert A. Brady of the Conference Board's Research Staff' (p. vii).
13. Hughes (2007), p. 210. A faith in the ability to monitor the performance of the divisions within large firms with financial measures probably reached a peak with the fashion for conglomerates in the 1970s (see Chapter 5). There then emerged an emphasis on firms pursuing their 'core competencies' and using, where possible, a comparison with market alternatives as a mechanism for judging the efficiency of the firm's diverse activities.
14. Jacob (1997), chapter 9 and Mokyr (2002), chapter 3.
15. Nelson and Wright (1992), p. 1941.
16. On the evolution of the role of science in technology since 1860, see Mowery and Rosenberg (1989), chapters 2 and 3.
17. Noble (1977). This issue will re-emerge in later chapters.
18. Gerschenkron (1962a).
19. 'Un jour M. de Fontanes [le Grand-Maître de l'Université] vantait à Napoléon Ier la centralisation admirable de l'organisation universitaire: "Sire, il est trois heures: eh bien, je puis assurer à Votre Majesté que dans ce moment même les écoliers de toutes les classes de quatrième de l'Empire font un thème latin" ' (Le Clère, 1864, p. 955).
20. The discussion below is reliant on Noble (1977), chapter 5, Hughes (2007), chapter 5 and Auerbach (1988), pp. 274–8 (and references therein).
21. Sawyer (1954). Its roots have been traced to the procedures of the eighteenth-century French arms-making industry: Friedel (2007), pp. 322–6.
22. Noble (1977), pp. 72–3; Wengenroth (1997), pp. 146–7.
23. Noble (1977), pp. 69–70; and see Smil (2005), pp.83–9, concerning Edison's (losing) battle to defend electrical transmission using direct current.
24. Adams (1919).
25. Alexander (1929); a brief biography of Alexander may be found in Noble (1977), pp. 52–4.
26. Hawley (1974), pp. 117–25; Noble (1977), pp. 81–3; see Alexander (1929), p. 11 and all of chapter 3.

27. Noble (1977), p. 79; Hughes (2007), p. 203.
28. Hughes (2007), pp. 204–5, 207.
29. Smil (2005), p. 126.
30. Kanigel (1997), pp. 494–9.
31. On the links between scientific management and cost accounting: Kaigel (1997), pp. 267–9, Alexander (1929), pp. 30–2 and Auerbach (1988), pp. 108–18.
32. In Marxian theory, the value of the labour power embodied in a pair of shoes is not linked to the number of labour hours that *happen* to be used in their fabrication, but to a *socially normed* accounting of the necessary labour hours, one that emerges through unspecified economic processes representing, presumably, 'typical' effort (enforced or voluntary) and manual facility.
33. Chandler (1977).
34. Coase (1937).
35. Williamson (1971), pp. 117, 122. Williamson's major statement on these questions is to be found in Williamson (1976).
36. Lamoreaux et al. (2002) put forth a new synthesis to account for the demise of the Chandlerian system in later decades, an issue to be discussed in the following chapters.
37. Chandler (1992), p. 87.
38. Chandler (1992), pp. 92–3.
39. Lazonick (1991), p.8.
40. Chandler (1992), pp. 86–7; the notion of learned routines was originally developed in Nelson and Winter (1982).
41. Chandler and Hikino (1997), p. 25.
42. Chandler (1992), p. 83.
43. McGraw (2007); Schumpeter (1911), p. 64.
44. See Baumol (2002), chapters 2 and 3.
45. Schumpeter (1928), pp. 384–6.
46. Schumpeter (1947), chapters VII and VIII; Hayek (1949a).
47. Rosenberg (1976), pp. 63–5; Auerbach (1988), pp. 265–7; Smil (2006).
48. Smil (2005), p. 11.
49. Wengenroth (1997), pp. 143–4.
50. Hughes (2007), pp. 150–1.
51. Friedel and Israel (1987), p. 117.
52. Smil (2005), p. 49; Friedel and Israel (1987), pp. 69, 227.
53. See Smil (2005), pp. 58–9 for sources of this quotation.
54. Smil (2005), p. 50 and Friedel and Israel (1987), p. 67.
55. Friedel and Israel (1987), pp. 52, 228.
56. Friedel and Israel (1987), p. 40.
57. Elbaum and Lazonick (1986a).

3 Technocratic Planning and the Emergence of a Socialist Orthodoxy

1. Bairoch (1993), pp. 32–51.
2. Cain and Hopkins (1993), pp. 209–25; Zebel (1967).
3. Stocking and Watkins (1948), p. 19.
4. See the discussion in Lazonick (1991), chapter 5.
5. As noted in Chapter 2, the present-day notion of perfect competition was still emerging in the 1920s.

6. Marshall (1922), p. 621.
7. Marshall (1920), p. 156.
8. Marshall (1920), pp. 321–2.
9. Marshall (1922), p. 316. A comparable 'common-sense' balancing can be found even later from one of Marshall's key successors – see Robinson (1931), chapters II and III.
10. Chamberlin (1933); Robinson (1933).
11. Cain and Hopkins (1993), p. 12.
12. As quoted in Hofstadter (1955), p. 45.
13. Steinmetz (1916). The key section used is entitled 'The Individualistic Era: From Competition to Co-operation'.
14. Burns (1936), pp. 8–9; a British parallel to Burns may be found in Levy (1936).
15. Hamlin (1930).
16. National Industrial Conference Board (1931) 'Rationalization of German Industry', pp. 6–7, as quoted in Mason (1931), pp. 641–2; the author of this quotation is identified as Mr Vaso Trivanovitch in Brady (1932), p. 30. Movements in the direction of cartelisation are reflected in the plans offered by Gerald Swope, president of General Electric, and from the US Chamber of Commerce, both in 1931: see Balisciano (1998), p. 163.
17. Alexander (1929), chapter XIV. In Brady (1933), chapter XII, in a book otherwise sympathetic to rationalisation, it is suggested that this process, as it had proceeded in Germany, might well have exacerbated the contemporaneous downturn. Even this example underlines the consideration being given in pre-Keynesian thinking to a link between microeconomic restructuring and business cycle fluctuations. The 'regularization' literature from 1924 on in the US was part of a movement to mitigate macroeconomic fluctuations through managerial regulation of microeconomic decisions – see Alchon (1985), pp. 124–5.
18. Brady (1932), p. 527.
19. Maier (1970), pp. 27–9.
20. Maier (1970), pp. 45–50.
21. Alexander (1929), pp. 32–3, passages slightly rearranged.
22. The major US (peacetime) venture in this direction took place under the New Deal, from 1933 to 1935: the failure of the National Recovery Administration (NRA) is summarised in Balisciano (1998), pp. 166–7.
23. As quoted in Porter (1995), p. 57.
24. Veblen (1924): see chapter V, 'The Pecuniary Standard of Living'. A prime example of the technocratic 'waste' tradition is Chase (1926).
25. Veblen (1904), pp. 47–8.
26. Veblen (1921), pp. 82–3; chapter 1 is entitled 'On the Nature and Uses of Sabotage'. See as well Hobson (1936), chapters 4 and 5.
27. Veblen (1923), pp. 372–3; note as well (p. 10) his favourable citation of Walter Rathenau's article on the 'new economy'.
28. Layton (1962); Noble (1977), chapter 4.
29. Weber (1922), volume II, pp. 973–4, 979–80, 987–8; emphasis in original.
30. Dardot and Laval (2013), p. 3; emphasis in original.
31. Dardot and Laval (2013), p. 84, footnote omitted.
32. For the linkage at the origin of capitalism, see Israel (1995), pp. 267–75, and Hoffman (2015).
33. The construction of the state apparatus in the US from what were, by Weberian criteria, weak foundations is developed in Skowronek (1982).

34. List (1841), from chapter IV: 'The English'; emphasis in original.
35. Marx (1845); emphasis in original. The fact that this article only surfaced long after Stalin's death (in Russian in *Voprosy Istorii* K.P.S.S. No. 12, 1971) may reflect the difficulty of reconciling Marx's words with the Soviet 'socialism in one country' doctrine emerging in the 1920s.
36. Lee (1991), p. 6.
37. Tooze (2014), p. 502.
38. Tooze (2006), chapter 4.
39. Tooze (2006), pp. 96–7, calls into question the objective reality of Nazi success in dealing with unemployment.
40. Sassoon (2010), p. 12.
41. See Sabel and Zeitlin (1985).
42. Sassoon (2010), pp. 6–8.
43. Slightly modified from Roth (1963), p. 201.
44. Bernstein (1899), pp. 90–7.
45. Engels (1877) and Engels (1880); emphasis in original.
46. Lenin (1917), pp. 119–22.
47. Ibid.
48. Lih (1992).
49. Engels (1877) and Engels (1880); emphasis in original.
50. Shanin (1983).
51. These quotations come from a series of articles originally published in *Vestnik Evropy* in 1915–16, which were then collected and published as Y. Larin, *Gosudarstvennii kapitalizm voennogo vremeni v Germanii* [*State Capitalism in Wartime Germany*], Moscow, 1928; the translations are from Auerbach et al. (1988). The page numbers in brackets are from the book published in Moscow; all emphases in the original.
52. For further elaboration, see Auerbach et al. (1988).
53. Feldman (1966), pp. 45–55, 169, 262–73.
54. See Merkle (1980), pp. 105–27.
55. Roberts and Stephenson (1968).

4   Socialist Theory and Practice

1. Szamuely (1974), pp. 34–5; the author (pp. 24–5) derives the Bolshevik approach directly from the Erfurt programme of the German Social Democratic Party in 1891, written by Karl Kautsky.
2. Szamuely (1974), p. 34; Malle (2002), pp. 165–7.
3. Gregory (2003), pp. 34–40; for an alternative but not incompatible discussion, see Allen (2003), pp. 78–87.
4. Zaleski (1971), p. 71.
5. Lieberman (1983); Harrison (1988).
6. Harrison (1998), p. 39; on Germany, Tooze (2006), pp. 584–9; Overy (1995), chapter 6.
7. Samuelson (1961), p. 830.
8. Allen (2003), p. 37.
9. Allen (2003), pp. 167–8; a similar argument had been made in Dobb (1966), pp. 22–5.
10. This conclusion is confirmed in Cheremukhin et al. (2013).
11. Allen (2003), pp. 202–11.

12. Smil (2006), chapters 2 and 3.
13. Maddison (1969), pp. 61–3, 129–30.
14. Gregory and Stuart (1994), pp. 211–16.
15. Wilhelm (1985).
16. Gregory (2003), pp. 117, 216–17.
17. Roberts (1971).
18. Barber and Harrison (1991), p. 189.
19. An important exception to this general proposition may well have been present in the agricultural sector. The residual effects of the Stalin-era antagonism to the enrichment of the peasantry and the focus on heavy industry impeded attempts to improve agricultural performance even after Stalin's death. Branco Milanovic (Milanovic, 2011, pp. 53–60), a World Bank researcher from the former Yugoslavia, makes some brief remarks on the disincentive effects of 'too much' equality in formerly socialist countries. These passing comments on this central issue (see Chapter 10) are likely to receive undue weight because of his prominence in research on worldwide inequality.
20. Gregory and Stuart (1994), p. 274.
21. Montias (1959), p. 972; Rutland (1986).
22. See Carr (1952), pp. 62–90, 224–9, for a discussion of the Bolshevik rejection of any important component of workers' control of enterprises during war communism, and the subsequent suppression of the Workers' Opposition Bolshevik faction.
23. Malle (2002), pp. 36–8.
24. Lenin's views on Taylorism and Fordism are summarised in Merkle (1980), chapter 4.
25. Siegelbaum (1988), p. 2.
26. See Merkle (1980), pp. 127–34, for the links between Taylorism and Stakhanovism.
27. Nove (1969), pp. 40–3; Siegelbaum (1988), pp. 42–3.
28. Siegelbaum (1988), p. 296.
29. Shmelëv and Popov (1989), pp. 88–9.
30. One unsympathetic discussion of planning from the pre-revolutionary period concludes: 'it is obvious how fantastic those doctrines are which imagine that production in the collectivist regime would be ordered in a manner substantially different from that of [capitalism]' (Barone, 1908, p. 289).
31. The recent summaries of this debate have been largely from an Austrian perspective, such as De Soto (2010).
32. Lange (1938), p. 97 note 50.
33. Roberts (1971a).
34. Heal (1973), pp. 79–80.
35. Stiglitz (1994), chapter 2.
36. Lavoie (1985); the argument is summarised on pages 20–4.
37. Neurath (1910).
38. Mises (1920).
39. See Chaloupek (2007).
40. Uebel (2004), p. 66 and Chaloupek (2007), p. 67.
41. Neurath (1910), pp.173, 163, 193; emphases in original.
42. Neurath (1917), pp. 238–9.
43. Gulick (1948), chapter XIV.
44. Gulick (1948), p. 153.
45. Keynes (1936).

46. Wilczynski (1972), pp. 129–30.
47. Nove (1969), p.188; see as well Zaleski (1971), chapters 2 and 3.
48. Kornai (1972).
49. Meek (1953).
50. See Gregory (2003), chapter 8.
51. A perspective which Nathan Rosenberg also attributes to Marx: see Rosenberg (1982), chapter 2.
52. Hayek (1945), pp. 82, 89–91.
53. Hayek (1945), pp. 85–6.
54. Hayek (1945), p. 79.
55. Hilferding (1910). All quotations are from chapter 15.
56. The accommodating, passive nature of credit extension to firms in the Soviet economy is indicated by the fact that 'automatic extension of credit was required ... to validate any distortion, whether it resulted from uncontrollable causes, administrative failures, misjudgement in planning, or mismanagement of real resources' (Garvy, 1977, p. 121).
57. Voznesensky (1948).

5 Ironies of History: Markets, Planning and Competition

1. Tinbergen (1952).
2. See Oulès (1966). Oulès was a professor of economics and former French civil servant.
3. Burnham (1941); Whyte (1956).
4. Baran and Sweezy (1966); Galbraith (1967).
5. Berle and Means (1932). Aspects of the exposition here follow from Auerbach (1988), chapter 5.
6. This new book acted in part as a replacement for his own earlier vision of the presence of forces of countervailing power constraining the activities of great firms; see Galbraith (1956).
7. Galbraith (1967), p. 40 note 6. For the difficulties empirical researchers find in disentangling the 'large' versus the 'monopoly' relationship to innovation, see Kamien and Schwartz (1982), chapter 2.
8. The book was published in 1969 as *Novoe Industrial'noe Obshchestvo* (The New Industrial Society), Moscow: Progress Publishers.
9. Galbraith (1958).
10. Lilienthal (1953); Berle (1965); Friedman (1970).
11. The doctrine of convergence in this relatively benign form was first exposited in Tinbergen (1961). More sinister versions of such a convergence can be found earlier in Burnham (1941) and George Orwell's *1984*.
12. Steindl (1952).
13. Cowling (1982). A general critique of this literature can be found in Auerbach and Skott (1988).
14. A Soviet variant of the same thesis can be found in Fedorovich (1979).
15. Phillips-Fein (2009).
16. Kolko (1963).
17. University of Chicago upholders of Marshallian orthodoxy rejected these innovations, claiming that they were empirically intractable: see Stigler (1949).
18. The revival of these doctrines at a later date had little to do with their initial impetus – to formalise and model the departure from an earlier age of

competition. Instead, as in the case of Paul Krugman's use of the model of monopolistic competition in international trade (Krugman, 1979), their role has been to facilitate the solving of particular problems in economic theory, rather than to function as a replacement for perfect competition as a general model of the functioning of the business economy.

19. The only exception I have been able to detect is an article in, admittedly, an obscure source: Nutter (1954).
20. See, for instance, Baumol (1959).
21. Servan-Schreiber (1968).
22. Auerbach (1988) pp. 1, 3–4; much of the material below follows from chapter 9.
23. Ritschel (1997), p. 4.
24. Notable in terms of the politics of the Conservative Party is Macmillan (1933).
25. Ritschel (1997), p. 25.
26. Ritschel (1997), pp. 110–12.
27. Barnett (1995).
28. On this period, see Chick (1998), especially chapter 2.
29. Chick (1998), pp. 83–4.
30. Panitch (1976), pp. 245–50.
31. Glyn and Sutcliffe (1972). See as well Armstrong et al. (1991).
32. The details here of the AES programme owe a good deal to Wickham-Jones (1994), especially chapter 3.
33. See Rowthorn and Wells (1987).
34. See Tomlinson (1996).
35. Crosland (1956); Holland (1975).
36. De Grauwe and Camerman (2003).
37. See Ietto-Gillies (1993).
38. See Auerbach (2007a).

6 Education and Economic Growth: The Statistical and Historical Record

1. Kiernan (1969).
2. Walsh and Gram (1980), chapters 1–4.
3. Harrod (1939); Domar (1946).
4. In Harrod's work in particular, this conclusion could be modified by the introduction of Keynesian issues of deficient demand and the potential instability of the equilibrium growth path (the 'warranted path', in Harrod's terminology).
5. Solow (1956); Solow (1957); Swan (1956).
6. Stone (1980). The main work under consideration is Denison (1979); Denison's original empirical research emerged earlier: Denison (1961).
7. A prime example is Romer (1990); a general review may be found in Aghion and Howitt (1998).
8. See Sianesi and Van Reenen (2003) for a general survey. A prominent example of those expressing doubts about the education–growth relationship is Pritchett (2001); a recent study claiming support for the relationship is Cohen and Soto (2007).
9. Note, for instance, the substantial variance in adult literacy scores between countries for given levels of educational attainment: OECD (2014), p. 52.
10. Sianesi and Van Reenen (2003), p. 163.

11. Representative examples include: Hanushek and Woessmann (2008); Hanushek and Woessmann (2010a); Hanushek and Woessmann (2010b). The last paper is of particular relevance to the role of education in rich countries. See as well Hanushek and Woessmann (2012).
12. See Hanushek and Woessmann (2008), table A1, p. 661.
13. Grek (2009).
14. Even the relatively simple 'years of schooling' variable has, as we have seen above, some ambiguous aspects, since it has a volitional component at levels beyond the compulsory requirement, and a signalling component; if we attempt to introduce even purer measures of the inputs devoted to school education, such as expenditure per pupil or teacher–pupil ratios, the links that these factors possess to the development of cognitive capacity are matters of significant controversy.
15. See Hanushek and Woessmann (2008), pp. 609–16; Hanushek and Woessmann (2010b), pp. 6–7.
16. Zeira (2009); Acemoglu (1998). And see the discussion in Hanushek and Woessmann (2010b), pp. 16–18.
17. Hayek (1960), p. 382, suggests that for 'maximum economic return from a limited expenditure on education [society] should concentrate on the higher education of a comparatively small elite'.
18. Hayek (1949a), pp. 95–6.
19. Womack et al. (2007), chapter 3. Mainstream economic orthodoxy concedes the possibility, in specific contexts, of violations of the presumption that available resources and technologies are used optimally on a universal basis, such as X-inefficiency on the part of monopolistic producers (Leibenstein, 1966) or the supposed 'advantages of backwardness' possessed by newcomers. But to an outsider to the economics profession, the orthodox notion that resources, to a first approximation, are always being used efficiently seems at odds with everything one knows about human existence and, less portentously, makes one wonder why vast resources have been allocated to the profession of management if this task is so readily accomplished.
20. Griliches (1996), pp. 11–12, suggests this possibility but does not necessarily endorse it.
21. Young (1995).
22. Young (1995), p. 675.
23. Krugman (1995). The exchange was discussing Krugman (1994a).
24. Nelson and Pack (1999).
25. Green (2013), p. 77. Footnote omitted.
26. Yoong-Deok and Kim (2000); see the comments by Ishrat Husain in the Krugman (1995) letter exchange, p. 173; Amsden (2001), pp. 17–19; Wade (1990), p. 38; Lee (1997).
27. Rosenberg (1976), pp. 63–5.
28. Edgerton (2008), pp. 100–2.
29. Edgerton (2008), p. 105.
30. 'By assigning so great a role to "technology" as a source of growth, the theory is obliged to assign correspondingly minor roles to everything else, and so has little ability to account for the wide diversity in growth rates we observe'; Lucas (1988), p. 15.
31. Nordhaus (1997), in Bresnahan and Gordon (1997), pp. 29–66.
32. See the review of climate change 'solutions' offered in Levitt and Dubner (2009) by Kolbert (2009).

33. Mandel (2004), p. 76.
34. Nelson and Wright (1992), pp. 1934–9; Edgerton (2008), pp. 109–13.
35. As argued in Gomory (2010) and Edgerton (2008), pp. 70–4.
36. '[A] simple, linear, modernization model of literacy as a prerequisite for development and development as a stimulant to increased levels of schooling, will not do. Too many periods of lags, backward linkages, setbacks, and contradictions existed to permit such cavalier theorizing to continue without serious challenge and criticism'; Graff (1987), p. 13.
37. Nicholas (1990) in Tortella (1990), pp. 47–67.
38. Cipolla (1969), p. 71. This statement has received support in Becker et al. (2011).
39. Easterlin (1981), appendix table 1 – primary school enrolment rates for various countries; Lindert (2004), chapter 5 on the popular basis of school expenditure; Goldin and Katz (2008), chapter 5 on the high school movement in the US.
40. Goldin and Katz (2008), pp. 172–81.
41. For a sample of the literature discussing the efficacy of education, especially of a vocational kind, for German economic development and the complaints in Britain about failures in this realm, see Lee (1978), pp. 453–59 and Sanderson (1999), chapters 2 and 3. A minority have dissented from this consensus, suggesting that, even for Germany, where supervisors and skilled labourers received scientific training, the most important skills were those they developed on the job; for the common worker, it is suggested that even minimal literacy was unnecessary: see Mitch (1990), pp. 33–4.
42. Nelson and Wright (1992), pp. 1940–1; Lazonick and O'Sullivan (1997) in Chandler et al. (1997), p. 499.
43. Lazonick and O'Sullivan (1997), pp. 500–4.
44. In this context, see Noble (1984), p. 146: 'The Darwinian ideology of technological progress…does not so much side with technical or economic superiority as with social power…it blinds society to the full range of possibilities available to it as well as to the realities of its own history, structure, and cultural make-up.' See as well Schumacher (1973).
45. Braverman (1988), pp. 102–3; emphasis in original.
46. A review can be found in Meiksins (1994).
47. Katz and Margo (2013).
48. Goldin and Katz (2008), pp. 102–18.
49. Clarke (1994), chapter 2; Goldin and Katz (2008), p. 40.
50. Morikowa (1997), pp. 321–6; Altshuler et al. (1984), pp. 205–10.
51. Solow and Temin (1978), p. 630 note 15.
52. Smil (2005) and Smil (2006). Only a few new technologies made an important impact in the first two decades after 1945, such as synthetic petroleum-based products and antibiotic drugs from the pharmaceutical industry: see Panitch and Gindin (2012), p. 85.
53. 'The capacity of a modern industrialized society is best measured by its steel production'; Crankshaw (1962), p. 28.

7   Education as a Social Process

1. Hofstadter (1948), pp. 68–92.
2. Becker (1962), pp. 28–9, and see the Marshall quotation in note 34.
3. See Becker (1962), p. 10, footnote 2 for citation of sources.

4. Fisher (1930); Becker and Mulligan (1997), p. 752 postulate a possible reverse causation by which wealth generates patience, one reason for which is that 'many investments in future-oriented capital may occur during childhood and richer parental households have more resources to make the investments'.

5. An example of a well-behaved situation is an investment in which outlays take place in the present, with an expectation of gaining net returns in the future: a simple two-stage process. By contrast, the pattern of returns for investing in a nuclear reactor is not well-behaved: substantial investment outlays take place in the present and there is an expectation of a net stream of returns subsequently, but then a large outlay has to be made several decades later when the reactor has to be decommissioned. The prospect of retirement makes decisions surrounding human capital somewhat of this messy type, with net outflows at both the beginning and the end of life.

6. Friedman (1962), p. 227; see as well his University of Chicago colleague: 'Concern about inequality … is emotional rather than rational', Johnson (1973), pp. 53–4.

7. Becker (1962), pp. 46–7.

8. Stiglitz (2013), pp. 134–5. The mobility advantages accruing to the well-off (partially in mitigating downward movements) are discussed in Reeves and Howard (2013) (for the US) and McKnight (2015) (for the UK).

9. A standard critique is that prohibitions on slavery and legal inhibitions on indenturing mean that the market in human capital is inevitably imperfect: Friedman (1956a), p. 8. Becker (1962), p. 43, denied that there is a problem of this nature specific to human capital, but latterly was willing to consider this issue: see the review in Björklund and Jäntti (2009), pp. 494–6. The presence of student debt in, especially, the US and the UK raises the question of whether de facto forms of indenturing of students' future incomes have been instituted.

10. Streeck (1989), pp. 92–3.

11. For a discussion covering mid-century UK, see Jackson and Marsden (1966), pp. 225–9.

12. Stigler (1966), p. 110.

13. See Sianesi and Van Reenen (2003), pp. 160–1 and Hanushek and Woessmann (2008), pp. 615–16.

14. Krueger and Lindahl (1999), p. 35; Acemoglu and Angrist (2001); Kling et al. (2007); Breton (2010) and as corrected in Breton (2010a). A small literature giving special prominence to externalities will be noted below.

15. This point is noted by Breton (2010), p. 68: 'The finding of a lagged effect on personal income is an indication that the external effects of schooling on national income also may occur with a lag. If there is a long lag, then even accurate estimates of the effect of changes in schooling over short periods will under-estimate the full effect, perhaps to a substantial degree.' In the research by McMahon (1999), p. 12, lags are considered that may be as long as 10 to 25 years. The time scales under consideration here can, in various historical contexts, extend much longer.

16. Pioneering efforts to elucidate these external effects may be found in Haveman and Wolfe (1984), pp. 382–6; see as well McMahon (1999) and Wolfe and Haveman (2002). General reservations about the kind of statistical modelling used in these studies have been expressed in Chapter 6.

17. The approach taken here has affinities with the 'diffusionist' approach to education and growth in the economic history literature: see Tortella and Sandberg (1990), pp. 10–11.

18. 'A nation's firms which lack sophisticated home buyers...face grave difficulties in innovating more rapidly than rivals who possess them' Porter (1990), p. 145.
19. De Waal (2001).
20. The generation of high-technology industry clusters of firms in recent decades has led to the notion that Marshall had pre-figured a successful alternative to the technocratic planning approach, one that emerged from market-based forms of firm interaction and co-ordination. Porter (1990), pp. 144, 166; Langlois (1992).
21. Lucas (1988), p. 39; emphasis in original.
22. The stations included commercial ones such as WNCN, WQXR, WEVD and WOR, the listener-sponsored WBAI, and non-commercial stations such as WRVR, WKCR and WNYC; the British equivalent of the latter would have been the output of the BBC, most especially the Third Programme.
23. See McMahon (1999), chapter 1.
24. Streeck (1989), p. 90.
25. Gould and Lewontin (1979).
26. Cipolla (1969), p. 92.
27. Tawney (1952), p. 19.
28. The literacy campaign of the Protestant king of Sweden Charles XI had as its major goals 'piety, civility, orderliness, and military preparedness'; Graff (1987), pp. 13, 149–50.
29. Cipolla (1969), p. 65.
30. Bowles and Gintis (1976), chapter 5.
31. Noble (1977), p. 170.
32. 'Some skills are "general": they can generate higher value wherever they are applied...Most skills are transferable among employers to some extent, but not "general". This fact implies that workers are unable to gain the full wage increase warranted by their increased skills, thus giving the employer an incentive to invest.' Green (2013), p. 85.
33. This is the fundamental message to be found in Wolf (2011); see pp. 7–12.
34. Study from the UK in 2004, cited in Barnard (2015).
35. Hillmert and Jacob (2002), pp. 329–32, raise the possibility that the availability of vocational training (as in Germany) could be a pathway steering young people (especially from the working class) away from university.
36. A prominent example for the US: Buckley (1951).
37. Lords Select Committee (2012).
38. A representative discussion for the US may be found in National Commission on Excellence in Education (1983).
39. Hirsch (2010), pp. 2–6, 24–5.
40. In Ravitch (2000), p. 15, p. 527 n. 6, a literature is cited that questions the extent to which progressive education was in fact implemented in American public schools. A critique similar to that of Ravitch had earlier been voiced by Antonio Gramsci against the class aspects of the (roughly contemporaneous) Giovanni Gentile reforms in fascist Italy: Gramsci (1935), pp. 71–4.
41. Dewey was, however, directly influential on Soviet educational developments: see Fitzpatrick (2002), p. 7.
42. Dewey (1915), pp. 23–4.
43. Dewey (1915), pp. 21–2.
44. Dewey (1902), pp. 118–19.
45. Dewey (1915), pp. 8–9; emphasis in original. Recent empirical studies seem to corroborate Dewey's approach in the context of science teaching at the university level: 'At the college level, the evidence is clear; science students learn less when

they are expected to listen passively': the scientist and educator Carl Wieman, quoted in Kantrowitz (2014), p. 60; similar claims are made for the efficacy of interactive learning methods in science teaching for young children (Wysession, 2015). Support for more traditional methods may be found in Paul (2015), which gives evidence for the efficacy of repeated testing for, especially, students from more deprived backgrounds.

46. Dewey (1902), p. 119.
47. Dewey (1915), pp. 19–20.
48. Dewey (1915), p. 24.
49. Dewey (1915), pp. 10–11.
50. Bowles and Gintis (1976), pp. 45–7, 181.
51. Hofstadter (1963), pp. 361, 367.
52. Ravitch (2000), p.95.
53. Bowles and Gintis (1976), p.59.
54. Ravitch (2000), pp. 51–2, 76, 169.
55. Ravitch (2000), p. 59.
56. Dewey (1915), pp. 19–20.
57. Ravitch (2000), p. 276; footnote omitted.
58. Nussbaum (2010), p. 18.
59. Gardner (2002), p. 24; this Harvard Professor of Cognition and Education feels it appropriate to cite the example of his own four-year-old children as representative of human learning processes.
60. Hirsch (2010), pp. 35–6, 163. On the cognitive efficacy of fact-rich learning, see Willingham (2006).
61. Hirsch (1987), p. xiii.
62. Hirsch (1987), pp. 124, 127, 134, 136.
63. Hirsch (1987), p. 11; see Bauerlein (2008), chapters 1 and 2; the complaint that there is a deficit of substantive knowledge in the US even among the university population is a long-standing one – see Barzun (1959), chapter 4. It is likely that Barzun was using his own superlative (elite) preparation as a vantage point from which to perceive a general decline in standards; overall, levels of academic achievement were increasing in the US and elsewhere. Similar complaints were made in the preface to Hindemith (1949), in a period in which technical proficiency among musicians was rising rapidly.
64. Ravitch (2002), pp. 17–19.
65. Kim (2005).
66. UK Department for Education (2013).
67. Gove links his policies to the writings of E. D. Hirsch, Jr, who identifies himself as an American liberal: O'Grady (2013), p. 5.
68. Researchers are quoted as justifying the study of the latter subjects on the basis that 'Much evidence suggests that students who study creative arts do better at more traditional academic subjects such as mathematics and computer science': Garner (2012).
69. Evans (2011).
70. *Guardian/Observer* (2013).
71. The latter being academies without a predecessor state school.
72. Such tendencies exist simultaneously with attempts to impose uniform national standards through regularised testing, as exemplified by the development of the Common Core programme in the US. Such tests, as we shall see below, are being used not only to monitor pupils' educational progress, but to discipline teachers by measuring their 'performance'.

73. Ladd (2002); Belfield and Levin (2005); Rouse and Barrow (2009).
74. Charter schools: *Economist* (2012); Academies: Department for Education (2015).
75. Adonis (2012), chapter 7; *Economist* (2011).
76. BBC News (2012).
77. Benn (2011a), pp. IX–X.
78. Angrist et al. (2013).
79. Center for Research on Educational Outcomes (CREDO) Stanford University (2013); Machin and Vernoit (2011); Machin (2012).
80. Ravitch (2010); Mansell (2015) claims that 60 per cent extra funds are received by England's free school pupils compared with the bulk of the state sector.
81. *Economist* (2012).
82. Hanushek (2005); Hanushek discussed the firing of teachers in the film 'Waiting for "Superman" ' (cited in Ravitch, 2012).
83. Marx (1873).
84. Bowles and Gintis (1976), pp. 27, 52.
85. Bowles and Gintis (1976), pp. 230–1, citing a range of contemporaneous authorities supporting these views.
86. Bowles and Gintis (1976), p. 114; and see p. 76.
87. Bowles and Gintis (1976), p. 246.
88. Bowles and Gintis (2002), p. 15.
89. Illich (1973), pp. 43–4.
90. Illich (1973), p. 70 (footnote omitted).
91. Illich (1973), p. 111.
92. Illich (1973), pp. 95, 100.
93. Illich (1973), p. 14.
94. Illich (1973), pp. 93, 90.
95. Illich (1973), pp. 103–4.
96. Illich (1973), p. 96.
97. Illich (1973), p. 57.
98. The school inspectors in the UK: Office for Standards in Education, Children's Services and Skills (2007).
99. Ravitch (2000), p. 393. In the early 1970s in the US, there was a movement for the teaching of African-American syntax in ghetto neighbourhoods using a lexicon containing a grammar, including verb conjugations, of African-American English. The practical role of this lexicon was to serve as a bridge for the teaching of English to these supposedly dialect-speaking children. Some purveyors of this approach suggested that, having established the legitimacy of this African-American dialect, the teaching of standard English to such children would be an oppressive, hegemonic act. Under such conditions, the ability of these children to function in the modern world was to be sacrificed at the altar of a political agenda in which it was questioned 'whether a command of the standard language is really necessary for educational purposes at all' (Torrey, 1970, as reprinted in Keddie, 1973, p. 73).
100. A case in point is interwar social democracy in Austria: Gulick (1948), chapters XIV–XVI.
101. OECD (2012); see the table on p. 5.
102. Sahlberg (2011), p. 100.
103. Sahlberg (2011), p. 101.
104. Sahlberg (2011), p. 127.

105. Sahlberg (2011), p. 134, slightly rearranged.
106. OECD (2014), pp. 207, 437.
107. Sahlberg (2011), p. 76.
108. Using US data, Chetty et al. (2014) claim empirical support for the efficacy of firing 'poorly performing' teachers on a regular basis.
109. Sahlberg (2011), p. 21.
110. Green (2013), chapter 9.
111. Sahlberg (2011), p. 118.
112. Ravitch (2012).
113. Andrews et al. (2014), pp. 1, 22–3.
114. Ravitch (2010), p. 24; Sahlberg (2011), pp. 45–7.
115. Green (2013), chapter 8 and references therein.

8 The Working and Living Environment

1. Bruner (1972), p. 69.
2. See Rose (2004), chapter 7. As Aditya Chakrabortty pointed out in his critique of Richard Florida and his focus on the 'creative class' as the source of economic renewal, 'what really stuck out was how Florida fenced off creative work. You were either a knowledge worker or a factory worker – as if the other stuff didn't require brains' (Chakrabortty, 2011).
3. Apologies here to the film 'Field of Dreams'. This notion reached perhaps its most articulate expression in Reich (1992), epitomised in a later quotation from him: 'Forget the debate over outsourcing. The real question is how to make Americans so competitive that all global companies — whether or not headquartered in the United States — will create good jobs in America': Reich (2012).
4. Chang (2010), pp. 135–6, 189.
5. Crump (2007), chapter 4.
6. Mokyr (2009), pp. 61–2.
7. Becker and Woessmann (2009); Cipolla (1969), pp. 72–4.
8. Allen (2009), pp. 10–11, referencing Mokyr (2002).
9. Mokyr (2009), pp. 111–12.
10. Epstein (2008), p. 80.
11. Fogel (1964).
12. Chandler (1977), chapters 3–5.
13. Some of the material below derives from Auerbach (2007).
14. As Alfred Marshall commented with reference to English industrial districts, 'The mysteries of the trade become no mysteries; but are as it were in the air, and the children learn many of them unconsciously' (Marshall, 1922, p. 271, as quoted in Sabel and Zeitlin, 1985, p. 152).
15. Easterlin (1981), p. 9 note 21; Veblen (1914), p. 312.
16. Rostowski and Auerbach (1986).
17. De Grazia (2005), p. 206.
18. This literature is reviewed in Acemoglu et al. (2014).
19. Vernon (1966).
20. Wiener (1981); Cain and Hopkins (1993).
21. Guagnini (1993), p. 37.
22. For the US, see Stein (2010).
23. Duhigg and Bradsher (2012).

24. President's Council of Advisors on Science and Technology (PCAST) (2004).
25. Panitch and Gindin (2012), p. 186; Van Reenen (2013).
26. Franco (2002); Bloom et al. (2012).
27. Panitch and Gindin (2012), p. 188.
28. Freeman (2007), p. 36.
29. Streeck (1989), p. 98; Grubb and Lazerson (2004), pp. 171–3; Green (2013), chapter 6.
30. OECD (2015a), first quarter 2015.
31. For a survey, see Røed (1997). Some writing in this area pursues a 'blame the victim' strategy: rather than focusing on skill and reputational deterioration from involuntary unemployment, one paper reviewed (p. 398) explains the hysteresis effect in terms of unemployment (more leisure in the past) cultivating a preference for leisure and thus the likelihood of future unemployment. Deleterious effects of unemployment on the economy's longer-term capacity are discussed in Stockhammer and Sturn (2012) and Reifschneider et al. (2013).
32. Eichhorst (2011), p. 49.
33. See Bennett and Kaufman (2004).
34. Pencavel (2005), pp. 70–1, 74.
35. Freeman (2005), p. 129.
36. Freeman (2007), pp. 4–16. As of 2012, a broad range of European Union countries have better records than the US (and the UK) in the generation of employment in the prime age group of 25 to 54 (OECD, 2013a): a point underlined in Krugman (2014).
37. Farber (2010), pp. 223–5. The quotation continues: 'Potential motivation for employers to implement such changes range[s] from a need for added flexibility in the face of greater uncertainty regarding product demand to avoidance of increasingly expensive fringe benefits and long-term obligations to workers.' Another possibility is that these changes simply result from increasing exploitation of workers in the present period. On changes in the bargaining power of capital vis-à-vis labour, see Schmitt and Jones (2012) and Kalleberg (2011).
38. Farber (2011).
39. Green (2006), chapters 6 and 7. Chakrabortty (2010) notes that 'management thinkers such as Tom Peters and Charles Handy have spent decades telling us that the workplace of the future is a shiny, hi-tech grotto where people are free to exercise initiative and innovate. Yet the reality is that innovation is imposed on staff and where initiative is encouraged it's within heavily circumscribed borders.'
40. International Labour Office (2013), pp. 4–5, 11–13, table B1: most statistics are for 2012.
41. International Labour Office (2010), p. 42; International Labour Office (2013), pp. 43–4.
42. See various approaches in Beecroft (2011), Mulligan (2013) and Farber and Valletta (2013).
43. A general survey can be found in Card et al. (2010).
44. Paul Osterman, quoted in Shapiro (2012). A subdued assessment of the effects of ALMP can be found in Lindert (2004), pp. 253–5.
45. The seriousness of the state of youth unemployment has, however, continued to evoke calls for initiatives that 'more tightly couple labor market demand with education and training': Sum et al. (2014), p. 1.
46. Green (2013), p. 81.

47. Dustmann and Schönberg (2012), p. 37.
48. Harhoff and Kane (1995), p. 4.
49. On early streaming, see Tremblay and Le Bot (2003), p. 7.
50. Green (2013), p. 86; footnote omitted.
51. Steedman (2011), pp. 95–6, 98–9.
52. Tremblay and Le Bot (2003), pp. 15–16.
53. Méhaut et al. (2010).
54. Despite the unsubstantiated claims in Wolff (2002), there is no sign, either from contemporaneous reports (including his son's extensive biographical sketch) or from the narrow and backward range of literature in his book collection (after having lived for decades in a city, Leipzig, famous for its book fair), that Bach was 'learned' or possessed intellectual curiosity about any area outside of music.
55. Powell et al. (2012), p. 255.
56. Hacker (2008), introduction and chapters 1 and 2. See, as well, Gottschalk and Moffitt (2009) for evidence of increasing wage instability for especially low-paid and male workers.
57. Borio (2007), p. 5.
58. Merton (2003), p. 23.
59. Carnoy et al. (1997), pp. 27–8, 47.
60. OECD (2011a), pp. 30–1. Coates and Lehki (2008) discuss the range of parameters that impinge upon the notion of job security, and their relationship to concepts of job flexibility and the notions of 'good work'.
61. Freeman (2005). Freeman notes (pp. 137–9) the extravagant claims that have been made by the IMF for the efficacy of such policies.
62. De Grauwe and Polan (2005), p. 119.
63. See Harmon and Oosterbeek (2003), where none of these considerations are dealt with.
64. Despite having high mobility in general (see Björklund and Jäntti, 2009, pp. 494–6), Sweden's 'intergenerational transmission of income is remarkably strong at the very top of the distribution...the most likely mechanism for this is inherited wealth': Björklund et al. (2012), p. 483.
65. Harmon and Oosterbeek (2003) focus on the possibility of children 'inheriting' from [highly educated] parents stronger tastes for schooling, lower discount rates and higher ability (p. 119).
66. The following story will not sound strange, or particularly amusing, to those from working-class backgrounds: 'The day that Leonard Susskind [the physicist] decided he was not going to follow his father into the family plumbing business, his parents were appalled. "My father was a tough guy," says Prof. Susskind with a chuckle. "He said: 'What do you want to be: a ballet dancer?' I said: 'No, I don't want to be a ballet dancer, I want to be a physicist.' He said: 'You aint going to work in no drugstore.' I said: 'No, not a pharmacist, a physicist.' He said: 'What's a physicist?' I said: 'Like Einstein.' That shook him and from that moment he got it. My mother was crying and saying, 'We're going to be broke,' and he just looked at her and said: 'Shut up – he's going to be Einstein.' " De Bertodano (2014).
67. Checchi et al. (1999), pp. 351–93.
68. See Duncan and Murnane (2011a), especially pp. 7–12. Some prominent contemporary research has questioned the notion that poor people are locked in a 'culture of poverty' that generates errors in decision making. The poor, to paraphrase the proverbial Scott Fitzgerald–Hemingway exchange, are very much like

the rest of us (in the rationality of their decision making), but they have less money. As a result, the consequences of bad decisions are particularly high: see Bertrand et al. (2004).

69. Becker and Tomes (1986) deal with differential wealth endowments and capital market imperfections, as well as cultural and genetic endowments. Galor and Zeira (1993) focus on the role of credit market imperfections in income distribution. Hacker (2008), chapter 3, underlines the risks for workers in the contemporary economy in 'investing' in skills for which a return may cease to be forthcoming.
70. Goldin and Katz (2008), pp. 351–2.
71. Bale and Greenshields (1978) and Anderson and Tyers (1987).
72. Li (2004).
73. Samuelson's textbook used this case to instance how such policies could impoverish a country. Samuelson (1964), chapter 20, especially p. 413.
74. Clarke (1992).

9   The US as Exemplar and Paradigm

1. World Bank (2015).
2. Wills (1999).
3. Hofstadter et al. (1967), pp. 266–7.
4. See Novak (2010) and Lind (2013).
5. Weinstein (1984), chapter 3.
6. In Lipset and Marks (2000), especially chapter 3, it is suggested that the failure of the Socialist Party to make a successful link with unions was central to the demise of socialism in the US.
7. Sombart (1906), pp. 116, 119.
8. Elements of unequal sacrifice were, of course, present, with riots from 1863 undoubtedly provoked in part by the provision that conscription could be avoided upon payment of $300 to the authorities: Hofstadter et al. (1967), p. 435.
9. Carpenter (2001).
10. Sombart (1906), p. 115.
11. Implementation of a secularist agenda in France has, on occasion, been used as an excuse for populist, anti-Muslim actions (such as the banning of head scarves) by the state; comparable actions in the US (the banning of 'Sharia law') have, as yet, been localised events.
12. Rossiter (1979), p. 242. George Washington had originally advocated the founding of a national agricultural department in 1796 (Carpenter, 2001, p. 179).
13. Rossiter (1979), p. 211.
14. Rossiter (1979), p. 213; Bowman (1962), p. 527.
15. Arrow (1962).
16. Ferleger and Lazonick (1993), p. 73; Evenson (1982), pp. 237–41.
17. Rasmussen (1962), pp. 588–90; Clarke (1994), chapter 1; Evenson (1982).
18. Rossiter (1979), p. 247.
19. Bowman (1962), p. 542.
20. Hounshell (1984), pp. 25–65.
21. Baran and Sweezy (1966), chapter 7.
22. Peck and Scherer (1962), especially chapters 16–19.
23. Tirman (1984a), especially pp. 5–13; Dunne (1990).
24. Abbate (2000).

25. The continued importance of the state in US technological development is underlined in Block and Keller (2011) and Mazzucato (2013), chapters 3 and 4.
26. '[T]he rhetoric of disruption [is] a language of panic, fear asymmetry, and disorder ... [it] is competitive strategy for an age seized by terror.' Lepore (2014), p. 31.
27. Schumpeter never used this example. He might have hesitated to do so, since AT&T was a quintessential example of the kind of managerially run firm that for Schumpeter augured the demise of capitalist entrepreneurial innovation.
28. This is the title of part I of Gilder (1989).
29. Wilson (1985).
30. Braun and Macdonald (1982), pp. 24, 36; Gertner (2012), pp. 83–91.
31. Levin (1982), pp. 58, 66–7; Flamm (1988), p. 16; Gertner (2012), chapter 4.
32. Braun and Macdonald (1982), p. 1; Riordan et al. (1999), p. S336.
33. Riordan et al. (1999), pp. S342–343; Braun and Macdonald (1982), pp. 43, 57–8. A rejection of this dichotomy in the context of the early history of modern science can be found in Roberts and Schaffer (2007).
34. Lécuyer (2006), chapter 1; Sturgeon (2000).
35. Sturgeon (2000); Lécuyer (2006), chapters 1 and 2 and pp. 292–4.
36. Schumpeter (1947), p. 84.
37. Rosenberg (1972), pp. 83–6.
38. Braun and Macdonald (1982), p. 75.
39. Lécuyer (2006), p. 77.
40. 'Silicon Valley owes its present configuration to patterns of federal spending, corporate strategies, industry-university relationships, and technological innovation shaped by the assumptions and priorities of Cold War defense policy.' Leslie (2000), p. 49.
41. Levin (1982), p. 13.
42. Lécuyer (2006), p. 139 (footnote omitted).
43. Levin (1982), p. 63, table 2.17.
44. Flamm (1988), p. 16.
45. Levin (1982), p. 67; Holbrook (1995), pp. 137–8.
46. Levin (1982), p. 67; Holbrook (1995), p. 137.
47. Lécuyer (2006), pp. 130, 160, 164–5.
48. Levin (1982), p. 65.
49. Holbrook (1995), p. 135; 'No major innovations emerged directly from government-funded R&D ... But ... when a breakthrough occurred in the private sector it found enthusiastic support and substantial aid.' Levin (1982), p. 73.
50. Levin (1982), pp. 47–57; Braun and Macdonald (1982), pp. 60–1.
51. Lécuyer (2006), pp. 167, 255–8.
52. Lécuyer (2006), p. 264; Kenney and Florida (2000), p. 100.
53. Lécuyer (2006), p. 165.
54. Levin (1982), p. 44.
55. Leslie (1993).
56. Lécuyer (2006), pp. 53–5; Levin (1982), pp. 47–9; Leslie (1993), chapter 1.
57. Dumas (1984), table 7–1, p. 130.
58. Goldin and Katz (2008), pp. 261–83; Braun and Macdonald (1982), p. 64; Levin (1982), p. 83.
59. Kenney and Florida (2000), pp. 98–123 and Suchman (2000).
60. Lindert (2004), pp. 115–22; Rosenberg (1972), pp. 35–9; Goldin and Katz (2008), p. 222.

61. Ueda (1987), chapter 7.
62. Transistor manufacture in the 1950s typically had yields of 20–30% (Braun and Macdonald, 1982, pp. 66–7); on manufacturing protocols, see Lécuyer (2006), pp. 220–38.
63. Abbate (2000), p. 183.
64. Lécuyer (2006), p. 1.
65. Gertner (2012), pp. 12–13.
66. Hacker (2009), p. 38.
67. Lécuyer (2006), pp. 81–2, 98–9, 123–8, 162–4, 264–5.
68. Riordan et al. (1999), p. S337; Stafeev (2010).
69. Johnson (1982), pp. 226, 277–80; Amsden (1989), pp. 81–5.
70. Block (2008); Lazonick (2009); Mazzucato (2013).
71. Atkinson et al. (2011), p. 49.
72. Tranter and Booth (2015) suggest that while climate change scepticism is high in the US, it is as high or higher in countries such as Australia, Norway and New Zealand.

10   Economic Growth and Inequality

1. See Kendrick (1970), especially pp. 304–9.
2. United Nations Development Programme (2015).
3. Baumol et al. (2007), p. 16.
4. Carey (1992), chapter 4.
5. OECD (2015). Prescott (2004) accounts for this change since the 1970s solely in terms of the lower marginal tax rates in the US generating greater incentives to work. Offer (2006), pp. 298–9, more plausibly attributes the exceptional levels of hours worked in the US to high and rising levels of economic insecurity, as discussed in Chapter 8.
6. Atkinson et al. (2011), pp. 9–10. By contrast, see Van Reenen (2013), where income distribution considerations are given a parenthetical consideration.
7. Stiglitz (2005), p. 128.
8. Hicks (1946), p. 172.
9. Parker and Harcourt (1969), pp. 1–30.
10. Kaletsky (2004), p. 56.
11. A range of approaches may be found to these issues: see the websites of the European Commission (2015a) and Creative Commons (2015).
12. Baumol et al. (2007), p. 18.
13. The contrary notion that the reconstruction of the urban environment to support the car in Los Angeles was part of a 'democratic impulse' is supported in Bottles (1987).
14. Data on growth rate per capita are from Maddison (2006), table A-j, p. 206.
15. Easterlin (1981), appendix table 1 – primary school enrolment rates for various countries; Hanley (1990); Ohkawa and Rosovsky (1973), chapter 1. The comparable figures for 1910 are 79 per cent in Germany and 88 per cent in France.
16. Sen (2006), p. 111, cites a source suggesting that 'Between 1906 and 1911, education consumed as much as 43 percent of the budgets of the towns and villages for Japan as a whole.'
17. The stresses of Westernisation in this period are discussed in Sukehiro (1989), pp. 496–8.

18. In another historical context, it has been claimed (Field, 2003) that the depression-era economic conditions in the US in the period from 1929 to 1941 have masked the fact that it was an era of substantial increase in economic capacity, being 'the most technologically progressive decade of the century'.
19. Goldman et al. (2008). In an analogous argument in the context of physical capital, Robert C. Allen (Allen, 2011, pp. 139–45 and references therein) suggests that large investments in physical assets in the agricultural domain in the pre-1978 period may have played a substantial role in the subsequent success of post-reform agriculture in China.
20. Playfair (1852).
21. Sandberg (1982): see table 1, p. 687. See also Easterlin (1981).
22. Nilsson and Pettersson (1990), pp. 209–22.
23. Maddison (2006); Myllntaus (1990).
24. Feldstein (1995).
25. Alvaredo et al. (2013), p. 6.
26. Brandolini and Smeeding (2009), especially pp. 82–97, Alveredo et al. (2015) and OECD (2011a).
27. See the contributions to Gautié and Schmitt (2010).
28. Piketty and Saez (2007), pp. 18–19. This question will be re-engaged with in Chapter 12.
29. Goldin and Katz (2008), especially part 1. In Murnane (2013), a reversal of the stagnation in US high-school graduation rates is reported for the twenty-first century, but no claim to full explanation is made.
30. Autor et al. (2003), p. 1279. A more recent contribution that emphasises the continuing bifurcation of the labour market as a result of technological change is Autor and Dorn (2013). A critique of an exclusive focus on technological explanations to explain these developments in a US context may be found in Mishel et al. (2013). Note, however, that even neutral technical change not biased in favour of those with higher skill levels will stretch out the wage distribution if employers can choose 'overeducated' workers in preference to those with lower skills: Skott and Auerbach (2004).
31. This is the approach to be found in Schumpeter (1939), pp. 137–50 from chapter IV, section D.
32. Glyn (2009). For the US, labour's share of business net value added moves decisively downward since the 1980s when the top 1 per cent of remuneration is omitted (p. 113). See as well European Commission (2015b); International Labour Organization (2013), pp. 43–4: adjusted labour shares for Germany, the US and Japan 1970–2010; and Karabarbounis and Neiman (2013). Claims that this tendency is largely a statistical artefact can be found in Bridgman (2014).
33. Bebchuk et al. (2002); Mishel and Sabadish (2012), p. 5; Smith and Kuntz (2013); Mishel and Bivens (2013); House of Commons Library (2009).
34. Jensen and Meckling (1976).
35. Skott and Guy (2013).
36. Freeman (2006). See also Autor et al. (2013).
37. Freeman (2009), p. 575.
38. Freeman (2009), p. 576.
39. Influential figures have also been willing to invoke the theory of monopoly capital (see Chapter 5) on fragmentary domestic evidence: 'increasing business concentration could be an important factor in stagnating demand for labor, as corporations use their growing monopoly power to raise prices without passing

the gains on to their employees'. Krugman (2012). Krugman cites as authority the sketchy presentation in Lynn and Longman (2010).

40. Richardson (1995), p. 51, and Krugman (1997), especially chapters 2 and 3; Krugman appears to have modified his position in recent times.

41. Okun (1975), pp. 1, 2, 89, emphasis added. An upgraded version of the equity–efficiency trade-off may be found in Mulligan (2012), pp. 253–6.

42. Kuznets (1955).

43. Galor and Moav (2004) suggest that, in the contemporary era, with human capital emerging as a prime engine of economic growth, economic equality alleviates the adverse effects of credit constraints on human capital accumulation and thereby stimulates the growth process.

44. The article by Trabandt and Uhlig (2009) tests the Laffer notion under the assumption that 'The government collects distortionary taxes on labor, capital and consumption and issues debt to finance government consumption, lump-sum transfers and debt repayments.' With all government expenditure (including on infrastructure and education) being classified as 'consumption', there is little surprise that some nations' tax rates reach a Laffer threshold of 'overly' high taxation. Even in this framework, US taxation rates are well beneath that threshold.

45. There are, however, serious claims that Jean Sibelius's relative compositional silence in the last three decades of his life was in part engendered by his success in paying off his debts and his increased income from the tightening of Finnish copyright laws: Sibelius (2015) and McKenna (2012).

46. Diamond and Saez (2011), p. 165.

47. Rawls (1999), pp. 65–6 and Rawls (1993), p. 6.

48. Lamont and Favor (2009), section 3.

49. Rawls (1999), p. 56.

50. Rawls (1999), pp. 118–23.

51. Nozick (1973), a slightly updated version (despite the publication dates) of the equivalent section in Nozick (1974) pp. 57–61, a section entitled 'How Liberty Upsets Patterns'.

52. Nozick (1973) says one million people (p. 57).

53. See Wilkinson and Pickett (2009). On the by-products of inequality, see, as well, Offer (2006), chapter 12.

54. Collins (2013).

55. For African-Americans and Hispanics in the US, the gap in living standards relative to other citizens results not only from differences in remuneration but in holdings of stocks of physical and financial wealth, including housing. In recent decades, the wealth gap has deteriorated much more egregiously than that for income. See Kochhar et al. (2011).

56. Berlin (1969), pp. 123, 131, 144.

57. Sen (2009), pp. 227–31. See as well Sen (1999), especially chapters 1 and 3, and Nussbaum (2011).

58. Conlisk (1974) indicates that such a conflict is unlikely to take place.

59. Nolan and Marx (2009), p. 325; Björklund and Jäntti (2009), p. 516. And see OECD (2009), Isaacs (2009) and Schütz et al. (2008).

60. OECD (2011b). And see Smeeding et al. (2011), especially Pfeffer (2011) and Zissimopoulos and Smith (2011) on wealth transfers and mobility, and Nolan et al. (2011) on the role of social institutions.

61. See Corak (2013). Chetty et al. (2014a) find intergenerational mobility to be stable in the US for birth cohorts born between 1971 and 1993, a period coincident with

rising inequality; other studies similarly confirm this stability for much of the postwar period. Putnam (2015), pp. 293–4, suggests that the general conclusion of a lack of change in mobility for the past several decades in the US, a period of increasing inequality, may be premature, given the presence of substantial lag effects in the registering of intergenerational mobility in the data. The 'socioeconomic gradient' (the level of intergenerational immobility), however, remains highest in the US when compared with a range of European countries, Australia and Canada (Ermisch et al., 2012a).

62. Schütz et al. (2008), pp. 304–5; OECD (2010), pp. 167–8. Critics of PISA (Carnoy and Rothstein (2013)) do not contest the latter result, but claim that 'Because social class inequality is greater in the United States that in any of the countries with which we can reasonably be compared, the relative performance of U.S. adolescents is better than it appears when countries' national average performance is conventionally compared' (p. 3). This defence of US educational standards is tempered by the statement that 'At all points in the social class distribution, U.S. students perform worse, and in many cases substantially worse, than students in a group of top-scoring countries (Canada, Finland, and Korea). Although controlling for social class distribution would narrow the difference in average scores between these countries and the United States, it would not eliminate it' (p. 4). A review of the literature on the education-inequality gradient in a US context can be found in Ladd (2012). The US ranked last in a survey of adult literacy among 23 nations considered for those with below secondary education, ahead of only Poland and Spain for those with non-tertiary education, and slightly below the average of the group for all levels combined (the UK was slightly above average for the combined levels): OECD (2014), p. 35.

63. Institute of Education Studies (IES) National Center for Education Statistics (2009).

64. OECD (2014), p. 13. Some studies have contested the notion that societies with greater economic mobility have better average results on standardised tests: Schütz et al. (2008), p. 305 and Institute of Education Studies (IES) National Center for Education Statistics (2009).

65. See Schütz et al. (2008), pp. 281, 304–5, and the discussion here in Chapter 11.

66. Domar (1957a), p. 151.

67. Osterman and Shulman (2011), pp. 11–12.

68. A discussion of the underserving poor may be found in Rector and Sheffield (2011). For a critique of this position, see Edsall (2013a).

69. United Nations Children's Fund (2007); Gould and Wething (2012); OECD (2011b).

70. Stigler (1945), updated in Stigler (1952), p. 2.

71. Mankiw (2008), p. 90: 'most people view doctor visits as a *necessity* and sailboats as a *luxury*. Of course, whether a good is a *necessity* or a *luxury* depends not on the intrinsic properties of the good but on the preferences of the buyer' [emphasis in original].

72. 'Nutrition, health and education are important for fuller labour utilization … They have been neglected because in advanced societies they count as consumption and have no effect on human productivity. The only exceptions that have been admitted in the literature until recently are some forms of education.' Streeten (2003), p. 95.

73. Townsend (1979), pp. 5–8.

74. Atack and Bateman (1992). The article on page 133 refers to various elements mitigating the harshness of steel work, but Costa (1998) underlines the presence of a class of low-paid workers working very long hours.

75. Friedman (1999), pp. 27–8.
76. ' "Having a low minimum wage is not a bad thing for this country," says billionaire Republican presidential candidate Donald Trump in phone interview on MSNBC. "We can't have a situation where our labor is so much more expensive than other countries that we can no longer compete. It's the United States against other places", where the taxes and wages are lower': Dodge (2015).
77. De Grauwe and Polan (2005), p. 105; the text is slightly rearranged in the quoted passage.
78. This is the conclusion reached in De Grauwe and Polan (2005).
79. Krugman (1994), p. 35.
80. Lindert (2004), pp. 227–45.
81. Lindert (2004), p. 227.
82. '[T]he especially large decline in labour share in the Nordic countries [in recent years] relates ... to the fact of their increasing integration into global capitalism and the consequent intensified competition among corporations and states anxious to attract or retain capital. States with a more egalitarian income chose, or were compelled — given those pressures and their commitment to globalization — to move more rapidly towards the international "norms." ' Sam Gindin, quoted in Edsall (2013b).
83. Sala-i-Martín et al. (2012), p. 4.
84. Sala-i-Martín et al. (2012), pp. 6–7.
85. Dustmann et al. (2014), p. 184.
86. Bilbao-Osorio et al. (2012), p. 58.
87. Baumol et al. (2007), pp. 24, 91.
88. Lindert (2004), pp. 233–5.
89. Baumol and Bowen (1965), p. 500.
90. Cowen and Tabarrok (2014), p. 519.
91. Vaitheeswaran (2007).
92. Krugman (2011).
93. Nussbaum (2010), p. 112; footnote omitted.
94. Arnold (1882).
95. Arnold (1875). Arnold is quoting his father in an excised portion from the 1875 edition.
96. Lindqvist (1997).
97. Brighouse (2006), pp. 2–4.
98. Sutton Trust (2010).
99. As in his poem 'Dover Beach'. A salubrious way of digesting the poem's toxic message is by consulting Samuel Barber's setting of it in the performance sung by the composer:http://www.youtube.com.
100. Tchougounnikov (1957).
101. Gordon (2012), pp. 12–14. This research has been extended in Gordon (2014).
102. Gordon (2000), pp. 50–7.
103. Gordon (2012), p. 20.
104. Gordon (2012), p. 21.
105. Daly (2011).
106. Manyika et al. (2013), p. 4.
107. Krugman (2013).
108. This issue will be re-engaged with in Chapter 12 in the context of the recent claims in Ford (2015) of an inexorable process by which human labour is being replaced by robots.

11 Education in a Free Society

1. Hayek (1982), volume 2, p. 84.
2. Hayek (1982), volume 2, p. 10.
3. Hayek (1982), volume 2, pp. 9–11.
4. Hayek (1982), volume 2, pp. 84–5; emphasis added.
5. See, for instance, Reporters without Borders (2015).
6. Hayek (1982), volume 2, pp. 70–4.
7. Hayek (1982), volume 2, p. 74.
8. A contemporary example is Mankiw (2013).
9. Burt (1957), pp. 64–5.
10. As quoted in Ravitch (2000), p. 133.
11. University of Pennsylvania (2011).
12. Gardner (1993); Goleman (1996).
13. Bouchard and McGue (2003); Bouchard (2004).
14. For the US: Ravitch (2000), p. 155 and Gould (1981), pp. 292–6; for the UK, Simon (1953).
15. For the UK, for instance, see Saunders (2010); the US case will be considered extensively below. On rare occasions (Bowles and Nelson, 1974, pp. 47–8), the IQ measure is used in the context of research concluding that 'the genetic inheritance of IQ is a relatively minor mechanism for the intergenerational transmission of economic and social status' [footnote omitted].
16. Clark (2008); Lynn and Vanhanen (2002).
17. Wintour (2013): '[T]he most influential adviser to the education secretary in the past five years [argues that] ... Education in England is no better than mediocre, and billions of pounds have been wasted on pointless university courses and Sure Start schemes for young children ... educationists need to better understand the impact of genetics on children' [slightly rearranged].
18. Jensen (1969).
19. Turkheimer et al. (2003).
20. His early notoriety was linked to his intervention in the race–IQ controversy in Herrnstein and Murray (1996). In recent years, this consistently held focus on biological endowment has been combined with admonitions to the [white] working class to behave itself: Murray (2012). He has been a prominent influence on a range of Republican contenders for the US presidency, including Mitt Romney and Jeb Bush.
21. Murray (2008b) and Murray (2007).
22. Murray (2008b).
23. Murray (2009).
24. Murray (2009).
25. Murray (2008b).
26. Murray (2009).
27. Murray (2008a).
28. Murray (2008a).
29. Lange (1938), p. 57.
30. Turkheimer et al. (2003).
31. Bouchard (2004), p. 149, and the critique in Richardson and Norgate (2006).
32. Caplan and Miller (2010).
33. Flynn (1978) as described in Flynn (2009a), chapter 2; Flynn (2009b); Ramsden et al. (2011).

34. Flynn (2009a), p. 41; see, as well, Horwitz et al. (2003).
35. Sternberg (2004); see also Nisbett et al. (2012).
36. Bateson and Mameli (2007), pp. 818–19.
37. Stiles (2009), p. 196.
38. Kolb et al. (2015).
39. Ericsson et al. (2007), p. 3.
40. Macnamara et al. (2014).
41. The early-twentieth-century pioneer against racism and biologistic determinism, Franz Boaz, never rejected the role of biology in heredity and human development; it is questionable whether any significant social thinker in modern times has ever dismissed the role of biology. See Degler (1991), pp. 80–2.
42. Smith (1776), p. 15.
43. Rose et al. (2009); Hoynes et al. (2012) claim to see a positive impact of the US food stamp programme from 1961 to 1975 on health and human capital in adulthood because of the resources provided earlier in utero and during childhood.
44. Lewontin (2012), p. 18.
45. Waldfogel and Washbrook (2010) and Fitzpatrick and Pagani (2012).
46. Gopnik (2010), p. 81.
47. Gopnik et al. (1999), p. 181.
48. Rubenstein and Heckman (2001) and Goodman and Gregg (2010).
49. Abel and Göncü (2009), p. 257.
50. Hart and Risley (2003), pp. 111–12.
51. Hart and Risley (2003), pp. 116–17.
52. Fernald et al. (2013).
53. Dickens et al. (2006) and Heckman (2008), Cunha and Heckman (2008), Chetty et al. (2011).
54. For the UK, see Bamfield (2007); for the US, Currie (2009).
55. Bouchard and McGue (2003), pp. 5–6.
56. Thus, at least some of the educational deficits accruing in parent–children relationships in Hart and Risley for the US do not appear in the same form in other countries: Canadian parents with low education read to their children as often as highly educated parents in the US, the UK and Australia (Bradbury et al., 2015, p. 58). More recent research comparable to that of Hart and Risley has found differences in linguistic facility linked to income at very young ages, but due to differences in the quality, rather than the quantity, of non-verbal and verbal interactions that children had received (Hirsh-Pasek et al., 2015).
57. Lareau (2003); Tudge (2008); Dreyer (2013).
58. Ladd (2012).
59. Kim (2011). Deming (2009) reaches a similar conclusion, but emphasises other positive aspects of the programme of a non-cognitive nature.
60. Positive cognitive results: North Carolina Abecedarian Project (2015); positive non-cognitive results: Day et al. (2012). Duncan and Magnuson (2013) find that the significant cognitive benefits from preschool programmes dissipate in subsequent years of schooling; the gains through young adulthood (greater likelihood of high-school graduation, less likelihood of arrest) are attributed to the behavioural and non-cognitive gains from such programmes.
61. A general critique of the irreversibility of early childhood deprivation may be found in Bruer (1999).
62. What we would call 'creativity' or 'imagination'. Bach might well have rejected our modern descriptions as being, respectively, sacrilegious or an indication of insanity.

63. David and Mendel (1966), pp. 37–9. On human 'musicality' in general, see Blacking (1976) and Ball (2010), especially chapters 1 and 2.
64. Chin and Phillips (2004), p. 185.
65. Such conditions have far from disappeared, even in rich countries: Quinn (2013).
66. Reynolds (2012).
67. Huntington (2000), p. xv.
68. Landes (1999), p. 29.
69. Huntington (2000), p. xiii.
70. Chang (2007), chapter 9.
71. Naipaul (1964). The one-sided view in the latter book may be contrasted with the nuanced approach taken to South Asian culture in Myrdal (1972): see the discussion of religion on p. 42.
72. Lewontin (1997).
73. See the examples in Hobsbawm and Ranger (1983).
74. Wright (2013).
75. Hofstadter (1963), p. 237.
76. Hofstadter (1963), p. 434.
77. Molotsky (1988).
78. Linn (2004), p. 1.
79. Steinberg and Kincheloe (2004a), pp. 11, 16.
80. Steinberg and Kincheloe (2004a), p. 18.
81. Steinberg and Kincheloe (2004a), pp. 23–4.
82. Basie (1987), pp. 41–68.
83. Heckman et al. (2013); for the UK, see Gorard et al. (2012).
84. Himmelstrad (2010).
85. Hamer and Fisher (2012)
86. See Chin and Phillips (2004); Stephens et al. (2014).
87. A phrase associated with the educational policies of interwar Social Democratic governments in Vienna. See Gulik (1948), pp. 509–29, 544–82.
88. This description is taken from Krueger (2002), p. 8.
89. Both sides of the debate may be found in the articles in Mishel and Rothstein (2002).
90. Chetty et al. (2011). A contrary conclusion had been reached using data from a recent Texas schools project: Rivkin et al. (2005).
91. Mishel and Rothstein (2002a), p. 6.
92. For the UK, we read: 'the available evidence...suggests that class size reduction policies are not the best option in terms of value for money to raising pupil attainment, compared to others such as increasing teacher effectiveness. Broadly, evidence suggests that class size reduction policies have an uncertain and diminishing effect on pupil achievement in the long run.' Department for Education (2011), p. 1.
93. Hanushek (2011); Krueger (2003). Possible cognitive and non-cognitive spillover effects are briefly mentioned on p. F59; Chetty et al. (2011).
94. Krueger (2003), p. F54.
95. Hanushek (2011), pp. 467–8.
96. Isenberg et al. (2009).
97. See the discussion in Chapter 7. For the UK, a recent example of this approach is Sutton Trust (2011).
98. Podgursky and Springer (2007).

99. Hanushek and Rivkin (2004), pp. 14–17.
100. McKinsey & Company (2010).
101. Hanushek and Rivkin (2004), pp. 21–5.
102. Haycock (2004), p. 241; footnote omitted.
103. Haycock (2004), p. 146.
104. OECD (2014), table D4.1, p. 484 'Organisation of Teachers' Working Time (2012)': column – working time required at school in hours.
105. The issues of classroom discipline and order are nowhere addressed in Haycock (2004).
106. Krueger (2003), F58–9.
107. Duncan and Magnuson (2011), p. 55.
108. Reardon (2011), pp. 91–2; note the dramatic expansion in recent decades in the US on 'enrichment expenditures' for the children of the well-off (Duncan and Murnane, 2011a, p. 58).
109. Niall Ferguson, BBC Reith lectures 2012, as quoted in Murray (2012).
110. Anderson and Ohm (2012) and Dixon (2013), table 8.
111. BBC News (2011); Chowdry and Sibieta (2011), figure 2, p. 7; and Stanford (2012).
112. Anderson (2013). Several anonymous comments on the situation described above found nothing to mock but only wished that these conditions were available for their own children: 'I am so unbelievably jealous of the education these kids are getting. Please note the lack of standardized testing – these kids are busy actually learning, going to museums, building, learning language, and at a 9 to 1 ratio. I wish, oh how I wish, that our public school kids could get an education like this. It would bring everyone up so much.'
113. Powell (1996), p. 42.
114. Lurie (2008), p. 31.
115. Anderson and Ohm (2012).
116. Benn (2011), p. 7.
117. Peshkin (2001), pp. 20–1.
118. Anderson (2013).
119. Anderson and Ohm (2012).
120. Green et al. (2011).
121. Wilby (2013).
122. Edemariam (2013), p. 31.
123. Powell (1996), p. 17.
124. Edemariam (2013), p. 31.
125. 'The school choice of private-independent schools in France, UK, USA and Japan is mainly driven by school characteristics, especially the school composition, student-teacher ratio and better resources in the private-independent schools.' Dronkers and Avram (2009), p. 906. In the UK, there has been a 'steady decline since before 1980 in the independent sector's pupil-teacher ratio, dipping below 1 in 10 by 2004.' Green et al. (2008), p. 392.
126. See Lightfoot (2010).
127. Green et al. (2008).
128. Tough (2012), p. xiv.
129. See Mighton (2007), especially pp. 46–7.
130. Questions surrounding excellence are issues of public concern: Sellgren (2013).
131. Kohn (1998).

132. OECD (2014), p. 230. The high figures for the US are partially accounted for by the unusually large percentage of the population under 15 in the US (20 per cent), compared with Finland's more representative figure for rich countries of 17 per cent (Eurostat, 2012).
133. Esping-Andersen (2008).
134. Corno and Xu (2004), p. 228.
135. France 24 International News 24/7 (2012).
136. 'Is homework one of the bad guys? Supporters of homework say that it's a way of getting parents involved in their children's education by bringing school into the home, and that has to be a good thing. But it's also likely (contrary to President Hollande's assumption) that the people most hostile to homework are affluent parents who want their children to spend their after-school time taking violin lessons and going to Tae Kwon Do classes – activities that are more enriching and (often) more fun than conjugating irregular verbs. Less affluent parents are likely to prefer more homework as a way of keeping their kids off the streets. If we provided after-school music lessons, museum trips, and cool sports programs to poor children, we could abolish homework in a French minute. No one would miss it.' Menand (2012).
137. In Houtenville and Conway (2008).
138. Paton (2013).
139. Mani et al. (2013).
140. See the frosty approach taken to these questions in Morozov (2013).
141. Huizinga (1938).

12   Equality and Democratic Control

1. For a review, see Skott (2015); a mainstream Keynesian approach may be found in Summers (2015).
2. Thornton (2012); *Official Journal of the European Union* (2012).
3. Bien (2015).
4. Bien (2015); Janson (2015) cites the prospect of persistent unemployment as the motivation for Swedish opinion supporting guaranteed income; see, as well, Caputo (2012a), p. 4.
5. Bargain and Doorley (2011) find a modest disincentive effect of a French minimum income scheme offered to uneducated single males over the age of 25. They note (p. 1097) that these results are of the same order of magnitude as previous estimates for the US labour market.
6. Caputo (2012).
7. Etzioni (2008), p. 4.
8. Janson (2015).
9. Murray (2015) p. 2.
10. Murray (2015), pp. 7–8.
11. Carnegy (2012).
12. Frase (2012).
13. Katz (2011).
14. Cingano et al. (2010).
15. See Kaboub (2007).
16. Kaboub (2007), p. 12.
17. Traub and Hiltonsmith (2013). In the UK, the public sector appears to have experienced a less extreme widening of pay differentials than private firms,

with the exception of local government and National Health Service remuneration. The latter conclusion has to be qualified because of opaqueness in the pay arrangements at upper levels of management: Hutton Review of Fair Pay (2011), pp. 13–19.

18. Bergholm and Bieler (2013).
19. This concept is explored in Kalleberg (2011), chapter 1, Osterman and Shulman (2011), chapter 1, and Coates and Lehki (2008), chapter 1.
20. Piketty (2014), pp. 481–2; Atkinson (2015), chapter 1.
21. Empirical studies (Kling et al., 2007 and Gibbons et al., 2013) plausibly suggest that short-term interventions, such as rezoning and housing vouchers, that involve a mere shuffling of cohorts are not likely to generate any exceptional improvements in a range of parameters (such as the test scores of the 11–14-year-olds involved in the first study). Substantive social intervention is likely to be of a long-term kind, effecting change simultaneously at the level of the household, school and neighbourhood. The methodological and empirical difficulties in isolating the impacts of neighbourhoods on the educational development of children are explored in Burdick-Will et al. (2011) and Harding et al. (2011).
22. Lerner (1943).
23. 'We do not believe that securitization alone caused the crisis, but by channelling money from investors to borrowers with ruthless efficiency, it may have allowed speculation on a scale that would have been impossible to sustain with a less sophisticated financial system…the inefficiency of a more traditional financial system might have proved a blessing during this time, as it could have prevented overly optimistic borrowers and investors from finding each other.' Foote et al. (2012), pp. 140, 174.
24. Schularick and Taylor (2012), p. 1057; and see Borio (2012).
25. Borio and Disyatat (2011).
26. Schularick and Taylor (2012), p. 1031 and Borio (2007), p. 6.
27. See, in general, the discussion in Shefrin and Statman (2012), and the quotation therein from Minsky, p. 121.
28. 'Certainly few would agree that a Soviet-type central planning system is likely to make better allocation decisions.' Malkiel (2012), p. 90.
29. See Barro (2009).
30. Dos Passos (1936); Steinbeck (1939); Packer (2014).
31. Schumpeter (1939), p. 173. A summary of Schumpeter's explanation for the overall causes of business cycles is on pp. 181–2. Hayek took different positions over time on the role of finance in business fluctuations, but in his most elaborate statement, his approach was congruent with that of with Schumpeter's real factors approach: 'though in the short run monetary influences may delay the tendencies inherent in the real factors from working themselves out, and temporarily may even reverse these tendencies, in the end it will be the scarcity of real resources relative to demand which will decide what kind of investment, and how much, is profitable…Ultimately, therefore, it is the rate of saving which sets the limits to the amount of investment that can be successfully carried through' (Hayek, 1941, p. 393).
32. Much of the discussion below follows from Auerbach and Siddiki (2004), sections 1 and 2.
33. Modigliani and Miller (1958); and see Auerbach (1988), pp. 163–7 and Gilchrist and Zakrajšek (2012), p. 40.
34. Pensieroso (2007), p. 135.

35. See the critical discussion of such doctrines in Sotiropoulos et al. (2013), chapter 7, especially p. 136.
36. See Auerbach (1988), pp. 226–9 and Winslow (1973).
37. See Steinherr (2000), especially chapters 1 and 5, and Borio (2007); this section borrows material from Auerbach (1988) pp. 188–201.
38. See Steinherr (2000), chapter 5.
39. A discussion of these events from a slightly different perspective may be found in Panitch and Gindin (2012), chapter 5.
40. Hodgman (1963).
41. For a contemporary manifestation of these developments, see Doidge et al. (2013).
42. Steinherr (2000), pp. 36–9.
43. Philippon and Reshef (2013), pp. 74–5.
44. The following uses material from Auerbach and Siddiki (2004), pp. 237–8.
45. It might be thought that such a saving of cash would increase the net supply of investable funds. But in a system of national fiduciary money, any such savings – increases in monetary velocity – are merely the equivalent of monetary creation, which can be done by governments at zero cost. By contrast, savings of non-fiduciary monies (such as silver) may increase national wealth by increasing net claims on foreign resources.
46. Steinherr (2000), chapters 7 and 8; Borio (2011).
47. Steinherr (2000), pp. 42–5, 202; Sotiropoulos et al. (2013), pp. 116–20.
48. '[T]he current approach to regulation and supervision of banks is rapidly becoming ineffective for the most important part of the financial system, namely the global risk-managing banking institutions.' Steinherr (2000), p. 207, and see pp. 132–3, 152–4; Panitch and Gindin (2012), p. 306 give the example of 'special investment vehicles' (SIVs) created by banks in the first part of the twenty-first century to avoid regulation by the Federal Reserve.
49. Steinherr (2000), pp. 221–6.
50. Jarrow (2012).
51. For a historical overview, see Allen (1993).
52. See Borio (2011) and Steinherr (2000), chapter 9.
53. De Grauwe and Ji (2013).
54. See, for instance, Alperovitz (2005).
55. A useful critical review of these doctrines can be found in Erturk et al. (2007).
56. Steinherr (2000), p. 279.
57. Steinherr (2000), pp. 103, 255; Shiller (2008), pp. 164–8; Shiller (2012), pp. 67, 117.
58. Shiller (2012), pp. xiv, 43–4; Shiller (2008), p. 126; emphasis added.
59. Shiller (2012), p. 5; emphasis added.
60. Shiller (2012), pp. 22, xvii.
61. All such activities will have to contend with the forms of lobbying and special interest pleading to be found in the contemporary world. Thus, recently proposed legislation in the US to set up a bank providing funds to state and local governments for infrastructural projects is likely to be compromised by tax concessions to multinationals contributing to its start-up financing. See Hungerford (2014).
62. Piketty et al. (2014), p. 232; Saez et al. (2012), p. 42 and table p. 45; McClelland and Mok (2012); Diamond and Saez (2011), p. 171; Mirrlees et al. (2011).
63. Atkinson et al. (2011), pp. 125–32.
64. Piketty and Saez (2007), pp. 11–13.
65. Atkinson et al. (2011), pp. 9–10.

66. In general, see Atkinson (2004) and Piketty and Saez (2007).
67. Lindert (2004), chapter 10; Piketty and Saez (2007), pp. 19–22.
68. See Roine et al. (2009), pp. 367–8.
69. Adema and Ladaique (2009), table A3.1.a p. 84; and see Fishback (2010).
70. Adema and Ladaique (2009), p. 28.
71. Adema and Ladaique (2009), pp. 14, 44.
72. Shaxson (2011), pp. 13, 45.
73. Atkinson et al. (2011), p. 40.
74. Rogers and Toder (2011), p. 1.
75. See McIntyre (2011) compared with Carter (2014).
76. Toder and Baneman (2012).
77. Burman (2013), pp. 589–90.
78. The enormous obstacles to limiting these exemptions are reviewed in Toder et al. (2013).
79. Piketty (2014), chapters 14 and 15. For reasons of simplicity alone, Piketty's scheme is to be preferred to other taxation regimes, such as taxes on consumption that make claim to greater efficiency (see Auerbach and Hassett, 2015, especially pp. 40–2).
80. See Piketty (2014), pp. 569–70.
81. Mayersohn (2014). And see Skocpol (2003).
82. Edsall (2014).
83. Henry (2012), p. 36.
84. Atkinson et al. (2011), p. 29, note the consistently lower shares for income for the top 1 per cent in survey data compared with tax records.
85. Bø et al. (2014). Since the beginning of 2011, access to the tax lists now takes place through a personalised log-in system for accessing online public services, which involves a pin-code and a password.
86. Shaxson (2011), p. vi.
87. Henry (2012), pp. 3–5.
88. Henry (2012), p. 20.
89. Henry (2012), p. 44.
90. Palan (2002), pp. 158–9, reviews a right-wing literature that justifies tax havens as protection against the monopolistic power of the state.
91. Picciotto (2012).
92. Henry (2012), p. 41.
93. Picciotto (2012), p. 14.
94. Johannesen and Zucman (2014), p. 65.
95. Tax Justice Network (2014).
96. Friedman (1962), p. 196.
97. Sala-i-Martín et al. (2012), pp. 4–5.
98. Decker (2013).
99. Financial Transparency Coalition (2014).
100. Piketty (2014), p. 570.
101. Boldrin and Levine (2013); see as well Lerner (2009).
102. Moser (2013).
103. See Boldrin and Levine (2013), pp. 4, 18–19.
104. Boldrin and Levine (2013), p. 3.
105. Stiglitz (2013a).
106. The head of a British drug company called an Indian manufacturer a pirate for coming out with a generic version of one of its AIDS drugs: see Goldacre (2009).

107. Hacker and Pierson (2010), p. 6. Such a view is now a fairly orthodox one: 'economic elites and organized groups representing business interests have substantial independent impacts on U.S. government policy, while average citizens and mass-based interest groups have little or no independent influence.' Gilens and Page (2014).

108. Bonica et al. (2013). Unsurprisingly, very rich people have a more tolerant attitude towards inequality than others. Surveys commonly indicate that the public views present-day inequalities to be too wide, especially at the top (Orton and Rowlingson, 2007, for the UK and Andersen and Yaish, 2012, covering 20 countries). But strong claims for a substantial gap between actual and desired distributions (Norton and Ariely, 2011) may partially reflect confusion among interviewees on the distinction between income distribution and the much more skewed wealth distributions with which they were confronted. In general, surveys asking the public to respond to abstract questions of this kind can only give a very partial indication of public attitudes towards inequality as part of a society's lived experience.

109. Thus, with cutbacks to public funding for research and growing wealth inequalities in the US, it has been suggested that scientific research is progressively being shaped 'by the particular preferences of individuals with huge amounts of money'. Steven A. Edwards, quoted in Broad (2014).

110. In Europe, alienation from political processes appears to be particularly strong among lower-income social groupings. See Stoker (2011), p. 12.

111. Hacker and Pierson (2010) suggest that 'To call [most US citizens'] knowledge of even the most elementary facts about the political system shaky would be generous', a fact that 'in serious political discourse it is usually considered to be bad manners to point out' (pp. 108–9). Whether such a generalisation is universally valid is less certain than the fact that elite groupings in most countries would perceive it to be so.

112. Stiglitz (2013), chapter 2. Stiglitz is also concerned with a range of market failures that will inherently emerge in contemporary capitalism, most especially because of the presence of asymmetric information between market participants.

113. Open Secrets (2015).

114. POGO (2013).

115. Ferguson et al. (2013).

116. Biegelsen (2011). For the UK, Hackett and Hunter (2015).

117. International Federation of Health Plans (2013).

118. Ornstein et al. (2014).

119. This literature is reviewed in Hacker and Pierson (2010), pp. 151–5.

120. Curran et al. (2009).

121. Curran et al. (2009), p. 22.

122. Freeman (2005), p. 137, suggests that it is now a consensus view that unions reduce inequality of pay, a view also held by Card et al. (2004).

123. See Western and Rosenfeld (2011) and Farber (2005).

124. Coats and Lehki (2008), pp. 38, 41–2.

125. Kocher et al. (2012); Pencavel (2005), pp. 86–7, discusses unions' role in worker grievances.

126. Freeman (2007), pp. 13–14, 93–4.

127. Pencavel (2005), p. 69.

128. Pencavel (2005), pp. 66–7, and Schmitt and Mitukiewcz (2012), pp. 1, 5–7. Note that there can often be, as in France, a broad gap between union membership

(less than 10 per cent) and union coverage in collective bargaining (90 per cent). Pontusson (2013), p. 800, cites Visser (2013) with data from 1960 to 2011 for 22 OECD countries, all showing a decline from peak levels of union density.

129. Freeman (2007), pp. 78–9, and Bryson and Blanchflower (2008).
130. Public sector unions remain the only large source of funds in the US acting as a countervailing force to right-wing political donations. The relevant information can be disinterred from Open Secrets (2015).
131. Baccaro and Howell (2011), p. 550: 15 advanced capitalist countries considered.
132. Bronfenbrenner (2009).
133. See Gross (2003a).
134. Freeman (2007), p. 11, fig. 1.2 indicates a positive relationship between collective bargaining coverage and social expenditure as a share of GDP for different countries. In Pontusson (2013), p. 813, it is suggested that the relationship between union density and both earnings inequality and redistributive policies has weakened since 1995; on pp. 807–10, a positive association between union density and electoral turnout across countries is reported.
135. Pontusson (2009). This typology is used by Pontusson to draw conclusions about the real-life efficacy of these regimes as they function in various countries. Here, these different categories are used more abstractly to characterise a range of relationships between capital and labour. The continental variant depicted here is perhaps particularly distant from the countries to which it is attached in the text.
136. Scandinavian social democracy's right-wing admirers have sometimes chosen to ignore the role of union involvement in its construction. See the reminder of this fact given by Schwartz (2013) in response to Wooldridge (2013). Recent decades have witnessed a decline in both the economic and the political role of unions in Scandinavia (with some variance between countries), though in both contexts they retain substantial power relative to other countries. The decline of the political power of trade unions is described in Allern et al. (2010).
137. The figures for all countries are from Schmitt and Mitukiewcz (2012).
138. Pontusson (2009), pp. 7–8.
139. It was, perhaps, dissatisfaction with the low level of worker influence over the destinies of firms in the Nordic model that led to the ultimately unsuccessful promotion in the 1970s by Rudolf Meidner of wage earner funds that would lead gradually to the transfer of the assets of the firm to its employees: see Sassoon (2010), pp. 706–15.
140. Note the discussions in Chapter 3 and see, for instance, Schweickart (1980).
141. Mill (1870), chapter VII, section 2(2), p. 537 and section 2 (6), p. 543.
142. Perhaps feeling defensive in this regard, supporters of capitalism have put forth a view of firm functioning as the voluntary interaction of a team. The central agent (the capitalist) typically hires workers to perform tasks, but it might just as well have been the other way around – workers could have hired a capitalist, whose specialised skills would facilitate team production: '[In] the classical firm … the central agent is called the firm's owner and the employer. No authoritarian control is involved. The contractual structure arises as a means of enhancing efficient organization of team production.' Alchian and Demsetz (1972), p. 794.

143. Kruse et al. (2010a) in Kruse et al. (2010), pp. 1–4. The discussion here is largely in the context of Employee Stock Ownership Plans (ESOPs) in the US, situations in which workers gain (some) ownership of the enterprise, and therefore a direct material interest in its fortunes, but do not, as a rule, formally control it.

144. Lazonick and Huzzard (2014). The range of 'employee involvement' ranges from ESOPs to co-determination (to be discussed below). These themes are expanded upon in Lippert et al. (2014).

145. Ward (1958), p. 575.

146. Vanek (1970), pp. 298–300.

147. Dow (2003), pp. 152–6, 236–8.

148. The important question of the state's role in the initiation of these techno-logical developments is discussed in Chapter 9.

149. Lécuyer (2006), pp. 98–9, 123–8, 192. The solution to this problem proposed by Dow (2003), p. 154, is for worker-managed enterprises to have a market in membership rights for the enterprise.

150. Dow (2003), p. 47.

151. See Wolff (2012).

152. Alperovitz (2013).

153. Alperovitz (2013).

154. Dow (2003), pp. 59–64.

155. Thomas and Logan (1982), pp. 35–6, 70.

156. The sources consulted on co-determination have included Dow (2003), pp. 83–91, Michel (2007), and Becker and Paulusma (2011) in Anderson et al. (2011), chapter 8.

157. Germany's employment ministry has banned its managers from calling or emailing staff out of hours except in emergencies: Vasagar (2013).

158. Hutchins (2014).

159. Feldstead et al. (2009), p. 5.

160. Hager (2004).

161. Colley et al. (2003).

162. Green (2006), chapters 6 and 7. Merkle (1980), chapter 2, had properly dismissed the notion that Taylorism was a once-and-for-all fashion to be exclusively iden-tified with the early twentieth century.

163. Ford (2015), pp. 252–3. Frey and Osborne (2013) suggest that around 47 per cent of total US employment involves jobs which 'could be automated relatively soon, perhaps over the next decade or two'. What remains the mainstream consensus view is less calamitous: 'journalists and even expert commenta-tors tend to overstate the extent of machine substitution for human labor and ignore the strong complementarities between automation and labor that increase productivity, raise earnings, and augment demand for labor' (Autor, 2015, p. 5).

164. Ford (2015), pp. 257–61.

165. See Ford (2015), chapter 9, 'Super-Intelligence and the Singularity', concerned with computers of the future that exceed human intelligence (whatever that means).

Conclusion

1. Israel (2006), pp. 15–26; Israel (2010), especially the preface and chapter 1.

2. Note, for instance, the widespread use of value-added measures to judge teacher performance based on changes in students' test scores from year to year, and between students: see Dillon (2010).
3. Fromm (1956).
4. Fromm (1956), p. 293.
5. Habermas (2015), p. 64.
6. Auerbach (1992), p. 35.

Bibliography

Abbate, J. (2000) *Inventing the Internet*. Cambridge, MA: MIT Press.

Abel, B. and Göncü, A. (2009) 'Activities of Children in Different Societies and Social Classes – Essay Review of the Everyday Lives of Young Children: Culture, Class, and Child Rearing in Diverse Societies by J. Tudge'. *Human Development* 52: 257–60.

Abraham, K. G., Spletzer, J. R. and Harper, M. (eds) (2010) *Labor in the New Economy*. Chicago: University of Chicago Press.

Acemoglu, D. (1998) 'Why Do New Technologies Complement Skills? Directed Technical Change and Wage Inequality?' *Quarterly Journal of Economics* 113(4): 1055–89.

Acemoglu, D. and Angrist, J. (2001) 'How Large Are Human-Capital Externalities? Evidence from Compulsory-Schooling Laws' in Bernanke and Rogoff (2001), pp. 9–74.

Acemoglu, D., Cantoni, D., Johnson, S. and Robinson, J. A. (2011) 'The Consequences of Radical Reform: The French Revolution'. *American Economic Review* 101(7): 3286–307.

Acemoglu, D., Gallego, F. A. and Robinson, J. A. (2014) 'Institutions, Human Capital and Development', *NBER Working Paper* No. 19933, February.

Acemoglu, D., Johnson, S. and Robinson, J. (2005) 'The Rise of Europe: Atlantic Trade, Institutional Change and Economic Growth'. *American Economic Review* 95(3): 546–79.

Adams, C. A. (1919) 'Industrial Standardization'. *American Academy of Political and Social Science* 82: 289–99.

Adema, W. and Ladaique, M. (2009) 'How Expensive Is the Welfare State?: Gross and Net Indicators in the OECD Social Expenditure DataBase (SOCX)'. *OECD Social, Employment and Migration Working Papers* No. 92, OECD Publishing, http://www.oecd-ilibrary.org (accessed September 2015).

Adonis, A. (2012) *Education, Education, Education: Reforming England's Schools*. London: Biteback Publishing.

Aghion, P. and Howitt, P. (1998) *Endogenous Growth Theory*. Cambridge, MA: MIT Press.

Alchian, A. (1950) 'Uncertainty, Evolution and Economic Theory'. *Journal of Political Economy* LVIII: 211–21.

Alchian, A. and Demsetz, H. (1972) 'Production, Information Costs, and Economic Organization'. *American Economic Review* 62(5): 777–95.

Alchon, G. (1985) *The Invisible Hand of Planning: Capitalism, Social Science and the State in the 1920s*. Princeton: Princeton University Press.

Alexander, M. (1929) *Industrial Standardization*. New York: National Industrial Conference Board, Inc.

Allen, R. C. (2003) *Farm to Factory: A Reinterpretation of the Soviet Industrial Revolution*. Princeton: Princeton University Press.

Allen, R. C. (2009) *The British Industrial Revolution in Historical Perspective*. Cambridge: Cambridge University Press.

Allen, R. C. (2011) *Global Economic History: A Very Short Introduction*. Oxford: Oxford University Press.

Allen, W. R. (1993) 'Irving Fisher and the 100 Percent Reserve Proposal'. *Journal of Law and Economics* 36(2): 703–17.

Allern, E. H., Aylott, N. and Christiansen, F. J. (2010) 'Scenes from a Marriage: Social Democrats and Trade Unions in Scandinavia', *Centre for Voting and Parties Department of Political Science University of Copenhagen*, http://www.cvap.polsci. ku.dk (accessed September 2015).

Alperovitz, G. (2005) *America beyond Capitalism: Reclaiming Our Wealth, Our Liberty, and Our Democracy.* Hoboken: John Wiley & Sons.

Alperovitz, G. (2013) 'Mondragón and the System Problem', 13 November, http://www.garalperovitz.com (accessed September 2015).

Altshuler, A., Anderson, M., Jones, D., Roos, D. and Womack, J. (1984) *The Future of the Automobile.* London: George Allen & Unwin.

Alvaredo, F., Atkinson, A. B., Piketty, T. and Saez, E. (2013) 'The Top 1 Percent in International and Historical Perspective', *NBER Working Paper* No. 19075, May.

Alveredo, F., Atkinson, A., Piketty, T. and Saez, E. (2015) *The World Top Incomes Database*, http://topincomes.parisschoolofeconomics.eu (accessed September 2015).

Amsden, A. (1989) *Asia's Next Giant: South Korea and Late Industrialization.* New York: Oxford University Press.

Amsden, A. (2001) *The Rise of 'the Rest': Challenges to the West from Late-Industrializing Economies.* Oxford: Oxford University Press.

Andersen, R. and Yaish, M. (2012) 'Public Opinion on Income Inequality in 20 Democracies: The Enduring Impact of Social Class and Economic Inequality'. Amsterdam Institute for Advanced Labour Studies (AIAS), *GINI Discussion Paper* 48.

Anderson, J. (2013) 'Is This the Best Education Money Can Buy?' *New York Times Magazine*, The Money Issue, 2 May, www.nytimes.com (accessed September 2015).

Anderson, J. and Ohm, R. (2012) 'Bracing for $40,000 at New York City Private Schools'. *New York Times*, 27 January, www.nytimes.com (accessed September 2015).

Anderson, K., Becker, F., Diamond, P., Eichhorst, W., Gusenbauer, A., Hassel, A., Hedborg, A., Hemerijck, A., Jameson, H., Lindh, T., Manning, A., Natali, D., Palier, B., Paulusma, P., Stoker, G. and Vandenbroucke, F. (2011) *Social Progress in the 21st Century: Social Investment, Labour Market Reform and Intergenerational Inequality.* London: Policy Network, Wiardi Beckman Stichting & Foundation for Progressive European Studies.

Anderson, K. and Tyers, R. (1987) 'Japan's Agricultural Policy in International Perspective'. *Journal of the Japanese and International Economies* 1(2): 131–46.

Andrews, P., Ryve, A., Hemmi, K. and Sayers, J. (2014) 'PISA, TIMSS and Finnish Mathematics Teaching: an Enigma in Search of an Explanation'. *Educational Studies in Mathematics* 87: 7–26.

Angrist, J. D., Pathak, P. A. and Walters, C. R. (2013) 'Explaining Charter School Effectiveness'. *American Economic Journal: Applied Economics* 5(4): 1–27.

Armstrong, P., Glyn, A. and Harrison, J. (1991) *Capitalism since 1945.* Oxford: Blackwell.

Armytage, W. H. G. (1955) *Civic Universities.* London: Ayer Publishing.

Arnold, M. (1875) *Culture and Anarchy*, second version. Cambridge: Cambridge University Press, edition of 1931.

Arnold, M. (1882) 'Literature and Science', lecture in 1882; electronic edition by Ian Lancashire, http://homes.chass.utoronto.ca (accessed September 2015).

Arrow, K. J. (1962) 'Economic Welfare and the Allocation of Resources for Invention' in Nelson (1962), pp. 609–28.

Arrow, K. J. (1963) *Social Choice and Individual Values*, second edition. New Haven: Yale University Press.

Atack, J. and Bateman, F. (1992) 'How Long Was the Workday in 1880?' *The Journal of Economic History* 52(1): 129–60.

Atkinson, A. B. (2004) 'Income Tax and Top Incomes over the Twentieth Century'. *Hacienda Pública Española / Revista de Economía Pública* 168(1): 123–41.

Atkinson, A. B. (2015) *Inequality: What Can Be Done?* Cambridge, MA: Harvard University Press.

Atkinson, A. B., Piketty, T. and Saez, E. (2011) 'Top Incomes in the Long Run of History'. *Journal of Economic Literature* 49(1): 3–71.

Auerbach, A. J. and Hassett, K. (2015) 'Capital Taxation in the Twenty-First Century'. *American Economic Review* Papers & Proceedings 105(5): 38–42.

Auerbach, P. (1988) *Competition: The Economics of Industrial Change.* Oxford: Basil Blackwell.

Auerbach, P. (1992) 'On Socialist Optimism'. *New Left Review* 192: 5–35.

Auerbach, P. (2007) 'US Decline in the Context of Formal Education and In Situ Learning'. *Journal of Economic Issues* XLI(2): 715–28.

Auerbach, P. (2007a) 'The Left Intellectual Opposition in Britain 1945–2000: the Case of the Alternative Economic Strategy'. London: Socialist History Society *SHS Occasional Paper* No. 23.

Auerbach, P., Desai, M. and Shamsavari, A. (1988) 'The Dialectic of Market and Plan: The Transition from Actually Existing Capitalism'. *New Left Review* 170: 61–78.

Auerbach, P. and Siddiki, J. (2004) 'Financial Liberalisation and Economic Development: An Assessment'. *Journal of Economic Surveys* 18(3): 231–65, sections 1 and 2.

Auerbach, P. and Skott, P. (1988) 'Concentration, Competition and Distribution – a Critique of Theories of Monopoly Capital'. *International Review of Applied Economics* 2(1): 42–61.

Auerbach, P. and Skott, P. (1992) 'Financial Innovation and Planning in a Capitalist Economy'. *Metroeconomica* 43(1–2): 75–102.

Autor, D. H. (2015) 'Why Are There Still So Many Jobs? The History and Future of Workplace Automation'. *Journal of Economic Perspectives* 29(3): 3–30.

Autor, D. H. and Dorn, D. (2013) 'The Growth of Low-Skill Service Jobs and the Polarization of the US Labor Market'. *American Economic Review* 103(5): 1553–97.

Autor, D. H., Dorn, D. and Hanson, G. H. (2013) 'The China Syndrome: Local Labor Market Effects of Import Competition in the United States'. *American Economic Review* 103(6): 2121–68.

Autor, D. H., Levy, F. and Murnane, R. J. (2003) 'The Skill Content of Recent Technological Change: An Empirical Exploration'. *Quarterly Journal of Economics* 118(4): 1279–333.

Baccaro, L. and Howell, C. (2011) 'A Common Neoliberal Trajectory: The Transformation of Industrial Relations in Advanced Capitalism'. *Politics and Society* 39(4): 521–63.

Bairoch, P. (1993) *Economics and World History: Myths and Realities.* Chicago: University of Chicago Press.

Bale, M. D. and Greenshields, B. L. (1978) 'Japanese Agricultural Distortions and Their Welfare Value'. *American Journal of Agricultural Economics* February: 59–64.

Balisciano, M. L. (1998) 'Hope for America: American Notions of Economic Planning between Pluralism and Neoclassicism, 1930–1950'. *History of Political Economy* 30 (Supplement): 153–78.

Ball, P. (2010) *The Musical Instinct*. London: Bodley Head.

Bamfield, L. (2007) *Born Unequal: Why We Need a Progressive Pre-Birth Agenda*. London: Fabian Society Policy Report no. 61.

Baran, P. and Sweezy, P. (1966) *Monopoly Capital*. Harmondsworth: Penguin Books.

Barber, J. and Harrison, M. (1991) *The Soviet Home Front*. London: Longman.

Bargain, O. and Doorley, K. (2011) 'Caught in the Trap? Welfare's Disincentive and the Labor Supply of Single Men'. *Journal of Public Economics* 95: 1096–1110.

Barnard, H. (2015) 'Raising Aspirations and Attainment'. *Joseph Rowntree Foundation*, http://amie.atl.org.uk (accessed September 2015).

Barnett, C. (1995) *The Lost Victory: British Dreams, British Realities, 1945–50*. London: Macmillan.

Barone, E. (1908) 'Il Ministro della Produzione nello Stato Collettivista'. *Giornale degli Economisti*, September–October, reprinted in English as 'The Ministry of Production in the Collectivist State' in Hayek (1935), pp. 245–90.

Barro, R. J. (2009) 'Rare Disasters, Asset Prices, and Welfare Costs'. *American Economic Review* 99(1): 243–64.

Barzun, J. (1959) *The House of Intellect*. Chicago: University of Chicago.

Basie, C. (1987) *Good Morning Blues: The Autobiography of Count Basie*, as told to Albert Murray. London: Paladin Books.

Bateson, P. and Mameli, M. (2007) 'The Innate and the Acquired: Useful Clusters or a Residual Distinction from Folk Biology?' *Developmental Psychobiology* 49: 818–31.

Bauerlein, M. (2008) *The Dumbest Generation*. New York: Jeremy P. Tarcher/Penguin.

Bauman, Z. (1976) *Socialism: The Active Utopia*. New York: Holmes & Meier.

Baumol, W. (1959) *Business Behavior, Value and Growth*. New York: Macmillan.

Baumol, W. (2002) *The Free-Market Innovation Machine: Analyzing the Growth Miracle of Capitalism*. Princeton: Princeton University Press.

Baumol, W. and Bowen, W. (1965) 'On the Performing Arts: The Anatomy of their Economic Problems'. *The American Economic Review* 55(2): 495–502.

Baumol, W., Litan, R. and Schramm, C. (2007) *Good Capitalism, Bad Capitalism and the Economics of Growth and Prosperity*. New Haven: Yale University Press.

BBC News (2011) 'What Does [sic] the Schools Spending Data Show?' 12 January, http://www.bbc.co.uk (accessed September 2015).

BBC News (2012) 'Teaching Evolution Key to Free School Funding Deal', 28 November, http://www.bbc.co.uk (accessed September 2015).

Bebchuk, L. A., Fried, J. M. and Walker, D. I. (2002) 'Managerial Power and Rent Extraction in the Design of Executive Compensation'. *University of Chicago Law Review* 69: 751–846.

Becker, F. and Paulusma, P. (2011) 'Hidden Depression in the Workplace' in Anderson et al. (2011), chapter 8.

Becker, G. (1962) 'Investment in Human Capital'. *Journal of Political Economy* 70(5) part 2: 9–49.

Becker, G. and Mulligan, C. B. (1997) 'The Endogenous Determination of Time Preference'. *Quarterly Journal of Economics* 112(3): 729–58.

Becker, G. and Tomes, N. (1986) 'Human Capital and the Rise and Fall of Families'. *Journal of Labor Economics* 4(3) part 2: S1–S39.

Becker, S., Hornung, E. and Woessmann, L. (2011) 'Education and Catch-Up in the Industrial Revolution'. *American Economic Journal Macroeconomics* 3(3): 92–126.

Becker, S. and Woessmann, L. (2009) 'Was Weber Wrong?' *Quarterly Journal of Economics* 124(2): 531–96.

Beecroft, A. (2011) *Report on Employment Law*, October, http://news.bis.gov.uk (accessed September 2015).

Belfield, C. and Levin, H. (2005) 'Vouchers and Public Policy: When Ideology Trumps Evidence'. *American Journal of Education* 111(4): 548–67.

Benn, M. (2011) 'At a Private School in Berkshire, Pupils Pay £30,000 a Year for Lessons in Happiness and a Golf Course, at an Inner London State School 75% of Pupils Are So Poor They Qualify for Free Meals'. *Guardian G2*, 17 August, pp. 6–9.

Benn, M. (2011a) *School Wars: The Battle for Britain's Education*. London: Verso.

Bennett, J. T. and Kaufman, B. E. (2004) 'What Do Unions Do? A Twenty Year Perspective'. *Journal of Labour Research* XXV(3): 339–49.

Bergholm, T. and Bieler, A. (2013) 'Globalization and the Erosion of the Nordic Model: A Swedish–Finnish Comparison'. *European Journal of Industrial Relations* 19(1): 55–70.

Berle, A. (1965) *The American Economic Republic*, revised edition. New York: Harcourt, Brace and World.

Berle, A. and Means, G. (1932) *The Modern Corporation and Private Property*. New York: Harcourt, Brace and World, revised edition 1968.

Berlin, I. (1969) 'Two Concepts of Liberty' in *Four Essays on Liberty*. Oxford: Oxford University Press.

Bernanke, B. and Rogoff, K. (eds) (2001) *NBER Macroeconomics Annual 2000, Volume 15*. Cambridge, MA: MIT Press.

Bernstein, E. (1899) *The Preconditions of Socialism*. Cambridge: Cambridge University Press, 1993.

Bertrand, M., Mullainathan, S. and Shafir, E. (2004) 'A Behavioral-Economics View of Poverty'. *The American Economic Review* 94(2): 419–23.

Biegelsen, A. (2011) 'Half the Members of Congress are Millionaires', Center for Public Integrity, http://www.publicintegrity.org (accessed September 2015).

Bien (Basic Income Earth Network) (2015) 'About Basic Income', http://www.basicincome.org (accessed September 2015).

Bilbao-Osorio, B., Blanke, J., Crotti, R., Drzeniek Hanouz, M., Fidanza, B., Geiger, T., Ko, C. and Serin, C. (2012) 'Assessing the Sustainable Competitiveness of Nations' in Schwab and Sala-i-Martín (2012), pp. 49–63.

Björklund, A. and Jäntti, M. (2009) 'Intergenerational Income Mobility and the Role of Family Background' in Salverda et al. (2009), pp. 491–521.

Björklund, A., Roine, J. and Waldenström, D. (2012) 'Intergenerational Top Income Mobility in Sweden: Capitalist Dynasties in the Land of Equal Opportunity?' *Journal of Public Economics* 96: 474–84.

Blacking, J. (1976) *How Musical Is Man?* London: Faber and Faber.

Blair, J. (1972) *Economic Concentration*. New York: Harcourt Brace.

Blinder, A. S., Lo, A. W. and Solow, R. (2012) (eds) *Rethinking the Financial Crisis*. New York: Russell Sage Foundation.

Block, F. (2008) 'Swimming against the Current: The Rise of a Hidden Developmental State in the United States'. *Politics & Society* 36(2): 169–208.

Block, F. and Keller, M. R. (eds) (2011) *State of Innovation: The U.S. Government's Role in Technology Development*. Boulder: Paradigm Publishers.

Bloom, N., Sadun, R. and Van Reenen, J. (2012) 'Americans Do IT Better: US Multinationals and the Productivity Miracle'. *American Economic Review* 102(1): 167–201.

Bø, E. E., Slemrod, J. and Thoresen, T. O. (2014) 'Taxes on the Internet: Deterrence Effects of Public Disclosure', *Statistics Norway, Research Department Discussion Papers* No. 770, January, http://www.ssb.no (accessed September 2015).

Boldrin, M. and Levine, D. K. (2013) 'The Case against Patents'. *Journal of Economic Perspectives* 27(1): 3–22.

Bonica, A., McCarty, N., Poole, K. T. and Rosenthal, H. (2013) 'Why Hasn't Democracy Slowed Rising Inequality?' *Journal of Economic Perspectives* 27(3): 103–24.

Borio, C. (2007) 'Change and Constancy in the Financial System: Implications for Financial Distress and Policy', *BIS Working Papers* No. 237, October.

Borio, C. (2011) 'Rediscovering the Macroeconomic Roots of Financial Stability Policy: Journey, Challenges and a Way Forward', *BIS Working Papers* No. 354, September.

Borio, C. (2012) 'The Financial Cycle and Macroeconomics: What Have We Learnt?' *BIS Working Papers* No. 395, December.

Borio, C. and Disyatat, P. (2011) 'Global Imbalances and the Financial Crisis: Link or No Link?' *BIS Working Papers* No. 346, May.

Bottles, S. (1987) *Los Angeles and the Automobile: The Making of the Modern City.* Berkeley: University of California Press.

Bouchard, T. J., Jr (2004) 'Genetic Influence on Human Psychological Traits – a Survey'. *Current Directions in Psychological Science* 13(4): 148–51.

Bouchard, T. J., Jr and McGue, M. (2003) 'Genetic and Environmental Influences on Human Psychological Differences'. *Journal of Neurobiology* 54(1): 4–45.

Bowles, S. and Gintis, H. (1976) *Schooling in Capitalist America.* New York: Basic Books.

Bowles, S. and Gintis, H. (2002) 'Schooling in Capitalist America Revisited'. *Sociology of Education* 75: 1–18.

Bowles, S. and Nelson, V. (1974) 'The "Inheritance of IQ" and the Intergenerational Reproduction of Economic Inequality'. *Review of Economics and Statistics* 56(1): 39–51.

Bowman, M. J. (1962) 'The Land-Grant Colleges and Universities in Human-Resource Development'. *Journal of Economic History* 22: 523–46.

Bradbury, B., Corak, M., Waldfogel, J. and Washbrook, E. (2015) *Too Many Children Left Behind: The US Achievement Gap in Comparative Perspective.* New York: Russell Sage Foundation.

Brady, R. (1932) 'The Meaning of Rationalization'. *Quarterly Journal of Economics* 46(3): 526–40.

Brady, R. (1933) *The Rationalization Movement in German Industry.* Berkeley: University of California Press.

Brandolini, A. and Smeeding, T. (2009) 'Income Inequality in Richer and OECD Countries' in Salverda et al. (2009), pp. 71–100.

Braun, E. and Macdonald, S. (1982) *Revolution in Miniature,* second edition. Cambridge: Cambridge University Press.

Braverman, H. (1988) *Labor and Monopoly Capital: The Degradation of Work in the Twentieth Century,* new edition 1988; originally published 1974. New York: Monthly Review Press.

Bresnahan, T. and Gordon, R. (eds) (1997) *The Economics of New Goods.* Chicago: University of Chicago.

Breton, T. R. (2010) 'Schooling and National Income: How Large Are the Externalities?' *Education Economics* 18(1): 67–92.

Breton, T. R. (2010a) 'Schooling and National Income: How Large Are the Externalities?: Correction'. *Education Economics* 18(4): 455–56.

Bridgman, B (2014) 'Is Labor's Loss Capital's Gain? Gross versus Net Labor Shares'. *Bureau of Economic Analysis,* October, http://bea.gov (accessed September 2015).

Brighouse, H. (2006) *On Education.* London: Routledge.

Broad, W. J. (2014) 'Billionaires with Big Ideas Are Privatizing American Science', *New York Times*, 15 March, http://www.nytimes.com (accessed September 2015).

Bronfenbrenner, K. (2009) 'No Holds Barred: The Intensification of Employer Opposition to Organizing', Briefing Paper, May, Washington, DC. Economic Policy Institute, http://www.epi.org (accessed September 2015).

Bruer, J. T. (1999) *The Myth of the First Three Years: A New Understanding of Early Brain Development and Lifelong Learning*. New York: The Free Press.

Bruner, J. (1972) *The Relevance of Education*. Harmondsworth: Penguin.

Bryson, A. and Blanchflower, D. (2008) 'The End of Trade Unionism as We Know It?' *Centrepiece*, Autumn, http://cep.lse.ac.uk (accessed September 2015).

Buckley, W. (1951) *God and Man at Yale*. South Bend: Gateway Editions, edition of 1977.

Burdick-Will, J., Ludwig, J., Raudenbush, S. W., Sampson, R. J., Sanbonmatsu, L. and Sharkey, P. (2011) 'Converging Evidence for Neighborhood Effects on Children's Test Scores: An Experimental. Quasi-Experimental, and Observational Comparison' in Duncan and Murnane (2011), pp. 255–76.

Burman, L. E. (2013) 'Taxes and Inequality'. *Tax Law Review* 66: 563–92.

Burnham, J. (1941) *The Managerial Revolution*. Bloomington: Indiana University Press, edition of 1962.

Burns, A. (1936) *The Decline of Competition*. New York: McGraw-Hill.

Burt, C. (1957) *The Causes and Treatments of Backwardness*. London: University of London Press, 4th edition, pp. 64–5, as cited in Indiana University 'Human Intelligence', http://www.intelltheory.com (accessed September 2015).

Cain, P. J. and Hopkins, A. G. (1993) *British Imperialism: Innovation and Expansion 1688–1914*. London: Longman.

Caplan, B. and Miller, S. C. (2010) 'Intelligence Makes People Think Like Economists: Evidence from the General Social Survey'. *Intelligence* 38: 636–47.

Caputo, R. K. (ed.) (2012) *Basic Income Guarantee and Politics: International Experiences and Perspectives on the Viability of Income Guarantee*. New York: Palgrave Macmillan.

Caputo, R. K. (2012a) 'Hopes and Realities of Adopting Unconditional Basic Income Guarantee Schemes' in Caputo (2012), pp. 3–16.

Card, D., Kluve, J. and Weber, A. (2010) 'Active Labour Market Policy Evaluations: A Meta-Analysis'. *Economic Journal* 120: F452–F477.

Card, D., Lemieux, T. and Riddell, W. C. (2004) 'Unions and Wage Inequality'. *Journal of Labor Research* XXV(4): 519–62.

Carey, J. (1992) *The Intellectuals and the Masses: Pride and Prejudice among the Literary Intelligentsia, 1880–1939*. London: Faber and Faber.

Carlisle, R. (1968) 'Saint-Simonian Radicalism: A Definition and a Direction'. *French Historical Studies*, 5(4): 430–45.

Carlisle, R. (1974) 'The Birth of Technocracy: Science, Society, and Saint-Simonians'. *Journal of the History of Ideas* 35(3): 445–64.

Carnegy, H. (2012) 'France's 35-hour Working Week Is Spared', *Financial Times*, 1 November, www.ft.com (accessed September 2015).

Carnoy, M., Castells, M. and Brenner, C. (1997) 'Labour Markets and Employment Practices in the Age of Flexibility: A Case Study of Silicon Valley'. *International Labour Review* 136(1): 27–48.

Carnoy, M. and Rothstein, R. (2013) 'What Do International Tests Really Show about U.S. Student Performance?' *Economic Policy Institute Report*. Washington, DC: EPI, 15 January.

Caro, Robert (1998) 'The City Shaper' [Robert Moses], *New Yorker*, 5 January, http://www.robertacaro.com (accessed September 2015).

Carpenter, D. (2001) *The Forging of Bureaucratic Autonomy: Reputations, Networks, and Policy Innovation in Federal Agencies, 1862–1928*. Princeton: Princeton University Press.

Carr, E. H. (1952) *The Bolshevik Revolution 1917–923*, Volume 2. Harmondsworth: Penguin.

Carter, B. (2014) 'Which Country Has the Highest Tax Rate?' BBC News, 25 February, http://www.bbc.co.uk (accessed September 2015).

Center for Research on Educational Outcomes (CREDO) Stanford University (2013) *Charter School Growth and Replication*, Executive Summary, 30 January.

Chakrabortty, A. (2010) 'Why Our Jobs Are Getting Worse'. *Guardian*, 31 August, http://www.guardian.co.uk (accessed September 2015).

Chakrabortty, A. (2011) 'Why Doesn't Britain Make Things Any More?' *The Guardian*, 16 November, http://www.guardian.co.uk (accessed September 2015).

Chaloupek, G. (2007) 'Otto Neurath's Concepts of Socialization and Economic Calculation and His Socialist Critics' in Nemeth et al. (2007), pp. 61–76.

Chamberlin, E. (1933) *The Theory of Monopolistic Competition: A Re-Orientation of the Theory of Value*. Cambridge, MA: Harvard University Press, eighth edition of 1965.

Chandler, A. (1977) *The Visible Hand: The Managerial Revolution in American Business*. Cambridge, MA: Belknap Press.

Chandler, A. (1990) *Scale and Scope*. Cambridge, MA: Belknap Press.

Chandler, A. (1992) 'Organizational Capabilities and the Economic History of the Industrial Enterprise'. *Journal of Economic Perspectives* 6(1): 79–100.

Chandler, A., Amatori, F. and Hikino, T. (eds) (1997) *Big Business and the Wealth of Nations*. Cambridge: Cambridge University Press.

Chandler, A. and Hikino, T. (1997) 'The Large Industrial Enterprise and the Dynamics of Modern Economic Growth' in Chandler et al. (1997), pp. 24–57.

Chang, H-J. (2007) *Bad Samaritans: Rich Nations, Poor Policies and the Threat to the Developing World*. New York: Random House.

Chang, H-J. (2010) *23 Things They Don't Tell You about Capitalism*. London: Penguin.

Chase, S. (1926) *The Tragedy of Waste*. New York: Macmillan.

Checchi, D., Ichino, A. and Rustichini, A. (1999) 'More Equal But Less Mobile? Education Financing and Intergenerational Mobility in Italy and in the US'. *Journal of Public Economics* 74: 351–93.

Cheremukhin, A., Golosov, M., Guriev, S. and Tsyvinski, A. (2013) 'Was Stalin Necessary for Russia's Economic Development?' *Vox*, October 2013, www.voxeu.org (accessed September 2015).

Chetty, R., Friedman, J. N., Hilger, N., Saez, E., Schanzenbach Whitmore, D. and Yagan, D. (2011) 'How Does Your Kindergarten Classroom Affect Your Earnings? Evidence from Project Star'. *Quarterly Journal of Economics* 126(4): 1593–660.

Chetty, R., Friedman, J. N. and Rockoff, J. E. (2014) 'Measuring the Impacts of Teachers II: Teacher Value-Added and Student Outcomes in Adulthood'. *American Economic Review* 104(9): 2633–79.

Chetty, R., Hendren, N., Kline, P., Saez, E. and Turner, N. (2014a) 'Is the United States Still a Land of Opportunity? Recent Trends in Intergenerational Mobility'. *Working Paper 19844 January*. Cambridge, MA: National Bureau of Economic Research.

Chick, M. (1998) *Industrial Policy in Britain, 1945–1951: Economic Planning, Nationalisation and the Labour Governments*. Cambridge: Cambridge University Press.

Chin, T. and Phillips, M. (2004) 'Social Reproduction and Child-rearing Practices: Social Class, Children's Agency, and the Summer Activity Gap'. *Sociology of Education* 77(3): 185–219.

Chowdry, H. and Sibieta, L. (2011) *Trends in Education and Schools Spending*. Institute for Fiscal Studies IFS Briefing Note BN121, October.

Chrystal, K. A. and Mizen, P. D. (2001) 'Goodhart's Law: Its Origins, Meaning and Implications for Monetary Policy'. Prepared for the Festschrift in honour of Charles Goodhart held on 15–16 November 2001 at the Bank of England, http://cyberlibris.typepad.com (accessed September 2015).

Chung, L.L.W. (1996) 'The Economics of Land Use Zoning: A Literature Review and Analysis of the Works of Coase'. *Town Planning Review* 65(1): 77–98.

CIA (2004) *The World Factbook*, https://www.cia.gov (accessed September 2015).

Cingano, F., Leonardi, M., Messina, J. and Pica, G. (2010) 'The Effects of Employment Protection Legislation and Financial Market Imperfections on Investment: Evidence From a Firm-Level Panel of EU Countries'. *Economic Policy* January: 117–63.

Cipolla, C. (1969) *Literacy and Development in the West*. Harmondsworth: Penguin.

Clark, G. (2008) *A Farewell to Alms: A Brief Economic History of the World*. Princeton: Princeton University Press.

Clarke, S. (1992) ' "Innovation" in U.S. Agriculture: A Role for New Deal Regulation'. *Business and Economic History* Second Series 21: 46–55.

Clarke, S. (1994) *Regulation and the Revolution in United States Farm Productivity*. Cambridge: Cambridge University Press.

Coase, R. H. (1937) 'The Nature of the Firm'. *Economica* New Series IV: 386–405.

Coase, R. H. (1960) 'The Problem of Social Cost'. *Journal of Law and Economics* 3(1): 1–44.

Coats, D. and Lehki, R. (2008) ' "Good Work": Job Quality in a Changing Economy'. *The Work Foundation*, http://www.theworkfoundation.com (accessed September 2015).

Cohen, D. and Soto, M. (2007) 'Growth and Human Capital: Good Data, Good Results'. *Journal of Economic Growth* 12: 51–76.

Colley, H., Hodkinson, P. and Malcom, J. (2003) *Informality and Formality in Learning: A Report for the Learning and Skills Research Centre*. London: Learning and Skills Research Centre, https://kar.kent.co.uk (accessed September 2015).

Collins, C. (2013) 'The Wealthy Kids Are All Right', *Prospect*, 28 May, http://prospect.org (accessed September 2015).

Conlisk, J. (1974) 'Can Equalization of Opportunity Reduce Social Mobility?' *American Economic Review* 64(1): 80–90.

Corak, M. (2013) 'Income Inequality, Equality of Opportunity, and Intergenerational Mobility'. *Journal of Economic Perspectives* 27(3): 79–102.

Corno, L. and Xu, J. (2004) 'Homework as the Job of Childhood'. *Theory into Practice* 43(3): 228–33.

Costa, D. (1998) 'The Wage and the Length of the Work Day: From the 1890s to 1991', *NBER Working Paper No. 6504*, Cambridge, MA: National Bureau of Economic Research, www.nber.org (accessed September 2015).

Cowen, T. and Tabarrok, A. (2014) 'The Industrial Organization of Online Education'. *American Economic Review* Papers & Proceedings 104(5): 519–22.

Cowling, K. (1982) *Monopoly Capitalism*. London: Macmillan.

Crankshaw, E. (1962) *Khrushchev's Russia*. Harmondsworth: Penguin, revised edition.

Creative Commons (2015) 'Genuine Progress – Moving beyond GDP', http://genuine-progress.net (accessed September 2015).

Cronin, J., Ross, G. and Shoch, J. (eds) (2009) *What's Left of the Left: Democrats and Social Democrats in Challenging Times*, http://read.dukeupress.edu (accessed September 2015).

Cronon, W. (1991) *Nature's Metropolis: Chicago and the Great West*. New York: W.W. Norton.

Crosland, A. (1956) *The Future of Socialism*. London: Jonathan Cape.

Crump, T. (2007) *A Brief History of the Age of Steam*. London: Constable & Robinson.

Cunha, F. and Heckman, J. J. (2008) 'Formulating, Identifying and Estimating the Technology of Cognitive and Noncognitive Skill Formation'. *Journal of Human Resources* 43(4): 738–82.

Curran, J., Iyengar, S., Brink Lund, A. and Salovaara-Moring, I. (2009) 'Media System, Public Knowledge and Democracy: A Comparative Study'. *European Journal of Communication* 24(5): 5–26.

Currie, J. (2009) 'Healthy, Wealthy, and Wise: Socioeconomic Status, Poor Health in Childhood, and Human Capital Development'. *Journal of Economic Literature* 47(1): 87–122.

Daly, H. (2011) 'A Catechism of Growth Fallacies', http://www.greanvillepost.com (accessed September 2015).

Dardot, P. and Laval, C. (2013) *The New Way of the World: On Neoliberal Society*. London: Verso.

David, H. T. and Mendel, A. (eds) (1966) *The Bach Reader: A Life of Johann Sebastian Bach in Letters and Documents*, revised edition (to be preferred to the subsequent edition). New York: W.W. Norton.

Day, C., Michelson, D., Thomson, S., Penney, C. and Draper, L. (2012) 'Evaluation of a Peer Led Parenting Intervention for Disruptive Behaviour Problems in Children: Community Based Randomised Controlled Trial'. *British Medical Journal (BMJ)* Open Access, March, www.bmj.com (accessed September 2015).

De Bertodano, H. (2014) 'The Man Who Proved Stephen Hawking Wrong'. *The Telegraph* (London). 27 February, http://www.telegraph.co.uk (accessed September 2015).

Decker, S. (2013) 'Apple and Samsung Win Ruling to Keep Financial Data Secret', Salon.com, 23 August, http://www.salon.com (accessed September 2015).

Degler, C. (1991) *In Search of Human Nature*. Oxford: Oxford University Press.

De Grauwe, P. and Camerman, F. (2003) 'Are Multinationals Really Bigger than Nations?' *World Economics* 4(2): 23–37.

De Grauwe, P. and Ji, Y. (2013) 'More Evidence That Financial Markets Imposed Excessive Austerity in the Eurozone'. *CEPS Commentary*, 5 February.

De Grauwe, P. and Polan, M. (2005) 'Globalization and Social Spending'. *Pacific Economic Review* 10(1): 105–23.

De Grazia, V. (2005) *Irresistible Empire: America's Advance through Twentieth Century Europe*. Cambridge, MA: Belknap Press.

Deming, D. (2009) 'Early Childhood Intervention and Life-Cycle Skill Development: Evidence from Head Start'. *American Economic Journal: Applied Economics* 1(3): 111–34.

Denison, E. (1961) *The Sources of Economic Growth in the United States*. New York: Committee for Economic Development.

Denison, E. (1979) *Accounting for Slower Economic Growth: The United States in the 1970s*. Washington, DC: Brookings Institution.

Department for Education (2011) *Class Size and Education in England*. Research Report DFE-RR169.

Department for Education (2013) *The National Curriculum in England*. Framework document for consultation, February, http://socialwelfare.bl.uk (accessed September 2015).

Department for Education (2015) 'Data, Research and Statistics – Numbers of Open Academies and Free Schools', http://www.education.gov.uk (accessed September 2015).

Descartes, R. (1637) *Discourse on Method and Meditations on First Philosophy* (translation Donald Cress), third edition. Indianapolis: Hackett, 1993.

De Soto, J. H. (2010) *Socialism, Economic Calculation and Entrepreneurship*. Aldershot: Edward Elgar.

De Vries, J. (1994) 'The Industrial Revolution and the Industrious Revolution'. *Journal of Economic History* 54(2): 249–70.

De Waal, F. (2001) *The Ape and the Sushi Master: Reflections of a Primatologist*. New York: Basic Books.

Dewey, J. (1902) *The Child and the Curriculum*. LaVergne, TN: BN Publishing.

Dewey, J. (1915) *The School and Society*. LaVergne, TN: BN Publishing.

Diamond, P. and Saez, E. (2011) 'The Case for a Progressive Tax: From Basic Research to Policy Recommendations'. *Journal of Economic Perspectives* 25(4): 165–90.

Dickens, W., Sawhill, I. and Tebbs, J. (2006) 'The Effects of Investing in Early Education on Economic Growth'. Brookings Institution, www.brookings.edu (accessed September 2015).

Dillon, S. (2010) 'Formula to Grade Teachers' Skill Gains in Use, and Critics'. *New York Times*, 31 August, www.nytimes.com (accessed September 2015).

Dixon, M. (2013) *Public Education Finances: 2011*. Governments Division Reports G11-ASPEF, US Department of Commerce Economics and Statistics Administration, US Census Bureau, May.

Dobb, M. (1966) *Soviet Economic Development since 1917*, sixth edition (revised). London: Routledge Kegan & Paul.

Dodge, C. (2015) 'Trump Says Low Minimum Wage 'Not a Bad Thing'. *Bloomberg Politics*, 20 August, http://www.bloomberg.com (accessed September 2015).

Doidge, C., Karolyi, G. A. and Stulz, R. M. (2013) 'The U.S. Left Behind? Financial Globalization and the Rise of Ipos outside the U.S.' *Journal of Financial Economics* 110: 546–73.

Dolphin, T. and Lanning, T. (eds) (2011) *Rethinking Apprenticeships*. London: Institute for Public Policy Research.

Domar, E. D. (1946) 'Capital Expansion, Rate of Growth, and Unemployment'. *Econometrica* 14(2): 137–47.

Domar, E. D. (1957) 'A Soviet Model of Growth' in Nove and Nuti (1972), pp. 149–72, reprinted from Domar (1957).

Domar, E. D. (1957) *Essays in the Theory of Economic Growth*. Oxford University Press.

Dos Passos, J. (1936) *U.S.A.* London: Penguin Classics, 2001 – a trilogy originally published between 1930 and 1936.

Dow, G. K. (2003) *Governing the Firm: Workers' Control in Theory and Practice*. Cambridge: Cambridge University Press.

Dreyer, B. P. (2013) 'To Create a Better World for Children and Families: The Case for Ending Childhood Poverty' APA Presidential Address 2012. *Academic Pediatrics* 13(2): 83–90.

Dronkers, J. and Avram, S. (2009) 'Choice and Effectiveness of Private and Public Schools in Seven Countries – A Reanalysis of Three PISA Data Sets'. *Zeitschrift für Pädagogik* 55(6): 895–909.

Duhigg, C. and Bradsher, K. (2012) 'How the U.S. Lost Out on iPhone Work'. *New York Times*, 21 January, http://www.nytimes.com (accessed September 2015).

Dumas, L. (1984) 'University Research, Industrial Innovation, and the Pentagon' in Tirman (1984), pp. 123–51.

Duncan, G. and Magnuson, K. (2011) 'The Nature and Impact of Early Achievement Skills, Attention Skills, and Behavior Problems' in Duncan and Murnane (2011), pp. 47–69.

Duncan, G. and Magnuson, K. (2013) 'Investing in Preschool Programs'. *Journal of Economic Perspectives* 27(2): 109–32.

Duncan, G. and Murnane, R. (eds) (2011) *Whither Opportunity?* New York: Russell Sage Foundation.

Duncan, G. and Murnane, R. (2011a) Introduction to Duncan and Murnane (2011), pp. 3–23.

Dunne, P. (1990) 'The Political Economy of Military Expenditure: An Introduction'. *Cambridge Journal of Economics* 14(4): 395–404.

Dustmann, C., Fitzenberger, B., Schönberg, U. and Spitz-Oener, A. (2014) 'From Sick Man of Europe to Economic Superstar: Germany's Resurgent Economy'. *Journal of Economic Perspectives* 28(1): 167–88.

Dustmann, C. and Schönberg, U. (2012) 'What Makes Firm-Based Vocational Training Schemes Successful? The Role of Commitment'. *American Economic Journal: Applied Economics* 4(2): 36–61.

Easterlin, R. (1981) 'Why Isn't the Whole World Developed?' *Journal of Economic History* 41(1): 1–19.

Economist, The (2011) 'The Great Schools Revolution'. 17 September, pp. 21–3.

Economist, The (2012) 'Charting a Better Course: Charter Schools Raise Educational Standards For Vulnerable Children'. 7 July, http://www.economist (accessed September 2015).

Edemariam, A. (2013) 'I Don't Feel Defensive about What We Do'. *The Guardian*, 9 February, pp. 31–2.

Edgerton, D. (2008) *The Shock of the Old: Technology and Global History since 1900.* London: Profile.

Edsall, T. B. (2013a) 'The Hidden Prosperity of the Poor'. *New York Times*, 30 January, http://opinionator.blogs.nytimes.com (accessed September 2015).

Edsall, T. B. (2013b) 'Hard Times, for Some'. *New York Times*, 21 August, http://opinionator.blogs.nytimes.com (accessed September 2015).

Edsall, T. B. (2014) 'In Defense of Anonymous Political Giving'. *New York Times*, 18 March, http://www.nytimes.com (accessed September 2015).

Eichhorst, W. (2011) 'Delivering on Valid Labour Market Policies' in Anderson et al. (2011), pp. 48–53.

Einstein, A. (1949) 'Why Socialism?' *Monthly Review* 61(1): May, http://monthlyreview.org (accessed September 2015).

Elbaum, B. and Lazonick, W. (eds) (1986) *The Decline of the British Economy.* Oxford: Clarendon Press.

Elbaum, B. and Lazonick, W. (1986a) 'An Institutional Perspective on British Decline' in Elbaum and Lazonick (1986), pp. 1–17.

Engels, F. (1877) *Anti-Dühring,* http://www.marxists.org (accessed September 2015).

Engels, F. (1880) *Socialism: Utopian and Scientific*, http://www.marxists.org (accessed September 2015).

Epstein, S. R. (2008) 'Craft Guilds, Apprenticeship, and Technological Change in Pre-Industrial Europe', in Epstein and Prak (2008), pp. 52–80.

Epstein, S. R. and Prak, M. (eds) (2008) *Guilds, Innovation, and the European Economy, 1400–1800*. Cambridge: Cambridge University Press.

Ericsson, K. A., Roring, R. W. and Nandagopal, K. (2007) 'Giftedness and Evidence for Reproducibly Superior Performance: An Account Based on the Expert Performance Framework'. *High Ability Studies* 18(1): 3–56.

Ermisch, J., Jäntti, M. and Smeeding, T. (eds) (2012) *From Parents to Children: The Intergenerational Generation of Advantage*. New York: Russell Sage Foundation.

Ermisch, J., Jäntti, M. and Smeeding, T. (2012a) 'Socioeconomic Gradients in Children's Outcomes' in Ermisch et al. (2012), pp. 32–52.

Erturk, I., Froud, J., Johal, S., Leaver, A. and Williams, K. (2007) 'The Democratization of Finance? Promises, Outcomes and Conditions'. *Review of International Political Economy* 14(4): 553–75.

Esping-Andersen, G. (2008) 'Childhood Investments and Skill Formation'. *International Tax and Public Finance* 15: 19–44.

Etzioni, A. (with Platt, A.) (2008) *The Social Contract Revisited: A Community-Based Guaranteed Income*. Oxford: The Foundation for Law, Justice and Society in collaboration with The Centre for Socio-Legal Studies, University of Oxford.

European Commission (2015a) *Beyond GDP – Measuring Progress, True Wealth, and the Well-being of Nations*, http://ec.europa.eu (accessed September 2015).

European Commission (2015b) *Economic and Financial Affairs*, http://ec.europa.eu (accessed September 2015).

Eurostat (2012) *Educational Expenditure Statistics*. Data from September, http://epp.eurostat.ec.europa.eu (accessed September 2015).

Evans, R. J. (2005) *Death in Hamburg*. London: Penguin Books.

Evans, R. J. (2011) 'The Wonderfulness of Us'. *London Review of Books*, 17 March, http://www.lrb.co.uk (accessed September 2015).

Evenson, R. E. (1982) 'Agriculture' in Nelson (1982), pp. 233–82.

Farber, H. S. (2005) 'Nonunion Wage Rates and the Threat of Unionization'. *Industrial and Labor Relations Review* 58(3): 335–52.

Farber, H. S. (2010) 'Job Loss and the Decline in Job Security in the US' in Abraham et al. (2010), pp. 223–62.

Farber, H. S. (2011) 'Job Loss in the Great Recession: Historical Perspective from the Displaced Workers Survey, 1984–2010'. *Forschungsinstitut zur Zukunft der Arbeit Institute for the Study of Labor* IZA DP No. 5696, May.

Farber, H. S. and Valletta, R. G. (2013) 'Do Extended Unemployment Benefits Lengthen Unemployment Spells? Evidence from Recent Cycles in the U.S. Labor Market'. *Princeton University Industrial Relations Section Working Paper #573*, April.

Fedorovich, V. A. (1979) *Amerikanskyi Capitalizm i Gosudarstvennoe Khozyaistvovanie [American Capitalism and State Management]*. Moscow: Nauk.

Feldman, G. (1966) *Army Industry and Labor in Germany 1914–1918*. Princeton: Princeton University Press.

Feldstead, A., Fuller, A., Jewson, N. and Unwin, L. (2009) *Improving Working as Learning*. London: Routledge.

Feldstein, M. (1995) 'The Effect of Marginal Tax Rates on Taxable Income: A Panel Study of the 1986 Tax Reform Act'. *Journal of Political Economy* 103(3): 551–72.

Ferguson, T., Jorgensen, P. and Chen, J. (2013) 'Party Competition and Industrial Structure in the 2012 Elections: Who's Really Driving the Taxi to the Dark Side?', http://www.rooseveltinstitute.org (accessed September 2015).

Ferleger, L. and Lazonick, W. (1993) 'The Managerial Revolution and the Developmental State: The Case of U.S. Agriculture'. *Business and Economic History* 22(2): 67–98.

Fernald, A., Marchman, V. A. and Weisleder, A. (2013) 'SES Differences in Language Processing Skill and Vocabulary Are Evident at 18 Months'. *Developmental Science* 16(2): 234–48.

Field, A. (2003) 'The Most Technologically Progressive Decade of the Century'. *American Economic Review* 93(4): 1399–413.

Financial Transparency Coalition (2014) 'European Parliament Gives Overwhelming "Yes" Vote to End Secret Corporate Ownership', 11 March, http://www.financial-transparency.org (accessed September 2015).

Fishback, P. V. (2010) 'Social Welfare Expenditures in the United States and the Nordic Countries: 1900–2003'. *NBER Working Paper No. 15982*, National Bureau of Economic Research, May.

Fisher, I. (1930) *The Theory of Interest as Determined by Impatience to Spend Income and Opportunity to Invest It.* Clifton, NJ: Augustus M. Kelley, 1974; a reworking of materials from the beginning of the century.

Fitzpatrick, C. and Pagani, L. S. (2012) 'Toddler Working Memory Skills Predict Kindergarten School Readiness'. *Intelligence* 40: 205–12.

Fitzpatrick, S. (2002) *Education and Social Mobility in the Soviet Union 1921–1934.* Cambridge: Cambridge University Press.

Flamm, K. (1988) *Creating the Computer: Government, Industry and High Technology.* Washington, DC: Brookings Institution.

Flynn, J. (1978) 'The Mean IQ of Americans: Massive Gains 1932 to 1978'. *Psychological Bulletin* 95: 29–51.

Flynn, J. (2009a) *What Is Intelligence?* Cambridge: Cambridge University Press.

Flynn, J. (2009b) 'Requiem for Nutrition as the Cause of IQ Gains: Raven's Gains in Britain 1938–2008'. *Economics and Human Biology* 7: 18–27.

Fogel, R. W. (1964) *Railroads and American Economic Growth: Essays in Econometric History.* Baltimore: Johns Hopkins Press.

Fogel, R. W. (2004) *The Escape from Hunger and Premature Death, 1700–2100: Europe, America, and the Third World.* Cambridge: Cambridge University Press.

Foote, C. L., Gerardi, K. and Willen, P. (2012) 'Why Do So Many People Make So Many Ex Post Bad Decisions? The Causes of the Foreclosure Crisis' in Blinder et al. (2012), pp. 136–86.

Ford, M. (2015) *Rise of the Robots: Technology and the Threat of a Jobless Future.* New York: Basic Books.

Fox, R. and Guagnini, A. (eds) (1993) *Education, Technology and Industrial Performance in Europe, 1850–1939.* Cambridge: Cambridge University Press.

France 24 International News 24/7 (2012) 'France's Hollande Promises Pupils "No More Homework" ', 10 October, http://www.france24.com (accessed September 2015).

Franco, L. G. (2002) 'Global Competition in the 1990s: American Renewal, Japanese Resilience, European Cross-Currents'. *Business Horizons* May–June: 25–38.

Frase, P. (2012) 'The Politics of Getting a Life'. *Jacobin* issue 6, http://jacobinmag.com (accessed September 2015).

Freedman, L. (2010) 'Do Academy Schools Really Work?' *Prospect*, 24 February, http://www.prospectmagazine.co.uk (accessed September 2015).

Freeman, R. (2005) 'Labour Market Institutions without Blinders: The Debate over Flexibility and Labour Market Performance' *International Economic Journal* 19(2) June: 129–145.

Freeman, R. (2006) 'The Great Doubling: The Challenge of the New Global Labor Market', August, http://emlab.berkeley.edu (accessed September 2015).

Freeman, R. (2007) *America Works: Critical Thoughts on the Exceptional U.S. Labor Market.* New York: Russell Sage Foundation.

Freeman, R. (2009) 'Globalization and Inequality' in Salverda et al. (2009), pp. 575–98.

Frey, C. and Osborne, M. A. (2013) 'The Future of Employment: How Susceptible Are Jobs to Computerisation?' *Oxford Martin School Working Paper*, September, http://www.oxfordmartin.ox.ac.uk (accessed September 2015).

Friedel, R. (2007) *A Culture of Improvement: Technology and the Western Millennium.* Cambridge, MA: MIT Press.

Friedel, R. and Israel, P. (with Finn, B.) (1987) *Edison's Electric Light: Biography of an Invention.* New Brunswick: Rutgers University Press.

Friedman, M. (ed.) (1956) *Studies in the Quantity Theory of Money.* Chicago: University of Chicago Press.

Friedman, M. (1956a) 'The Quantity Theory of Money: A Restatement' in Friedman (1956), pp. 3–21.

Friedman, M. (1962) *Price Theory: A Provisional Text.* Chicago: Aldine.

Friedman, M. (1970) 'The Social Responsibility of Business Is to Increase Its Profits'. *New York Times Magazine*, 13 September.

Friedman, T. (1999) *The Lexus and the Olive Tree.* London: HarperCollins.

Fromm, E. (1956) *The Sane Society.* London: Routledge & Kegan Paul, 1991.

Fukuda-Parr, S. and Shiva Kumar, A. K. (eds) (2003) *Readings in Human Development.* Oxford: Oxford University Press.

Galbraith, J. K. (1956) *American Capitalism: The Concept of Countervailing Power*, revised edition. Cambridge, MA: Houghton Mifflin.

Galbraith, J. K. (1958) *The Affluent Society.* Boston: Houghton Mifflin Harcourt, edition of 1998.

Galbraith, J. K. (1967) *The New Industrial State.* New York: Signet Books.

Galor, O. and Moav, O. (2004) 'From Physical to Human Capital Accumulation: Inequality and the Process of Development'. *Review of Economic Studies* 71: 1001–26.

Galor, O. and Zeira, J. (1993) 'Income Distribution and Macroeconomics'. *Review of Economic Studies* 60: 35–52.

Gandy, M. (1999) 'The Paris Sewers and the Rationalization of Urban Space'. *Transactions of the Institute of British Geographers*, New Series 74(10): 23–44.

Gans, H. (1968) *People and Plans: Essays in Urban Problems and Solutions.* New York: Basic Books.

Gardner, H. (1993) *Multiple Intelligences.* New York: Basic Books.

Gardner, H. (2002) 'Contemporary Consciousness and the Study of the Humanities'. *Daedalus* 131(3): 22–5.

Garner, R. (2012) 'Tory Grandee Attacks Gove's "Huge Mistake" on New Exams'. *The Independent*, Thursday, 27 December, http://www.independent.co.uk (accessed September 2015).

Garvy, G. (1977) *Money, Financial Flows, and Credit in the Soviet Union.* Cambridge, MA Ballinger.

Gautié, J. and Schmitt, J. (eds) (2010) *Low Wage Work in the Wealthy World.* New York: Russell Sage Foundation.

Gerschenkron, A. (1962) *Economic Backwardness in Historical Perspective.* Cambridge, MA: Belknap Press.

Gerschenkron, A. (1962a) 'Economic Backwardness in Historical Perspective' in Gerschenkron (1962), pp. 5–30.

Gertner, J. (2012) *The Idea Factory:* Bell Labs and the Great Age of American Innovation. New York: Penguin Press.

Gibbons, S., Silva, O. and Weinhardt, F. (2013) 'Everybody Needs Good Neighbours? Evidence from Students' Outcomes in England'. *Economic Journal* 123: 831–74.

Gide, C. and Rist, C. (1948) *A History of Economic Doctrines from the Time of the Physiocrats to the Present Day,* second English edition. London: George G. Harrap & Company Ltd.

Gilchrist, S. G. and Zakrajšek, E. (2012) 'Credit Supply Shocks and Economic Activity in a Financial Accelerator Model' in Blinder et al. (2012), pp. 37–72.

Gilder, G. (1989) *Microcosm: The Quantum Revolution in Economics and Technology.* New York: Simon & Schuster.

Gilens, M. and Page, B. (2014) 'Testing Theories of American Politics: Elites, Interest Groups, and Average Citizens'. *Perspectives on Politics* 12(3): 564–81.

Glyn, A. (2009) 'Functional Distribution and Inequality' in Salverda et al. (2009), pp. 101–26.

Glyn, A. and Sutcliffe, B. (1972) *British Capitalism, Workers and the Profits Squeeze.* London: Penguin.

Goldacre, B. (2009) 'Please Give Us All Your Money'. *The Guardian,* 5 September, http://www.badscience.net (accessed September 2015).

Goldin, C. and Katz, L. (2008) *The Race between Education and Technology.* Cambridge, MA: Belknap Press.

Goldman, C. A., Kumar, K. B. and Liu, Y. (2008) 'Education and the Asian Surge: a Comparison of the Education Systems in India and China'. Rand Center for Asia Pacific Policy, http://www.rand.org (accessed September 2015).

Goleman, D. (1996) *Emotional Intelligence: Why It Can Matter More than IQ.* London: Bloomsbury Publishing PLC, new edition.

Gomory, R. (2010) 'The Innovation Delusion'. *The Huffington Post,* 2 March, http://www.huffingtonpost.com (accessed September 2015).

Goodman, A. and Gregg, P. (eds) (2010) 'Poorer Children's Educational Attainment: How Important Are Attitudes and Behaviour?' Joseph Rowntree Foundation, March, www.jrf.org.uk (accessed September 2015).

Gopnik, A. (2010) 'How Babies Think'. *Scientific American,* July: 76–81.

Gopnik, A., Meltzoff, A. and Kuhl, P. (1999) *How Babies Think: The Science of Childhood.* London: Weidenfeld & Nicolson [US edition entitled *The Scientist in the Crib*].

Gorard, S., See, B. H. and Davies, P. (2012) 'The Impact of Attitudes and Aspirations on Educational Attainment and Participation'. Joseph Rowntree Foundation, April, http://www.jrf.org.uk (accessed September 2015).

Gordon, R. J. (2000) 'Does the "New Economy" Measure Up to the Great Inventions of the Past?' *Journal of Economic Perspectives* 14(4): 49–74.

Gordon, R. J. (2012) 'Is U.S. Economic Growth Over? Faltering Innovation Confronts the Six Headwinds'. *NBER Working Paper 18315.* Cambridge, MA: National Bureau of Economic Research, August.

Gordon, R. J. (2014) 'The Demise of U.S. Economic Growth: Restatement, Rebuttal, and Reflections'. *NBER Working Paper Series 19895.* Cambridge, MA: National Bureau of Economic Research, February.

Gottschalk, P. and Moffitt, R. (2009) 'The Rising Instability of U.S. Earnings'. *Journal of Economic Perspectives* 23(4): 2–24.

Gould, E. and Wething, H. (2012) 'U.S. Poverty Rates Higher, Safety Net Weaker than in Peer Countries'. Washington, DC: Economic Policy Institute Issue Brief N. 339, 24 July.

Gould, S. J. (1981) *The Mismeasure of Man*. New York: W.W. Norton & Company.

Gould, S. J. and Lewontin, R. (1979) 'The Spandrels of San Marco and the Panglossian Paradigm: A Critique of the Adaptationist Programme'. *Proceedings of the Royal Society of London Series B* 205(1161): 581–98.

Graaff, J. de V. (1967) *Theoretical Welfare Economics*. Cambridge: Cambridge University Press.

Graff, H. (1987) *The Legacies of Literacy: Continuities and Contradictions in Western Culture and Society*. Bloomington: Indiana University Press.

Gramsci, A. (1935) 'From the "Prison Notebooks" '. *Daedalus* 131(3): 71–83, 2002; written between 1929 and 1935.

Green, F. (2006) *Demanding Work: The Paradox of Job Quality in the Affluent Society*. Princeton: Princeton University Press.

Green, F. (2013) *Skills and Skilled Work: An Economic and Social Analysis*. Oxford: Oxford University Press.

Green, F., Machin, S., Murphy, R. and Zhu, Y. (2008) 'Competition for Private and State School Teachers'. *Journal of Education and Work* 21(5): 383–404.

Green, F., Machin, S., Murphy, R. and Zhu, Y. (2011) 'The Changing Economic Advantage from Private Schools'. *Economica* 79: 658–79.

Gregory, P. (2003) *The Political Economy of Stalinism*. Cambridge: Cambridge University Press.

Gregory, P. and Stuart, R. (1994) *Soviet and Post-Soviet Economic Structure and Performance*. New York: HarperCollins.

Grek, S. (2009) 'Governing by Numbers: the PISA "Effect" in Europe'. *Journal of Education Policy* 24(1): 23–37.

Griliches, Z. (1996) 'Education, Human Capital and Growth: A Personal Perspective'. Cambridge, MA: *NBER Working Paper 5426*, January.

Gross, J. A. (ed.) (2003) *Workers' Rights as Human Rights*. Ithaca: Cornell University Press.

Gross, J. A. (2003a) 'A Long Overdue Beginning – The Promotion and Protection of Workers' Rights as Human Rights' in Gross (2003), pp. 1–22.

Grubb, W. N. and Lazerson, M. (2004) *The Education Gospel: The Economic Power of Schooling*. Cambridge, MA: Harvard University Press.

Guagnini, A. (1993) 'Worlds Apart: Academic Instruction and Professional Qualifications in the Training of Mechanical Engineers in England, 1850–1914' in Fox and Guagnini (1993), pp. 16–41.

Guardian/Observer, The [no author given] (2013) 'Michael Gove's reform agenda: some good school work, but must do better', 10 February, http://www.guardian.co.uk (accessed September 2015).

Gulick, C. (1948) *Austria from Hapsburg to Hitler, Volume 1, Labor's Workshop of Democracy*. Berkeley: University of California Press.

Habermas, J. (2015) *The Lure of Technology*. Cambridge: Polity Press.

Hacker, A. (2009) 'Can We Make America Smarter?' *New York Review of Books* LVI (7): 37–40.

Hacker, J. (2008) *The Great Risk Shift*. Oxford: Oxford University Press.

Hacker, J. and Pierson, P. (2010) *Winner Take All Politics*. New York: Simon & Schuster.

Hackett, P. and Hunter, P. (2015) 'Who Governs Britain? A Profile of MPs in the New Parliament'. Smith Institute, www.smith-institute.org.uk (accessed September 2015).

Hager, P. (2004) 'The Competence Affair, or Why Vocational Education and Training Urgently Needs a New Understanding of Learning'. *Journal of Vocational Education & Training* 56(3): 409–33.

Halliday, S. (2007) *The Great Filth: The War against Disease in Victorian England*. Stroud: Sutton Publishing.

Hamer, M. and Fisher, A. (2012) 'Are Interventions to Promote Physical Activity in Children a Waste of Time?' *BMJ*: 345, http://www.bmj.com (accessed September 2015).

Hamlin, S. (ed.) (1930) *The Menace of Overproduction*. Freeport, NY: Books for Libraries, Press edition from 1969.

Hanley, S. (1990) 'The Relationship of Education and Economic Growth: The Case of Japan' in Tortella (1990), pp. 69–87.

Hanushek, E. (2005) 'The Economics of School Quality'. *German Economic Review* 6(3): 269–86.

Hanushek, E. (2011) 'The Economic Value of Higher Teacher Quality'. *Economics of Education Review* 30: 466–79.

Hanushek, E. and Rivkin, S. (2004) 'How to Improve the Supply of High-Quality Teachers' in Ravitch (2004), pp. 7–25.

Hanushek, E. and Woessmann, L. (2008) 'The Role of Cognitive Skills in Economic Development'. *Journal of Economic Literature* 6(3): 607–68.

Hanushek, E. and Woessmann, L. (2010a) 'The Economics of International Differences in Educational Achievement'. Cambridge, MA: *National Bureau of Economic Research Working Paper 15949*, April.

Hanushek, E. and Woessmann, L. (2010b) 'How Much Do Educational Outcomes Matter in OECD Countries?' *CESifo Working Paper No. 3238*, November.

Hanushek, E. and Woessmann, L. (2012) 'Do Better Schools Lead to More Growth? Cognitive Skills, Economic Outcomes, and Causation'. *Journal of Economic Growth* 17: 267–321.

Harding, D., Gennetian, L., Winship, C., Sanbonmatsu, L. and Kling, J. (2011) 'Unpacking Neighborhood Influences on Educational Outcomes: Setting the Stage for Future Research' in Duncan and Murnane (2011), pp. 277–96.

Harhoff, D. and Kane, T. (1995) 'Is the German Apprenticeship System a Panacea for the U.S. Labor Market?' Zentrum für Europaische Wirtschaftsforschung GmbH *Discussion Paper No. 95–19*.

Harmon, C. and Oosterbeek, H. (2003) 'The Returns to Education: Microeconomics'. *Journal of Economic Surveys* 17(2): 115–55.

Harrison, L. and Huntington, S. (eds) *Culture Matters: How Values Shape Human Progress*. New York: Basic Books.

Harrison, M. (1988) 'Resource Mobilization for World War II: The U.S.A., U.S.S.R., and Germany, 1938–1945'. *Economic History Review* New Series 41(2): 171–92.

Harrison, M. (1998) 'The Economics of World War II: An Overview' in Harrison, M. (ed.) (1998) *The Economics of World War II: Six Great Powers in International Comparison*. Cambridge: Cambridge University Press, 1998, pp. 1–42.

Harrod, R. (1939) 'An Essay in Dynamic Theory'. *Economic Journal* 49(193): 14–33.

Hart, B. and Risley, T. R. (2003) 'The Early Catastrophe'. *Education Review* 17(1): 110–18.

Haveman, R. H. and Wolfe, B. L. (1984) 'Schooling and Well-Being: The Role of Nonmarket Effects'. *Journal of Human Resources* 19(3): 377–407.

Hawley, E. (1974) 'Herbert Hoover, the Commerce Secretariat, and the "Associative State," 1921–1928'. *Journal of American History* 61(1): 116–40.

Haycock, K. (2004) 'The Elephant in the Living Room' in Ravitch (2004), pp. 229–47.

Hayek, F. A. (ed.) (1935) *Collectivist Economic Planning*. Auburn: Ludwig von Mises Institute, 2009.

Hayek, F. A. (1941) *The Pure Theory of Capital*. London: Macmillan and Co.

Hayek, F. A. (1944) *The Road to Serfdom*. Chicago: University of Chicago Press.

Hayek, F. A. (1945) 'The Use of Knowledge in Society' in Hayek (1949), pp. 77–91. Reprinted from the *American Economic Review* XXXV(4) September 1945: 519–30.

Hayek, F. A. (1949) *Individualism and Economic Order*. Routledge & Kegan Paul.

Hayek, F. A. (1949a) 'The Meaning of Competition' in Hayek (1949), pp. 92–106, from a lecture given in 1946.

Hayek, F. A. (1952) *The Counter-Revolution of Science*. Indianapolis: Liberty Fund.

Hayek, F. A. (1960) *The Constitution of Liberty*. London: Routledge and Kegan Paul.

Hayek, F. A. (1960a) 'Why I Am Not a Conservative', postscript to Hayek (1960), pp. 397– 411.

Hayek, F. A. (1977) *The Denationalization of Money*. London: Institute of Economic Affairs Hobart Papers.

Hayek, F. A. (1982) *Law, Legislation and Liberty: A New Statement of the Liberal Principles of Justice and Political Economy*, one volume edition from 1993. London: Routledge & Kegan Paul.

Hayek, F. A. (2011) *The Fatal Conceit: The Errors of Socialism*, posthumously edited by W. W. Bartley, III. Chicago: University of Chicago Press.

Heal, G. M. (1973) *The Theory of Economic Planning*. Amsterdam: North Holland.

Heckman, J. (2008) 'Schools, Skills, and Synapses'. *NIH Public Access*; published in final edited form as: *Economic Inquiry* 46(3): 289–324, http://www.ncbi.nlm.nih.gov (accessed September 2015).

Heckman, J., Pinto, R. and Savelyev, P. (2013) 'Understanding the Mechanisms through Which an Influential Early Childhood Program Boosted Adult Outcomes'. *American Economic Review* 103(6): 2052–86.

Henry, J. S. (2012) 'The Price of Offshore Revisited – New Estimates for "Missing" Wealth, Income, Inequality, and Lost Taxes'. *Tax Justice Network*, July.

Herrnstein, R. J. and Murray, C. (1996) *The Bell Curve: Intelligence and Class Structure in American Life*. New York: Simon & Schuster.

Hicks, J. (1946) *Value and Capital*, second edition. Oxford: Clarendon Press.

Hilferding, R. (1910) *Finance Capital: A Study of the Latest Phase of Capitalist Development*. London: Routledge & Kegan Paul 1981. Accessed from http://www.marxists.org (accessed September 2015).

Hillmert, S. and Jacob, M. (2002) 'Social Inequality in Higher Education – Is Vocational Training a Pathway Leading to or away from University?' *European Sociological Review* 19(3): 319–34.

Himmelstrad, J. (2010) 'Are Swedish State Family Policies Delivering?' 25–27 May, http://www.mireja.org (accessed September 2015).

Hindemith, P. (1949) *Elementary Training for Musicians*, second edition. London: Schott & Co. Ltd.

Hirsch, E. D., Jr (1987) *Cultural Literacy: What Every American Needs to Know*. Boston: Houghton Mifflin.

Hirsch, E. D., Jr (2010) *The Making of Americans: Democracy and Our Schools.* New Haven: Yale University Press.

Hirsh-Pasek, K., Adamson, L. B., Bakeman, R., Owen, M. T., Golinkoff, R. M., Pace, A., Yust, P. K. S. and Suma, K. (2015) 'The Contribution of Early Communication Quality to Low-Income Children's Language Success'. *Psychological Science* 26(7): 1071–83.

Hobsbawm, E. and Ranger, T. (eds) (1983) *The Invention of Tradition.* Cambridge: Cambridge University Press.

Hobson, J. A. (1936) *Veblen.* Fairfield: Augustus M. Kelley, 1991.

Hodgman, D. (1963) *Commercial Bank Loan and Investment Policy.* Champaign: University of Illinois.

Hoffman, Philip T. (2015) *Why Did Europe Conquer the World?* Princeton: Princeton University Press.

Hofstadter, R. (1948) *The American Political Tradition.* New York: Vintage Books.

Hofstadter, R. (1955) *Social Darwinism in American Thought*, revised edition. Boston: Beacon Press.

Hofstadter, R. (1963) *Anti-Intellectualism in American Life.* New York: Random House.

Hofstadter, R., Miller, W. and Aaron, D. (1967) *The United States: The History of a Republic*, second edition. Englewood Cliffs: Prentice Hall.

Holbrook, D. (1995) 'Government Support of the Semiconductor Industry: Diverse Approaches and Information Flows'. *Business and Economic History* 24(2): 133–65.

Holland, S. (1975) *The Socialist Challenge.* London: Quartet Books.

Horwitz, A. V., Videon, T. M., Schmitz, M. F. and Davis, D. (2003) 'Rethinking Twins and Environments: Possible Social Sources for Assumed Genetic Influences in Twin Research'. *Journal of Health and Social Behavior* 44: 111–29.

Horwitz, M. J. (1977) *The Transformation of American Law, 1780–1860.* Cambridge, MA: Harvard University Press.

Hounshell, D. (1984) *From the American System to Mass Production.* Baltimore: Johns Hopkins University Press.

House of Commons Library (2009) 'Executive Remuneration in UK Banking'. Standard Note: SN/BT/04970, www.parliament.uk (accessed September 2015).

Houtenville, A. and Conway, K. S. (2008) 'Parental Effort, School Resources, and School Achievement'. *Journal of Human Resources* XLIII(2): 437–52.

Hoynes, H. W., Schanzenbach, D. W. and Almond, D. (2012) 'Long Run Impacts of Childhood Access to the Safety Net'. National Bureau of Economic Research *NBER Working Paper No. 18535*, November.

Hughes, T. (2007) *American Genesis: A Century of Invention and Technological Enthusiasm.* Chicago: University of Chicago.

Huizinga, J. H. (1938) *Homo Ludens: A Study of the Play-Element in Culture.* New York: Beacon Press, edition of 1992.

Hungerford, T. L. (2014) 'How *Not* To Fund An Infrastructure Bank'. *Economic Policy Institute*, Policy Memo #203, February.

Huntington, S. (2000) 'Cultures Count' in Harrison (2000), pp. xiii–xvi.

Hutchins, G. (2014) 'Work Like a German'. *New York Times*, 14 March, http://www.nytimes.com (accessed September 2015).

Hutton Review of Fair Pay (2011) *Hutton Review of Fair Pay in the Public Sector*, Final Report, March, http://webarchive.nationalarchives.gov.uk (accessed September 2015).

Ietto-Gillies, G. (1993) 'Transnational Companies and UK Competitiveness: Does Ownership Matter?' in Hughes, K. (ed.) (1993) *The Future of UK Competitiveness and the Role of Industrial Policy.* London: Policy Studies Institute.

Illich, I. (1973) *Deschooling Society*. Harmondsworth: Penguin.

Institute of Education Studies (IES) National Center for Education Statistics (2009) 'Closer Look 2009 U.S. Performance across International Assessments of Student Achievement: How Much Does Performance within the United States Vary by School Poverty?' http://nces.ed.gov (accessed September 2015).

International Federation of Health Plans (2013) '2013 Comparative Price Report', http://www.ifhp.com (accessed September 2015).

International Labour Office (2010) *Global Employment Trends for Youth: Special Issue on the Impact of the Global Economic Crisis on Youth*. Geneva: ILO.

International Labour Office (2013) *Global Employment Trends for Youth 2013: A Generation at Risk*. Geneva: ILO.

International Labour Organization (2013) *Global Wage Report 2012/13: Wages and Equitable Growth*. Geneva: ILO.

Isaacs, J. B. (2009) 'International Comparisons of Economic Mobility' in Isaacs et al. (2009), pp. 37–46.

Isaacs, J. B., Sawhill, I. V. and Haskins, R. (2009) *Getting Ahead or Losing Ground: Economic Mobility in America*. Washington, DC: The Brookings Institution. http://hdr.undp.org (accessed September 2015).

Isenberg, E., Glazerman, S., Bleeker, M., Johnson, A., Lugo-Gil, J., Grider, M., Dolfin, S., Britton, E. and Ali, M. (2009) *Impacts of Comprehensive Teacher Induction: Results from the Second Year of a Randomized Controlled Study*. US Department of Education NCEE 2009–4072, August.

Ishikawa, T. (1997) 'Growth, Human Development and Economic Policies in Japan: 1955–1993'. *UNDP Occasional Paper 23*, sections 3 and 5,

Israel, J. (1995) *The Dutch Republic: Its Rise, Greatness, and Fall 1477–1806*. Oxford: Oxford University Press.

Israel, J. (2006) *Enlightenment Contested*. Oxford: Oxford University Press.

Israel, J. (2010) *A Revolution of the Mind: Radical Enlightenment and the Intellectual Origins of Modern Democracy*. Princeton: Princeton University Press.

Israel, J. (2011) *Democratic Enlightenment: Philosophy, Revolution, and Human Rights 1750–1790*. Oxford: Oxford University Press.

Jackson, B. and Marsden, D. (1966) *Education and the Working Class*, revised edition. Harmondsworth: Penguin.

Jacob, M. (1997) *Scientific Culture and the Making of the Industrial West*. Oxford: Oxford University Press.

Jacobs, J. (1961) *Death and Life of Great American Cities*. London: Jonathan Cape.

Jansen, M. B. (ed.) (1989) *The Cambridge History of Japan Volume 5: The Nineteenth Century*. Cambridge: Cambridge University Press.

Janson, P. (2015) 'Basic Income and the Swedish Welfare State', http://www.basicincome.org (accessed September 2015).

Jarrow, R. (2012) 'The Role of ABSs, CDSs, and CDOs in the Credit Crisis and the Economy' in Blinder et al. (2012), pp. 210–34.

Jensen, A. (1969) 'How Much Can We Boost IQ and Scholastic Achievement?' *Harvard Educational Review* 39(1): 1–123.

Jensen, M. C. and Meckling, W. H. (1976) 'Theory of the Firm: Managerial Behavior, Agency Costs and Ownership Structure'. *Journal of Financial Economics* 3(4): 305–60.

Johannesen, N. and Zucman, G. (2014) 'The End of Bank Secrecy? An Evaluation of the G20 Tax Haven Crackdown'. *American Economic Journal: Economic Policy* 6(1): 65–91.

Johnson, C. (1982) *MITI and the Japanese Miracle: The Growth of Industrial Policy, 1925–1975*. Stanford: Stanford University Press.

Johnson, H. (1973) 'Some Micro-Economic Reflections on Income and Wealth Inequalities'. *The Annals of the American Academy of Political and Social Science* 409(1): 53–60.

Josephson, P. (2002) *Industrialized Nature: Brute Force Technology and the Transformation of the Natural World*. Washington: Island Press Shearwater Books.

Kaboub, F. (2007) 'Employment Guarantee Programs: A Survey of Theories and Policy Experiences'. *Working Paper No. 498*, Levy Economics Institute, May.

Kaletsky, A. (2004) 'Dark Clouds Gather above Our Golden Pillars of Growth'. *The Times* (London). 16 November, p. 56.

Kalleberg, A. (2011) *Good Jobs, Bad Jobs*. New York: Russell Sage Foundation.

Kamien, M. and Schwartz, N. (1982) *Market Structure and Innovation*. Cambridge: Cambridge University Press.

Kanigel, R. (1997) *The One Best Way: Fredrick Winslow Taylor and the Enigma of Efficiency*. London: Abacus.

Kantrowitz, B. (2014) 'The Science of Learning'. *Scientific American* 311(2): 59–63.

Karabarbounis, L. and Neiman, B. (2013) 'The Global Decline of the Labor Share'. *NBER Working Paper Series, Working Paper 19136*. Cambridge, MA: National Bureau of Economic Research, June.

Katz, L. F. (2011) 'Invest in Workers'. *New York Times*, 6 September, http://www.nytimes.com (accessed September 2015).

Katz, L. and Margo, R. A. (2013) 'Technical Change and the Relative Demand for Skilled Labor: The United States in Historical Perspective'. *NBER Working Paper No. 18752*, February.

Keddie, N. (ed.) (1973) *Tinker, Tailor…The Myth of Cultural Deprivation*. Harmondsworth: Penguin.

Kendrick, J. (1970) 'The Historical Development of National-Income Accounts'. *History of Political Economy* 2(2): 284–315.

Kenney, M. (ed.) (2000) *Understanding Silicon Valley*. Stanford: Stanford University Press.

Kenney, M. and Florida, R. (2000) 'Venture Capital in Silicon Valley: Fueling New Firm Formation' in Kenney (2000), pp. 98–123.

Keynes, J. M. (1936) *The General Theory of Employment Interest and Money Volume 7: The General Theory v. 7* (Collected works of Keynes). London: Palgrave Macmillan; edition of 1973.

Kiernan, V. G. (1969) *The Lords of Human Kind: European Attitudes towards the Outside World in the Imperial Age*. London: Weidenfeld & Nicolson.

Kim, K. H. (2005) 'Learning from Each Other: Creativity in East Asian and American Education'. *Creativity Research Journal* 17(4): 337–47.

Kim, Y-J. (2011) 'Head Start, 4 Years after Completing the Program'. *Education Economics*, http://www.tandfonline.com (accessed September 2015).

Kling, J. R., Liebman, J. B. and Katz, L. F. (2007) 'Experimental Analysis of Neighborhood Effects'. *Econometrica* 75(1): 83–119.

Kocher, E., Klose, A., Kühn, K. and Wenckebach, J. (2012) *No Accountability without Transparency: Legal Instruments for Corporate Duties to Disclose Working and Employment Conditions*. Friedrich Ebert Stiftung, June, http://library.fes.de (accessed September 2015).

Kochhar, R., Fry, R. and Taylor, P. (2011) 'Wealth Gaps Rise to Record Highs between Whites, Blacks, Hispanics Twenty-to-One'. Pew Research Center, *Pew Social & Demographic Trends*, http://www.pewsocialtrends.org (accessed September 2015).

Kohn, A. (1998) 'Only for My Kid – How Privileged Parents Undermine School Reform'. *Phi Delta Kappan*, April, http://www.alfiekohn.org (accessed September 2015).

Kohn, A. (2007) 'Rethinking Homework'. *Principal*, January/February, http://www.alfiekohn.org (accessed September 2015).

Kolb, B., Gibb, R. and Robinson, T. (2015) 'Brain Plasticity and Behavior'. *Association for Psychological Science*, www.psychologicalscience.org (accessed September 2015).

Kolbert, E. (2009) 'Hosed – Is There a Quick Fix for Climate Change?' *New Yorker*, 16 November, http://www.newyorker.com (accessed September 2015).

Kolko, G. (1963) *The Triumph of Conservatism: A Reinterpretation of American History, 1900–1916*. Chicago: Quadrangle Paperbacks.

Kornai, J. (1972) *Rush versus Harmonic Growth*. Amsterdam: North-Holland.

Krueger, A. (2002) 'Understanding the Magnitude and Effect of Class Size on Student Achievement' in Mishel and Rothstein (2002), pp. 7–35.

Krueger, A. (2003) 'Economic Considerations and Class Size'. *Economic Journal* 113: F34–F63.

Krueger, A. and Lindahl, M. (1999) 'Education for Growth in Sweden and the World' *NBER Working Paper 7190*, June.

Krugman, P. (1979) 'Increasing Returns, Monopolistic Competition and International Trade'. *Journal of International Economics* 9(4): 469–79.

Krugman, P. (1994) 'Competitiveness: A Dangerous Obsession'. *Foreign Affairs* 73(2): 28–44.

Krugman, P. (1994a) 'The Myth of Asia's Miracle'. *Foreign Affairs* 73(6): 62–78.

Krugman, P. (1995) quoted in an exchange of letters in *Foreign Affairs* (1995) 74(2): 177.

Krugman, P. (1997) *Pop Internationalism*. Cambridge, MA: MIT Press.

Krugman, P. (2011) 'Springtime for Toxics'. *New York Times*, 25 December, http://www.nytimes.com (accessed September 2015).

Krugman, P. (2012) 'Robots and Robber Barons'. *New York Times*, 9 December, http://www.nytimes.com (accessed September 2015).

Krugman, P. (2013) 'Sympathy for the Luddites'. *New York Times*, 13 June, http://www.nytimes.com (accessed September 2015).

Krugman, P. (2014) 'Europe's Secret Success'. *New York Times*, 25 May, http://www.nytimes.com (accessed September 2015).

Kruse, D. L., Freeman, R. and Blasi, J. P. (eds) (2010) *Shared Capitalism at Work: Employee Ownership, Profit and Gain Sharing, and Broad-Based Stock Options*. National Bureau of Economic Research Conference Report. Chicago: University of Chicago Press.

Kruse, D. L., Freeman, R. and Blasi, J. P. (2010a) 'Introduction' in Kruse et al. (2010), pp. 1–37.

Kula, W. (1986) *Measures and Men* (translated by R. Szreter). Princeton: Princeton University Press.

Kunstler, J. H. (2001) *The City in Mind*. New York: The Free Press.

Kuznets, S. (1955) 'Economic Growth and Income Inequality'. *American Economic Review* XLV(1): 1–28.

Ladd, H. (2002) 'School Vouchers: A Critical View'. *Journal of Economic Perspectives* 16(4): 3–24.

Ladd, H. (2012) 'Education and Poverty: Confronting the Evidence'. *Journal of Policy Analysis and Management* 31(2): 203–27. Reprint of Presidential Address to the Association for Public Policy Analysis and Management, Washington, DC.

Lamont, J. and Favor, C. (2009) 'Distributive Justice'. *Stanford Encyclopedia of Philosophy*, spring edition, http://plato.stanford.edu (accessed September 2015).

Lamoreaux, N., Raff, D. and Temin, P. (2002) 'Beyond Markets and Hierarchies: Towards a New Synthesis of American Business History'. *NBER Working Paper Series Working Paper 9029*, July.

Landes, D. (1983) *Revolution in Time*. Cambridge, MA: Belknap Press.

Landes, D. (1999) *The Wealth and Poverty of Nations*. London: Abacus.

Lange, O. (1938) 'On the Economic Theory of Socialism' in Lange and Taylor (1964) *On the Economic Theory of Socialism*. New York: McGraw-Hill, pp. 57–143.

Lange, O. and Taylor, F. (1964) *On the Economic Theory of Socialism*. New York: McGraw-Hill.

Langlois, R. (1992) 'External Economies and Economic Progress: The Case of the Microcomputer Industry'. *Business History Review* 66(1): 1–50.

Lareau, A. (2003) *Unequal Childhoods: Class, Race and Family Life*. Berkeley: University of California Press.

Lavoie, D. (1985) *Rivalry and Central Planning: The Socialist Calculation Debate Reconsidered*. Cambridge: Cambridge University Press.

Layton, E. (1962) 'Veblen and the Engineers'. *American Quarterly* 14(1): 64–72.

Lazonick, W. (1991) *Business Organization and the Myth of the Market Economy*. Cambridge: Cambridge University Press.

Lazonick, W. (2009) *Sustainable Prosperity in the New Economy: Business Organization and High-Tech Employment in the United States*. Kalamazoo: W.E. Upjohn Institute.

Lazonick, W. and Huzzard, T. (2014) 'Why Everyone Does Better When Employees Have a Say in the Workplace'. *Alternet*, 6 March, http://www.alternet.org/economy (accessed September 2015).

Lazonick, W. and O'Sullivan, M. (1997) 'Big Business and Skill Formation in the Wealthiest Nations: The Organizational Revolution in the Twentieth Century' in Chandler et al. (1997), pp. 497–521.

Le Clère, J. (1864) 'Chronique du mois'. *Revue d'économie chrétienne* new series, 5th year, tome VI.

Lécuyer, C. (2006) *Making Silicon Valley: Innovation and the Growth of High Tech, 1930–1970*. Cambridge, MA: MIT Press.

Lee, J. J. (1978) 'Labour in German Industrialization' in Mathias and Postan (1978), pp. 442–91.

Lee, J-W. (1997) 'Economic Growth and Human Development in the Republic of Korea'. United Nations Human Development Report Office *Occasional Paper 24*, hdr.undp.org (accessed September 2015).

Lee, W. R. (1991) *German Industry and German Industrialisation*. London: Routledge.

Leibenstein, H. (1966) 'Allocative Efficiency vs. X-Efficiency'. *American Economic Review* 56(3): 392–415.

Lenin, V. I. (1917) *The State and Revolution*. Peking: Foreign Language Press, 1970.

Leonard, T. (2009) 'American Economic Reform in the Progressive Era: Its Foundational Beliefs and Their Relation to Eugenics'. *History of Political Economy* 41(1): 109–41.

Lepore, J. (2014) 'The Disruption Machine – What the Gospel of Innovation Gets Wrong'. *New Yorker*, 23 June, pp. 30–6.

Lerner, A. P. (1943) 'Functional Finance and the Federal Debt'. *Social Research* 10(1): 38–51.

Lerner, J. (2009) 'The Empirical Impact of Intellectual Property Rights on Innovation: Puzzles and Clues'. *American Economic Review* Papers & Proceedings 99(2): 343–8.

Leslie, S. (1993) *The Cold War and American Science: The Military-Industrial-Academic Complex at MIT and Stanford*. New York: Columbia University Press.

Leslie, S. (2000) 'The Biggest "Angel" of Them All: The Military and the Making of Silicon Valley' in Kenney (2000), pp. 48–67.

Levin, R. (1982) 'The Semiconductor Industry' in Nelson (1982), pp. 9–100.

Levitt, S. and Dubner, S. (2009) *Superfreakonomics*. New York: William Morrow.

Levy, H. (1936) *The New Industrial System: A Study of the Origin, Forms, Finance and Prospects of Concentration in Industry*. London: George Routledge & Sons.

Lewontin, R. (1997) 'Billions and Billions of Demons' a review of Sagan, Carl *The Demon-Haunted World: Science as a Candle in the Dark*. New York Review of Books, 9 January, http://www.nybooks.com (accessed September 2015).

Lewontin, R. (2012) 'Is There a Jewish Gene?' *New York Review of Books* LIX(19): 17–19.

Li, C. (2004) 'China's Northeast: From Largest Rust Belt to Fourth Economic Engine?' *China Leadership Monitor* 2004 No. 9. Hoover Institution, Stanford University, http://www.hoover.org (accessed September 2015).

Lieberman, S. (1983) 'The Evacuation of Industry in the Soviet Union during World War II'. *Soviet Studies* XXXV(1): 90–102.

Lightfoot, L. (2010) 'Pupil Numbers: Is Class Size That Critical?' *Financial Times*, 19 March, http://www.ft.com (accessed September 2015).

Lih, L. (1992) Introduction to Lih et al. (1992), pp. 1–61.

Lih, L., Naumon, O. and Khlevniuk, O. (eds) (1992) *Stalin's Letters to Molotov*. New Haven: Yale University Press.

Lilienthal, D. (1953) *Big Business: A New Era*. New York: Harper.

Lind, M. (2013) *Land of Promise: An Economic History of the United States*. New York: Harper.

Lindert, P. (2004) *Growing Public Social Spending and Economic Growth since the Eighteenth Century, Volume 1*. Cambridge: Cambridge University Press.

Lindqvist, S. (1997) *Exterminate All the Brutes: One Man's Odyssey into the Heart of Darkness and the Origins of European Genocide*. London: Granta Books.

Linn, S. (2004) *Consuming Kids: The Hostile Takeover of Childhood*. New York: New Press.

Lippert, I., Huzzard, T., Jürgens, U. and Lazonick, W. (2014) *Corporate Governance, Employee Voice, and Work Organization: Sustaining High-Road Jobs in the Automotive Supply Industry*. Oxford: Oxford University Press.

Lipset, S. M. and Marks, G. (2000) *It Didn't Happen Here: Why Socialism Failed in the United States*. New York: W.W. Norton & Company.

List, F. (1841) *The National System of Political Economy*, reprint of English translation published in London by Longmans Green & Co. in 1909 of *Das Nationale System der Politischen Oekonomie*, http://oll.libertyfund.org (accessed September 2015).

Lords Select Committee (2012) 'UK Must Produce More High Calibre Science Graduates to Secure Economic Growth'. 24 July, http://www.parliament.uk (accessed September 2015).

Lucas, R. (1988) 'On the Mechanics of Economic Development'. *Journal of Monetary Economics* 22(1): 3–42.

Lurie, A. (2008) 'The Message of the Schoolroom'. *New York Review of Books*, 4 December: 31–3.

Lynn, B. C. and Longman, P. (2010) 'Who Broke America's Jobs Machine? Why Creeping Consolidation Is Crushing American Livelihoods', http://www.washingtonmonthly.com (accessed September 2015).

Lynn, R. and Vanhanen, T. (2002) *IQ and the Wealth of Nations*. London: Greenwood.

Machin, S. (2012) 'Academies: Old Research Is Being Wrongly Used to Validate Them. The Coalition's Academy Programme Is Not the Same as Labour's, So Why Is Our Old Research Being Used to Support Them'. *The Guardian*, 9 April, http://www.guardian.co.uk (accessed September 2015).

Machin, S. and Vernoit, J. (2011) 'Changing School Autonomy: Academy Schools and Their Introduction to England's Education'. London School of Economics Centre for the Economics of Education, CEE DP 123, April, http-//cep.lse.ac.uk (accessed September 2015).

Macmillan, H. (1933) *Reconstruction: A Plea for National Policy*. London: Macmillan.

Macnamara, B. N., Hambrick, D. Z. and Oswald, F. L. (2014) 'Deliberate Practice and Performance in Music, Games, Sports, Education, and Professions: A Meta-Analysis'. *Psychological Science* 25(8): 1608–18.

Maddison, A. (1969) *Economic Growth in Japan and the USSR*. London: George Allen & Unwin.

Maddison, A. (2006) *The World Economy: A Millennial Perspective*. Paris: OECD.

Maier, C. (1970) 'Between Taylorism and Technocracy: European Ideologies and the Vision of Industrial Productivity in the 1920s'. *Journal of Contemporary History* 5(2): 27–61.

Malkiel, B. (2012) 'The Efficient-Market Hypothesis and the Financial Crisis' in Blinder et al. (2012), pp. 75–98.

Malle, S. (2002) *The Economic Organization of War Communism, 1918–1921*. Cambridge: Cambridge University Press.

Mandel, M. (2004) 'In Praise of Heady Growth'. *Business Week*, 17 May, pp. 76–81.

Mani, A., Mullainathan, S., Shafir, E. and Zhao, J. (2013) 'Poverty Impedes Cognitive Function'. *Science* 341(6149): 976–80.

Mankiw, N. G. (2008) *Principles of Economics*, fifth edition. Boston, MA: South-Western College Publishers.

Mankiw, N. G. (2013) 'Defending the One Percent'. *Journal of Economic Perspectives* 27(3): 21–34.

Mansell, W. (2015) 'The 60% Extra Funds Enjoyed by England's Free School Pupils'. *Guardian*, 25 August, http://www.theguardian.com (accessed September 2015).

Manyika, J., Chui, M., Bughin, J., Dobbs, R., Bisson, P. and Marrs, A. (2013) *Disruptive Technologies: Advances That Will Transform Life, Business, and the Global Economy*. McKinsey Global Institute, May.

Marshall, A. (1920) *Industry and Trade*, third edition. London: Macmillan and Co., Ltd.

Marshall, A. (1922) *Principles of Economics*, eighth edition. London: Macmillan.

Marx, K. (1845) Comment on Friedrich List's book *Das Nationale System der Politischen Oekonomie*, March (fragment). Source: MECW (Marx's collected works, USSR), volume 4, p. 265, http://www.marxists.org (accessed September 2015).

Marx, K. (1867) *Capital*, volume I (translation Ben Fowkes). Harmondsworth: Penguin, edition of 1976.

Marx, K. (1873) 'Political Indifferentism', http://www.marxists.org (accessed September 2015).

Mason, E. S. (1931) 'Saint-Simonism and the Rationalisation of Industry'. *Quarterly Journal of Economics* 45(4): 640–83.

Mathias, P. and Postan, M. M. (eds) (1978) *The Cambridge Economic History* volume VII, part I. Cambridge: Cambridge University Press.

Mayersohn, A. (2014) 'Transparency Is Not the Government's Responsibility'. *Boston Review*, 23 January, http://www.bostonreview.net (accessed September 2015).

Mazzucato, M. (2013) *The Entrepreneurial State: Debunking Public vs. Private Myths.* London: Anthem Press.

McClelland, R. and Mok, S. (2012) 'A Review of Recent Research on Labor Supply Elasticities'. *Congressional Budget Office Working Paper 2012–12,* October.

McGraw, T. (2007) *Prophet of Innovation: Joseph Schumpeter and Creative Destruction.* Cambridge, MA: Belknap Press.

McIntyre, B. (2011) 'America's Tax System Is Not as Progressive as You Think'. *Citizens for Tax Justice,* April.

McKenna, M. (2012) 'Who Stopped the Music – How Jean Sibelius Ran Out of Notes'. *The Monthly* 84, November, http://www.themonthly.com (accessed September 2015).

McKinsey & Company (2010) *How the World's Most Improved School Systems Keep Getting Better.* Report, 29 November, pp. 70–6, http://www.tes.co.uk (accessed September 2015).

McKnight, A. (2015) 'Downward Mobility, Opportunity Hoarding and the "Glass Floor" '. Centre for Analysis of Social Exclusion (CASE), London School of Economics Research Report, June, https://www.gov.uk (accessed September 2015).

McMahon, W. (1999) *Education and Development: Measuring the Social Benefits.* Oxford: Oxford University Press.

Meek, R. (1953) 'Stalin as Economist'. *Review of Economic Studies* 21(3): 232–9.

Méhaut, P., Berg, P., Grimshaw, D. and Jaehrling, K., with van der Meer, M. and Eskildsen, J. (2010) 'Cleaning and Nursing in Hospitals: Institutional Variety and the Reshaping of Low-Wage Jobs' in Gautié and Schmitt (2010), pp. 319–66.

Meiksins, P. (1994) 'Labor and Monopoly Capital for the 1990s: A Review and Critique of the Labor Process Debate'. *Monthly Review* November: 45–59.

Menand, L. (2012) 'Today's Assignment'. *New Yorker,* 17 December, http://www.newyorker.com (accessed September 2015).

Merkle, J. (1980) *Management and Ideology: The Legacy of the International Scientific Management Movement.* Berkeley: University of California Press.

Merton, R. (2003) 'Thoughts on the Future: Theory and Practice in Investment Management'. *Financial Analysts Journal* 59(1): 17–23.

Michel, H. (2007) 'Co-Determination in Germany: The Recent Debate'. Johann Wolfgang Goethe-Universität Frankfurt, March, http://www.uclouvain.be (accessed September 2015).

Mighton, J. (2007) *The Myth of Ability: Nurturing Mathematical Talent in Every Child.* Toronto: Anansi Press.

Milanovic, B. (2011) *The Haves and the Have Nots: A Brief and Idiosyncratic History of Inequality.* New York: Basic Books.

Mill, J. S. (1870) *The Principles of Political Economy with Some of Their Applications to Social Philosophy* (ed. William James Ashley). London: Longmans, Green and Co., based on Mill's seventh edition of 1870, oll.libertyfund.org (accessed September 2015).

Mirrlees, J., Adam, S., Besley, T., Blundell, R., Bond, S., Chote, R., Gammie, M., Johnson, P., Myles, G. and Poterba, J. (2011) 'Tax by Design: The Mirrlees Review'. Institute for Fiscal Studies, http://www.ifs.org.uk (accessed September 2015).

Mises, L. von (1920) 'Economic Calculation in the Socialist Commonwealth' in Hayek (1935), pp. 87–130.

Mishel, L. and Bivens, J. (2013) 'The Pay of Corporate Executives and Financial Professionals as Evidence of Rents in Top 1 Percent Incomes'. Economic Policy Institute *Working Paper no. 296,* 20 June.

Mishel, L. and Rothstein, R. (eds) (2002) *The Class Size Debate.* Washington, DC: Economic Policy Institute.

Mishel, L. and Rothstein, R. (2002a) 'Introduction' to Mishel and Rothstein (2002), pp. 1–6.

Mishel, L. and Sabadish, N. (2012) 'CEO Pay and the Top 1%: How Executive Compensation and Financial-Sector Pay Have Fueled Income Inequality'. *Economic Policy Institute Issue Brief* no. 331, 2 May.

Mishel, L., Shierholz, H. and Schmitt, J. (2013) 'Don't Blame the Robots: Assessing the Job Polarization Explanation of Growing Wage Inequality'. Economic Policy Institute *Working Paper*, 13 November.

Mitch, D. (1990) "Education and Economic Growth: Another Axiom of Indispensability? From Human Capital to Human Capabilities' in Tortella (1990), pp. 29–45.

Modigliani, F. and Miller, M. (1958) 'The Cost of Capital, Corporation Finance and the Theory of Investment'. *American Economic Review* 48: 261–97.

Mokyr, J. (2002) *The Gifts of Athena: Historical Origins of the Knowledge Economy.* Princeton: Princeton University Press.

Mokyr, J. (2009) *The Enlightened Economy: Britain and the Industrial Revolution 1700– 1850.* London: Penguin.

Molotsky, I. (1988) 'Reagan Vetoes Bill Putting Limits on TV Programming for Children'. *New York Times*, 7 November, http://www.nytimes.com (accessed September 2015).

Montias, J. M. (1959) 'Planning with Material Balances in Soviet-Type Economies'. *American Economic Review* 49(5): 963–85.

Morikowa, H. 'Japan: Increasing Organizational Capabilities of Large Industrial Enterprises' in Chandler et al. (1997), pp. 307–35.

Morozov, E. (2013) *To Save Everything, Click Here: Technology, Solutionism and the Urge to Fix Problems That Don't Exist.* London: Allen Lane.

Moser, P. (2013) 'Patents and Innovation: Evidence from Economic History'. *Journal of Economic Perspectives* 27(1): 23–44.

Mowery, D. and Rosenberg, N. (1989) *Technology and the Pursuit of Economic Growth.* Cambridge: Cambridge University Press.

Mulligan, C. (2012) *The Redistribution Recession: How Labor Market Distortions Contracted the Economy.* Oxford: Oxford University Press.

Mulligan, C. (2013) 'Hidden Costs of the Minimum Wage'. *Economix*, 13 March, http://economix.blogs.nytimes.com (accessed September 2015).

Murnane, R. J. (2013) 'U.S. High School Graduation Rates: Patterns and Explanations'. *Journal of Economic Literature* 51(2): 370–422.

Murray, C. (2007) 'Intelligence in the Classroom'. American Enterprise Institute, January, http://www.aei.org (accessed September 2015).

Murray, C. (2008a) 'Are Too Many People Going to College?' American Enterprise Institute, September, http://intelligencesquaredus.org (accessed September 2015).

Murray, C. (2008b) 'We Can't All Make the Grade'. *Standpoint*, October, www.standpointmag.co.uk (accessed September 2015).

Murray, C. (2009) 'Intelligence and College'. American Enterprise Institute, October, www.aei.org (accessed September 2015).

Murray, C. (2012) *Coming Apart: The State of White America, 1960–2010.* New York: Crown Publishing.

Murray, C. (2015) *The Social Contract Revisited: Guaranteed Income as a Replacement for the Welfare State.* Oxford: The Foundation for Law, Justice and Society in collaboration with The Centre for Socio-Legal Studies, University of Oxford, http://www.fljs.org (accessed May 2015).

Murray, J. (2012) 'Why I Sent My Child to a Private School'. *The Guardian*, 23 July, http://www.guardian.co.uk (accessed September 2015).

Myllntaus, T. (1990) 'Education in the Making of Modern Finland' in Tortella (1990), pp. 153–71.

Myrdal, G. (1972) *Asian Drama: An Inquiry into the Poverty of Nations*; abridged in one volume. London: Penguin Press.

Naipaul, V. S. (1964) *An Area of Darkness*. New York: Vintage, edition published in 2002.

National Commission on Excellence in Education (1983) *A Nation at Risk: The Imperative for Educational Reform*. A Report to the Nation and the Secretary of Education, United States Department of Education, April, http://datacenter.spps. org (accessed September 2015).

Nelson, R. (ed.) (1962) *The Rate and Direction of Inventive Activity: Economic and Social Factors*. Princeton: Princeton University Press.

Nelson, R. (ed.) (1982) *Government and Technical Progress: A Cross-Industry Analysis*. New York: Pergamon Press.

Nelson, R. and Pack, H. (1999) 'The Asian Miracle and Modern Growth Theory'. *The Economic Journal* 109(457): 416–36, pp. 418–19.

Nelson, R. and Winter, S. (1982) *An Evolutionary Theory of Economic Change*. Cambridge, MA: Belknap Press.

Nelson, R. and Wright, G. (1992) 'The Rise and Fall of American Technological Leadership: The Postwar Era in Historical Perspective'. *Journal of Economic Literature* XXX: 1931–64, 1934–9.

Nemeth, E., Schmitz, S. and Uebel, T. (eds) (2007) *Otto Neurath's Economics in Context*. Vienna: Springer.

Neurath, O. (1910) 'War Economy' in Uebel and Cohen (2004), pp. 153–99.

Neurath, O. (1917) 'State Cartels and State Trusts as Organisational Forms of the Future' in Uebel and Cohen (2004), pp. 235–61.

New York Times Editorial Board (2013) 'Even Gifted Students Can't Keep Up in Math and Science, the Best Fend for Themselves'. *New York Times*, 15 December, http://www.nytimes (accessed September 2015).

Nicholas, S. (1990) 'Literacy and the Industrial Revolution' in Tortella (1990), pp. 47–67.

Nilsson, A. and Pettersson, L. (1990) 'Some Hypotheses Regarding Education and Economic Growth in Sweden during the First Half of the Nineteenth Century' in Tortella (1990), pp. 209–22.

Nisbett, R. E., Aronson, J., Blair, C., Dickens, W., Flynn, J., Halpern, D. F. and Turkheimer, E. (2012) 'Intelligence: New Findings and Theoretical Developments'. *American Psychologist* January: 1–29.

Noble, D. (1977) *America by Design*. Oxford: Oxford University Press.

Noble, D. (1984) *Forces of Production: A Social History of Industrial Automation*. Oxford: Oxford University Press.

Nolan, B. and Marx, I. (2009) 'Economic Inequality, Poverty, and Social Exclusion' in Salverda et al. (2009), pp. 315–51.

Nolan, B., Esping-Andersen, G., Whelan, C., Mâitre, B. and Wagner, S. (2011) 'The Role of Social Institutions in Intergenerational Mobility' in Smeeding et al. (2011), pp. 331–67.

Nordhaus, W. (1997) 'Do Real-Output and Real-Wage Measures Capture Reality? The History of Lighting Suggests Not' in Bresnahan (1997), pp. 29–66.

North, D. and Thomas, R. P. (1973) *The Rise of the Western World*. Cambridge: Cambridge University Press.

North Carolina Abecedarian Project (2015) http://www.promisingpractices.net (accessed May 2015).

Norton, M. I. and Ariely, D. (2011) 'Building a Better America – One Wealth Quintile at a Time'. *Perspectives on Psychological Science* 6(1): 9–12.

Novak, W. J. (2010) 'The Myth of the "Weak" American State'.*American Historical Review* 115(3): 766–7.

Nove, A. (1969) *An Economic History of the U.S.S.R.* Harmondsworth: Penguin.

Nove, A. and Nuti, D. M. (eds) (1972) *Socialist Economics*. Harmondsworth: Penguin.

Nozick, R. (1973) 'Distributive Justice'. *Philosophy & Public Affairs* 3(1): 45–126.

Nozick, R. (1974) *Anarchy, State and Utopia*. New York: Basic Books, Inc.

Nussbaum, M. (2010) *Not for Profit: Why Democracy Needs the Humanities*. Princeton: Princeton University Press.

Nussbaum, M. (2011) *Creating Capabilities*. Cambridge, MA: Belknap Press.

Nutter, G. W. (1954) 'Is Competition Decreasing in Our Economy?' *Journal of Farm Economics* 36: 751–8.

OECD (2009) *Economic Policy Reforms: Going for Growth*, part II, chapter 5, 'A Family Affair: Intergenerational Social Mobility across OECD Countries'. Paris: OECD, www.oecd.org (accessed September 2015).

OECD (2010) *PISA 2009 Results: Overcoming Social Background: Equity in Learning Opportunities and Outcomes*, volume II. Paris: OECD.

OECD (2011a) *Divided We Stand: Why Inequality Keeps Rising: an Overview of Growing Income Inequalities in OECD Countries*, www.oecd.org (accessed September 2015).

OECD (2011b) *Social Justice in the OECD – How Do Member States Compare? Sustainable Governance Indicators*, http://www.sgi-network.org (accessed September 2015).

OECD (2012) *PISA 2012 Results in Focus: What 15-Year-Olds Know and What They Can Do With What They Know*, http://www.oecd.org (accessed September 2015).

OECD (2013) 'Unemployment Rates' in *OECD Factbook 2013 Economic, Environmental and Social Statistics*. Paris: OECD Publishing, http://www.oecd.org (accessed September 2015).

OECD (2013a) 'Employment/Population Ratios by Selected Age Groups', *Employment Outlook 2013*, table B, http://www.keepeek.com (accessed September 2015).

OECD (2014) *Education at a Glance*. Paris: OECD, http://www.oecd.org (accessed September 2015).

OECD (2015) 'Average Annual Hours Actually Worked per Worker for Various Countries, 1980 and 2009', StatExtracts, http://stats.oecd.org (accessed September 2015).

OECD (2015a) 'Harmonised Unemployment Rates'. *Short Term Labour Market Statistics*, https://stats.oecd.org (accessed September 2015).

Offer, A. (2006) *The Challenge of Affluence*. Oxford: Oxford University Press.

Office for Standards in Education, Children's Services and Skills (2007) 'Summerhill School Independent School Standard Inspection Report', reports.ofsted.gov.uk/index (accessed September 2015).

Official Journal of the European Union (2012) 'Protocol No. 4: On the Statute of the European System of Central Banks and of the European Central Bank', http://www.ecb.europa.eu (accessed September 2015).

O'Grady, J. (2013) editorial, *The Week*, issue 914, 6 April, p. 5.

Ohkawa, K. and Rosovsky, H. (1973) *Japanese Economic Growth*. Stanford: Stanford University Press.

Okun, A. (1975) *Equality and Efficiency: The Big Tradeoff*. Washington, DC: The Brookings Institution.

Oleson, A. and Voss, J. (eds) (1979) *The Organization of Knowledge in Modern America 1860–1920*. Baltimore: Johns Hopkins University Press.

Open Secrets (2015) Lobbying Database, http://www.opensecrets.org (accessed September 2015).

Ornstein, C., Sagara, E. and Grochowski, R. (2014) 'As Full Disclosure Nears, Doctors' Pay for Drug Talks Plummets'. *ProPublica*, March, http://www.propublica.org (accessed September 2015).

Orton, M. and Rowlingson, K. (2007) *Public Attitudes to Economic Inequality*. York: Joseph Rowntree Foundation.

Osterman, P. and Shulman, B. (2011) *Good Jobs America: Making Work Better for Everyone*. New York: Russell Sage Foundation.

Oulès, F. (1966) *Economic Planning and Democracy*. Harmondsworth: Penguin.

Overy, R. (1995) *Why the Allies Won*. New York: W.W. Norton.

Packer, G. (2014) *The Unwinding: Thirty Years of American Decline*. London: Faber & Faber.

Palan, R. (2002) 'Tax Havens and the Commercialization of State Sovereignty'. *International Organization* 56(1): 151–76.

Panitch, L. (1976) *Social Democracy and Industrial Militancy: The Labour Party, the Trade Unions and Incomes Policy, 1945–1974*. Cambridge: Cambridge University Press.

Panitch, L. and Gindin, S. (2012) *The Making of Global Capitalism: The Political Economy of the American Empire*. London: Verso.

Parker, R. H. and Harcourt, G. C. (eds) (1969) *Readings in the Concept and Measurement of Income*. Cambridge: Cambridge University Press.

Paton, G. (2013) 'Eton Head in Drive for Network of State Boarding Schools'. *Daily Telegraph*, 26 May, http://www.telegraph.co.uk (accessed September 2015).

Paul, A. M. (2015) 'A New Vision for Testing'. *Scientific American* August: 45–51.

Peck, M. and Scherer, F. M. (1962) *The Weapons Acquisition Process: An Economic Analysis*. Boston: Harvard University.

Pencavel, J. (2005) 'Unionism Viewed Internationally'. *Journal of Labor Research* XXVI(1): 65–97.

Pensieroso, L. (2007) 'Real Business Cycle Models of the Great Depression: A Critical Survey'. *Journal of Economic Surveys* 21(1): 110–42.

Peshkin, A. (2001) *Permissible Advantage: The Moral Consequences of Elite Schooling*. Mahwah, New Jersey: Lawrence Erlbaum Associates.

Pfeffer, F. (2011) 'Status Attainment and Wealth in the United States and Germany' in Smeeding et al. (2011), pp. 109–37.

Philippon, T. and Reshef, A. (2013) 'An International Look at the Growth of Modern Finance'. *Journal of Economic Perspectives* 27(2): 73–96.

Phillips-Fein, K. (2009) *Invisible Hands: The Making of the Conservative Movement from the New Deal to Reagan*. New York: W.W. Norton.

Picciotto, S. (2012) 'Towards Unitary Taxation of Transnational Corporations'. *Tax Justice Network*, December, http://www.taxjustice.net (accessed September 2015).

Piketty, T. (2014) *Capital in the Twenty-First Century*. Cambridge, MA: Belknap Press of Harvard University Press.

Piketty, T. and Saez, E. (2007) 'How Progressive is the U.S. Federal Tax System? A Historical and International Perspective'. *Journal of Economic Perspectives* 21(1): 3–24.

Piketty, T., Saez, E. and Stantcheva, S. (2014) 'Optimal Taxation of Top Labor Incomes: A Tale of Three Elasticities'. *American Economic Journal: Economic Policy* 6(1): 230–71.

Playfair, L. (1852) 'The Chemical Principles Involved in the Manufactures of the Exhibition as Indicating the Necessity of Industrial Instruction', in *Lectures on the Results of the Great Exhibition of 1851*, as quoted in Armytage (1955), p. 195.

Podgursky, M. J. and Springer, M. G. (2007) 'Teacher Performance Pay: A Review'. *Journal of Policy Analysis and Management* 26(4): 909–49.

POGO (Project on Government Oversight) (2013) *Dangerous Liaisons: Revolving Door at SEC Creates Risk of Regulatory Capture*. Washington, DC: The Project on Government Oversight, February, http://www.pogo.org (accessed September 2015).

Polanyi, K. (1944) *The Great Transformation*. Boston: Beacon Press.

Policy Network (2011) *Social Progress in the 21st Century: Social Investment, Labour Market Reform and Intergenerational Inequality*, www.policy-network.net (accessed September 2015).

Pontusson, J. (2009) 'Once Again a Model: Nordic Social Democracy in a Globalized World' in Cronin et al. (2009).

Pontusson, J. (2013) 'Unionization, Inequality and Redistribution'. *British Journal of Industrial Relations* 51(4): 797–825.

Porter, M. (1990) *The Competitive Advantage of Nations*. London: Macmillan.

Porter, R. (1999) *The Greatest Benefit to Mankind: A Medical History of Humanity from Antiquity to the Present*. London: Fontana Press.

Porter, T. (1995) *Trust in Numbers*. Princeton: Princeton University Press.

Powell, A. G. (1996) *Lessons from Privilege: The American Prep School Tradition*. Cambridge, MA: Harvard University Press.

Powell, J. W., Bernhard, N. and Graf, L. (2012) 'The Emergent European Model in Skill Formation: Comparing Higher Education and Vocational Training in the Bologna and Copenhagen Processes'. *Sociology of Education* 85(3): 240–58.

Prescott, E. C. (2004) 'Why Do Americans Work So Much More than Europeans?' *Quarterly Review, Federal Reserve Bank of Minneapolis* 28(1): 2–13, http://www.minneapolisfed.org (accessed September 2015).

President's Council of Advisors on Science and Technology (PCAST) (2004) *Report on Information Technology, Manufacturing and Competitiveness*, January, http://www.ostp.gov (accessed September 2015).

Pritchett, L. (2001) 'Where Has All the Education Gone?' *World Bank Economic Review* 15(3): 367–91.

Putnam, R. D. (2015) *Our Kids: The American Dream in Crisis*. New York: Simon & Schuster.

Quinn, B. (2013) 'Thousands of Children as Young as Five Act as Family Carers, Figures Show'. *Guardian*, 16 May, http://www.guardian.co.uk (accessed September 2015).

Ramsden, S., Richardson, F. M., Goulven Josse, M. S., Thomas, C., Ellis, C., Shakeshaft, C., Seghier, M. L. and Price, C. J. (2011) 'Verbal and Non-Verbal Intelligence Changes in the Teenage Brain'. *Nature* 479: 113–16.

Rasmussen, W. (1962) 'The Impact of Technological Change on American Agriculture, 1862–1962'. *Journal of Economic History* 22: 578–91.

Ravitch, D. (2000) *Left Back*. New York: Simon & Schuster.

Ravitch, D. (2002) 'Education after the Culture Wars'. *Daedalus* 131(3): 5–21.

Ravitch, D. (ed.) (2004) *Brookings Papers on Education Policy*. Washington, DC: Brookings Institution.

Ravitch, D. (2010) 'The Myth of Charter Schools'. *New York Review of Books* 11 November, pp. 22–4.

Ravitch, D. (2012) 'Schools We Can Envy', review of Sahlberg (2011) in the *New York Review of Books*, 8 March, http://www.nybooks (accessed September 2015).

Rawls, J. (1993) *Political Liberalism*. New York: Columbia University Press.

Rawls, J. (1999) *A Theory of Justice*. Oxford: Oxford University Press, revised edition 1999; original edition 1971.

Rector, R. and Sheffield, R. (2011) 'Air Conditioning, Cable TV, and an Xbox: What Is Poverty in the United States Today?' *Backgrounder* Executive Summary No. 2575, 18 July, Washington, DC: Heritage Foundation.

Reardon, S. F. (2011) 'The Widening Academic Achievement Gap between the Rich and the Poor: New Evidence and Possible Explanations' in Duncan and Murnane (2011), pp. 91–115.

Reeves, R. V. and Howard, K. (2013) 'The Glass Floor: Education, Downward Mobility, and Opportunity Hoarding'. *Centre on Children and Families at Brookings*, November, http://www.brookings.edu (accessed September 2015).

Reich, R. (1992) *The Work of Nations – Preparing Ourselves for 21st Century Capitalism*. New York: Vintage Books.

Reich, R. (2012) 'Outsourcing isn't the problem'. Salon.com, 19 July, http://www.salon.com (accessed September 2015).

Reifschneider, D., Wascher, W. L. and Wilcox, D. (2013) 'Aggregate Supply in the United States: Recent Developments and Implications for the Conduct of Monetary Policy'. Paper presented at the 14th Jacques Polak Annual Research Conference Hosted by the International Monetary Fund, Washington, DC, 7–8 November.

Reporters without Borders (2015) *World Press Freedom Index 2015*, https://index.rsf.org (accessed September 2015).

Reynolds, G. (2012) 'Do Exercise Programs Help Children Stay Fit?' *New York Times*, 3 October, http://well.blogs.nytimes.com (accessed September 2015).

Richardson, D. (1995) 'Income Inequality and Trade: How to Think, What to Conclude'. *Journal of Economic Perspectives* 9(3): 33–55.

Richardson, K. and Norgate, S. (2006) 'A Critical Analysis of IQ Studies of Adopted Children'. *Human Development* 49: 319–35.

Riordan, M., Hoddeson, L. and Herring, C. (1999) 'The Invention of the Transistor'. *Reviews of Modern Physics* 71(2) Centenary: S336–S345.

Ritschel, D. (1997) *The Politics of Planning: The Debate on Economic Planning in the 1930s*. Oxford: Clarendon Press.

Rivkin, S., Hanushek, E. and Kain, J. F. (2005) 'Teachers, Schools, and Academic Achievement'. *Econometrica* 73(2): 417–58.

Roberts, L. and Schaffer, S. (2007) Preface to Roberts et al. (2007), pp. xiii–xxvii.

Roberts, L., Schaffer, S. and Dear, P. (eds) (2007) *The Mindful Hand: Inquiry and Invention from the Late Renaissance to Early Industrialisation*. Amsterdam: Koninklijke Nederlandse Akademie van Wetenschappen.

Roberts, P. C. (1971) 'Marx's Classification of Economic Systems and the Soviet Economy'. *Soviet Studies* 23(1): 96–102.

Roberts, P. C. (1971a) 'Lange's Theory of Socialist Planning'. *Journal of Political Economy* 79(3): 562–77.

Roberts, P. C. and Stephenson, M. (1968) 'Alienation and Central Planning in Marx'. *Slavic Review* 27(3): 470–4.

Robinson, E. A. G. (1931) *The Structure of Competitive Industry*. London: Cambridge University Press.

Robinson, J. (1933) *The Economics of Imperfect Competition*. London: Macmillan, second edition 1969.

Røed, K. (1997) 'Hysteresis in Unemployment'. *Journal of Economic Surveys* 11(4): 389–418.

Rogers, A. and Toder, E. (2011) 'Trends in Tax Expenditures, 1985–2016'. *Urban-Brookings Tax Policy Center*, September.

Roine, J., Vlachos, J. and Waldenström, D. (2009) 'The Long-Run Determinants of Inequality: What Can We Learn from Top Income Data?' *Journal of Public Economics* 93: 974–88.

Romer, P. (1990) 'Endogenous Technical Change'. *Journal of Political Economy* 98(5) Part II: S71–S102.

Rose, M. (2004) *The Mind at Work: Valuing the Intelligence of the American Worker*. New York: Viking.

Rose, S. A., Feldman, J. F. and Jankowski, J. J. (2009) 'Information Processing in Toddlers: Continuity from Infancy and Persistence of Preterm Deficits'. *Intelligence* 37(3): 311–20.

Rosenberg, N. (1972) *Technology and American Economic Growth*. New York: M.E. Sharpe.

Rosenberg, N. (1976) *Perspectives on Technology*. Cambridge: Cambridge University.

Rosenberg, N. (1982) *Inside the Black Box*. Cambridge: Cambridge University Press.

Rossiter, M. (1979) 'The Organization of Agricultural Sciences' in Oleson and Voss (1979), pp. 211–48.

Rostowski, J. and Auerbach, P. (1986) 'Storming Cycles and Economic Systems'. *Journal of Comparative Economics* 10: 293–312.

Roth, G. (1963) *The Social Democrats in Imperial Germany*. Totowa, New Jersey: Bedminster Press.

Rouse, E. and Barrow, L. (2009) 'School Vouchers and Student Achievement: Recent Evidence and Remaining Questions'. *Annual Review of Economics* 1: 17–42.

Rowthorn, R. E. and Wells, J. R. (1987) *De-Industrialisation and Foreign Trade*. Cambridge: Cambridge University Press.

Rubenstein, Y. and Heckman, J. (2001) 'The Importance of Noncognitive Skills: Lessons from the GED Testing Program'. *American Economic Review* Papers & Proceedings 91(2): 145–9.

Rutland, P. (1986) 'Productivity Campaigns in Soviet Industry' in Lane, D. (ed.) (1986) *Labour and Employment in the USSR*. Brighton: Wheatsheaf, pp. 191–208.

Sabel, C. and Zeitlin, J. (1985) 'Historical Alternatives to Mass Production: Politics, Markets and Technology in Nineteenth-Century Industrialization'. *Past & Present* 108: 133–76.

Saez, E., Slemrod, J. and Giertz, S. H. (2012) 'The Elasticity of Taxable Income with Respect to Marginal Tax Rates: A Critical Review'. *Journal of Economic Literature* 50(1): 3–50.

Sahlberg, P. (2011) *Finnish Lessons: What Can the World Learn from Educational Change in Finland?* New York: Teachers College, Columbia University.

Sala-i-Martín, X., Bilbao-Osorio, B., Blanke, J., Crotti, R., Drzeniek Hanouz, M., Geiger, T. and Ko, C. S. (2012) 'The Global Competitiveness Index 2012–2013: Strengthening Recovery by Raising Productivity' in Schwab and Sala-i-Martín (2012), pp. 3–48.

Salverda, W., Nolan, B. and Smeeding, T. (eds) (2009) *The Oxford Handbook of Economic Inequality*. Oxford: Oxford University Press.

Samuelson, P. (1961) *Economics*, fifth edition. New York: McGraw-Hill.

Samuelson, P. (1964) *Economics*, sixth edition. New York: McGraw-Hill.

Sandberg, L. (1982) 'Ignorance, Poverty and Economic Backwardness in the Early Stages of European Industrialization: Variations on Alexander Gerschenkron's Grand Theme'. *Journal of European Economic History* 11(3): 675–97.

Sanderson, M. (1999) *Education and Economic Decline in Britain, 1870 to the 1990s*. Cambridge: Cambridge University Press, chapters 2 and 3.

Sassoon, D. (2010) *One Hundred Years of Socialism: The West European Left in the Twentieth Century*. London: L.B. Tauris & Co. Ltd.

Saunders, P. (2010) *Social Mobility Myths*. London: Civitas.

Sawyer, J. (1954) 'The Social Basis of the American System of Manufacturing'. *Journal of Economic History* XIV: 361–79.

Schmitt, J. and Jones, J. (2012) 'Where Have All the Good Jobs Gone?' Washington, DC: Center for Economic and Policy Research, July.

Schmitt, J. and Mitukiewcz, A. (2012) 'Politics Matter: Changes in Unionisation Rates in Rich Countries, 1960–2010'. *Industrial Relations Journal* 43(3): 260–80.

Schularick, M. and Taylor, A. (2012) 'Credit Booms Gone Bust: Monetary Policy, Leverage Cycles, and Financial Crises, 1870–2008'. *American Economic Review*, 102(2): 1029–61.

Schumacher, E. F. (1973) *Small Is Beautiful: A Study of Economics as if People Mattered*. London: Blond & Briggs.

Schumpeter, J. (1911) *The Theory of Economic Development*. New Brunswick: Transactions Publishers, 2008.

Schumpeter, J. (1928) 'The Instability of Capitalism'. *Economic Journal* 38(151): 361–86.

Schumpeter, J. (1939) *Business Cycles*. New York: McGraw-Hill Book Company, abridged edition 1964.

Schumpeter, J. (1947) *Capitalism, Socialism and Democracy*, third edition. New York: Harper & Row.

Schütz, G., Ursprung, H. W. and Woessmann, L. (2008) 'Education Policy and Equality of Opportunity'. *Kyklos* 61(2): 279–308.

Schwab, K. (ed.) and Sala-i-Martín, X. (chief advisor) (2012) *Global Competitiveness Report 2012–2013*. Geneva: World Economic Forum.

Schwartz, J. M. (2013) 'Democracy for Centrists'. *Dissent*, 19 March, http://www. dissentmagazine.org (accessed September 2015).

Schweickart, D. (1980) *Capitalism or Worker Control? An Ethical and Economic Appraisal*. New York: Praeger.

Scott, J. C. (1998) *Seeing like a State*. New Haven: Yale University Press.

Sellgren, K. (2013) 'Schools Fail to Challenge the Brightest, Warns Ofsted'. BBC News, 3 June, http://www.bbc.co.uk (accessed September 2015).

Sen, A. (1999) *Development as Freedom*. Oxford: Oxford University Press.

Sen, A. (2006) *Identity and Violence*. New York: W.W. Norton.

Sen, A. (2009) *The Idea of Justice*. London: Allen Lane.

Servan-Schreiber, J.-J. (1968) *The American Challenge*. New York: Scribner.

Setterfield, M. (ed.) (2004) *Interactions in Analytical Political Economy: Theory, Policy and Applications*. Armonk, NY: M.E. Sharpe.

Shanin, T. (1983) *Late Marx and the Russian Road*. New York: Monthly Review Press.

Shapiro, A-L. (1982) 'Social Space and Social Control'. *French Historical Studies* 12(4): 486–507.

Shapiro, L. (2012) ' "Skills Mismatch" Causing High Unemployment? Not Quite'. *Huffington Post*, 22 February, http://www.huffingtonpost.com (accessed September 2015).

Shaxson, N. (2011) *Treasure Islands*. London: Vintage Books.

Shefrin, H. and Statman, M. (2012) 'Behavioral Finance in the Financial Crisis: Market Efficiency, Minsky, and Keynes' in Blinder et al. (2012), pp. 99–135.

Shiller, R. (2008) *The Subprime Solution*. Princeton: Princeton University Press.

Shiller, R. (2012) *Finance and the Good Society*. Princeton: Princeton University Press.

Shmelëv, N. and Popov, V. (1989) *Na Perelom: Ekonomicheskaya Perestroika v CCCP*. Moscow: Novosti. English translation: *The Turning Point*. London: I.B.Tauris & Co. Ltd, 1990.

Sianesi, B. and Van Reenen, J. (2003) 'The Returns to Education: Macroeconomics'. *Journal of Economic Surveys* 17(2): 157–200.

Sibelius (2015) 'Sibelius's Debts and Assets', http://www.sibelius.fi/english (accessed September 2015).

Siegelbaum, L. (1988) *Stakhanovism and the Politics of Productivity in the U.S.S.R. 1935–1941*. Cambridge: Cambridge University Press.

Simon, B. (1953) *Intelligence Testing and the Comprehensive School*. London: Lawrence and Wishart.

Simons, H. C. (1948) *Economic Policy for a Free Society*. Chicago: University of Chicago.

Skocpol, T. (2003) *Diminished Democracy: From Membership to Management in American Civic Life*. Norman, OK: University of Oklahoma Press.

Skott, P. (2015) 'Public Debt, Secular Stagnation and Functional Finance', presented as a keynote address at The Third Nordic Post-Keynesian Conference, Aalborg, 22–23 May 2014.

Skott, P. and Auerbach, P. (2004) 'Skill Asymmetries, Increasing Wage Inequality and Unemployment' in Setterfield (2004), pp. 27–54.

Skott, P. and Guy, F. (2013) 'Power, Luck and Ideology – Technological and Institutional Parameters of the Agency Problem for CEOs'. *Review of Radical Political Economics* 45(3): 323–32.

Skowronek, S. (1982) *Building a New American State: The Expansion of National Administrative Capacities, 1877–1920*. Cambridge: Cambridge University Press.

Smeeding, T., Erikson, R. and Jäantti, M. (eds) (2011) *Persistence, Privilege and Parenting: The Comparative Study of Intergenerational Mobility*. New York: Russell Sage.

Smil, V. (2005) *Creating the Twentieth Century: Technical Innovations of 1867–1914 and Their Lasting Impact*. Oxford: Oxford University Press.

Smil, V. (2006) *Transforming the Twentieth Century: Technical Innovations and Their Consequences*. Oxford: Oxford University Press.

Smith, A. (1776) *An Inquiry into the Nature and Causes of the Wealth of Nations*. New York: Modern Library, edition of 1937.

Smith, E. B. and Kuntz, P. (2013) 'CEO Pay 1,795-to-1 Multiple of Wages Skirts US Law', *Bloomberg*, 30 April, http://www.bloomberg.com (accessed September 2015).

Solow, R. (1956) 'A Contribution to the Theory of Economic Growth'. *Quarterly Journal of Economics* 70(1): 61–94.

Solow, R. (1957) 'Technical Change and the Aggregate Production Function'. *Review of Economics and Statistics* 39(3): 312–20.

Solow, R. and Temin, P. (1978) 'Introduction: The Inputs for Growth' in Mathias and Postan (1978), pp. 1–27.

Sombart, W. (1906) *Why Is There No Socialism in the United States?* English translation. London: Macmillan, 1976.

Sotiropoulos, D. P., Milos, J. and Lapatsioras, S. (2013) *A Political Economy of Contemporary Capitalism and its Crisis: Demystifying Finance*. London: Routledge.

Sowell, T. (1980) *Knowledge and Decisions*. New York: Basic Books.

Spencer, H. (1843) 'The Proper Sphere of Government' in Spencer (1982), pp. 181–264.

Spencer, H. (1853), 'Over-Legislation' in Spencer (1982), pp. 265–330.

Spencer, H. (1857) 'Representative Government – What Is It Good For?' in Spencer (1982), pp. 331–84.

Spencer, H. (1982) *The Man versus the State: With Six Essays on Government, Society, and Freedom*. Indianapolis: Liberty Fund.

Stafeev, V. I. (2010) 'Initial Stages of the Development of Semiconductor Electronics in the Soviet Union (60 Years from the Invention of the Transistor)'. *Semiconductors* 44(5): 551–7.

Stanford, P. (2012) 'Private Education: What Price Excellence?' *Daily Telegraph*, 26 April, http://www.telegraph.co.uk (accessed September 2015).

Steedman, H. (2011) 'Challenges and Change: Apprenticeships in German-speaking Europe' in Dolphin and Lanning (2011), pp. 93–105.

Stein, J. (2010) *Pivotal Decade: How the United States Traded Factories for Finance in the Seventies*. New Haven: Yale University Press.

Steinbeck, J. (1939) *The Grapes of Wrath*. London: Penguin Classics, 2000.

Steinberg, S. and Kincheloe, J. L. (eds) (2004) *Kinderculture: The Corporate Construction of Childhood*, second edition. Boulder: Westview Press.

Steinberg, S. and Kincheloe, J. L. (2004a) 'Introduction – Kinderculture, Information Saturation, and the Socioeducational Positioning of Children' in Steinberg and Kincheloe (2004), pp. 1–46.

Steindl, J. (1952) *Maturity and Stagnation in American Capitalism*. New York: Monthly Review Press, 1976.

Steinherr, A. (2000) *Derivatives: The Wild Beast of Finance*. Chichester: John Wiley and Sons.

Steinmetz, C. P. (1916) *America and the New Epoch*. Memphis: General Books.

Stephens, N. M., Markus, H. R. and Phillips, L. T. (2014) 'Social Class Culture Cycles: How Three Gateway Contexts Shape Selves and Fuel Inequality'. *Annual Review of Psychology* 65: 611–34.

Sternberg, R. J. (2004) 'Culture and Intelligence'. *American Psychologist* 59(5): 325–38.

Stigler, G. (1945) 'The Cost of Subsistence'. *Journal of Farm Economics* XXVII: 305–14.

Stigler, G. (1949) 'Monopolistic Competition in Retrospect' in Stigler, G. *Five Lectures on Economic Problems*. London: London School of Economics, 1949.

Stigler, G. (1952) *The Theory of Price*. New York: Macmillan.

Stigler, G. (1957) 'Perfect Competition, Historically Contemplated'. *Journal of Political Economy* LXV(1): 1–17.

Stigler, G. (1966) *The Theory of Price*, third edition. New York: Macmillan.

Stiglitz, J. (1994) *Whither Socialism?* Cambridge, MA: MIT Press.

Stiglitz, J. (2005) 'The Ethical Economist', review of Benjamin Friedman *The Moral Consequences of Economic Growth*. *Foreign Affairs*, 84(6): 128–34.

Stiglitz, J. (2013) *The Price of Inequality: How Today's Divided Society Endangers Our Future*. London: W.W. Norton.

Stiglitz, J. (2013a) 'How Intellectual Property Reinforces Inequality'. *New York Times*, 14 July, http://opinionator.blogs.nytimes.com (accessed September 2015).

Stiglitz, J. (2014) 'Inequality Is Not Inevitable'. *New York Times*, 27 June, http://opinionator.blogs.nytimes.com (accessed September 2015).

Stiles, J. (2009) 'On Genes, Brains, and Behavior: Why Should Developmental Psychologists Care about Brain Development?' *Child Development Perspectives* 3(3): 196–202.

Stockhammer, E. and Sturn, S. (2012) 'The Impact of Monetary Policy on Unemployment Hysteresis'. *Applied Economics* 44: 2743–56.

Stocking, G. and Watkins, M. (1948) *Cartels or Competition?* New York: Twentieth Century Fund.

Stoker, G. (2011) 'Anti-Politics, Social Progress and Re-Energising Citizenship' in Policy Network (2011), pp. 10–14.

Stone, R. (1980) 'Whittling Away at the Residual: Some Thoughts on Denison's Growth Accounting: A Review Article'. *Journal of Economic Literature* 18(4): 1539–43.

Streeck, W. (1989) 'Skills and the Limits of Neo-Liberalism: The Enterprise of the Future as a Place of Learning'. *Work, Employment & Society* 3(1): 89–104.

Streeten, P. (2003) 'Shifting Fashions in Development Dialogue' in Fukuda-Parr and Shiva Kumar (2003), pp. 92–105.

Sturgeon, T. (2000) 'How Silicon Valley Came to Be' in Kenney (2000), pp. 15–47.

Suchman, M. (2000) 'Dealmakers and Counselors: Law Firms as Intermediaries in the Development of Silicon Valley' in Kenney (2000), pp. 71–97.

Sukehiro, H. (1989) 'Japan's Turn to the West' in Jansen (1989), pp. 432–98.

Sum, A., Khatiwada, I., Trubskyy, M. and Ross, M. with McHugh, W. and Palma, S. (2014) 'The Plummeting Labor Market Fortunes of Teens and Young Adults'. *The Brookings Institution*, March, http://www.brookings.edu (accessed September 2015).

Summers, L. (2014) 'America Risks Becoming a Downton Abbey Economy'. *Financial Times*, 16 February, p. 11.

Summers, L. H. (2015) 'Demand Side Secular Stagnation'. *American Economic Review* Papers and Proceedings 105(5): 60–5.

Sutton Trust (2010) 'Comprehensive Pupils Outperform Independent and Grammar Pupils in University Degrees'. 3 December, http://www.suttontrust.com (accessed September 2015).

Sutton Trust (2011) 'Improving the Impact of Teachers on Pupil Achievement'. September, http://www.suttontrust.com (accessed September 2015).

Swan, T. (1956) 'Economic Growth and Capital Accumulation'. *Economic Record* 32: 334–61.

Szamuely, L. (1974) *First Models of the Socialist Economic Systems*. Budapest: Akadémiai Kiadó.

Tawney, R. H. (1952) *Inequality*. London: George Allen & Unwin, first edition 1931.

Tax Justice Network (2014) 'OECD Information Exchange Standard: Watershed Moment for Fighting Offshore Tax Evasion?' March, pp. 1–2, http://www.internationaltaxreview.com (accessed September 2015).

Tchougounnikov, S. (1957) 'M. Bakhtin's Circle and the "Stalinist Science" '. *Toronto Slavic Quarterly*, originally published 1957, http://www.utoronto.ca (accessed September 2015).

Thomas, H. and Logan, C. (1982) *Mondragon: An Economic Analysis*. London: George Allen & Unwin.

Thornton, D. L. (2012) 'The Dual Mandate: Has the Fed Changed its Objective?' *Federal Reserve Bank of St. Louis Review* 94(2): 117–33.

Tinbergen, J. (1952) *On the Theory of Economic Policy*. Amsterdam: North-Holland Publishing Company.

Tinbergen, J. (1961) 'Do Communist and Free Economies Show a Converging Pattern?' *Soviet Studies* XII(4): 333–41.

Tirman, J. (ed.) (1984) *The Militarization of Technology*. Cambridge, MA: Ballinger.

Tirman, J. (1984a) 'The Defense-Economy Debate' in Tirman (1984), pp. 1–32.

Toder, E. and Baneman, D. (2012) 'Distributional Effects of Individual Income Tax Expenditures: An Update'. *Urban-Brookings Tax Policy Center*, 2 February, http://www.taxpolicycenter.org (accessed September 2015).

Toder, E., Rosenberg, J. and Eng, A. (2013) 'Evaluating Broad-Based Approaches for Limiting Tax Expenditures'. *National Tax Journal* December 66(4): 807–32.

Tomlinson, J. (1996) 'Inventing "decline": The Falling Behind of the British Economy in the Post-war Years'. *Economic History Review* XLIX(4): 731–57.

Tooze, A. (2006) *Wages of Destruction: The Making and Breaking of the Nazi Economy*. London: Penguin.

Tooze, A. (2014) *The Deluge: The Great War and the Remaking of Global Order*. London: Penguin.

Torrey, J. (1970) 'Illiteracy in the Ghetto'. *Harvard Educational Review* 40(2): 253–9.

Tortella, G. (ed.) (1990) *Education and Economic Development since the Industrial Revolution*. València: Generalitat Valenciana.

Tortella, G. and Sandberg, L. (1990) 'Education and Economic Development since the Industrial Revolution: A Summary Report' in Tortella (1990), pp. 3–28.

Tough, P. (2012) *How Children Succeed: Grit, Curiosity, and the Hidden Power of Character*. Boston: Houghton Mifflin Harcourt.

Townsend, P. (1979) *Poverty in the United Kingdom*. Harmondsworth: Penguin.

Trabandt, M. and Uhlig, H. (2009) 'How Far Are We from the Slippery Slope? The Laffer Curve Revisited'. *NBER Working Paper No. 15343*. Cambridge MA: National Bureau of Economic Research, September, http://www.nber.org (accessed September 2015).

Tranter, B. and Booth, K. (2015) 'Scepticism in a Changing Climate: A Cross-National Study'. *Global Environmental Change* 33: 154–64.

Traub, A. and Hiltonsmith, R. (2013) *Underwriting Bad Jobs: How Our Tax Dollars Are Funding Low-Wage Work and Fueling Inequality*. New York: Demos May.

Tremblay, D-G. and Le Bot, I. (2003) 'The German Dual Apprenticeship System: Analysis of Its Evolution and Present Challenges'. Québec: Télé-université Université du Québec, http://www.teluq.uquebec.ca (accessed September 2015).

Tudge, J. (2008) *The Everyday Lives of Children: Culture, Class and Child Rearing in Diverse Societies*. Cambridge: Cambridge University Press.

Turkheimer, E., Haley, A., Waldron, M., D'Onofrio, B. and Gottesman, I. (2003) 'Socioeconomic Status Modifies Heritability of IQ in Young Children'. *Psychological Science* 14(6): 623–8.

Turkheimer, E., D'Onofrio, B. M., Maes, H. H. and Eaves, L. J. (2005) 'Analysis and Interpretation of Twin Studies including Measures of the Shared Environment'. *Child Development* 76(6): 1217–33.

Uebel, T. (2004) 'Introduction: Neurath's Economics in Critical Context' in Uebel and Cohen (2004), pp. 1–108.

Uebel, T. and Cohen, R. (eds) (2004) *Otto Neurath: Economic Writings Selections 1904–1945*. Dordrecht: Kluwer Academic Publishers.

Ueda, R. (1987) *Avenues to Adulthood: The Origins of the High School and Social Mobility in an American Suburb*. Cambridge: Cambridge University Press.

United Nations Children's Fund (2007) *Child Poverty in Perspective: An Overview of Child Well-Being in Rich Countries*. Innocenti Report Card 7. Florence: UNICEF Innocenti Research Centre.

United Nations Development Programme (2015) *Human Development Reports*, http://hdr.undp.org (accessed September 2015).

University of Pennsylvania (2011) 'Penn Research Demonstrates Motivation Plays a Critical Role in Determining IQ Test Scores', http://www.upenn.edu (accessed September 2015).

Vaitheeswaran, V. (2007) 'Something New under the Sun', A Special Report on Innovation. *The Economist* 13 October, p. 22.

Vanek, J. (1970) *The General Theory of Labour-Managed Market Economies*. Ithaca: Cornell University Press.

Van Reenen, J. (2013) 'Mrs Thatcher's Economic Legacy'. *Vox*, 11 April, http://www.voxeu.org (accessed September 2015).

Vasagar, J. (2013) 'Out of Hours Working Banned by German Labour Ministry'. *Daily Telegraph*, 30 August, http://www.telegraph.co.uk (accessed September 2015).

Veblen, T. (1904) *The Theory of Business Enterprise*. New Brunswick: Transactions Books, 1978.

Veblen, T. (1914) *The Instinct of Workmanship and the State of the Industrial Arts*. New York: Augustus M. Kelley Reprints of Economic Classics, 1964.

Veblen, T. (1921) *The Engineers and the Price System*. New York: Harcourt, Brace & World 1963.

Veblen, T. (1923) *Absentee Ownership and Business Enterprise in Recent Times*. New York: Augustus M. Kelly, 1964.

Veblen, T. (1924) *The Theory of the Leisure Class: An Economic Study of Institutions*, originally published 1899. London: Allen & Unwin.

Vernon, R. (1966) 'International Investment and International Trade in the Product Cycle'. *Quarterly Journal of Economics* 80: 190–207.

Visser, J. (2013) *ICTWSS: Database on Institutional Characteristics of Trade Unions, Wage Setting, State Intervention and Social Pacts in 34 Countries between 1960 and 2012*. Version 4 – April, http://www.uva-aias.net (accessed September 2015).

Voth, H.-J. (2003) 'Living Standards during the Industrial Revolution: An Economist's Guide'. *American Economic Review* Papers and Proceedings 93: 221–6.

Voznesensky, N. (1948) *The Economy of the USSR during World War II*. Washington, DC: Public Affairs Press.

Wade, R. (1990) *Governing the Market*. Princeton: Princeton University Press.

Waldfogel, J. and Washbrook, E. (2010) 'Low Income and Early Cognitive Development in the U.K.' A Report for the Sutton Trust, February, www.suttontrust.com (accessed September 2015).

Walsh, V. and Gram, H. (1980) *Classical and Neoclassical Theories of General Equilibrium*. Oxford: Oxford University Press.

Ward, B. (1958) 'The Firm in Illyria: Market Syndicalism'. *American Economic Review* 48(4): 566–89.

Weber, M. (1922) *Economy and Society*, posthumous publication. Berkeley: University of California, 1978.

Weinstein, J. (1984) *The Decline of Socialism in America 1912–1925*. New Brunswick: Rutgers University Press.

Wengenroth, U. (1997) 'Germany: Competition Abroad – Co-operation at Home, 1870–1990' in Chandler et al. (1997), pp. 139–75.

Western, B. and Rosenfeld, J. (2011) 'Unions, Norms, and the Rise in American Wage Inequality', March, http://faculty.uml.edu (accessed September 2015).

Whyte, W. (1956) *The Organization Man*. Harmondsworth: Penguin, 1963.

Wickham-Jones, M. (1994) *The Political Economy of the Alternative Economic Strategy*. PhD dissertation, University of Manchester.

Wiener, M. (1981) *English Culture and the Decline of the Industrial Spirit*. Cambridge: Cambridge University Press.

Wilby, P. (2013) 'They Stole Our Name' [referring to the term 'free school']. *Guardian*, 28 May, p. 34.

Wilczynski, J. (1972) *The Economics of Socialism*, second edition. London: George Allen.

Wilhelm, J. (1985) 'The Soviet Union Has an Administered, Not a Planned Economy'. *Soviet Studies* XXXVII(1): 118–30.

Wilkinson, R. and Pickett, K. (2009) *The Spirit Level: Why More Equal Societies Almost Always Do Better.* London: Allen Lane, and their website The Equality Trust 'Why More Equality?' http://www.equalitytrust.org.uk (accessed September 2015).

Williamson, O. (1971) 'The Vertical Integration of Production: Market Failure Considerations'. *American Economic Association Papers and Proceedings* LXI(2): 112–23.

Williamson, O. (1976) *Markets and Hierarchies: Analysis and Antitrust Implications.* New York: Free Press.

Willingham, D. (2006) 'How Knowledge Helps – It Speeds and Strengthens Reading Comprehension, Learning – and Thinking'. *American Educator* Spring 2006, as reprinted at http://www.readingrockets.org (accessed September 2015).

Wills, G. (1999) *A Necessary Evil.* New York: Simon and Schuster.

Wilson, J. W. (1985) *The New Ventures: Inside the High-Stakes World of Venture Capital.* Reading: Addison-Wesley Publishing.

Wingert, P. (2012) 'Building a Better Science Teacher'. *Scientific American* 307(2): 48–55.

Winslow, J. (1973) *Conglomerates Unlimited.* Bloomington: Indiana University.

Wintour, P. (2013) 'Genetics Outweighs Teaching Gove Advisor Tells Boss'. *Guardian*, 11 October, http://www.theguardian.com (accessed September 2015).

Wolf, A. (2011) 'Review of Vocational Education'. Royal Commission, March, https://www.gov.uk (accessed September 2015).

Wolfe, B. L. and Haveman, R. H. (2002) 'Social and Nonmarket Benefits from Education in an Advanced Economy', bostonfed.org (accessed September 2015).

Wolff, C. (2002) *Johann Sebastian Bach: The Learned Musician.* Oxford: Oxford University Press.

Wolff, R. D. (2012) 'Yes, There Is an Alternative to Capitalism: Mondragon Shows the Way'. *Guardian*, 24 June, http://www.theguardian.com (accessed September 2015).

Womack, J., Jones, D. and Roos, D. (2007) *The Machine That Changed the World*, new edition. New York: Simon & Schuster.

Wooldridge, A. (2013) 'Special Report: The Nordic Countries: Northern Lights'. *The Economist*, 2 February, http://www.economist.com (accessed September 2015).

World Bank (2015) 'GDP Per Capita, PPP (Current International $)', http://data.worldbank.org (accessed September 2015).

Wright, D. C. H. (2013) *The Associated Board of the Royal Schools of Music: A Social and Cultural History.* Woodbridge: Boydill Press.

Wysession, M. (2015) 'Kids Are Scientists Too'. *Scientific American* August: 52–3.

Yoong-Deok, J. and Kim, Y. (2000) 'Land Reform, Income Redistribution, and Agricultural Production in Korea'. *Economic Development and Cultural Change* 48(2): 253–68.

Young, A. (1995) 'The Tyranny of Numbers: Confronting the Statistical Realities of the East Asian Growth Experience'. *Quarterly Journal of Economics* 110(3): 641–80.

Zaleski, E. (1971) *Planning for Economic Growth in the Soviet Union, 1918–1932.* Chapel Hill: University of North Carolina.

Zebel, S. (1967) 'Joseph Chamberlain and the Genesis of Tariff Reform'. *The Journal of British Studies* 7(1): 131–57.

Zeira, J. (2009) 'Why and How Education Affects Economic Growth'. *Review of International Economics* 17(3): 602–14.

Zissimopoulos, J. and Smith, J. (2011) 'Unequal Giving: Monetary Gifts to Children across Countries and over Time' in Smeeding et al. (2011), pp. 289–328.

Index

academy schools *see* schools, academy and charter schools

accounting *see* giant firms, cost accounting

Active Labour Market Policies (ALMP), 238–9, 389–90, 448 n44

Adams, C.A., 51–2

Adams, John Quincy, 251

advertising *see* marketing and advertising

advertising to children, 281, 338–40

African-American syntax, teaching of, 446 n99

agricultural and 'rustbelt' subsidies, 245–7

Alchian, Armen, 466 n142

Alexander, Magnus W., 52

Allen, Robert C.
on British industrialisation, 228
on Chinese agricultural development, 453 n19
on Soviet economic development, 102–5

alleviationist policies, 1–2, 143, 373–4

Alternative Economic Strategy (AES), 8, 143–56 *see also* Labour Party (Britain)
and Holland, Stuart, 150–5
policy programme, 147–9

American system of manufactures *see* standardisation

American Telephone and Telegraph Company (AT&T), 59, 186–7, 263–6, 268, 451 n27

anarchists, 85

antitrust policies *see* United States

Arnold, Matthew, 310–11

Asian tigers, 102–104, 141, 172–5, 337

assembly line, 7, 62–3, 76 *see also* Ford, Henry

Associated Board (UK), 337

Attenborough, David, 338, 340

Attlee, Clement *see* Labour Party (Britain)

Austrian Social Democratic Party, 114

Bach, Johann Sebastian, 333, 449 n54, 458 n62

backward bending labour supply curve, 298

Bacon, Francis, 18

Barone, Enrico, 438 n30

Baran, Paul, 109
and Sweezy, Paul *Monopoly Capital*, 130, 134–6, 262, 281

basic (guaranteed) income, 367–9, 420

Basie, William James (Count), 340

Bauer, Otto, 86

Bauman, Zygmunt, 22

Baumol, William
Baumol's law; Baumol cost disease, 307–8, 311, 373
Business Behavior, Value and Growth, 440 n20
income distribution and, 307

Becker, Gary, 192–3, 443 n4–9

Bell Labs *see* American Telephone and Telegraph Company (AT&T)

Berle, Adolf
American Economic Republic, 133
and Means, Gardiner *Modern Corporation and Private Property*, 130–1, 137

Berlin, Isaiah, 301

Bernstein, Eduard, 73, 88, 91–2, 94, 134

Binet, Alfred, 323 *see also* IQ

Bolsheviks *see* Lenin, Vladimir

Bowles, Samuel, 212–15

Braverman, Harry
deskilling, 181–2
technology, social influences upon, 240–1

Breton, Theodore, 443 n15

Brighouse, Harry, 310–11

British industrial revolution *see* First Industrial Revolution

Bryan, William Jennings, 253, 272

Bukharin, Nikolai, 93, 98, 100

bureaucracy, growth in, 40, 48–9, 75, 78–82, 90, 180

Burke, Edmund, 18
Burnham, James, 130
Burt, Cyril, 323 *see also* IQ

Calhoun, John C., 191–2, 199–200
Carnegie, Andrew, 71
Carr, Edward Hallett, 109
cartels
  and monopolistic restriction, 67
  and rationalisation, 72, 74, 84, 144,
    436 n16
Ceauşescu, Nicolae, 29
central planning, 1, 6, 37, 97, 126 *see
    also* Soviet economy
CEO remuneration, 293–4
Chakrabortty, Aditya, 447 n2, 448 n39
Chamberlain, Joseph, 67, 144
Chandler, Alfred DuPont, 39–40, 58, 69,
    138–9, 180 *see also* giant firms
  managerial innovations, giant firms,
    39–40, 49
  giant firms as fulcrums of planning,
    54–8
  railroads, 42–5, 229–30
  and the separation of ownership and
    control, 138–9
Chang, Ha-Joon, 226–7, 230
charter schools *see* schools, academy
    and charter schools
Chartists, 19
China, 128, 232, 289, 294, 426
Chomsky, Noam, 196
citizenship *see* education
city planning *see also* Jacobs, Jane and
    Haussmann, Georges-Eugène
  absence of spontaneous solutions to,
    35, 286
  Coasian approaches to, 30–1
  as a model for planning in general,
    18, 20
  Hayek's attitude towards, 30–1
  and state coercion, 28–9
Clarke, Sally, 246–7
classical dichotomy of real and financial
    sectors, 48, 122–3, 381–3
climate change, 6, 12, 125, 258, 273,
    275, 286, 377, 391, 421, 426, 429,
    430
Coase, Ronald
  external effects, 30–1, 32

theory of the firm, 55–6, 69
Common Core State Standards
    Initiative, 445 n72
Communist Manifesto (Marx and Engels),
    19, 38, 117, 118–19, 157
competition
  acceleration of, 136–7, 139–43, 384
  in Marxian economics, 134
competition for government contracts,
    377
competitiveness, international, 305–7,
    428–9
Comte, Auguste, 26
Confucian ethic, 141, 336–7
conglomerates, 383
consolidation in industry *see*
    rationalisation of industry
cooperative ventures, 85–6, 269, 394,
    413–5, 422
corporate social responsibility doctrine,
    133–4
creative displacement, 264
Crédit Mobilier, 20
crisis of, 207–8, 235–7, 239, 242, 279,
    292–3, 296–7, 367, 379, 382–3, 390,
    406
creative destruction *see* Schumpeter,
    Joseph
Crosland, Anthony, 147, 150–1
cultural studies perspective, 338–40
culture as a social determinant, 335–41

De Grauwe, Paul, 244
deindustrialisation (Britain), 149
democracy, 5–6, 365–6, 399–400,
    405–7, 426
  and civic groups, 400
  information, free flow of, 399–401,
    404–5
  and special interests, 400, 406
  and voter ignorance, 406–7
  at work, 407–8, 417, 423
Democratic Party (US) 2, 133, 253, 406
Demsetz, Harold, 466 n142
Department of Defense, US (DOD), 104,
    186, 188, 261–2, 265–6, 391
Descartes, René, 17–19, 26, 28
de-schooling *see* Illich, Ivan
de-skilling *see* Braverman, Harry
Deutscher, Isaac, 109

Dewey, John
  educational practice, influence on,
    203–9, 222, 338, 419
  Soviet education, influence on, 204
dirigisme, 129, 130
Domar, Evsey, 163, 302–4
Drucker, Peter, 131

early childhood intellectual
    development, 330–33, 342, 458 n56
economic growth *see also* national
    income
  environmental considerations, 286,
    290
  irreversibilities, 286–7
  lags in, 10, 158, 168, 179, 196–7, 285,
    290–1
  as maximand, 4, 161–4, 277–82,
    308–10, 390
  and population growth, 283
economic income, 283–5
  and education, 284–5, 287–91
  and infrastructure, 285
economic inequality *see* income
    distribution
economic mobility *see* income
    distribution
economic orthodoxy, 7, 16, 20, 54–5,
    66–70, 78, 81–2, 122, 432 n10 *see*
    also Marshall, Alfred
Economist, 211, 219, 274, 308
Edison, Thomas, 179
  as myth, 130, 249–50, 255
  as systems builder, 61–2, 130, 252
Edsall, Thomas, 400
education, 2–4, 9, 423 *see also* schools
  citizenship, training in, 5, 241–2,
    357–9, 361
  cognitive and non-cognitive aspects
    of, 350, 352–3, 357
  community-centred education, 203,
    205, 210–11
  competition, role in, 360–1
  consumption benefits of, 169
  differences between Catholic and
    Protestant education, 199, 228
  differences linked to class, 193,
    200–1, 205–6, 216–7, 244–5
  elite standards as benchmark, 11,
    311–12, 334–5, 339–40, 346–56

elite vs. broadly diffused, 167, 179–81
expenditure on, 351
external (spillover) effects, 9, 168, 179,
  193–8, 287–9
and Gove reforms (UK), 208–10
and government loan schemes, 193
higher and post-high school (tertiary)
  education, 254–6, 268, 356–7, 363,
  371–2
and homework, 351–2, 362
and income distribution, 166–7, 291,
  301–2
and industrial revolutions, 178–83
lags in effects of, 9–10, 158, 167–8,
  172, 179, 195–7, 283–5, 290–1, 442
  n36, 443 n15
left and Marxist tendencies, 203,
  212–13, 218, 340–1
lifetime learning, 363, 372
managerialist approaches to, 343–46,
  360
narrow versus broad-based learning,
  168, 189, 199–201, 419
non-economic motivations for, 198–9
preschool programmes, 332–3, 342,
  346, 350–1, 357, 361
reform programmes for, 361–3, 371–2,
  423
and STEM subjects (Science,
  Technology, Engineering and
  Mathematics), 202
and streaming ('tracking'), 220–1, 423
and teacher quality, 211, 344–5
traditional versus progressive, 202–3,
  205, 206–8, 340–1
vocational skills, 180–1
vouchers, 166, 210, 216–7
and white collar work, 180, 182
Education Act 1944 (Great Britain), 15,
  146, 206
education and economic growth, 8,
  41–2, 116, 161–75, 178–84, 188,
  195–6
efficiency, presumption of, 170–7
Einstein, Albert, 13, 361
Eisenhower, President Dwight, 262
electronics industry, 10, 177, 250, 263–7
  competition in, 268–70
  cooperative ventures in, 269, 415
  finance in, 266–7

electronics industry – *continued*
  and the internet, 268
  role of the state, 186–8, 250, 262–3,
    265–7, 270
  semiconductor in, 186
  and Silicon Valley, 197
  and universities, 183, 186, 188, 261,
    263–70
employer of last resort (ELR)/
  employment guarantee
  programmes, 367, 370–1, 377
employment protection legislation
  (EPL), 367, 370
endogenous growth theory *see* new
  growth theory
Engels, Friedrich, 89, 133
Enlightenment, the, 17–18, 22, 169, 170,
    199, 203, 250, 272
  and the First Industrial Revolution,
    227, 228
  and planning, 6, 22, 33–35, 157
entrepreneur, myth of, 177, 250, 268–9
  see also Edison, Thomas
Etzioni, Amitai, 368
European Central Bank, 367
European Union (EU)
  single currency, 389
  unemployment in, 236–7
Evans, Richard, 209
expert performance, 330

Fabian Society, 91, 144–5
Farber, Henry, 448 n37
fascism, 66, 84, 101
Federal Reserve (US), 367
Feldstein, Martin, 292, 395
finance *see also* giant firms
  and avoidance of regulation, 384–5,
    387–8, 463 n48
  and capitalist dynamism, 62, 122–3,
    185, 234–5, 379, 383–4
  and economic instability, 279, 379–80
  entrepreneurial forms of, 185, 187,
    380, 383
  and euro single currency, 389
  financial bubbles, 379–81
  financial derivatives, 384–6, 388
  financial innovation, 379, 383–9
  industrial banks, 20
  and junk bonds, 385
  liquidity paradoxes in, 386–7
  Modigliani and Miller theorem, 381
  as regulator of economic activity, 388–9
  securitisation of, 383
  in socialism, 366, 382–3, 385–6, 388,
    391–2, 394–5
  and technocratic planning paradigm,
    58, 379, 382
  and Tobin tax, 387
financial crisis of, 207–8, 235–9, 279,
    292, 296, 367, 379, 382–3, 390, 406
Finland
  education in, 218–23, 290–1
  and GERM critique, 219–20
  PISA and TIMSS performance, 218,
    222–3
  teachers' status in, 220
  teacher training in, 220
First Industrial Revolution, 37–8, 179,
    181
  education in, 178–9, 228
  income growth in, 38
  scientific literacy of inventors in, 227–8
Fisher, Irving
  banking reforms, 387–8
  and investment decisions, 192
flexibility *see* labour flexibility
Flynn effect *see* IQ
Fogel, Robert, 229, 230
Ford, Henry, 7, 37, 40, 45, 49, 52–3,
    54, 59, 62, 76, 252, 255 *see also*
    assembly line
Ford, Martin, 420–1
France, Anatole, 33
free schools *see* Summerhill
French Revolution (1789), 19
Friedman, Milton, 128, 216
  and corporate social responsibility,
    133–4
  as follower of Alfred Marshall, 68
  on inequality, 192–3, 296, 299, 402–3
Friedman, Thomas, 305
Fromm, Erich, 429–30
full employment
  as a socialist goal, 3, 5, 11, 318, 341–2,
    364, 366–7, 372, 378–9, 389–95,
    409, 421–3, 427–9
  as a presumption in economic
    modelling, 163, 170
functional finance, 367, 377

'g' measure of intellectual capacity *see* IQ measure

Galbraith, John Kenneth, 58–9, 135, 137
  Affluent Society, 133, 211, 280–1, 302
  New Industrial State, 71, 130–33, 139–42, 151, 153–4
Galileo [Galilei], 18
Gantt chart, 41
Garvey, George, 439 n56
GDP *see* national income
General Motors (GM)
  diversified output of, 50–1
  New Industrial State, as exemplification of, 131–2, 139–41
gentlemanly capitalism, 69
German Social Democratic Party (SPD), 85–7, 94
German war economy (First World War) *see* Larin, Yuri
Germany, 20, 39, 41, 60, 68, 69, 236–7, 252, 307
  as antipode to British liberalism, 73, 76, 83–87
  and First World War economy, 93–4
  and rationalisation, 73, 74–6
  and the role of science in industry, 51, 60
Gerschenkron, Alexander, 50–1, 120
giant firms *see also* Chandler, Alfred
  cost accounting in, 43–5, 50
  diseconomies of scale in, 48–9, 138
  financing of, 42, 47–8, 58, 62
  and innovation, 40–1, 46–7, 58–61
  and labour, 46, 51
  managerial challenges of, 39–46, 64
  as monitoring stations, 120–1
  management innovations in, 42, 45–6, 48–51, 55, 407
  and market expansion, 39
  and modernity, 39, 40, 49, 54
  and planning, 7, 40, 54–5, 60–4
  professionalisation of personnel in, 42, 47, 49–51, 60, 138–9, 180
  and vertical integration, 55–7
Gilens, Martin, 465 n107
Gindin, Sam, 456 n82
Gintis, Herbert *see* Bowles, Samuel
Glass-Steagall Act (US), 279
Glyn, Andrew, 147
Golden Age of Capitalism (1947–1971), 2, 102, 104, 127–8, 140, 278–9, 292

Goldin, Claudia, 245, 293, 295
good job, concept of, 372
Gorbachëv, Mikhail, 102
Gordon, Robert J. 313–4
Gove, Michael, 208–10
government procurement and wage setting, 376–8
Graff, Harvey, 442 n36
Gramsci, Antonio, 208, 444 n40
Great Transformation, 7, 37–8, 69, 180
Green, Francis, 174, 444 n32
guaranteed income schemes *see* basic income
guilds *see in situ* learning

Habermas, Jürgen, 431
Hacker, Jacob, 242, 465 n111
Hanushek, Eric, 165–6, 189, 211, 343
Harrod, Roy, 163, 440 n4
Hart and Risley study, 331–2, 458 n56
  see also early childhood intellectual development
Haussmann, Georges-Eugène, 20, 28–9, 31
Haydn, Joseph, 330
Hayek, Friedrich, 6, 21–3, 116, 119, 128, 171, 215, 296, 379, 432 n8, 462 n31
  and the constructivist fallacy, 24–7, 34, 36, 275, 424–5
  democratic decision making, 121–2
  dynamic approach to competition, 105–6, 153, 171
  on equality of opportunity, 319–20
  knowledge, inherent limitations in, 23–6, 320
  legal systems, 23–5, 27–8, 32–3
  planning critique, 22–3, 26–7
  'Road to Serfdom' argument, 321
  and socialist calculation debate, 112–113, 118–22
  and social justice, 34
  and spontaneous order, 6, 23–8, 32–5, 170, 319–22, 328, 424–5
  unintended consequences, 25–6
  and the urban environment, 30–1
Head Start programme (US), *see* education, preschool programmes
Hegel, Georg Wilhelm Friedrich, 26, 90
Hilferding, Rudolf, 91, 123–4, 134, 135
Hirsch, Eric Donald, Jr., 207–8

Hofstadter, Richard, 338
Holland, Stuart *see* Alternative Economic Strategy
homework *see* education
Hoover, Herbert *see* standardisation
households
  as fulcrums of planning, 10, 223–4, 345–6, 370
  influence on learning, 4–5, 159, 190, 244–5, 291, 342, 365
  and insecurity, 3, 158, 159, 223–4, 242–5, 247, 272, 364, 370
human assets
  compared with human capital theory, 193–195
  depreciation of, 302–5
  and inequality, 297, 302–3
human capital theory, 9, 191–4
Humboldt, Wilhelm von, 169
Hume, David, 18
Huntington, Samuel, 336

Illich, Ivan, 215–17, 355
imperfect and monopolistic competition, 69, 136–7, 439–40 n18
income distribution, 3, 10–11, 166–7, 193, 235, 271–2, 282, 285, 292–3
  changes since Thatcher and Reagan years, 270–1, 292–5
  and economic mobility, 271–2, 301–2, 454–5 n61
  ethical approaches to, 321–3
  and Hayek's spontaneous order, 27–8, 320–2
  international competition and, 294–5
  international labour market expansion and, 294
  political effects of inequality, 366, 399–400
  public policy and, 294–6
  technological change and, 293–5
  and wealth distribution, 400–1, 454 n55
India, 232, 294, 336
industrial banks, 20
Industrial Revolution (Britain) *see* First industrial Revolution
industrious revolution, 37, 433 n1
industry clusters, 197, 234, 444 n20
inequality *see* income distribution

innovation, 158
  role of competition, 58
  and finance, 58, 62
  giant firms and planned innovation, 40–1, 60–1
  link to marketing, 40, 59–60
  role of science in, 46–7, 141–2
  role of the state in, 186–89
  in situ learning, 9, 175, 181, 187, 219, 225–7, 342, 373
  advantages accruing to rich countries, 229–32
  dissipation of advantages accruing to rich countries, 232–4
  in the general environment, 230
  and guilds, 228–9
  at work, 5, 9, 231–2, 239–40, 418–19, 423
intellectual property rights (IPRs), 47, 142, 187, 404–6
International Labour Organization, 428
IQ (Intelligence Quotient) measure, 3, 11, 166, 206–7, 282, 322–334, 346
  and Binet, Alfred, 323
  and brain plasticity, 330–1
  Burt, Cyril, 323
  and Education Act 1944 (Britain), 325
  Flynn effect, 329
  and the 'g' measure of intellectual capacity, 323–4
  and Jensen, Arthur, 325
  Minnesota twins studies, 324, 328
  and motivation, 323–4, 331
  and Murray, Charles, 325

Jackson, Andrew, 251
Jacobs, Jane
  city planning, attitudes towards, 29–30, 32, 35, 374
  Hayek's attitude towards, 30
Japan, 171, 197, 236, 296
  agricultural protection, 246
  education in, 183
  managerial innovations in, 141, 142, 171
  economic development in, 102–104, 116, 188, 287–90
jazz, 249, 256, 340
Jensen, Arthur *see* IQ
jobs worth doing programme, 367, 372–8, 390, 420, 423

junk securities, 384–5
just-in-time system (Japan), 386

Kalecki, Michał, 135
kanban, 171
Katz, Lawrence, 293, 295
Kautsky, Karl, 91, 94
Kellogg's, 59–60
Keynes, John Maynard, 82, 114–15, 124
Keynesian macroeconomic planning *see* planning
khozrachët see Soviet economy
Khrushchëv, Nikita, 108, 163, 185
Kohn, Alfie, 350–1
Kolko, Gabriel, 136
Kornai, János, 118 *see* Soviet economy, soft budget constraint
Krueger, Alan, 343
Krugman, Paul, 314–15, 420, 439–40 n18, 453–4 n39
Kunstler, James, 29
Kuznets, Simon, 296

labour flexibility, 189, 224, 207, 220, 224, 236, 240, 243, 245–7, 279, 306, 333, 359, 372, 374–5, 411–12, 417,
labour market regimes, 410–13
Labour Party (Britain), 2, 215, 410
Attlee government of 1945, 15, 145–6, 218
and nationalised industries, 145–7, 150
and planning, 144–5
labour unions *see* unions
Laffer, Arthur, 292, 297, 395
Landes, David, 336
Lange, Oskar, 110–12, 114, 122, 153, 171, 328, 382 *see also* socialist calculation debate
Larin, Yuri, 92–4
Lassalle, Ferdinand, 87
Lavoie, Don, 112–13, 116, 119–20, 122, 185 *see also* socialist calculation debate
Lazonick, William, 57
Le Corbusier (Charles-Édouard Jeanneret-Gris), 29, 30, 31
Lenin, Vladimir, 87, 92, 94, 98, 110, 121–3, 158
and electrification, 61–2

planning, 89–90, 99, 110
scientific management, 89, 95, 107–8, 247
and workers' control, 89, 95, 107–8
Lewontin, Richard, 337
liberalism, economic *see* economic orthodoxy
Liberman, Evsei, 117
Lilienthal, David, 133
Lindert, Peter, 397, 412
List, Friedrich, 76, 83–4, 92, 130
Little, Tony, 352
Luxemburg, Rosa, 91, 98

macroeconomic fluctuations, pre-Keynesian approaches, 72–3
mainstream economics *see* economic orthodoxy
mainstream responses to New Economy approach, 130, 137–8
Mandel, Michael, 177–8
Mankiw, N. Gregory, 455 n71
marketing and advertising, 40, 58–9, 90, 338–40
Marshall, Alfred, 68–9, 104, 136, 192, 447 n14
Marx, Karl, 33, 130–1, 135–6, 162, 191, 192, 203, 223, 301, 393, 429–30
and central planning, 87–9, 92
on education, 213
and finance, 91–2
labour, productive and unproductive, 90
and planning, 17, 19, 2
slavery and free labour, 191–2,
and the state, 83–4, 87–9, 92
maximum hours worked legislation, 367, 369–70
Maxwell, James Clerk, 62
McKinsey Global Institute, 308, 314
Means, Gardiner *see* Berle, Adolf
Menand, Louis, 461 n132
Milanovic, Branko, 438 n19
military-industrial complex, 262
Mill, John Stuart, 319, 413
minimum wage legislation, 279, 298, 378, 395, 409, 456 n76
Minsky, Hyman, 124
and employment guarantee programme, 370
and financial bubbles, 379

Mises, Ludwig von, 110–11, 113–14, 117, 128, 328 *see also* socialist calculation debate
Mississippi Delta blues, 177
modern corporation approach, 130–1
Modigliani and Miller theorem *see* finance
Mokyr, Joel, 227–8
Mondragón cooperative *see* workers' control
monopoly capital theory, 8, 127, 134–6
Monopoly Capital see Baran, Paul
monopolies, ubiquity of, 41, 67, 71–2, 127, 151–3
Moore's law, 265–6, 268
Morris, William, 70
Moses, Robert, 29, 31, 286, 374
Mozart, Wolfgang Amadeus, 330, 360
multinationals
    and the dissipation of *in situ* advantages, 232–3
    and US economic success, 234
Murray, Charles, 325–8, 368–9
    see also IQ

National Health Service (UK), 143, 145, 255, 285, 461–2 n17.
national income, 10 *see also* economic growth
    accounts, 277
    as aggregate demand measure, 278–80
    as capacity measure, 282–6, 302–3
    as welfare measure, 278–82
    and working hours, 281
    environmental critiques, 281, 286, 290
National Recovery Administration (NRA), 436 n22
nationalisation *see* Labour Party (Britain)
necessities and luxuries, 304, 455 n71
neighbourhoods, 9, 29–30, 357, 374–6, 421, 462 n21
Nelson, Richard R., 173
neoclassical theory of growth, 163–4, 172
neoliberalism, 28, 81, 292
Neurath, Otto, 110, 113–15
New Deal (US), 130, 246–7, 249, 253, 260, 436 n22

New Economic Policy (NEP) *see* Soviet economy
New Economy perspective, 126–7, 130, 134
new growth theory, 164
Noble, David, 240, 442 n44
North, Douglass, 223
Nove, Alec, 118
Nozick, Robert, 217, 299, 322

Okun, Arthur, 295–6, 319
Oliver, Jamie, 337
optimism, 2, 431
ordoliberalism, 81
Organisation for Economic Co-operation and Development (OECD), 236–8, 242–3
Osterman, Paul, 238
Orwell, George, 130
over the counter (OTC) financial offerings, 384, 388, 390–1

Pack, Howard, 173
Page, Benjamin, 465 n107
Paine, Thomas, 18
Pareto optimality, 27, 31, 33, 137, 299
patents *see* intellectual property rights (IPRs)
Pauli, Wolfgang, 136
Pickett, Kate, 300
Pierson, Paul, 465 n111
Piketty, Thomas, 398, 404
Pigou, Arthur Cecil, 30, 82, 146
PISA (Programme for International Student Assessment), 165, 218–9
planning
    firm level, 54–8, 61–2, 75–8, 120–1, 129–30, 132–3
    Keynesian macroeconomic planning, 2, 114–115, 126, 128–30, 278–9
    indicative planning, 129
    as mode of economic regulation, 6, 8, 22, 72, 74–5, 126–7
    rationality, links to, 17–19, 22, 33–5
Playfair, Lyon, 289
Polan, Magdalena, 244
Polanyi, Karl, 32–3, 366
political contributions by the rich *see* United States
Pontusson, Jonas, 410, 412, 466 n135

Preobrazhensky, Evgenii, 98, 100
preschool programmes *see* education
private property, inviolability of, 402–5
private schools *see* schools
privatisation of public services, 376
production function, presumption of
   universal efficiency, 170–4
productive and unproductive labour, 90
productivity
   growth in, 307–9, 313–15
   measurement of, 307–9
Progressive movement (US) 40, 67
Project Star, 343
Proudhon, Pierre-Joseph, 19, 85
public health reforms *see* state
   intervention
public transportation, 376

Radio Corporation of America (RCA),
   261
railways (railroads) *see also* Chandler,
   Alfred and Fogel, Robert
   and cost accounting, 43–4
   and human capital development,
      229–30
   challenges facing, 42–5
   creation of management structures,
      44–5, 48–9
   and market extension, 39
Rathenau, Emil, 61, 130
Rathenau, Walter, 61, 73
rationalisation of industry, 67, 72–4, 84,
   436 n17
Ravitch, Diane, 206–7, 208, 217–18, 222,
   444 n40
Rawls, John, 298–300
Reagan, Ronald, 136, 234, 292, 295, 338
real business cycle theory, 381
Rehn-Meidner plan, 411
Reich, Robert, 447 n3
research and development (R&D) *see*
   technological change
revolving door between public and
   private sectors, 376–7
Ricardo, David, 19, 83, 122, 135, 162,
   124, 381, 429
Roberts, Paul Craig, 111
robotic displacement of labour, 292,
   420–1
rock 'n' roll, 256

Rockefeller, John D., 63, 67, 71
Roosevelt, Theodore, 67
Rosenberg, Nathan, 176

Sagan, Carl, 337
Saint-Simon, Henri de *see* Saint-
   Simonian ideology
Sahlberg, Pasi, 218–20
Saint-Simonian ideology, 19–20, 28, 83
Samuelson, Paul, 101, 133
Schoenberg, Arnold, 256
schools *see also* education
   academy and charter schools, 210–11,
      219
   classroom size (teacher-student ratios),
      343–4, 353, 358–9, 460 n125
   competition in, 360–1
   computer use in, 361–2
   discipline in, 5, 353–4, 362
   private schools, 169, 199, 220, 311,
      346–50, 353
Schumpeter, Joseph, 9, 10, 58–9, 131–2,
   167, 171, 176, 185–6, 462 n31
   competition and monopoly in
      innovation, 58–9
   and creative destruction, 10, 158, 229,
      263–4, 293, 381
   finance in innovation, 62, 381
   innovation as discontinuous
      thunderbolt, 58, 119, 171, 176
   managerially-directed firms, attitude
      towards, 59, 451 n27
science, commercial use of, 46–7, 60–1,
   179–80
science to craft ratio, 46–7, 141–3,
   186–7, 197, 232, 268–70
scientific management, 51, 53–4, 179,
   181, 247, 407
   and cost accounting, 45–6, 53, 63
   and labour autonomy, 46, 54, 181–2,
      419–20
   and mitigation of economic
      fluctuations, 73
   and the Soviet economy, 95, 107–8
Second Industrial Revolution, 38–9, 47,
   179–81 *see also* giant firms
secrecy *see* democracy, information
security *see* households
semiconductor *see* electronics industry
Sen, Amartya, 300–1, 304

separation of ownership and control,
42, 130–1, 137–9, 151
Servan-Schreiber, Jean-Jacques, 140
Shiller, Robert, 392–4
Silicon Valley *see* electronics industry
slavery *see* United States (US)
Smith, Adam, 6, 26, 162, 330
social Darwinism, 16, 41, 66, 71, 84,
121, 272, 296, 318, 322, 328, 425–6
social democracy, 1, 275
socialism
alternative conceptions, 1, 4, 15–16,
85–6, 341–2, 364–5, 422–4
and solidarity, 6, 82, 159, 275, 318,
350, 405, 417, 426–8
and technocratic planning paradigm,
7, 85–7, 155–6
socialist calculation debate, 7, 110–114,
119–22; *see also* Hayek, Friedrich,
Lavoie, Don, Mises, Ludwig von and
Neurath, Otto
Solow, Robert, 133, 163
Sombart, Werner, 252–5
South Korea, 102, 105, 116, 120, 141,
173, 174, 188, 296 *see also* Asian
tigers
Soviet economy, 1, 7, 58–9, 76, 133
admiration for, 74–5, 84, 101
agriculture in the, 99–100, 109, 116–7
campaigns in the, 118–19
and Cold War pressures, 103–5
economic growth in, 101–4, 185
and egalitarianism, 106–7
five year plans, 100, 105–6
foreign trade with centrally planned
economies
and human development, 108–9
and *khozrachët*, 99, 117
military expenditure as a drain on
development, 104–5
New Economic Policy (NEP), 99–100
orthodox economic analysis of,
116–18
and planning, 105–6, 133
and the Second World War, 101, 106,
108
soft budget constraint, 102–3, 118–9
Stakhanovite movement, 107–8, 119
storming in, 106–7
war communism, 98–9

and workers' control, 107–8
spandrels in human capital
development, 198
Spencer, Herbert, 21, 34, 71, 309
spillover effects to cognitive
development *see* education, external
effects
Spinoza, Baruch (Benedict De), 26, 301
spontaneous order *see* Hayek, Friedrich
Stalin, Joseph, 82, 91, 100–1, 108, 116
and the law of value, 118–9
and linguistics, 312
standardisation, 40, 45, 51–3, 58, 63, 74
and American system of
manufactures, 51, 53, 260
British failures in, 63
consumer goods, 40, 142–3
and the Ford Motor Company, 40, 52,
62, 76
Hoover, Herbert, 52
protocols of production, 40, 141–2
weights and measures, 19
state, the
and bureaucracy, 75, 81–3
central planning, role in
and economic development, 19, 71,
78–84, 120–2, 186–9, 270
Marx and, 83–4
military dimension, 81–2
and socialism, 82–3, 87, 91
US view of, 251–2
state intervention
and market creation, 19, 33–4, 384
opposition to, 21
and public health reforms, 20–2, 38
Steindl, Josef, 135
Steinherr, Alfred, 392–3
Steinmetz, Charles P., 71–2
STEM subjects (Science, Technology,
Engineering and Mathematics) *see*
education
Stigler, George, 31
efficacy of competition, 360
external effects of education, 195
follower of Alfred Marshall, 68
subsistence consumption, 303–4
Stiglitz, Joseph, 282
Stravinsky, Igor, 256
suburbs, 374–5
Summerhill, 217–8, 348, 359

Summers, Lawrence, 3
Supreme Court (US), 403–4
Sutcliffe, Bob, 147
Swan, Trevor, 163
Sweden
    economic development and literacy,
        290–1
    labour market policies in
Sweezy, Paul *see* Baran, Paul
syndicalists, 85

tariff rates, US, 67
taxation, 306, 375–6, 423
    and income equalisation, 395–7
    Norway, public disclosure of tax
        returns in, 401
    supply side approaches, 292
    tax expenditures, 396–8
    and tax havens and avoidance, 6, 294,
        366, 396–404
    and transfer pricing, 401
    on wealth, 395–398
tax credits for job creation, 367, 370
Taylor, Fredrick Winslow and Taylorism
    see scientific management
technical training *see* vocational
    training
technocratic planning paradigm, 7,
    57–8, 66, 70–1, 75, 126–7
    deleterious effects for socialism, 94–6,
        124–5, 155–6
    engineering perspective, 19, 71, 75–8
    finance and marketing as peripheral,
        40, 90–1, 122–5
    and Marx, 87–92
    and political radicalism, 94, 143
    principles of, 70–1
technological change, 8–9, 158, 175–8
    see also Schumpeter, Joseph
technocracy *see* Veblen, Thorstein
    as discontinuous thunderbolt, 171
    and economic growth, 163–4, 178,
        184–5
    elixir, as an, 7, 177–8, 184
    research and development (R&D),
        176–8
    role of the state, 186–8, 265–7
    social aspects of, 240–1
Thatcher, Margret, 2, 146–7, 150, 154–5,
    234, 282, 292, 295, 302, 410

TIMSS (Trends in International
    Mathematics and Science Study),
    222
Tinbergen, J.
    convergence between west and east,
        133
    On the Theory of Economic Policy,
        128–9
trade unions *see* unions
trade-off between equality and
    efficiency, 3, 10–11, 158, 224,
    295–300, 402
transactions costs approaches, 56–7, 69
transistor *see* electronics industry,
    semiconductor
Trivanovitch, Vaso, 73
Troksky, Leon and Trotskyism, 98, 109,
    126–7, 134
Trump, Donald, 456, n76

unemployment, 1, 225–6, 236–7, 367,
    378, 408–9
uniformity of output *see*
    standardisation
    hysteresis effect, 236
    long term, 236
    for young people, 225–6, 236–8
unions
    and the Labour Party (Britain), 146–7,
        410
    and political action, 400, 407–8,
        410–11
    and unemployment, 236, 408–9
    and wage compression, 395, 407–8
    and worker rights, 366, 407–10
    and working conditions, 408
United States (US), 10
    agricultural development in, 259–60
    antitrust policies, 67, 133, 266
    citizenship, concept of, 251–2, 254,
        257, 271
    creationism in, 249, 253, 272–3
    cultural and political continuity in,
        257–8
    cultural dominance, 250, 252, 256,
        274–5
    entrepreneur, myth of, 130, 249–50,
        255, 258, 263
    income distribution in, 270–2, 310–2
    opportunity in, 254–5, 271, 301–2

United States (US) – *continued*
  per capita income in, 249
  political contributions by the rich,
    272
  school education in, 198, 254–6, 268,
    273, 293
  slavery in, 191–2, 251–2
  socialism, absence of, 252–4
  state role in economic development,
    251–2, 254, 258–62, 267
  tariff levels, 67, 260
  university (college) education in, 49,
    183, 186, 188, 254, 261–8, 270, 273,
    293
unskilled work *see* work
urban planning *see* city planning

Veblen, Thorstein, 76–8, 113, 132
  The Higher Learning in America, 201,
    267
  The Theory of the Leisure Class, 77
  engineering perspective and, 77–8
venture capital *see* finance,
    entrepreneurial forms of
vocational training, 180–1, 238–40
  broad-based vs. focused, 238–9
  German approaches, 181, 239–40
voting paradox, 433 n44
vouchers *see* education
Voznesensky, Nikolai, 125

Walras, Léon, 111
war communism *see* Soviet economy
Weber, Max, 49, 78–82, 90, 228
wealth distribution *see* income
    distribution
Whyte, William, 130
Wilder, Billy, 130
Wilkinson, Richard, 300
Williamson, Oliver *see* transactions
    costs approaches
Woessmann, Ludger, 165–6, 189
work
  hand and brain distinction, 226, 419
  unskilled, 226
worker representation, typology of
    regimes of, 410–13, 416–7
worker rights *see also* unions
workers' control, 85, 423
  efficacy of, 413–5, 418
  and the Mondragón cooperative,
    415–6
  in Soviet economy, 107
  and worker councils, 416–8
working conditions and socialism, 430
working hours, 281, 304
workplace learning, 418–20, 423
workplace learning *see in situ* learning
World Economic Forum (WEF), 306–7

Young, Alwyn, 172–3